THE ELDERLY AS
MODERN PIONEERS

THE ELDERLY AS MODERN PIONEERS

EDITED BY

PHILIP SILVERMAN

INDIANA UNIVERSITY PRESS
Bloomington and Indianapolis

Manufactured in the United States of America

Library of Congress Cataloging-in-Publication Data

The Elderly as modern pioneers.

Bibliography: p.
Includes index.
1. Gerontology.   I. Silverman, Philip.
HQ1061.E37   1988   305.2'6   86-43047
ISBN 0-253-31904-8
0-253-20463-1 (pbk.)

1 2 3 4 5 92 91 90 89 88

CONTENTS

PREFACE

In 1975 a colleague and I jointly developed an undergraduate course in gerontology. For the two of us, an anthropologist and a psychologist with background in biology, it was our first effort at teaching a course on aging. It was also the first time that a gerontology course was offered on our campus. I suspect similar developments were occurring on a number of campuses in this country at about that time. Gerontology was coming of age as an academic discipline.

One of the first problems we faced was finding a suitable text. We wanted one that provided a broad, comprehensive background in the field. Ideally, we sought material that would furnish upper division students interested in human development, regardless of their major, with a greater understanding of the nature and problems of old age. At the same time, we wanted it to be relevant to aspiring professionals and paraprofessionals who expected to work with the elderly and needed background in gerontology as part of their career development. We also looked for material reflecting a coherent theoretical framework for organizing the diverse findings in the field. It might be only a tentative framework, but some integrating conceptual scheme remained a primary consideration. None of the textbooks we examined fulfilled these needs.

We brazenly made the decision to write the book we sought in vain to find. In an initial flurry of activity, a manuscript of approximately one hundred pages of preliminary material was prepared. But before we had the opportunity to concentrate our attention on the project, almost a decade had passed. As we began anew, our original plan still seemed appropriate, but by now the volume of literature had become overwhelming and the nature of the information increasingly technical. The task appeared forbidding in its scope. Eventually, other commitments absorbed the attention of my colleague. The project was redefined when I decided to edit a volume that would essentially cover the same ground by bringing together the specialized knowledge of a number of scholars. Thus, all the chapters in this book are original contributions.

Gerontology is an extraordinarily rich field. It draws generously from a number of disciplines in both the natural and social sciences. This book brings together within an interdisciplinary framework the research from four of these disciplines—biology, psychology, anthropology, and sociology. The conceptual scheme most appropriate for integrating this material is the life course perspective. Basically, this views the life course as multidetermined, with change occurring within the various interrelated levels—the social, psychological, and biological.

In addition, we give emphasis to comparative material where appropriate. Partly because the greater proportion of research on the aged has been done in the United States, most overviews in gerontology focus almost exclusively on studies of North American elderly. Despite the importance of this research, we chose a broader perspective by including relevant findings from other societies. The majority of contributors to this volume are anthropologists who have worked in North America as well as other Western and non-Western societies. Cross-cultural and even cross-species comparisons play an essential part in their understanding of human behavior, and this is reflected in much of the material.

The contributors were asked to summarize the most important recent findings in their area of concern in a manner that would be understandable to a general college-level audience. Some material may still present a challenge to students, for many chapters do assume basic knowledge of the vocabulary in the various disciplines covered. The intent was to be selective but still thorough in the literature covered. Contradictions in the findings and areas that still lack adequate empirical work were not to be ignored or glossed over. The contributors to this volume will have achieved a measure of success if they have presented the research enterprise as struggling to make sense of some difficult matters. Though often revealing gaps in our knowledge or even incoherent results, the material also includes new and provocative findings which occasionally have practical implications.

In many cases, the chapters represent excellent overviews of the current state of the art within the respective research areas. Some contributors define the direction that future research might take in order to clarify present findings or fill in the more evident gaps in our knowledge. In this sense, the volume goes beyond standard textbooks for undergraduates or beginning graduate students, and should be useful to gerontologists and professionals working with the elderly who are seeking a summary of research areas outside their expertise.

I wish to thank all the contributors for responding seriously to editorial suggestions. Diane Rykken, the author of the chapter on sexuality, was involved in the original conceptualization of the book. M. Powell Lawton, J. Daniel McMillin, Kenneth Nyberg, and Corinne Nydegger were kind enough to comment on various chapters. Alana Patris Loyér, Robert J. Maxwell, and Eleanor Krassen Maxwell read all of the editor's chapters and made many useful suggestions. Finally, I am indebted to the able clerical assistance of Jacki Lawson and Linda Masi.

Philip Silverman

THE ELDERLY AS
MODERN PIONEERS

I

INTRODUCTION

THE LIFE COURSE PERSPECTIVE

Philip Silverman

> . . . the life-cycle revolution . . . is a
> dramatic assertion of the later life stages
> as a time for renewed activity, and crea-
> tiveness. Nothing like it has ever hap-
> pened in America—or anywhere else.
>
> —Max Eastman (as quoted in Blau 1981, 1)

Who Are the Modern Pioneers?

The title of this book is taken from a quote by David Plath who writes: "The aged are among the true pioneers of our time, and pioneer life is notorious-ly brutal" (Plath 1972, 150). He goes on to point out that modern society has bestowed longevity, but the maps it has provided those who achieve it are medieval, "full of freaks and monsters and imaginary harbors" (ibid, 150). Truly, a dramatic change in this century has led to unprecedented aging in the populations of industrial countries. Because of the de-velopments in science and technology over the past one hundred years, such factors as disease, famine, and even complications occurring in as natural a process as childbirth no longer sweep most people away before they reach old age. At present the proportion of elderly in the population is higher than it ever has been in human history, and the trend is expected to continue well into the next century. We find ourselves in the midst of an extraordinary revolution, one that has been unheralded and thus easily ignored, but one that will have the profoundest effects on the nature of our lives.

It is the recognition of this extensive reshaping of society now taking place that has led others to hit upon the pioneer theme. In her important summary of research on older people and their families, Shanas (1980)

1

subtitled her paper "The New Pioneers." And in an overview of anthropological approaches to aging Keith writes:

> The [old people] are also actors, and the actions that old people in industrial societies take now will have a profound influence on the roles of old people in the future. Because it is a new phenomenon in the history of humanity for a large proportion of a population to enjoy a long period of life in old age, the meaning of that new life stage is not yet defined. The role models for that life stage are the old-age pioneers who are exploring it now, and their experiments in community formation, or political organization, are active sources of social change (Keith 1982, 6).

This book will allow some assessment of what pioneer life is like for those presently living it. The major purpose, however, is to summarize what we presently know about the nature of old age. In another sense the term modern pioneers is appropriate in reference to those who contributed to this volume. Gerontology is rapidly coming of age as an academic discipline. New course offerings abound, even curriculum guidelines and standards are on the horizon. Concomitantly, the amount of research grows furiously. In this fluid situation, the contributors to this volume work in a field to which they are relatively recent arrivals. They represent for the most part younger professionals in the field. Their contributions attempt to carry forward the fruitful elements of earlier work in gerontology, while also exploring important new directions in the field.

Evident in this volume is a somewhat different philosophy from much of the earlier writing in gerontology. In the two decades following World War II, the generation of scholars who formed the first professional association in gerontology was very conscious of the pejorative stereotypes that this society imposed on the elderly. In attempting to combat this ageism, there was a tendency to sentimentalize and idealize old age in the hope that, by pointing out all the negative myths of aging, it would improve the treatment of the elderly by the larger society (Rosow 1982). In extreme cases aging as an inevitable biological process that necessarily involved physical decrements was practically ignored.

Many myths still exist which portray old people as essentially incompetent, decrepit, and desexualized humans. Where these procrustean stereotypes are still inflicted upon the elderly, they need to be exposed, and the diversity that is now known to exist must be reaffirmed. But this should not lead to glossing over that part of aging which does involve loss and inevitable decline in function. We have now reached the point where reacting to these myths need not color the interpretation of research findings. Both the potentials as well as the burdens of growing old deserve recognition. The contributors to this volume present a more balanced picture of the enormous variability to be found among the aged, both biologically and socially, and thus move beyond both the pejorative stereotypes and the moral outrage in reaction to these myths.

Defining Old Age

Defining the subject of this book—old age—is by no means a trivial task. A great deal of disagreement still exists regarding how this stage in the life cycle should be determined. For the most part, a chronological boundary has been accepted as the beginning of old age. Because of its historical importance in defining retirement, most studies of the elderly use sixty-five as the boundary, although one also encounters studies using sixty or some other age boundary as the cutoff year. For purposes of this volume, the terms old age, aged, elderly, and so forth refer to anyone sixty-five or older, unless otherwise specified.

Although we accept the sixty-five-plus convention, it clearly is not an adequate marker for old age. Gerontologists are aware that chronological age often says very little about the individual or about how different societies impinge on individuals. It would be preferable to have an objective biological marker, or a functional one based on what people can or cannot do. Functional determinations of old age are commonly used in non-Western societies rather than chronological definitions (Holmes 1980). But since these are definitions appropriate only within a given cultural context, the criteria are difficult if not impossible to generalize to other settings. As yet, there is no universal criterion, including chronological age, which identifies major shifts in aging. Indeed, for many purposes it is misleading to select a single age break to identify the elderly population (Griffith 1985). Nevertheless, chronological age still remains the predominantly used criterion.

Several of the contributors to this volume point out the increasing variability that occurs with age (see especially the chapter on biological theories by Peter Mayer). Because of this recognition, and the increasing number and proportion of longevous people, it has become less meaningful to treat everyone sixty-five and over as members of a single cohort. Within this volume, the reader will find different boundaries for delineating stages of old age. Peter Uhlenberg discusses two categories, the young-old, those sixty-five to seventy-four, and the old-old, those over seventy-four. Colleen Johnson refers to the old-old as eighty and older. Andrea Sankar focuses her chapter on the oldest old, those eighty-five and older. And finally, there are those who prefer to construe overlapping age categories, as does David Chiriboga in his discussion of Levinson's "eras" of personality development. Readers are cautioned to recognize this diversity of usage, one that is unavoidable in the present state of the art.

Because of the dissatisfaction with chronological age, there have been attempts to go beyond this unidimensional view of aging. In the chapter on demography, Peter Uhlenberg provides a useful discussion of the definition of old age and suggests some alternatives to using an individual's sixty-fifth birthday as the marker of old age. Others are seeking culturally sensitive techniques for identifying life cycle transitions, such as age status graphing in the work of Christine Fry (1983). There is also an emerging theoretical perspective that attempts to embrace the multifaceted nature of aging. This is the approach that gives conceptual coherence to the material in this volume. The life course perspective is arguably the dominant paradigm in contemporary gerontology. This perspective is introduced in the next section, followed by a critique.

The Life Course Perspective: A Theoretical Framework

Since its emergence around 1970, the life course perspective has had a major impact on the social and behavioral sciences concerned with aging. Although it has roots in psychology that can be traced to the nineteenth century, the most immediate precursors are Havighurst (1948) and Erikson (1963); the seminal contributions of both are discussed in David Chiriboga's chapter on personality. Around 1970, as a result of the work of people in the area of adult development and aging, a new crystallization of these early ideas took place. It included concepts from a number of disciplines, including sociology, demography, history, and anthropology. Not everyone agrees yet on what this perspective should be called. Many use life-span development, which is preferred by some psychologists, whereas others talk of life cycle and life events in referring to very similar notions. But there is agreement on the fundamental point that aging is a complex phenomenon that is multidetermined and cannot be understood within the scope of a single disciplinary approach. The major premises of the life course perspective are summarized by Matilda White Riley:

> (1) Aging is a life-long process of growing up and growing old. It starts with birth (or with conception) and ends with death. Thus no single stage of a person's life (childhood, middle age, old age) can be understood apart from its antecedents and consequences. . . .
>
> (2) Aging consists of three sets of processes—biological, psychological, and social; and these three processes are all systematically interactive with one another over the life course. . . .
>
> (3) The life-course pattern of any particular person (or cohort of persons all born at the same time) is affected by social and environmental change (or history). . . .
>
> (4) New patterns of aging can cause social change. That is, social change not only molds the course of individual lives but, when many persons in the same cohort are affected in similar ways, the change in their collective lives can in turn also produce social change (Riley 1979, 4–5).

The first premise goes beyond the narrow view of conventional developmentalists who saw growth and differentiation restricted essentially to the early stages or were content to focus their attention on only one stage of the life cycle. In the newer formulation, development is seen as a life-long process involving both continuities and discontinuities with prior stages. Sensitivity to the complex relationship that exists between ongoing adaptations and earlier life events or stages is stressed. Brim and Kagan (1980) have characterized how this premise differs from earlier conceptualizations:

> The view of human nature emerging from this work sees a capacity for change across the entire life span and questions the traditional idea that the experiences of the early years . . . constrain the characteristics of adolescence and adulthood. . . . [T]he consequences of the events of early childhood are continually being transformed by later experiences, making the course of human development more open than many have believed (quoted in Schlossberg 1981, 4).

It has been exceedingly difficult to realize an understanding of the life course as a process. Several helpful concepts are those of development, socialization, and adaptation (Clausen 1986). Development involves typical processes of growth of the organism's potentials. The rate of this growth and the circumstances that influence it are clearest during the initial years of life, especially in the biological realm. Once maturity is reached, growth and differentiation have been far less recognized, and the process becomes more difficult to delineate. Because the biological growth model has dominated the thinking about development, understanding of cognitive and social development has been hindered. Baltes (1979) points out that behavior change may not have the same characteristics as biological change, which unfolds in a sequential, unidirectional, and irreversible pattern. Most importantly, recent research has shown that novel processes can emerge at many points along the life cycle, including during old age.

Socialization refers to the ways individuals learn to function in society. It focuses on the demands members of society make on an individual so that behavior, values, and feelings conform to the expectations of the larger society (Featherman 1981). It is a process now considered to extend throughout the life cycle. Finally, adaptation refers to responses to the physical and social environment by modifications in habitual behavior. It expresses the scope of choice available to individuals coping with changing circumstances.

The second premise stated by Riley recognizes the lifelong interaction among the three realms of existence: the biological, the psychological, and the sociocultural. This holistic vision does not mean that human behavior can be factored into so much of one and so much of the other component. Rather, the interaction among the three leads to emergent properties. No one of the components should be thought of as more basic, as some would prefer, since it is not possible to add up the attributes of the various components and give a weight to each. The nature of the system is too complex for such determinations. There is an interpenetration of components that does not allow simply dissolving one from the other. Difficult as this interdependence is to penetrate analytically, it is nevertheless crucial for an appreciation of the life course approach.

Each realm consists of a number of domains of interest. The biological component may focus on any one of several systems, including the musculoskeletal, cardiovascular, endocrine, and central nervous systems. Or a number of physical attributes may be considered, such as strength, height, stamina, and susceptibility to disease. Finding some correspondence between biological aging and chronological age has been fundamental to the study of human development and adaptability (Beall 1984). Biological age can be assessed for each of the several physiological systems mentioned above. Although inherently more difficult, this is also possible for more elusive biological attributes such as temperament, beauty, intelligence, and physical capacities used in games of physical skill. It is in the nature of these latter attributes that psychological and sociocultural components are heavily implicated.

The psychological realm involves the sensory, perceptual, cognitive, and personality systems. Some of the most persuasive and challenging research in the life course has come from life-span developmental studies in psychology, especially in the area of cognitive studies. In this volume Deirdre Kramer's chapter on cognition demonstrates how studies of adults and the elderly are expanding our understanding of the variety of cognitive skills employed through the life course. It is this perspective that is leading to a broader, contextual approach to psychological phenomena that traditionally have been studied within more restricted experimental designs.

Psychologically oriented research has given a great deal of attention to life satisfaction in old age. Two theories offered opposing views in addressing this issue. The first, disengagement theory (Cumming and Henry 1961), sparked heated controversy among gerontologists for a number of years. This theory stated that normal and successful aging involves a mutual withdrawal between the aging person and the rest of society. This allows the aging person to prepare psychologically for the inevitability of death, a process that requires introspection and reflection. At the same time, it allows society to find alternative incumbents for the social positions once actively filled by the aging person, so that when death does occur, the disruption it may cause will be minimized. Both society and the aging individual are winners in this presumably inevitable and universal later life adaptation.

These assumptions were countered by activity theory, which insisted that only through active engagement in social life, however modified by the constraints imposed by one's age, could the elderly find satisfaction and a sense of personal dignity. Although each theory is useful in understanding the circumstances of particular individuals, both suffer from ethnocentric bias. A broader conceptualization is necessary, one that is informed by both cross-cultural and historical analyses (Maddox and Campbell 1985). Despite the saliency of this debate over the past quarter century, it has probably run its course. In the material of this volume, disengagement theory is mentioned rarely and only in passing (see the chapters by David Chiriboga and Linda Cool).

The sociocultural realm concentrates on how societies use age as a basis for organizing and defining people. Because of the prominence of age transitions in many nonindustrial societies, anthropologists were among the first to study the differing cultural conceptualizations of age and life cycle periods (Fry and Keith 1982). Sociologists, however, provided the first theoretical framework for the sociocultural realm with the development of age stratification theory by Matilda White Riley and her associates (see especially Riley, Johnson, and Foner 1972; Riley 1985). In this formulation every society has two structural elements relevant to age:

(1) Age strata. All societies are divided into strata based on groups of people of similar age. The individuals who comprise each stratum, or cohort, have a distinct subculture because of their unique experiences. Exposure to historical events occurred at approximately the same time period in their lives, and this gives them a perspective different from other age cohorts in society. In some cases, a sense of solidarity can develop with other age peers. This may occur because of particular sociopolitical circumstances, as in the 1960s in this country, when a familiar shibboleth was: "Don't trust anyone over thirty!" Or it may be built into the social structure, as in the age-set societies known especially in Africa (discussed by Rhoda Halperin in chapter 13).

Cohorts cannot be thought of as undifferentiated strata. Those who make up the same cohort can experience very different life cycles based on an individual's location in the social structure. Factors that influence this include gender, social class, ethnic group membership, and (in larger societies) geographical region. Each factor can have a different effect on how age is evaluated in terms of the prestige hierarchy of the society.

(2) Age structure of roles. Each society creates a sequence for entering new roles and relinquishing old ones. Most social positions have more or less clearly defined norms regarding the age one assumes a role and at what point one should abandon it. This can be precisely defined, as is the age one becomes a voter, or there may be various degrees of flexibility in defining the norms, such as the appropriate age to marry or to give up wearing certain clothing styles. Despite the openness of some age boundaries, Neugarten and Datan (1973) demonstrate that people have a

very clear notion of age-appropriate behavior, including what constitutes being "late" or "early" in assuming or abandoning a given role.

Elder (1985) discusses two concepts useful in gaining a dynamic view of the social component of the life course: transition and trajectory. Transitions are changes that occur over short time spans and involve specific life events. Getting married, obtaining a divorce, becoming a parent, and changing jobs are good examples of transitions that are significant life events. In chapter 7, David Chiriboga draws upon anthropological and psychological theories in order to relate key life cycle transitions to personality development. Trajectories are longer term changes in which the transitions are embedded. These can be construed as various "careers" that make up a person's life, each having their own trajectory but influenced by the others. For example, work careers and family careers have been studied over the life course. Less attention has been paid, however, to the leisure-time career or what we might call the "convoy career" of an individual. A convoy, or personal network, consists of all the people to whom one gives and from whom one receives support. The size, composition, functions, and other characteristics of a convoy can change radically as one moves through the life course. It is a trajectory that deserves much greater attention (Kahn and Antonucci 1980).

Elder also distinguishes a "subjective career" referring to how a person views his or her own life. To varying degrees people engage in some form of introspective monitoring of themselves as physical and social beings. As part of this evaluation process, considered particularly intense during transition periods in a person's life, commonly accepted (i.e., normative) definitions of age-appropriate behavior play an important role in assessing one's self-concept and self-esteem (Neugarten and Datan 1973). As a result, the life course changes reflect a negotiation process that occurs between the individual and the social context in which the individual is embedded. Thus, Elder (1981) refers to the life course as both contextual and transactional, and Lerner and Busch-Rossnagel (1981) refer to individuals as producers of their own development by the reciprocal relations existing between the active person and the active context. Here we are in an area where the psychological and the sociocultural realms clearly interpenetrate.

In their important paper on the life cycle, Neugarten and Datan (1973) distinguish three dimensions of time: (1) Life time—the chronological age of the individual; this is closely related to biological changes. (2) Social time—the system of age grading and age expectations discussed in the previous paragraphs. (3) Historical time—the succession of social, political, economic and environmental events through which individuals live.

This last dimension of time is of concern in the third and fourth premises of the life course perspective. Every person's life is anchored in the epoch-making events of particular historical periods. Such events as wars, revolutions, economic depressions, and natural disasters impact on people depending on their age and position in society. Momentous social changes can affect the way society structures the life course and provide new definitions of age-appropriate behavior. And at the same time, as cohorts move through the life cycle and are replaced by others with different life experiences, society in turn is changed (Riley 1976).

In conclusion, one may think of the life course as consisting of an immense number of rhythms (Bohannon 1980). Our bodies and our communities create biological, psychological, and cultural rhythms, all of which occur within the context of various environmental rhythms occurring daily, monthly, and seasonally. The cultures studied by anthropologists each have their unique rhythms, yet in any given culture these may change over time. Neugarten and Datan (1973) claim, for example, that data from 1890 to 1966 show that the rhythm of the family cycle in American culture had accelerated as a major life event, as marriage occurred much earlier in life. Bohannon suggests that a certain dysrhythmia can affect social relations between different age cohorts so that their interactions do not mesh well. All too frequently this can also occur when people of different cultures must communicate with one another. Only by studying the life course both historically and cross-culturally can the rhythmic and dysrhythmic within and between societies be understood.

Critique of Theory

In many disciplines concerned with the study of aging, the life course perspective represents an encouraging theoretical development. Much of the promise, however, is still to be realized. For this reason, the term perspective is used rather than life course theory. Generation of testable hypotheses, one of the three purposes of theory discussed by Peter Mayer in the next chapter, has been extremely rare so far. There are a number of reasons for this.

First, most research has not been guided by a methodology adequate to handling process, which is central to the perspective. This is an old problem in the social sciences and is not likely to be easily resolved in the foreseeable future. In the previous section, the more process oriented concepts have been given the most attention, but they are technically difficult to work with. For example, it has been much easier to describe the differences between cohorts in the same society rather than explain the process leading to these differences.

Second, although the holistic approach makes one sensitive to the totality of factors affecting the aging process, it has not been possible to take into account all the possible variables that are relevant. According to Nydegger (1982), not only are there too many variables to consider throughout the life span, but there are no clear guidelines as to how they should be winnowed. Also, there is still a dearth of developmental theory beyond childhood which could help target the more promising variables.

In anthropology a holistic approach has been preferred and often considered a critical element in shaping the distinctive contribution of the field. As a result, cultural anthropologists have been more willing to trade off precision for insightful understanding; for the price paid for working with a broad, multi-deterministic approach is the loss of the methodological rigor made possible when a limited number of variables is isolated for examination. Thus, some gerontologists have expressed concern that the quest for a more holistic interpretation raises the specter of creating a fuzzy conceptual framework too complex and all-embracing for precise empirical inquiry (Rowles and Ohta 1983). It remains to reconcile these two very different research styles in order to fulfill the promise of a life course theory.

Third, the holistic approach is difficult to realize because of the limited expertise of any one researcher. Few can be conversant with the massive literature and diverse techniques within any one realm, let alone across the biological, psychological, and sociocultural ones. Since the characteristic training within disciplines tends to create expertise in increasingly narrower domains, this perspective suggests a rethinking of how scholars can best prepare themselves for life course research. In the meantime, an interdisciplinary team approach provides the best strategy for overcoming these limitations.

Fourth, there are inherent difficulties associated with longitudinal research. In the next section the importance of longitudinal strategies to the life course approach is discussed. Here, we recognize the practical problems such research creates. An obvious limitation is the life span of the researcher who perforce must work within the same spatio-temporal framework as the subjects who ideally would be followed from birth to death. Long-term research designs do not provide for timely payoffs that are a practical necessity for anyone working within modern institutional structures. As a result, compromises are made in the scope and the nature of the strategies employed.

Related to this time dimension is the problem of measuring certain variables over different life stages or sociohistorical situations. Nydegger (1982) has raised some difficult questions regarding the operationalization of variables in longitudinal studies. Does a measure regarding sexual activity have the same meaning in adolescence as in late middle age? Does a measure of life satisfaction mean the same during a depression (or war) as in a period of affluence (or peacetime)? Nydegger suggests several strategies for resolving these and other difficulties with the life course approach. She offers a "mid-ground" solution whereby the extremes are avoided. Thus, a person's life course can best be understood by avoiding the extremes of unidimensional and grand holistic strategies. Variables need to be operationalized somewhere between narrow specificity and unmeasurable openness. Thinking along these lines may lead to solutions for some of the more intractable problems.

Despite all these limitations, the life course perspective does facilitate the posing of relevant questions, encourage certain data analysis techniques, and suggest ways to interpret findings (Abeles and Riley 1976–77). In time, one can expect a more rigorous, holistic model to emerge. We now turn to an examination of some of the methodological challenges presented by this approach.

Methodological Issues

It should be clear from the foregoing discussion that the life course approach requires a data base over extensive time periods. The major methodological concern in gerontology in recent years has been to find ways to isolate the various factors that cause change over the life course (Maddox and Campbell 1985). There are three major factors, or "effects" as they are called, which can explain differences between individuals or in the same individual over time.

(1) Maturational (or age) effect. The differences are due to chronological age. This is essentially the result of biological aging.

(2) Cohort effect. The differences are due to the experiences and circumstances unique to the particular cohort a person belongs to. One of the difficulties in determining the impact of this effect is the lack of agreement on the time depth which defines a cohort. Should only those people born in a single year be included in the same cohort? That sounds a bit too narrow. Or should one take a twenty year span? Some might consider that too broad. There may not be a cohort time span relevant to all research issues, in which case a variable answer is the best one. This issue still needs to be resolved.

(3) Period (or time of measurement) effect. The differences are due to the impact of events (whether social, environmental, or otherwise) at the time the information is obtained from an individual. The difficulty here is specifying which event or combination of events is affecting behavior and to what degree.

Analytically, researchers have attempted to identify and separate each of the three types of effects. But this cannot be done easily because all three effects are logically confounded. That is, any one effect is a function of the other two. For example, cohort membership can only be defined by a person's chronological age and the period of observation. Thus, in order to interpret findings, researchers have assumed that one of the factors has had no effect on the results, justifying this, if at all, by resorting to extraneous information or some theoretical stance (Foner 1986).

There are no easy solutions to these methodological problems. A number of strategies have been suggested to disentangle these time-confounded effects (Nydegger 1981a) and to assign more specific meaning to the cohort and period factors (Schaie 1984). The details of these and other arcane methodological efforts need not concern us here. Eventually, methods may emerge that can account for both the separate and combined effects of all these factors as they interpenetrate in the actual lives of people. Meanwhile, it is important to be familiar with the various kinds of study designs presently employed to make statements about the changes that occur over time.

One can divide the various study designs into two broad categories: cross-sectional and longitudinal. A cross-sectional design compares people of different ages during a single time period. Based on the differences found between the respondents of different age groups, conclusions are drawn regarding changes over the life course. But there is no way to determine if the results are due to maturational or cohort effects. It is also possible that an actual difference due to maturational effects is cancelled or weakened by the cohort effect in the opposite direction. Thus, interpretation of such data is hazardous, as was the case in some of the early studies of intelligence (see Deirdre Kramer's chapter on cognition). Nevertheless, cross-sectional studies have the advantage of being relatively inexpensive and quick to do, and thus the payoff is more easily realized than in longitudinal designs.

Longitudinal studies compare data collected over different time periods. Such data are generally considered superior to cross-sectional data and of particular importance in life course analyses. But they have the disadvantage of being relatively expensive, requiring a long-term commitment with a payoff that demands years of patience. There are several longitudinal designs that must be distinguished:

(1) Panel design is perhaps the most typical. This involves interviewing or testing a sample of the same individuals over several time periods, whether of two, five, or ten year intervals. The results obtained from each individual over each wave of data collection are then compared. If the sample selected includes individuals from the same cohort, then the confound between maturational and cohort effects is not eliminated. Nevertheless, these studies are considered superior because at least the changes occurring in the same individual can be followed. One problem with this design is the test effect; that is, the differences found in an individual's responses at different time intervals may be due to the experience of having had the exposure previously. Given the opportunity to practice,

people can become very sophisticated at responding to questions and taking tests. A further complication of this design is the need to track down everyone in the sample for each subsequent wave; this invariably leads to sample losses that may seriously distort the results. In her chapter on sexuality, Diane Rykken provides a useful discussion of these and other limitations in the samples now available.

(2) Cohort design refers to a sample of respondents from whom data are collected over different time intervals, but they are not the same individuals. For each wave, a different sample is selected from the same cohort. Thus, one can follow the changes occurring in the same cohort over time without the need to track down the same individuals. Because the same individuals are not interviewed or tested, it also eliminates any impact that the test effect might have.

(3) Longitudinal sequence design was developed to overcome some of the limitations of the preceding types. In this design data are collected from the same individuals over several time intervals, but the sample includes respondents from at least two cohorts and there is a minimum of three waves of data collection. The researcher can then employ techniques of data analysis which allow better control over both cohort and maturational effects.

The various methodological issues discussed above are the concern of survey research and studies in which test protocols are used on relatively large samples of people. These techniques provide a large fraction of the data base now available on the elderly. But increasingly there have been calls for research designs that are more holistic and provide contextually sensitive data of greater importance in gaining insight into a number of life course issues. Neugarten (1985) argues that the results of survey data and the preoccupation with clarifying maturational, cohort, and period effects are unlikely to inform us of how particular historical, social, or economic events affect the individual life course. It might be more useful to concentrate on small samples of people and bring into the analysis data from a much broader range of variables.

Essentially, Neugarten is calling for greater use of the ethnographic techniques cultivated by anthropologists. This would allow a closer look at how cultural patterns mold the behavior of particular individuals. The performance of any social role allows for some options and some violations of norms. Contextually sensitive data provides insights into how individuals manipulate these options to their own best advantage, or how they fail to take advantage of opportunities provided by the options. One such ethnographic approach that allows for detailed retrospective data on a person's life course is the life history technique (Frank 1980). The contextual detail inherent in this technique may lead to the uncovering of important principles of behavior. How do people react to specific historical events and life crisis events, such as death and divorce? How do people actively manipulate their environment as they grow old, and what resources do they use to satisfy their needs?

These techniques have their own methodological pitfalls. When data are collected in a variety of observational and informal interview contexts, there tend to be difficulties with validity and reliability. Clausen (1986) points out the retrospective bias that exists in accounts of earlier periods in a person's life. For example, he cites a study which demonstrates that retrospective accounts of a relationship tend to be heavily influenced by the status of the relationship at the time the account is given. Of course, if the goal is to get at a person's subjective understanding of their life course, this may not be a serious problem. The truthfulness or falseness of an account is less important than the patterning of beliefs and the determining of one's conceptualization of past events. However, this kind of analysis requires interpretive skills that are rarely objectified clearly.

Much needs to be done to develop more explicit techniques for qualitative designs. Yet the power of this research approach lies not in attempts to achieve rigorous quantitative proofs, but rather in the marshalling of rich contextual detail to provide support for the interpretations that will give insight into people's lives.

Guide to Chapters

It is neither possible nor helpful to summarize the content of the chapters in a volume of this breadth. More importantly, one should be aware of the logic in terms of which the material is ordered and some of the basic threads running through the material. It would be difficult to separate the chapters along traditional disciplinary boundaries. Such a procedure would have little relevance to the interdisciplinary thrust of the life course perspective. Any one chapter may draw materials from several disciplines. For example, nursing homes have been studied by anthropologists, psychologists, and sociologists (among others), and this is reflected in the material covered by Colleen Johnson in chapter 17. The influence of social class and ethnicity on the elderly have been of concern to both sociologists and anthropologists, as is reflected in the studies covered by Linda Cool in chapter 12. This eclecticism can be found in most of the chapters.

It will be evident in the ordering of the material that each chapter is dominated by one of the three realms of existence, with the sequence moving from the biological, through the psychological, to the sociocultural. The major emphasis in the next three chapters is the biological realm, beginning with a thorough overview of the many competing biological theories of aging by Peter Mayer, then the long-term evolutionary and demographic changes that have occurred in the human life span by Mary

Jane Moore, and finally the determinants of longevity in modern populations by Cynthia Beall.

Chapters 5 through 8 are concerned primarily with the psychological realm, and chapters 9 through 14 with the sociocultural realm. It should be noted, however, that the transition chapters between the different levels reflect most clearly the interpenetration of the various realms. For example, in chapter 4 Cynthia Beall deals with factors in all realms that affect longevity. In chapter 5, Dana Plude is concerned with the biopsychological frame for information processing. Diane Rykken's treatment, in chapter 8, of later life sexuality deals with factors crossing the three realms.

The chapters concentrating on sociocultural matters are introduced by Peter Uhlenberg's overview in chapter 9 of the demographic transition that has so dramatically altered the structure of modern populations. Most of the material in the chapters on family life, community settings, and social class and ethnicity deal with research on U.S. society with some cross-cultural references. Chapters 13 and 14 bring to gerontology the broad perspective of anthropological studies with a consideration of an evolutionary and a comparative view of the elderly, and thus complete the section concerned with the sociocultural realm.

The final four chapters deal with some of the serious problems facing people in old age. In chapter 15, Andrea Sankar focuses on the fastest growing segment of the elderly, those eighty-five and older. The chapter presents a unique situation in human history, with large numbers of people still alive who are freighted with the most pejorative evaluations by the rest of society. In chapter 16, J. Neil Henderson focuses on what has been called the disease of the twenty-first century, Alzheimer's disease, and the "biopsychosocial" environment which affects the course of this severe form of dementia. In chapter 17, Colleen Johnson characterizes the situation of those elderly no longer residing in communities, those who have been forced or have chosen to live in the controlled environment of an institution. Most of these elderly will spend their last days in a nursing home, geriatric hospital, or similar institutional setting. With inexorable logic the volume concludes with an overview of the final stage of life, death and dying.

Aside from the fact that all the contributors seek to provide a life course perspective, there are several thematic threads that run through the material. The need for contextural data in understanding the life course is apparent from the discussion in the chapters on cognition, family life, and community settings. Only such data can yield information on the distinctive capacities and social strategies used by individuals in later life. A second, related theme is the emphasis several contributors give to evocative but often methodologically elusive concepts. Andrea Sankar organizes her material around the notion of the cultural construction of aging; Colleen Johnson shows how basic American values color our views of the dependency situation in which many old people find themselves; and Linda Cool finds the role of ethnicity can be understood with reference to concepts like worldview, belief systems, and, again, values.

A third theme running through the volume is the importance of group solidarity in providing elderly people with more secure living contexts. The terminology may differ here, but the group behavior being characterized is very similar. Linda Cool's explanation of ethnicity as a possible source of support is similar to Rhoda Halperin's use of organic solidarity to account for the contributions of the old in preindustrial societies. Similar concepts include the creation of a distinct "we-feeling" among the elderly in certain kinds of community settings, as discussed in chapter 11, and social rigidity as an aspect of community life, as discussed in chapter 14. Finally, certain issues cause sufficient concern that they are raised in several contexts. For example, concern over the availability of sexual partners for older women is expressed in the chapters on sexuality, demography, and family life.

From the earliest development of gerontology the accumulation of knowledge through research has developed alongside an abiding commitment to improve the quality of life for all old people. In more recent years, theoretical and methodological issues have become more prevalent in gerontology than social problem issues. Nevertheless, program and policy issues occupy a prominent place in the literature. A number of chapters deal with the policy implications of the findings, most especially the last four chapters. Although political implications are not dealt with in any detail, Peter Uhlenberg does include a useful discussion of elderly political power and potential generational conflict.

A person who has spent her later years dedicated to changing policy toward the elderly in this country is the convener of the Gray Panthers, Maggie Kuhn. Her work for a senior organization represents an emerging role, possibly one that could take on increasing importance in a rapidly aging society. As an example of a modern pioneer who provides a role model for many people, both old and young, this impressive woman captures the spirit of an expansive old age:

> This is indeed a New Age—an age of liberation and self-determination. I'm glad to have reached seniority at this time. I feel free to speak out and act in ways that I was not able to when I was younger.—Maggie Kuhn (quoted in Dychtwald 1981, 256)

II

BIOLOGICAL THEORIES OF AGING

Peter J. Mayer

It has been said that there are as many biological theories of aging as there are biogerontologists. While this is an exaggeration, the statement does partly reflect the truth of the matter. That there have been numerous theories proposed to explain biological aging is a function of both the nature of aging and the state of biological gerontology.

For one thing, biological aging refers to a large number of processes, any one of which can be investigated and about which theories can be formulated. For another thing, these processes are complex, and they occur at many different levels of biological organization, from the molecular and cellular up to the whole animal (see Table 2.1). (In this chapter we restrict our consideration to animals, especially higher animals, and focus most of our attention on mammals, including, of course, human beings.) Thus, the aging processes one chooses to study (e.g., biochemical, genetic, physiological) will in large part determine the level of theoretical explanation. Furthermore, since the processes within each level are complex, many causal and contributing factors will be isolated and identified. These factors, either independently or in concert, can then be generalized in order to formulate a theory of aging.

That there are many biological theories of aging is not solely due to the complexity of aging processes. To a lesser extent it is also due to the relative "immaturity" of the field. For example, the Gerontological Society of America was founded as recently as 1945. Moreover, unlike the case of developmental biology, which can serve as an appropriate comparison, there has not been a modern institutional recognition of the field, nor have we seen a proliferation of specialized researchers. The fact that the National Institute on Aging, which is the major source of research support in the biology of aging, was established only a decade ago (in 1974) serves to reinforce the point.

Yet it would be a mistake to think that scientific study of the biology of

TABLE 2.1. **Levels of Biological Organization**

Species
Strain
Population
Individual (whole animal)
Physiological System
Organ
Tissue
Extracellular Matrix
Cell
Organelle (e.g., nucleus)
Macromolecule (e.g., DNA, protein)
Molecule (e.g., nucleotide, amino acid)

aging began after the Second World War. For example, "wear and tear" theories can be traced back to Weissman (1882), the rate of living theory to Rubner (1908), developmental theories to Baer (1864), theories based on growth to Minot (1908), and genetic theories of inherited longevity to Beeton and Pearson (1900). All of these references are listed in Comfort (1979), where a more detailed and thorough survey of the history of biological theories of aging can be found.

What follows is as much a guide to ways of thinking about biological theories of aging as it is a brief survey of the more significant of those theories.

What Is Biological Aging?

As mentioned above, aging refers to many biological processes that occur simultaneously in a living organism, albeit at different rates and with differing consequences. While aging is an extraordinarily general term, a viable definition of aging must be able to differentiate two related and more specific sets of processes, namely, senescence and disease (especially age-associated disease such as osteoporosis, cataracts, and diabetes). With this in mind, those processes that are universal, irreversible, cumulative, sequential, and progressive constitute aging. Let us consider each of these qualities in turn.

To say that aging is universal is really to make a statement about the biological attributes of an entire species of multi-cellular animals (and plants)—including, of course, *Homo sapiens*. On a simple level we observe that animals exhibit different maximum life spans in zoos (essentially our only source of such data), and from this fact we infer that they age at different rates. On a more complex level, there are good evolutionary reasons why this may be so. All species of animals have discrete ecological niches, usually accompanied by geographical boundaries, which limit their distribution in the natural world. Adaptation to a niche involves internal physiological adjustments to climate, food, altitude, and so forth, as well as temporal adjustments such as the timing of mate selection, reproduction, and weaning. Seasonality, competition (from other species as well as from members of the same species), temperature, humidity, terrain, and a host of other external factors also determine the range of a species' "lifestyle" or adaptation.

In general, it can be argued that rates of aging in different species are strongly linked to their adaptation to specific ecological niches. For example, polar bears live in a barren environment (the Arctic) where they must hunt to survive and reproduce; successful hunters are not only big and fast, but must also have learned where to find prey and how to track, stalk, and kill "potential meals" once they are found. This learning takes practice and experience, and so the age at which a bear cub is weaned (approximately four months), the age at which it reaches sexual maturity (two to four years), and its maximum life span (about thirty-five years) all reflect, in part, the time necessary to acquire successful hunting skills.

In contrast, the maximum life span of a hamster is approximately four years. In order to survive and reproduce it must learn how to avoid becoming a predator's meal. Its own food requirements are met relatively easily by foraging in a local environment abundant in a variety of edible grasses, shoots, nuts, seeds, and berries. Thus, a hamster needs first of all to be fast (in order to escape potential predators)—success is less dependent on learning than on innate speed and quick reflexes. Hamsters are weaned and become sexually mature adults at a relatively early age (approximately two months). To the extent that aging begins at adulthood (see below), then hamsters age relatively more rapidly (in less than four years) than polar bears (during more than thirty years). To put it another way, polar bears live nearly ten times longer than hamsters because they age more slowly. Both of these traits (maximum longevity and rate of aging) can be related, at least in theory, to the adaptations of a species.

The rates of aging and the maximum life spans of hamsters and polar bears are characteristic for each species, and reflect their different evolutionary histories in terms of adaptation to specific ecological niches. (This is not to say that we have in any way explained *how* the differences arise; we have merely illustrated in an oversimplified manner the observation that among mammals, larger body size and brain weight are closely related to longer life span.) It is in this sense that aging can be said to be universal among members of a species, in much the same way that short tails and cheek pouches are universal among hamsters or that a white coat of fur is universal among polar bears.

For *Homo sapiens*, which has come to inhabit nearly the entire land mass of the earth, we consider adaptation through culture to be a universal and primary characteristic. This of course distinguishes us from all other living animals. Yet because adaptation through culture has its own long evolutionary history, which is intimately related to changes in biology, we recognize that human biological characteristics such as rate of aging and maximum longevity can be studied in much the same way that aging among hamsters (or any other rodent) is studied. The fact that human beings have come to occupy a wide range of geographic areas does not negate our identity as one species. Indeed, what it does is to demonstrate the great variability of our cultures and attest to the biological diversity of one species. Looked at in another way, the geographic distribution and cultural diversity of *Homo sapiens* provide a world-wide laboratory of successful "experiments" in adaptation. This variability provides the best evidence to ascertain what is truly species-specific (universal) in human aging, as opposed to what is merely local, regional, or specific to one culture.

The universal nature of biological aging helps to distinguish it from disease, especially age-associated disease processes. For example, if all members of a species that attain a certain age undergo a decrease in reaction time when presented with a well-defined stimulus, then that behavioral change could be considered a consequence of biological aging. If, however, only a subset of the species demonstrate such a decline, and others demonstrate no change with age, then the behavioral decrease is not a parameter of aging. Most likely the decline is due to some local condition such as a nutritional deficiency, an environmental toxin, or a specific disease. One widespread finding in aging research, which is almost axiomatic, is that among individual organisms there is increased variability with increasing age. This general result strongly suggests that regular aging processes can be positive or negative, since in becoming more variable some individuals may gain while others lose.

The tragic suffering caused by Senile Dementia of the Alzheimer Type (SDAT), a growing problem among highly industrialized societies, provides an excellent case in point. On the one hand, senility used to be considered a nearly inevitable consequence of aging (as the name suggests), whereas current data indicate that approximately 1 in 25 of those aged sixty-five or older are afflicted with SDAT (see chapter 16 for more details). Moreover, the memory loss, confusion, and disorientation associated with the disease, the loss of mental faculties properly embodied in the term senility, do not afflict all old people. In fact, many mental processes show no decline with age, and some abilities may even improve with adult age (see chapters 5 and 6). Finally, and this is the focus of much current research, it is quite possible that many of the effects of SDAT can be counteracted, if not reversed (see chapter 16). This characteristic, reversibility, is a second major distinction between aging processes and those of disease.

Aging processes and changes are irreversible, whereas pathological processes can be ameliorated, at least in theory. The rate of aging processes can be accelerated, for example by radiation, or decelerated, for example by dietary restriction (see below). However, rejuvenation has yet to be scientifically documented: there is no cure for aging. What may be required is a change in perception: clinicians or researchers may need to redefine changes assumed to be inevitable consequences of aging—to redefine these changes as disease, which is amenable to therapeutic intervention. Osteoporosis among postmenopausal women may provide another good example of a presumptive aging change that, upon investigation, turns out to be a medical condition subject to treatment. Immune system decline, which regularly accompanies aging may, in part, be an indirect consequence of malnutrition or other factors rather than an inevitable result of growing old.

We can consider the remaining three qualities more briefly. Biological aging changes are sequential, cumulative, and progressive; that is, later events depend on earlier changes, effects accumulate over time, and individuals (of the same species) progress through a regular, predictable order of changes. In fact, one of the goals of gerontology is to document these changes in such a way that patterns emerge and, ultimately, mechanisms of action are understood. Aging is also progressive in that it represents a series of processes that are continuous and connected, and that advance the organism closer to death.

This last criterion of aging shades into the realm of senescence, which refers to that subset of aging processes that are deleterious to the organism. Senescence comprises those processes and changes that link aging to mortality. Some definitions of biological aging focus on the increased likelihood of death with advancing age. In fact, evolutionary theory demonstrates that senescence is inevitable among populations subject to natural selection that exhibit variability in age-specific rates of birth and death. Yet to equate aging with senescence is to decide a priori that all changes and processes associated with increased age are deleterious, and this is clearly not the case. It eliminates many biological processes that maintain a plateau in level of functioning and dictates an unduly pessimistic view of gerontology. It may stem, in part, from the influence of geriatric medicine, which is quite rightly concerned with deterioration and debility in old age, and which has not yet fully established the viewpoint of preventive practice.

It is important to emphasize that animals can age without undergoing senescence. On the one hand, the developmental or life cycle approach to gerontology suggests that aging ultimately begins at conception, whereas no one would sensibly argue that senescence does. On the other hand, some components of cellular or physiological systems might undergo "senescence," while other components compensate for the decline such that there is no overall loss of function with age. At the cellular level, for example, there may be a decrease with age in the number of receptor binding sites that is compensated by an increased sensitivity of the remaining sites. At the physiological level, complex compensatory interactions are reported to maintain an adequate level of cardiac output in active community-living adults free from coronary heart disease. In fact there are two components of senescence to consider, age of onset and rate of decline.

The age of onset of senescence is highly variable, both among members of the same species and for different physiological systems within each organism. For example, in human beings substantial loss of hearing for low frequencies may not begin until the seventh, eighth, or ninth decade, whereas for higher frequencies acuity starts to decline steeply in the third or fourth decade. (See chapter 5 for more examples.) The rate of senescence may also vary among members of the same species, especially when the aging changes under study are strongly influenced by environmental and behavioral factors. Few biological theories of aging discuss in detail age of onset (of either aging or senescence) or treat the question of rate. This is due to the great variability inherent in these two components and to the relative lack of knowledge in biological gerontology.

A number of terms that have been used throughout this introductory section require specific definitions. As we have emphasized, aging refers to processes and changes—to dynamic phenomena which are measurable in theory if not always in practice—while longevity and life span refer to static numbers. Although often used interchangeably, longevity and life span can be defined so that each refers to a different concept. Longevity refers to length of life of one or a few individual organisms; it is often used in the phrase maximum longevity or maximum achievable longevity, where it refers to the highest recorded age at death, usually of animals in captivity or under laboratory conditions (see chapters 3 and 4). Life span, in contrast, connotes a more generic attribute of a population (e.g., mean life span of dietarily restricted rats), and often measures the average response or characteristic of a group (as opposed to the extreme of maximum longevity seen in one or a few group members). Life span is conceptually related to average life expectancy and other demographic indicators of aging; it is a quantity well-known for numerous populations of *Homo sapiens* (see chapter 3) but rarely collected for populations of animals under natural conditions. Because it is derived from a large number of individual organisms, life span is a more legitimate indicator of rates of aging when comparing different populations or species; but because maximum longevity is much easier to ascertain, it is used more widely. However, it is also more suspect. For example, the documented maximum longevity of a species could reflect the age at death of only one or a few individual animals that happened to live an extraordinarily long time. By definition, then, such exceptional organisms are not representative, although they may warrant study for other reasons.

Longevity and life span are the "endpoints," if you will, but they do not necessarily reflect the underlying processes and consequences of aging. On the one hand, there are certainly a host of aging changes that do not affect longevity (e.g., graying of hair, wrinkling of skin, decrease in stature, reduced sleeping time, decrease in acuity of taste and smell). On the other hand, life span is determined by the interaction of genetic and environmental influences, so that accidents and natural catastrophes, which can strike at any age, reduce longevity and yet clearly do not constitute biological aging. Thus a very important but often overlooked point is that, paradoxically, death does not necessarily indicate the finality of aging; death is often a nonspecific event that, in fact, "interrupts" ongoing aging processes. That death certificates (for *Homo sapiens*) are notoriously inaccurate, and that, clinically speaking, people rarely die of "old age," support the argument.

What Is a Biological Theory?

A useful biological theory serves at least three purposes: (1) it organizes and integrates a set of scientific observations; (2) it abstracts a few concepts and general principles from many observations; and (3) it generates testable hypotheses or predictions. Theories are usually formulated inductively, that is, derived from a series of established facts and repeated observations. The observation, cited above, that among a wide range of mammals there is a very strong correlation between increased brain and body size and increased species' longevity, taken together with more basic information about neurology and physiology, might lead to a theory that relates metabolic rate and homeostatic control to aging rate. One prediction of the theory, as applied only to mammals, is that for two species of approximately equal body weight (e.g., the genet, a small cat-like carnivore, and the capuchin monkey), the species with the larger average brain size (genet = 16 grams, monkey = 70 grams) will exhibit a greater maximum longevity (genet = eighteen years, monkey = forty-six years). (See chapter 3 for more examples.)

A more complicated and potentially interesting approach would be to try to determine *how* differences in body weight or brain weight affect life span, by manipulating one or the other parameter and seeing if this affects longevity. A simple test of this sort might involve a colony of laboratory rodents divided into two groups, one fed a normal diet and one restricted in the amount of calories consumed (so that the mean body weight of the second group came to be significantly lower than that of the first group). When this type of experiment is performed, the dietarily restricted group consistently outlives the group fed a normal diet. This result is contrary to the theory's prediction—namely, that higher body weight is related to increased longevity—and leads to a number of possible conclusions: (1) the original theory is wrong and should be abandoned (but what about the valid observation that increased brain size and body weight is associated with increased species' longevity?); (2) the test was not valid because members of the same and not different species were compared (true: even though dietary restriction increases longevity in a number of species, the test was not a critical one); or (3) the theory needs to be refined in order to account for the new observations.

The most productive conclusion is to develop a model of the effects of metabolic or homeostatic parameters on aging and longevity. A model in this case would refer to a detailed understanding of the baseline character-istics of nonexperimental rodents (not dietarily restricted) and to a cata-logue of those metabolic or homeostatic factors (e.g., caloric versus protein restriction, hormone levels, enzyme levels and activities, effects of ex-ercise, and genetic background) known to influence or not to influence life span in dietarily restricted animals. The value of the model—a well-defined experimental system relevant to a theory or set of theories—lies both in testing predictions from theory and in exploring additional parameters of possible relevance to the theory.

The choice of models in biological aging research depends upon practical matters as well as on scientific interest and reasoning. If one is ultimately interested in human aging, three types of experimental models are avail-able. The first is laboratory animals such as rodents. Laboratory rodents are, of course, a hallmark of experimental biology, in part because they are relatively easy to maintain in large numbers yet possess many biological features common to all higher mammals (including *Homo sapiens*). Higher nonhuman primates (monkeys and apes) offer the indisputable advantage of being our evolutionarily and genetically closest living relatives; so stud-ies involving them are of the most immediate biological relevance and significance. Yet this benefit is balanced by the high costs of maintenance, the endangered status of many species, and the long life span (e.g., the great apes, orangutan, chimpanzee, and gorilla, can live forty-five to fifty-five years in captivity, thereby probably exceeding the productive period in any gerontologist's research career), not to mention ethical concerns.

A second set of models appeals to researchers at the other end of the scale of biology, namely, cellular models of aging. Skin cells (fibroblasts) from a number of mammals, including *Homo sapiens*, undergo only a limited number of cell divisions (mitoses) when they are cultured under laboratory conditions. Populations of these human cells—obtained from skin biopsies and maintained in glass dishes (hence the term *in vitro* model)—will double in size every few days until they have achieved about fifty to seventy doublings, at which point they cease proliferating and eventually die. Human fibroblasts obtained from older donors tend to attain fewer total population doublings than fibroblasts from younger donors. More remarkable, perhaps, is the additional observation that when human fibroblasts that have been frozen in liquid nitrogen (at −70°C) for years are thawed and cultured again *in vitro,* they "remember" how many population doublings they have "used up," so that their total is still about fifty to seventy doublings. Basically these three observations— finite proliferative capacity, inverse correlation between donor age and proliferative potential, and consistent number of total population dou- blings—constitute the fundamental evidence that supports the *in vitro* model of aging.

A third model of aging, and one that spans all levels of biological investigation, involves so-called "experiments of nature." By this term is meant genetic "accidents" or events such as mutations and chromosomal aberrations that happen rarely and cause marked abnormalities in human beings. A subset of these genetic abnormalities (approximately 7%) com- prise syndromes of premature or accelerated aging, which manifest some of the following characteristics relevant to the pathobiology of aging: de- mentia, premature graying or loss of hair, diabetes mellitus, autoimmuni- ty, hypertension, osteoporosis, cataracts, degenerative vascular disease. Interestingly enough, the one genetic abnormality that expresses the great- est number of features of these "segmental progeroid syndromes" is tri- somy 21 or Down's Syndrome, a condition commonly associated with developmental abnormalities. (Other syndromes referred to include Hutchinson-Guilford progeria, Werner's syndrome, and ataxia telangiecta- sia.) Moreover, analysis of these genetic abnormalities leads to the conclu- sion that perhaps as many as seventy genes (out of approximately one hundred thousand in *Homo sapiens*) have major effects on the biology of human aging.

Genetic syndromes of premature or accelerated aging provide models of complex processes that occur in less exaggerated form, or at an older age, in normal populations. Perhaps the clearest example is progeria (Hutch- inson-Guilford syndrome) in which growth is stunted, baldness appears, skin is thin and wrinkled, and other changes in appearance occur to such an extent that teenagers suffering from progeria look strikingly like little old men or women. They die by age twenty or so, usually from heart disease or atherosclerosis. Moreover, in support of the cellular model of aging, fibroblasts from progeria patients (as well as from other accelerated aging syndromes) have a significantly reduced "life span" in culture. The reasons for the loss of proliferative potential *in vitro* are unknown. Never- theless, because it is known that these premature aging syndromes occur in association with genetic defects, analysis at many levels of biological organization is possible. Thus, these models can provide evidence for a wide range of researchers to use in formulating and testing biological theories of aging.

In thinking about scientific theories it is important to recognize the logical context of a theory. That is to say, research can *disprove* a theory with one or a few unambiguous, contradictory results, but it is much more difficult to actually prove that a theory is correct. What usually happens is that sufficient evidence in support of a theory is accumulated over time such that it comes to be accepted. It continues to be accepted until either its assumptions are proved to be wrong (often by new methodological approaches) or it is replaced by a more inclusive theory.

How Do Organisms Age Biologically?

As we have stressed throughout this chapter, aging processes occur simultaneously at all levels of biological organization. This complexity is both an obstacle and a challenge to gerontologists because it means that ultimately any one set of results, no matter how conclusive, will supply only one piece of the puzzle. It also means that theories have been formulated (and tested) at different levels of organization using different experimental approaches and model systems. Theories that come closest to the truth encompass the largest number of facts and observations, without ignoring any major or consistent contradictory data. Below we summarize the most enduring and significant of these theories (significant in terms of stimulating productive research—after all, most good research raises more questions than it answers), from the genetic to the organismal. Following this research-oriented approach we will consider conceptual categories (e.g., developmental, evolutionary) which cut across levels of biological organization to reveal a few general themes common to many of the theories.

Genetic Level Theories

A few scientific studies, as well as much anecdotal information, demonstrate that human longevity runs in families. (The inheritance of species-specific life spans, mentioned above and discussed further below, also requires the existence of longevity-influencing genes.) Investigations of monozygotic twins (clones from the same fertilized egg) confirm that human life span is inherited (also see chapter 3). All the evidence taken together indicates that perhaps 10–15% of variation in age at death is genetically determined in *Homo sapiens*, leading to the common advice that wisely choosing one's grandparents is a good start to a long life. But the actual mechanisms involved have yet to be elucidated. A number of theories have arisen to explain how changes in DNA could lead to differential rates of aging.

Program Theories

The simplest genetic theory of aging postulates that the program that directs embryogenesis, growth, and development eventually runs out of information, with the result that the organism dies. This nonspecific idea invokes no mechanism and implies that survival into and beyond adulthood requires some additional message or instructions. In fact, such is not the case because adult organisms survive and reproduce quite adequately. Moreover, it implies that longer-lived species have more genetic information than shorter-lived species (which is certainly not true) and that polyploid organisms (e.g., plants with 4N, 8N, etc., genomes) outlive diploid members of the same species (also contrary to observation). (Genome refers to all of the genetic material in each cell of an organism, comprised of DNA and organized into chromosomes in higher organisms.)

The converse of this theory has also been postulated, namely, that gene redundancy (repeated DNA sequences) protects against loss or mutation of genetic information and thus reduces the rate of aging. The available evidence comparing species longevity and redundant DNA does not support the theory, although gene amplification (an epigenetic process) has not been ruled out.

The most straightforward "theory" of programmed aging is based on the argument that aging is merely a continuation of the genetic processes of embryogenesis, growth, and development. The idea that "in our beginning is our ending" is intuitively appealing, aesthetically pleasing (symmetrical, life coming full circle, one turn of the mandala, alpha = omega, etc.), and without assumptions: it denies the "artificial" distinction between aging and that which precedes aging (i.e., pre-aging? living? growing? developing? younging?—there is no term in English to denote the time in an organism's life cycle when it is not aging).

More empirical grounds for the developmental view of aging can be found in comparisons of evolutionarily close species that nevertheless differ substantially in life span. The best examples are two mouse species (*Mus musculus* and *Peromyscus leucopus* with a life span difference of 250%) and two species of higher primates (*Pan troglodytes* and *Homo sapiens* with a life span difference of 220%). In the latter case DNA hybridization studies indicate that chimpanzees and human beings have greater than 99% genetic similarity. This observation, plus morphological, anatomical, and developmental homologies, suggest that regulatory genes account for differences between the two species. The inference to aging, then, is that similar regulatory processes and similar developmental events also account for the twofold difference in life span. Such processes and events have been detailed conceptually, but the genes and actual mechanisms have yet to be demonstrated.

Three related theories of aging, which also lack empirical mechanisms or experimental verification in mammals, have been developed from evolutionary theory: early-acting beneficial genes, delay in action of detrimental genes, and pleiotropic genes. Natural selection could act to favor genes that improve survival early in the life span over genes that improve survival later in the life span. Conversely, natural selection could act to prevent genes with detrimental effects from having an effect until late in the life span. The result in either scenario is to increase survival at younger ages and decrease survival at older ages. The difference between the two is that the first assumes that senescence is due to the absence of beneficial genes, whereas the second assumes that senescence is due to the presence of deleterious genes. While this is ultimately an empirical question, and both sorts of genes may exist, it also reveals one's philosophical bias: is the cup half empty (i.e., senescence means a decrease in positive factors) or is the cup half full (i.e., senescence means an increase in negative factors)?

Pleiotropic genes produce a wide range of phenotypic effects, some of which may be distant in time as well as space. (Phenotype refers to the observable properties of an organism, developed through the interaction of genotype and environment. It is contrasted with genotype, the genetic constitution of an organism.) Thus, selection may act such that genes with both advantageous and disadvantageous effects will produce the beneficial products earlier in the life span and the deleterious products later in life. The consequence of this evolutionary process would be to delay the deleterious effects of any pleiotropic genes until late in life, at which point they are defined as senescence. In other words, vigor gained in youth is at the expense of vigor lost later in life. Such genes have not yet been identified in mammals, although there is some evidence for their existence in fruit flies.

Somatic Mutation

The somatic mutation theory of aging postulates that changes in the genetic information of nongerminal cells (i.e., all cells not involved in the production of spermatozoa and ova) lead to the death of cells, and subsequently to dysfunction of tissues and organs. Based initially on observations that sublethal doses of radiation lead to life-shortening in experimental animals, it was later established that even in the absence of radiation there is an age-related accumulation of chromosomal abnormalities that presumably lead to cell dysfunction or death. (For the purposes of this discussion, a chromosomal aberration such as a deletion, insertion, translocation, duplication, or loss can be considered a "macromutation.")

Closely related to the somatic mutation theory is the "hit" theory of aging which proposes that genetic information is lost, and the cell thus becomes ineffective, when both alleles of a gene (one on each chromosome) undergo damage or receive a "hit" (e.g., from background radiation sources). Since cells can inherit a "fault" in one allele, each gene does not have to be "hit" twice. Once a critical fraction of cells has been rendered dysfunctional by "hits," the animal dies. The theory is essentially a mathematical analysis of survival curves (see chapter 3) and suggests no real mechanism. Like the somatic mutation theory, the "hit" theory proposes that random loss of genetic information throughout the body could cause the organism to become a mosaic of cells, each with a different set of genetic instructions. Much experimental evidence has been collected, and it does not support the theory, although subtle, as yet undetected, changes ("hits" or mutations) may occur.

Both theories are static in that they assume that a gene or chromosome has either been "hit" (mutated) or not, and that once damaged, a cell's status does not change. The fact that some cells in the body actively proliferate (e.g., skin, blood, liver, gut) while others never divide (e.g., nerve cells, cardiac muscle cells and skeletal muscle cells, cells of the eye lens, cells of artery and vein walls) presents a difficulty for both theories. Moreover, evidence accumulated since the theories were first proposed indicates that in fact the situation is quite fluid and dynamic because cells can repair damage induced in DNA.

DNA Damage and Repair

The fact that cells can repair damage to their DNA—both chemical damage and radiation damage—does not disprove the somatic mutation or the "hit" theory of aging. Rather, it helps to elaborate possible mechanisms cells may have evolved to deal effectively with the damage predicted by theory. Yet it also makes it very difficult to test those theories, since it introduces a whole new level of control and influence; mutations or "hits" could in fact lead to cell dysfunction or death, but it might be due to misrepair rather than to the original damage.

DNA repair systems, of which at least four are known to be active in mammalian cells, could act to modulate either the extent, location, or timing of DNA damage, and could do so differently in different cell types. Both germinal and somatic cells, as well as dividing and nondividing types, are capable of DNA repair. If chemical or physical damage of DNA could be shown to be repaired less completely or accurately as organisms age, thereby causing differential rates of cell dysfunction or death, then interindividual and interspecies differences in life span could be partially explained. Rates of aging, according to this idea, would depend in part on levels, activity, and fidelity of DNA repair enzymes. This is currently a promising but complicated area of research, in part because four biochemical processes are involved in repair: recognition of the damage, its removal, insertion of the correct genetic information, and resealing of the reconstituted DNA molecular strands. Evidence regarding change in DNA repair capacity with *in vitro* aging is contradictory, although it appears that there probably is no decline. Evidence regarding *in vivo* aging is even more complicated because it involves differences in type of damage, type of repair, tissue and organ as well as strain or species.

Longevity Determinant Genes

Based on the fact that species have characteristic longevities, it has been proposed that there exists a relatively small set of genes that determine the biological potential for longevity. (Based on a number of assumptions and limited data, the size of this set of genes was estimated at 0.6% of all genes in hominids.) Among mammals these genes code for enzymes involved in a number of mechanisms postulated to affect aging and longevity: DNA repair, superoxide dismutase (a free radical scavenger [see below]), detoxification processes (which render potentially lethal toxins, including precarcinogens, harmless), uric and ascorbic acid (antioxidants which, for example, keep fats from becoming damaged or going rancid), heavy metal chelating agents (which safely remove potentially harmful metals from the body), and others. These genes are called structural because they code for enzymes that are regularly involved in cellular metabolism.

Other genes are called regulatory because they regulate the expression of structural genes. These regulatory genes could account for species differences in aging rate and longevity by controlling the timing of expression of the structural genes that directly determine the potential for longevity. Thus, there are two proposed levels of a collection of longevity determinant genes: the higher level controls the operation of the lower level; the lower level, in turn, operates to counteract two types of "biosenescent" processes, one that is intermittently acting and developmentally linked, and one that is continuously acting and metabolically linked. These two types of "biosenescent" processes act to increase the likelihood that a cell will become "dysdifferentiated," that is, nonfunctional.

The notion of longevity determinant genes is not a theory so much as it is an attempt to organize and subsume a number of other, more detailed theories. It encompasses a wealth of data and generates myriad predictions about species differences in "antibiosenescent" properties. The emphasis on the timing and degree of expression of specific genes is important because it allows specific hypotheses to be tested. Yet perhaps because it attempts to be so inclusive, it is more of a comprehensive collection of potential pleiotropic gene mechanisms than an independent theory of aging.

Cellular Level Theories

Genes, encoded in DNA molecules, determine the identity of cells (cell differentiation), direct their functional activity (cell metabolism), and reproduce themselves (cell proliferation). DNA is directly transcribed into RNA, RNA translates the genetic information into enzymes and other proteins, and these molecules, in turn, produce or direct the biochemistry of the cell. There are, of course, many complex feedback mechanisms and interactions operating among all of these types of molecules. One can say that ultimately DNA is responsible for the life of all cells, and in this sense the genetics of aging determines the biology of aging. Heredity is not destiny, however (at least not 85–90% of destiny, as shown above), because DNA exists in a complex cellular environment, because in multi-celled organisms cells act in a coordinated fashion as tissues and organs, and because the entire organism regulates the functions of its constituent parts. Thus we must consider biochemical and other intracellular processes that have been invoked in biological theories of aging.

Wear and Tear

One of the oldest and most enduring theories locates the cause of aging in the mechanical processes of living itself. This idea, in various guises, blames loss of function and death on the wearing out of irreplaceable parts. The cell is seen as a highly complex, exquisitely ordered piece of machinery, much like a finely tuned automobile. It is not perfect or built to last forever (and who would want to be cursed with immortality, anyway?). The goal of experiment is to identify those parts (organelles) which give out first. Some organisms live longer than others of the same species because, like automobiles of the same make, model, and year, they were driven more slowly, maintained more carefully, or protected more assiduously.

There are a number of problems with this theory. One is that it proposes no mechanisms, no testable hypotheses, other than the biochemistry of living itself—so that one ends up saying that organisms wear out (age and die) because they live too long! A second is that it does not differentiate between dividing cells, which are continuously renewed, and nondividing cells, which are not. If aging is caused by the former, then it must involve DNA (since that is essentially the only continuity within a cell lineage), and we should seek the answer at the genetic level. If aging is caused by the latter, then our investigation is limited to the central nervous system (CNS), the heart, the skeletal muscle system, and the eye (some of which are discussed below). Finally, the theory ignores the fact that cells can repair damage caused by wear and tear, so that one's focus must shift from the model of a static, mechanical machine to a dynamic information and energy transfer system.

Error Cascade

Cells are not flawless in their myriad operations, and as a consequence errors occur. Despite elaborate DNA repair systems briefly outlined above, some of these errors will remain undetected or uncorrected. At the level of DNA, such an error could lead to a mutation; at the level of RNA, errors can lead to a mistranslation of the genetic code such that an incorrect amino acid molecule is added to a growing protein chain; at the level of protein synthesis, an error could lead to a faulty enzyme. By itself a faulty enzyme (or pool of identical faulty enzymes) might not be critical to the cell's continued functioning inasmuch as the reaction(s) in which the enzyme is involved might merely be slowed down, or there may exist alternative metabolic pathways. Furthermore, both RNA molecules and proteins (including enzymes) are continuously being degraded and re-synthesized so that, unlike DNA, the consequences of an error may be only temporary. However if they are not temporary but persist, these errors could, in theory, be the cause of cell aging and death.

A more mechanistic theory of aging elaborates the possible con-sequences of accumulated errors beyond the level of DNA. The central idea of this theory—that imperfection of the cell's synthesizing apparatus will accelerate functional decline in a time-dependent manner—is simple, straightforward, and intriguing. If a faulty enzyme is part of the molecular complex (RNA plus proteins) that functions to synthesize other proteins and enzymes, then a relatively minor initial error will be multiplied and will result in a series of errors that cascade throughout the cell. For tissues comprised of nondividing or slowly dividing cells, this "error catastrophe" could eventually be fatal. On the other hand, tissues comprising cells that proliferate rapidly would most likely not accumulate a fatal level of errors since defective cells could be "diluted out" by intact cells. The error cascade theory has generated many research investigations because predictions of the theory are eminently testable. On one level this in itself bespeaks the success of the theory, whether it is actually confirmed or rejected. Yet the theory has fallen out of favor, in part because results have been con-tradictory: alterations do accumulate with age in some, but by no means all, proteins. Whether the altered proteins found are a cause or a conse-quence of cellular aging is unknown. In short, the predicted "error catas-trophe" has not been established, despite much research activity.

Free Radicals

Another theory that has fluctuated in popularity focuses on very specific biochemical entities—free radicals. Free radicals are highly reactive by-products of the normal metabolic processes of respiration, which a cell uses to generate energy. They are chemical species that contain oxygen in a highly activated state (due to an unpaired electron) that will react with any nearby molecule, thereby altering that molecule's structure and hence its function. Because free radicals are continuously generated by living cells and yet are potentially so disruptive, cells also produce molecules specifi-cally designed to minimize the potential damage. These protective mole-cules are enzymes called free radical scavengers (e.g., superoxide dis-mutase, catalase, peroxidase) and, as it turns out, their levels in a range of mammalian species correlate very strongly with the maximum life spans of those species.

The free radical theory of aging was formulated three decades ago and it continues to generate interest. In part this is due to the fact that free radicals are a ubiquitous by-product of cells in oxygen breathing organisms, all of which age. In part it can be attributed to the range of experimental approaches that can be productively pursued when investigating free radical chemistry and aging. And in part it is due to the fact that the biochemistry of free radical formation is an integral part of other biological theories of aging: wear and tear theory infers the existence of cellular constituents with potentially damaging consequences to cellular machinery; rate of living theory (see below) places central consideration on the role of energy metabolism; and theories that cite radiation damage implicitly invoke free radicals since these chemicals are the major mediators of radiobiological effects in cells.

Cross-linking

Either spontaneously or due to reactive chemical intermediates, large molecules (macromolecules) can form cross-linkages between separate parts of the same molecule, such as the two strands of the DNA double helix, or between separate molecules, such as the extracellular protein elastin. Because cross-linking can alter the structure and function of macromolecules in a way that is biochemically very stable (and thus can accumulate over time), the deterioration and dysfunction associated with aging may be caused by cross-linking.

While DNA-DNA and DNA-protein cross-linking have been reported in cultured mammalian cells, the best evidence for the predicted association between cross-linking and aging is found in the extracellular matrix. Collagen is a long-chained protein constituent of the matrix that surrounds cells of the skin and blood vessels (as well as many other body tissues, accounting for about 25% of total body weight). The stiffening and loss of elasticity of these tissues with increasing age is due to the formation of collagen cross-links. Thus a molecular process at the cellular level has demonstrated physiological consequences and may, speculatively, affect an even wider range of functions in the aging body. However, it is difficult to see how rates of accumulation of cross-linking can account for the wide range of life spans seen among mammals. Parenthetically, cross-linking does not appear to increase with *in vitro* aging of human fibroblasts.

Accumulation of Wastes

As a general principle one would expect that cells have evolved the capacity to deal effectively and safely with the waste products of their metabolism. Like theories of damage and wear and tear, theories of waste product accumulation at the cellular level infer that the cell is a passive, static machine with little or no ability to monitor its own condition and thus effect self-repair or other maintenance functions. While we know that this is not the case, there is in fact consistent evidence that so-called "age-pigment," generally referred to as lipofuscin, does accumulate over time *in vivo* and *in vitro*. This yellow-brown granular substance increases with age in mammalian tissue, both post-mitotic (e.g., neural and cardiac muscle) and dividing (e.g., prostate and spleen). Lipofuscin has been reported in the literature since the turn of the century, and yet its origin is still unknown. More significantly, perhaps, its effect on cellular function is also unknown, and so whether it is a cause or a consequence of aging remains a mystery.

Codon Restriction

The three letter genetic word that directs the next link to be added to a growing protein chain (the nucleotide triplet that codes for a specific amino acid) is called a codon. There are sixty-four possible codons but only twenty amino acids for which they code—the so-called redundancy of the genetic code. Thus some proteins could be encoded by only a very specific string of codons, whereas other proteins have greater flexibility in the words (codons) which are used to direct their synthesis. (DNA codons are first transcribed into messenger RNA, and it is the sequence of mRNA that is translated into amino acid chains.)

In the codon restriction theory it is assumed that different cell types have different capacities to read the genetic message, that is, to translate a sequence of codons into the string of amino acids that comprise a protein. It is further assumed that in the course of cellular development and aging, some codons become untranslatable in some cell types whereas other codons, previously unreadable by a cell, subsequently become readable. Finally, it is assumed that some proteins can inhibit the translation of specific codons, whereas others can inhibit a wide range of codons. According to the theory, cell aging is a by-product of the genetically programmed inhibition that occurs sequentially during the life span of a cell. In other words, the genetic code originally common to all the cells in an organism eventually causes each cell type to inhibit differentially its own genetic message. Cellular dysfunction and death are not caused by any error, but are inherent in the gene-directed protein-synthetic machinery itself. Evidence in support of the theory has been reported, although the data are also compatible with a number of alternative hypotheses.

Caveat

Before leaving the level of the cell it is important to realize that not all researchers accept the cellular model of aging as valid. Some believe that fibroblasts (and other cell types) cease proliferation in culture because they are "differentiated to death" and this terminal differentiation is conceptually distinct from aging. On the one hand, it is undoubtedly clear that *in vitro* conditions are artificial: it must be demonstrated (and not just assumed) that processes and changes observed *in vitro* are also seen *in vivo*. For example, the proliferative life span of human fibroblasts in culture far exceeds the maximum longevity of 110–120 years: we do not die because all of our cells cease dividing. On the other hand, because of its very artificial-ity (i.e., human-created simulation), "aging under glass" offers theoretically complete experimental control to the investigator. This scientifically optimal situation, impossible *in vivo*, greatly simplifies a highly complex reality and thus can lead to definitive results. Interpretation of these results for the *in vivo* equivalents, and generalization from one or two cell types to the multiplicity of tissues found in multicellular organisms, are problematic. There exists a wide gap between human cells in culture and our cultural human selves. Fortunately it is filled, in part, by a range of theories at the level of the tissue or organ.

Tissue and Organ Level Theories

Whether the declines in physiological functioning that generally accompany aging are disease processes or senescence is ultimately an empirical question: Are they reversible or treatable? Are they universal and inevitable? Yet precisely because they are age-associated, meaning that older organisms have a deficit relative to younger organisms, it becomes very difficult to distinguish causes of aging (antecedent changes and predisposing conditions) from effects of aging (subsequent changes and negative consequences). The best recourse is to longitudinal studies, which follow the same individuals over time, taking repeated measures as they age. Whether such studies involve human beings or laboratory animals, they provide the most valid empirical data. They also require the greatest commitment of time and resources. Yet they are invaluable for continually testing and refining theories of aging at the tissue and organ level.

At one time or another it seems that nearly every tissue and organ system in the mammalian body has been invoked to explain aging. Without going into a lot of detail (the literature is vast, complex, and often contradictory), we will briefly review the concepts behind the major theories.

Sex Glands

Probably because human male sexual potency declines with age, and because until fairly recently all investigators were male, it was proposed that deterioration of the sex glands was a primary cause of aging. Initially, and for several centuries, attempted rejuvenation of aging humans involved the use of transplanted gonads or extracts from animal testicles. Eventually, purified hormones were administered under more scientific conditions. However, for males the side effects of exogenous testosterone, which can lead to the development of prostrate cancer, clearly outweigh the dubious "invigorating" results anecdotally reported. Moreover, "encouraging" results due to placebo effects and culturally mediated symbolism are impossible to confirm without controlled studies, hyperbolic testimonials notwithstanding.

For postmenopausal women, however, endocrinologists successfully prescribe female sex hormones to counteract the bone-thinning (osteoporosis) related to normally reduced secretions by the ovary. Yet here, too, there can be an increased risk of ovarian (and possibly breast) cancer so that treatment must be short-term, at low levels, and carefully monitored. For both sexes there is no indication that attempts to reverse "sexual aging" yield any general, beneficial consequences for biological aging.

Thyroid

Due to its declining activity during adulthood and its central role in controlling cellular metabolism throughout the body, gerontologists have logically postulated that changes in the thyroid gland might cause aging. The physiological effects of thyroid hormone (thyroxine) at the cellular level include protein synthesis, enzyme activity, and cell membrane permeability. Evidence in support of the theory comes from individuals who suffer hypothyroidism, because some of their symptoms mimic senescence: hair loss, skin wrinkling, slowed reaction time, and decreased basal metabolic rate (oxygen consumption). Yet when these patients are administered exogenous thyroid stimulating hormone, which is ordinarily supplied endogenously by the pituitary gland, their thyroids respond normally: they produce thyroxine, which in turn increases metabolic rate. The utility of hypothyroidism as a possible model of aging decrements in cellular oxygen uptake was undermined by studies demonstrating that tissue loss—not impaired oxygen uptake—accounted for reduction in basal oxygen uptake as a function of increased age.

Cardiovascular System

Cardiovascular disease has been the leading killer of adults over fifty in industrialized countries such as the United States since 1900. Its increasing incidence is especially sharp among the elderly. For these reasons changes in the cardiovascular system have been proposed as the primary cause of aging. However, the proposal can be dismissed on a number of grounds. For reasons detailed in an earlier section, age-associated disease processes, even if the leading causes of death among the elderly, are not conceptually equivalent to aging. Moreover, under the cardiovascular theory, historical and cross-cultural comparisons of causes of death among the elderly would lead one to conclude that most of the human race (across space and through time) have not experienced aging. Finally, even among populations where cardiovascular disease is the leading killer, many people age and die apparently without suffering coronary heart disease or atherosclerosis.

Hypothalamus and Pituitary

The hypothalamic-hypophysial axis (hypophysis is the anterior part of the pituitary) regulates the activity of a range of endocrine organs (e.g., thyroid, adrenals, sex glands) and continually monitors the blood level of the hormones they secrete. The fundamental physiological control maintained by this system makes it an attractive candidate for the role of "aging pacemaker." Physiological declines with age in functions influenced by the hypothalamic-hypophysial axis have been documented. However, much more needs to be known before definitive details and tests of the theory can be completed. One major area of active investigation in this regard concerns the question of target-tissue responsiveness in aging organisms.

Since hormones act by binding to cell membranes and affecting cellular function, the number, location, turnover, stability, affinity, etc., of binding sites in organisms of different ages are variables critical to hormone response in target organs and tissues. A second focus is on possible changes with age in the sensitivity of the central control, monitoring tissues. Thus, increased physiological variability in older animals might result from less sensitive control by parts of the hypothalamic-hypophysial axis. These realms of research comprise highly complex interactions between physiology, on the one hand, and molecular and cell biology, on the other. Neuroendocrine theories of aging (see the following section on CNS) represent a vast, exciting, and potentially promising field of investigation. One proposal, for example, suggests that the same neuroendocrine mechanisms that operate during organismal development produce a "regulatory cascade" of effects during aging. Should this turn out to be even partly correct, then much of the wealth of data collected by developmental biologists will be applicable to questions of biological gerontology.

Central Nervous System (CNS)

Similar to the central role of the hypothalamic-hypophysial system in regulating endocrine function, the central nervous system (CNS) coordinates a wide array of processes and behaviors. Locating an aging "clock" in the brain is thus a tempting theoretical speculation, and it enjoys some empirical support. For example, declines with aging have been reported for breathing capacity, heart rate, temperature regulation, and maximum work performance. Arguably these may be due more to a reduction in coordination and integration, to a decrement in rate of performance, than to decreased organ or motor function per se. Similarly, many of the multiple age-related changes in physiological function (see chapters 5, 6, 15, and 16) may reflect slower response, diminished integration of functions, or less effective central control. The anatomical site of such control, however, is not known, which of course obviates investigation of neurophysiological or morphological alterations in it with age.

While there are differential rates of nerve cell loss in human beings, the often repeated "fact" that human beings lose one hundred thousand neurons daily has never been established: rather it is an extrapolation from cross-sectional studies that determined that between the thirties and the nineties there occurs a neuronal decrease and a 10% reduction in cerebral cortex surface area. The rate and variability of the processes that lead to this loss are unknown. Clearly much more research is needed in this area since even the well diagrammed clock theory merely postulates a concept in search of CNS incarnation.

Immune System

The immune system represents a promising focus of biological aging theories for a number of reasons: (1) many aspects of immune function in adults decline regularly with age; (2) this decline may be causally related to many kinds of age-associated diseases (e.g., infectious, neoplastic or cancerous, autoimmune); (3) cellular components of the immune system become terminally differentiated *in vivo* (and can be stimulated to do so *in vitro*); (4) the immune system is readily accessible for assay, manipulation, and intervention; and (5) therapeutic intervention has the potential to delay or reverse many age-related diseases. The primary key to decline in normal immune function with age is involution and atrophy of the thymus shortly after sexual maturity. Theories of thymic involution include a genetic program of limited proliferation, as modeled by fibroblasts in culture; changes in genetic information through viral genome integration, DNA damage and misrepair, or somatic mutation; and some form of error cascade at the non-DNA level. Thus, specific physiological and pathological changes with age might be due to more general cellular and molecular mechanisms of aging. Alternatively a signal might be sent to the thymus from some other "aging pacemaker," for example, the hypothalamic-hypophysial circuit (see discussion of clocks below), causing its functional decline and atrophy.

Whether due to the marked and consistent immunodeficiency associated with aging, or independent of it, there is substantial evidence of increased autoimmunity with increased adult age. Eventually this means that there is a change in the ability of the organism to distinguish between self—which is not to be attacked, inactivated, or destroyed—and nonself—that is, foreign invaders and substances such as bacteria, viruses, fungi, and toxins. This change is obviously harmful not only because immunological attack against self is "suicidal," but also because one's declining immune system is "distracted" from attacking the real enemy, namely, potentially pathogenic invaders. The situation is complicated by the fact that the healthy organism must maintain constant vigilance against "treasonous" cells of its own, namely, tumor cells or mutant clones.

Breakdown in the exquisitely regulated system of immune surveillance could be due to the reappearance of "forbidden clones" as a result of somatic mutation. According to this theory, autoreactive immune cells (T lymphocytes) that had been selected against during embryological development arise in adulthood because of mutations; these "forbidden clone" T cells successfully proliferate in an aging immune system in which the normal suppression of such clones is reduced. In addition, the reduced suppression of "mutant" lymphocytes could lead to increased tolerance of abnormal cells such as those that are precancerous. Thus, the decline in immune function with age (thymic involution) "allows" infectious disease, cancer, and autoimmune diseases to cause increased morbidity and mortality among the aged (breakdown of immune surveillance) primarily because of somatic mutation.

In addition to the regular decline in immune function with age, there is an increase in autoantibodies in the blood. These can interfere not only with the immune system itself but also with tissues and organ systems throughout the body. Moreover, there are similarities between a number of immune-related diseases (e.g., rheumatoid arthritis, arteritis, maturity onset diabetes, thyroiditis, certain anemias, amyloidosis, Parkinson's disease, mysasthenia gravis, and osteoporosis) and characteristics of normal aging in human beings. These observations support an autoimmune theory of aging, although the greater incidence of autoimmune disease in women, who are nevertheless longer-lived in industrialized societies, contradicts it. Compared to theories of thymic involution, autoimmune theories of aging have the significant advantage of being testable with a number of genetically specific rodent models. The fact that these animal models manifest increased variability with age adds to their value (and to experimental difficulties) as useful research tools.

Postscript

In general terms theories of aging at the level of the tissue or organ must ultimately consider the question of peripheral versus central effect. The neuroendocrine system exerts its effects by stimulating the cells of target organs with chemical messengers (e.g., hormones). Age-related change in the production or effectiveness of these messengers, or in the monitoring and regulation of their availability, would be a central effect. In contrast, a peripheral effect would involve decline with age in target cells themselves. Such decline could be due to a wide range of factors such as receptor binding, level or activity of intracellular (secondary) messenger, or degree of intracellular responsiveness (due, in turn, to other metabolic, biochemical, or genetic changes). Thus, the decline in homeostasis that is a characteristic of senescence may be explicable by biological theories of aging that involve tissue or organ changes. The immune and the neuroendocrine systems are the most promising in this regard since they affect nearly every cell in the body. However, if homeostatic decline is ultimately a cellular phenomenon, then central aging changes may be secondary to or caused by peripheral aging changes. Focus on cellular mechanisms of aging may be particularly illuminating because studies of any eucaryote are potentially applicable to all eucaryotes. (Eucaryotes are organisms whose cells divide and reproduce by mitosis, and that have a nuclear membrane.

They are contrasted with procaryotes such as bacteria which have nuclear material, e.g., DNA, dispersed throughout the cell.) Alternatively, it is quite possible that both types of changes are causally involved: it is this idea, in part, that has led to investigation of higher order phenomena, namely, whole animal or organismal theories of aging.

Organismal and Whole Body Theories

We now consider theories of aging that are the most interdisciplinary and general. In one sense, these theories assume that the organism is greater than the sum of its parts, so that coordinated regulation of functions and the integration of tissues and organ systems are the primary focus. In another sense, these theories developed from observations of the effects of particular experimental manipulations or environmental conditions. Thus, they encompass a range of experimental techniques and general concepts that share an emphasis on aging in the unitary, complete, intact organism.

Radiation

The effects of radiation appear to mimic those of aging. Whole-body ionizing radiation (produced by X-rays, gamma-rays, neutrons) is known to shorten the life span of a range of mammals and appears to accelerate the appearance of all diseases. That radiation-induced life-shortening causes a general, systemic decline argues strongly against the idea that only one or a few age-related diseases (e.g., cancer) are involved. (This is critical because it has been known since X-rays were discovered that ionizing radiation causes cancer.) Moreover, the short-term toxic effects of radiation are more pronounced in aged as opposed to younger rodents. In human beings the most obvious effects of nonionizing radiation, due to years of exposure to ultraviolet radiation from the sun, comprise excessive wrinkling and premature aging of the skin. More generally, ionizing irradiation of animals results in the following changes: graying of hair, early appearance of cataracts, decrease in activity, progressive reproductive dysfunction, generalized residual injury, and alterations in body tissues and fat accumulation, which resemble normally observed aging. Thus it would appear that radiation (especially of the ionizing type) causes premature aging.

Yet the increase in mortality caused by irradiation is not necessarily equivalent to accelerated aging. For example, an infectious epidemic, massive food poisoning, or famine would each increase mortality but would not be considered to accelerate aging. Thus it becomes a question of analyzing biological mechanisms—are radiation-induced processes equivalent to aging processes? Is the physiological decline produced by irradiating animals similar to senescence in those animals?

Reanalysis of the original animal data, which had seemed to indicate that all causes of death occur earlier in irradiated populations, indicates that in fact only one noncancer disease (a kidney ailment) occurs at younger ages. Moreover, not even all types of fatal cancer appear earlier. Studies of radiologists and of Japanese atomic bomb survivors, upon reexamination, extended these conclusions to human beings. In addition, studies of collagen biochemistry, age-pigment accumulation, neuromuscular performance, and behavioral changes associated with aging in nonirradiated rodents, monkeys, and human beings failed to show that radiation either mimicked or accelerated these changes. Finally, detailed studies of cataracts, hair graying, and fertility decline reveal that either radiation does not produce an accelerated age-related effect or does so by a different mechanism.

Thus, even though it remains true that whole-body radiation increases the mortality rate (and shortens the life span), in almost every detail it does not accelerate the rate of aging. What radiation does do, at low to moderate doses, is to accelerate a set of age-related diseases, namely, certain types of cancer. The fact that cancer is currently a leading cause of death among middle-aged and older members of industrialized populations, and that human cells in culture that are transformed to overcome their limited "life span" may eventually become cancerous, suggest a commonality between aging and cancer. Other data support this idea, and researchers in both fields share many techniques, models, hypotheses, and insights. Yet the recent (mid-1970s) reappraisal of the original radiation data suggests three caveats: (1) cancer is not the equivalent of aging; (2) analysis of mortality rates, taken alone, may not be a good criterion for aging; and (3) later reanalysis of earlier data can be invaluable.

Rate of Living

Stated most simply, the rate of living theory of aging postulates a direct causal relationship between energy expenditure (e.g., metabolic rate) and aging rate. Thus, the higher the metabolic rate, the faster an animal ages and the sooner it dies. Conversely, slowing down the rate of aging and increasing longevity will be the result of a lower metabolic rate (all other things being equal, especially, for example, physical activity). In organisms that adjust their body temperature to the environment (cold-blooded animals or poikilotherms) such as fruit flies, there is good evidence to support the theory. For example, *Drosophila* (fruit flies) live longer when reared in colder temperatures and die sooner at warmer temperatures. In the case of homeotherms (warm-blooded animals), however, the situation is complicated by the fact that internal temperature is maintained within a constant, narrow range despite external conditions. This has led researchers to use dietary manipulation as a means of investigating the rate of living theory in mammals.

Dietary restriction of laboratory rodents—by means of either reduced caloric intake or intermittent fasting—has very consistently led to increased life span. Both mean and maximum longevity increase 10–300% when compared to *ad libitum* (freely) fed control animals. (One word of caution in interpreting these and other data concerns control animals: since these experiments involve studying the effects of a treatment relative to un-treated [i.e., control] subjects, it can be logically argued that the *ad libitum* fed animals die sooner because they overeat. In other words, dietarily restricted animals do not demonstrate extended life span but are merely appropriately meeting their nutritional needs, whereas the *ad lib* fed groups suffer from a sub-optimal diet which leads to accelerated aging and a reduced life span. The issue of appropriate and valid control populations in experimental studies is a matter of continual discussion and debate.) In addition to increased survival, the age-associated pathology usually observed (e.g., tumor incidence, immune system decline, kidney failure) is reduced or delayed in food restricted animals.

These kinds of results were first reported fifty years ago and have been observed over the last decade in rats, mice, and hamsters. It is important to note that dietarily restricted animals receive appropriate levels of all es-sential nutrients (e.g., proteins, vitamins, minerals, fat, fiber). This has led to the concept of *under*nutrition without *mal*nutrition (as suggested for human beings in Walford 1983).

While the many recent studies of dietary restriction seem to support the rate of living theory of aging, more detailed testing of the hypothesis may cast some doubts. For example, when metabolic rate is actually measured in these animals, it seems that longer-lived (restricted) groups burn *more* calories than "normal-lived" (*ad libitum* fed) animals. These data are in direct contradiction to predictions of the theory, and suggest that more complicated relationships account for the observed beneficial results. In addition, the role of physical activity must be assessed since metabolic rate is but one component of energy expenditure. As you can see, even the most promising results usually raise more questions than they answer. Among the mechanisms most likely to account for the life-extending effects of food restriction are: the hypothalamic-pituitary system (since it produces endocrine and metabolic effects); slowing down the decline in protein turnover (meaning that degradation of proteins doesn't exceed synthesis of proteins by quite so much); and reducing the damage caused by free radicals.

Stress

Hans Selye has applied his General Adaptation Syndrome (G.A.S.) to the biology of aging. The three stages of the G.A.S. are: (1) the alarm reaction, in which an organism's defensive forces (immune, neuroendocrine, car-diovascular, muscular) are induced, and adaptive processes are initiated; (2) the stage of resistance, during which the organism adjusts itself to the changes induced by the alarm reaction (e.g., by means of hypertrophy, accumulation of reserves, and returning to homeostatic balance); and (3) the stage of exhaustion, in which resources are drained, the organism can no longer respond and the acquired adaptation is lost (resulting in death). These three stages are taken to be analogous to aging inasmuch as the first resembles childhood, the second is like adulthood, and the third is reminiscent of senescence. Because each encounter with a stressor is thought to leave some residual deficit, the accumulation of stress during the organism's lifetime (i.e., aging) ultimately leads to loss of adaptive capacity and the decline of senescence.

Application of the G.A.S. to biological aging is really just an organism-level generalization of the wear and tear theory. As Selye has written, "at the end of a life under stress, [there] was a kind of premature aging due to wear and tear" (Selye 1956, 274). Looked at in one way this means that investigation at the cellular level is a necessary adjunct to testing the theory. However, since the "stress theory of aging" is specifically formulated as a physiological or systemic explanation, it must be evaluated at the level of the whole animal. We know, for example, that the stress of exercise seems to protect against some kinds of age-related diseases (e.g., cardiovascular, pulmonary, skeletal). But it is more likely that reversal of the usual decline in physical activity with age is more directly responsible. Indeed, the value of Selye's work lies more in highlighting the relationship between stress and disease than in proposing any specific mechanism of aging. Moreover, there may be physiological problems associated with "under-stress" (i.e., lack of stimulation or use) as well as with "over-stress."

Loss of Coordinated Regulation

A living multicelled organism is a vastly complex system of genetic, biochemical, and physiological functions designed to evade, for a limited time, the second law of thermodynamics. The coordinated regulation of all of these functions need not be perfect; it need only stay one ordered step ahead of chaos. Put another way, just as long as an organism is able to adapt to an ever-changing environment, it will continue to exist.

One hallmark of aging is a decrease in the performance of numerous physiological processes such as temperature regulation, maximum breathing capacity, kidney function, peak heart rate, and pancreatic function. The more deleterious of these we have termed senescence, but even excluding senescent changes there is clearly a decrease with age of integrated response in nervous, cardiovascular, respiratory, and muscular systems. The theory of aging as loss of coordinated regulation focuses on these system decrements in the whole animal. However, it is more of a theoretical approach than a well-articulated theory inasmuch as central control mechanisms are invoked but no detailed model of action emerges. For example, the loss could be due to cellular changes within each organ system, to changes in the signals that circulate to coordinate functions, to changes in the reception and processing of signals by target organs, or to other phenomena. Loss of coordinated regulation and integration of physiological systems is a conclusion (based on inductive reasoning) about, rather than a testable theory of, aging.

Central Clock Hierarchy ("Clock of Clocks")

In much the same way that there are neuroendocrine "pacemakers" of growth and development, so too there may exist locations in the brain that fundamentally influence aging. The regular timing of such complex physiological events as puberty and menopause (in human beings) means that central control is species-wide and species-specific. Moreover, the physiological mechanisms responsible for puberty appear to be common among mammals. Furthermore, the cellular and genetic effects of mammalian neuroendocrine signals (e.g., hormones and peptides) share a great many features in common. These three generalizations—species-specific timing, common mammalian mechanisms, shared effects of signals—derive from a substantial amount of research on developmental as well as aging processes. They strongly suggest the idea that central timing mechanisms exist in the brain (the hypothalamus is most often mentioned), and that these act coordinately—perhaps in a controlling fashion—with peripheral mechanisms outside the brain.

The brain itself, of course, is a highly complex organ comprising billions of cells. Soon after birth (by about age three in human beings) these cells (neurons) cease dividing and become known as fixed post-mitotic cells, although they may continue to make new interconnections until the organism dies. Although their DNA no longer replicates, as with all living cells genes are transcribed, proteins are synthesized and degraded, free radicals are generated, waste products accumulate, and errors in metabolism occur. In other words, any or many of the genetic and cellular theories outlined above could be responsible for changes in a central clock; the clock, in turn, could then affect peripheral organs, tissues, cells, or genes, with highly complex feedback loops and interactions occurring. A cascade could thus ensue, at different rates in different tissues, with some cells dying, some organs declining in function, and the deterioration of senescence setting in here and there. One can plausibly imagine a sequence of changes, set in motion by a central control mechanism, that comprises all that we know of biological aging. So in effect, the central clock hierarchy is at once the simplest (conceptually) and the most complex (empirically) theory: its hierarchical nature effectively subsumes all other models and hypotheses.

Conceptual Categories of Aging

The theories discussed above are considered within the framework of biological organization as outlined in Table 2.1. Roughly speaking these levels correspond to traditional academic disciplines as seen, for example, in the structure of academic departments within colleges and medical schools. An alternative and more synthetic approach cuts across levels by focusing on one guiding concept or on one central criterion. This concept or criterion can be used to think about theories in a new way, to combine theories that operate at different levels, and to integrate levels in ways that suggest new theories, hypotheses, models, and research. In the following three subsections each category is of the A versus B type; such dichotomies oversimplify information in order to fit complex and subtle ideas into an artificial (but useful) grouping. Yet too much damage is done to theories if they are forced too doggedly into preconceived categories (and a bruised theory is a dangerous thing indeed!). So a second, complementary approach uses one general principle (e.g., evolution) to help structure and critically evaluate theories of biological aging. This approach allows one to choose the guiding principle a priori on some grounds external to gerontology. The merit in this approach is that one's bias is independent of aging, although one could as easily be close-minded in choosing the principle. As valuable as the following may be, to see any of these conceptual categories as more than potentially useful heuristic devices is to mistake the key for the treasure. (See Table 2.2.)

Intrinsic versus Extrinsic

Intrinsic theories of aging locate the primary processes or causes of aging within the organism itself. Genetic program theories represent the best example of intrinsic mechanisms since the DNA presumed to be responsible for aging is constitutionally present from the moment of fertilization. Extrinsic theories of aging cite various agents in the environment as primary. These agents range from cosmic rays and other sources of background radiation, to general adaptation to the environment, for example, rate of living or stress.

As mentioned, this dichotomy is exaggerated inasmuch as the phenotype of aging (in any organism) is the product of the interaction of genotype and environment. There is no purely intrinsic or extrinsic theory, process, or mechanism of aging. Yet the distinction is useful because it establishes a range of possibilities and defines the two end points of a continuum. Some theories are indeed more intrinsically focused, and thereby require testing in environments as constant and equivalent as possible. Genetic studies of animal life spans, for example, are most valid and valuable when all environmental variation is minimized so that differences in longevity can be ascribed to differences in genes (and not to temperature, food, activity, etc.).

Conversely, testing theories that are based on extrinsic factors ideally involves genetically identical animals that are studied under a range of environmental conditions. The environmental conditions represent the

TABLE 2.2.   **Theories of Aging in Conceptual Categories**

Intrinsic
genetic programs
somatic mutation
DNA repair
error cascade
wear and tear (adjustment to internal
   environment)
free radicals (due to metabolism)
cross-linking (due to metabolism)
codon restriction
longevity determinant genes
chromosome "hits"
accumulation of wastes

Extrinsic
radiation
stress
DNA damage

wear and tear (adjustment to external
   environment)
free radicals (due to diet)
cross-linking (due to diet)

Deterministic
pleiotropic genes
immunological (e.g., thymic
   involution)
DNA repair
codon restriction
longevity determinant genes
rate of living
hierarchy of clocks
disposable soma
life history theory
genetic programs

Stochastic
somatic mutation
autoimmunity
loss of genetic information
error cascade
accumulation of wastes
wear and tear
free radicals
cross-linking
radiation
stress

Homeostatic
organ level theories
stress
loss of coordinated regulation
central clock hierarchy

Metabolic
genetic programs
accumulation of wastes
wear and tear (cellular)
DNA repair
somatic mutation

Developmental
codon restriction
longevity determinant genes
life history theory
disposable soma
growth or body size
cell differentiation

Postdevelopmental
thymic involution
cardiovascular
autoimmunity
loss of coordinated regulation
CNS
loss of genetic information

Neutralist
wear and tear
accumulation of wastes
cross-linking
autoimmunity
error cascade
loss of coordinated regulation
stress
free radicals
somatic mutation
loss of genetic information

Selectionist
genetic programs
disposable soma
DNA repair
physiological theories
hierarchy of clocks
longevity determinant genes
life history theory
codon restriction
pleiotropic genes
rate of living

extrinsic factors under study—for example, diet, stress, or exercise. Nearly all investigations of physiological theories use animals of one or another genetic strain, from which there are dozens to choose for any particular species. This means that different genetic backgrounds (intrinsic factors) must be considered in terms of the hypothesis being tested (extrinsic factors). In short, despite theoretical simplification one cannot avoid the complex interplay of both intrinsic and extrinsic effects on aging.

Deterministic versus Stochastic

Deterministic theories of aging propose that specific mechanisms and processes are the direct causes of aging in a regular and predictable manner. In contrast, according to stochastic theories it is not single events or processes that predetermine aging but rather an accumulation of random, often indirect effects. As this accumulation is variable among individuals, stochastic theories generate probabilities of aging changes—"if one thing doesn't get you, another will"—while deterministic theories predict that all individuals will be affected by the same mechanisms of aging, which are programmed into each organism. To take an example, somatic mutation theory is random because there is no exact relationship between locations of mutations (i.e., which genes, on which chromosomes, in which cells) and rates of aging. In contrast, the theory of DNA repair postulates that the efficacy of repair processes directly determines the life span of cells (and ultimately organisms) in a regular, predictable way. In stochastic theories aging differences among individuals are caused by differences in sites of action or rates of processes that fluctuate by chance. In deterministic theories, aging differences among individuals are caused by differences in the program of aging. That individuals become more variable with age (more different from one another) suggests either that deterministic mechanisms become less influential or that processes proposed by random theories are expressed more fully.

In general, genetically-based theories are deterministic whereas nongenetically-based theories are stochastic. This is due to the simple fact that the program in deterministic theories must ultimately be stored in the structure of DNA, even if the program operates at a higher level (e.g., as a CNS clock). That there is a heritable component to longevity within a species, and that different species regularly demonstrate different life spans, strongly support deterministic theories. But this is not to say that many aging processes might not be the result of random effects, be they internal, external, or both. There may be more variability in aging than is dreamed of in deterministic theories.

Homeostatic versus Metabolic

Homeostatic theories of aging essentially integrate intrinsic and extrinsic, deterministic and stochastic mechanisms into one body (literally). They postulate that genes determine a physiologically normal range within which bodily functions operate in order to maintain an organism in a healthy or viable state. When the organism is stimulated, challenged, or stressed by random factors in the external environment, it responds with internal processes that act to regain equilibrium and return the organism to its normal range. However, should the random environmental stimuli cause the organism to exceed its normal range, and should the internal processes fail to regain equilibrium, the organism would die. Senescence, in such a scenario, refers either to narrowing the normal range (essentially lowering the threshold to death) or to diminished restorative powers. Aging is produced by the interaction of programmed (genetic) and random (environmental) factors as they affect the internal, central structures and processes which maintain homeostasis.

In one sense all physiological theories of aging are homeostatic, because they postulate that eventually the heart or the hypothalamus, for example, is unable to respond adequately to the organism's demands. However, in another sense there are many possible homeostatic theories of aging—each of which might postulate one from among a variety of interrelationships among specific cells, tissues, and organs as the key to aging. As more data are collected at numerous levels of biological organization, homeostatic theories can be specifically formulated, tested, and refined.

Metabolic theories represent the molecular counterpart of homeostatic theories. Whereas homeostatic theories propose that a central mechanism(s) controls the cascading effects of aging, metabolic theories postulate peripheral mechanisms as primary. Metabolic theories focus on biochemical events and processes, for example, DNA replication, protein synthesis, or free radical generation, which occur in all cells. However, in different cell types these events and processes occur at different rates and may be subject to different control signals (e.g., hormones, peptides, neurochemicals). Because of these sources of variability, metabolic theories seek general biological processes in specific cell models (e.g., fibroblasts, retinal cells, hepatocytes). They encounter the problem that observations made with one cell type may not be valid in another cell type—which raises again the larger question of whether cellular aging and senescence are simply a matter of "differentiation to death." Metabolic theories suggest that aging processes are cellular, diffuse, and general, whereas homeostatic theories suggest that aging processes are physiological, central, and organ-specific.

Developmental

Developmental theories of aging conceive the life span as a continuum of processes and changes beginning at conception and ending at death. They are uniformitarian (as opposed to catastrophic) and deterministic. Early theories along these lines suggested that senescence begins when growth ceases or that length of life is limited by "growth inhibitors" which delimit body size (in land vertebrates). Evidence gathered more recently indicates that body size is specified more by the number of body cells than by their size, so that cessation of cell division determines species' body size and therefore might determine longevity. As we have already seen, among mammals adult body size is in fact positively correlated with species' longevity; thus, developmental and growth processes might be common determinants of morphology and aging. However, the correlation is strengthened if species' metabolic rate and brain size are included in the equation, suggesting that such nondevelopmental factors as diet, activity, ecological environment, cellular physiology, learning, and CNS homeostatic control are also involved.

Two further propositions at the cellular level derive from these ideas: (1) that the very process of cellular differentiation inevitably causes dysfunction and death, a postulate supported by observations that precancerous cells are both "dedifferentiated" and "immortal"; and (2) that the same processes or programs that delimit an organism's size, by ending cell proliferation, cause the physiological deterioration of senescence. Support for this possibility comes from studies in which two different cells are fused together: results indicate that senescent fibroblasts produce a substance that inhibits the otherwise unlimited proliferation of precancerous cells. Since cells that are fully differentiated and cease to divide nevertheless continue to metabolize actively and to function viably (e.g., neurons, cardiac and skeletal muscle), the two propositions are not identical. In fact they represent two major avenues of current cell biology research.

Theories that are based on a definition of aging as beginning in adulthood or after reproduction clearly ignore the earlier periods of the life cycle. Such postdevelopmental theories, for example thymic involution and cardiovascular deterioration, often derive from observations that rates of decline in a particular tissue or organ do not begin until adulthood. These theories find support in the fact that, biologically, the adult organism differs more from the newborn than the old differs from the adult. Hence adulthood and aging represent a different field of study from growth and development. The regularity of normal biological development ensures that mature phenotypes exhibit a fairly narrow range of variation; this channeling of growth stands in sharp contrast to the biological diversity seen in older animals. This contrast is exemplified by the theory that aging is due to the loss of coordinated regulation of physiological functions. However, it is important to realize that growth limitation may not be due to any material substance or genetic program at all—it could be caused by environmental conditions (e.g., fibroblasts in culture cease to proliferate when hemmed in by their neighbors, so-called contact inhibition) or by fundamental physico-chemical properties. To the extent that this is true, aging and senescence probably are not approachable or understandable from the perspective of developmental theories.

Evolutionary

Evolution is the prevailing paradigm in modern biology, meaning that it unites and informs all of biology, and provides the central theme and theoretical core of the discipline. Consequently all biological theories of aging can be evaluated within the conceptual framework of evolutionary theory. One convenient way of doing this involves a currently active debate in evolutionary biology—namely, the question of non-Darwinian or "neutral" evolution. To put it most simply, non-Darwinian processes refer to changes in genes that are neutral with respect to natural selection, meaning that they have no direct effect on reproduction or survival. For a number of reasons, such processes are most likely to act at the molecular and biochemical level and least likely to act at the level of tissues, organs, and physiological systems. Thus, biological theories of aging classified as "neutralist" will involve mechanisms that operate at the cellular and sub-cellular levels of organization. In addition the neutralist category includes any nongenetic theory such as wear and tear, stress, or accumulation of wastes.

The contrasting category of aging theories is termed "selectionist" because the mechanisms involved directly affect survival and reproduction. Moreover, such theories must have a genetic basis if natural selection is to evolve differences in the aging rates and longevities of species. Selectionist theories do not require that aging be adaptive; for example, the pleiotropic gene theory postulates that there is a trade-off between improved vitality at early ages and diminished vitality at later ages. This theory explicitly invokes natural selection while emphasizing the senescent aspects of aging. Similarly, developmental theories suggest that aging processes may be the inevitable outcome of mechanisms that are required at some prior period in the life cycle. A recent idea along these lines, the disposable soma (literally the "body") theory, posits an evolutionary compromise between investment in survival and investment in reproduction. Given a finite amount of energy and material resources available to each organism for its life, there is a trade-off between investing more or less in growth and maintenance of the soma—and investing less or more in reproduction. The theory assumes that damage is the immediate cause of aging, so that natural selection will optimize the balance between repair of the soma and reproduction of the genes which produce the soma (via offspring).

In general, selectionist theories propose that aging is an evolved trait upon which natural selection has acted to generate species differences in rates of aging and longevity. Selection may act by postponing deleterious processes (for example, delaying immune system decline) or by accelerating benefical processes (for example, improving DNA repair capabilities). In contrast, neutralist theories argue either that aging and senescence are the indirect consequences of otherwise adaptive traits, or that the force of natural selection diminishes with age such that it eventually is too weak to counteract age-related deterioration. In short, the neutralist perspective assumes that aging and senescence are "invisible" to natural selection.

One final point implicit in this discussion, and throughout this chapter, deserves explicit recognition: that the evolutionary perspective is, at heart, a comparative perspective. It is based on the premise that cross-species analysis can reveal patterns and common mechanisms that might be less obvious if only intraspecies differences are studied. For *Homo sapiens* especially, the higher primates (monkeys and apes) offer an invaluable resource for insights into our own processes of biological aging.

Why Do Organisms Age Biologically?

The answer to the question "Why do organisms age biologically?" must be framed within the context of evolution since this is the prevailing paradigm in biology. Ultimately this means that aging must be discussed with reference to differential fertility and differential mortality (reproduction and survival of the "fitter"). Even without a background in evolutionary biology, we can imagine three possible, mutually exclusive perspectives: irrelevance, error, inevitability. Each will be briefly considered.

The argument that aging is irrelevant to evolution rests on the definition of aging as postreproductive senescence and asserts that in the wild, senescence has no evolutionary consequences. Such an assertion could be true if those organisms that undergo senescence do so only after finishing reproduction, at which time they essentially disappear without affecting other members of the species, other species, or the environment. This "aging in a vacuum" is clearly an empty proposition, for every living creature exploits resources in its environment and exists in an intricate web of biological relationships with parasites, predators, and prey. Moreover the notion that aging is irrelevant to evolution effectively eliminates human beings from consideration by asserting that aging as senescence (or postreproductive senescence) is, historically, a very recent phenomenon. (This issue is discussed in chapter 3.)

The idea that aging is due to error indicts the "imperfection" of evolutionary processes for failing to produce either immortal creatures or species' members that all die at the same age. In a way this approach makes aging a design problem of Nature, inasmuch as it infers that aging is the consequence of something gone wrong. The error can be internal or external, programmed or random, homeostatic or metabolic. Different organisms age and are subject to senescence for either the same or different reasons. There may be order in aging phenomena, despite the obvious complexities, or the complexities may mask a hidden chaos. This may sound hopeless, yet the perspective of error is really an optimistic one, because it suggests that where there are flaws there may be corrections, that aging may represent a series of extremely difficult problems that are nevertheless solvable. Perfection may not be of this world, but improvement is always a possibility.

The proposition that aging is evolutionarily inevitable requires that there be some genetic factor responsible for aging at some level, to some extent. This is a requirement because it is genes that maintain the continuity of species and it is changes in genes upon which evolution ultimately operates. This is not to exclude higher levels of biological organization as predominant in aging, although in order to be compatible with a genetic basis the theories involved would have to be intrinsic and programmed rather than extrinsic and stochastic. Moreover, the relevant theories could be homeostatic or metabolic. And in some aspect they must be developmental or at least related to development at the genetic level.

This last criterion is a requirement because the argument for the inevitability of biological aging rests on the theory of life history. The concept of life history refers to the characteristic pattern of growth, development, maturation, reproduction, adult maintenance, and senescence of a species; a life history strategy refers to the adaptive consequences of such a pattern in the constant struggle of evolutionary competition. For example, species A might be best adapted to its environment if it develops quickly (to a small size), reproduces abundantly (if only once), and dies soon thereafter. This life history strategy is known as the "big bang," for obvious reasons. Organisms subject to high predation and periodic drought or famine might do best as short-lived but prolific breeders. Species B, in contrast, might be best adapted as a larger, long-lived organism that reproduces rarely (but repeatedly) with only a few offspring; it invests a lot of time and energy rearing its few offspring to ensure that they reach adulthood and in turn reproduce. This life history strategy could be called the "long haul" because it requires a much more enduring commitment in order to be successful. Such a species might be a predator, which must learn a lot about its environment and its prey in order to be successful. (Hamsters are a good example of species A and polar bears of species B.)

Clearly, these two life histories are polar opposites, and will include remarkably different rates of aging. Yet in both cases the overall pattern is determined by evolutionary processes. Moreover, the pattern is determined not for "the good of the species" (as too many biologists have misunderstood) but because individuals which follow better adapted life histories out-reproduce (and out-survive) other members of the species. It is often written that senescence evolved in order to minimize competition between the generations (e.g., for food, mates, etc.) by eliminating older cohorts. According to Darwinian theory this scenario would occur only if the offspring of more senescent individuals directly benefitted from their own parents' deterioration or demise.

It is important to remember that natural selection acts on *individual* differences in reproduction and survival (although under very special and rare conditions it may be able to act on group differences). Among these individual differences we can include rates of aging and length of life, as well as rates of growth and length of development. Aging is inevitable, then, because it is built into each species in much the same way as body size, metabolic rate, number of teeth, mode of locomotion, means of reproduction, etc. Like birth, death, and the myriad processes in between, aging is a biological property of living.

III

THE HUMAN LIFE SPAN

Mary Jane Moore

At first glance, the term life span appears to be a relatively simple concept—how long an individual lives from birth to death. However, there are several ways to view life span. When dealing with populations, the terms *mean* or *average life span* and *maximum life span* are often used. The average life span is the life expectancy at birth of individuals in a population. The life expectancy at birth is the average number of years a person is expected to live from day of birth. For example, the mean life span in the United States is currently seventy-five years. (See Acsadi and Nemeskeri [1970] for details in calculating demographic parameters.) If one follows the population until the last individual dies, the age of that individual defines the maximum life span of the population. Usually maximum life spans are determined for species and mean life spans for populations.

This chapter will discuss both the mean life span and the maximum life span of human populations within a demographic and evolutionary framework. While both environmental and genetic factors contribute to the length of life span, the genetics of longevity will be reviewed here, and a more detailed discussion of environmental and sociocultural factors will be explored in the next chapter.

Survival Curves

A reflection of mean life span for populations can be seen in survival curves. Theoretical survival curves showing the effect of environmental stress on longevity were first proposed by Pearl and Miner in 1935. Figure 3.1 shows four possible curves illustrating life spans of individuals that are determined solely by environmental factors or solely by genetic factors. In each case, two conditions, stress or stress-free, are superimposed. Curve 1(a) occurs when only environmental factors determine longevity in a stress-free environment. In this case, individuals are immortal. Curve 1(b)

54

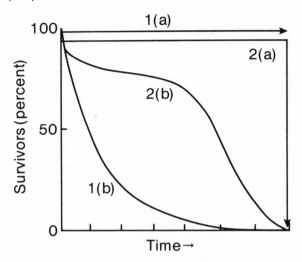

FIGURE 3.1. **Theoretical survival curves.**

describes the situation where only environmental factors determine longevity in a stressful environment. In this case population members are not subject to senescence and are exposed only to random overall mortality. They die from causes that would have killed them at any age. Curve 2(a) illustrates longevity that is due only to genetic factors in a stress-free environment. In other words, all individuals of the population live to the same age. This curve reflects a species-specific life span that is genetically programmed, and its full potential is realized by each member of the population. Curve 2(b) represents longevity determined by genetic factors in an environment with stress. This curve best fits the human survival curve.

Figure 3.2 shows how survival curves of different human populations at different times approximate curves 2(a) and 2(b) of Figure 3.1. The estimated survival curve for early prehistoric human populations reflects genetically programmed longevity in an environment of many hazards and stresses. Gradually, as sanitation improved, and housing, antiseptics, public health, hygiene, immunization, antibiotics, and improved medical practices enter the picture, the survival curve approaches the rectangular curve 2(a). Everyone is approaching the maximum life span for the species.

Maximum Life Spans

If both environmental and genetic factors contribute to average life span it is important to ask what is determining the maximum life span of a species. The great diversity of maximum life-span lengths throughout the animal

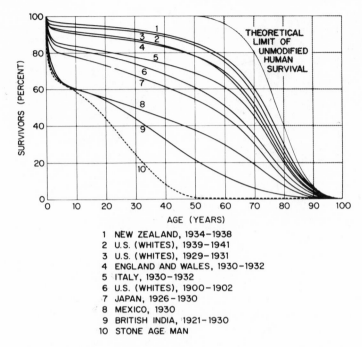

FIGURE 3.2. **Historical changes in the human survival curve.**

SOURCE: Reprinted by permission of the publisher from *The biology of senescence* by A. Comfort. © 1979 Elsevier Science Publishing Co., Inc.

kingdom is evident in Table 3.1. The longevities reported for both domestic animals and those in the wild depend upon the accuracy of records, how many animals have been studied, and how they fare in captivity. One can see that each group of animals has both long and short lived species. Why should different species of animals have finite, fixed maximum life spans? Recent work by Sacher (1975, 1976) and by Cutler (1975, 1978) have discussed some of the underlying biological factors that may be governing maximum life-span potentials (MLP). They have looked at how a species' body size and brain size relate to MLP through a regression equation given by Sacher (1957). Table 3.2 illustrates how closely the predicted MLP obtained from the equation compares to the observed maximum life span. The relationship between body and brain size and MLP can account, statistically, for over 80% of the observed variation in mammal life-span values.

Besides body size and brain size, a species' basal specific metabolic rate (SMR) is also related to maximum life-span potential. In general there is a negative correlation, in that the higher the SMR, the shorter the life span. These data show a strong correlation between rate of oxygen consumption per body weight and aging rate, suggesting that oxygen utilization may be

TABLE 3.1. **Maximum Recorded Life Spans for Selected Mammals, Birds, Reptiles, and Amphibians**

	Scientific Name	Common Name	Maximum Life Span (years)
Primates	*Macaca mulatta*	Rhesus monkey	29
	Pan troglodytes	Chimpanzee	44
	Gorilla gorilla	Gorilla	39
	Homo sapiens	Man	115
Carnivores	*Felis catus*	Domestic cat	28
	Canis familiaris	Domestic dog	20
	Ursus arctos	Brown bear	36
Ungulates	*Ovis aries*	Sheep	20
	Sus scrofa	Swine	27
	Equus caballus	Horse	46
	Elephas maximus	Indian elephant	70
Rodents	*Mus musculus*	House mouse	3
	Rattus rattus	Black rat	5
	Sciurus carolinensis	Gray squirrel	15
	Hystrix brachyura	Porcupine	27
Bats	*Desmodus rotundus*	Vampire bat	13
	Pteropus giganteus	Indian fruit bat	17
Birds	*Streptopelia risoria*	Domestic dove	30
	Larus argentatus	Herring gull	41
	Aquila chrysaëtos	Golden eagle	46
	Bubo bubo	Eagle owl	68
Reptiles	*Eunectes murinus*	Anaconda	29
	Macroclemys temmincki	Snapping turtle	58+
	Alligator sinensis	Chinese alligator	52
	Testudo elephantopus	Galapagos tortoise	100+
Amphibians	*Xenopus laevis*	African clawed toad	15
	Bufo bufo	Common toad	36
	Cynops pyrrhogaster	Japanese newt	25

SOURCE: Kirkwood, T.B.L. 1985. Comparative and evolutionary aspects of longevity. In *Handbook of the biology of aging*, 2d ed., C. E. Finch and E. L. Schneider, eds. New York: Van Nostrand Reinhold.

TABLE 3.2. **Prediction of Maximum Life-Span Potential on Basis of Body and Brain Weight for Some Common Mammalian Species**

Common name	Cranial capacity (cm^3)	Body weight (g)	Maximum life-span potential (yr)	
			Observed	Predicted*
Nonprimate species				
Pigmy shrew	0.11	5.3	1.5	1.8
Field mouse	0.45	22.6	3.5	3.2
Opossum	7.65	5000	7.0	5.8
Mongolian horse	587	260 kg	46	38
Camel	570	450	30	33
Cow	423	465	30	27
Giraffe	680	529	34	35
Elephant (India)	5045	2347	70	89
Mountain lion	154	54	19	23
Domestic dog	79	13.4 ↓	20	21
Primate species				
Tree shrew	4.3	275	7	7.7
Marmoset	9.8	4.3	15	12
Squirrel monkey	24.8	630	21	20
Rhesus monkey	106	8719	29	27
Baboon	179	16,000	36	33
Gibbon	104	5500	32	30
Orangutan	420	69,000	50	41
Gorilla	550	140,000	40	42
Chimpanzee	410	49,000	45	43
Man	1446	65,000	95	92

*The equation used to predict MLP is MLP = 10.839 (brain wt, g)$^{0.636}$ × (body wt, g)$^{-0.225}$.

SOURCE: Cutler, R. G. 1978. Evolutionary biology of senescence. In *The biology of aging*, J. A. Behnke, C. E. Finch, and G. B. Moment, eds. New York: Plenum Press. Reprinted with permission.

related to the processes of aging. There are abundant data describing the toxicity of by-products of oxygen metabolism (Armstrong et al. 1984). For example, oxygen metabolism produces free radicals, aldehydes, and a wide range of peroxides that are highly toxic and could therefore be important in the aging process. There are a number of defense and protective mechanisms in the cell that protect the organism against the toxic side effects of normal oxygen metabolism. Cutler (1984) has collected data on various antioxidants that combat the harmful effects of oxygen metabolism and evaluated them as possible determinants of maximum life span. Superoxide dimutase (SOD) is one of the most important enzymes that counteracts the toxic effect of oxygen metabolism. Figure 3.3 demonstrates

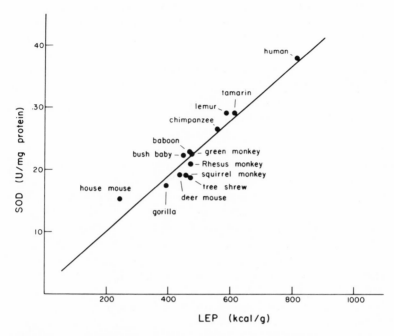

FIGURE 3.3. **Correlation of SOD activity per LEP in liver.** Correlation coefficient, r = .952; p < .001.

SOURCE: Cutler, R. J. Antioxidants, aging and longevity. In *Free radicals in biology, Vol VI,* W. A. Pryor, ed. Academic Press, New York, 1984. Reprinted with permission.

a very close correlation (r = .952, p < .001) between SOD and life-span energy potential (LEP). LEP is derived from the specific metabolism rate times life span potential (SMR × LSP). In addition to superoxide dimutase, Cutler and his associates have demonstrated with nine other cellular anti-oxidants that in general, the longer the life span, the higher the level of antioxidant (Cutler 1984).

Theories on the Evolution of Aging

In order to understand the diversity of maximum life span that abounds in vertebrates, it is relevant to ask how these survival patterns evolved. There are two contrasting types of theories on the evolution of aging. The first sees aging as advantageous and essential to set a finite limit to the life of the individual. This kind of theory is termed *adaptive* and suggests that aging has been selected for by natural selection. The second, a *nonadaptive* kind of theory, argues that senescence is detrimental to the reproductive fitness of the individual and is not selected for directly.

The adaptive theory is based on three assumptions: (1) natural selection is operating; (2) there is age structure in populations; and (3) there are genes affecting longevity and age-specific reproductive rates. Implied in these assumptions is the corollary that the reproductive pattern of a population affects the evolution of senescence within it such that life span should be *shorter* in a population with a relatively earlier average age of reproduction and *longer* in a population with a relatively later age of reproduction. According to Rose and Service (1985), these assumptions and corollaries appear to be valid.

Two of the main nonadaptive theories are (1) the force of natural selection declines with age and is eventually too weak to prevent senescence and (2) aging is a by-product of other adaptive traits. A possible genetic mechanism for the first nonadaptive theory is the maintenance of deleterious genes by mutation pressure. These mutations have such late effects (they occur late in the reproductive period or even postreproductively) that natural selection has little impact on them (Medawar 1952). With this explanation, senescence is nothing more than the result of random accumulation of deleterious mutations with late age-specific effects.

Williams (1957) proposed the second nonadaptive theory through the action of antagonistic pleiotropy. Here, natural selection favors genes that have beneficial effects early in life. However, these genes are pleiotropic (genes having more than one effect) and have deleterious effects later in the life span. Since the harmful effects are late in life, selection against such pleiotropic genes will be outweighed by the positive selection for their beneficial properties. A hypothetical example is a mutation which has a favorable effect on the calcification of bones during development but later results in calcification of the arteries.

Evolution of the Human Life Span

In order to determine which theory of the evolution of aging best applies to humans, we need to look at the primate order and examine possible variables that contribute to maximum life span. Table 3.3 illustrates the relationship between body weight, cranial capacity, and life span in living primate species. The predicted maximum life span is calculated using the same regression equation that was used in Table 3.2. The superfamilies, Lorisoidea, Lemuroidea, and Tarsioidea are considered the lower primates and are grouped in the suborder, Prosimii. The Ceboidea (New World monkeys) have evolved separately from the Cercopithecoidea (Old World monkeys) and do not have fossil representatives in the human ancestral line. The Old World monkeys and the Hominoidea (apes and humans) are the primates more closely related to modern humans. The overall trend in length of maximal life span is that the lower primates (galagos, lemurs,

TABLE 3.3. **The Relationship between Body Weight, Cranial Capacity, and Life Span in Living Primate Species**

Superfamily and genus/species	Average Body Weight (g)	Average cranial capacity (cc)	Life span (yrs)	
			Observed	Predicted
LORISOIDEA				
Perodicticus potto				
(potto)	1,150	14.0	12	12
Galago crassicandatus				
(greater galago)	850	10.3	14	11
Galago senegalensis				
(lesser galago)	186	2.8	25	9
LEMUROIDEA				
Hepalemur griseus				
(grey gentle lemur)	1,300	9.5	12	9
Lemur macaco fulvus				
(black lemur)	1,400	23.3	31	16
TARSIOIDEA				
Tarsius syrichta				
(tarsier)	87.5	3.63	12	9
CEBOIDEA				
Saguinus oedipus				
(tamarin)	413	9.8	15	12
Saimiri sciureus				
(squirrel monkey)	630	24.8	21	20
Cebus apella				
(black-capped capuchin)	2,400	75	40	29
Cebus capucinus				
(white throated capuchin)	3,765	74	40	26
CERCOPITHECOIDEA				
Presbytis entellus				
(langur)	21,319	119	22	24
Macaca mulatta				
(rhesus)	8,719	106	29	27
Papio hamadryas				
(baboon)	16,000	179	36	33
HOMINOIDEA				
S. syndactylus				
(siamang)	11,100	126	16	29
Hylobates lar				
(gibbon)	5,500	104	32	30

TABLE 3.3.   *(continued)*

Superfamily and genus/species	Average Body Weight (g)	Average cranial capacity (cc)	Life span (yrs) Observed	Life span (yrs) Predicted
Gorilla gorilla (gorilla)	140,000	550	40	42
Pan troglodytes (chimpanzee)	49,000	410	45	43
Pan t. paniscus (pygmy chimpanzee)	38,500	356	40+	42
Pongo pygmaeus (orangutan)	69,000	415	50	41
Homo sapiens modern	65,000	1,446	95	92

NOTE: Based on the regression, due to Sacher: life span = 10.839 (cranial capacity)$^{0.636}$ × (body weight)$^{-0.225}$. *Galago senegalensis, Lemur macaco fulvus, Cebus apella,* and *Cebus capucinus* have life spans significantly longer than predicted, attributed by Cutler to metabolic traits.

SOURCE: Data from Cutler (1976) as cited in Weiss, K. M. Evolutionary perspectives on human aging. In *Other ways of growing old: Anthropological perspectives* edited by Pamela T. Amoss and Stevan Harrell with the permission of the publishers, Stanford University Press. © 1981 by the Board of Trustees of the Leland Stanford Junior University.

tarsiers) have a shorter life span than the higher primates (chimpanzees, orangutans, and gorillas). In the middle, the New World and Old World monkeys show a diversity of life-span lengths. The major variable is body size, which is a good indicator of development rates and metabolism. However, cranial capacity is a more important factor when comparing the predicted life spans between the great apes and humans.

The increase in brain size and accompanying behavioral changes that occurred in human evolution have led anthropologists to look for clues as to the beginning of life-span expansion in humans. Washburn (1981) has outlined three phases of the primate life span as preparation, adaptation, and decline (Table 3.4). Preparation, which includes infancy and juvenile periods, can be determined by tooth eruption patterns. The adaptation or the reproductive period is defined by the eruption of the third molar and completed with the union of the proximal epiphysis of the humerus (maturation of bone calcification). This period of adaptation is roughly twice the length of preparation. The period of decline exists where it is possible for animals to grow old where there are less hazards in the environment: lower predator pressure, fewer food shortages, and less habitat disturbance, to name a few. In most primates living in the wild, this period of aging is very short or nonexistent. The range in the table takes into consideration life spans of captive animals.

TABLE 3.4. **Length of Phases of Primate Life Span in Years**

	Preparation (Immaturity)			Adaptation (Maturity)	Decline (decreasing effectiveness)
	Eruption of molars:				
	First	Second	Third		
Human	6	12	18	18–45	45–75
Chimpanzee	3	6	10	10–30	30–50
Macaque	2	4	6	6–20	20–35

SOURCE: Washburn, S. L. 1981. Longevity in primates. In *Aging—Biology and behavior*. J. L. McGaugh and S. B. Kiesler, eds. New York: Academic Press. Reprinted with permission.

The juvenile period (preparation) has received recent attention by Lancaster (1985), who focused on its role in the evolution of the hominid life cycle. Primate studies have shown that when there are fluctuating food supplies, on the average only one in eight monkeys born survive to adulthood. In the more slowly developing baboon and chimpanzee, one in three survive to reproductive maturity. The loss of offspring during early infancy is common and varies little from species to species. But there is much variation during the juvenile period. When food supplies are poor, the young subordinate animals suffer disproportionately because of their disadvantage in finding and competing for food. Unlike these primates, human juveniles do not have to forage for themselves. Thus, the intense selection pressure during which poor food supply selects out juveniles has been eliminated. In fact, data show that human hunter and gatherer groups with occasional food scarcity have similar survivorships to adulthood as nonhuman primate groups with no food limitations (those provisioned by humans).

As a rule, the infant and juvenile periods tend to be more or less equal in the individual life cycles of nonhuman primate species (Lancaster 1985). For example, an infant chimpanzee may be nursed four to five years and spend the same period as a juvenile living close to its mother before it reaches reproductive maturity. In contrast, a human infant may be nursed for as long as four years in hunter-gatherer societies but will not reach reproductive adulthood for another twelve years. The delay of the onset of reproductive maturity would be selected for only if it enhanced the reproductive success of the individual or the species as a whole. This prolonged dependence brings with it a greater vulnerability to starvation and predation and the postponement of reproduction. However, the longer juvenile period considerably lengthens the time for learning. According to Lancaster, early hominids might have evolved two major behavioral patterns:

TABLE 3.5. **Life Span and Stages in Hominid Evolution**

Genus/species	Est. avg. body wt. (kg)	Est. avg. cranial cap. (cc)	Predicted life span (yrs)	Time of appearance (yr × 10⁻⁶)
Ramapithecus punjabicus	32	300	42	14
Australopithecus africanus	32	450	51	3
Australopithecus robustus	40.5	500	52	2.5
Australopithecus boisei	47.5	530	52	2
Homo habilis	43	660	61	1.5
Homo erectus javanicus	53	860	69	0.7
Homo erectus pekinensis	53	1,040	78	0.25
Homo europaeus pre-Wurm	—	1,310	89	0.1
Homo neanderthalensis europaeus	—	1,460	93	0.045
Homo sapiens europaeus Wurm	—	1,460	94	0.015
Homo sapiens recens	—	1,460	94	0.01
Homo sapiens modern	63.5	1,410	91	present

NOTE: This table is taken directly from Cutler to illustrate the trend; no claim is made that taxonomic assignment, weight, or cranial capacity estimates are exact. This area is somewhat controversial at the moment, however, the trend is in general not affected. Cutler's data are from various primary sources.

SOURCE: Data from Cutler (1975) as cited in Weiss, K. M. Evolutionary perspectives on human aging. In *Other ways of growing old: Anthropological perspectives*, edited by Pamela T. Amoss and Stevan Harrell with the permission of the publishers, Stanford University Press. © 1981 by the Board of Trustees of the LeLand Stanford Junior University.

their feeding of juveniles and the creation of a protected environment in which to learn—a home base. In this way juvenile survivorship is maximized and more time is available for young hominids to spend in play, object manipulation, and learning hunting and gathering skills. Thus, increased parental investment along with delayed reproductive maturation may have later led to our long life span—the longest among the primates.

What is actually known about the maximum life spans of our hominid ancestors? Table 3.5 gives estimates that Cutler (1975) has calculated using the same regression equation previously described. Although there is inherent error in estimating average cranial capacity and body size for ancestral species based on fragmentary fossils, the MLP for early hominids prior to one million years ago was about fifty years. The australopithecines are considered the first hominids. It appears that most of the changes in MLP occurred during the period when they evolved into Homo erectus (from about four to one million years ago). The estimates in Table 3.5 illustrate that the changes in MLP have been fairly rapid and there has been essentially no change in MLP since the appearance of Homo sapiens one hundred thousand years ago.

There is evidence that at the australopithecine period of human evolu-

TABLE 3.6. **History of Human Life Expectancy (Approximate values in years)**

Cultural group	General range of life expectancy
Australopithecines	±15
Neanderthals	±18
"Hunters" through the Neolithic	19–25
Early agriculturalists and horticulturalists	20–27
Westerners of the classical and medieval periods	22–29
Living primates	22–29
Sweden 1780	38
United Kingdom 1861	43
Guatemala 1893	24
Sweden 1905	55
Sweden 1965	76

SOURCE: Weiss, K. M. Evolutionary perspectives on human aging. In *Other ways of growing old: Anthropological perspectives,* edited by Pamela T. Amoss and Stevan Harrell with the permission of the publishers, Stanford University Press. © 1981 by the Board of Trustees of the LeLand Stanford Junior University.

tion the maturation rate had slowed down. In other words, the expansion of the juvenile period had already begun. Mann (1975) has shown through X-rays that in humans the eruption of the permanent teeth has slowed. The second molar has not undergone calcification at the time the first molar erupts. However, in apes, the tooth that is about to erupt next is calcified by the time the preceding tooth has erupted. These data suggest that sexual maturation came at a later time in the australopithecines since studies of tooth eruption patterns show that sexual maturity is close to the time of the eruption of the second molar (Washburn 1981).

If the human maximum life span had essentially reached the current MLP one hundred thousand years ago, how has the *average* life span changed during human evolution? Table 3.6 provides a summary of the work focused on the history of human longevity. Although the early data are based on fragmentary materials, Weiss (1981) concludes that for early hominids through early agricultural populations, life expectancy at birth was only about twenty to thirty years. This short average life span reflects heavy infant mortality. Those who survived infancy would probably live through their thirties. Figure 3.4 shows a survivorship curve of a pre-contact American Indian population, the Libben of Ohio. This skeletal study included 1289 burials and is probably one of the more reliable

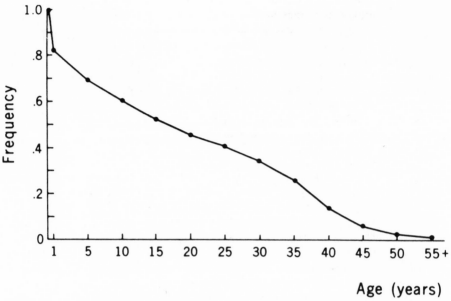

FIGURE 3.4. **Survivorship curve for the total Libben population.**

Source: Data from Lovejoy et al., 1977 as cited in Washburn, S. L. Longevity in primates. In *Aging—Biology and behavior*, J. L. McGaugh and S. B. Kiesler, eds. Academic Press, New York, 1981. Reprinted with permission.

paleodemographic studies available. Here the average life span is about fifteen years. These modern *Homo sapiens* hunter-gatherers had essentially the same *average* life span as the australopithecines. Note how this survival curve relates to curves 1(b) and 2(b) of Figure 3.1.

Genetics of Longevity

If one operates on the assumption that natural selection is selecting for a longer life span (adaptive theory), then there must be genes affecting longevity. Almost everyone is familiar with the simple observation that longevity "runs in families." Pearl and Pearl (1934a) published results of a study in which they attempted to look for a familial component in longevity by comparing the ages at death of the parents and grandparents of long-lived individuals (ninety or over) with ages at death of persons bearing the same relationships to control subjects. Recently, Abbott and colleagues (1974, 1978) conducted a follow-up analysis of the descendents of the Pearls' study. They found with a sample of 9,205 progeny a small positive correlation between the average age at death of the descendents and the original subjects. Two interesting aspects of this study were that parents who died at any age of eighty-one or older had offspring who lived on the average some five to seven years longer than offspring of parents who died at sixty or younger. In the correlation between parent and offspring, the relationship between mother and child was closer than that between father and child.

Perhaps the best evidence for genetic factors that influence human longevity is Kallman and Sander's work in 1948. They compared over nine hundred pairs of monozygotic and dizygotic twins and found that the mean difference in longevity between the dizygotic pairs (78.3 months) was twice that between monozygotic pairs (36.9 months). Kallman and Sander noted in their paper that in cases where adult identical twins lived apart in different environments, many of them aged identically. They stated, "The similarities often included the degree of general enfeeblement or its absence, the graying and thinning of hair, the configuration of baldness and senile wrinkle formation, and the types and extent of eye, ear, and tooth deficiencies" (Kallman and Sander 1948, 353).

While it is widely recognized that there are probably genetic components in longevity, the mechanism through which these factors work still eludes investigators. Certainly there are many examples of single gene traits that cause early death, but so far there is no single gene known in humans that prolongs life. Abbott and his coworkers (1978) suggest that the genetic component of longevity operates not through specific genes for longevity but through an absence of deleterious genes leading to premature death. But recent research in heart disease and immunology has brought promising findings that indicate some single genes may be operating in longevity after adulthood. A growing body of research suggests that high-density lipoproteins (HDL) protect against heart attacks. Glueck and his colleagues (1976, 1977) have identified two groups of people who are genetically endowed either with high HDL or low LDL (low-density lipoproteins) concentrations. High concentrations of LDL have been linked to an increased risk of heart attack or stroke. Those people with the high HDL or low LDL levels rarely have arteriosclerosis and have life spans as much as five to twelve years longer than average.

The other area of interest, the immune system, is becoming one of the most promising systems being investigated in both basic and applied aging research (Makinodan 1977). It is involved with many of the diseases of the aged and offers potential in minimizing the deteriorative processes of aging. There is an increasing amount of data demonstrating an association between the histocompatibility complex (HLA) and a variety of disease states. The HLA system (human leukocyte antigens) is a genetic system in which the antigen groups on white blood cells are inherited. There are at least four genes that code for the HLA antigens: A, B, C, and D. The four genes are closely linked together on the same chromosome, and the alleles (alternative genes at the same locus) for these genes produce many kinds of linkage groups in individuals. The HLA-A1-B8-Dw3 linkage group has been associated with decreased immune cell function and decreased survival in women (Greenberg and Yunis 1978). Yarnell and colleagues (1979) reported a significant increase in frequency of HLA-B40 in the over-seventy age group of a population they studied for HLA differences related to the absence or presence of ten chronic diseases. The excess HLA-B40 was found in the disease-free group.

Sex differences in longevity are well established facts. In most countries around the world, women outlive men and can have increased average life spans of as much as seven to eight years. However, there are at least ten countries where male life expectancies equal or exceed female life expectancies at birth (see Table 3.7). It is possible that genes carried on the X chromosome may decrease vulnerability to degenerative diseases. And it may be possible that genes on the Y chromosome may exert life-shortening effects in addition to their main function. In other words, genes on the X and Y chromosomes may have pleiotropic effects. Most researchers point to the more hazardous environment (occupation) of the male as the culprit for his shorter life span. However the male sex is the shorter-lived in most animal species (Hayflick 1982). After studying the data of various researchers who were measuring the heritability of longevity, Jacquard, a population geneticist, came to the conclusion that the variation seen in longevity was better explained by environmental factors than by genetic factors (Jacquard 1982). Whatever may be operating in the genes, women appear to be more successful in the interaction of environment and their genetic makeup. (For additional discussion of sex differences in longevity, see the chapters by Beall and Uhlenberg.)

Theories of Evolution of Human Life Span

Let us turn our attention back to the two basic theories of the evolution of aging. If we consider the adaptive theory first, we remember that there is some evidence of genetic factors playing a part in longevity. Cutler (1980) accounts for the evolutionary changes in the primate life span as a result of point mutations occurring in the regulatory genes. He cites work of other researchers that points to the lack of correlation between the rate of change in amino acid sequences of proteins and nucleotide sequences of DNA with the rate of change occurring in morphology and the appearance of new species. It has been previously recognized that much of the change in morphology in primates with increasing maximum life spans can be explained by a general retardation of development, a process called neotany. When comparing human and chimp, we are more fetal and childlike at all stages of development. Cutler has suggested that different sets of regulatory genes cause a common set of structural genes to be expressed at

TABLE 3.7. **Life Expectancies at Birth, Birthrates, Fertility, Death Rates, and Infant Mortalities in Nations Where Male Life Expectancy Equals or Exceeds Female Life Expectancy at Birth**

Nation	Life expectancy		Births/1000	Fertility	Death/1000	Infant mortality/1000
	Male	Female				
Upper Volta	32.10	31.10	48.5	197.0	25.8	182.0
Bangladesh	35.80	35.80	49.5	231.7	2.8	. . .
Nigeria	37.20	36.70	49.3	217.8	22.7	. . .
India	41.89	40.55	34.5	136.7	14.4	122.0
Kampuchea	44.20	43.30	46.7	143.1	19.0	127.0
Liberia	45.80	44.00	49.8	161.2	20.9	159.2
Sabah Malaysia	48.79	45.43	35.0	179.4	14.4	31.6
Indonesia	47.50	47.50	42.9	175.7	16.9	125.0
Pakistan	53.72	48.80	36.0	174.8	12.0	124.0
Jordan	52.60	52.00	47.6	206.6	14.7	36.3
Industrial Nations of High Life Expectancy						
Canada	69.34	76.36	15.8	61.6	7.2	15.0
U.S.A.	68.70	76.50	14.7	58.5	8.9	15.1
Denmark	71.10	76.80	12.9	61.3	10.7	10.3
France	69.00	76.90	13.6	72.0	10.5	10.4
Netherlands	71.20	77.20	12.9	53.9	8.3	10.5
Japan	72.15	77.35	16.4	62.6	6.3	9.3
Sweden	72.09	77.65	11.9	56.4	11.0	8.7
Norway	71.50	77.83	13.3	64.1	9.9	11.1
Iceland	73.00	79.20	19.4	81.9	6.9	11.7

SOURCE: United Nations (1978) as cited in Stini, W. A. Growth rates and sexual dimorphism in evolutionary perspective. In *The analysis of prehistoric diets*, R. I. Gilbert and J. H. Mielke, eds. Academic Press, New York, 1985. Reprinted with permission.

different times and degrees to affect the morphological changes seen between nonhuman primates and humans. A different set of regulatory genes, then, would also change the expression and time of the structural genes that determine aging rate. He estimates that there are 40 to 250 amino acid substitutions per fourteen years of increased maximum life potential per one hundred thousand years to produce the current human life-span period of one hundred years.

Although Cutler's estimates are interesting, we still do not know how natural selection selects for these regulatory gene changes. Currently primate behavioral studies have provided data to support the role of inclusive fitness as a mechanism by which older members of a population may be selected for. Hrdy (1981) defines fitness as the genetic contribution an individual makes to the next generation. In other words, the more offspring one has, the greater reproductive fitness that individual possesses. Inclusive fitness not only involves an individual's fitness but also any contribution the individual's behavior makes to the reproductive success of his or her close relatives. Hrdy cites data of her own and those of other researchers that describe old female monkeys (macaques and langurs) exhibiting caretaking behavior toward related individuals. Because there are few old males in monkey populations in the wild, the focus of the role of inclusive fitness is on aged females. The old females are among the first to defend their grandchildren and other related kin and may serve as important repositories of information in times of emergencies such as severe drought. Thus, investment in kin by postreproductive females may be one way a longer life span could be selected. If this kind of behavior is genetically determined, then those genes will increase in frequency in the population if the inclusive fitness is greater in individuals who exhibit altruism toward their kin.

This pattern of behavior has been examined in studying the evidence of inclusive fitness in human life-span research. Mayer (1982) studied four New England genealogies that totaled 1,890 women born between 1675 and 1874. Those who died postmenopausally had greater inclusive fitness than those who died premenopausally. Mayer suggests that the women who lived beyond menopause could help in the caretaking of their grandchildren and other close kin and thus increase the probability of these relatives' reproductive success. He goes on to suggest that this constitutes an evolutionary advantage of the menopause. He proposes that postreproductive women could be infant carriers. This would enhance population growth through shorter birth intervals among mobile hominid groups.

Washburn (1981) and Weiss (1981) believe the modern human life span can be explained by a nonadaptive theory of evolution. Washburn views old age as a by-product of adaptation at younger ages. Selection for genes that maximize reproductive fitness during the younger years provides the possibility of a long period of old age if the environment is optimal.

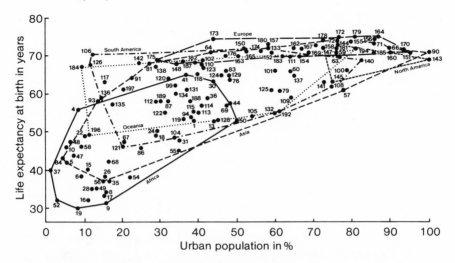

FIGURE 3.5. **Life expectancy at birth in years and percentage of urban population in different countries of six continents.** *Africa:* 1, Algeria; 4, Botswana; 5, Burundi; 6, Cameroon; 8, Central African Empire; 9, Chad; 10, Comoros; 13, Egypt; 15, Ethiopia; 16, Gabon; 17, Gambia; 18, Ghana; 19, Guinea; 22, Kenya; 24, Liberia; 26, Madagascar; 28, Mali; 30, Mauritius; 31, Morocco; 35, Nigeria; 36, Reunion; 37, Rwanda; 41, Seychelles; 44, South Africa; 47, Swaziland; 48, Tanzania; 49, Togo; 50, Tunisia; 52, Upper Volta; 54, Zaire; 55, Zambia. *Asia:* 56, Afghanistan; 57, Bahrain; 58, Bangladesh; 59, Bhutan; 60, Brunei; 63, Taiwan; 64, Cyprus; 66, Hong Kong; 67, India; 68, Indonesia; 69, Iran; 71, Israel; 72, Japan; 76, Republic of Korea; 79, Lebanon; 81, Malaysia; 83, Mongolia; 84, Nepal; 86, Pakistan; 87, Philippines; 90, Singapore; 91, Sri Lanka; 93, Thailand; 94, Turkey. *Latin America:* 99, Antigua; 100, Argentina; 101, Bahamas; 102, Barbados; 104, Bolivia; 105, Brazil; 106, British Virgin Islands; 108, Chile; 109, Colombia; 110, Costa Rica; 111, Cuba; 112, Dominican Republic; 114, Ecuador; 115, El Salvador; 117, Grenada; 118, Guadeloupe; 119, Guatemala; 120, Guyana; 121, Haiti; 122, Honduras; 123, Jamaica; 124, Martinique; 125, Mexico; 126, Montserrat; 128, Nicaragua; 129, Panama; 131, Paraguay; 132, Puerto Rico; 134, Saint Christopher-Nevis-Anguilla; 135, Saint Lucia; 136, Saint Vincent; 137, Surinam; 138, Trinidad and Tobago; 140, Uruguay; 141, Venezuela; 142, Virgin Islands. *North America:* 143, Bermuda; 144, Canada; 145, Greenland; 147, United States. *Europe:* 148, Albania; 150, Austria; 151, Belgium; 152, Bulgaria; 154, Czechoslovakia; 155, Denmark; 156, Faroe Islands; 157, Finland; 158, France; 159, German Democratic Republic; 160, Federal Republic of Germany; 162, Greece; 163, Hungary; 164, Iceland; 165, Ireland; 167, Italy; 169, Luxembourg; 170, Malta; 172, Netherlands; 173, Norway; 174, Poland; 175, Portugal; 176, Romania; 178, Spain; 179, Sweden; 180, Switzerland; 181, United Kingdom; 182, Yugoslavia; 183, Soviet Union. *Oceania:* 184, American Samoa; 185, Australia; 187, Fiji; 188, French Polynesia; 189, Gilbert Islands and Tuvalu; 192, New Caledonia; 194, New Zealand; 196, Papua New Guinea; 197, Samoa.

SOURCE: Wolanski, N. Urbanization and life span. *Current Anthropology* 23: 579–80. © 1982, University of Chicago Press. Reprinted with permission.

However he does not propose how this is done. Weiss argues that one does not need to involve inclusive fitness in explaining the evolution of the maximum life span of people today. He considers the existence of an aging clock calibrated with the variables of body size and metabolism to be operative and the only way to extend the calculated life span is through change in the environment. In this case, the change in the environment is human culture. Our technology (tools, weapons, medicine, etc.) has allowed the once rare elder to become an increasingly common occurrence.

The role of culture in the increasing average life span of populations will be developed in more detail in chapter 13. However, a few points can be made here. There is no doubt that level of nutrition, health care, and sanitation is correlated with increasing life span. Wolanski (1982) has plotted life expectancy at birth and degree of urbanization of over one hundred countries to show that urban conditions have a positive effect on life span (Figure 3.5). The relationship is strongest in countries of Africa and Asia but less prominent in Oceania and South America. The relationship is negligible in the countries of North America. Thus, there is a certain optimal degree of urbanization, which he found to be 40–50%. Fry (1985) brings up another point that relates to the gender difference in life spans discussed earlier. She asks if the sex roles that men and women have during their earlier years may be factors in how men and women age in their culture. For example, in a given society or culture, women may have more flexibility to deal with age-related role losses.

Both biological and sociocultural aspects of aging must be examined if the evolution of the human life span is to be understood. Perhaps the importance of the two are best seen as an interaction in which biological factors emerge first in importance and then sociocultural conditions are present that permit the individual to live his or her full potential life span (Moore 1981). For example, if one has a family history of an unusual amount of heart disease and cancer, he or she will have a low probability of reaching an advanced age. Yet another individual, whose family history lacks the predisposition for these diseases, may need the positive effect of high social status and the sense of continuity to reach his or her full life span. Thus, a sort of genetic bottleneck may be operating in populations that screens out those individuals who have genetic tendencies for fatal adult diseases. This screening provides the background for sociocultural factors to maximize life span.

IV

STUDIES OF LONGEVITY

Cynthia M. Beall

Longevity refers to a long duration of individual life, measured as chronological age. Scientific interest in longevity centers on identifying biological, sociocultural, and environmental concomitants of survival to advanced age. This chapter describes the major approaches to studying longevity and some of the commonly studied influences. In the process, it also illustrates some of the methodological intricacies of these studies.

The Classical Anthropological Approach

The classical anthropological approach to longevity compares diverse populations in order to detect common denominators. Well-known, but poorly executed, applications of this approach are the source of popular and scientific misconceptions about longevity. Indeed, this chapter must begin by debunking the notion that there are some remote populations characterized by extreme longevity. Three populations, Hunza in Pakistan, Vilcabamba in Ecuador, and Abkhasia in the Soviet Union, have received widespread attention owing to reports from a series of visits and studies seeking to determine the biological, sociocultural, or environmental determinants of their reputed longevity (Benet 1974; Davies 1975; Halsell 1976; Leaf 1973a and b; Pitskhelauri n.d., translated in 1982). However, before seeking the cause of their longevity, it is necessary to establish whether these populations are in fact longevous. The following discussion evaluates the published evidence and shows that there is no substance to claims that these societies are characterized by unusual longevity.

Longevity may be measured at the individual and the population level. Stating that a group is characterized by extreme longevity could mean any or all of the following: that some members are exceptionally old, that an especially large number of its members are old, that its old members have an unusually good chance of surviving to even older ages. Each of these meanings can be evaluated for the three reputedly longevous populations.

73

One line of evidence for unusual longevity is the presence of individuals of extraordinarily old age. Ages of 120–140 years have been reported in each of these three populations (Davies 1975; Halsell 1976; Leaf 1973a and b; Pitskhelauri n.d., translated in 1982). However, these reported ages do not withstand close scrutiny. For one of the three reputedly long-lived populations, the Hunza, ages are simply not known because there are no written records or censuses to independently verify individuals' stated ages. They will not be discussed further. For the other two (Vilcabamba and Abkhasia), age exaggeration has been established unequivocally. This was detected differently in the two areas.

In Catholic, Spanish-speaking Vilcabamba, the presence of written church records lent a spurious sense of accuracy to the initial reports of extraordinarily old residents. Authors gave isolated examples of documenting reported ages by finding in these records individuals of the "right" name born around the "right" time. These were offered as evidence for the authenticity of reported ages (e.g., Leaf 1973a and b; Davies 1975). However, these authors did not present a systematic verification of all claimed ages. Furthermore, since they did not use the records properly, even the supposedly authentic ages are inaccurate. The most recent, and the only thorough, scientific, assessment of age and longevity detected age exaggeration in Vilcabamba. It found that determining accurate ages there hinged upon correctly linking individuals in the community with individuals in the records (Mazess and Foreman 1979). Constructing extensive genealogies revealed that there are relatively few different personal and family names in this community, and therefore many individuals have all or some of the same names. Because the earlier researchers in this community were apparently unaware of this, they often associated individuals with the wrong records of birth or baptism. Thus, many exaggerated ages had been "verified" erroneously when living individuals were linked incorrectly with the records of parents, aunts, uncles, and older deceased siblings, or even unrelated persons with the same name or with some of the same names (Leaf 1982; Mazess and Foreman 1979). The following paragraph describes one scientist's realization that he had been misled this way.

> Micaela Quezada's case is another that typifies the difficulties encountered in determining ages. She claimed to be 106 years old. I had seen her baptismal record prominently underscored by local officials in the book of birth records. She was born in 1870 and it was then 1974, so the documented age of 104 was not too inconsistent with her claim of 106 years. However, on questioning we found her father's name to be Benino Quezada, and her mother's, Maria de los Angeles Mendietta. A return visit to the baptismal records revealed that the Micaela Quezada listed there as born in 1870 had parents named Juan Quezada and Maria Mercedes Patino. This revelation was disconcerting. Clearly the entry in the baptismal record was of a person

with different parents from those of our living Micaela Quezada. When confronted directly by these facts, Senorita Quezada said, "Oh, yes, of course, that's my cousin who lived in San Pedro (a village some three miles away). She was older than me and died thirty or forty years ago." Thus we had been misled by accepting a baptismal record that our Ecuadorian friends had mistaken for that of the living Micaela Quezada. Since the same names were used repeatedly, one had to make certain that the name in the baptismal record was of the same generation as that of the living person (Leaf 1982, 485).[1]

This was not done systematically until the Mazess and Foreman findings were published in 1979. Though Leaf knew in 1974 that there was a problem with age accuracy and thus the findings of his 1973 articles, he did not publish this until 1982, three years after Mazess and Foreman's work appeared.

Leaf was not the only author who detected discrepancies and ignored or passed them off as unimportant. For example, one credulous reporter was frustrated to find discrepancies between supposedly documented ages and stated ages. Citing a case where a document indicated 110 and the individual claimed 127 years of age, the reporter responded to this frustration by concluding that the Vilcabambans "may not know their exact ages but in all cases are very old" (Halsell 1976, 16). She went on to write a monograph on the "very old." Subsequently, others determined that the individual in question was 91 years old.

Constructing genealogies enabled Mazess and Foreman to identify individuals accurately by their patronyms, matronyms, and relatives' full names. Since records of births, baptisms, deaths, and marriages frequently mentioned the participants and witnesses by full name, age, and relationship, individuals could be positively identified and their reported age noted at several times during their lives. This procedure revealed that individuals generally gave approximately correct ages during young adulthood but began exaggerating their ages around 70 and exaggerated even more with increasing age. For example, one man who had given an age of 50 at one time, died 22 years later at the reputed age of 95 (Mazess and Foreman 1979). Another man who gave his age as 121 in 1970 claimed to be 131 in 1974 (Leaf 1982). His age was not verified at the time because the relevant pages of the birth records had been torn out (Leaf 1982), and other records were apparently not consulted. Using genealogies to unequivocally identify individuals several times in the various types of available records revealed that all the purported centenarians had exaggerated their ages. The oldest was 96 and their average age was 86. All of the purported nonagenerians had exaggerated their ages too. The oldest was

1. Reprinted with permission from the American Geriatric Society. Long-lived populations: Extreme old age, by A. Leaf, *Journal of the American Geriatric Society* 38:485–87.

88 and their average age was 82. Therefore, there were no centenarians in Vilcabamba (Mazess and Foreman 1979).

Accurate ages for the Abkhasians in the USSR were determined recently by using genealogies and tying individual life histories to dated events. These methods showed that age exaggeration occurs there too. Just 38% of a group of 115 people who claimed to be over 90 years of age actually were that old, and the oldest was 110 (Palmore 1984).

An earlier study describing the lives of the "longliving" (over 90) in Abkhasia devotes only one page to age verification and apparently accepted as true the stated ages of the participants, although the text is not completely clear on this point (Benet 1974, 14–15). The monograph discusses in general terms what Soviet medical teams had done to assess ages, gives one numerical example of constructing an Abkhasian's age using undocumented life history events, notes that Abkhasians are age conscious, and refers to a report describing a survey of old people. However, the monograph does not state whether individuals' reported ages or the Soviet medical team's assessment of ages were used (nor is there any mention of the degree of correspondence between these two). In addition, having noted the importance of age in determining status, it rather naively infers that this is conducive to good memory and equates that with accurate reporting. One could just as easily assume the opposite and infer that this would be conducive to carefully crafted and remembered stories supporting exaggerated ages. Furthermore, the cited report by an American sociologist who interviewed Soviet demographers about the nationwide Soviet survey of people who claimed to be over 80 says there was age exaggeration and that this was more frequent in some parts of the country, such as the Georgian Republic where Abkhasia is located (McKain 1967). Despite this weak support for accepting stated ages, the author went on to give ages as high as 134 years. Undocumented statements of extreme age as well as falsely documented ages, often involving individual misidentification (e.g., using parent's papers so as to appear above draftable age), are common sources of erroneous ages in this area (Medvedev 1974).

Thus in these two communities where the question of age accuracy has been investigated intensively, the oldest individuals were actually 97 (Vilcabamba) and 110 (Abkhasia)—old, but not mythically old as believed previously. It is interesting to note that age exaggeration is not a recent phenomenon in either community. It is not clear why this was done in Vilcabamba's past, although the attention received presently by individuals and communities appears to be an incentive to maintain the practice (Leaf 1982; Mazess and Mathisen 1982). Numerous social and political motivations have been described for age exaggeration in Abkhasia where it is easy to do because of lack of documentation. These include high local status and national attention accorded very old people, as well as Stalin's official fostering of the notion that people from this area are longevous, done in an effort to convince people of his potential for long life (Medvedev 1974).

While it seems obvious that accurate information on chronological age is essential to studies of longevity, these studies illustrate that this can be difficult to obtain. It will become easier as time passes and more societies accumulate good documentation with greater time depth, but will remain problematic for quite a while in many parts of the world. Documents must be used appropriately in order to realize their potential. In their absence, alternative techniques must be employed, such as assembling genealogies, triangulating the ages of everyone in the community, associating life events with dated historical events, and using local traditions of age assignment which can be translated into Western ages (e.g., Van Arsdale 1981; McKain 1967; Palmore 1984). Rigorous age verification should be undertaken for *all* study participants. The assumption that illiterate respondents are motivated to report accurately or that they are not capable of the numerical agility necessary to concoct a convincing story (McKain 1967) has been shown to be completely false (e.g., Mazess and Foreman 1979; Medvedev 1974). Familiarity with the culture and the motivations and opportunities it provides for age overstatement (and understatement) is essential.

Despite the absence of individuals of extreme age, these three populations could be characterized as longevous if they had an unexpectedly large number of old people. A second line of evidence used to support the claim of extreme longevity in these populations is a high proportion of elderly in the total population. While there are no data on the Hunza, this claim can be evaluated for the other two populations. The 11.4% of the 1970 resident Vilcabamba population over 60 years of age is higher than the regional average of 6%—unless account is taken of the high rate of outmigration of young adults. When this is done the proportion over 60 is 7%, no different from other regions (Mazess and Foreman 1979).

A different proportional measure is offered to support claims of a high density of longevous people in Abkhasia. The "index of longevity" is the proportion of those over 60 years of age who are over 90 years of age. After correcting for age exaggeration, the "index of longevity" of the Abkhasian population is 0.3% compared with 0.2% for the entire USSR (Koslov 1984). Unfortunately, proportions such as these are difficult to interpret because they are dependent upon other demographic parameters including migration (illustrated by the Vilcabamba example), mortality at all ages, and fertility. For example, a population with low fertility will have a small proportion of youths and a relatively large proportion of elderly. The "index of longevity" (number 90+/number 60+) of the Abkhasian population could be inflated relative to the whole USSR if Abkhasian infant mortality, out-migration, or death were high in the cohort of people born sixty to ninety years ago. There is evidence that each did occur. For example, mortality in this cohort was greatly affected by World War II (Palmore 1984). The result is a smaller denominator in the "index of longevity" and a higher value.

Thus the evidence for an unusually high proportion of elderly is deceptive in Vilcabamba and unconvincing in Abkhasia due to the nature of proportional measures. Because populations may have different proportions of elderly due to factors other than the chances of survival to old age or the mortality rates of old people, commonly used population comparisons based on proportions are likely to be misleading.

A third line of evidence used to support the claim of extreme longevity in these populations is increased life expectancy of the elderly. Life expectancy is the average number of additional years of life for an individual who has survived to a particular age. It is calculated from age specific mortality rates; lower mortality rates yield longer life expectancies. Vilcabambans have a *shorter* life expectancy than people living in the United States at all ages. For example, in the time span 1966–1979, the Vilcabamba life expectancy at 60 was 15.1 years and at age 80 was 4.2 years compared with 18.4 and 7.1 years respectively in the United States in 1969–1971 (Mazess and Mathisen 1982; *Nutrition Week* 1984).

Thus each time anecdotal claims of extreme longevity have been evaluated, they have been disproven. There is no currently known remote population characterized by well-documented extreme longevity. This hyperborean ("beyond the forests") theme of aging, that somewhere far away people do not age, has been persistent (Barash 1983), and the mistaken identification of the Hunza, Vilcabamba, and Abkhasian societies as longevous has sustained it. However, it remains mythical and, importantly, distracts attention from societies with more and better data on longevity. These are the industrial societies, where age is relatively well-documented and features associated with survival are much better studied. Even so, age exaggeration occurs there, too: the U.S. Bureau of Census estimates that 95% of the reported centenarians in the 1970 census were actually younger than 100 (Rosenwaike 1979). It occurs at earlier ages, too, as the following demonstrates.

Claims of unusual longevity of the Puerto Rican population have been made recently on the basis of high expectation of long life in adults. For example, the life expectancy of forty-five-year-old Puerto Rican males was thirty years compared with twenty-seven years for all U.S. males, and resulted from apparently very low mortality and therefore an unexpectedly high number of survivors among the elderly (Rosenwaike and Preston 1984). However, age exaggeration among people over fifty accounts for this spurious finding. Comparing changes in the size of age cohorts between the 1960 and the 1970 censuses while taking into account the age specific death rates during the intervening years enabled detection of the age exaggeration among Puerto Ricans. For example, there were 19,717

Puerto Rican males over seventy-five in the 1960 census. According to the known death rates there should have been 18,230 deaths from 1961 to 1969 leaving 1,487 males over eighty-five still alive at the 1970 census. However, the census enumerated 8,419 males claiming to be over eighty-five, nearly six times the expected number of people (Rosenwaike and Preston 1984, 520)! Massive age exaggeration adds new members erroneously to these older age cohorts while subtracting them from younger cohorts. The result is the false impression of a low death rate in the younger age categories as these deaths are counted in older age categories. This illustrates again that the accuracy of any measure of longevity rests on the accuracy of ages.

The Actuarial Approach

In addition to the anthropological approach, a second approach to the study of longevity is an actuarial one dealing with two aggregate measures of longevity—survival and life expectancy. This approach uses a formal analysis called the life table method, so called because of the convention of presenting data in the form of a table containing standardized information on mortality and survivorship. The most widely used is the "current life table method" which considers a hypothetical group of people born at one time (a cohort) experiencing the age-specific mortality rates observed for an actual population during a particular period. For example, the U.S. current life table for 1982 assumes a hypothetical cohort of one hundred thousand people subject throughout its lifetime to the age specific mortality rates for the actual U.S. population in 1982 (National Center for Health Statistics 1985). (Another method is the "generation life table method" which follows a cohort of people from birth through each consecutive year until the death of the last member, a data collection method that would take over a century and would not yet be complete for the cohort born in 1880!)

An abbreviated form of the current life table for U.S. white females in 1982 is presented in Table 4.1. A life table may be summarized graphically by drawing curves of age-specific mortality rates (column 2 of Table 4.1) and survivorship (column 3 of Table 4.1), and numerically by calculating life expectancy (last column of Table 4.1) to produce a "snapshot" of the mortality/longevity experience. The age-specific mortality rates for U.S. white females (lower curve) and U.S. "all other" females (other than white, upper curve) in 1982 plotted in Figure 4.1 illustrate the shape of mortality rate curves in all populations: a relatively high infant mortality rate is followed by lower mortality rates during childhood, adolescence, and young adulthood and then by a noticeable increase in mortality rate beginning about age forty-five to fifty and continuing exponentially thereafter. This general pattern is common to most populations although the level of mortality varies. For example, today's developing countries have

TABLE 4.1. Abbreviated Version of Abridged Life Tables, White Females: United States, 1982

| Age interval | Proportion dying | Of 100,000 born alive | | Average remaining lifetime |
Period of life between two exact ages stated in years	Proportion of persons alive at beginning of age interval dying during interval	Number living at beginning of age interval	Number dying during age interval	Average number of years of life remaining at beginning of age interval
0–1	0.0089	100,000	888	78.8
1–5	0.0019	99,112	185	78.5
5–10	0.0011	98,927	108	74.6
10–15	0.0010	98,819	102	69.7
.	.	.	.	.
.	.	.	.	.
.	.	.	.	.
75–80	0.1831	69,337	12,697	12.0
80–85	0.2899	56,640	16,419	9.0
85 and over	1.0000	40,221	40,221	6.7

SOURCE: National Center for Health Statistics: 1985, p. 7.

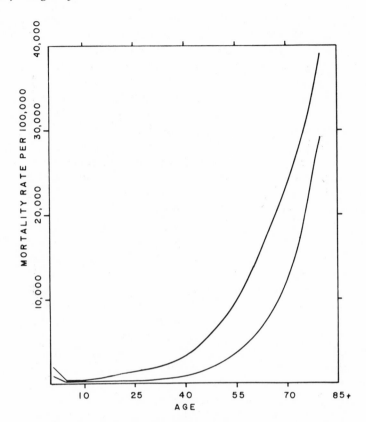

FIGURE 4.1. **Age specific mortality rates for U.S. white females (lower curve) and U.S. "all other" males (upper curve),** 1982.

Source: National Center for Health Statistics, 1985.

higher age-specific mortality rates than those in Figure 4.1. Deaths during the period of accelerating mortality are considered deaths due to aging and the underlying events and processes are the focus of longevity studies. Earlier deaths are attributed to other phenomena (Lints 1978), and while they greatly influence summary statistics, they are not of primary interest to gerontology.

A survivorship curve translates this summary of a cohort's death experience into a summary of its longevity experience. The top panel of Figure 4.2 presents survivorship curves for two U.S. populations. Beginning with a cohort of one hundred thousand at birth, the upper curve depicts how many or what proportion of that cohort would remain alive (survive) at each age thereafter, based on 1982 death rates for U.S. white females (whose mortality rates are plotted by the lower curve of Figure 4.1). A small initial dip represents infant mortality, the long plateau represents the subsequent period of low mortality, and the downward curve represents the accelerating mortality rate. The lower curve in this panel depicts the survivorship of U.S. white females born in 1900–02. The much larger initial dip reflects the high infant and early childhood mortality at that time, and the shallow downward slope to age fifty reflects the higher mortality rates at all ages, followed by the acceleration of mortality rates after fifty. Survivorship curves can be generated for any population or subgroup for which age-specific mortality rates are available. The middle panel of Figure 4.2 illustrates that a larger proportion of U.S. white males than "all other" males remains alive at each age and that the difference decreases with advancing age. The lower panel of Figure 4.2 illustrates that a larger proportion of U.S. white females than males remains alive at each age and that the difference increases with advancing age.

Mortality rate and survivorship curves may be summarized with single numbers called life expectancies, defined as "average number of additional years remaining to individuals of a certain age." The life expectancy at birth is simply the average of the age at death of each member of the cohort. For U.S. white females this was 78.8 years in 1982, compared with 51.8 years in 1900–02 (National Center for Health Statistics 1985). Comparing their survivorship curves in the top panel of Figure 4.2, it is evident that the main reason for the low life expectancy at birth in 1900–02 is the high infant mortality rate, which lowers the average age at death. When a low value is reported for life expectancy at birth, it is frequently misinterpreted to signify that there are no or few old people in the population. This is untrue: the survivorship curve shows that slightly over half the 1900–02 cohort remained alive at age sixty. There has been a substantial increase in the proportion of the cohort reaching the older ages: 76% of the 1982 cohort will remain alive at age sixty. More members of the later cohort die at older ages and this yields a higher life expectancy at birth. Historically the major determinant of increases in life expectancy at birth has been improvements in infant mortality (Yin and Shine 1985). Because life expectancy at birth is so influenced by events prior to the aging process, it is not a very useful measure for comparing populations' longevity experience. However, it is frequently reported and misrepresented, and it is important to be aware of the actual meaning of life expectancy at birth. This measure does not provide information about the ages of the most long-lived in a population.

Life expectancy can be calculated for any age. For example, life expectancy at fifty is the average number of additional years of life for individuals who have survived to fifty. A 31.3 year life expectancy for fifty-year-old, U.S., white females in 1982 means that based on 1982 death rates, women who survive to fifty live an average of 31.3 more years. A 21.9 year life expectancy for fifty-year-old, U.S., white females in 1900–02 means that based on 1900–02 death rates, women who survived to age fifty lived an average of 21.9 more years. Life expectancies in the age range of

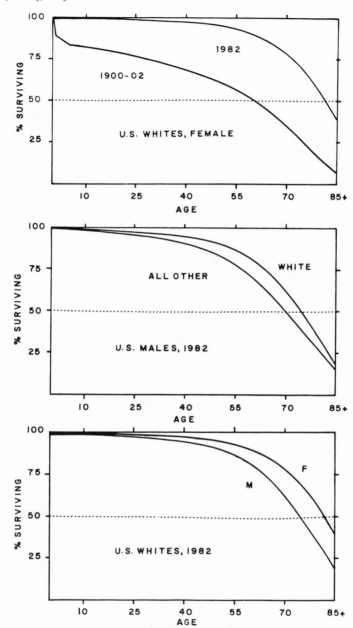

FIGURE 4.2. **Upper panel: Survivorship curves for U.S. white females in** 1982 **and in** 1900–02. **Middle panel: Survivorship curves for U.S. white and "all other" males in** 1982. Lower panel: Survivorship curves for U.S. white females and males in 1982.

SOURCE: National Center for Health Statistics, 1985.

accelerating mortality may be the most appropriate ones for aging studies to consider. Of course an individual must survive to fifty in order to have the opportunity to survive to eighty. However, the causes of mortality are different for infants and young adults than for middle-aged and old adults, and, therefore, focus on the latter age range is more meaningful for aging studies.

Comparing life expectancy at each age from birth to eighty-five for U.S. white and "all other" males in 1982 reveals an interesting phenomenon. Although white males have a higher life expectancy than "all other" males from birth to age sixty-five, the two curves cross at about seventy and thereafter "all other" males have a higher life expectancy. White male life expectancy at birth is 71.5 years compared with 66.8 years for "all other" males. This 4.7 year advantage decreases progressively to 3.5 years at age thirty-five, 0.4 years at age sixty-five, and then reverses direction. At age seventy "all other" males' life expectancy is 0.1 years longer, and at age eighty-five it is 0.5 years longer. This is called a "mortality crossover": the population which had the higher mortality rate and lower survivorship and life expectancy at earlier ages has lower mortality rate and higher survivorship and life expectancy at later ages among those who do survive. This reversal of population differences in life expectancy is observed when U.S. white and "all other" females are compared and when U.S. whites are compared with U.S. blacks and Native Americans (e.g., Markides and Machalek 1984).

There are at least two possible explanations for this mortality crossover. Theoretically it could be that higher mortality rates in early life removed the less robust and left a larger proportion of very healthy old with a better chance of surviving longer (e.g., Manton et al. 1979; Markides and Machalek 1984). An alternative explanation of the mortality crossover is age exaggeration in the "all other" population. This occurs to a greater degree in some of the "other" groups (for example, the Puerto Rican and black populations), than in the white population (Rosenwaike 1979; Rosenwaike and Preston 1984). If death certificates report exaggerated ages, then falsely low mortality rates will be calculated for true ages, and life expectancy will be inflated artificially. These alternative explanations could be evaluated with information on health and age accuracy in these subpopulations. (Chapter 12 also addresses this topic.)

The Epidemiological Approach

A third approach to the study of longevity is an epidemiological one. It seeks to explain the distribution of longevity and survivorship in populations. That is, it compares groups within a cohort in order to identify characteristics of those likely to live longer than others or those more likely to survive a specified time interval. These characteristics serve as markers that predict likelihood of survival to a future time. Biological markers include attributes that are unmodifiable and lifelong, such as genotype and sex; attributes that are established during growth, such as adult height; and attributes that may fluctuate during adulthood, such as weight and blood pressure. Sociocultural markers include attributes such as marital status and lifestyle. The following examples illustrate some of the wide range of research designs embraced by the epidemiological approach.

Evidence of genetic contributions to longevity is provided by population and twin studies demonstrating that individuals with greater genetic similarity have more similar life spans. A population study found that the life spans of siblings differed by an average of fourteen years while those of random pairs of people differed by an average of thirty-nine years (Swedlund et al. 1983). Similarly, a study of twin pairs who had survived to at least age sixty found that the life spans of monozygotic twins differed by an average of fifty-nine months while the life spans of dizygotic, opposite sexed twins differed by an average of 102 months (Jarvik et al. 1960). Genealogies also reveal family patterns in longevity. Parents who lived longer than average had children who did the same in populations as diverse as fourteenth to nineteenth-century China, seventeenth to nineteenth-century Finland and Sweden, and eighteenth to nineteenth-century United States (Yuan 1933; Pearl and Pearl 1934a; Lints 1978; Meindl and Swedlund 1982). For example, analyzing one U.S. genealogy revealed that if both parents survived to eighty then their offspring survived to an average age of fifty-three, whereas if neither parent survived to sixty their offspring survived to an average of just thirty-three years (Bell 1918, cited in Lints 1978). In a sample of families selected because one parent had lived to at least ninety, the longevity of the other parent also had an effect on offspring survival. In the subsample of sons whose fathers had survived to ninety or more, there was a five year difference in the average length of the life span. Those whose mothers survived past eighty survived to an average age of seventy-three, while those whose mothers did not survive past sixty survived to an average age of sixty-eight (Murphy 1978). The interpretation of these familial patterns is unclear. This is because siblings, parents, and offspring share environments (e.g., life-style, health practices) as well as genes, and genealogical studies demonstrating familial patterns do not measure the relative contributions of genes and environment to family similarities.

A genetic contribution to sex differences in longevity has been considered. Females live longer than males in virtually all populations studied. The lower panel of Figure 4.2 illustrates greater female survivorship throughout the life cycle in the United States in 1982. As long as U.S. vital statistics have been available, males have had higher mortality rates (Verbrugge 1985). This occurs in virtually all countries and at nearly all ages.

The female life expectancy at age sixty was greater than the male in all seventy-seven countries reporting this value in the 1983 United Nations Demographic Yearbook. Sixty-year-old females' life expectancies averaged 19.4 years compared with 16.2 years for males (United Nations 1983). The unanswered, intriguing question is whether this consistent female advantage is due to intrinsic biological sex differences in fitness or to extrinsic sociocultural sex differences in behavior/environment, or both. Theoretically, biological determinants of differences in survivorship could arise from X- or Y-chromosome linked or regulated genes, sex hormones, or inherent sex differences in reproductive physiology and anatomy. For example, X-linked genes appear to confer greater female resistance to infectious disease, and female hormones may reduce the risk of some diseases (Waldron 1983). However, many sociocultural determinants of survivorship operate to reduce male survival more than female. For example, many cultural values generate sex differences in life-style (e.g., smoking and alcohol consumption, occupational health hazards, preventive and health seeking behavior) that tend to put males at higher risk of dying (see Verbrugge 1985).

Evaluating the relative contributions of biological and sociocultural determinants of sex difference in survival is difficult because it requires constructing appropriate study designs holding constant one set of factors while varying the other. That is, to detect the effect of chromosomes or hormones, only sex or hormonal status should vary while life-style should not. "Natural experiments" provide an opportunity to do this. For instance, the association between the hormone testosterone and shorter male survivorship was examined by comparing castrated and intact male inmates of a Kansas institution for the mentally retarded. Among white males who survived to age forty, the average length of life of castrates was longer than that of noncastrated men, and the earlier the castration the greater the length of life. Men castrated between eight and fourteen years of age survived an average of 76.3 years, 3.4 years longer than those castrated between fifteen and nineteen years of age, and 6.7 years longer than those castrated between twenty and twenty-nine years of age. These groups of castrates survived five to twelve years longer than the intact group, who survived an average of 64.7 years (Hamilton and Mestler 1969). This was interpreted as evidence of detrimental effects on survival of exposure to testosterone and testicular function. This supports the reasoning that there are biologically based differences in survival.

On the other hand, some life-style differences, such as generally lower alcohol consumption and smoking, favor greater female survival. A genealogical study of one lineage of Amish (farmers who do not smoke or drink alcohol) found that forty-year-old males and females survived similar lengths of time afterward (Miller 1980), and a population study of male and female nonsmokers found no sex differences in life expectancy (Miller and

Gerstein 1983). Smoking differences account for a proportion of sex differences in survival in some populations. This supports the reasoning that there are socioculturally based determinants of the difference.

Statistical analysis provides another opportunity to take sex differences in behavior into account by controlling for or removing their effect mathematically so as to compare males and females with the same life-style. One study controlled statistically for sixteen demographic, social, psychological, health, and behavioral risk factors and found that females still retained a sizable survival advantage over a nine year period. Male mortality was 70% higher than female after controlling for these factors (Wingard 1982). Because this complex issue has major social consequences (there are very few very old men compared to women) it will continue to be studied intensively (Hazzard 1985). A recent review of the topic concludes that sex differences in survival are principally the outcome of different roles, stress, life-styles, and preventive health practices (Verbrugge 1985). The magnitude of the difference in male and female longevity varies tremendously from one historical time to another and from one country to another (see Madigan 1959; United Nations 1983), and this argues for strong sociocultural influence on intrinsic biological characteristics.

Other biological markers associated with likelihood of survival have been studied epidemiologically using a prospective study design that follows a cohort for a certain time. The typical study design to detect an association between survival and a biological attribute (*a*) surveys a cohort for some continuously varying characteristic such as weight, height, blood pressure, (*b*) divides the cohort into subgroups called strata, (*c*) counts the deaths in the cohort during the follow-up period, and (*d*) determines whether deaths are evenly distributed or occur disproportionately in some strata. This design is exemplified by a national survey of 1.8 million Danes that measured height, weight, and age, and gathered information on mortality over a sixteen year period (Waaler 1984). A simple measure of obesity called Quetelet's Index ($QI = weight/height^2$) was calculated, the population subdivided into strata of QI, and the sixteen year mortality rate for each QI stratum was calculated. Especially lean and especially obese men have higher mortality than men in the middle of the obesity distribution. This is illustrated by the survivorship curve in Figure 4.3 describing the experience of three QI strata among fifty- to fifty-four-year-old men. This shows that 80% of the fifty- to fifty-four-year-olds with a QI of 27 are alive after sixteen years, compared with 74% of those with a QI of 35 (obese), and 64% of those with a QI of 17 (lean). (A man 1.83 meters [six feet] tall, weighing 90.4 kg [200 pounds] has a QI of 27, one weighing 57 kg [125 pounds] has a QI of 17 and one weighing 117.2 kg [258 pounds] has a QI of 35.)

Figure 4.4 illustrates in another way that some QI have greater survivorship. The distribution of QI for males forty to forty-four years old and sixty

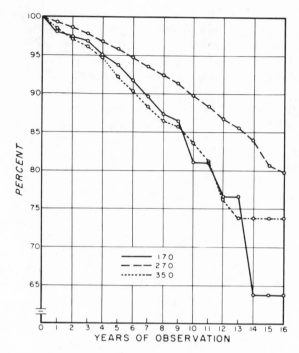

FIGURE 4.3. **Sixteen year survivorship curves of fifty- to fifty-four-year-old Danish men in three strata of Quetelet's Index.**

SOURCE: Waaler, H. T. Height, weight, and mortality; The Norwegian experience. *Acta Medica Scandinavica Supplementum* 679(1984):25. Reprinted with permission.

to sixty-four years old at entry into the study indicates a greater percentage of sixty-year-old men in the higher, more obese QI strata. The average QI for sixty-year-olds was 25.3 compared with 24.9 for the forty- to forty-four-year-olds (Waaler 1984). The mortality rate curves for both age categories and each obesity stratum in the upper panel of Figure 4.4 are roughly U-shaped. That is another way of indicating that especially lean and obese men both have higher mortality than men in the middle of the obesity distribution. While the general pattern of mortality is similar in the two cohorts, there are some important age differences: sixty- to sixty-four-year-olds have higher mortality at all obesity categories, along with shorter arms and a wider trough of the U-shaped curve. That is, irrespective of level of obesity, older men have a higher risk of dying. The shorter arms of the U-shaped curve reflect a smaller difference in risk of dying between the extreme and the middle categories of QI among the sixty-year-olds. The wider trough of the U means that a wider range of QI is relatively favorable, and a greater departure from the average is required to elevate mortality risk among sixty-year-olds. Findings such as these are generating controversy over the "ideal" or "optimum" levels of weight relative to

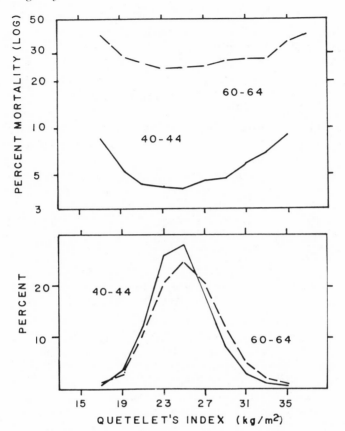

FIGURE 4.4. **Lower panel: Frequency distribution of Quetelet's Index among Danish men forty to forty-four and sixty to sixty-four years old.** Upper panel: Percent mortality rate (log scale) for each value of Quetelet's Index in the same age groups of Danish males.

SOURCE: Waaler, H. T. Height, weight, and mortality; The Norwegian experience. *Acta Medica Scandinavica Supplementum* 679(1984):19,20. Reprinted with permission.

height, that is, the QI associated with the lowest mortality. These Danish data suggest that the optimum may not be the same for forty-year-olds and sixty-year-olds. One U.S. study confirms this by reporting that the weight associated with greatest survivorship increases with age and there is a progressively broader range of weights associated with high survivorship in older age categories (Andres 1985). The interpretation of these data is controversial. One point in the controversy is whether weight gain is associated with survival or whether the susceptible obese and lean individuals are weeded out (die) earlier in life. This latter alternative argues that those who survive to sixty are a selected group relatively resistant to the deleterious effects of obesity/leanness or who enjoy the protection of other unmeasured characteristics lowering mortality risk. If this is the case, then conclusions that survival is enhanced by weight gain throughout adulthood would be in error.

The Danish study is one of many studies of European, North American, and Far Eastern populations reporting optimal levels of body fatness (see Simopoulous and Van Itallie 1984; Beall n.d., for discussion). The optimum differs somewhat in each study, illustrating the dependence of optimal weight on other life-style and environmental factors. For example, within a population, the survivorship at a given stratum of QI is influenced by smoking or hypertension or type of disease contracted (Garrison et al. 1983; Lew and Garfinkel 1979; Waaler 1984). While QI is a marker for survival, there may not be a single optimum for the human species under all conditions and at all ages.

Applying this study design to the relationship between blood pressure and survival has yielded similar results. The optimal blood pressure for survival among the very old may differ from that for younger adults. Among younger adults there is an inverse relationship between blood pressure and survival, yet 45% of a sample of men eighty-five and older with blood pressures of 110–129 mm Hg survived a two year follow-up period while only 15% of men with lower systolic blood pressure did so (Rajala et al. 1983). It is not clear whether this means that higher blood pressure itself prevents or protects against some causes of death, or whether those at risk of death related to hypertension had already been removed from the population due to earlier mortality, or whether those who have survived to that age with hypertension enjoyed the protection of some other unmeasured risk-lowering factor (Burch 1983). This is another illustration of the complexity of determining what is optimal for survival and longevity at different ages. Intuitively, it seems likely that an individual who has survived to a great age may differ from one who succumbed earlier. However, the problem of how to take this into account in study design and interpretation remains to be solved.

Certain sociocultural characteristics, such as marital status and life-style, are markers of current status that predict survival (Blackfield-Cohen and Brody 1981). For example, men aged fifty to seventy-nine married to spouses up to twenty-four years younger than themselves tend to live longer than men married to spouses up to fourteen years older than themselves. The overall mortality rate of husbands with younger wives was only 87% of the mortality rate for the general population of U.S. white married men, whereas that for husbands with wives the same age or older was 120%. This could be due to premarital selection factors (healthier, more vigorous men marry younger women) or postmarital personal interactions that are somehow beneficial (Foster et al. 1985). The transition from married to widowed is a stressful status change that may influence survival. A sample of widowed males aged fifty-five to seventy-four had

61% higher mortality rates than married males of the same age span; 78% of the married and just 69% of the widowed men fifty-five to sixty-four years old remained alive twelve years later (Helsing and Szklo 1981). This could be due to married men receiving better care than unmarried, a factor that may be crucial to survival in a population with high morbidity such as the elderly population (Brenner et al. 1985). It could also be due to association with other people. Widowers with social support networks have better survival chances and widowers' mortality rate drops after remarriage to that for married males (Helsing and Szklo 1981, 1985).

The relationship between life-style and survival has been investigated frequently. For example, the effects of smoking on longevity are well documented (Brackenridge 1985). A study of a large sample of adult Californians of all ages illustrates some of the myriad life-style characteristics that influence survival in some situations. Using participants' responses to a questionnaire inquiring about health practices, the association of a number of health practices with nine year survival has been demonstrated (Belloc 1973; Breslow and Enstrom 1980). Responses categorized as healthy practices are: (1) usually sleep seven or eight hours; (2) eat breakfast almost every day; (3) eat between meals once in a while, rarely, or never; (4) weight for men between 5% under and 19.99% over desirable weight for height; weight for women not more than 9.99% over desirable weight for height; (5) often or sometimes engage in active sports, swim or take long walks, or often garden or do physical exercises; (6) drink not more than four drinks at a time; and (7) never smoked cigarettes. These are associated with survival. Nearly 95% of men and women who responded positively to all seven items survived the follow-up period compared with 80% of men and 88% of women who responded positively to just 0–3 of the items (Breslow and Enstrom 1980). This pattern held throughout adulthood. Statistical analysis identified four items as having significant independent associations with greater survival: never smoking, physical activity, low alcohol consumption, and seven to eight hours' sleep (Wingard et al. 1982). For example, 92% of men who reported seven to eight hours of sleep a night survived the nine year follow-up period compared with 68% of those reporting six or fewer hours and 89% of those reporting nine or more (Wingard and Berkman 1983). This study also found an association between social ties and survival that was independent of health practices (Berkman and Syme 1979).

A replication of this study limited to people over sixty-five in Massachusetts found that none of these health practices were related to five year survival of elderly men and just one (smoking) related to survival of elderly women (Branch and Jette 1984). This appears to be an example of the same phenomenon reported for biological markers: that the relationship between levels of markers and survival may be different at different ages. The authors of this study comment, "If gerontology has a central message, it is that those who have survived to old age often represent a special case" (Branch and Jette 1984, 1128).

Summary and Conclusions

In summary, this chapter considers approaches to the challenging task of studying longevity and illustrates some of the difficulties. Three general approaches to studying longevity are (1) cross-cultural investigations of populations purportedly characterized by extreme longevity, (2) actuarial investigations of the survival and life expectancy of populations or sub-populations, and (3) epidemiologic investigations of the characteristics of individuals more likely to survive than others.

There are several important considerations for applying any of these approaches. (1) The need for accurate age information is fundamental, and obtaining this may demand considerable ingenuity, time, and effort. An alternative to documented chronological age would be a biological measure of chronological age that is uninfluenced by environment or life-style and simply reflects the passage of time. Although the existence of such biological clocks has been postulated, none has been identified so far (Reff and Schneider 1982). (2) Moving from the individual to the population level, measures of longevity require caution because of the potential ambiguity of some measures—for example, the proportion in an age range and life expectancy at birth. (3) While in principle there is no reason to limit the study of longevity to the study of events in adulthood, it is generally considered that the underlying causes of earlier mortality are different and best considered separately. For this reason, longevity studies find it meaningful to concentrate on life expectancy, survival, and biological markers assessed during adulthood. (4) Once population, cultural, sub-cultural, sex, genotypic, and other differences in survival and life expectancy are detected, the next step is to identify the causes. This requires study of biological and sociocultural markers influencing survival. Studies assessing the impact on survival of some form of intervention (e.g., anti-hypertensive treatment, education about life-style risk factors) may be especially informative. (5) The study of longevity is complicated by the practical necessity of choosing to assess just a few markers in an unavoidably selected, perhaps biased, sample of individuals who survived long enough to be included in the study. The older the sample, the more selected it is. Thus, the biological and life-style characteristics of survivors of the fifth decade often differ from those of survivors of the ninth decade of life. Longitudinal studies are extremely important in this context. The complication of having a selected sample can be overcome by such studies, in which survivors of different ages can be compared.

The information in this chapter derives primarily from Western, industrialized societies. The extent to which it generalizes to non-Western, nonindustrial settings where the majority of the elderly live, is unknown. Some findings, such as family patterns and female advantage in the length of the life span, repeat in many cultures and historical periods. Other findings, such as the optimal QI or marital status, may vary across cultures and environment. Other potential influences on longevity include the level of public health, the type of diseases prevalent, the health care system, family structure, and rapid modernization. Thus, factors conducive to longevity may vary from one society to another. For example, characteristics promoting survival in an environment where malaria is the leading cause of death may differ from those in an environment where heart disease is the leading cause of death. The consequences of widowhood may differ for those expecting to live out their lives in joint versus stem versus nuclear families. Identifying markers of longevity in a variety of societies will require sociocultural knowledge, good demographic and public health information, and well-designed epidemiological studies.

V

SENSORY, PERCEPTUAL, AND MOTOR FUNCTION IN HUMAN AGING

Dana J. Plude

A life-course perspective in the study of adult development and aging acknowledges that aging is not necessarily synonomous with decline (Birren and Renner 1977). However, in examining sensory, perceptual, and motor processes that depend extensively on physiological structures and their functions, a decrement model is difficult to reject. Probably in no other area of psychological investigation are the findings so clear-cut and consistent: Sensory, perceptual, and motor processes do not function as efficiently in older adults as they do in younger people. Biological processes decline with advancing age (see, for example, Finch and Schneider 1985), and the anatomical structures and physiological systems underlying sensorimotor function decline concomitantly.

It is important to note, though, that the magnitude of decline varies greatly between individuals and even between (and within) components of different sensory and motor systems. Furthermore, many of the decrements commonly associated with advancing age can be offset by physical prostheses, such as corrective lenses and hearing aids. Age decrements can also be compensated by re-allocating attentional resources or by increasing reliance on experience-based knowledge that is accumulated over the life course. But not all decrements can be compensated, and compensation itself exacts a toll by reducing either the factuality of perceptual analysis or the capacity available to support performance; but that is getting ahead of the story. Thus, although the main theme of this chapter is age-related decline, it must be emphasized that the majority of older adults are able to function quite adequately in everyday life despite decrements in sensory,

Preparation of this chapter was supported in part by a General Research Board Award from the Graduate School of the University of Maryland, College Park.

perceptual, and motor function. It is likely that because of their gradual onset over the life course many decrements are offset by a series of relatively minor adjustments in activities and behavior, such as cupping one's hand about the ear to enhance speech perception. But the sensory, motor, and perceptual decrements are no less real.

It is important to determine the extent of age-related change in sensory, perceptual, and motor function because of the consequences of such changes for even the most basic aspects of everyday life, from recognizing common objects to executing practiced skills in complex problem solving. The Human Information Processing framework (Howard 1983; Lachman, Lachman, and Butterfield 1979; Lindsay and Norman 1977) is used to organize this chapter. Its basic tenets are summarized before reviewing the gerontological literature on sensory, perceptual, and motor function. The concluding section integrates the diverse findings and points up the important contribution of central aspects of information processing to age-related change.

Human Information Processing

Simplistically, humans can be considered information processors who take in environmental stimulation, transform it to a code that can be analyzed and elaborated, and prepare and execute behavioral responses. Figure 5.1 depicts such a system schematically. Although the flow of information in the figure is unidirectional, it is probably more accurately conceived as a completely interactive process whereby processes later (or "higher up") in the sequence of processing feed back onto earlier (or "lower level") processes. Thus, there are probably many more interconnections in the system than suggested in this diagram. What this means is that the perception of (and response to) even the simplest stimulus is saturated with knowledge. For example, upon seeing a book lying on a tabletop the experience is one of beholding a familiar object—even though this particular book may never before have been seen—rather than an array of environmental energy comprising colors, angles, shadows, and so on. Furthermore, the object perceived is usually embedded in a context of other objects (actors, settings, situations) that also influences the perception of the object. Thus sensory, perceptual, and motor processes are interactive and should be considered in parallel in any analysis of human performance (see Neisser 1976). Nevertheless, these aspects of human behavior can be decomposed to determine the nature of age-related change in each. And the Human Information Processing framework provides a heuristic for such a decomposition.

Within the information processing framework, age limitations can be partitioned into two classes. Peripheral limitations affect information pro-

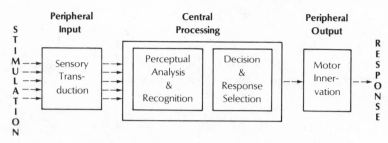

FIGURE 5.1. **Schematic of the basic components of the human information processing system.** (See text for distinction between "central" and "peripheral" components of performance.)

cessing at input by reducing the integrity of the sensory signal, and at output by restricting the functional range of overt response. Central limitations affect all aspects of information processing by reducing the speed, efficiency, or allocation of limited resources available to support performance. In one sense, peripheral limitations are less severe than central limitations because the former are less pervasive and more amenable to correction by prostheses of one sort or another. This argument is made more forceful by reference to specific examples in subsequent sections. Suffice it to say that the distinction between peripheral and central limitations can be useful in delineating age differences in sensory, perceptual, and motor functioning. Age-related changes in peripheral sensory function are discussed first.

Sensory Function

Age-related reductions in peripheral sensory function impose data limitations on input into the information processing system (Hoyer and Plude 1982). The measurement of sensory function is basically concerned with the sensitivity of sensory systems to variations in environmental stimulation and the discriminatory capability of the senses. Before examining evidence bearing on age limitations in sensory sensitivity and discriminability, three points must be emphasized. First, this section consists of a selective review of only some of the many age-related changes that characterize sensory systems. Very little is said about the myriad structural changes that occur at the physiological-anatomical level (see, for example, Corso 1981), and the psychophysical data that are discussed represent only a sampling of the growing literature on sensory aging.

Second, it is beyond the scope of the present chapter to elaborate on the substantial problems involved with quantifying not only the physical stimuli to which the senses are directed, but also (and perhaps more importantly) the variable of age. Even in what is ostensibly a rather precise and restricted domain, there are tremendous differences among same-aged adults in the range of sensitivity and discriminability of sensory systems. Thus, using chronological age as a metric for delineating age limitations in sensory function is at best imprecise, but in the absence of a meaningful alternative, for example, some functional age measure (Dempster 1972; Nuttall 1972), it will have to suffice. Related to the metric problems of chronological age are the problems attending the application of the cross-sectional method (see Nesselroade and Reese 1973), which is the most common design used in gerontological research (see, for example, Abrahams et al. 1975; Hoyer, Raskind, and Abrahams 1984).

Third, and finally, the measurement of sensitivity is not as straightforward as the purist might hope. Every sensory experience consists of (at least) two components: the transduction of physical energy by sensory receptors, and the interpretation of the transduced energy by an observer. In the parlance of psychophysics, these components are labeled "sensitivity" and "criterion," respectively. The study of sensory functioning has as its primary goal the assessment of sensitivity, but this goal can only be realized by relying on an observer's reported sensory experience. Differences between observers (or even between observations) can derive from either or both components of the sensory experience. In studying age-related sensory function it is imperative to distinguish the relative contributions of each, because apparent age-related decrements in sensory sensitivity may reflect a criterion bias on the part of older observers, who may be reluctant to report sensory experiences about which there is uncertainty. The interested reader is referred to recent applications of the Theory of Signal Detection (Green and Swets 1966) to the study of sensory aging (e.g., Harkins and Chapman 1976; Hertzog 1980; Williams 1980). Also, because space does not permit a detailed description here, the interested reader should consult Gescheider's (1985) recent text on psychophysical methods used in assessing sensory function.

The Visual System

To a great extent, ours is a visual world. We rely extensively on our sense of sight in nearly every aspect of our waking life, from gathering information about the world to carrying out mundane chores. Recently, Cogan (1979) found that the loss of vision was second only to cancer as the most dreaded consequence of aging. Perhaps because of our dependence on this sensory system, the age-related changes that occur in it are both dramatic and pervasive. Vision is by far the most well-researched of the sensory systems, and the age-related changes that occur over the entire life span are well-documented. In general the changes can be partitioned into two classes: changes in optical structures, and changes in the retina. The

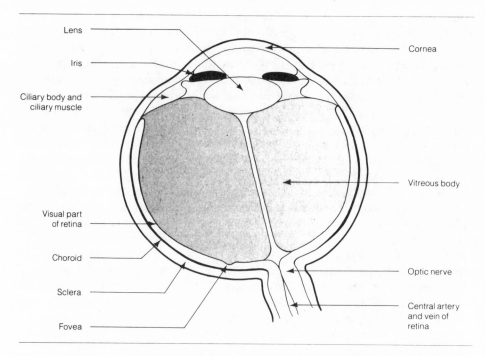

FIGURE 5.2. **Diagram of the major structures and sense receptors of the human eye.**

former class of changes begins to have prominent effects on visual function in middle age (around the fourth decade of life), whereas the latter do not significantly affect visual function until later in life (around the sixth decade).

Changes in the optical structures affect the transmissiveness and accommodative power of the eye, producing difficulties in distance vision, binocular depth perception, and color sensitivity as well as sensitivity to glare (among other things). Four specific optical structures can be singled out for their contributions to age-related changes in vision (refer to Figure 5.2).

(1) The cornea is the principal refracting surface of the eye and serves a protective function as well. It undergoes three principal age-related changes: (*a*) loss of lustre—which probably reflects changes in the refractive power and a decrease in the amount of fluid bathing the corneal surface; (*b*) development of an opaque gray ring around its outer edge (arcus senilis)—which results from an accumulation of fatty constituents that leak from the blood vessels of the eye; and, (*c*) decreased curvature and increased thickness—one result of which is increased astigmatism and blurred vision.

(2) The ciliary muscles attach to the lens and contort it to focus vision at different viewing depths. The primary change in the ciliary muscle is

atrophy, which leads to reduced accommodative power in the lens, producing difficulty especially in seeing objects at close distances (presbyopia).

(3) The lens lies between the anterior and posterior chambers, just behind the iris (the colored part of the eye that surrounds the pupil). It is a flexible biconvex structure that has as its primary function the refraction of light onto the retina. With age the amount of light reaching the lens is reduced due to the decrease in diameter of the pupil (Birren, Casperson, and Botwinick 1950), and the lens itself becomes less flexible (Weale 1963, 1982) due to a variety of physical changes (see Kuwabara 1975). These changes result in decreased accommodative power (and increased presbyopia), and also reduce the amount of light (and even its composition) transmitted through the lens. In addition, the lens is the site of significant pathology in the form of cataracts which, because of their opacity, interfere further with its transmissiveness.

(4) The anterior and posterior chambers are the fluid-filled spaces surrounding the lens. The aqueous fluid in the anterior chamber bathes the lens with nutrients obtained from the blood vessels of the eye. An obstruction of the aqueous flow results in glaucoma, one of the most prevalent visual diseases in middle and late adulthood. The posterior chamber accounts for 80% of the total volume of the eye and is filled with a gelatinous fluid (vitreous humor) which helps to retain the shape of the eyeball. With age the vitreous humor becomes thinner, and fibrous segments break off and are free to float about causing the appearance of floating specks. These segments are not a serious threat to visual function, though they can be distracting when large.

In general, the presbyopia resulting from these structural changes in optical components can be offset by corrective lenses. However, the reductions in transmittance and refractive characteristics are not so readily compensated. Increased lighting would seem sufficient to overcome reduced transmissiveness, however there is increased susceptibility to glare with increasing age too (see Fozard et al. 1977), so caution must be exercised in designing environmental interventions to compensate these kinds of visual changes.

The second class of visual changes involves the retina. Although this too is an optical structure in the strict sense, it deserves separate treatment because it is the sensory surface of the eye that interfaces with the central nervous system. The retina lines about two-thirds of the interior at the sides and back of the eyeball, with the receptors most densely packed toward the rear and especially concentrated at the focal point of vision, in a region called the macula. At the center of the macula is the fovea, where light is focused for detailed acuity, as, for example, when reading. There are a variety of age-related disease processes that result in macular degeneration (see, for example, Lewis 1979), but they will not be described here. There are also a variety of changes in retinal function that accompany normal aging, and it is to these changes that discussion now turns.

Retinal function can be assessed by measuring the ability to detect changes in light energy or the ability to discriminate between visual patterns. Many studies have used threshold detection measures to assess age-related changes in retinal function. With age there is a decrease in the sensitivity of dark-adapted vision (McFarland and Fisher 1960), which is to say that the threshold for detecting a test flash of light (after sitting in the dark for thirty minutes) is higher for older observers compared to younger observers. Not only is the final level of dark-adapted vision less sensitive, but there is a progressive increase with age in the time required to achieve this level (Wolf 1960), and in the time required to recover from it (Domey, McFarland, and Chadwick 1960). The size of the functional visual field diminishes with increasing age, with the extent of peripheral sensitivity decreasing and the size of the "blind spot" (i.e., the area of the retina where the optic nerve connects) increasing (Wolf 1967).

The ability to discriminate independent flashes of light diminishes with age as demonstrated in measures of Critical Flicker Frequency, wherein the rate of successive light and dark periods is varied until they appear steady rather than as a flickering light (McFarland, Warren, and Karis 1958). Thus, with increasing age there is a tendency to experience fusion at progressively slower rates of alternation. In a similar vein, there is evidence that visible persistence, that is, the continued sensation that follows the termination of a physical stimulus, increases with advancing adulthood age (see Kline and Birren 1975; Kline and Szafran 1975). Mundy-Castle (1953) documented electrophysiological evidence of an age-related increase in visible persistence (see Botwinick 1978; and Kline and Schieber 1985, for reviews). These kinds of findings may be attributable to a decrease in the speed of operation of the retina or to age changes in different cell assemblies in the retina (e.g., DiLollo, Arnett, and Kruk 1982).

Finally, there is evidence that visual acuity, or the ability to discriminate between visual patterns, declines with advancing age, particularly in the sixth decade of life. For example, in performance on a Snellan test, wherein an observer is asked to identify characters (or other symbols) that are listed in progressively smaller fonts, there is a steady decline in acuity commencing around age twenty, but with particular acceleration between ages sixty and ninety (Richards 1977). In sum, both the functional receptive surface of the retina and its processing speed decrease with age. Consequently, in combination with the changes in optical structures described above, the retinal changes contribute to senescent declines in the size and function of the visual "perceptual window."

The Auditory System

Hearing impairment is a concomitant of normal aging, and the term "presbycusis" is widely used to encompass senescent changes in auditory functioning. Hinchcliffe (1962) identified impairments in pure-tone thresholds (especially high frequencies), frequency discrimination, temporal discrimination, spatial localization, speech discriminability, and auditory recall as part of the spectrum of changes in auditory function associated with presbycusis (Olsho, Harkins, and Lenhardt 1985). There may be four types of presbycusis: (1) sensory, consisting of atrophy and degeneration of the hair cells (and their supporting cells); (2) neural, consisting of a loss of neurons in the auditory pathway; (3) metabolic, consisting of a diminished supply of nutrients to the cells of the cochlea; and (4) mechanical, consisting of atrophy and stiffening of the vibrating structures within the cochlea. Although these four types have been found to have different rates of incidence (12%, 31%, 35%, and 23% respectively), rarely do they occur in isolation (Schuknecht 1974).

Generally, presbycusis refers to hearing loss due to normal age-related changes in the various major structures of the ear (see Figure 5.3). These changes encompass: (1) changes in the resonance characteristics of the outer ear (pinna and auditory canal); (2) changes in the transmission and amplification characteristics of the middle ear (the ossicular chain bounded laterally by the eardrum and promontory of the basal cochlear turn); and (3) changes in the transduction characteristics of the inner ear (the cochlea, oval window, round window, basilar membrane, etc.). For example, thickening of the eardrum, stiffening of the ossicles, and degeneration in the structures of the inner ear (e.g., stiffening of the basilar membrane) produce impairments like those specified above. But these changes also manifest themselves in other age-related hearing problems, such as tinnitus, a ringing sound in the ears, and recruitment, a condition in which the range of intensities between sounds heard as soft and loud is shortened, producing an age difference in the subjective intensity (loudness) of low-intensity but not high-intensity sounds (Welford 1980). The behavioral consequences of these kinds of changes are manifested in two primary ways: (1) reduction of pure-tone sensitivity, and (2) decreased ability to discriminate speech.

Auditory sensitivity is typically assessed with pure-tone threshold techniques, such as the standard hearing test in which tones of different frequencies are played through headphones with the listener indicating the channel (left/right) containing the tone. With increasing adulthood age there is a decline in pure-tone sensitivity that is at first gradual but which accelerates around the fifth decade of life (e.g., Corso 1977, 1984). The magnitude of hearing loss is typically greater for males than for females (Robinson and Sutton 1979; Spoor 1967), but the contribution of occupational "noise pollution" to the sex difference is not known. Importantly, some of the known declines associated with presbycusis can be compensated by hearing aids, especially if two are worn and balanced for each ear separately (Welford 1980).

A basic component of successful speech discrimination is the ability to

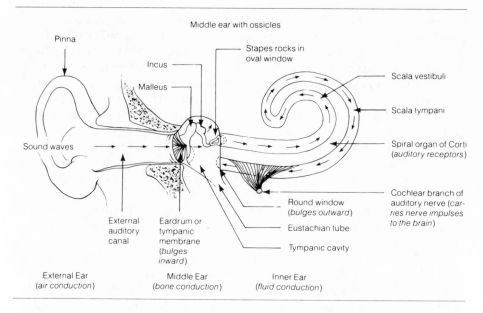

FIGURE 5.3. **Diagram of the major structures and sense receptors of the human ear.**

discriminate between sounds on the basis of frequency or intensity (e.g., Botwinick 1978; Corso 1981). Olsho, Harkins, and Lenhardt (1985) have reviewed the literature on age effects in discriminating tones of differing frequencies and intensities and conclude that there is insufficient evidence to clearly conclude an age deficit. The reader is referred to that work (and also Marshall 1981) for additional evidence bearing on auditory discriminability using masking and critical bandwidth measures.

In regard to speech perception per se, that is, when spoken words serve as the stimuli to be discriminated, there is a gradual decline in the accuracy of performance commencing around the third decade of life, with accelerated decline around the fifth decade (see, for example, Jerger 1973). In general, speech discrimination deteriorates in the elderly when the speech is altered in any way, such as accelerated speech (Bergman 1971) and filtered speech (Jokinen 1973). However, the magnitude of deterioration may depend on the meaningfulness of the speech (as demonstrated recently by Wingfield et al. 1985), and on the context within which the speech act occurs.

In sum, it can be concluded that: (1) in most elderly adults there is a decline in absolute sensitivity to pure tones; (2) the decline is larger for men than for women; and (3) speech perception deteriorates with age, but the magnitude of decline depends on the presence of noise, the distortion of the speech, and the context within which perception occurs.

The Cutaneous, Vestibular, and Proprioceptive Systems

The cutaneous system mediates tactile sensitivity (mechanoreception), temperature sensitivity (thermoreception), and pain sensitivity (nociception). The vestibular system (in the inner ear) and the proprioceptive system (whose receptors are located in the joints and muscles) provide important information for the control of bodily orientation in space, and are particularly important for maintaining a sense of balance. Compared to the visual and auditory systems, relatively little is known about sensory processes in these systems and even less about age changes therein (see, for example, Kenshalo 1977). Perhaps this reflects the lack of severe limitations in these modalities relative to the afflictions of blindness and deafness. Nevertheless, there is a growing literature on age-related changes in these systems, which can be briefly summarized.

The measurement problems outlined in the introduction of this part of the chapter are particularly poignant in regard to the cutaneous system. The skin is the largest sensory organ in the human body, and it is composed of a variety of receptor cells that have highly specialized functions (see Figure 5.4).

Vibrotactile sensitivity diminishes with age, but the magnitude of decline depends on (among other factors) the vibrating frequency of the test stimulus, skin temperature, and the specific site tested (e.g., Verillo and Verillo 1985). Age-related changes in temperature sensitivity are less clearly defined. In two of the three studies cited by the Verillos a decline in thermoreception was obtained, but much more research is needed before conclusions can safely be drawn.

Finally, much the same can be said of age-related changes in pain sensitivity although somewhat more research has been conducted, perhaps because of the age-related incidence of complaints about chronic pain. Pain is a complex experience, comprising not only sensory processing, but emotional, social, and motivational factors as well (Melzack 1973; Sternbach 1978). The studies that have been conducted have either shown no age difference in pain sensitivity (e.g., Harkins and Chapman 1976, 1977), or a decrease with age (e.g., Schluderman and Zubek 1962). Verillo and Verillo conclude their review of this literature with the statement that "no definitive statement can be made at this time with regard to the relationship between age and the threshold of pain, the ability to tolerate pain, or the effect of analgesic agents in the control of pain" (1985, 23).

The control of bodily orientation is particularly important for older adults, given their susceptibility to serious injury from falls. Vertigo (dizziness) is a worrisome complaint of older adults, and the maintenance of balance is governed by input from the visual, vestibular, and proprioceptive systems. Age-related changes in the visual system were described above.

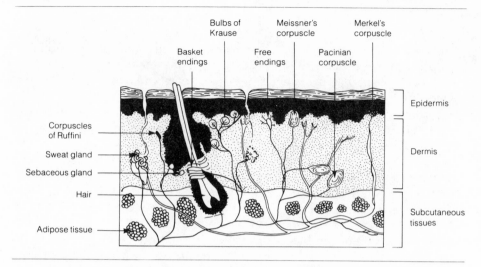

FIGURE 5.4. **Diagram of the major structures and sense receptors of the human skin.**

The vestibular system is located in the inner ear and is intimately related to the anatomical structures of the auditory system, though its receptors are attuned primarily to dynamic changes in head position and to gravity (see Precht 1979). Age-related degeneration within specific vestibular receptor systems, known collectively as "the organ of equilibrium" (Ross 1979), has been linked to age-related increments in vertigo and consequent falling (Verillo and Verillo 1985). The few psychophysical studies that have examined age effects have indicated substantial decline after the sixth decade of life in nystagmic activity, a drifting of the eyes, after the body stops spinning (Van der Laan and Oosterveld 1974), and a substantial increase in the amount of energy expended in maintaining erect posture (Black 1979). Both sets of findings suggest that reduced vestibular functioning is a significant factor in postular instability among the elderly (Verillo and Verillo 1985).

The receptors of the proprioceptive system are located within specialized fibers of the skeletal muscles and tendons and within the joints, and provide feedback about body position and movement. Age-related decrements in active movement (e.g., touching one's nose with eyes closed) but not in passive movement (e.g., detecting the amount of displacement of an extremity), and in the accuracy of discriminating between lifted weights under speeded-response but not self-paced conditions have been reported (see Verillo and Verillo 1985). These age changes in vestibular and proprioceptive function, though not particularly overwhelming in isolation, contribute to age-related difficulties in body control. Age-related changes in the central nervous system may exacerbate these changes too, but that is a topic for the last section.

The Gustatory and Olfactory Systems

Psychophysical studies of taste and smell are prone to significant stimulus quantification problems. Both must use substances in solution, presenting additional problems for stimulus presentation and control. As with the other sensory systems, studies have been designed to evaluate age-related changes in both threshold detection and stimulus discrimination.

The gustatory system mediates sensitivity to soluble substances, and its receptors are located in different concentrations in the taste buds of the tongue. Although perhaps as many as two-thirds of the taste buds atrophy in old age, Bradley (1979) has cautioned that many other anatomical changes (in the salivary glands, teeth, and gums, for example) contribute to age-related changes in gustatory function. There are four basic taste qualities: salty, sour, bitter, and sweet. In general, the research indicates that there is a decline in sensitivity to all four basic tastes, with sensitivity to sweet perhaps suffering the greatest decline (see, for example, Murphy 1979). However, there is evidence that nonsmokers preserve gustatory function well into later life, whereas smokers show significant decline (Kaplan, Glanville, and Fischer 1965). It is important to note that the magnitude of deterioration in gustatory sensitivity is relatively small, and, in fact, the ability to discriminate between the four basic tastes remains intact even in elderly adults who complain of losses in taste capacity (Cohen and Gitman 1959). It is likely that odor contributes substantially to the appreciation of flavor, and perhaps its role increases with age.

The olfactory system mediates sensitivity to gaseous substances, and its primary receptors are located at the roof and to the rear of the nasal cavity (see Graziadei 1971). Naessen (1971) has documented a variety of changes in anatomical structures in the olfactory system, and, most notably, has reported that in some cases the olfactory receptors are completely atrophied by the sixth decade of life! Though they are replete with methodological difficulties, psychophysical studies of olfactory sensitivity and discriminability indicate age-related decline, but whether it is gradual in onset or precipitates in later life is unclear (Engen 1977). A common complaint among the elderly is that "the flavor of foods is 'not what it used to be' " (Verillo and Verillo 1985, 30). Schiffman (1979) has suggested that this complaint is prompted by decrements in olfactory function, and more recently Schemper, Voss, and Cain (1981) have suggested that a cognitive deficit exacerbates the sensory deficit. Despite the need for more careful psychophysical investigation, it is clear that the olfactory and gustatory systems interact in the taste experience, and it appears that decrements in each are interrelated.

Perceptual Function

The research on sensory function reviewed above indicates some degree of age-related decline in sensitivity and discriminability across all the senses. The detection and discrimination of simple sensory events makes up only part of the input in the sequence of information processing. Typically, simple signals are organized into meaningful or recognizable units, decisions are made about them, and often, some response follows, such as naming, classifying, categorizing, or the like. The recognition aspect of information processing is commonly subsumed under the rubric of "perception." Formally, perception refers to the interpretation of sensory information in light of past experience (e.g., Solso 1979). Although sensation and perception can be differentiated conceptually and experimentally, in everyday life they are fully interactive: Perception depends upon sensory input, but sensation depends equally as much on experience, because sensation in the absence of recognition is not meaningful (Neisser 1976). Furthermore, the acquisition of experience (or skill) can enhance the discriminatory capability of the observer as, for example, in skilled radiologists who are adept at detecting tumors on photographic plates that to the untrained eye appear no different than random smudges (Swenson 1980).

Some evidence bearing on age differences in auditory (speech) perception was reviewed already, and much of the research reviewed on the gustatory and olfactory systems involves perception (i.e., the recognition of foods) more than sensation in the strict sense (no pun intended). However, most of the research on perceptual function has been in the area of vision, and the age-related effects observed are presumed to generalize to the other sense modalities.

One of the clearest findings in the domain of visual perception is that with age there is an increase in the time required to recognize information. For example, studies that have employed visual masking, wherein a target stimulus is displayed briefly followed at some interval by a second stimulus (the mask), have indicated that the length of the intervening interval required for successful target identification increases with advancing age (for review, see Kline and Schieber 1985). Older adults are also less accurate than younger adults at recognizing target patterns that are degraded, as in identifying incomplete figures (e.g., Verville and Cameron 1946). The magnitude of age-related deficit, however, has been shown to decrease with increasing familiarity of the stimulus materials. For example, Poon and Fozard (1978) found that age-related slowing in the time taken to name pictured objects was reduced when the objects were common rather than unique to contemporary culture (e.g., teacup versus micro-cassette player), and, in fact, reversed when the objects were unique to the elderly's cohort (e.g., butter churn). (see Figure 5.5.)

Presumably, familiar materials are more expediently connected to their

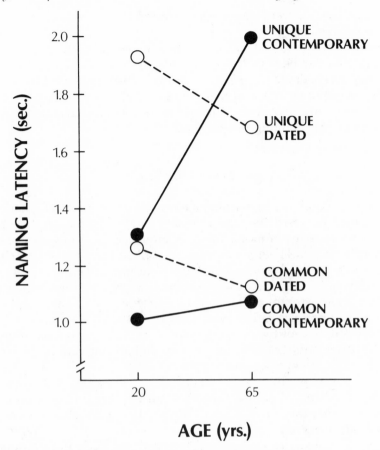

FIGURE 5.5. **Average time (sec.) to name pictured objects for adults in three age groups as a function of the datedness and uniqueness of the object.**

ADAPTED FROM L. W. Poon and J. L. Fozard, Speed of retrieval from long-term memory in relation to age, familiarity, and datedness of information, *Journal of Gerontology* 33 (1978).

referents stored in memory. Various hypotheses have been put forth to account for the particular advantage this serves the elderly. For example, Welford (1984) has proposed a signal-detection hypothesis in which familiarity acts to enhance the memory trace of information stored in long-term memory, making it stand out more prominently from background "noise" which increases with age. Layton (1975) proposed a perceptual noise hypothesis wherein familiarity acts to reduce uncertainty about which of the many possible responses associated with different stimuli should be selected. Birren and others (Birren 1965; Cerella, Poon, and Williams 1980; Salthouse 1982, 1985) posit a speed-of-processing model in which familiarity reduces the number of processes (or stages) required for recognition, thereby reducing the number of age-slowed processes involved. Other researchers have proposed that familiarity minimizes the demand on attention, which diminishes in capacity—the amount of information that can be attended (e.g., Craik and Byrd 1981)—or allocation—how attention is deployed (Hoyer and Plude 1980, 1982)—with advancing age. But these hypotheses address more central limitations on age-related performance, and there is another set of peripheral limitations to be discussed before elaborating further.

Motor Function

Age-related reductions in peripheral motor function impose limitations on performance by restricting the intensity and speed of overt response. Age-related changes in motor function are caused not only by senescent changes in the central nervous system (described later) but also by changes in various phases of metabolism within the muscular, respiratory, and circulatory systems that reduce the supply of oxygen to the muscle tissue (see Mortimer, Pirozzolo, and Maleeta 1982, for a comprehensive review). Motor function is also influenced by various other age limitations such as increased stiffness of the joints, which act to reduce muscular efficiency, and arthritic conditions, which may cause pain during certain movements. Thus the assessment of age-related changes in peripheral motor function is by no means a straightforward affair.

Tests of maximal muscular strength indicate that peak performance is achieved during the early twenties, followed by gradual decline, until by age sixty muscular strength is reduced by as much as 35% (Welford 1977). Loss of muscle tissue may account in part for such decline, but it is exacerbated by age-related losses in neural cells, interconnections, and neurotransmitters in the brain, spinal cord, and afferent nerves to the muscles (Spirduso 1982). In addition, Scheibel (1978) has suggested that loss of muscular receptor cells responsible for inhibiting sets of opposing muscles contributes to age-related decline in strength because the muscles involved in the voluntary action must work against the opposing force. It should be noted that the magnitude of decline tends to be less for muscle groups involved with endurance rather than with speed (Spirduso 1982).

Evidence of age-related changes in the speed of muscular response comes from studies that decompose simple responses into "premotor" and "motor" components. The premotor component (primarily determined by central processes, such as decision and preparation) is measured by the latency of initiating a movement in response to a simple signal, such as a tone or flash of light. The motor component (or peripheral motor time) is measured by the time taken to carry out some simple action, such as moving a finger from one response key to another. The consensus among these kinds of studies involving elderly participants (see Welford 1984, for a review) is that both components show age-related slowing, with the premotor component demonstrating proportionally larger effects of aging. Thus, the speed of peripheral motor function declines with age, but the limitations imposed by it are less severe than the limitations imposed by more central aspects of performance.

Age-related reductions in peripheral motor strength and speed are probably of little consequence in everyday functioning because most daily tasks impose less than maximum workload. However, they may well be important factors limiting energetic pursuits and work involving heavy muscular effort by older adults, and especially when such activity must be engaged in swiftly and maintained over a period of time. The possibility that age-related reductions in muscular strength and speed can be avoided by, or at least compensated by, regular exercise is a topic of active research (e.g., Larsson 1982). Spirduso (1975, 1980) has found that the difference in speed of simple movement between exercised (i.e., regular participants in sports) and unexercised individuals is nearly twice as great among the elderly as among young adults (see Figure 5.6). Although many factors may distinguish between people who engage in regular exercise and those who do not (e.g., various personality traits, diet, etc.), the positive effect of exercise on cardiovascular fitness underscores its importance in maintaining adequate peripheral motor function throughout the adult years. Maintaining motor function is especially important in light of the potential consequences of disuse: Muscular disuse may lead to neuronal atrophy which, in turn, reduces muscular coordination and power which, in turn, results in even greater disuse, and so on.

The Control of Information Processing

In the foregoing sections various age-related changes in peripheral aspects of human performance were reviewed, and it was shown that the data argue overwhelmingly for at least some amount of decrement at least by the sixth or seventh decade of life. A major question is whether peripheral decrements alone can account for age-related changes in performance. And here the answer is a resounding "No!" But the question warrants careful consideration because peripheral or "data" limitations may mimic central or "resource" limitations on information processing (Norman and Bobrow 1975).

For example, Cerella (1985) recently articulated the consequences of age-related reductions in the size of the "perceptual window" for various perceptual tasks. Cerella first demonstrated that the elderly show a deficit of about one-third compared to young adults in the speed and accuracy of letter identification as the letter is moved away from the fovea. This decline

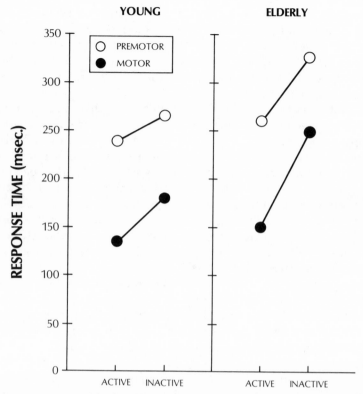

FIGURE 5.6. **Premotor and motor response times (msec.) for active and inactive adults in two age groups.** (See text for definition of premotor and motor responses.)

ADAPTED FROM W. W. Spirduso, Reaction and movement time as a function of age and physical activity level, *Journal of Gerontology* 30 (1975).

in extrafovea letter recognition had a direct impact on the amount of interference caused by to-be-ignored characters in a visual display. Elderly adults exhibited less interference than young adults, provided the characters fell outside their "perceptual window," replicating earlier findings of age-related equivalence in a visual "filtering" task (Wright and Elias 1979). However, when the nontarget characters were adjusted in size for extrafovea discriminability, older adults exhibited larger interference effects than did younger adults. According to Cerella, this age-associated data limitation may also account for a variety of performance decrements previously ascribed to age-related changes in central processing components, such as reduced attentional capacity, and even to decrements previously ascribed to different neural pathways (sustained versus transient) in the visual system (Kline and Schieber 1981, 1985).

While Cerella's findings point up the importance of assessing the contribution of age-related limitations in peripheral processes to decrements in performance, recent findings obtained by Plude and Hoyer (1986) indicate that aging is associated with important limitations in central aspects of information processing as well. Young and elderly adults participated in two conditions of a letter recognition task that differed in the number of display locations (one versus five) monitored to detect a given target character. As shown in Figure 5.7, the elderly exhibited a deficit relative to young adults in interference produced by nontarget characters when multiple locations were monitored, but not when a single location was relevant, and this obtained even when performance was equated for foveal acuity. Thus, it is clear that peripheral limitations contribute to age-related decrements in information processing, but they do so in interaction with central processes that are responsible for controlling the flow of information between input and output.

The study of attention is concerned with limitations on the control of information processing and with information selection processes. Attentional processes determine in part which of the many bits of sensory information reach consciousness, and they govern the selection and initiation of action appropriate to that information. The concept of attention has been used in reference to a variety of central processes including alertness and arousal (Posner and Boise 1971), search and selection (Shiffrin and Schneider 1977), and preparedness and expectancy (for review, see Parasuraman and Davies 1984). Although these are overlapping (and fuzzily defined) processes, it is useful to view attention as a complex process involving at least these aspects.

There has been considerable research devoted to assessing age-related changes in these various aspects of attention, and each has been shown to contribute to age-related differences in performance on a wide variety of tasks (see, for example, Hoyer and Plude 1985; Kausler 1982; Plude and Hoyer 1985), but many of these age-related limitations can be attenuated, and sometimes even eliminated completely, by capitalizing on past experience with particular (familiar) stimulus materials (e.g., Poon and Fozard 1978; Thomas, Waugh, and Fozard 1978) or response contingencies (Plude, Hoyer, and Lazar 1982; Simon 1968), or by fostering the development of "automaticity" which bypasses limitations on central processing (e.g., Madden and Nebes 1980; Plude and Hoyer 1981; Plude et al. 1983).

The precise nature of the age-related difference underlying these effects is a topic of heated debate. As noted in the section on perceptual function, there are (at least) four prominent hypotheses about the nature of central limitations in aging, but they are not necessarily mutually exclusive. Salthouse (1980, 1982) has suggested that the speed-of-processing and attentional-capacity hypotheses cannot be distinguished from one another, at least not with current experimental methodology. Welford (1984, 1985) has suggested that a signal-detection problem lies at the root of the pro-

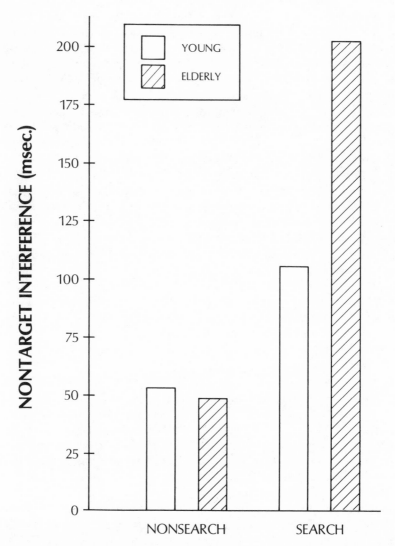

FIGURE 5.7. **Magnitude of nontarget interference (msec.) in detecting a target letter for adults in two age groups as a function of focused (nonsearch) and divided (search) attention.** (Target acuity was equated between conditions.)

ADAPTED FROM D. J. Plude and W. J. Hoyer, Age and the selectivity of visual information processing, *Journal of Psychology and Aging,* 1 (1986):4–10.

cessing-speed hypothesis; that is, difficulty in signal processing results in slower processing speed. And Layton's (1975) perceptual-noise hypothesis emphasizes the difficulty in selecting among responses (rather than signals). Clearly, much more careful research is needed to decide which of these models (alone or in combination) provides the best account of age-related changes in information processing. The final form of the model must accommodate potentially different developmental courses for peripheral and central components of information processing, and the best model will apply to the entire life span (see Pollack and Atkeson 1978, for one such example).

Despite the controversy over the theoretical interpretation of age-related changes in information processing, the gradual ascendance of the life-course perspective has spurred investigators to examine the ecological significance of laboratory findings (e.g., Bronfenbrenner 1977; Schonfield 1974; Labouvie-Vief and Chandler 1978), and to consider the impact of a life-long accumulation of knowledge on sensory, perceptual, and motor function. It is likely that with advancing age there is increased reliance on "higher-order" information, that is, conceptual knowledge, in offsetting "lower-order" sensory and motor limitations commonly associated with senescence. Certainly this thesis is not new (Hoyer and Plude 1980, 1982; Plude and Hoyer 1985), but recent advances in mainstream cognitive psychology provide the theoretical framework for investigating the application of real-world knowledge in perceiving, comprehending, remembering, and responding to objects and events in everyday life (Bobrow and Norman 1975; Schank and Abelson 1977). This orientation to the study of age-related changes in sensory, perceptual, and motor function will no doubt reveal the truly interactive nature of these processes, and their role in the maintenance of everyday performance on the part of the great majority of elderly adults.

VI

COGNITION AND AGING
THE EMERGENCE
OF A NEW TRADITION

Deirdre A. Kramer

All these things and a thousand more are embodied in me, the good years
and the bad, the wide rings of growth and the narrow. One's past is not
something we leave behind but something we incorporate. . . . Outwardly I
am eighty-three years old, but inwardly I am every age, with the emotions
and experience of each age period. (Coatsworth 1976, xiv–xv)

These words, taken from the autobiography of an eighty-three-year-old
author, were also echoed in a touching poem written anonymously by an
elderly woman on a geriatric ward. That woman concluded her poem by
stating that if what the nurses saw was a "crabbed" old woman, dribbling
and unwise, they were not really looking at her, for she was more than
that; in fact, she encompassed all the experiences her life had offered.

Do psychologists really look at the elderly when we study them? Like
nurses, we too are subject to biases, and each psychologist sees through a
particular lens that brings certain aspects of behavior into focus while it
blurs others. Is it possible to live for seventy years without changing,
growing? Or does one absorb the fruits of all his or her years, as suggested
in these quotes? In dealing with these questions we will see that the lens
we use substantially affects the answers we find.

This chapter deals with cognitive development in adulthood. Cognition,
broadly speaking, represents awareness of the world, and incorporates
such wide-ranging phenomena as perception, learning, memory, intelligence, and a broad array of problem-solving skills. In the author's
view, cognition arises as a result of adapting to the environment, and thus,

The author would like to thank Lillian Troll for her comments on an earlier version of this
chapter.

114

should be understood in relation to the individual's life experiences. The wealth of seventy years' experience must translate into potential growth. Not all psychologists hold this view, however.

In this chapter, cognition in aging will be considered from the perspectives of two disparate kinds of lenses, or world views. These are the traditional, mechanistic world view and the adult-centered, organismic world view, respectively. The traditional, mechanistic approach seeks to reduce cognition to its most basic elements and study these in an isolated manner in the laboratory, in an attempt to eliminate real-world confounds. Such an approach generally results in a picture of aging characterized almost exclusively by decline. However, findings generated by this perspective result in some puzzling questions, mostly pertaining to strong effects of content material on performance. These questions might be resolved if we adopt an adult-centered organismic world view, or lens. In this approach, all cognitive activity is purposeful and adaptive, and must be construed as inseparable from the everyday context in which it occurs. Hence, it would be useless to break cognition down to its basic components and study these in an isolated manner in the lab as if they would be unaffected by real-life experiences. Such an approach generally produces a more favorable picture of the aging process and resolves the dilemma of content effects, since the context becomes a focus of analysis. However, it raises difficulties of its own, most evidently those pertaining to measurement precision. It is suggested that the traditional, mechanistic approach may underestimate age-related growth, while the adult-centered, organismic perspective may underestimate age-related decline. These approaches, or lenses, will be described in greater detail, followed by a consideration of major findings from the areas of learning and memory, intelligence, logical reasoning, and creative problem solving. It will be demonstrated that the traditional and adult-centered approaches yield divergent conclusions, respectively, about the fate of these cognitive processes in later life.

The Traditional versus the Adult-Centered Approach

For many years, developmental psychology was considered by most to be virtually synonymous with child psychology. In recent decades, however, there has been increasing interest in the entire life span (Baltes, Reese, and Lipsitt 1980). One precursor of this orientation was the burgeoning field of gerontology. Much of the empirical and theoretical work on aging, however, contributed few new developmental principles about cognitive processes. Constructs and measurements designed for use with children and college students were almost blindly applied to the study of aging adults.

Such tests have little demonstrated relevance to the study of adulthood (Labouvie-Vief 1977), and were often used with the explicit purpose of demonstrating regression of cognitive function in later life. Researchers are finally making headway in developing adult-centered models and measures of cognition (see, for example, Baltes, Dittmann-Kohli, and Dixon 1984; Berg and Sternberg 1985; Commons, Richards, and Armon 1984; Labouvie-Vief 1982, 1985).

What is meant by an adult-centered model of cognition? Such a model would focus on the kinds of concerns that actually confront adults, that is, the kinds of thought processes used in solving real-life problems. This seems simple enough and, indeed, adults generally report that the kinds of problems that typically confront them are of a practical and social nature (Newman, Attig, and Kramer 1983; Sinnott 1984). It is also believed that much of adult problem solving occurs with problems that are not clearly defined and structured (i.e., *ill-structured* problems), such as those confronting parents where there is not one right solution with a known outcome (Kitchener 1983; Wood 1983). Yet, in a recent survey of the problem-solving tasks used in studies published in four major developmental journals in the past five years (Kramer and Dittmann-Kohli 1984) it was found that only 36% of the tasks used with adults were in the social realm, and only 25% were ill-structured problems which occur outside an educational setting.

Cornelius and Kenney (1982) found that, while academic forms of intelligence are believed by the layman to be at their peak in early adulthood, social and practical forms of intelligence are believed to develop later in life. Such continued development makes intuitive sense—imagine living for fifty or sixty years beyond the age of twenty and learning nothing! That would take a great deal of hard work! But, while the majority of problems adults have to solve are considered practical, social, and ill-structured in nature, only a minority of studies employ such problems. Kramer and Dittmann-Kohli (1984) argued that by testing adults with the kinds of processes that most typify childhood, adolescence, and early adulthood, we are developing a distorted view of the aging process, one that is particularly damaging to our conception of aging. In this chapter, an adult-centered model of aging will be compared with the traditional approach to aging research to highlight the divergent conclusions drawn from the two perspectives with respect to the development of memory, intelligence, logical reasoning, and creativity in later life.

The traditional and adult-centered views typically tend to reflect assumptions of different *world views*, variously labeled as mechanistic versus organismic (Overton and Reese 1973; Reese and Overton 1970), analytic versus synthetic (Pepper 1942), and linear versus nonlinear (Labouvie-Vief and Schell 1982), respectively. These are delineated as follows.

The Traditional, Mechanistic Approach

The traditional mechanistic approach views human behavior as machine-like, so that if we break the machine down to its basic parts we can understand the working of the whole. Such an approach can also be considered analytic or linear. A component may be a physiological process, a behavior, a skill, or a specific type of problem-solving activity. In carrying out this kind of research program, we would have to make sure that we *do* separate these basic components—that is, that they are not confounded with each other or with other factors. We want to study each component as purely as possible. Therefore, it is best to isolate such basic processes in a highly controlled laboratory setting, and make sure to separate the process under study from the other variables and life experiences that are confounded with it and, hence, might obstruct its pure measurement. As a result, the focus has generally been to use academic tests with abstract content which are as far removed from real-life experiences as possible in order to avoid such confounds.

The Adult-Centered, Organismic Approach

In contrast, an adult-centered, organismic model views cognition as inseparable from its environment, or from the life course of the individual. The human being is an active, purposeful organism (thus, it is an organismic, rather than mechanistic, perspective), rather than a machine programmed by others, whose problem solving is geared toward the solution of real-world problems and life tasks. Such problems are inherently motivating. Failure to test people on problems that are inherently meaningful or motivating to them may result in nonoptimal problem-solving performance, and thus produce an artificial picture of cognitive processes. As Scribner (1984) so eloquently stated, the difference here is one of viewing problem solving as either an end in itself (the traditional approach) or as a means to some desired end (the adult-centered approach). In real life, problem solving is generally a means to some end; in the lab it is usually the end. In the adult-centered view the organism undergoes continual growth as he or she actively adapts to the environment, and it would take a tremendous amount of effort to try to impede that growth. Since problem solving cannot be separated from the environment and processes cannot be decomposed into finite parts, such a view is considered synthetic, or nonlinear. Everything in a system is related to everything else in that system.

The Role of World Views

It has been pointed out that a scientist cannot denounce one world view as wrong and herald the other as right. They simply represent different lenses

(Overton and Reese 1973; Reese and Overton 1970). Nor can the two be resolved, since they operate from incompatible sets of assumptions and are different "languages," so to speak. They employ different criteria for what constitutes a truth, different measurement strategies, and different explanations. For example, the traditional, mechanistic researcher would never admit to the validity of assessing psychological processes amidst the confounding influence of real-life factors. Such an approach would be nonscientific, imprecise. Likewise, the adult-centered, organismic researcher would argue that such isolation of variables would trivialize the phenomenon under investigation and render it nongeneralizable to real-life problem solving. There is no real resolution of these two approaches. There is a necessary trade-off between precision and generalizability, of which there is no "true" solution (Labouvie 1975). Therefore, work conducted under the auspices of each of these two programs will inevitably produce different pictures of the same phenomena. The scientist must determine whether the picture generated allows accurate predictions to be made about the development. In the following pages, the author will compare and contrast these two approaches to the study of various cognitive processes, and demonstrate some of the range and limits of each approach. The discussion will begin with memory.

Learning and Memory

Much of the literature on aging as it concerns learning and memory has proceeded from the assumptions and methods of the traditional mechanistic model. A common approach to the study of learning and memory has involved the learning of lists. In such an approach, lists containing either pairs of words or single words are presented to the individual, who is required to memorize them. The manner in which he or she recalls the lists, and the kinds of words best recalled allow the researcher to infer the organizational strategies underlying more complex forms of learning and retention. For example, people often recall words from the same category together—such as all fruit or all vegetables—rather than in the order in which they were originally presented by the experimenter. Thus, we can infer that people organize material to be remembered conceptually. Such an approach has resulted in a very negative picture of the aging process. Older adults generally show poorer retention for such lists, and do not spontaneously generate the organizational strategies most expedient for learning them, although they are shown to be capable of using such strategies when instructed to do so (Craik 1977). How often do people have to memorize lists of words though? Further, are the processes that underlie list learning really the same as those underlying everyday memory processes? A number of researchers think not (e.g., Cavanaugh 1983; Labouvie-Vief and Schell 1982; Sinnott 1985).

Not only may one question whether such tasks capture the processes used in everyday life, but one may also question whether they arouse the interest and motivation of elderly subjects who, unlike the college sophomores with whom they are typically compared, are probably no longer accustomed to taking school-like tests. In fact, Hulicka (1967) found that 80% of her older subjects refused to participate in a paired-associates study when they learned what the task would be! This is an astounding percentage. Yet sadly, too few researchers have questioned whether the reason elderly subjects find such tests unpalatable and why they do not spontaneously produce the strategies of which they are capable is that they find them irrelevant. Such findings alone should be most informative about the validity of using such tests with the elderly.

One traditional approach to the theoretical conceptualization of the development of memory is that of information processing. In an information processing model, the person is viewed as similar to a machine, and an attempt is made to isolate a small number of basic components, or processes, that comprise his or her memory. The model with which the reader is most likely to be familiar refers to short-term and long-term memory, and a somewhat similar distinction has been made between primary, secondary, and tertiary memory. Primary memory is seen as limited capacity information storage in which information is still "in mind," has not yet been committed to more permanent memory storage. The most common means of assessing primary memory is the "digit span," requiring the reproduction of as many digits as possible. The maximum number of digits the individual can reproduce is presumed to represent maximum information processing capacity; for most individuals this is approximately seven digits. Primary process memory shows little or no age-related differences, suggesting no basic capacity differential between the young and the old (Craik 1977; Poon 1985).

Secondary memory is seen to be an unlimited, relatively permanent store of recently acquired information, such as a list just learned, or what was eaten for lunch. Tertiary memory includes information that has been permanently committed to memory, such as where one went to high school, who one's first boyfriend or girlfriend was, and so on. Like primary memory, tertiary memory shows no apparent decline with age. Secondary memory, on the other hand shows age-related deficits (Craik 1977; Poon 1985). Secondary memory involves the acquisition of new information and is believed to require processing the information in a deep, meaningful manner if it is to be retained in permanent storage. Older adults do not spontaneously use the organizational strategies necessary for encoding such information efficiently. However, even secondary memory does not always show such decline. Consequently, many are skeptical about the utility of any model that attempts to show a "locus" of decline, or about traditional models that attempt to break memory down to its basic "components," to study components free from the context in which they are embedded (Labouvie-Vief and Schell 1982; Poon 1985). A few relevant findings will be described briefly to illustrate this point.

Performance on a number of memory tasks—as wide-ranging as list learning and memory for prose passages—show content effects. In essence, when one measures content that is familiar and/or interesting to older adults, age differences vanish and sometimes older adults perform better than young adults on such tasks (e.g., see Hultsch and Dixon 1983; Poon 1985). For example, when Cavanaugh presented adults with television material, using a variety of formats, he found no difference in the retention of either details or the overall gist between young and older adults matched for high verbal skills (Cavanaugh 1983, 1984). Thus, when the material is interesting, older adults remember as well as young adults, making one question just why it is that they do not remember well on less interesting tasks. A key to this question might be found in a provocative anecdote told by a memory researcher, Cameron Camp, of an old woman who announced to her daughter one morning that it was time to die because she had already learned everything there was to learn.

> She called for her daughter to make her one last cup of tea. The daughter went over to the cold fireplace in the mother's cabin and scooped up a handful of ashes. "Why are you doing that?" asked the older woman. "My fireplace still has some hot coals," said the daughter. "I will go to my cabin, put a coal on top of these cold ashes, and carry it over to your fireplace without getting burned. Then I can start a fire to make some tea." Upon hearing this, the old woman got out of bed. "I've never heard of that before," she said. "I guess I won't have to die today" (Cavanaugh et al. 1985, 146–47).

Information new and captivating to a college student may be old hat to an elderly person. Work by Camp and his colleagues suggests that older adults sometimes remember difficult and unusual sentences more readily because they have greater novelty and distinctiveness compared to easier or less interesting materials, and force the older adults to pay attention to otherwise uninteresting material (reported in Cavanaugh et al. 1985). Thus, if the material to be learned is already irrelevant, then it had better be unusual (and, hence, "mind-grabbing") if it is to be remembered by the old.

There is reason to believe that the content which most interests older people deals with abstract generalizations, principles, and morals (Blanchard-Fields 1981; Labouvie-Vief and Schell, 1982). If one sees cognition as adaptive, then such processing makes sense in light of the life tasks that are faced in later life. According to Erik Erikson (1968) a major task of old age is to reflect on one's life in order to try to carve a meaning from it, make sense of it. Butler (1963) has termed it "life review." The poem by the older nursing home patient who stated that she was inwardly reliving all of the years of her life, reexperiencing joys and pains, and reflecting upon them reflects this theme. An individual may look back on his or her life and weigh the balance of deeds accomplished and those left undone, maintaining a sense of integrity in the face of imminent death—achieving a feeling of having lived a life, which, while not perfect, was well-lived. Alternatively, one may conclude that one's life was not well-lived, or that there were some major tasks left undone, resulting in a sense of despair. It is interesting that one of the "deeds undone" which the author's grandmother regretted before her death was that of writing a family history. According to Erikson (1968, 1969) it is with history—the history of one's life, the continuity between past, present, and future generations—that middle-aged and older adults are most concerned. In line with this, assessment of memory in later life needs to consider the type of content that is intriguing to the aging individual and the kinds of cognitive processes that are necessary to achieve desired goals.

Gisela Labouvie-Vief and her colleagues have found that the information processing of older adults is more abstract in nature, being more concerned with drawing inferences from material presented than with faithfully reproducing details. This can be seen most readily with memory for prose passages, where older adults are more likely to recall the meaning of a passage at the expense of details, and are more likely to draw inferences, especially those having to do with moral lessons (Labouvie-Vief and Schell 1982). Work conducted by Camp (1981) has also shown that older adults engage in more inferential processing, suggesting that the abstraction of meaning and pattern is a characteristic feature of thought in later life. Such abstraction certainly could serve the individual's goals in solving late-life personality tasks, where themes that give continuity to one's life must be inferred. Work by the author on categorization of everyday social situations also suggests that some older adults do more inferencing than young adults (Kramer and Woodruff 1984).

In summary, research that arises from a traditional mechanistic framework suggests that older adults show a predominant pattern of decline or, at most, stability in certain kinds of memory processes with age. The presumed deficit is at the level of processing new information, or secondary memory. However, as shown, such processes cannot be neatly separated, as they show strong context or content effects. A more advantageous approach to the study of memory in the adult years may be an adult-centered one, which attempts to place the memory processes in the broader ecological context of the individual's life. When such an approach is utilized, there may be certain memory processes—in particular those having to do with higher-order, abstract, inferential processes—that continue to grow across the life span, while others, less useful to the adult's overall life goals, may drop out. There may be a trade-off in order to develop the broader, more abstract style; it may be necessary to give up some on details. Birren (1969) referred to this process as the "race between the bit and the bite." Older adults give up the bit for the bite.

Intelligence

The earliest work on psychometric intelligence (i.e., IQ tests) suggested that it begins to decline after about the age of nineteen. If that is so, most of those reading this book are already over the hill. However, we may all take comfort. That early work was *cross-sectional* in nature, which means that at a given point in time people of one age were being compared to people of another, and age *differences* that were seen to occur were presumed to represent actual age *declines* on the part of the older subjects. This was a false assumption. Older adults are, on the average, in each preceding generation, less educated than younger adults, and differ from them on a number of other dimensions as well that may be relevant to IQ test performance. Chances are they *never* would have scored higher on that test, even as young adults, as research has borne out (e.g., Schaie and Parham 1977).

When one follows a group of people from their early adulthood into old age, a quite different pattern emerges. To briefly summarize these findings: (1) whatever apparent declines occur, they occur much later in life, sometimes even into the late seventies (Botwinick 1977; Dixon, Kramer, and Baltes, 1985; Schaie and Parham 1977); (2) the declines are small enough to make one question their significance in terms of real-life functioning (Schaie and Parham 1977); (3) there are strong generational, or cultural effects—stronger than the age effects (Schaie and Parham 1977); and (4) a complex pattern of age-related trends occurs, where different kinds of intelligence show different patterns and rates of growth and decline (Baltes, Dittmann-Kohli, and Dixon 1984; Dixon, Kramer and Baltes 1985; Willis and Baltes 1980).

For example, a distinction has been made between fluid and crystallized intelligence (Horn 1976). *Fluid intelligence* presumably represents pure learning ability unaffected by experience. It is the ability to perceive new patterns and acquire new knowledge, and shows the earliest age-related decline. *Crystallized intelligence*, on the other hand, represents accumulated knowledge, and shows much later, if any, decline and sometimes even growth. However, even fluid intelligence has been shown to be trainable in older adults, bringing into question its presumed decline (Plemons, Willis and Baltes 1978; Bliezsner, Willis, and Baltes 1981). It, too, has been shown susceptible to content effects on performance suggesting that it is not a pure process or entity separable from the context in which it occurs (Gonda, Quayhagen, and Schaie 1979).

Crystallized intelligence has been considered less relevant to the overall notion of intelligence by its originators. Yet, when one takes a life-course or adult-centered approach to the study of intelligence, it is exactly that form of intelligence which relies on accumulated experience that sets the elderly apart from other age groups in their potential for continued growth. Cognitive growth in the latter half of the life span is likely to be related to reorganization and application of previously acquired knowledge. Once again, the adoption of the more traditional, mechanistic approach to the study of intelligence in aging, which construes it as an entity separable from the environment in which it occurs, results in a predominantly negative view of the aging process. This is not to deny that there is intellectual decline in later life—much evidence points in that direction; the intent is merely to show that by adopting such models we are led down a path of nearly complete and inevitable decline in later life. By taking a different path we might be led to a contrasting set of conclusions about aging.

An adult-centered model of aging and intelligence would attempt to specify the kinds of intelligence that would most likely develop in older individuals. As noted earlier, adults identify the practical and social realms as the loci of intellectual activity. When intelligence tests are designed to include social and practical information, older people have sometimes scored higher than younger adults (Demming and Pressey 1957; Gardner and Monge 1977). Correspondingly, increasing attention is now being devoted to the issue of practical and social intelligence in later life with some favorable results (Berg and Sternberg 1984; Cornelius and Kenney 1982).

Another promising avenue for the study of adult-centered forms of intelligence in later life concerns the concept of wisdom. Wisdom, while enjoying various definitions, is generally believed to represent insight into human nature and the life cycle (Brent and Watson 1980; Clayton 1982; Clayton and Birren 1980; Dittmann-Kohli and Baltes, n.d.; Moody 1983). While there are differences among the various conceptions, there is general agreement that wisdom involves an awareness of the subjectivity or ill-defined nature of real-life problems, and would recognize the fact that one cannot impose one's solutions on others. A solution that is appropriate for one person in one situation may not extend to another. Rather, one must find a solution tailored to the individual's own life situation, and the task of the wise person is to aid in this discovery (Kramer 1984). In addition, wisdom is believed to involve an integration of affect and cognition: to be able to apply one's principles in the context of an emotionally arousing

experience, yet without losing sight of the emotions themselves, or com-
passion. This is indeed a most difficult task (e.g., see Janis and Mann 1977).

Roodin, Rybash, and Hoyer (1984) feel that it is precisely this integration
between cognition and affect which characterizes adult development. If
that is indeed the case, then a life-course approach, where intelligence is
explicitly placed in the context of solving life tasks, would be most useful.
One such model was offered by Schaie (1977–78). He postulated five stages
of adult intelligence that are centered on the kinds of tasks facing individuals at different times in their lives. Adolescents and young adults
face tasks centering on acquisition of new knowledge and skills, resulting
in problem-solving strategies uniquely suited to the acquisition of novel
information, or fluid intelligence. Middle-aged and older adults, who must
manage the society and make meaning of their lives, respectively, would
develop unique styles of processing information that rely more on pattern
recognition and the use of old information to solve new problems. Unfortunately, there has been thus far no attempt to operationalize Schaie's
model and hence, validate it. In a more positive vein, the increasing
acceptance and adoption of adult-centered approaches to the study of
aging is likely to result in such attempts. Let us now proceed with this
analysis to the study of logical reasoning, where more vigorous attempts
are being made to chart an adult-centered course of cognitive growth.

Logical Reasoning

One of the major theories of childhood cognitive development has centered on the development of logical reasoning and was developed by Jean
Piaget. Piaget traced the development of knowledge about the world from
infancy through adolescence. His theory was an organismic one, in which
he defined intelligence as adaptation to the environment. He saw children
as naturally developing through qualitatively different levels in their reasoning about the world. In other words, at each stage, or level, the child
has a characteristic style or mode of seeing the world that differs qualitatively from those at the stages above and below. There are four such
stages in his model. During the first, the *sensori-motor period*, lasting from
birth until around age two, the child "thinks" with his or her actions,
rather than with mental images and words. In the second, the *preoperational
period*, which lasts until about age seven, the child thinks with mental
images and other symbols, but cannot think logically. During middle
childhood, in the *concrete operational period*, which lasts until about age
eleven or twelve, the child thinks logically but only about the concrete
world—he or she cannot think abstractly or in terms of the hypothetical. It
is during the final stage, the *formal operational period*, which occurs in

adolescence, that the child can think abstractly, hypothetically, and scientifically.

Piaget was revolutionary in his approach. Convinced that there was a logic behind the often incorrect answers given by young children to IQ tests, he became a keen observer of children and discovered that at different ages, children had vastly different ways of understanding the world. There has yet to be a Piaget of adulthood, though some promising moves have been made in this direction. Early attempts to extend his theory to adult development proceeded mostly along the traditional lines thus far described in this chapter—atheoretical, non-adult-centered. They involved the administration of concrete—and formal—operational tasks to older adults, perhaps comparing their performance with that of younger adults, and concluding that older adults have lost their ability to think logically (Hooper, Fitzgerald, and Papalia 1971; Papalia and Bielby 1974). Actually, such studies were cross-sectional and, thus, subject to all of the confounds due to cohort changes. More recent research with better-educated older adults has questioned the validity of the age-related deficit (e.g., Chance, Overcast, and Dollinger 1978; Kramer and Woodruff 1986; Kuhn, Pennington, and Leadbeater 1983; Papalia-Finlay et al. 1980–81; Protinsky and Hughston 1978; Schaier and Cicirelli 1976). However, methodological criticism merely begs the more general issue of why such tests were given to older adults in the first place. For one thing, such tests are subject to the same content effects mentioned earlier (e.g., Newman, Attig, and Kramer 1983; Sinnott 1975). Further, a recent review by Reese and Rodeheaver (1985) points out that such tests are given in a manner totally incongruent with the basic principles of Piagetian theory.

If one were to adopt the principles of Piagetian theory, one would define intelligence as adaptation to the environment, and hence set out to study the kinds of problems that are likely to uniquely confront older adults (i.e., an adult-centered approach). Then one would want to posit the modes of thinking used specifically by older adults to solve such problems. This approach reflects the adult-centered view described above. In such a view there is no rationale for merely giving older adults tests designed for children and comparing their performances to those of young adults. Such an approach is totally atheoretical. What is needed is the identification of the kinds of problem-solving and cognitive styles uniquely employed by older individuals. There is a body of literature emerging that attempts to extend Piaget's stage theory to incorporate one or more stages of adult reasoning, referred to as "post-formal operations." A foremost proponent of such work is Gisela Labouvie-Vief, who sees adult thought as being more pragmatic in nature than that of youth. The latter is highly idealistic, as yet untempered by the realities and contradictions of everyday life.

The author's own work has centered largely on this issue. She concluded that models of postformal thought contain several common features which converge on two possible levels of postformal thought. These are, respectively, relativism and dialecticism (Kramer 1983a). *Relativism* involves the awareness that the context from which one views a phenomenon influences how one sees it, and therefore, since different contexts may produce contradictory, yet equally valid kinds of information, contradiction is an inherent feature of reality. All phenomena are seen as constantly changing as the surrounding environment or culture changes, and there is no way to predict such change. An example of a relativistic response given by an older subject in a study by Kramer and Woodruff (1986) is as follows:

> There is no such thing as just because my parents or grandparents were raised in that way for generations that I have to continue. They lived in a different world than I do, and I have to adjust myself. That's very—being able to adjust—without remorse, without fear, and without blame . . . it has been said that the only permanent thing in life is change—and that is so true. Because there is no such thing as an everlasting thing (Kramer 1983b, S-15).

With *dialectical* reasoning, there is also an emphasis on the changing, evolving nature of phenomena, but in such a view things change in a systematic, forward-directional manner. As things progress, they become more encompassing and stable. Such progress occurs because every state or event carries along with it its contradiction, and thus we seek to find a better solution to eliminate that contradiction, by somehow incorporating the contradictory elements and perhaps redefining them. Once such a synthesis is achieved, knowledge has progressed, but new contradictions will arise—the synthesis will bring about its own set of problems and the cycle continues indefinitely. An example of this kind of thinking can be seen in the following response by a middle-aged female: "There will always be problems arising. If he would suggest, uh, one thing, then that might lead to something else and then he would have to solve that and so forth, and so on, and so on. There is no true solution" (Kramer 1983b, S-58).

Such reasoning is presumably adaptive for the adult. Ideally, it should result in greater tolerance of differences among individuals and groups, greater acceptance of the imperfections both within the self and in others, and greater skill at resolving conflict among disagreeing parties (due to a better ability to accept and integrate contradictory perspectives). The greater acceptance of imperfection within the self may explain why older people have been shown to have higher self esteem as they age (e.g., Bengston, Reedy, and Gordon 1985). A quote from a highly dialectical individual in one of the author's studies, a sixty-year-old woman, demonstrates this idea:

You know, the worst part about being really young is being out of control and always feeling that everybody else is smarter than you. As you get older you find—and it's disillusioning too, because the presidents don't seem as smart to you and the corporations don't seem so smart to you but . . . um . . . you feel—it also gives you the feeling of being on par with them which is nice . . . everybody is sort of floundering. There's a lot of floundering going around . . . it's disillusioning but it does make you feel better about yourself. (author's notes)

It is the author's contention that this form of reasoning develops in later life. There is evidence for such development (Kramer and Woodruff 1986) and more systematic work is currently under way to assess this hypothesis further (e.g., see Kramer 1985). When prototypical, relativistic, and especially, dialectical responses are given, they generally come from middle-aged or older adults, though not all middle-aged and older adults show such reasoning (see Sinnott 1985, for a discussion of such disparities in developmental trends). Such a development would be in keeping with the general theme developed earlier in this chapter—that a task of aging is to reflect on one's life experiences in order to infer continuity across the sum of one's experiences. Relativistic and dialectical thought are both integrative forms of thinking that integrate across contexts, even contradictory ones. Dialectical thought, in particular, construes all phenomena as interrelated. An example of this interrelationship can be seen in the following quote about imperialism and war by an older woman:

We're all interlaced, and we're all gonna sink or swim together, I think, and I think that we have, as the arrogant brat for too long taken that attitude. And uh, we just can't be the big kid on the block. Therefore, I think you've got to be understanding and cooperative (Kramer 1983b, S-1).

The awareness of the interrelatedness of all phenomena may be at the heart of aging, and integration is a good metaphor for understanding aging. A student of the author once summarized these ideas very aptly by comparing the aging process to walking up a hill. The higher up one goes the broader the view. The broader view of the aged may afford them greater perspective, although the greater distance that accompanies this perspective might result in a blurring of detail. Just as nurses and psychologists wear specific lenses, people in general may wear different lenses as they become older.

One note of caution. The author highly doubts that relativistic and dialectical thought do, indeed, represent qualitatively distinct stages of *logic* beyond Piaget's formal operations. According to philosophers, it is highly dubious that dialectics can maintain the status of a "logic" (e.g., Popper 1963), and there is good reason to assume some similarities between formal operational reasoning and both relativistic and dialectical thought (Kramer 1983a, 1985). However, the study of relativistic and dialectical thought as unique levels of thinking in adulthood in and of themselves constitutes an interesting and important area of investigation, one which the author is pursuing (Kramer 1985). However, the debate about whether these can be seen as postformal operational Piagetian stages continues (Commons, Richards, and Armon 1984; Commons et al. n.d.), and in the years to come we are likely to witness a major expansion of this revolutionary way of construing adult thought. As a final illustration, let us now proceed to the topic of creativity.

Creativity and Creative Productivity

There is much speculation among both laymen and scientists alike about whether old people continue to be creative. Does creativity flourish in later life, or does it dry up? Depending on whether one adopts the traditional or the adult-centered approach, once again the answer to this question may vary. Creativity is generally conceived as the ability to generate novel perspectives and solutions to existing problems. Studies using tests of creativity, which tend to be relatively academic in nature (e.g., requiring subjects to generate a variety of uses for common objects), paint a rather depressing picture of the aging process: older adults do not appear as creative as young adults on such tests (Alpaugh and Birren 1977; Bromley 1967). However, the test used by Bromley was one known to be highly correlated with IQ; thus, its validity is seriously questioned (Kogan 1973). Furthermore, well-known creative geniuses, such as Einstein, are known to have reported that what motivated them was an intense interest in the particular questions for which they sought answers (e.g., see Clark 1971). If that is the case, then once again, in order to fully explore the creative potential of an individual, we must assess his or her creativity in the context of the content that captures that individual's greatest interest. Needless to say, we cannot have a separate test for every individual, and such an approach raises difficult issues.

An alternative solution has been to study the creative output of people throughout their careers. The earliest and best-known work along these lines is that of Lehman (1953). Lehman found that in most fields, creativity peaked in the thirties, for a few fields in the forties, and declined thereafter. However, Lehman's findings have been subject to criticism on a number of methodological grounds. First, he did not take into account the longevity of his subjects. He plotted the amount of productive output of individuals from each age group, comparing these. However, since there were more geniuses alive at thirty than at seventy, it is not surprising that there were also more creative products in that age group (Dennis 1966). Second, Lehman's data referred to "superior" works only, an idea laden with value judgments. What is considered highly significant at one point in history may not be at another point, and vice versa. Third, Lehman did not allow for category changes in later years (e.g., switching from scientific or artistic work to writing one's memoirs) or for the assumption of administrative duties, which comes later in a career (Butler 1967; Roe 1972).

Dennis (1966) set out to ameliorate these flaws, and found much later peaks for creative output. For most, the forties was a highly productive decade, the highest for a number of professions, especially scientific. However, novelists peaked in their fifties, with the sixties pulling a close second. Historians, philosophers, botanists, and inventors peaked in their sixties. Mathematicians showed equal productivity in their thirties, forties, and sixties, with the fifties lagging only slightly behind. In just about every case, creative output was lowest in the twenties, which makes sense in light of the fact that the individual spends most of the twenties becoming trained, and has not yet the knowledge base and the foundation for great discovery. For the scholars (i.e., historians, humanists, and philosophers) the seventies was a productive decade as well: they increased their preceding number of books by 25%. Likewise, scientists increased their preceding number of articles by 18%, while artists showed the lowest level of productivity in this decade, increasing their works by only 6%. Nevertheless, even the latter figure is hardly paltry, if one is a Leonardo da Vinci or Michelangelo.

The fact that philosophers, historians, and scholars showed the highest degree of productivity in very late life is not surprising if one places creative productivity in the context of life tasks. If old age is indeed a time for reflection, in particular reflecting on one's past, seeking historical continuity and searching for the greater meaning of life, it makes good sense that a major contribution would occur in these fields in later life. There have been a number of lines of evidence to indicate greater concern with historical, spiritual, and philosophical matters among creative geniuses, as well as ordinary people, in later life (e.g., Funk 1985; Koplowitz 1984; Moody 1983). Thus, major gains are likely to be made late in life in fields of inquiry maintaining continuity with those themes. Maduro (1974) found that in India, it is believed that one cannot be creative until later life, when one may cast aside the responsibilities of family and friends, and go off to meditate. In our country, as pointed out by Roe (1972), quite the opposite is true: it is older adults who take on more administrative duties, or put aside their research to write their auto-biographies, or to compile the lifetime collections of their work. Simonton (1983) found that time spent in one's career (career age) is a more important predictor of creative productivity than is chronological age. Thus, if we

Jon Serl, primitive artist, born 1894: Jon started painting at about fifty-five. His paintings have been shown extensively in the United States and abroad. He lives in Lake Elsinore, California and continues to work every day. (Photographer: G. Pasha Turley)

place the creative process in the context of the life course, a quite different picture emerges, suggesting continued potentials for creativity in later life.

A most interesting study, which places creativity within the life course perspective, is one conducted by Jaques (1970) on creative geniuses throughout the centuries. His analysis suggested that something akin to a midlife crisis dramatically altered the creative output of such artists. Such change took different forms for different individuals. A dramatically high number of creative geniuses died between the ages of thirty-five and thirty-nine (e.g., Chopin, Baudelaire, Mozart, Raphael); in contrast, the rest of the population showed a greater number of deaths in the ensuing decade. A number of creative geniuses stopped being creative, either permanently or for a span of many years (e.g., Ben Jonson, Michelangelo, Racine, Rossini). Finally, a number of creative geniuses did not begin their creative careers until this age period (e.g., Bach, Gauguin).

However, more fundamental changes occurred in the products of those who continued to be creative. First, the works shifted from reflecting a more optimistic, perhaps satirical outlook on life to that of a more melancholy, pessimistic outlook which is characterized by an awareness of the sinister, destructive forces of human nature as well as the good forces. For example, Shakespeare wrote all of his comedies before the age of thirty-five; he began his tragedies in his thirties; Dickens's career took a similar path. Second, the output went from a "hot-from-the fire" sort of creativity to a more "sculpted" form of creativity. Younger geniuses produced greater abundance, but the products themselves were not as carefully worked-through. Older geniuses were more concerned with the quality of the product—with perfecting it—while they were less interested in the amount of output.

Personality researchers have described feelings of limitless potential for productivity by people in their twenties. It is not until the presumed midlife crisis that an awareness of finitude, limitations, and imperfection emerges (Gould 1978; Levinson 1978). One cannot buy immortality by producing great abundance, and the shift in creative productivity may reflect this shift in emotional awareness. Whether one construes such a change as due to the midlife crisis, due to cognitive advances described in the previous section (i.e., toward relativistic and dialectical thought), simply as a result of the lesser need of the older, more established artist to prove his or her talent, or even as a reflection of expanding competencies, the crucial point is that in order to fully understand the path that creative productivity takes in adulthood, it is essential to place it within the context of the broader life course. The interference of more worldly concerns such as establishing a home, family, and career, or the resolution of personality tasks across the life span—all of these will influence the nature, form, and output of one's creative work. If we want to have a more complete understanding of what becomes of creativity in later life, we must understand the whole life context in which that work is embedded.

Conclusions

Based on this review, what may we conclude about the process of cognitive aging? Most importantly, just as the author does not wish to portray an overly negative view of the aging process, neither does she wish to convey an unrealistically optimistic one. There are undoubtedly cognitive losses with age. This is indicated by the difficulty with which older adults perform many cognitive tasks given them. However, the degree of difficulty is strongly modified by variations in the task situation, and are not as pervasive or far-reaching as might have been imagined. Furthermore, as a more adult-centered approach indicates, the losses are accompanied by probable gains as well, and these may be more related to the kinds of integrative and reflective processes that occur in later life. An exciting trend in the field can be seen in recent chapters in major handbooks on aging and intelligence, where more contextualized, adult-centered approaches are being offered, and hence will become major forces in shaping our views of aging research (e.g., Dixon, Kramer, and Baltes 1985; Labouvie-Vief 1985; Poon 1985).

The purpose of this review was to show that there are at least two distinct lenses through which to view the aging process. One, employing a more traditional, mechanistic approach to theory and measurement, yields a picture of aging that is characterized by inevitable decline or, at most, stability. The second, an adult-centered one, results in a much more optimistic picture of aging, where certain cognitive processes continue to grow with age. Both are simply lenses: one brings into greater focus the limitations of the aging organism, while the other emphasizes its strengths with equal force. One seeks more rigorous control over confounding variables in the test situation, while the other seeks greater generalizability to the real-life situation. Neither completes the picture; each contains a kernel of truth, and each represents some aspect of the aging process. The former has dominated much of the thinking about adult cognition throughout the years, while the latter is just beginning to feel its force.

VII

PERSONALITY IN LATER LIFE

David Chiriboga

In this chapter we consider what has been called the "essence" of the human being: the personality—that particular grouping of characteristics that makes each one of us a unique and identifiable person. We will begin with some thoughts on life-span issues relevant to the study of personality, move on to talk about some theorists whose works are central to any evaluation of personality in later life, present the issue of continuities and discontinuities in personality, and then finish with a discussion of two social phenomena that help us to understand how and why individuals change or remain constant over time: stress and transitions.

On the Nature of Personality

Although the nature of personality has been the subject of debate since the times of Plato and Aristotle, there is no agreement concerning what the term means, nor is there any single acceptable definition. A long time ago, one of the major theorists in psychology, Gordon Allport (1937) tracked down at least fifty definitions that were currently in use. More recently, Corsini (1977) has identified seventy-eight distinct personality theories, and probably more are used today. Even more diversity can be found in how the concept is measured.

With so little agreement concerning either definition or measurement, one may legitimately question whether we can say anything at all about personality in late life, let alone devote a whole chapter to it. As it turns out, however, there are indeed certain points about which personality researchers agree. One is the basic content of what is being studied. It involves both the way that people view themselves, and the way scientists, presumably with more objectivity, view these people. In fact, there is some agreement that personality can be broadly defined as the objective component of the individual's self concept (see, for example, Bengston, Reedy, and Gordon 1985).

That is, each of us carries around a self-image, or set of images about the self, that make up what we see as the self. While these images may appear highly individualized and perhaps chaotic, to the social scientist there are certain patterns and regularities that can be identified and assessed. These patterns and regularities, which extend beyond self-image to include the organization and function of the self, constitute the individual's personality.

Another point of agreement centers on the fact that most theorists and researchers view personality as something that is relatively stable over time, or at least that changes in predictable, nonrandom ways. How much stability and how much change are currently topics of heated debate, and we will examine this issue in a later section. But first, we need to consider some of the basic ways in which personality theories attempt to assess stability and change, and then actually look at some of the major theories themselves.

Models of Development

Nearly all research on adult personality and behavior has addressed itself directly or indirectly to the question of stability over time. One school of thought emphasizes the stability of personality. As William James once stated, by the age of thirty an individual's personality "has set like plaster and will never soften again" (James 1950, 121). On the opposing side are those who suggest that life in modern society promotes discontinuity. Lifton (1971), for example, sees the pace and fragmentation of modern life to result in what he calls "Protean Man," an individual with a chameleon-like ability to change persona in midstream.

A more moderate position, and one that reflects the thinking of many developmental researchers, is voiced by Margaret Clark and Barbara Anderson, members of a small but growing number of anthropologists who consider themselves to be gerontologists as well:

> A person is not a pile of stone, no matter how artfully arranged, laid down in concrete early in life. . . . Personality is rather an ongoing process of interaction between the sociocultural world and the internal life of the individual—a process that continues throughout the life cycle (Clark and Anderson 1967, 63).

Research evidence for or against stability is inconclusive, even though the results consistently point in the direction of greater stability. In part, the lack of definite answers is due to the state of the art in life-span studies, which are few in number and which take many years to complete. There are few studies that cover the period extending from childhood or adolescence to later life (or, for that matter, even shorter periods of time); the same instruments are rarely used across studies; and social scientists sometimes resort to highly inferential strategies to impute stability or change.

To illustrate this latter point, in some research involving children and adults different measures are employed at different times in order to measure the same underlying characteristic (see, for example, McKee and Turner 1961; Kagan and Moss 1962). The problem faced by such researchers, of course, is that it is often impossible to administer the same instrument, say for example an intelligence test, both to very young children and to adults. Other researchers will infer "genotypic" continuity if personality characteristics measured at one point in time predict different personality characteristics at another point in time (e.g., Livson 1973; Maas and Kuypers 1974).

One reason behind the continuing lack of closure in stability research may be that we have simply been asking the wrong questions. It is probably not a matter of whether there is any evidence *for* stability, because there usually is. At issue is *how much* stability exists across personality attributes, and how much evidence for stability is required before we can legitimately say that a given behavior or personality attribute is stable over time. Perhaps more importantly, under what conditions can we predict the degree of stability of these attributes?

In order to better appreciate the question of stability, we will next consider the ways in which various types of developmental theories handle the question of stability versus change in personal functioning.

Templates of Personal Change

From a historical perspective, studies of personality in middle and later life have generally followed one of three underlying models of development. As originally outlined by Gergen (1977), the most widely used of these models is one he calls the "Stability Template." Theorists who employ this model are committed to the principle of stability in adult life; change is thought to exist only as a reflection of the continued development of some already-existing characteristic. The work of Freud and his colleagues representing the classic psychoanalytic perspective serves as a good illustration of this model since most of them believed that the trajectory of personal development was relatively fixed by the age of five or six.

A somewhat different orientation can be found in Gergen's (1977) second model, that of "Orderly Change." Theories following this model view development as a progression of orderly and perhaps invariant changes over time. This is another way of saying that they usually are stage theories, one of the most popular ways of conceptualizing personality development. The reader may be familiar with the works of Piaget, Loevinger, and Kolhberg, whose stage theories of childhood and adolescent development are well accepted among developmental psychologists. The theories we will be covering in this chapter generally represent a blending of both orderly change and stability template models, since most theories of personality in later life view the individual as grounded in the past but interacting with the present and possible futures.

There is, finally, a more recently developed model that emphasizes the role of chance in our lives. Labeled the "Random Change" model, its central thesis is that human beings run out of genetic programming by late adolescence. Thereafter, the role of chance factors, such as exposure to major stress conditions or transitions, becomes more important as a shaper of personality. Support for this model can be found in the stress research of developmental scientists such as Klaus Riegel, Werner Schaie, Paul Baltes, and Bernice Neugarten. From the mainstream of psychological research, the research of Mischel (1979) also emphasizes the importance of the situational context in determining levels of stability in personality. Unfortunately, no well-formulated theories of personality have yet been developed that follow this model.

Templates: A Critique

Although the three templates or models of change we have presented are not really contradictory to each other, they are often treated that way by their proponents. That is, they are often treated as if in fact only one model really could hold true, and so evidence against the favored model is often dismissed or reinterpreted.

For example, consider a hypothetical situation in which a researcher has asked people to complete a self-concept inventory twice over a ten year period. The data are analyzed by means of the standard Pearson correlation coefficient and correlations of the magnitude of .50 are found. To a researcher committed to the stability model, this might be viewed as convincing evidence of stability: "After all," the individual might say, "this correlation is much larger than is usually found in social science research." On the other hand, a researcher committed to the random nature of later development might counter with the argument: "Gee, a .50 correlation only accounts for 25% of the variance. How can that be evidence for stability, when 75% of the variance is not accounted for?"

While such a conversation might seem rather far-fetched, in point of fact it represents as close an approximation as I can recall to an actual encounter I overheard at a recent Gerontological Society of America conference. The topic of the conversation was the implications of a longitudinal study conducted by Grant (1969), where correlations over time in personality characteristics averaging .50 had been reported.

At present, there is a resurgence of interest in evidence for stability of personality and behavior over the adult life course. This interest has been sparked by the extensive amount of evidence that has accrued in support of stability (see, for example, Sears 1977; Block 1971; McCrae and Costa 1984; Peskin and Livson 1981), and it is not surprising that the last five years have seen a renewed concern with trait psychology.

Normative and Nonnormative Change

How best to attack the problem of identifying and studying the dynamics of stability and change remains an open question. However, in a review of life-span developmental research conducted over the past one hundred years, Paul and Margaret Baltes (1980) have developed a multi-causal framework for development that shows promise. They identify three major sources of change: the normative age-graded sources, which include factors such as biological maturation and early socialization practices; the normative history-graded sources, which include events such as the Great Depression, World War II, or fads, which often play a role in establishing cohort differences; and the nonnormative sources, which include unscheduled events such as divorce, unemployment, unexpected illness, or death of a child.

This framework for the study of sources of stability and change expands on Gergen's (1977) distinction between models predicated on orderly change and those predicated on random change, since both types of normative change agents can be construed as orderly in nature, while the nonnormative by definition includes the random or unscheduled situations.

There is considerable research now available on both normative and nonnormative sources of change, although not all of it is relevant to studies of personality in later life, and most of it has focused on either normative life transitions or social stressors. We will look at these two phenomena in detail somewhat later in this chapter, but will present an overview here.

The source of normative change most frequently studied has been the transition. The importance for personal functioning of the orderly, expectable transitions of life has received extensive attention. Although several studies report that these transitions do affect personal makeup (e.g., Chiriboga 1984; Golan 1986), other studies report little impact. One reason may be that the same normative transition may have extremely different implications for the lives of different people. For example, Pearlin (1980) reports that men and women respond in opposing ways to both the advent of the first child and the departure of the last child—they respond so differently that when the sexes are combined the impact of the transition in question is canceled out.

Standing in contrast to the regular and expectable conditions of everyday life are those chance circumstances that seem relevant to Gergen's random change model of development. Perhaps the most common way of studying such circumstances is through what is called "life events." Life events are potentially disruptive experiences, such as divorce, bereavement, or even a vacation, that upset the day-to-day routine in some way. Using the forty-two-item Schedule of Recent Events developed by Holmes and Rahe (1967), or any of dozens of variations, countless researchers have examined the incidence of discrete, more or less nonnormative events that occur in the lives of individuals at any age.

As far as knowledge about later life is concerned, this massive research effort has done little beyond establishing that older persons may experience fewer events, whether conceived as positive or negative in nature. According to a number of investigators, however, the life event approach to studying change is of particular salience to life-span developmental research (e.g., Brim and Ryff 1980; Chiriboga and Cutler 1980). For the moment, please keep in mind that both life events and transitions refer to changing conditions in the social environment. How individuals react to such changes has often been considered to be of major consequence by life-span theorists. It is also thought that the changes themselves impose demands for readjustment on the part of the individual that can be considered as developmental tasks if they occur at regular points along the life course.

Personality and the Tasks of Life

One approach to studying personality from a life-span perspective is to consider how the demands of each stage of the life course impact on the person and help to shape the structure and functioning of the self. The adherents of this approach follow the "Orderly Change" model outlined by Gergen (1977), and are generally viewed as "stage" theorists because of the progressive changes, over the course of human life, that they portray in personality characteristics. Here we will review the works of five theoreticians whose ideas have been especially influential in the study of late-life personality: Carl G. Jung, Robert J. Havighurst, Erik H. Erikson, David L. Gutmann, and Daniel Levinson. In presenting these theories of personality in later life, we shall try to highlight both their similarities and their differences.

The Developmental Theory of Carl Jung

Departing from his preceptor, Sigmund Freud, on the issue of when the primary thrust of development ended, Jung divided psychological development into two phases, with the break between the two occurring at about age forty. According to Jung, up until the forties, men and women tend to be primarily concerned with meeting obligations that revolve around the dual responsibilities of raising a family and establishing one's place in society. The expectations and demands created in the push to meet these obligations shape the directions in which personality develops. A gender difference emerges. Men, for example, often focus on the instrumental and achievement-oriented side of their personalities in consequence of their need for outward success in the employment arena. Women, in contrast, were seen to focus on the more expressive and nurturant dimensions of personality, as a result of the greater salience of their parenting role.

The cost of this one-sided development may not be immediately obvious to the individual:

> The nearer we approach to the middle of life, and the better we have succeeded in entrenching ourselves in our personal attitudes and social positions, the more it appears as if we had discovered the right course. . . . We overlook the essential fact that the social goal is attained only at the cost of a diminution of personality (Jung 1960, 772).

As the demands of the family lessen, and at about the age of forty, individuals become more free to balance their hitherto uneven development. The initial stages of this development are heralded by what Dr. Robert Butler has labeled the "life review" but which Jung simply described as a period of stocktaking:

> Instead of looking forward one looks backward, most of the time involuntarily, and one begins to take stock, to see how one's life has developed up to this point. The real motivations are sought and real discoveries are made. The critical survey of himself and his fate enables a man to recognize his peculiarities (Jung 1954, 331).

One hallmark of later life, according to Jung is the tendency—perhaps even the duty—to consider the inner self. In this, Jung anticipates Neugarten's (1964) concept of "interiority," a concept developed on the basis of empirical studies of her pioneering work in Kansas City during the late 1950s and early 1960s. This inner involvement, according to Jung, stands in opposition to the early years: "For a young person it is almost a sin, or at least a danger, to be too preoccupied with himself; but for the ageing person it is a duty and a necessity to devote serious attention to himself" (Jung 1960, 785).

The growing introspection may prompt recognition of an essential imbalance within oneself. Earlier demands on men and women to devote their time and energy to perform as providers, parents, and spouse may have quenched unconventional desires and aspirations. The desire, for example, of a young mother to excell as a tennis champion or stockbroker. But now that society's demands have begun to peak, or even to diminish, middle-agers may find the time to give expression to the suppressed side of their personalities. They achieve this "union of opposites" by paying greater heed to the inner world, and by bringing parts of this world to consciousness.

This confrontation with the inner world may be a threatening experience, since it involves giving up an identification with immortal youth and recognizing the finitude of life. The transition to an inner orientation is therefore often associated with a period of "storm and stress" and is a transition people often attempt to avoid, preferring instead to continue with the increasingly inappropriate life-style of the first half of life. Unfortunately, this balancing out is not only a possibility afforded by the growing freedom from obligations and social demands but is also a requirement for successful adjustment during the middle and later years.

Concerning the relationship of personal development to adjustment, Jung suggests that one of the major causes of neurosis among persons in the second half of life is the preservation of an inappropriate life-style:

> They cling to the illusion of youth or to their children, hoping to salvage in this way a last little scrap of youth. One sees it especially in mothers, who find their sole meaning in their children and imagine they will sink into a bottomless void when they have to give them up (Jung 1953, 114).

In describing the need to withdraw from old involvements with the world, Jung here foreshadows the theory of disengagement expressed so eloquently by Cumming and Henry (1961), in which a distinction is also drawn between psychological and social involvement.

If the individual successfully completes the transition to an inner orientation, she or he can continue to grow and thrive. Acquiring a mature sense of responsibility for oneself also involves developing a feeling of responsibility to the community, and the balanced person in later life often becomes a spiritual or social leader. At the same time, however, an awareness of the inner world sensitizes one to the beginnings of the aging process. Once again relating personality to adjustment, Jung (1953) portrays acceptance of diminishing capacity and increasing losses as a first step toward coping with the problems, as well as the potentials, of later life.

Havighurst and Developmental Tasks

Unlike Jung and many other theorists of personality in adult life, Robert J. Havighurst is not a clinician, nor is he oriented to psychoanalysis. His initial training, in fact, was in engineering, although he subsequently pursued careers in education and gerontology. But like his distinguished Viennese counterpart, Havighurst also proposed a model of personal development that suggests that successful resolution of past challenges helps in future adjustment. Both theorists also felt that resolution of the tasks of life enhanced an ability to play an effective and influential role in society.

For Havighurst, each phase of life is associated with a set of "developmental tasks" that confront the individual. Although recognizing that the actual tasks that confront an individual arise from relatively unique combinations of biological, psychological, and social forces, Havighurst provides lists of developmental tasks that generally must be addressed at different stages of life. Of interest to us are those tasks that pertain to the middle and later years.

During the middle years, which for Havighurst (1952) encompassed roughly the period from age thirty to sixty, the tasks were to:

(1) Achieve adult civic and social responsibility
(2) Establish and maintain an economic standard of living
(3) Assist teenaged children to become responsible and happy adults
(4) Develop adult leisure-time activities
(5) Relate to one's spouse as a person
(6) Accept and adjust to the physiological changes of middle age
(7) Adjust to aging parents

We can see that the first three "tasks" outlined by Havighurst reflect the kinds of social obligations considered by Jung as exerting more dominance in the first half of life, while the remainder come close to what Jung (if asked) might have referred to as the tasks of the second half of life.

In the tasks that Havighurst outlined for the later years of life, or from approximately age sixty onward, the orientation becomes more and more focused on confronting losses in the social and physical spheres:

(1) Adjust to decreasing physical strength and health
(2) Adjust to retirement and reduced income
(3) Adjust to death of one's spouse
(4) Establish an explicit affiliation with one's age group
(5) Adopt and adapt social roles in a flexible way (an expansion in family, community, or hobbies, a slowdown in all activities, etc.)
(6) Establish satisfactory physical living arrangements

A perusal of the literature on later life published during the thirty-eight years since Havighurst first published his model demonstrates its continuing vitality. Some tasks, such as that of adjusting to aging parents, have only recently begun to receive extensive attention from researchers. Others, such as the use of leisure, are still awaiting the attention they deserve.

At the same time, the reader should be cautioned that: (1) the lists of tasks provided by Havighurst were not meant to be exhaustive, but only to provide guidelines; (2) since it was developed nearly two generations ago, the social context and demands may have shifted significantly; and (3) these tasks may vary substantially in type, number, and meaning across various ethnic and cultural groups, across gender, and also across age cohorts.

Erikson's Life Cycle Theory of Personality

Trained as a child analyst, and steeped in the psychoanalytic tradition of Freud, Erik Homberger Erikson's theoretical formulations were heavily influenced by his years as a clinician and by his involvement in the studies of child development conducted at the Institute of Human Development, University of California, Berkeley. It is not altogether surprising, therefore, to find that although Erikson made a landmark break with the classic Freudian position in proposing a theory of personality change that encompassed the entire life course, his principal emphasis—at least in the original formulations (Erikson 1963)—was on the period from childhood to young adulthood.

In fact, Erikson originally devoted only a few paragraphs to the later stages of life, a fact upon which he has commented recently: "Take this last stage: It was in our middle years that we formulated it—at a time when we certainly had no intention of (or capacity for) imagining ourselves as really old" (Erikson 1982, 62).

A pervasive theme in Erikson's writings concerns the relationship of the individual's personal life evolution to the historical period and to the society in which one lives (Erikson 1975, 1978). Essentially, Erikson sees personality development over the life course as a series of transactions between the developing organism and the social order: "Personality can be said to develop according to steps predetermined in the human organism's readiness to be driven toward, to be aware of, and to interact with, a widening social radius, beginning with the dim image of a mother and ending with mankind" (Erikson 1980, 54).

The interactive "steps" take the form of a series of eight developmental crises, during each of which the individual is confronted by opposing tendencies to either grow or decline. These stages occur in a predetermined and sequential ordering that draws on biological and psychosocial maturation, as well as interactions with society. Following what Erikson refers to as an "epigenetic" principle, the way in which one stage is resolved lays the groundwork, good or bad, for resolution of any further crises.

As presented by Erikson (1980), the basic principle of epigenesis has its intellectual roots in the biological principle that development of an embryo proceeds according to an overall ground plan. Within this plan each distinct organ has its own time of maximum growth and differentiation, until all parts have developed sufficiently to form an integrated, functional whole.

Other assumptions made by Erikson include: (1) each of the eight psychosocial characteristics exists in interrelation to the rest; (2) the viability of each characteristic is dependent on its emergence at the appropriate time in development; (3) each characteristic exists in some precursor stage prior to the time of special ascendance, and continues in yet another form after that time; and (4) that the crisis that surfaces around each characteristic cannot be resolved successfully without experiencing some elements of the less successful side. As an example of this last point, an individual must experience distrust to fully establish trust, but once trust or any other quality is established, it continues to operate in relation to other qualities.

Erikson based his eight stages in personality development over the life course on the classic psychosexual stages of development outlined by Freud, but incorporated additional psychosocial stages. The stages are described as follows:

(1) *Basic Trust versus Basic Mistrust.* During the first year of life, infants either develop confidence or trust in the environment's ability to satisfy basic needs, or they develop mistrust. To the extent that trust is established, the infant lays the groundwork for the manifestation of the ability to hope. This stage is roughly equivalent to what Freud (1965) called the "oral" stage.

(2) *Autonomy versus Shame and Doubt.* Comparable to Freud's "anal" period, this stage reaches its crisis point as infants develop control over their muscles, including sphincters. With basic trust established in the first stage, the child now attempts to develop a sense of personal control over the world. A sense of personal will is created. If thwarted in this attempt, the child may react with feelings of shame and self-doubt.

(3) *Initiative versus Guilt.* Given a grounding in trust and autonomy, the child reaches a stage where planful action is undertaken with an abundance of spirit. The negative side is a sense of guilt over one's undertakings or desires. Infantile sexuality must gradually be diverted from parental objects. When accomplished successfully, one later result is a sense of purpose in life.

(4) *Industry versus Inferiority.* During the early school years the child faces the need to establish control over the energies of past stages and to begin to focus them onto productive endeavors. For Erikson, this symbolized the beginnings of becoming a worker, and could lead to a sense of competence in later life, or immediately result in the beginnings of feelings of inadequacy.

(5) *Identity versus Identity Diffusion.* Marking the end of childhood and the beginning of youth, this stage is marked by the crisis of identity—the discovery of self. To the extent that the stage is resolved successfully (sometimes after a psychosocial moratorium during which the youth may try on a variety of identities), the framework for an integrated sense of self is established. This lays the ground work for a spirit of fidelity in later

years. The danger is a growing sense of confusion over personal identity, marked by a lack of integration of the role identities that have been tried out and incorporated.

(6) *Intimacy and Distantiation versus Self-Absorption.* The first of the three stages of adulthood proposed by Erikson, this stage is marked by attempts to merge one's newly achieved personal identity with that of another person. The capacity for intimacy lays the groundwork for the expression and capacity to love, but also for the ability to distance oneself from others or from situations that are harmful: it provides the ability to say "no" as well as "yes."

(7) *Generativity versus Stagnation.* Calling generativity the stage that subsumes "the evolutionary development which has made man the teaching and instituting as well as the learning animal" (Erikson 1963, 266), Erikson hypothesized that the older generations develop an interest in both creating and guiding their own offspring as well as future generations. This stage draws from the capacity for intimacy and leads to an expansion of ego interests beyond the immediacy of self. The essential accomplishment of the stage of generativity is the developed capacity to care for others. Failure to develop generativity may lead to an increasing focus on self-indulgence that masks a sense of impoverishment.

(8) *Integrity versus Despair and Disgust.* When an individual has successfully resolved the challenges presented by the preceding stages, the stage is set for the establishment of an acceptance of one's self and the life one has led, coupled with a sense of kinship with others and belongingness. It is often marked by an increased concern with inner life. In later works, Erikson spoke of this stage as providing the development of wisdom.

A few additional words are in order concerning the last two stages: Erikson (1982) has recently reconsidered the significance of these two stages from the perspective of both a changing society and his own advanced age (in 1982 he was eighty years old). For example, he extends the notion of sexuality past Freud's genital stage to include procreativity in adulthood and "generalized sensuality" in later life. He also begins to speak of the last stage of life in terms of a quest for coherence and wholeness, a sense of kinship not just with one's family but with the past and future world. This amounts to an extended sense of the generativity that plays an important role in an earlier stage.

Gutmann and Ego Mastery Styles

A clinical psychologist with training in anthropological techniques, David L. Gutmann has devoted over two decades to the examination of systematic changes in personality across middle and later life. His studies led him to consider the middle-aged and elderly residents of Kansas City, the Navajo of Arizona, the Highland and the Yucatan Maya of Mexico, and nomadic Druze living in Giliean and Syrian territories of the Middle East. For each group, Gutmann used a combination of projective tests, in-depth interviews, and dream analysis to record and assess common themes of middle-aged and older men and women.

One of Gutmann's (1964) earliest findings was the existence of three apparently universal ways in which individuals of different ages relate to demands placed upon them. He refers to these ways as ego mastery styles, since the overt or covert behaviors he assessed seemed rooted in the ego processes. The three styles are as follows:

(1) *Active Mastery.* Persons with this ego mastery style tend to take an active and assertive stance toward their environment. They try to change conditions in the outer world rather than change themselves, and pursue their goals aggressively.

(2) *Passive Mastery.* People with this ego mastery style are characteristically accommodative. They give in to the situation. Typically, they do not see themselves as being in positions of power, and hence try to change themselves rather than the situation.

(3) *Magical Mastery.* Use of this ego mastery style is indicated by a distortion of reality. Individuals attempt to cope with situations by means of denial or by redefining the situation, for instance, rather than taking some action to actually change it. This style is considerably less common than the other two.

Gutmann (1977) has found that across all the cultures he has studied there seems to be a nearly universal progression from one style to another. Men in the middle years, for example, typically display characteristics associated with Active Mastery, but Passive Mastery becomes a more common style in the later years. In contrast, women tend to move from Passive Mastery styles in early middle age toward Active Mastery in later middle age and in old age. Few men and women act in ways associated with Magical Mastery, but when they do, it typically is in extreme old age.

The shifts in mastery styles clearly overlap with Jung's postulated "balancing out" of personality characteristics. Gutmann (1975) has also postulated social obligations as playing a pivotal role in determining both the sex differences and the developmental trajectory. For Gutmann these social obligations have traditionally centered on parental responsibilities. Men sacrifice their needs for comfort and emotional expression in the interest of enhancing aggressive and competitive characteristics needed to fulfill their role as breadwinners; women sacrifice the more aggressive characteristics in order not to alienate the breadwinner or psychologically damage the vulnerable child. But as parental responsibilities lessen in midlife, a change takes place:

Particularly for women aging paradoxically brings new beginnings. As parents enter middle age, and as children take over the responsibility for their own security . . . the sex-role reversals that shape our transcultural data occur. . . . Both sexes can afford the luxury of living out the potentials and pleasures that they had to relinquish early on, in the service of their particular parental task (Gutmann 1975, 181).

Gutmann's point is that what we typically consider to be "masculine" and "feminine" behavior tends to be associated not only with gender but with period of the life course. He hastens to add that in today's society, with its new life-styles and parenting styles, changes in what we traditionally have viewed as male or female personality styles and behavior may change.

Levinson and the Seasons of a Man's Life

Basing his work on a study of forty men aged thirty-five to forty-five who were originally interviewed in 1969 and then reinterviewed approximately two years later, Daniel J. Levinson and his colleagues have developed a theory of personal development that blends ingredients of Jung's developmental perspectives, Havighurst's notions of developmental tasks, and more recent work on critical life transitions.

A critical postulate of Levinson's work is the existence of five eras within the course of a human life, each of which represents a relatively stable time of life with its own distinctive characteristics. Each era is also said to occur within a relatively restricted age range, although proof of this age-linked progression is not furnished. The eras are as follows:

    (1) Childhood and adolescence era   (birth to age 22)
    (2) Early adulthood era   (age 17 to 45)
    (3) Middle adulthood era   (age 40 to 65)
    (4) Late adulthood era   (age 60 to 85)
    (5) Late late adulthood era   (age 80 and over)

During each of these five eras, the individual builds a life structure or life-style that is predicated on: (1) the social context, (2) social interactions, and (3) personal characteristics such as personality, talents, and abilities. Bridging the eras are what Levinson calls "cross-era transitional periods," each of which lasts on the average up to four or five years:

    (a) Early adult transition   (age 17 to 22)
    (b) Midlife transition   (age 40 to 45)
    (c) Late life transition   (age 60 to 65)

Although the eras do not reflect simply a stage of personality development, Levinson's theory draws heavily on the work of C. G. Jung in considering the developmental issues faced by individuals in different eras. In the following comments, Levinson's description of men facing certain critical issues as they approach age sixty is reminiscent not only of Jung, but of Erikson and Havighurst as well:

> The developmental task is to overcome the splitting of youth and age, and find in each season an appropriate balance of the two. . . . During the Late Adult Transition, a man fears that the youth within him is dying and that only the old man—an empty dry structure void of energy, interests or inner resources—will survive for a brief and foolish old age. His task is to sustain his youthfulness in a new form appropriate to late adulthood (Levinson et al. 1978, 35).

Unfortunately, Levinson's sample of men were too young to present any refined consideration of eras and transitions specific to later life. The issues that are raised, however, reflect the concern all the theorists discussed here share in how the individual—man or woman—attempts to discover personal identity. For example, one kind of self-questioning that Levinson sees as becoming central during the midlife transition asks, "What have I done with my life? What do I really get from and give to my wife, children, friends, work, community—and self?" (Levinson et al. 1978, 60).

In reviewing and evaluating Levinson's theoretical contribution, it becomes clear that he differs from the other theorists presented thus far in that he does not see any specific personality qualities as being linked to the successive stages. An "empty" theory in terms of these qualities, he nevertheless views personal style as being impacted by certain regularities associated with each successive stage of life. He also makes use of a term, "transition," which has a long history in the social sciences and has been of increasing interest to gerontologists. Transitions will be covered later in this chapter.

Sources of Continuity and Change in Personality

We have seen that underlying the divergent views and opinions held by theorists of adult personality, there are certain recurring themes and issues. In the remaining sections of this chapter, we will devote ourselves to a consideration of one fundamental issue that pervades theories and research on personality in both earlier and later life. That issue is the degree of continuity or discontinuity in personality that can be found as the individual moves along the life course. The general objective is to identify those social and personal conditions that lead to continuities during later life, and those that lead to discontinuity and change.

The concern with the shapers of continuities and discontinuities in old age has arisen in reaction to a controversy of the last fifteen to twenty years between those who adhere to a stability or continuity model of development and adherents of change. Like the old "nature versus nurture" controversy that provided intriguing dinner-table conversation among developmentalists of the 1930s and 1940s, continuity and discontinuity as metaphors for adult development have provided the basis for rhetoric perhaps more worthy of pulpit than podium. Here a plea is made for an end to the "controversy" and for a quest for those factors that underlie both, for assuredly there is ample evidence for both in the developmental literature.

The quest for greater understanding of the dynamics of continuity and change begins with a scrutiny of publications concerned with adulthood. Some consistency is found in the issues that appear to obscure or highlight these dynamics. They are four in number:

(1) *The lack of life-span perspectives on continuity and change.* There is a growing recognition in the developmental community that the trajectory of the life course may vary by life stage. McCrae and Costa (1984), in an article on age differences in personality characteristics of men ranging from twenty-five to eighty-two, report intriguing suggestions of "developmental" differences: young men are open to feelings, middle-aged men are more dominant in the thinking sphere, while older men tend to integrate the two. At the same time, the authors rightly concluded that there may be cohort as well as age differences: only sequential and longitudinal approaches can rule out the possibility that, for example, the older men, who were in their twenties and thirties during the Depression and World War II, were deeply moved in the "feeling" sphere by those circumstances and continued to be so throughout their lives.

Theoretical perspectives have tended to emphasize the existence of continuity. That change may occur throughout adulthood is a fact that a majority of clinicians overlook. Traditional psychoanalytic theory, for example, has focused on childhood and adolescence, and the premise has been that adulthood is a stable era in which developmental processes have a minor role. But that view has come under increasing attack. Today many recognize that the normative crises of midlife can serve as an impetus to further growth. Heightened awareness of physical decline, for example, may prompt redefinitions of body-image. And the inevitable awareness of time left to live may serve as a stimulus for a realistic reordering of goals, one that takes into account current energy and resources (Colarusso and Nemiroff 1979). One consequence of this recognition is that therapists are beginning to describe therapeutic approaches that match the needs of persons at different stages of the life course. One typical report on the psychological problems of older adults emphasized the importance of a developmental approach. The authors saw a special need for therapeutic strategies unique to the conditions of later life, ones that would target the unique resources and strengths of older patients (Gutmann, Grunes, and Griffin 1980).

(2) *The need for a process orientation.* In order to understand development in all its complexity, it is agreed that what we have to do is look at the process of change (or continuity). Michael Lewis (1980), a psychologist whose specialty is educational testing, noted that study of the individual from a *process* perspective has been grossly neglected. The reason for this neglect lies in part in the tremendous range of circumstances that seem to affect process. Growing older in our society varies not only by gender but by educational and socioeconomic circumstances, temperament, perceptions of social norms, life events, values, goals, and interpersonal contexts.

Given this diversity of effects, one developmental scientist, Eisdorfer (1983), concludes that we need many models for growing older; no single one will suffice. Appropriate models and paradigms must be used and, within each, process and reciprocal interactions among major domains of living should have priority. The more common antecedent/consequence approach is lacking in any provision for assessing these dynamics of living through time. The theoretical orientations presented earlier, especially those of Erikson and Jung, emphasize reciprocity, and therefore are partly in accord with Eisdorfer's contention. They are also compatible with the idea, voiced many years ago by Gordon Allport (1937) and seconded more recently by Bandura (1982), that personality theories should pay equal heed to the actor and the environment. According to Bandura: "People are not only perceivers, knowers, and actors. They are also self-reactors with capacities for reflective self-awareness that are generally neglected in information-processing theories based on computer models of human functioning" (Bandura 1982, 356).

(3) *The need for complementary data to those drawn from elitist samples.* Many of the longitudinal studies of the adult life course that exist are continuations of contact with elitist or above average children or college students: Terman's gifted children, later studied by Robert Sears (1977) and Pauline Sears and Ann Barbee (1977); the Grant studies of Harvard undergraduates, subsequently followed-up as adults by George Vaillant (1977); and Harold Jones's studies of children in Berkeley and Oakland who turned out to be above average. These children and their parents have been studied by successive cohorts of scholars representing several disciplines (e.g., Jones et al. 1971; Haan 1981; Maas and Kuypers 1974). Many rather optimistic theories of adult development have emerged from these studies, and one can only hope to balance them with a "mainstream" sample.

(4) *Randomness as an emerging force in adulthood.* Several theorists in recent years have postulated that social stressors, or what are often called "non-

normative" events may play an increasingly important role in later life. Gergen (1977), for example, suggests that one model that underlies developmental research is one of random or "adventitious" factors. In line with this, the distinguished child psychologist Flavall has gone so far as to state categorically that there can be no developmental psychology of later life because development at that time is completely at the mercy of random conditions. Other specialists of the life span have argued that the conditions that shape later life may exhibit certain regularities that warrant further investigation.

Stress and the Adult Life Course

The focus we shall take in this section is to consider the potential of a phenomenon that has been proposed as a critical ingredient for personal change: social stressors. This potential has only recently come to be recognized among life-span social scientists. Up until the last ten to fifteen years or so, stress research remained the province of clinicians and those interested in the immediacies of mental health problems. Questions were asked primarily about whether a recent exposure to loss or other life events, or the presence of some enduring strain, produced an elevation or onset of psychological symptomatology. At the same time, clinicians were beginning to recognize that the health consequences of life stressors might continue for significant periods of time. Bereavement, for example, was often found to set the stage for chronic, and possibly life-long, depression (e.g., Brown and Harris 1978; Parkes 1972).

Among life-span scientists, interest in stressors was sparked by the work of several scholars who sought to identify the sources of change in adulthood. One such source, appearing repeatedly but independently in their thinking, was the exigencies of chance occurrences of life. As was mentioned earlier in this chapter, various theorists today are portraying social stressors as a key ingredient to both stability and change in adult life. In the next few paragraphs, we will explore some of the characteristics of stressors themselves: their incidence and type. We then turn to an examination of the role of stressors as agents of change.

The Longitudinal Study of Transitions and Stress

From 1969 to 1980, a study was conducted of the stress experiences of men and women who were aged sixteen to sixty-five at the initial contact. The sample consisted of 216 individuals who at their first contact were each facing one of four normative transitions: subjects included high school seniors facing graduation from high school, newlyweds who were facing decisions about parenthood, middle-aged parents facing the departure of their youngest child from their home, and workers facing retirement.

While the intent of the study was to examine the impact of transitions on the lives of people at different points along the life course, a life events inventory and other measures of stress were also included. The findings both supported and extended previous reports on the stress exposure of older people. For example, support was found for previous reports that, overall, older adults apparently did report fewer life events than younger adults (Lowenthal and Chiriboga 1973).

At the same time, there was also evidence that older respondents were reporting more life events in certain specific areas of life, especially the areas of health, finances, and family (Chiriboga and Cutler 1980). The reason for the discrepancy between our findings and those of others rested in part on the fact that we had developed a life event inventory that contained items appropriate to all stages of life (see Lowenthal, Thurnher, and Chiriboga 1975). In contrast, life event inventories generally are de-signed for younger populations and contain many items that are not appropriate for older and retired populations. For example, events such as "child born" or "promotion" are relatively infrequent for persons aged sixty-five and over. On inventories that contain mostly events appropriate to younger stages of life, it is impossible for older adults to receive a high score.

As the research continued over an eleven year period, we began to find that social stressors included not only life events but nonevents (for ex-ample, you did not have a grandchild), experiencing life transitions off schedule (for example, getting married for the first time at forty instead of in the early twenties), waiting for some anticipated problems to occur (such as waiting for retirement day), and the minor hassles of everyday life.

As we looked at the impact of all these stressors on the lives of respon-dents, we began to identify some important characteristics of stress con-ditions (Chiriboga 1984; Fiske and Chiriboga 1985). For example, life events and other stressors are not necessarily random conditions. At least for some people, there is continuity over time. That is, some people seem to continually have more than their share of stressors. Others have far less.

In another series of analyses, it was found that components of the personality such as dimensions of the self-concept, life satisfaction, and interpersonal style were relatively stable over the entire eleven years dur-ing which we followed the subjects (Chiriboga 1984). Despite the stability or lack of stability in personality, however, life stressors were found to tell us a lot about how people change over the life course.

In order to pursue this matter in more detail, the first step was to obtain the characteristic stress loads of individuals over the entire eleven years of the study. This was done by adding up their stress scores for each of four interviews and then finding the average score. The next step was to divide everybody into two groups: those who seemed to have more than their share of stress experiences during the course of the study (the "high" group), and those who seemed to be below average in stress exposure (the "low" group). This permitted the examination of an important question: do

TABLE 7.1. **Stress and Personality Change**

Correlations between baseline interview status and status at all follow-up interview rounds, for selected measures of personal functioning. Drawn from the Longitudinal Study of Transitions, with subjects subdivided into those with High (N = 75) and Low (N = 75) stress exposure.

Measure		Correlation with Interview Round			
		2	3	4	5
Affect Balance (Bradburn)	H	.15*	.28***	.13	−.03
	L	.43***	.43***	.36***	.35***
Negative Affect (Bradburn)	H	.10	.22**	.16*	.12
	L	.39***	.43***	.46***	.31***
Positive Affect (Bradburn)	H	.35***	.40***	.33***	.33***
	L	.28***	.48***	.47***	.35***
CSC-42 (Symptoms Total)	H	.57***	.39***	na	.39***
	L	.52***	.53***	na	.51***
Health Status (self R)	H	.34***	.34***	na	na
	L	.52***	.56***	na	na
Negative Self Image	H	.54***	.41***	na	.35***
	L	.61***	.60***	na	.63***
Positive Self Image	H	.69***	.60***	na	.44***
	L	.62***	.53***	na	.59***
Assertiveness (Image)	H	.63***	.56***	.46***	.34***
	L	.63***	.66***	.65***	.69***
Hostility (Image)	H	.52***	.37***	.50***	.44***
	L	.58***	.58***	.62***	.66***

*Correlation nearly significant (p = .10)
**Correlation moderately significant (p = .05)
***Correlation strongly significant (p = .01)
na means data not available
SOURCE: D. A. Chiriboga. 1985. Stress and personal continuity. Paper presented at annual meeting of the Gerontological Society of America, November, San Antonio, Texas.

people who experience less stress also show less change in their personalities?

As shown in Table 7.1, the results indicate that people who experience less stress also are less likely to change on a personal level (Chiriboga 1985). The table shows what are called "Pearson" correlations, and generally the higher the number after the decimal point, the more stable the personality measure being looked at. In each case, the score of the sample at the first contact in 1969 is being compared to scores for the second contact (two years later), the third contact (five years later), the fourth contact (seven years later) and the fifth and final contact in 1980.

Not only are the less stressed more stable, but it also appears that different domains of personal functioning vary inherently in stability, regardless of stress exposure. For example, measures of morale, such as the indicators of Affect Balance, Negative Affect, and Positive Affect, show a basically lower level than measures pertaining to physical and mental health, which in turn demonstrate a lower stability than measures of self concept. This is an interesting finding, one that has not been discussed in the literature before.

Summing Up the Evidence for Social Stressors

On the basis of the theoretical considerations that were presented earlier in this chapter, there seems to be a strong suggestion that seemingly adventitious or "random" circumstances can drastically affect our lives. And not just for a short time.

One implication of the random change model was that, in order to really study the issues involved with continuity and change, we must go beyond the kind of global analyses that have been used in prior research. That is, considering evidence for change by looking at people of the same age, or at any large and heterogeneous group, is probably too crude methodologically. We need to group people as to their different exposures to stress conditions that have the potential to create change or to induce stability.

When we looked at the role of stress conditions, we found that while a number of early life course studies suggested that older people experience fewer life events presumed to be stressful, other studies find indications that, in fact, seniors simply experience different kinds of stressors than do younger people. Their evaluations of stresses experienced also vary considerably from senior to senior, depending on their internal and external resources. For example, two older people suffering from painful chronic arthritis may have opposite reactions, one considering him/herself lucky in comparison with others in the same age group, the other feeling depressed and defeated.

And when we turned to the actual role of stressors in affecting personal functioning, we found evidence to support the contention that life circumstances play a major role in determining how individuals play out their own personal drama of the life course. The conclusion that can be drawn is that seemingly random conditions of life may affect our personal development in later life. At the same time, the more expectable, developmental transitions also affect our lives.

Transitions and Continuity

The concept of transitions is frequently invoked to help explain how individuals progress through periods of major change in their lives. What is a transition? Often used merely as a synonym for "role change," transitions can also be understood as a complex process. Dictionaries generally provide at least two definitions of a transition: (1) the process of changing from one form, state, activity, or place to another; and (2) passage from one subject to another, as in discourse. From a social science perspective, one of the earliest applications of transitions theory is van Gennep's ([1906] 1960) consideration of how agrarian societies attempt to smooth the passage between such potentially conflicting status sets as childhood and adulthood.

Van Gennep outlined three successive stages in what he called "rites of passage." Central to these rites, at least in primitive society, is the fact that individuals experience them as part of a group all of whom are undergoing the same transition, and also that each stage is marked by public ceremony. In the stage of segregation, the intent is to separate the individual from his or her former way of life by breaking the physical and spiritual bonds with the past, often by physical removal from the community for some specified period of time. In the liminal or transitional stages the individual is trained in the knowledge and behaviors suitable for the new status. In the last stage the individual is aggregated back into society.

The middle stage, that of liminality, is especially important from the point of view of self-concept and personality research. Victor Turner (1967) has called this the "betwixt and between" phase of a transition, a phase during which the individual may have lost critical elements of involvement with society that provide not only meaning but personal identity. It is the in-between stage because during it individuals are transiting from one place in society to another, and exist outside the normal framework of status constraints. Consequently, they tend to be unsure of their identity, of what their role in life will be. Perhaps more importantly, no one else knows, either.

This ambiguity in selfhood can be troubling to all parties. How should the liminal person, in the midst of a role passage, be addressed, what status in the pecking order will he or she assume? Consider, for example, a person who is in the process of a divorce. Do you act as if the person is still married, or as if he or she is now single? Either way can cause problems.

Transitions in modern societies stand in some contrast to the traditional rite of passage. Whether the transition involves marriage or divorce or retirement, it tends to be experienced on a less public and more individuated basis. This becomes increasingly true over the life course. For example, while transitions into and out of school may be experienced as part of a larger cohort, the timing of transitions marked by marriage, parenthood, divorce, or retirement tends to be increasingly idiosyncratic. One individual may become a grandparent at age thirty-nine, another at age sixty-nine. As Bernice Neugarten (1977) has commented, being off time in major normative transitions can raise havoc with one's sense of self, although any role passage has major consequences for personal development.

Modern societies are experiencing marked changes in the meanings and rituals attached to normative transitions. Also newer transitions are emerging that are fast becoming normative. Many of these affect the lives of our more senior citizens. For example, let us consider some of the transitions faced by older women today. Some of the more common or normative transitions are: (1) the empty nest, (2) the widow, and (3) the survivor. But there are new and emerging transitions as well: (1) the "caught in the middle" generation, (2) older woman as worker, (3) older woman as retiree, (4) when a spouse enters a nursing home, and (5) entry into a retirement community, nursing home, etc.

A problem with all these transitions, both new and old but especially for the newer ones, is that we have no rituals to help ease the transition, and to explain what is expected in the new roles. This creates greater hardships for those undergoing the transition, and may make it more difficult for individuals to make the new roles part of themselves.

To an individual experiencing a transition one key experience is a challenge to his or her usual way of viewing the world. A middle-aged woman, for example, finds that her role as mother must change after her youngest child leaves home. A retiring steelworker begins to question the need to occupy himself with work eight hours a day. Transitions research underscores the importance, for an individual's adaptation, of recognizing that change is taking place and of reformulating a view of oneself in relation to the transformed world.

Transitions as a Dialectic

Life-span scientists often emphasize the interactive nature of development. Development is portrayed as codetermined by the inner structure and outside sociocultural circumstances, with both gradual and sudden changes in either creating the conditions for developmental change. Some theorists have gone on to suggest that individuals move from periods of relative equilibrium, through periods of turmoil and change, toward new or restored equilibrium. Certain of these periods of change may bespeak normative transitions that fall at predictable points of the life course, such as those that surround a "timely" marriage or retirement. We have already mentioned, for example, that Daniel Levinson and his colleagues (1978) portray development in terms of four periods of relative stability (childhood and adolescence, early adult era, middle adult era, late adult era), each heralded by a normative transition.

Other transitions may reflect the impact of chance, as when an individual is widowed in early adulthood or is paralyzed as a result of some accident. But whether normative or non-normative, transitions confront the individual with a challenge to his or her habitual ways of living. The challenge however will vary in intensity. Most research indicates that normative transitions, possibly because they are expectable and occur gradually over a long period of time, exert less of an impact than non-normative transitions (e.g., Pearlin and Lieberman 1979).

Periods of Stability and Transition

Most of the well-known theories of development, whether they be focused on early or later life, view development in terms of progressive stages. There is little agreement concerning either the characteristics or the duration of periods of stability, and the mechanics of how an individual progresses from one stage to another are almost universally omitted. Some theorists have suggested that, especially after the main sweep of biological maturation draws to a close, points of stability and change may be highly dependent on chance exposure to disruptive life events (e.g., Marris 1974; Riegel 1975).

Transitions theory may provide some of the bridges between points of stability. Parkes (1972), for example, has developed a theory predicated on the idea that out of our unique set of experiences, each of us develops an "assumptive world" that guides our commerce with the environment. Assumptive worlds may succeed one another. Unlike stage theorists, however, Parkes sees the nature of these world views as being highly dependent on the life circumstances of the individual, and continuity is not assured. When we lose some significant component of the structure that underlies our assumptive world, the figurative walls come tumbling down.

From a less extreme perspective, others have used the concept of transitions as a vehicle for illustrating continuity over time. The family life cycle for example is often charted in terms of transitions between sequential role gains and losses (e.g., Duvall 1977), as well as between overlapping social epochs (e.g., Elder 1974; Hareven 1978). Continuities in individual development to late adulthood have also been charted from the perspective of transitions (e.g., Hareven and Adams 1982). Common to all such treatments is the perspective that life unfolds as a dialectic between the individual and the environment.

Transitions as Stressors

In considering the personal and social disruption often accompanying transitional periods, findings from the field of stress have provided useful information. There is, for example, the suggestion that transitions may consist of a chaining of life events over a relatively brief period of time, where one event precipitates the next. In one comparison of persons experiencing either normative transitions or divorce, for example, it was found that the divorcing persons were more likely to experience both positive and negative changes in nearly all areas of life, not simply the marital (Fiske and Chiriboga 1985). Another finding of particular interest is the importance of an individual's own perception of potential stressors, including chained stressors such as transitions, in determining health outcomes. It may be for this reason that many clinically oriented life-span scientists are beginning to develop intervention strategies to help individuals resolve transitions at all stages of the adult life course (e.g., Golan 1986; Schlossberg 1984).

Personality in Later Life: Concluding Comments

After exposure to such a broad spectrum of information on how theorists and researchers view personality in later life, the reader may be wondering what, if anything, she or he ought to be coming away with. One of the disconcerting aspects of personality research in adulthood and aging, as Neugarten (1977) remarked a decade ago, is that very little of it seems to support the theories that have been proposed. For example, although theorists seem to be quite taken with the notion that distinct stages exist in the development of personality during adulthood, there is, in fact, very little empirical evidence for a sequential unfolding of stages.

Instead, what we generally find is that while the characteristics associated with the so-called stages may in fact exist and cohere, they generally do not seem to progress in a preordained and sequential manner. Take, for example, Erikson's portrayal of ego integrity as the last stage in his epigenetic sequence. One individual may have become immersed in issues related to self-acceptance and a basic acceptance of life quite early, perhaps as a result of an "off-schedule" confrontation with death or a religious conversion. Another may have achieved ego integrity in a "timely" fashion, only to find his or her entire worldview called into question by dramatically changed circumstances. In short, situational conditions may exert a strong influence not only on the stability but on the unfolding of personality characteristics.

The lack of research support for stage theories, however, does not necessarily mean that such theories should be ignored. One exciting area for future research involves a melding of the three underlying models of personality, those involving stability, orderly change, and random change. As we begin to ascertain the different dimensions in which personality demonstrates greater or lesser stability, the dimensions in which ordered change seems more predominant, and the dimensions in which there is greater responsivity to the physical and social environment, we shall finally begin to understand the nature of personality development in later life.

VIII

SEX IN THE LATER YEARS

Diane E. Rykken

Attitudes Not Attributes

A seventy-one-year-old retired fireman and his seventy-year-old wife, both healthy, appeared in a doctor's office one day. They were troubled by a problem so "unnatural" and "abnormal" that they felt medical attention was necessary. After fourteen children and many, many years of marriage, they still liked to have intercourse at least once a day (Freeman 1971).

How do you the reader respond to this story? With amusement? Disbelief? Sympathy? A shake of the head? Does it sound like a joke? The sexual revolution has come and gone, but still most people in our society are likely to have two views about sex and our senior citizens. First, old people aren't interested in sex, and second, if they are, they shouldn't be.

This prejudice comes out in many ways. In the very recent past we penalized older individuals who dared to remarry by reducing their social security and censured those who committed the sin of cohabitation to evade our punishment (Dean 1966).

Lonely old men are regarded with extreme suspicion if they attempt to show affection to small children. Yet, in all countries for all races criminal behavior drops dramatically with age (Hirschi and Gottfredson 1983), and the crimes of the elderly are most commonly drunkenness, vagrancy, and gambling (McCreary 1979). Child molesters, by self-report, start at sixteen on the average, and are most likely to be in their late twenties when identified (Groth and Hobson 1985). Even so, legal prosecution of the elderly may be more likely because of intolerance of sexuality in aged men (Groth and Hobson 1985; McCreary 1979), and they may not receive fair treatment in the courts (Sex Information and Education Council of the U.S. 1970).

Most of the time we do not even allow the elderly a distorted form of sexuality. Broderick (1978) writes that when he tried to give a report on Rubin's book *Sexual Life after Sixty* to a professional audience of psychologists, social workers, and psychiatrists, he could not calm the mirth for

158

fifteen minutes, and even then, most never could be entirely serious about such a "hilarious" topic.

This attitude has hampered research in the area. Even when the elderly are willing, relatives may insist that they withdraw from such studies (Pfeiffer 1977b). Professionals are not immune. Administrators and personnel of community centers serving senior citizens frequently discouraged Starr and Weiner (1981) in their work. Sometimes these researchers were allowed to give their presentation and questionnaire only if "sex" was removed from its title.

Even assessments of public attitudes toward sex and the older individual have been sparse and sometimes indirect. In an extensive survey by the National Council on Aging (1975) only a single question dealt with sexuality. A cross-section of adults of all ages was asked how well they thought the phrase "sexually active" described the elderly. While 41% of the public thought that the old were "very physically active," only 5% thought they were "very sexually active." La Torre and Kear (1977), in a study using students and personnel at a nursing home, did not find negativity so much, as lack of credibility for stories which involved sexual activity and the elderly.

Brandeis University students (aged seventeen to twenty-three) almost all saw the sex life of the elderly as past, negligible, or nonexistent (Golde and Kogan 1959). Jokes (Davies 1977; Palmore 1971; Richmond 1977) and humorous birthday cards (Denos and Jacke 1981) poked fun at a lack of sexual ability in elderly men or used surprise that the ability is not gone. Usually the woman used as a foil was young. Those targeted at women were generally more negative and used ugliness and a lack of sex appeal as the point of the joke. The most common types were age concealment and old maid jokes.

The sexual revolution has had some effect. Arluke and colleagues (1984) compared advice books on the elderly published before and after 1970. Only 20% of those before approved of sexual activity, but 56% of those published after did. The latter books also contained a larger quantity of sexual information, and more of them were written for the elderly rather than for their children and relatives. Still, the stereotype has not disappeared.

Why do people have these views of old people? Is it because they correctly reflect the true state of affairs? Before examining the evidence for this "true state of affairs," it is useful to point out some reasons that might lead people to think of the elderly as sexless, regardless of the facts.

To begin with, we in America have come out of a social fabric that has strongly emphasized religion. One of the religious principles that has been held—especially in the past—is that sex is for procreation and not recreation. If younger people were held to this principle, over-population problems would be even worse than they already are. But for younger people it is easy to rationalize, conceal, or gloss over the recreational aspect of their behavior. With an older couple the purpose of their sexual activity is immediately and unmistakably clear (Pfeiffer 1977b).

Secondly, incest is the most universal taboo of the human race. In childhood, presumably because of the Oedipal or Electra conflict, children suppress the knowledge of parental sexuality—a suppression that lasts into adulthood and is generalized to the generation of elders. By making the idea of sex and the elderly ridiculous, laughable, ugly, and perverse, the offspring generation protects itself against incest and potential sexual competitors (Pfeiffer 1977b; Berezin 1978).

Finally, societal attitudes toward sex and the elderly can be seen as one more form of ageism. Like the objects of other forms of prejudice, the elderly are seen as ugly, inferior, worthless—and sexless (Kuhn 1976). Particularly pervasive is the reduction of the elderly to the status of small children (Arluke and Levin 1984). Many of those who serve the elderly feel that their clients should be protected like children (Starr and Weiner 1981). This often includes shielding them from sexuality.

Surveys and Speculations

Surveys of older people on sexuality are few and usually biased in one way or another. For that reason these studies should be examined carefully. One important consideration is the nature of the populations sampled. Affluent males, women in nursing homes, clinic patients, couples, and community volunteers have all been used. Generalizations to the general population may or may not be valid. The methodology used is important, too. Longitudinal versus cross-sectional techniques are beginning to yield very different results. To give some idea of the range of problems, a few of the more commonly quoted studies are described briefly below.

Kinsey

This pioneering work is truly monumental in its scope. Thousands of men, women, and children from all parts of the country were personally interviewed on their sexual behavior. Even though the two volumes (Kinsey et al. 1948, 1953) which came out of the study are almost forty years old, it is still one of the most quoted works on sex. Even so, Kinsey has been criticized for his sampling methods. Minority groups and elderly persons are grossly under-represented compared to their numbers in the population. Only 106 men and 56 women were sixty years or over, and of these only 31 women and 48 men were over sixty-five. Kinsey admits his statements about the older population, particularly women, are partially based on extrapolation from younger age groups.

Duke Longitudinal Studies

This massive program includes a large study on sexuality. Many researchers have reported on this project (e.g., Newman and Nichols 1960; Pfeiffer 1969; Pfeiffer and Davis 1972; Pfeiffer, Verwoerdt, and Davis 1972; Pfeiffer, Verwoerdt, and Wang 1968; George and Weiler 1981). It is a longitudinal design, although some of the data come from cross-sectional comparisons. The project began in 1954 with 260 community volunteers aged sixty or over. About half were men and half women. These people were given follow-up interviews every three to four years for at least ten years and some longer. The number of subjects eventually dwindled, and a second study consisting of 502 women and men, aged forty-five to sixty-nine was started in 1969.

A group of persons who actively volunteer for a time-consuming study lasting years probably is drawn from the healthy and less isolated segment of the population. The study is unusual in including some black subjects and some individuals of lower socioeconomic class, even though these two are partially confounded (Newman and Nichols 1960). That, plus its longitudinal design, help compensate for biases it might have.

Sexology Survey

While it is one of the larger surveys done with elderly men, it was not meant to be a typical cross-section of people. Potential subjects were selected from the book, *Who's Who in America*. As a consequence, the respondents are a group of highly successful and distinguished men. Only 14% of those asked responded and the subjects are biased for occupation. Their ages averaged sixty-nine, ranging from sixty-five to ninety-two. The majority (677 out of 832) were married (Rubin 1963).

Masters and Johnson

Where Kinsey asked, Masters and Johnson actually observed and measured sexual activity. This work, combined with therapeutic work on sexual dysfunction, provided a wealth of new information. Unfortunately, the number of older subjects was small (39 men aged fifty-one to eighty-nine and 34 women up to seventy-eight years old, with most in their fifties and sixties). Almost all of these were white with few lower-class individuals. Some were drawn from the clinic setting. In spite of these drawbacks, the information Masters and Johnson (1966, 1970) gained is unique, and their work is widely quoted.

Starr-Weiner Report

These researchers recruited subjects by delivering a talk, "Love, Intimacy, and Sex in the Later Years," at places that served the elderly. Questionnaires were distributed after the talk and mailed back to the researchers. Their average return rate was 14% with some talks yielding rates as high as 30%. Some responses were obtained by colleagues who distributed the questionnaires without the talk.

Subjects consisted of 800 adults between sixty and ninety-one. Thirty-five percent were male and 65% female. While all parts of the U.S. are represented, the largest proportion (47%) is from the Northeast with the next most frequent from the West and Northwest (27%). Most of the sample is white although some blacks and Hispanics were included.

The authors feel that their respondents were not especially interested in sex, but were those who usually attended events at these centers. However, the educational level of their subjects was somewhat higher than the general population of elderly.

The subjects in any research are going to be a limited sample of the population of interest. Only insofar as the sample is representative can the researcher say that such and such is true of the population. The elderly in America are often treated as if they were a monolithic group instead of the racial and socioeconomic multiplicity that they represent. The subjects so far studied have not been very representative of that diversity. In some cases subjects are deliberately picked from a select group, as in the Sexology Survey above. In other cases it just happens.

One of the reasons for this is the nature of large surveys. A reasonable rate of return is about 14%. This means that for every 100 subjects participating, around 600 do not respond. Chances are, the ones who do not participate are going to be different from those who do. Often it is not clear what this difference is. What follows is a discussion of where some of the weaknesses in subjects lie.

The broad studies of sexuality that look at people across the life span have had few subjects in older age categories. This is typical. *The Hite Report* (Hite 1976), for example, has age information on 1066 women. Only 19 were sixty and over. A mere 6 of these were in their seventies. This is often true even of studies specifically targeted for the elderly. As a general rule, the older people are, the less likely they are to respond to a questionnaire on sex. In order to get an even distribution Hegeler and Mortensen (1977) had to send out twice as many questionnaires to the oldest groups.

Even though there are many more elderly women than men, women are often underrepresented. Furthermore, because of a tendency to choose either men or couples, married women appear in a much higher proportion than in the general population. This has been changing, but at present less is known about the sex lives of unmarried older women than other segments of the population.

Education and occupation are frequently biased. Out of a selected group of 832 highly successful men, no less than 245 were educators in the

Sexology Survey (Rubin 1963). Although half of the women in the Wasow and Loeb (1978) study of women in a nursing home were over eighty and from a much less educated time, 25% of them had some college or professional experience or both. This is well over twice the national average for women at the time the study was done.

Although socioeconomic levels affect virtually any characteristic under investigation, studies have been heavily weighted toward white, middle-class subjects. Even when others are included, their numbers are not great. Starr and Weiner (1981) found groups of working-class elderly were very enthusiastic and asked intelligent questions, but returned unusually small numbers of questionnaires. Cross-cultural studies are likewise rare, with Winn and Newton (1982) being virtually the only example.

With such limited information it is even difficult to tell how these biases affect results. Available data, scant as it is, indicate that these factors do make a difference. Elderly married women tend to have a higher frequency of intercourse, but a lower incidence of masturbation than unmarried women. Newman and Nichols (1960) found lower socioeconomic elderly were considerably more active sexually than their middle-class group. Winn and Newton (1982) showed great cross-cultural differences in the sexuality of the elderly.

Studies that concentrate on a single group are not necessarily bad, as long as the findings are not generalized outside of that group. However, even within a single class of subjects biases caused by low rates of returns can destroy the validity of results. Perhaps those who are sexually active are more likely to answer; the others may feel they don't have anything to say. On the other hand, maybe the sexually inactive are more likely to answer because they have nothing to hide.

A picture of sexuality in the aging is emerging, but at present it is not a clear one. Some of the latest research differs drastically from older data. The next section, will give a brief overview of the directions that research has taken.

Percentages and Frequencies

Almost all studies show that for some individuals sexual activity never stops no matter what their age. It continues through the seventies, eighties, and on through the nineties (Kinsey et al. 1948, 1953; Pfeiffer and Davis 1972; Rubin 1963; Starr and Weiner 1981). Even if the ability (in men) does disappear, interest lingers on (Pfeiffer and Davis 1972; Pfeiffer et al. 1968; Verwoerdt et al. 1969a). Those still active show as wide a range of sexual behavior as at any other time. This is true for frequency and amount, and for any specialized tastes acquired earlier in life. This might be a preference for a certain type of partner, or the more esoteric forms of sexuality such as sadism, masochism, fetishism, or the like (Benjamin 1963).

One study (Clark and Anderson 1967) did find that sexual desire in both sexes and potency in males almost disappears between seventy-five and eighty. However, only 79 subjects were questioned on sexual behavior, and half of these were a hospital group. There were only 14 intact couples. Since the commonest reason given for ceasing sexual activity in both males and females is lack of a partner (Clark and Anderson 1967; Pfeiffer et al. 1968; Wasow and Loeb 1978), there may not have been enough healthy older individuals with a partner to test the hypothesis.

Overall though, most studies show a drop in sexual involvement over time. This change may be measured by tabulating the percentage of people still active or by looking at the frequency of activity for those still involved. Cross-sectional studies show decreases in both. Curves for these changes are not entirely consistent. Some show a steady decline. Others show critical changes around fifty or in the seventies (see reviews in Corby and Solnick 1980; Solnick 1978; White 1982).

One problem with cross-sectional studies is that age changes are confounded with cohort effects. Cohort effects are the result of being part of a particular generation. The elderly were raised before the sexual revolution of the sixties. Misconceptions such as weakening of sexual strength by excessive activity and the dangers of masturbation were pervasive in earlier times. Possibly sexual frequencies were lower for young adults then than they are today, and our elderly reflect these lower frequencies.

The Duke Longitudinal Studies initially confirmed a decline in sexuality. However, after the first round of studies in the sixties, a new set of subjects coming from a different generation has been followed. Research on this set shows, not decline, but a pattern of stability in frequency of intercourse. This stability is maintained until some event such as death of a partner or serious illness intervenes. At this time sexual activity ceases abruptly and frequently is not resumed (George and Weiler 1981; Starr and Weiner 1981; Weiler 1981). Even when the frequency of coitus itself declined, a substantial minority of people reported increases in sexual activity and satisfaction (Adams and Turner 1985). The majority of these were women.

There is other evidence of a cultural or cohort effect on sexual expression in the elderly. At the time of the Kinsey report the elderly adults studied by Starr and Weiner (1981) were in their forties. Kinsey found frequencies of 1.4 times a week for a forty-year-old married woman and 2.0 for a forty-year-old married man. Starr and Weiner found a current frequency of 1.4 for their subjects. Also pointing toward psychological factors is the fact that profession makes a difference. Rates of impotency are disproportionately high in certain professions—namely, editors, publishers, journalists, and physicians (Rubin 1963).

Finally, though quantitative data are meager, cross-cultural comparisons show great differences in the sexuality expected and obtained from older individuals. In cultures where the elderly are expected to remain active, the sexual behavior of the elderly is either maintained or diminishes quite modestly (Winn and Newton 1982). This is true even in cultures with high rates of intercourse. For example, Merriam (1971) found the rate of intercourse in 11 Bala men of Africa ranged from 1.9 to 1.2 times per day. Although the youngest was twenty-three, these men were not particularly youthful. Two were in their sixties. The oldest at sixty-six, had a rate of 1.5 times per day.

Separating age and cohort effects is not always easy, and these questions have not yet been decisively answered. However, if the cohort effect is as strong as the above evidence suggests, then some radical changes can be expected in the behavior of the elderly as the cohorts who reached maturity during the sexual revolution of the sixties and seventies age.

In the next section these age-related changes will be examined in more detail. Since men and women have been found to differ quite radically, and of course, women, a priori, are not going to suffer from impotency, the two will be discussed separately.

The Aging Woman

Physical changes

Women, unlike men, show a distinct and dramatic change in their reproductive functioning. Notice that reproductive, not sexual, function, is indicated. This is the change of life or climacteric. During this time, the ovaries drastically reduce the amount of female hormones (estrogen and progesterone) produced, menstruation ceases, and the woman becomes incapable of bearing children. Although often used interchangeably, menopause and the climacteric are different. Menopause refers to a single event, the cessation of menstruation; the climacteric refers to the whole complex of events occurring for the years before and after the last period.

The reduction in female hormones causes readjustments in other systems of the body besides the reproductive organs. For example, since the female hormones are controlled by certain pituitary hormones (gonadotrophins) via a feedback loop, the pituitary compensates for the decrease in female hormones by increasing the level of gonadotrophins until their concentration in the blood becomes quite high and stays that way.

These changes in the body can cause a variety of temporary symptoms. The most dramatic of these are "hot flashes" and night sweats in which vasodilation causes a feeling of intense heat accompanied by perspiration and flushing. They do not last long, but can cause considerable discomfort. The mechanism of the hot flash is still mysterious. A synchronized pulse of the gonadotrophin, Luteinizing Hormone (LH), from the pituitary is associated with them, but does not appear to be sufficient as a cause (Barzel et al. 1983).

These symptoms and others are not universal, but figures on how many women may expect to have problems vary widely from author to author—from 25% up to 85%. However, a much smaller number, perhaps 10–15%, will have symptoms severe enough to seek medical attention. In most cases hot flashes last less than a year, but for some women they may continue for a number of years. The intensity continuously diminishes during this period of time.

Older women who achieved orgasm earlier in their life remain orgasmic. Many women are capable of multiple orgasms. This ability is not lost with age (Kaplan and Sager 1971). However, there are some changes in physical response. These include differences in breast enlargement, diminished frequency of the sex flush, fewer orgasmic contractions, and rarity of rectal sphincter contractions during orgasm (Masters and Johnson 1966, 1970).

While the above are harmless, other changes can cause problems. Vaginal lubrication during sexual excitement may be delayed, and less is produced. As estrogen diminishes, the uterus shrinks in size and the walls of the vagina become thin, inelastic, and fragile. Both the vaginal barrel and outlet become constricted. These changes may cause intercourse to be accompanied by irritation and a burning pain, a susceptibility to urinary tract infections, and even tears and rips in the vaginal wall. Normally, vagina and uterus contract rhythmically during an orgasm. A few women develop a spastic rather than a rhythmic contraction in some of their experiences. This can cause pelvic pain, sometimes quite severe, which may radiate down as far as the legs (Masters and Johnson 1966, 1970).

The worst problems are seen in women who have not had sexual relations regularly after menopause. When such women remarry, "Widow's Syndrome" can cause unexpected problems, which may take six weeks to three months to reverse (Masters and Johnson 1981). On the other hand, older women who had intercourse regularly once or twice a week over the years maintained adequate lubrication, had vaginas of normal size, and climaxed with rhythmic and painless uterine contractions (Masters and Johnson 1966). This may account for the fact that 84% of Starr and Weiner's (1981) respondents did not report any physical discomfort during intercourse.

Aside from its physical symptoms, the climacteric has a bad reputation. It is often thought to be the end of attractiveness, sexuality, and femininity. Its reputation is worse among younger women than among those who have experienced it (Neugarten et al. 1968). In fact, these untrue stories may become a self-fulfilling prophecy for the woman who believes them.

Sexuality should not be affected by the climacteric since it is not controlled by female hormones. Aside from psychic factors which are not questioned, there is some controversy over exactly what does control it. Many researchers believe with reasonably good evidence that androgens influence sexuality in women as well as men (Money and Ehrhardt 1972; Schon and Sutherland 1963). Both sexes produce male and female hormones. In women the adrenal glands and ovaries produce androgens under the control of the pituitary. After menopause the ovaries continue to produce some androgens (Barzel et al. 1983). Together with adrenal production, ratio of androgens to estrogens actually increases with age.

Whether or not androgens are important in female sexual behavior, pituitary and adrenal glands are more critical than reproductive organs for maintenance of libido. If health is regained, a woman can lose uterus, ovaries, Fallopian tubes, and breasts without affecting sexual desire. If she does report loss, then it is usually because of psychological loss or the reaction of a spouse.

Of course unpleasant symptoms or painful intercourse caused by lack of estrogen can diminish desire. Giving estrogen will relieve all these symptoms, and doctors initially prescribed it liberally. Women remained on the hormones for years after the end of the climacteric. When a link was found between cancer and estrogen (Hoover et al. 1976; Smith et al. 1975; Weiss et al. 1976; Ziel and Finkle 1975), usage dropped. More recent studies seem to indicate that a cyclical use of low dosage estrogen combined with progesterone for the last week or so of the cycle is not associated with increased risk of cancer (Barzel et al. 1983). This more limited use seems more justifiable.

Interest and performance

Information on the sexuality of older women appears paradoxical. They generally express much less interest than males of the same age; many fewer are engaged in sexual activity; and if sexual activity stops, it does so at a much younger age (age sixty compared to sixty-eight for men) (Pfeiffer et al. 1968; Pfeiffer and Davis 1972). At all stages of life the average interest and frequency of outlets is less for women than for men, but the drop-off with age is still greater for women. For example, at the beginning of the Duke Longitudinal Studies, 80% of the men were still interested and active, but only 33% of the women admitted interest with even fewer (20%) still active. Kinsey noted a gradual decline in the frequency of coition for women between the ages of twenty and sixty, which parallels the decline in men.

However, some data show very little decrement, and even enhancement of sexuality with age. When measures independent of their partners are used, aging seems to have only a small effect on the sexuality of women (Christenson and Gagnon 1965; Kinsey et al 1953). Masturbation, for example, shows little change until women are quite old (Kinsey et al. 1953).

Starr and Weiner (1981) point out that, according to Kinsey, the orgasmic level of younger women increases with years of marriage. In their study, 72% of their women reported they had an orgasm always or most of the time; 27% sometimes had an orgasm; only 1.5% stated they never had orgasms. This did not change over the age span they studied—not even for those over eighty. Most respondents said that the frequency of orgasm was either the same (66%) or higher (20%) than when they were younger. Similarly Hite (1976) found that her middle-aged women felt that sexual pleasure had actually increased with age.

While there is much variation from culture to culture, it is common for women to become more sexually aggressive with age. This is expressed by sexual jokes, gestures, dress, and behavior. Aged males might do this too, but examples are more striking and more frequent for women. While women may be less active in America, cross-culturally elderly women are more often sexually active than elderly men. The partners for these women are often much younger men or even boys (Winn and Newton 1982).

These paradoxes can be resolved fairly easily. Kinsey and his colleagues (1953) interpreted the decreases in intercourse as an effect of aging on her partner, not the woman herself. When asked directly why sex had stopped, women blamed their partners. The men blamed themselves (George and Weiler 1981; Pfeiffer 1977b).

The reduction in the number of active women over time has a similar explanation. Earlier it was stated that the most common reason for terminating coital activity in both sexes was a lack of partner. Women in the United States outlive men by approximately seven years, but traditionally men are expected to marry women younger than themselves. A husband is, on the average, about four years older than his wife. So a woman can expect eleven years of widowhood. As a result, the number of widows is quite high compared to the number of widowers. Between the age of sixty-five and seventy-four, 39.1% of the women are widowed, but only 8.9% of the men. For ages seventy-five and over the figures are 66.9% and 23.8% respectively (Bureau of the Census 1985).

The most important factors in determining whether an older woman is sexually active are first and foremost, the presence of a *sanctioned* partner and second, past enjoyable sexual experiences. A sanctioned partner was not a factor for men at all (Pfeiffer and Davis 1972). If the death of a husband is not to mean the end of sexual life, then a widow must look for a new one. Some women do not care to do this. Others are constrained for economic reasons, loyalty to their dead husbands, and ties to in-laws and children who are sometimes fiercely opposed to a second marriage.

Even if an older woman wants to find a new partner, there are handicaps. Our society puts a heavy premium on youth, with the elderly getting the image of ugliness and unattractiveness. Elderly men influenced by this stereotype choose younger partners. Elderly women often do not feel attractive or desirable and may be reluctant to invite rejection. Furthermore, they were raised in another time that did not accept sexually assertive women. The combination of these factors makes it very hard for many older women to compete for marriage partners.

Yet compete they must. The number of available partners is very limited. Using data from the Bureau of the Census (1985) to calculate the ratio of unmarried women to unmarried men gives 3.6 for ages sixty-four to seventy-four, and 5.4 for seventy-five and over. Pfeiffer (1978) reports that one housing project for the elderly had 75 men and 300 women. Only two men were single. With such limited opportunities, many women will give up altogether, and even their interest will dwindle.

Given an opportunity, then, women show little impairment of sexuality with age. Because of early training, societal expectations, and lack of opportunity, however, women are handicapped in maintaining this sexuality. As Freeman (1961) has said, "Old men tend to get married while old women tend to get lonesome."

The Aging Man

Physical changes

Some professionals talk of a male climacteric in which there is a decline in the male hormones (Benjamin 1963; Weg 1978). Others (Kinsey et al. 1948) doubt its existence at all, and blame social and psychological factors for the "midlife" crises of men. Futterweit and colleagues (1984) suggest that while a male climacteric occurs it is rarer, less severe than women, and associated with certain problems such as Klinefelter's Syndrome, chronic orchitis resulting from mumps, or surgical procedures that have damaged the testicular blood supply.

Unfortunately, determining the relationship between age and testosterone, the most powerful of the androgens, is not straightforward. Levels measured in blood do not always correspond to the amount assayed in urine. Aging causes the circadian rhythm of its production to change, so that a difference between young and old men may show up if testosterone is measured in the morning, but not in the afternoon. There is an inactive form which the body must convert to the active, effective form. Testosterone level might be quite adequate, but perhaps conversion is defective or testosterone receptors are no longer sensitive to the hormone. Finally, many conditions, such as obesity, high alcohol consumption, certain illnesses, use of certain medications, depression, and heavy exercise may reduce testosterone independent of age.

In any case, the evidence for relationship between testosterone and sexuality seems conflicting. Young men reach a peak of sexual activity when testosterone levels are still rather low. By the time testosterone levels are at their highest, between twenty-six and thirty (Hermanova 1983), sexual activity is already declining, and continues to do so while testosterone stays steady. The hormone level does begin decreasing from fifty to fifty-five (Nieschlag 1979), but it happens slowly, with no abrupt changes. Barzel, Gambert, and Tsitouras (1983) found that if care is taken to eliminate from the sample men with conditions that reduce testosterone, there is no change with age.

Older men with high testosterone levels do tend to be more sexually active than those with lower levels, but there is a great deal of overlap (Tsitouras et al. 1982). It is possible that high sexual activity maintains testosterone level rather than the other way around (Barzel et al. 1983). Testosterone treatment for impotence has a definite placebo effect, but the results otherwise are uncertain. In any case, rather low levels appear to be adequate for erection and ejaculation to occur (Hermanova 1983; Nieschlag 1979), and the drop with age is not enough to destroy fertility. Viable sperm have been found in men in their nineties.

Regardless of the role of testosterone, a variety of physical changes have been documented for men. For example, the angle of the erect penis to the abdominal wall increases to 90 degrees. It takes longer to get an erection than when a man was younger and, although adequate, it is less firm. Erections during sleep become less frequent. The refractory period (the time it takes after ejaculation before the man can get another erection) becomes longer. Older men may even have what Kaplan and Sager (1971) call a paradoxical refractory period. That is, if the man loses his erection during a long foreplay, twelve to twenty-four hours may pass before he can have another. During intercourse itself, there is not the same urgency for orgasm and the man may not even feel the need to ejaculate at every intercourse. When ejaculation does occur, the amount of semen produced is less and may not be expelled with as much force (although there are great differences even in young men). After an orgasm there is an immediate loss of erection so that the penis, "literally falls out of the vagina" (Comfort 1980; Corby and Solnick 1980; Masters and Johnson 1966, 1970).

Using penile response to an erotic movie shown in private to their subjects, Solnick and Birren (1977) showed even greater age differences than Masters and Johnson. Although there is great overlap between the two, younger men responded rapidly; the older ones more slowly. Younger men partially lost an erection, then regained it rapidly. Older men were not only slower to respond, but slower to rebound when an erection was partially lost.

Although easily misinterpreted, these changes do not physically harm potency. From the woman's point of view, they are even beneficial since a man may now have more control than he ever did in his youth. More serious may be a loss of penile sensitivity. Edwards and Husted (1976) found a very large correlation (–57) between sexual activity and the threshold of response to vibration applied to the penis, with the older men being less sensitive.

Even so, this is not a barrier to potency. Edwards and Husted (1976) suggest development of chemical agents to enhance sensitivity. In the meantime education is another possibility. The use of fantasy is quite low in elderly of both sexes (Starr and Weiner 1981). Yet this can be a powerful compensatory tool. Solnick (1978) trained a group of men aged forty-five to fifty-five in the use of sexual fantasy. This training not only improved erectile response, but increased the rate of intercourse. The effect continued at least for a period of two weeks after the training was over.

Interest and performance

None of the physiological effects of normal aging mentioned above are enough to cause impotency. Nonetheless, most studies find a larger number of sexually inactive men among the older population. The older the group, the higher the proportion of impotent men. Kinsey and colleagues (1948), for example, found that at age sixty, only one in 5 could no longer perform sexual intercourse, but at age eighty, the number was 3 out of 4. Rubin's study (1963) found an impotency rate starting at 16% for ages sixty-five to sixty-nine, and ending with 43% for ages seventy-five to ninety-two. In the Duke Longitudinal Study 40–65% were still active in the age range of sixty to seventy-eight, but only 10–25% in the age group seventy-eight and over. Danish men showed a steady drop with 94% active at ages fifty-one to fifty-five, 36% from seventy-six to eighty, and only 3% in the ninety-one to ninety-five age group (Hegeler and Mortensen 1977). Masters and Johnson (1970) notice an upsurge in secondary impotence after age fifty.

For the group that does remain active, there is also a decline in the frequency of sexual activity (Clark and Anderson 1967; Kinsey et al. 1948; Pfeiffer et al. 1968). According to Kinsey, the median number of outlets per week for married men was 2.81 for men between twenty-one and twenty-five. This dropped to 0.79 per week for men between fifty-six and sixty years of age. De Nigola and Peruzza (1974) found that men sixty-two to seventy-one were coitally active an average of twice a week. The older group, from seventy-two to eighty-one, were least active at 3 times a month.

Whether this decrease in frequency is due to old age per se is unclear. Kinsey's figures show a gradual decline, which begins in late adolescence and continues throughout life. The rate of decline in old age is no greater than it is between thirty and sixty, and physiological changes—except for loss of penile sensitivity—do not seem to parallel changes in performances. Generally, the frequency of genito-urinary problems is the same in potent and impotent men (Bowers et al. 1963; Finkle et al. 1959). The men themselves do not perceive physical problems as the root of the problem. When men were asked why the frequency of sex had decreased, the vast majority did not even mention physical disability (Tarail 1962).

This kind of decline is not found universally. Weiner and Starr (1981) found 83% of their males (aged sixty to ninety-one) were still active and maintained the same frequency. George and Weiler (1981) noted stability in level of activity until some event such as illness or loss of partner causes sexual activity to cease suddenly. Verwoerdt and colleagues (1969b) found four different patterns in men which showed up over a period of years. One of these was a steady level of sexual interest; another was an increase in sexual activity. Twenty percent of the men fell into the latter category. If the groups were divided into age categories, the older the men, the higher the percentage who fell into the inactive and the declining patterns, but at no age did the other two patterns disappear.

Cross-cultural data show great variation. In some cultures there is decline and inactivity with age. Attitudes toward this loss range from despair to relief. In other cultures sexual activities continue to extreme old age in both men and women (Winn and Newton, 1981).

Studies that show declines in activity usually show decrements in sexual interest as well, but the latter is much milder. For example, only 44% of seventy-one to seventy-five-year-olds in the Hegeler and Mortensen study (1977) were still sexually active, but 86% were still interested. The gap between interest and activity increases with age (Pfeiffer 1977b). Since the surplus of women gives ample opportunities for men, the gap probably indicates some kind of potency problem for many men. The next section will deal with the sexual problems of older individuals. Because of the nature of the differences between males and females, we will discuss mainly males with comments on females.

Sexual Difficulties

Sometimes lack of sexual activity is not a problem. Ours is a sex-obsessed society, and it is assumed that young people, especially males, are going to be extremely interested in sex. But people do not come out of factories built to uniform standards. Many people of both sexes welcome old age if only because it gives them an excuse to give up something they never were terribly interested in. Naturally this attitude causes difficulties if a spouse feels differently. But such people are not necessarily abnormal, and if there is no partner problem, then there is no reason why they should have to change.

It is also an error to impose inflated standards of the young on the elderly. It is no help to drop the stereotype of the sexless old, if "normality" demands that they must perform marathon feats of eroticism to feel adequate.

More common than either of these extremes is a gap between the desire and the capacity to perform. Since nothing in the normal aging process terminates sexual capacity, reasons must be sought elsewhere. What then are the causes of late-life impotency?

An active youth and "over-indulgence" in sex is *not* a cause. The idea that a man can burn himself out by too early and too much sex goes back generations. It is a myth and a dangerous one. Two factors correlate with sexual activity late in life—a high level of sexual activity and continuity throughout life (Masters and Johnson 1970; Newman and Nichols 1960; Pfeiffer 1978; Pfeiffer and Davis 1972; White 1982). Opinion is divided on whether these findings support the "use it or lose it" position or whether they mean that men with a stronger biological drive start sexual behavior earlier, practice more frequently, and continue longer than those with a weaker drive. Whichever is true, libido is a renewable, not a limited resource, and need not be hoarded.

Actual causes of impotency can be divided roughly into organic and psychological causes. There is no hard and fast line between these two. Men can retain potency against all reason and lose it for insufficient reason. One man of sixty-two, castrated and given female hormones in treatment for cancer, continued having intercourse 15 times a week (Ellis and Grayhack 1963). For others, a small, inconsequential problem may cause complete impotence.

For treatment purposes it is important to know if there is a physical problem contributing to impotence. This can be done by examining involuntary erections. During sleep, from infancy to death, people cycle through several phases. During REM (rapid eye movement) phases, usually associated with dreaming, both sexes show signs of sexual arousal. Men develop involuntary erections and frequently awake with one. If these are present and normal, then nothing physical is preventing erection. If they are absent or inadequate then some organic cause should be sought. Penile plethysmography which measures penile dimensions during the night, can give precise information about this problem (Karacan et al. 1977).

Much less attention has been paid to sexual dysfunction of women. However, Corby and Solnick (1980) suggest that a device developed by Heiman (1976) which assesses the vasocongestion of the vagina may be used for a similar purpose.

Organic Problems

Health Problems

The great majority of the elderly are not so crippled with infirmities that they are either incarcerated in rest homes or house bound. About 89% are healthy enough to function in the community. Nonetheless, older people have more chronic health problems, which may account for some of the sexual problems. Hermanova (1983) states that diabetes, hypertension, and heart disease cause about 30% of the sexual difficulties in men aged forty and over.

Heart and circulatory diseases are now the number one killers in the United States. When coronary disease appears, it has a great impact on sex life. Bloch, Maeder, and Haissly (1975) found that their 100 patients drastically reduced the frequency of sexual intercourse. While there may be a direct effect on sexual function (Bancroft 1983), the main cause is not so much a physical problem, but depression, and the fear of relapse and death.

In all but the most severe cases, these fears are not justified. Hellerstein and Friedman (1969) showed that marital relations as measured by heart-rate were no more strenuous than climbing stairs or walking briskly. Work experiences on a sedentary job increased heart rate more, and worst of all were arguments and other frustrating situations. Some heart patients showed symptoms during coitus, but after a course of planned and super-vised exercise, these symptoms disappeared in most patients. The same exercise program, incidentally, also increased the frequency and improved the quality of marital relations.

Sudden death associated with intercourse or masturbation (Malik 1979; Massie et al. 1969) is known to coroners' offices everywhere, but it is not conspicuously common. The one systematic study found death during or shortly after intercourse to occur in only 0.6% (34 out of 5559) cases of sudden death (Ueno 1963). Such deaths are almost certainly un-derreported, but even so sexual activity does not cause heart disease. It is only one of many, many environmental triggers that can set off a condition already present.

Because of frustration, depression, and other painful emotions resulting from abstinence, many physicians believe that forbidding sexual activity may actually do more harm than good in all but the most severe coronary cases. Naturally no physician would recommend the procedure of one hospitalized patient who managed to consummate marital relations within the very first week of his coronary (Hellerstein and Friedman 1969), but most patients with doctor's advice can probably resume sexual activity after a period of six to eight weeks.

Sensible precautions need to be taken. Intercourse should be avoided during stressful situations such as after quarreling, overeating, or over-exerting, or when the temperature is extreme. Having a telephone and a supply of nitroglycerin nearby may be wise. And perhaps patients should also keep the ideal of marital fidelity fixed firmly in their minds. The majority of cases of sudden death during intercourse (about 80%) occur in illicit situations, generally after overeating and drinking (Hellerstein and Friedman 1969; Rupp in Massie et al. 1969; Ueno 1963).

Sudden death during or after coitus have not been reported for women (Malik 1979), perhaps because heart disease is rare in women before menopause, and the incidence increases only slowly after that. By the time the risk is appreciable a woman has probably been a widow for some time. If a woman does have heart disease, the same precautions used for men should be taken whether or not she plays an active role in the sex act. Autonomic arousal is more important than physical activity and this can be high even when the woman is completely passive.

Diabetes can occur at any age, but its incidence increases steadily with age. It is also the commonest cause of impotency. About 50% of diabetic men will have some trouble with erection (Corby and Solnick 1980). The exact mechanism is not clear, but the damage appears to be neurological. Effects in women are not obvious. A lack of vaginal lubrication may be a problem (Weg 1978), but there is also negative evidence of this (Bancroft 1983). Libido is not affected in either sex.

The *prostate* is a large gland located between the bladder and the base of the penis. Its secretions are in part voided into the urine and in part contribute to semen. The gland tends to become enlarged in men past middle age. No one is quite sure why, although several tentative hypotheses have been suggested—such as a relationship to testosterone production, zinc deficiency, abstinence, or some combination of these. When enlargement does occur it constricts the neck of the bladder. This causes pain or difficulty in urinating. Severe cases can lead to serious bladder and kidney complications, and surgery may be required to correct the problem. Fortunately, although 20–50% of older men have enlarged prostates, only about 35% of those who do will require surgery.

Prostate surgery, like menopause, has a bad reputation. According to rumor, a prostate operation can mean the end of sexual life. Fortunately the surgery does not live up to its reputation. The primary way that such an operation could affect potency is by damaging the nerves that control erection. Four methods are used—transurethral resection, subrapubic prostatectomy, retropubic prostatectomy and perineal prostatectomy (Rowan 1985). The first three methods do not approach the critical nerves. The fourth one is likely to cause nerve damage, but it is only used in extreme conditions such as cancer. Even so, some still recover sexual function.

Rowan (1985) gives several "rules of thumb" on the sexual effect of prostate surgery. The net effect is rather small. The majority of patients remain either active or inactive just as they were before. A man whose sex life was already declining probably will not recover. A few will experience an improved sex life. Spengler (cited by Hermanova 1983) felt that the patient's reaction, not age, was the significant factor in determining whether sexual contacts were resumed.

There can be some complications such as bleeding or pain with intercourse. Most of these are temporary, but retrograde ejaculation is permanent and may be frightening if the patient is not expecting it. In this condition ejaculation is backwards into the bladder instead of forward out of the penis. Although this sounds strange, it is harmless and does not diminish the physical sensation of orgasm.

Colonic and rectal operations may also cause sexual difficulties. Aso and Yasutomi (1974) found that their Japanese patients, mostly in their sixties or seventies, usually did not resume sexual intercourse after such operations. With men, the reason for this seemed to be an impairment of ejaculation. Most of the women felt personal embarrassment with the artificial abdominal anus. Corby and Solnick (1980) in their review found little impairment for women, while for men, the amount of rectum removed was important, but even so only a certain percentage developed impotence.

While the above are the most common there are *other conditions* that affect sexual functioning. A reversible impotency may be the presenting symptom for hypothyroidism (Morley 1984). Priapism (a non-erotic and involuntary erection) of even a few hours duration may cause impotence which is difficult to reverse. It can be caused by sickle cell anemia, certain tumors, prostatic inflammations, and other problems. A high proportion of both male and female patients with chronic renal failure have sexual problems.

Even in cases where the cause of the impotence is organic, many physicians recommend sex therapy and counseling. If potency cannot be restored, Comfort (1980) recommends instruction in techniques that do not require a full erection. As a last choice, a penile prosthesis can be surgically inserted. Although space does not permit an evaluation, several types are available. A prospective patient should consider options carefully since each has its advantages and disadvantages. Most leave the man with a permanent erection; however, one inflatable type with an hydraulic system does not (Furlow 1977). While it has been used quite successfully, it does require more complicated and delicate surgery.

Overeating and fatigue

Even strenuous activity will not cause problems to a person accustomed to a certain level of activity. However, sedentary men who abruptly go on a binge of arduous recreation may find that aching muscles are not the only symptoms. Temporary loss of potency may result. Overeating can have the same effect. Except for psychological effects, these temporary problems are not particularly serious.

Drugs

Older people with chronic ailments frequently take multiple medications that may interact with each other unexpectedly. The elderly are particularly vulnerable to these effects. Even for a single type of drug, their sensitivity differs from that of younger people, and the elderly more often react paradoxically (Lamy and Kitler 1971). This applies both to therapeutic and recreational drugs such as alcohol. More data are available on drug-related impotency, but adverse affects on the libido of women are also common.

Alcohol is particularly notorious in causing sex problems. It is a central nervous system depressant which affects nervous control of erection. This may cause temporary impotence, which may be misinterpreted by the man. Subsequent failures reinforce psychogenic impotence. Several authors suggest psychogenic causes as the primary problem (e.g., Finkle 1976). However, alcoholism may cause irreversible impotency via damage to the nervous system (Lemere and Smith 1973). In addition, chronic heavy use impairs liver function so that the estrogens produced by the adrenal glands are not broken down. These in turn suppress the production of testosterone. This affects not only potency but fertility and in extreme cases can lead to feminization of the man (Rossman 1978). Effects on women are less studied, but it appears to delay orgasm (Hermanova 1983).

Nicotine also acts on potency via the nervous system, but in a different way than alcohol does. It causes the blood vessels to constrict. This includes those that must fill with blood to cause an erection. While not as powerfully affected as alcoholics, heavy chronic smokers may have some problems (Cendron and Vallery-Masson, cited by Rossman 1978).

Recreational use of drugs other than alcohol and tobacco probably is not high in older people. Therapeutic drugs are far more important in affecting potency. Comprehensive lists of drugs affecting potency are available elsewhere. Here only general classes likely to be important will be mentioned.

Older people usually sleep more lightly and for shorter periods than they did when they were younger. This is normal, but may cause the elderly to resort to *barbiturates* in the form of sleeping pills. Alcohol and barbiturates are related drugs and have roughly similar effects on potency.

Tranquilizers and *anti-depressants*, both major and minor, may affect both men and women, though exactly what happens differs from drug to drug.

Arteriosclerotic diseases which increase blood pressure are more common in older people. It is vital to control this increase, and *anti-hypertensive drugs* are usually prescribed to do this. Many of these drugs can have the side-effect of impotency or drop of libido in women. It is rarely necessary to put up with these side-effects. Often the physician can change the dosage, the drug used, or sometimes switch to a combination of drugs so that the sex life is not affected.

Some elderly couples are tempted to resort to *aphrodisiacs* if the husband has potency problems. There are only a few drugs that can affect the libido directly. Either placebo effects or indirect mechanisms are usually responsible for any positive results. Effective drugs are likely to be dangerous. Cantharides (Spanish fly) in very small doses acutely irritates the urogenital tract. In males this produces priapism (an uncontrollable and constant erection), and, if interpreted this way, an increased libido in females. It is a very dangerous toxin. Even moderate doses can result in agonizing death. Amyl nitrate, prescribed for angina pectoris, is sometimes used in a misguided attempt to enhance intercourse. It has been known to result in coronary occlusions (Steffl 1978).

Yohimbine has been used medically as an aphrodisiac. There is considerable doubt about its effectiveness, and it is a prescription drug that must be used under a physician's care. Two drugs, L-dopa and PCPA, which are used to treat Parkinson's disease and other motor disorders, have been reported to increase sexual behavior. Although most of the evidence comes from rats, some effects have been reported in human males (Goodwin 1971), but evidence is too slim for a definitive connection (Waltzman and Karasu 1979). In any case, these are powerful agents that act directly on the nervous system, and are not to be used lightly.

Psychogenic Factors

Monotony and an Aging Partner

In mice and rats the male who has become sexually satiated can be rejuvenated by presenting a novel female. In aging humans, more sexual problems seem to arise from active and long-standing enmity than from boredom (Berman and Lief 1976). Still, many middle-aged women in the Hite Report (Hite 1976) whose husbands had become unexciting over the years found orgasm and excitement in extramarital affairs. A man impotent in his marriage may be potent in an illicit affair—temporarily. Perhaps boredom is as much in the mind as in the environment. As the adventure of the new alliance wears off, rats, mice, and men return to their usual frequency, and impotency very often recurs.

The problems may be more than boredom. Griffitt (1981) showed that arousal in both sexes enhances the sexual attraction of physically attractive persons of the opposite sex, but diminishes that of physically unattractive people. Since our standards of beauty are strongly youth-oriented, aging partners may find each other less interesting and even distasteful. This effect will be stronger for men than women since the perceived sexual attractiveness of women is more closely tied to physical attractiveness than it is for men.

A variety of solutions can be suggested for increasing sexual interest. The details are beyond the scope of this chapter; however, some suggestions might be sensate focus techniques (Masters and Johnson 1970), training in fantasy (Solnick 1978), pornography (Benjamin 1963), or ideas drawn from books on sexual techniques (Weiner and Starr 1981).

Learned Patterns of Impotency

Masters and Johnson found a common pattern in the production of secondary impotency. The man has a temporary failure of erection. The failure might be due to any number of factors—fatigue or negative emotions such as anger, fear, or guilt. If the man correctly interprets the cause, then no particular harm ensues. If he thinks it is a personal failure that is likely to happen again, then he will approach his next opportunity with a certain anxiety, an anxiety that may produce the very thing he's worried about. With each unsuccessful attempt, his confidence drops and his certainty of failure increases until permanent impotency results.

Earlier, the stereotype of sexlessness that our society imposes on elderly people was discussed. At what age does the virile young man become the impotent old one? The myth sets no dates. The older man must figure it out for himself. What a younger man may shrug off, the older man interprets as the sign he's been waiting for—the beginning of the end.

The older man also has more things to misinterpret. There are genuine effects of aging on sexual physiology: the reduction in the amount of ejaculation, the sudden loss of erection after orgasm, the delay in erection after arousal, the longer refractory period. None of these cause impotency in and by themselves, but again, if the man doesn't know they can happen to him, he may see these changes as ominous.

Retirement and Loss of Status

Retirement poses special problems to elderly men. Not only does it mean a change in economic status, but men, particularly the older generations, often have their sense of self-worth and self-esteem tied to their jobs. In many species, less dominant males do not breed. While this is not necessarily true for humans, retirement occasionally may have a disastrous and unexpected effect on the sexual relationship. A significant minority (17%) in the Starr–Weiner Report indicated there had been a decrease in sexual activity after retirement.

Oddly enough women, even career women, do not seem to have a tie either between self-worth and job or between self-worth and sexuality. As a consequence, retirement does not seem to affect their sexuality. At present there is more emphasis on women's careers and more performance pressure on women in the area of sexuality. Whether this will eventually lead to similar retirement problems for women will have to be answered by the next generation of researchers.

Pfeiffer and Davis (1972) found that having some form of status was correlated with late-life sexuality, but it did not have to be of a particular kind. While a feeling of worth might come from a job, it could also be from community standing or even a valued place in the family. This suggests that alternate sources of status could and should be developed even before retirement.

Negative Emotions

Fear of physical harm occasionally plays a role. Clark and Anderson (1967) reported several men in their study were afraid of "physical depletion."

One even told stories about "old men who remarried only to die shortly afterward." This belief is compounded if the man has a physical problem such as a heart or prostate condition. If the man misinterprets the doctor's instructions or nothing has been explicitly said about sexual activity, then he may be afraid sex will harm him. Obviously a man is not going to perform well during intercourse if he believes he is likely to drop dead at any moment.

There is an increased amount of stress in the life of the older person because of inevitable loss (Berman and Lief 1976). There are losses of physical power or health, loss of role or status, losses due to death, relocation, or withdrawal of persons close to the individual. All of these produce stress and depression, which severely affect sexual behavior. Rossman (1978) points out that loss of libido is a classic symptom of depression.

The elderly are not only susceptible and sensitive to the societal stereotypes, but they were also raised in a time when sex was not spoken of. The impact of this is hard to imagine for those of us raised in more permissive times, but as Wasow and Loeb (1978, 161) remark in their survey of sexuality in nursing homes, "It really says something about our Victorian era when 80-year-olds are asking, 'Just what is a homosexual?' 'Do normal people masturbate?' " Ignorance and negative feelings about sex may also be a problem, not only in causing dysfunction, but also in preventing the elderly from seeking help.

Often multiple factors may be involved, as in Widower's Syndrome (Comfort 1980; Masters and Johnson 1981) which can occur after remarriage. The man is particularly vulnerable when his first wife had a long terminal illness during which he was abstinent. The break in his sex life combined with anxiety, stress, and possibly guilt causes the problem.

Although the incidence of impotence in older men is higher than in younger, they are not quick to seek treatment. In the Sexology Survey of a very affluent, well-educated group, only 8 out of 134 married impotent men had sought help (Rubin 1963). The proportion of men over fifty who come in with sex difficulties is rather small and dwindles further for men in their sixties and seventies (Hermanova 1983). Yet Masters and Johnson (1970) found the same techniques used for younger couples were useful with older ones, and the success rate is about the same.

It does appear that couples with the best chances for successful therapy are those with a good relationship, a past satisfying sexual relationship, and difficulties less than six to eight years old (Berman and Lief 1976). However, even the most long-standing cases are not absolutely hopeless (Hamilton 1939). Women particularly have reported experiencing orgasm for the first time in their seventies or even eighties. Havelock Ellis, the great sexologist, did not overcome life-long impotency until he was in his sixties (Calder-Marshall 1960).

Conclusions and Recommendations

In the beginning, the point was made that a stereotype of sex and the elderly exists in our society—one which says that older individuals are not and should not be interested in sex. While many remain interested and involved in the face of cultural expectations, others may be harmed by this stereotype. It may distort interpersonal relations in marriage and cause quarrels with children and relatives when an older person wishes to remarry. By causing people to cut off sexual behavior against their inclination we may be depriving them of a necessary source of reinforcement. People are born with a need for touch, physical contact, and expressions of love and affection that are never outgrown. As other sources of satisfaction such as job, community involvement, relatives, and friends are lost, sex may become even more important.

Sexual activity can prevent or ameliorate congestive prostatitis in men (Butler and Lewis 1976; Kent 1975). It increases the amount of cortisol, an adrenal cortical hormone which may have a beneficial effect on arthritis (Butler and Lewis 1976; Steffl 1984). By slowing the decline of estrogens in the woman, female sexual problems may be helped (Corby and Solnick 1980). It provides affirmation of self, a means of self-assertion, romance, and sensual growth (Butler and Lewis 1976).

"What do you expect at your age!" should not be the answer to the sexual difficulties of the elderly. Many problems are easily solved. If a drug is causing problems, their doctor can be asked for a change of prescription. If the woman has the greater desire, the man can ejaculate only every two or three experiences (Masters and Johnson 1970). Lubricants, topical creams, or estrogen can be used for painful intercourse caused by a dry vagina. A rubber doughnut from a sex shop or even a rubber band can be used to help maintain an erection (Steffl 1984). Noncoital methods of sexual satisfaction can be explored. Fantasy training and sex manuals can be used to dispel boredom.

Even if the problem is harder to solve, sex therapy can be effective for older couples as it is for younger. Clearly, anyone seeking help for sexual difficulties must be cautious. Far too many sex clinics have inadequately trained staff or are actually fraudulent. Nevertheless, older couples have the same right to seek treatment as they did when they were twenty, thirty, or any other age.

For women who have lost their partners, answers are not so easy. Often radical solutions are suggested—polygyny (Kassel 1966), group marriages and lesbian relationships (Cavan 1973), or younger partners (Sviland 1978). However, the elderly women of this generation are not radical. Snyder and Spreitzer (1976) found that age is the strongest predictor of intolerance for nontraditional sexual behavior. Only about 10% of the elderly asked to suggest solutions for the imbalance of men and women gave unusual ones like those above (Starr and Weiner 1981).

There are other problems. Polygyny assumes the elderly man is capable of servicing several women. Even with the aid of a penile prosthesis, this is a dubious proposition. Lesbian relationships assume humans can easily shift their sexual orientation. Perhaps it is possible. Weiner and Starr (1981) found an unusually high amount of homosexual experience among women (20% by age forty). However, this generation of elderly is unlikely to find the idea congenial.

For some individuals, a younger partner works. As a general solution, it would require an overhaul of societal stereotypes and conceptions. Whatever Women's Lib does to change the qualities that women are valued for, it will probably not be soon enough for the present generation of older women. While older individuals endorsed the idea enthusiastically, few of the elderly (less than 4%) spontaneously suggest this solution (Starr and Weiner 1981).

The one viable alternative, masturbation, causes discomfort among these generations. Even though the older persons themselves commonly suggest this as a possibility, they are most reluctant to admit that they themselves do such things (Starr and Weiner 1981). Aside from the old ideas of masturbation, the elderly may be sensitive to outside opinion. Staff and students of a facility for the aged rated stories which involved an elderly person masturbating more "disgusting" than such a person having coitus (La Torre and Kear 1977).

Perhaps the best that can be done at present is to make these older women comfortable with the idea of masturbation. To assure them that this is neither a childish, harmful, nor despicable practice. If they cannot accept or find other solutions, it may be the only practical alternative to painful abstinence.

The ultimate remedy is a society where individuals could choose abstinence or activity freely without having to feel they are abnormal or immoral. One that does not say that only the young are beautiful, valuable, and sexually attractive. There would be more nursing and old age homes that not only respect the privacy of their guests, but even provide opportunities for it. More nurses and doctors would be sympathetic and aware of the sexual needs and problems of their patients. Until that time those older individuals who are content with their sex life, or its absence, are well advised to continue on with what they are doing without guilt or anxiety.

IX

A DEMOGRAPHIC PERSPECTIVE ON AGING

Peter Uhlenberg

Each year a new group of individuals enters the phase of life labeled "old age." Using the most common marker of old age, these new entrants into the older population are all of those who celebrated their sixty-fifth birthdays that year. Who are these individuals entering the final stage of the life course? They are the survivors of all babies born sixty-five years earlier, and they are collectively referred to as a *birth cohort*. If our interest is in the older population of the United States, then the new entrants are the survivors of the U.S. birth cohort of sixty-five years ago who are still living in this country, plus surviving immigrants who were born somewhere else sixty-five years ago. In 1985 there were approximately 2.045 million people in the United States who entered old age.

The total older population of a country is composed of all survivors of the cohorts who have entered old age over the preceding forty years or so. Those who entered forty years ago are now age one hundred and five, those who entered twenty years ago are age eighty-five, and those who entered in the past year are age sixty-five. Obviously there is a wide range of ages and birth cohorts within the older population. To somewhat reduce this heterogeneity, it is sometimes useful to divide the older population into two categories, the *young-old* (aged sixty-five to seventy-four) and the *old-old* (aged seventy-five-plus). In 1985 there were 28.6 million older people in the United States—16.9 million were young-old and 11.7 million were old-old.

The older population of a country continuously changes in composition as new members enter the community by crossing the age threshold marking old age, while some previous members depart by dying. The rate at which the older population is changing is determined by the difference in the number and characteristics of newcomers compared to those who are dying. Throughout the history of the United States the annual number arriving at old age has exceeded the number of deaths of people over age sixty-five, so the size of the older population has grown constantly larger. In 1985 the number of people over age sixty-five who died was approximately 1.430 million, so the size of the older population increased by 615 thousand (2,045,000 – 1,430,000 = 615,000).

Not only did the new entrants into old age in 1985 exceed in quantity the number exiting, but also they differed from them in a number of important characteristics. Compared to the more senior members of the older population, the newcomers were born more recently and, hence, lived out the earlier portion of their life course under more modern conditions. Thus, the new members, on average, had more education, more urban experience, and different occupational histories than those who were dying. The significance of these and other changes occurring within the older population as a result of the process of cohort flow is discussed more fully later in this chapter. It is important at this point to recognize how the process of change in the older population occurs—those joining the older population (not necessarily by choice) differ from those exiting via death (also, not necessarily by choice). Approximately 60% of the older population in 1985 had entered old age within the last ten years. Clearly then, within one decade there is a substantial turnover in the individuals who comprise the older population.

Numbers and Proportions of Older Persons

The U.S. Bureau of the Census conducts a census of the population once each decade and conducts a number of sample surveys of the population each year. The basic data regarding the size, composition, and distribution of the older population come from these past censuses and surveys. The Census Bureau also makes projections of the population by age, sex, and race for years to come. These projections provide a basis for discussing what the older population of the future might look like. We start by examining the most basic demographic fact, the size of the older population.

Number and Growth

As already mentioned, the size of the older population has continuously grown larger, and it will continue to grow over the next one hundred years (barring some major catastrophe). Table 9.1 provides information on the number of old people in the population for the years 1900 through 2050. During the first eighty-five years of this century the number of older people increased almost ten-fold: from 3 million in 1900 to nearly 30 million in 1985. The rate of growth up to 1985 was steady and very rapid (the average annual rate of growth being 2.6%). Between 1985 and 2010 the size

TABLE 9.1. **Absolute and Relative Size of the U.S. Older Population: 1900–2050**

Year	Number over 65	Percent Old	Rate of Children to Old
	(in 1,000s)	(pop. aged 65+) × 100 tot. pop.	(pop. aged 0–17) × 100 pop. aged 65+
1900	3,099	4.1	10.4
1920	4,929	4.7	8.5
1940	9,031	6.9	4.8
1960	16,675	9.2	3.9
1980	25,714	11.3	2.5
1990	31,697	12.7	2.0
2000	34,921	13.0	1.9
2010	39,196	13.8	1.7
2030	64,580	21.2	1.0
2050	67,412	21.8	1.0

SOURCES: U.S. Bureau of the Census, Historical Statistics of the United States: Colonial Times to 1970; Current Population Report, serial p-25, No. 952.

of the older population is expected to grow by about 10 million, but the rate of growth will be much slower than in the past (averaging only 1.3% per year). Then a most remarkable surge of growth will occur for the next two decades. In the twenty years between 2010 and 2030 the older population will increase by 25 million. After the year 2030 the older population is expected to grow at a very slow pace (about 0.2% per year).

Why does the rate of growth vary so much in different time periods? Obviously, the amount of growth in a particular year is the difference between the number entering and the number leaving the population of older people. The size of a cohort entering old age is determined by three factors: the number born sixty-five years earlier, the proportion of those who were born who survived to age sixty-five, and the number of immigrants who joined this cohort over the past sixty-five years. On the other side, the number of deaths to people over age sixty-five is determined by the size of the older population and the death rate it experiences. A brief overview of how these various demographic processes have changed provides the answers to the question of why growth rates vary as they do over time.

First, death rates have declined continuously since 1835 (the year of birth of those reaching age sixty-five in 1900), so over this century an increasing proportion of all babies born in successive cohorts have survived to old age. Given the death rates existing around 1900, only 40 out of every 100 newborns would survive to age sixty-five. By the mid-1980s almost 80 of every 100 babies born are expected to reach old age. If the annual number of babies born in earlier years had been constant, the annual number of people reaching old age would be increasing as a result of this dramatic decline in mortality.

But the number of babies born each year has not been constant. Up until 1915 the annual number of births in the United States was increasing each year. After 1915 the size of birth cohorts stopped growing, and during the Depression years of the 1930s the number of babies being born actually declined. This period of low fertility was followed by the baby boom, lasting from 1945 until the early 1960s. Finally, after 1962 the annual number of births declined significantly and in recent years has leveled off. These past swings in fertility are reflected in the changing rates of growth of the older population that were described above. The rapid growth of the older population up until 1980 reflects the increasing size of birth cohorts up to 1915. The growth rate is slower from 1985 to 2010 as the smaller birth cohorts from 1920 through 1945 reach old age. Then a burgeoning of the older population occurs between 2010 and 2030 as the baby boom cohorts enter old age. Finally, after 2030 the growth rate subsides, reflecting the smaller cohorts born after 1965.

Until recently, the cohorts entering old age were significantly augmented in size by immigrants who had come to the United States as young adults some years earlier. Through the first half of this century one-fourth or more of the population reaching old age each year were foreign born. But the era of heavy immigration ended in the 1920s, so the addition of immigrants to cohorts born after about 1900 (the young adults of the 1920s) became much smaller. Currently more than 90% of those entering old age were born in the United States. Thus, while immigration played an important role in the past growth of the older population, it is not a major factor now nor will it be over the next fifty years.

As the number of people entering old age has increased, it is not surprising that the number of deaths of older people has also increased. The death rate at older ages, however, has declined and is continuing to decline. This means that a smaller *proportion* of those at any particular age are dying in that year. This declining rate of loss of older persons, combined with the growing number entering old age, has produced the observed changes in the size of the older population.

To appreciate how large the older population of the United States has become in absolute number, perhaps a couple of comparisons are useful. There are more people over age sixty-five living in the United States today than there were people of all ages in this country in 1850. Or, for what it is worth, the older population of the United States is roughly equivalent in size to the combined total populations of Norway, Sweden, Denmark, and the Netherlands. But, to keep things in perspective, the number of babies born in India in 1985 was also roughly equal to the total number of old people living in the United States.

Proportion Old

Not only has the size of the older population increased, but also it has increased more rapidly than the size of the non-old population. Consequently, there has been an "aging of the population"; that is, an increasing proportion of the total population is old. Two measures of age composition of the U.S. population shown in Table 9.1 indicate the magnitude of this change.

First, the proportion of the population over age sixty-five increased from 4% in 1900 to almost 12% by 1985, and it will continue to increase until it exceeds 21% by the year 2030 (assuming the middle-range projection by the Census Bureau accurately anticipates future demographic trends). The second measure is equally interesting; it answers the question of how many old people there are for every 100 children under age eighteen in the population. The population in 1900 was truly "young," as there were only 10 old people for every 100 children (grandparents were in short supply!). By 1985 the population reached a "mature" status, with 46 old for every 100 children. By 2030, when the number of old people actually exceeds the number of children, the population can surely be called "old" (and grandchildren will be in short supply). Clearly, such a dramatic shift in the age structure of the population requires major changes in societal institutions and in the allocation of resources. In contemporary society neither children nor old people are expected to be in the labor force and, hence, both groups are dependent on the working-age population for support. But the mechanisms for supporting these two dependent groups are different. Private families are expected to meet most of the economic needs of children; the government and various pension programs are expected to meet most of the economic needs of old people.

The most important cause of population aging is the declining rate of childbearing that has occurred since about 1800. In the early 1800s American women were, on average, bearing 8 or 10 children each. By 1900 the average had dropped to 3.6, and it is currently only 1.8. When fertility rates fall, the number of children in the population grows more slowly than the number of older people (who were born during the higher fertility era that existed earlier). Hence, the proportion of the population that is old, as well as the ratio of old people to young people, increases.

Changes in mortality rates also tend to affect the age structure, but to a much lesser extent than changes in fertility. If death rates at each age declined by a uniform amount, the age composition of the population would not change at all (each age group would be affected equally). What actually happens when mortality is declining is that different age groups in the population are affected differently. In the early stages of declining mortality, the largest reductions in death rates occur among infants and children. The effect of this change is to make a population somewhat younger than it otherwise would be. Once death rates for infants and children are reduced to very low levels, however, as they are in the United States now, any further significant mortality declines must occur at the older ages. When death rates are declining primarily among older people, the result is a further aging of the population, since there are more old people living than there would be if death rates had not declined.

Composition

If we are told only that an individual is old, we know that he or she has lived more than a certain number of years, for example, sixty-five. Beyond that we know essentially nothing about this person. The individual may be sixty-five or one hundred and five, male or female, black or white or Asian, educated or uneducated, healthy or sick, Republican or Democrat, Protestant or Catholic or Jew or Atheist, married or unmarried, and so on. The tremendous diversity existing within the older population suggests that age alone is a very poor predictor of what any particular older person is like. However, it is interesting and useful to know what the aggregate characteristics of the older population are and how they are changing. Indeed, an accurate statistical profile of the older population is an important starting place both for understanding common problems of old age and for designing programs to alleviate these problems.

The composition of the older population today differs remarkably from what it was in 1900, or even in 1950. Further, the older population of the future will differ in a variety of important ways from the current one. The significance of compositional changes in the older population is discussed later. In this section the goal is to describe accurately the most basic changes that are occurring. Data showing the composition of the older population at several different time periods are presented in tables 9.2 and 9.3.

Age

Not only has the population as a whole grown older over this century, but also the older population itself has aged. This means that the proportion of all old people who are in the old-old category has increased. Between 1930 and 1985 the proportion of the elderly who were over age seventy-five increased from 29 to 41%. The old-old category will continue its rapid growth through the remainder of this century, resulting in almost half of

TABLE 9.2. **Composition of the Older Population by Age, Sex, and Race: 1900–2030**

Characteristic	Year					
	1900	1930	1960	1985	2000	2030
Age: % 65+	100.0	100.0	100.0	100.0	100.0	100.0
65–74	71.0	71.2	66.3	58.9	50.6	53.5
75–85	25.1	24.7	28.1	31.7	35.3	33.2
85+	4.0	4.1	5.6	9.4	14.1	13.3
Sex Ratio: (males/females) × 100						
65+	102	101	82	67	65	72
85+	—	—	64	40	38	40
Race: % Total	100.0	100.0	100.0	100.0	100.0	100.0
White	91.1	94.1	92.4	90.1	89.1	84.5
Black	8.5	5.6	7.1	8.1	8.5	11.3
Other	0.4	0.3	0.5	1.8	2.3	4.1

SOURCE: Ibid.

TABLE 9.3. **Percent Distribution of the Older Population on Selected Socioeconomic Characteristics: 1900–2000**

Characteristic	Year				
	1900	1930	1960	1985	2000
Marital Status: Females					
single	6	8	9	6	5
married	35	35	37	39	36
widowed/divorced	59	57	54	55	59
Marital Status: Males					
single	6	8	8	5	5
married	71	64	71	79	76
widowed/divorced	24	28	21	16	19
Labor Force Participation Rate					
male	63	54	33	17	13
female	8	7	11	8	6
Educational Attainment					
less than high school	—	—	81	54	36
high school	—	—	19	46	64
Nativity Status					
foreign born	31	25	19	11	—
native born	69	75	81	89	—
Poverty Status	—	—	35	14	—

SOURCES: Ibid.; Current Population Report p-23, No. 138.

189

all older people being over age seventy-five by the year 2000. As the baby boom cohorts enter the young-old ages after 2010, there will be a temporary "younging" of the older population, but this reversal will not last for long. These same baby boom cohorts will subsequently enter old-old age, swelling the numbers in this category.

Two factors account for the rapid aging of the older population in the last half of this century. First, the successive cohorts entering old age are not much larger in size than those that preceded them by ten years. Hence, the number of young-old persons is not growing very rapidly (the number aged sixty-five to seventy-four in 2000 will be only 4.5% larger than it was in 1985). Second, the size of successive cohorts entering old-old age is continuing to increase and the average number of years lived by those entering old-old age is increasing as death rates among the very old decline. As a result, the number of persons aged seventy-five and older will be 47% larger in 2000 than in 1985.

Sex

The older the age group, the fewer males there are relative to females. At birth, males outnumber females by a ratio of 105 to 100 (a *sex ratio* of 105). But from birth onward the death rates for males exceed those for females, so that by age sixty-five females significantly outnumber males. Currently, the sex ratio for those aged sixty-five to sixty-nine is about 80 (i.e., 80 males for every 100 females). Among the eighty-five and over population the domination of females is quite striking as they outnumber males by 2.5 to 1.

The excess of females relative to males in old age has not always been the case. Up until 1930 the sex ratio of the older population was above 100. The old prior to 1930 were members of cohorts born before 1865, and they lived out the earlier portion of their life course under mortality conditions that were less advantageous for females. Among these earlier cohorts a significant number of females died in their young adult years due to complications of childbirth. Also, the immigrants, who comprised a larger proportion of the older population in the early part of this century, were more often males than females. For cohorts entering old age now and in the future, however, lower death rates for females at every age and the declining significance of male immigrants are combining to produce a large surplus of older females.

Race

The black population of the United States has a younger age distribution than the white population, primarily due to higher fertility among blacks. Thus, while 12% of the total population is black, only 8% of the older population is black. Over the next fifty years the older black and older "other non-white" populations will grow more rapidly than the older white population. The proportion of older persons who are white is expected to decline from 90% in 1985 to less than 85% by 2030. Aging for members of minority groups may differ significantly from that of whites. It has been suggested that blacks may face a double jeopardy as they grow old—the greater risks of disadvantage associated with their minority status in addition to the greater risks of loss more generally associated with old age. Given the continuing relatively disadvantaged position of younger blacks in American society, it appears likely that blacks in the future will continue to bring fewer economic resources with them into old age.

The discussion of the composition of the older population has so far focused on the biological variables of age, sex, and race. While each of these characteristics is defined in biological terms, each also takes on particular social significance because of the cultural meaning attached to it. The older population is also differentiated on the basis of a large number of other purely social and economic variables. The distribution of some of these characteristics within the older population is especially relevant for understanding the social meaning of old age at different points in time. To further elaborate the changing profile of the older population, attention is directed toward the following socioeconomic characteristics: marital status, labor force status, poverty status, and educational status.

Marital Status

It has been relatively uncommon for men and women in the United States who live out a full life course to never marry. Over this century the proportion never-married among older people has averaged 6% and has not fluctuated too widely from this figure at any time. The current marital status of an old person who is not a bachelor or spinster must be either "married," "widowed," or "divorced." Of course, an older person who is married may have been previously widowed or divorced and be in a second or third marriage; a widowed person may have been previously divorced, etc. The information on current marital status available from a census or survey simply gives us a cross-sectional picture of the situation at that particular point in time.

The proportion of older people who are in the category of "divorced" is now about 4%, and this is the highest it has ever been. There are two reasons why this marital status has been even more uncommon than never-married. First, the cohorts who entered old age prior to 1980 experienced much lower divorce rates than cohorts who are currently in the young adult years of life. For example, only 15% of those reaching age sixty-five in 1980 had ever divorced, compared to a projected 45% for those who will enter old age in 2020 (Cherlin 1981). Second, a majority of those who divorce do not remain in that status for long, but rather they remarry. Since cohorts that will enter old age in the future are experiencing higher divorce rates and since the rate of remarriage among divorced people has been declining since 1975, the proportion of older people classified as "divorced" will increase substantially in the future.

If few old people are either divorced or never-married, then most must be either married or widowed. The most interesting aspect of these marital statuses is the striking contrast between males and females. A majority of older men are married; a majority of older women are widowed. The combination of women outnumbering men in old age and of women experiencing higher rates of widowhood produce the situation where there are five times as many widows as widowers in the United States today. The much greater likelihood of men being married in old age is a consequence of different mortality rates (women on average living 7.5 years longer than men), differences in age at marriage (wives are on average a couple of years younger than their husbands), and differences in probability of remarriage after the death of a spouse (the remarriage rate is eight times higher for older men than older women).

Since a long period of widowhood at the end of life may be an unhappy prospect for most women, we might consider possible ways to avoid this situation. The traditional Hindu custom of *suttee*, where the widow flings herself upon her husband's funeral pyre, would solve the problem, but is unlikely to gain much popularity. The odds of a husband and wife dying at about the same time could be achieved by another means—have women marry men who are seven or eight years younger than themselves. But twenty-three-year-old women might object to selecting their husbands from the group of fifteen-year-old boys. There is still another option for reducing the large number of widows—polygyny. If older men were allowed and encouraged to have several wives each, the surplus of older unmarried women could be reduced (assuming, that is, that these women would agree to such an arrangement). If none of the above options is chosen, it might be most fruitful to focus attention on how to improve the quality of life for older widows who will be a large and growing proportion of our population in the years ahead.

Employment and Income

Only a minority of men and women continue to work after age sixty-five; in fact, most now opt for an early retirement (before sixty-five). Individuals entering old age in recent years have increasingly viewed retirement as a right they have earned. But this contemporary view of retirement as a normal life course transition is rather recent. In 1900, almost two-thirds of the men over age sixty-five were still in the labor force, and most of those who retired were physically unable to continue working. The introduction of the social security system in 1935 and the expansion of other pension programs, combined with discrimination against older workers in the labor force, have produced the situation where retirement before age seventy is nearly universal. In 1981, only 17% of the males over age sixty-five remained in the labor force, and less than half of these men were employed full-time. However, as the proportion of the population that is old increases and as the average number of years lived past sixty-five increases, the societal cost of supporting the retired elderly population will grow ever larger. It is likely that pressure to reverse recent trends and to move back the normal age for retirement may increase in coming years. A first step in this direction was taken in the 1983 changes of the social security system, which call for gradually increasing the age at which a retired person is eligible for full benefits to sixty-seven.

Upon retirement, the income that an individual directly receives for working at a job ceases. For most older people, replacement income (coming from social security, pensions, etc.) does not equal their preretirement income. One recent study found that upon retirement, median after-tax income falls to only 55% of what it was before retirement. Thus, most people find that retirement is accompanied by a decline in standard of living. Despite this drop in income generally experienced when entering old age, the economic position of the older population is much better now than it was in the past. When the concept of an official poverty index was first introduced by the Census Bureau in 1959, 35% of the population over age sixty-five had incomes below the poverty line. By 1977 the proportion in poverty had dropped to 14%, and it has remained at approximately this level in recent years.

It seems clear that cohorts entering old age in recent years have experienced much higher aggregate incomes than cohorts that preceded them. It cannot be concluded, however, that most old people now have a comfortable retirement income. A significant number of old people who are not officially in poverty are barely above the poverty line. In 1981, about 15% of the elderly were "poor," but another 10% had incomes that were less than 25% above poverty. Thus, one-fourth of the older population falls into the category of poor or near poor. Furthermore, certain segments of the older population are particularly disadvantaged. The poverty rate for older females is 80% higher than it is for males (18% versus 10%), and more than one-half of the elderly poor are nonmarried females. The poverty rate among elderly blacks is three times greater than it is for whites (34% versus 11%), and about a quarter (26%) of the older Hispanic population is poor. So, while the overall economic plight of the elderly has improved, it is premature to celebrate an end to poverty among older Americans.

Educational Attainment and Nativity Status

A brief note on two additional variables, years of school completed and country of birth, completes the discussion of the changing composition of the older population. Each cohort entering old age in the twentieth century has exceeded the preceding one in level of educational attainment. As recently as 1960 less than 20% of all older people had graduated from high school, reflecting the limited educational opportunities available to those who were children before World War I. By the year 2000 nearly two-thirds (64%) of the elderly will have completed four years of high school. Furthermore, the gap in educational attainment between the older population and the middle-aged population is rapidly being closed.

As already noted, a smaller proportion of each cohort entering old age over this century has been born outside the United States. In 1900, 31% of all older people were foreign born, by 1985 this had declined to 11%. In coming years foreign-born people will comprise an even smaller proportion of the older population. Given the change in countries of origin of migrants to the United States since World War II, the older foreign-born population will be increasingly Hispanic and Asian rather than European.

An overview of the composition of the older population during the twentieth century reveals some striking changes. The number of older Americans grows from 3 million in 1900 to 35 million in 2000, and the percentage of the population that is old increases from 4 to 13. Females and old-old persons comprise a growing proportion of the older population. Dramatic changes occur in retirement patterns, economic position, educational attainment, and nativity status. Before discussing further the significance of these major social and demographic changes, let us inquire into the distribution and living arrangements of the elderly.

Distribution and Living Arrangements

In addition to size and composition, a demographic perspective on aging also focuses on the geographic distribution and living arrangements of older people. The needs and quality of life experienced by older people are affected by their places of residence. Further, the pattern of distribution of older people across geographic areas has social, economic, and political implications for regions, states, and local areas. Three aspects of where people live are discussed in this section: urban versus rural residence, regional distribution and redistribution, and household composition.

Urban and Rural

Throughout this century the proportion of the American population living in urbanized areas has increased while the proportion in rural areas (places

TABLE 9.4. **Rural-Urban Distribution of the Older Population: 1920–1983**

	Percent Living in:			
Year	Urban	Rural Non-Farm	Rural	Total
1920	47	25	28	100
1960	70	22	8	100
1983	75	22	3	100

SOURCE: U.S. Censuses of Population, 1920 and 1960; Current Population Report, series p-27, No. 57.

with a population under 2,500) has declined. The older population has followed the same pattern as the rest of the population, as successive cohorts entering old age have been more urban than those which preceded them. In 1920, a majority of the elderly were still living in rural areas, and over one-fourth of them were on farms. By 1980, the older farm population had nearly disappeared (only 3% were living on farms), and three-fourths were living in urban areas (see Table 9.4). The rural-to-urban transformation of the older population has now been completed, as the percentage urban is no longer increasing. In the 1970s there were actually more older people moving from metropolitan to nonmetropolitan areas than vice versa.

The elderly living within metropolitan areas are not spread evenly across all residential areas. Rather, there is a substantial clustering of older people in what some call "gerontic enclaves." These enclaves are neighborhoods in which 20% or more of the residents are old, and they are generally located in the older sections of the central city. Typically, these "gray ghettos" slowly evolve as older persons stay in houses they own while their children grow up and move to suburban areas as they begin their own families. There are also older suburban areas developed after World War II that now contain a high percentage of older people who have aged in place. Correspondingly, the elderly are relatively underrepresented in the newer suburban areas that are predominantly attracting young families.

Through the early 1970s most research on the elderly was done in urban settings and most aging policy had an urban bias. More recently, however, a good deal of attention has been directed toward the quarter of the older population residing in rural areas, and new insight into their special needs and distinctive aging experience has been gained. Stereotypes of the idyllic life of old people on farms and in small towns are being destroyed by these research findings. Compared to their urban counterparts, the rural elderly tend more often to be poor, to live in more substandard housing, to exhibit more health problems, and to have less access to health care and other human services (Coward and Lee 1985). Interestingly, despite being disadvantaged on these objective measures of well-being, the rural elderly appear to be slightly more satisfied with their lives than the urban elderly. Do the diminished threat of crime and other advantages of rural environments compensate for the greater socioeconomic disadvantages? Perhaps the children's story of the city mouse and the country mouse captures the contrast pretty well: the country mouse loves the quiet of the country and finds the city a frightening place; the city mouse loves the excitement of the city and finds the country boring. It is likely that neither rural nor urban older people would find the quality of their lives improved by changing places with the other. (For a more detailed discussion of differences in rural and urban environments, see chapter 11 on community.)

Regional and State Variations

Florida, with over 17% of its population being over sixty-five, is the state with the highest concentration of older people. (While Florida's population is "old" by contemporary standards, it is provocative to remember that in the future over 21% of the total U.S. population will be over age sixty-five.) The popular notion that Florida attracts retirement-aged migrants is correct—more than one-fourth of all older interstate migrants are choosing Florida as their destination. The second most popular destination state, California, by comparison attracts only 9% of the older migrants. The other most popular states for those moving after retirement are also located in the Sun Belt—Arizona and Texas.

Climate, recreational opportunities, and other retirement amenities of the Sun Belt states clearly are attractions to many older people living in the Snow Belt states. The extent of retirement migration from the North to the South and West should not, however, be overemphasized. Of all age groups, the elderly are the *least* mobile. The rate of interstate migration for the old is less than half that of the non-old population. Because most old people age in place, those states that experience the higher rates of out-migration are generally the states with the oldest populations. Sustained out-migration of younger people from the Midwest (Iowa, Kansas, Missouri, Nebraska, South Dakota, and Arkansas) and the Northeast (Maine, Massachusetts, and Rhode Island) over the past couple of decades has left these areas with an above average proportion of old people. By contrast, the youngest states are those that have grown most from in-migration in recent years (Alaska, Hawaii, Utah, Wyoming, Colorado, Nevada, and New Mexico). It is interesting that the South and the West, the regions with the largest number of elderly in-migrants, are younger than the North and East, the regions of largest out-migration of older persons. The reason, again, is that an even larger proportion of younger adults is leaving the North and East for the South and West.

Does an influx of retirement-aged people have a positive or negative economic effect on an area? This is not a question with a simple answer. In the short run, the effect of attracting retired people seems to be advantageous for a community. The elderly who migrate tend to be above average in wealth and health, and have a variety of positive economic consequences for the place of destination: "They are not likely to compete for local jobs; they become consumers of retail, medical, and recreational service institutions; and they broaden the tax base" (Bryant and El-Attar 1984, 637). However, the long-term impact of older in-migrants may be quite different, as the number of the old-old, more dependent people increases. The provision of health and support services for an increasingly large dependent older population may create a financial strain on the community's budget.

Living Arrangements

The myth that most old people in the United States live in nursing homes or old folks' homes is widely believed. In fact, only 5% of the elderly are currently living in institutions; 95% are living in households. In discussions of the living arrangements of the old, nursing homes often receive a disproportionate share of attention. Perhaps this occurs because nursing homes have such a negative image and because billions of dollars of government money are spent to maintain them (primarily through Medicaid). It should also be noted that the proportion of old people who will live in a nursing home at some time before their death greatly exceeds the proportion who are living there at any point in time. About 25% of the older population eventually enters a nursing home.

For the 95% of the older population living in households, a common pattern has emerged in recent years. Married individuals generally live with their spouses in households containing no other members; unmarried individuals tend to live alone. The emergence of these two types of living arrangements over this century can be seen from the data in Table 9.5. In 1900, less than 30% of the older couples were living in private households—a majority (58%) had at least one child present. By 1975, 85% of the couples had neither a child nor any other person sharing their households. Similarly, among the unmarried, living alone moved from an uncommon arrangement (11%) in 1900 to the dominant pattern (66%) by 1975.

At present neither old people nor their children prefer or expect to share households with each other. In 1900, most of those approaching old age must have expected to live in a household with a child, but it is not obvious that this was the preferred arrangement. Lacking public opinion data for the early portion of this century, we cannot know how much change has occurred in attitudes regarding most desirable living arrangements in old age. But we do know that the possibility (and necessity) of achieving an

TABLE 9.5. **Living Arrangements of the Older Population by Marital Status, 1880, 1900, and 1975**

	Marital Status and Year					
Living Arrangement	Married			Unmarried		
	1880	1900	1975	1880	1900	1975
with spouse only	25	29	84	—	—	—
alone	—	—	—	9	11	66
with child	57	58	12	64	65	17
with other relative	10	7	4	12	13	13
with non-kin	7	6	2	15	11	3
Total	99	100	102	100	100	99

SOURCE: Daniel Scott Smith. 1981. Historical change in the household structure of the elderly in economically developed societies. In *Aging: Stability and change in the family*, edited by Robert W. Fogel et al. New York: Academic Press. Reprinted with permission.

independent household in old age has increased. The significant increases in income of the elderly have enabled a growing number to afford living separately from children or others. At the same time, the number of children potentially available to live with older persons has declined as the more recent cohorts entering old age have borne fewer children.

The recent growth of single-person households has occurred among all adult age groups, but the pattern in old age is distinctive. Of the nearly 8 million older people living alone, 80% are women. The sex differences in longevity and age at marriage combine to produce the situation where most women are widowed at the end of their lives, while most men are married at the time of their deaths. Thus, whatever problems may be associated with living alone in old age, it is primarily women who experience them.

Significant Issues Related to Demographic Change

The demographic perspective on aging developed thus far provides a description of the size, composition, distribution, and living arrangements of the older population and an explanation of how change occurs over time. This information is crucial to an understanding of old age in modern society. Further, the demographic perspective contributes to an understanding of why several particular issues related to aging are emerging as especially significant at this time. Three important issues related to demographic change are discussed in this section.

Defining "Old Age"

It is possible to define old age as beginning when an individual crosses an arbitrarily chosen age boundary, such as sixty-five. Indeed, this is the most common definition, and the one used for convenience in this chapter. Age sixty-five was selected as the official marker of old age by the Social Security Act of 1935, and has subsequently become enshrined in other legislation and in official statistics. Nevertheless, it is abundantly clear that chronological age is a very poor indicator of an individual's physical, mental, psychological, economic, or social condition. If by "old" we mean something other than number of years lived, then we need some new measure.

It is not only individual variations in the process of aging that limit the usefulness of a definition of "old age" based on chronological age. Cohorts arriving at sixty-five in different historical time periods have very different aggregate characteristics. As discussed above, a large proportion of those in more recent birth cohorts survive to age sixty-five, and the average number of remaining years of life after age sixty-five is increasing. Further, those arriving at age sixty-five now, compared to those aged sixty-five in 1935, are generally healthier, wealthier, and better educated. Thus, the old stereotypes that portray the elderly as feeble, poor, and mentally slow badly misrepresent the condition of the vast majority of people who are officially labeled "old." In a real sense, cohorts now approaching later life are modern pioneers who are redefining what the last stage of life is.

One alternative to defining old age as beginning after a person has lived a fixed number of years since birth is to establish some functional criteria based on capacity for work and ability for self-maintenance. Under this scheme, each person would be assessed individually to determine whether or not he or she was "old." Of course, exactly what functional criteria should define old age and how they could be measured present a challenging problem.

An alternative proposal is to define old age as beginning for a cohort when the average number of remaining years of life are ten or fifteen. This approach allows for the marker of old age to begin at increasingly higher ages as life expectancy increases. Using life tables for the U.S. population, this type of calculation is possible and has been done. If ten years of average remaining lifetime is used as the criterion, a person would have entered old age at 69.1 in 1930 and 75.9 in 1980. This approach could also be made sex specific, in which case males would enter old age at a much earlier chronological age than females (72.6 years versus 77.6 years in 1980).

Recent Changes in Well-Being of Young and Old

As noted above, two groups in the United States, children and old people, are excluded from participation in the productive labor force. These two groups, therefore, depend on mechanisms other than employment to provide them with resources necessary for the purchase of goods and services. Two major social arrangements exist for caring for dependent members of society—the family and the government. In the United States, the family has primary responsibility for supporting children, while government programs (social security, medicare, tax benefits, etc.) provide support for older people.

It is interesting to note how these two age groups, at opposite ends of the life course and dependent on different sources of support, have fared in recent years. Since 1970 the economic well-being of children has deteriorated, as indicated by the increasing number of children under age fourteen living in poverty. The proportion of children in poverty rose from 16% in 1970 to 23% in 1982. Over this same period, the elderly experienced impressive economic gains as the percentage in poverty fell from 24 to 15. The contrasting experience of children and older people is related to the different mechanisms used for their support.

Two changes in the family, the primary source of support for children, have caused an increasing number of children to experience economic hardship. One is the large increase in illegitimacy (from 5.3% in 1960 to 18.4% in 1980), which means that an increasing number of children enter single-parent families after birth. The other change is the dramatic increase in the proportion of children experiencing the divorce of their parents. Increasing divorce also leads to more children living in families without a father. Since poverty for children is closely associated with living in a female-headed household, poverty among children has been increasing.

These changes in the family behavior of young and middle-aged adults, which have so significantly affected children, have relatively little impact on the economic position of older people. The old are not seriously affected because little economic aid flows directly from adult children to their parents. Rather, economic aid is transferred from the working population to the older population via federal expenditures. Between 1960 and 1980 these federal expenditures on the elderly sharply increased, leaving the old better off at the later date. In addition, the economic position of the elderly has also improved due to increasing eligibility for work-related pensions among those who are retiring.

In light of the worsening fate of children and the improving fate of the old, why have government expenditures continued to favor the old? Part of the answer to this question is found in recent demographic changes. Continuing low fertility and increasing longevity have resulted in children comprising a smaller proportion of the population while the old are a larger proportion. Since federal expenditures are determined by a political process that is responsive to the relative power of competing groups, those groups with increasing size are likely to gain increasing benefits. As the younger population declines in relative size, there are fewer adults who have a direct concern for their welfare. In contrast, the growing size of the older population increases their political strength. Furthermore, the middle-aged adult population is motivated to support political programs favoring the old for two reasons. First, this is a way of improving the lives of their parents, and an increasing proportion of adults have parents who are still alive. Second, by improving the support programs for older people, the middle-aged are working in favor of programs that might improve their own welfare as they grow old in the future. Thus, we see how demographic change can affect the well-being of different age groups in different ways. For a more complete discussion of this argument, see Preston (1985).

Conflict Between Age Groups

Since the valued resources and roles in society are never distributed equally across all age groups, there is always a potential for conflict to erupt between cohorts at different stages of the life course. The potential and actual conflict between adolescents, who are excluded from significant economic and political roles, and their parents is discussed frequently. But the possibility of conflict between the old and middle-aged in society has not received much attention. Perhaps this type of conflict is seldom considered because, in fact, there has not been much conflict. But the absence of conflict in the past does not ensure a tranquil future. Reasons for expecting conflict to develop in the future are given below, but first we must ask why there has been so little age-based conflict up to the present.

Three things have limited the emergence of conflict between the old and the middle-aged. First, the older population has been a relatively small and politically weak segment of the total population. It was not until after 1970 that the sixty-five and over population amounted to as much as 10% of the total population. Further, its political effectiveness was limited by very low levels of education of the old relative to the young. Second, family ties between the old and their adult children have mitigated the potential conflict of interest that exists between the age groups. That is, mutual concern of adult children and their older parents for each other's welfare has worked against cleavages along age lines. Third, since all individuals will become old themselves if they live long enough, there may be a hesitation on the part of younger adults to behave in ways that will jeopardize their own future well-being.

Given such strong reasons for cooperation between age groups, why might the future see the emergence of conflict? Once again, the changing demographic structure of the population has significant social and economic implications. To see how different the future will be, we need only go forward to the year 2030, when the baby boom cohorts will occupy the older ages. Several very significant changes will occur between now and then:

1. The proportion of the population that is old will almost double. The middle range projection by the U.S. Bureau of the Census shows that 21% of all Americans will be over age sixty-five by the year 2030—an unprecedented situation. If mortality rates in old age continue to decline rapidly, as they have in recent years, the proportion old could be even higher and the length of the retirement stage of the life course could grow even longer.
2. The old in 2030 will be better prepared to engage in effective political activity. They will have much higher levels of education than the current old and will have lived their adult years in an urban, bureaucratically complex society. Through their adolescent and young adult years, these cohorts have observed and participated in groups organized to further their self-interest through political action.
3. Cohorts that will be old in 2030 are likely to expect a continuing or increasingly affluent life-style throughout their later years. The recent major increases in social security benefits, health insurance, and other benefits of old age form a minimum level of expectations for subsequent cohorts. Already expectations of a comfortable retirement are being institutionalized.
4. The relative size of the working population will decline sharply so that the ratio of workers to retirees will fall from its current level of 3.4:1 to 2:1. Thus, to maintain the same level of benefits, the working population would have to pay much higher taxes than currently exist.
5. The high rate of divorce characterizing current cohorts of young adults might imply a weakening of parent-child bonds when they reach old age. In particular, will adult children feel obligations toward fathers who left their families when they were young?

Of course no one knows what the future holds; any number of plausible scenarios might be proposed. But at a minimum, the combination of the changes noted above suggests that future conflicts between age groups is a possibility. The bases for conflict appear to be increasing while the mechanisms leading to cooperation are weakening. Because the old have become dependent on the government for their support, their future welfare will necessarily be a political issue.

Aging in International Perspective

Although the focus of this chapter has been on aging in the United States, the same process of successive cohorts moving through the life course is occurring in every country. The age structure of the U.S. population is similar (but not identical) to that found in Canada, Australia, New Zealand, Japan, and European countries. These countries, collectively referred to as the more developed countries (MDCs), all have relatively low birth

TABLE 9.6. **Absolute and Relative Size of the Older Population for Major Regions of the World, 1980–2025**

Area	Pop. Ages 65+ (in millions)			Percent of Pop. Ages 65+		
	1980	2000	2025	1980	2000	2025
World	259.4	402.9	760.6	5.8	6.6	9.3
More Developed	127.8	166.0	230.3	11.3	13.0	16.7
Less Developed	131.7	236.9	530.4	4.0	4.9	7.8
Europe	63.0	74.4	94.9	13.0	14.3	18.2
North America	26.2	3.1	54.8	10.6	11.1	15.9
East Asia	68.2	116.0	232.4	5.8	7.9	13.6
Southeast Asia	43.8	84.2	195.1	3.1	4.1	6.9
Latin America	15.5	7.9	61.9	4.3	4.9	7.2
Africa	14.3	27.3	65.9	3.0	3.2	4.3

SOURCE: United Nations population projections, as reported in George C. Myers. 1985. Aging and worldwide population change. In *Handbook of aging and the social sciences*, 2d ed., edited by Robert H. Binstock and Ethel Shanas, 181. New York: Van Nostrand Reinhold. Reprinted with permission.

rates, low death rates, and high standards of living. The proportion over age sixty-five in the collective population of MDCs in 1980 was 11.3%, almost identical to the proportion old in the United States. While MDCs have only one-fourth of the world's population, they contain approximately one-half of the world's older population (see Table 9.6).

Countries in Asia (except Japan), Africa, and Latin America, the less developed countries (LDCs) of the world, have populations that are young. Only 4% of the people living in LDCs are over age sixty-five. As discussed earlier in this chapter, the primary determinant of a population's age structure is its past fertility level. Thus, the relative scarcity of old people in LDCs is a direct consequence of their high fertility levels in recent years. The youngest populations of the world are found in Africa (45% children and only 3% old), the region with the highest fertility rates. The oldest populations are found in Western Europe (22% children and 13% old), the region with lowest fertility rates over the past several decades.

Since everyone who will be entering old age over the next sixty-five years is already born, we have a fairly good basis for projecting the future size of the older population around the world. All that is necessary is that we assume that no global disaster will occur (such as a nuclear war) and that mortality rates will continue to decline in a predictable way. Under these assumptions, the number of old people in MDCs will almost double between 1980 and 2025, while the number in LDCs will quadruple. The difference in absolute growth of older persons reflects the current, very large differences in number of children and young adults between MDCs and LDCs. Thus, we should expect that less than one-third of the world's older population will be living in MDCs by 2025.

Despite this shift toward more of the world's older population living in LDCs, the LDCs will continue to have much younger populations than the MDCs. Population projections to 2025 show that 17% of the MDC population will be over age sixty-five, compared to 8% of the LDC population. Because fertility declines are starting late in LDCs, the younger population of LDCs will continue to grow rapidly over the next several decades. Nevertheless, reproductive rates and population growth rates are declining throughout the world, with the consequence that populations everywhere are now growing older.

How scarce resources should be distributed across the various age groups of a population and what roles old people should play in society are almost certainly going to be of growing concern in countries in all regions of the world over the next fifty years. The changing demographic structure of the world's population forces our attention to these issues. How these questions are answered will have tremendous significance for the lives of the growing number of old people who will inhabit the planet Earth in coming years.

X

FAMILY LIFE

Philip Silverman

The family life of elderly people has been a major concern of social gerontology. There are several reasons for this. It has been argued that nothing is more important in shaping the behavior of individuals than their experiences within the family, and this is especially true for the elderly who typically have been less active participants in other institutional spheres (Strieb and Thompson 1960). Furthermore, there has been considerable concern over the presumed inadequacy of the American family in fulfilling the traditional responsibilities toward the elderly. As young people enjoy increasing opportunity to determine their own lives, obligations toward older parents are reduced and the solidarity engendered by kinship is weakened (Steere 1981). As a result, the present unhappy situation of old people can be attributed to the dominant preference for nuclear family living, which leads to growing isolation in a societal context that does not provide adequately for its aged members.

At least part of this argument is incompatible with recent historical research. A Golden Age in which the aged were active, valued members of an extended family was simply not typical during the preindustrial era in Western society (Laslett 1976). Most would agree, however, that the broad social changes wrought by modernization bring about serious problems for old people (Little 1983). Indeed, much of the literature in gerontology has focused on these problems and what conditions alleviate them, thus allowing the elderly to enjoy greater life satisfaction.

What evidence do we have that adult family members neglect, ignore, and even abuse their aged relatives? To answer this question, research on the family has been concerned with the frequency and nature of interaction between the aged and their family members. The assumption is clear if often unstated: this interaction is a crucial component in the psychological well-being of the elderly person (Morgan 1981). Whether or not that is the case is an empirical question difficult to answer, but one that cannot be ignored by a life course perspective.

205

Of the various theoretical approaches used in the study of family life, developmental theory reflects most closely the concerns of a life course perspective. Developmentalists view the family as a system in which individuals at different stages in the developmental cycle interact and mutually influence each other. As people mature, they are affected by differing sources of change. Biological development predominates early in life, whereas sociopsychological forces are more important during later stages. Because of these and other differences of perspective and need, each person has a distinct "developmental stake" in his or her relations with other family members. As a result, there is a dynamic of inevitable conflict (Kuypers and Bengston 1984).

Another element of the developmental approach sensitizes one to the fact that change in the role content of one position necessarily brings about modifications in the other family positions (Hill and Mattessich 1979). Thus, it is important to account for the continuities in relations among family members through the various stages of the family life cycle and also the changing nature of role content as differing age norms are imposed on various positions over time. To demonstrate the validity of these assumptions remains an ongoing task, one that can be best accomplished by longitudinal-type research.

Our review of the research in this area will focus on the American family, for which the literature is richest. We will look at the following areas of concern: family relations, postparental marriage, grandparenthood, retirement, widowhood and divorce, remarriage, and requiring a caretaker. We also bring in comparisons with other industrialized or industrializing countries in order to put the American experience in a broader context. The concluding section summarizes a controversy regarding Japanese family life.

Family Relations

Our discussion of family relations will concern itself with the frequency and nature of interaction among family members. We may view this interaction as a means of determining the extent to which social solidarity is characteristic of family life. Briefly, social solidarity has to do with how society holds together by creating and maintaining cohesive bonds among people. Although this concept has enormous significance in much sociological analysis, accurate measurement of it remains problematic. Its complexity does not yield easily to the available techniques, and as we shall see, this can lead to contradictory results.

According to Bengston, Olander, and Haddad (1976), social solidarity has three components: (1) associational solidarity—the patterns of interaction among family members or, more precisely, the frequency of interaction; (2) affectional solidarity—the nature and extent of positive senti-ment (or feeling) among people; and (3) consensus solidarity—the extent of similarity in personal and social values, opinions, and beliefs. We deal with each of these types in turn, beginning with associational solidarity because it has been the least problematic to measure, and as a result the available data are the richest.

Associational Solidarity

The area of family relations given the most attention by gerontologists has been the nature of contact between elderly people and their adult children. Despite the stereotype of extreme isolation and loneliness of the aged in our society, there is substantial evidence of contact between them and their offspring. An important, early study that supports this conclusion is Rosow (1967), who found that most elderly people have frequent contact with their children. That this may be a general pattern in industrial soci-eties is suggested by the cross-national survey conducted in Great Britain, Denmark, and the United States (Shanas et al. 1968). The authors found that despite evidence of contraction in "peripheral" social relationships, such as with occupational colleagues, there was little change in the number of "central," meaning family, relationships as one ages. A significant proportion of the elderly actually lived with one of their children—20% in Denmark, 28% in the United States, and a hefty 42% in Great Britain. In addition to those living intergenerationally, the remaining proportion often lived within thirty minutes' journey of one or more of their children. Those falling in this category include 40% in Great Britain, 49% in the United States, and 55% in Denmark. In all of these countries, approximate-ly two-thirds of the elderly reported seeing one of their children the same or the previous day, and another one-fifth in the previous week.

Although the percentage of elderly living with their adult children had declined somewhat, a subsequent national survey undertaken in 1975 in the United States essentially confirmed these earlier results (Shanas 1980). In the 1981 Harris poll, based on a carefully drawn national sample, only 12% of all elderly were living with their children, although blacks at 20% and Hispanics at 29% remained considerably higher (National Council on the Aging 1981). Even though intergenerational common residence is clear-ly not preferred in our contemporary society, the amount of contact is frequent while still allowing for independent living when feasible. Cohler (1983), among others, has referred to this arrangement as a modified extended family in which considerable exchange of resources occurs, a situation called in the literature "intimacy at a distance," (Rosenmayr and Koeckeis 1963).

With nearly 40% of older women and about 15% of older men living alone in 1981 (figures that reflect continuing increases over earlier U.S.

census readings), it would be Pollyannaish to conclude that isolation and loneliness are not problems for the elderly (or other people, for that matter). But to demonstrate the extent to which such a situation exists through careful research has been a difficult task. One reasonable estimate by Rosenmayr (1968) suggests that, taking into account European data as well, about 5% of the aged can be considered extremely isolated. More recently, the 1981 Harris poll in the United States found that 13% of people sixty-five or older experienced loneliness as a very serious problem (National Council on the Aging 1981).

Who is more likely to be involved with an aging parent, a son or a daughter? In looking at sex role distinctions, a number of researchers have found that the task of maintaining kinship ties belongs to women. In general, daughters are more likely to come to the support of their aging parents (Sussman 1976), and more specifically, one study of attitudes of filial responsibility among students found that youngest daughters were most likely to favor supporting their parents (Wake and Sporakowski 1972). Sons might offer financial and other material support, but it is more common for daughters to come forth to offer the more demanding and time-consuming custodial care or emotional support. Similar results have been found in British surveys (Bowling and Cartwright 1982).

Perhaps this gender difference can be attributed to the fact that the mother-daughter tie tends to be stronger than the mother-son tie in adulthood. Despite this sex-linked difference in parent-child relations, the role of women as the instigators of family contacts could undergo substantial change as they enter the workforce in greater numbers and in an increasing variety of professions. Related to this tendency for women to maintain family contacts, extended families tend to be linked along matrilateral lines. In other words, to the extent that one has contact with extended kin, they tend to be on the mother's side. But not all studies find this. For example, Albrecht (1962) found in a sample of 252 middle-class, extended families that there was no preference for sharing rituals with either side of the family.

Some studies provide data which more readily allow a life course perspective on intergenerational interaction. Troll (1971) has suggested that the physical proximity of children responds to varying tasks in the family life cycle. When parents are in middle age and their children are in the early stages of their own family development, the two generations may be in a period of maximum geographical distance. As the parents grow older they may move nearer to one of their children, or possibly the latter will attempt to move closer to the parents if work commitments make it feasible.

The direction of intergenerational contact also differs according to the particular stage in the family cycle. Aldous and Hill (1965) report that 70% of the young married adults in their sample saw their parents weekly, but only 10% saw their grandparents as often. Among the middle-aged cou-

A Five Generation American Family: The first photograph was taken in August 1966. Standing in the back is Minnie Lane Yearout, born April 28, 1882. Seated left to right are Virginia Gable, granddaughter of Minnie, born June 26, 1923; Nancy Grona, daughter of Virginia, born October 18, 1941; and Jewell McCauley, daughter of Minnie and mother of Virginia, born June 23, 1899. The children in front are the daughters of Nancy, Emily Davis, born June 12, 1964 and Kate Davis, born May 15, 1966.

The second photograph was taken in December, 1985. Standing in the rear from left to right are Kate and Emily. Seated are Virginia, Jewell, and Nancy. Minnie died in 1976, but the five generation family is maintained with the birth of Megan McAtee, daughter of Kate, on September 30, 1985. (Two photos from Jim Davis)

ples, of whom 70% saw their children weekly, only 40% were seeing their own parents as often. Thus, for middle-aged adults the heaviest interaction is with the descendent generation where the strongest commitment can be found.

We now turn to a consideration of contacts among the siblings of elderly people. Given recent trends in American family life, the importance of siblings can be expected to have greater significance. For it is quite clear from demographic studies that there is a trend toward fewer couples having children and fewer children for those who do. Presently, 20% of all noninstitutionalized aged do not have living children. Given the low fertility of cohorts born after World War II, the proportion without children can be expected to increase after the turn of the century (Cherlin 1983). Thus, it may be a critical issue in the future to know the nature of the contacts that older people have with kin other than children. For the most part, there is little research in this area. Yet siblings and others can often play a critical role in the life of the elderly, especially if one has never married or has no children (Shanas et al. 1968).

In the cross-national study mentioned earlier (Shanas et al. 1968), questions were also asked regarding contacts with siblings. Although in all three countries fewer than 5% of the elderly lived with their siblings, contact with them remained reasonably common. Thus, one-third reported seeing a sibling in the previous week; significantly, this proportion increased substantially among those who had no children or who had children but saw them infrequently.

The intensity of the sibling relationship over the family life cycle tends to fluctuate in accordion-like fashion. One is normally close—perhaps painfully so—to siblings while growing up, then there tends to be an attrition of contacts with most kinsmen while establishing a family of procreation and raising children. But once the children are launched, it is possible to become more closely involved with siblings again in the later years. The strongest link between siblings is the sister-sister one, followed by sister-brother, with the weakest being brother-brother (Cumming and Schneider 1961). The gender differences in sibling relations can be explained by the fact that sisters are more likely to share household tasks and not be such a burden to one another. On the other hand, males are less inclined to carry out such tasks, so brothers can expect little support from one another. Men tend to seek out a female relative or a spouse to provide them with the household services to which they have become accustomed. It would be hazardous to expect this service luxury to continue indefinitely in the future.

Affectional and Consensus Solidarity

The second kind of solidarity to be considered is affectional, which has to do with the nature and extent of positive sentiment among family members. In the kind of survey research typically undertaken by sociologists, the measure of affectional solidarity considered most useful is helping behavior. Based on such studies, Bengston, Olander and Haddad (1976) conclude that affectional bonds between the aged and their children are strong. Just who gets how much of different kinds of supportive help is necessarily complicated. The type of help varies according to different classes and during different stages in the family life cycle. Overall, however, the help given to adult children by their aging parents is probably greater than the other way around. In fact, Streib (1965) found in his sample of 291 families with parents in their sixties and adult children, that parents gave financial help to their children far more often than they were the recipients of such help. In the 1981 Harris poll only 5% of elderly received financial help from their children (National Council on Aging 1981). Be that as it may, it is possible to document considerable reciprocity in helping behavior, although this is necessarily influenced by residential propinquity and the dependency needs of those involved (Cantor 1975).

Consensus solidarity—that is, the similarity in values, opinions, and beliefs—has received the least attention of the three. The limited results do indicate that, to the extent family members of different generations were born in this country and share educational, occupational, and peer group experiences, not surprisingly there is greater consensus solidarity (Bengston et al. 1976). However, the extent of this solidarity may vary greatly across cultures. A German study found much greater consensus between generations in the U.S. families than in the European ones. The West Germans in particular proved to have an especially large gap between the generations. These differences covered a variety of content areas, including moral, religious, political, and sexual matters (Noelle-Neumann 1984). The greater trauma experienced by European society during World War II may explain in part this striking generational discrepancy in values.

A study by Nydegger and Mitteness (1979) is marginally related to this kind of solidarity, but is especially relevant for its life course implications. They interviewed 250 fathers between the ages of forty-five and eighty and found a number of patterned changes in parenting behavior as their children grew older. Such functions as showing authority, teaching, and providing are dropped by the father as his children move toward middle age. Only one function invariably remains—that of friendship; although for some men counseling and companionship also remain viable. By the time the children reach middle age, there is also a convergence in the roles played by mother and father. What emerges is a transformation from status inequality to one of friendship between peers. How widespread is this pattern? That remains unclear, for the Nydegger and Mitteness sample was limited to men with above-average education and economic well-being.

Regarding all three types of solidarity Bengston and colleagues conclude that they are all strongly intercorrelated and sufficiently common in this society to falsify the popular belief in a "generation gap." But the literature is far from unequivocal on this matter. It is not at all clear that frequency of contact is associated with positive affect. For example, Troll and Smith (1976) have found family bonds are characterized more by obligation than by common interests, and thus may be maintained despite the presence of negative affect.

It is one thing to have some notion of the frequency of interaction, but quite another to be able to specify the quality of that interaction, as is implied by affectional and consensus solidarity. Some time ago Rosow (1967) lamented the absence of data that would allow some specification of the emotional bond between parent and child over various stages of the family career cycle. A similar concern was expressed by Rosenmayr (1968). The situation has not changed substantially since these complaints were registered.

To the extent we do have studies based on qualitative approaches, the accounts of family life in our society tend to describe a setting far from congenial to older people. For example, Simiĉ (1982) argues, based on the work of Bronfenbrenner, that both the family and society have failed to provide mechanisms and institutions for the integration of families intergenerationally. On the contrary, American values lead away from such integration, with the emphasis on independence, self-determination, and individuality, rather than toward a familial corporate entity characterized by strong emotional bonds among all family members. Where there is a dominant value of strong family orientation typical of European agrarian society, and even some modern, industrializing societies like Yugoslavia, Simiĉ found evidence of intense reciprocity between young and old, with clearly defined age and sex roles available throughout the life cycle. Part of this includes the duty to care for parents in old age, regardless of what is available through the state. These characteristics are consistent with Halperin's discussion of the preindustrial family in chapter 13. By contrast, the aged in our society contribute to their loneliness and exclusion by normally expressing support for the very values that lead to their own alienation—"I like to be on my own," or "I don't want to be a burden to the kids. They have their own life to lead," and so on. Although persuasively argued, Simiĉ presents little systematic data in support of his characterization of American family life.

Thus, there appear to be different views regarding the integration of the aged in the family life of industrial societies, and they seem to be based on different kinds of data. Those who are looking at various levels of interaction based on survey data find evidence of a lot more contacts with the elderly than was previously supposed. But those who are looking at the nature of the relationship between generations by employing more qualitative methods typically find the elderly in our society at a severe disadvantage. Insofar as the more holistic approach uncovers the subtleties of

basic values and the emotional tone behind social relationships, the usefulness of qualitative research is obvious. But, we still have few systematic
studies of a qualitative type, so that an accurate assessment of the emotional bonds between the aged and their family members still remains a critical
research goal.

Postparental Marriage

Given the preference for nuclear family households in our society, practically all elderly people who are married live in separate households. In
1981, 77% of the men and only 33% of the women sixty-five or older were
married and living with spouse (U.S. Bureau of the Census 1984). Because
of several demographic trends, the nature of postparental marriage is
becoming increasingly important in the family life cycle. The increase in life
expectancy during the twentieth century has had an impact on family life
in a number of ways. Most important for marriage has been the number of
years that a couple may live together after all children have left home, a
transition that is increasingly occurring at an earlier age. Porcino (1983)
reports that presently the last child leaves home when the mother is, on
the average, only forty-seven years old. That means almost half of her life
is still in front of her, and if she is married, she can expect some twenty or
thirty years remaining with her spouse. Clearly, this is historically an
unprecedented situation involving both obvious opportunities but also
potentially painful consequences.

How does marital satisfaction vary through the family life cycle? Prior to
1960, most studies showed a continual decline in marital satisfaction
through the life cycle, but since then researchers are more likely to find a
curvilinear pattern. It is high during the blissful, preparental years, then a
progressive disenchantment is reported through the child-rearing period,
but eventually greater satisfaction reemerges in the postparental years
(Cole 1984). Some have suggested that this later life increase in satisfaction
may be nothing more than having made a "devitalized" or "passive-
congenial" adjustment to a long marriage (Cuber and Harroff 1963). Along
similar lines, Spanier, Lewis, and Coles (1975) have argued, employing
cognitive consistency theory, that older people may see themselves as
happier in their marriages than younger cohorts because of the considerable investment they have made in the marriage. Not to value the time and
energy one has put into the relationship would imply a terrible waste of
resources, a situation that may be too painful for most to admit.

But there may be a simpler solution to this problem. Most of the studies
we now have are based on cross-sectional data. It could be that the changes
found are not due to fluctuations in the marital satisfaction for any given
couple over time, but are instead a result of the changing composition of

the married cohort in the later years. By the time people have reached their fifties, the least satisfying marriages have ended in divorce. Thus, those who have remained married represent the most satisfying unions of the earlier period. Campbell (1981), however, doubts this explanation, but lacks any longitudinal data to support his argument. Instead, he is inclined to attribute the increased satisfaction to the improved life circumstances, which occasion less stress, and the moderation of expectations, which evolves as couples move through the life cycle. Similarly, in a study of seventy-six older couples in the San Francisco area, Colleen Johnson characterized the responses to open-ended questions on marital satisfaction in the following way:

> . . . the criteria for a successful marriage in old age is neither a romantic relationship nor one laden with positive or negative emotions. Instead, there is a muted quality in these responses, where the fact of the marriage's mere survival connotes success. The many years of shared experiences, of hardships as well as successes, are usually viewed as a source of cohesion (Johnson 1985a, 171).

In general, older people have higher morale if married rather than single, and this seems especially true of men. Lee (1978) found that men prefer the marital bond regardless of the level of satisfaction they derive from it. On the other hand, the morale of women is more significantly tied to marital satisfaction. For the husbands, health and career satisfaction were much more important to their morale. Be that as it may, there are conditions under which marital status ceases to have an impact on morale. For example, the lower the income of a person, the more likely are such attitudes as dissatisfaction with life, unhappiness, feelings of loneliness, and worry—and this held regardless of marital status (Hutchinson 1975). Poverty has a way of brutally simplifying the problem; it overpowers all other relationships.

There is little evidence of an "empty nest" crisis overwhelming parents as their children are launched into the world. Although this requires a shift of focus from the children to each other, usually followed before too long by the need to incorporate retiring husbands into the daily routine of the household, this transition appears to be made without any abrupt changes (Troll 1971). Using survey data based on probability sampling of all Americans over eighteen, Campbell (1981) claims that parents at most may express some nostalgia for the days when children were still around, but there is no indication of any sadness associated with this. He finds this postparental period to be the time of greatest harmony and tranquility in the marriage. Why this overwhelmingly positive evaluation of marriage after the launching of children into the world? At least part of the answer is suggested by Deutscher (1964) who found 79% of the women in his sample considered the postparental phase better than earlier ones because there is greater freedom from responsibility and more opportunity to express one's personality.

A number of unanswered questions remain regarding this phase of the life cycle. Are the inconsistent findings related to the problem of varied and inadequate measures of marital satisfaction (Ade-Ridder and Brubaker 1983)? How are marital adjustment and the subsequent relationship with adult children affected by the age at which this postparental phase begins? To phrase it more generally, we know little about the relationship between age and the onset of various critical events in the family life cycle. Of possibly greater consequence, but even less well understood, is the impact of various sequences in the unfolding of these events.

Several researchers have even delineated stages of the family life cycle during the postparental years (Thompson and Strieb 1961; Feldman 1964). This might be overformalizing what is in reality a more fluid structure, but it does call attention to some of the most significant of these events, such as grandparenthood, retirement, widowhood, the possibility of remarriage, and finally the need for a caretaker. We now turn to an examination of these issues.

Grandparenthood

There is not a great deal of literature on grandparenting, perhaps because it only recently became a role that a significant number of people will attain. The notion of grandmother as a sweet, white-haired, old lady who enjoys pressing her grandchildren to her bosom while showering them with wet, unappreciated kisses and stuffing them with delicious cookies is for the most part an anachronism. Instead, it is more likely today that grandparenthood will be first experienced when one is still in middle age. Johnson (1983a) reports that at the birth of the first grandchild, the median age of women is forty-five. In other words, a relationship with a grandchild may last for over thirty years, and may commence at a point in the life cycle when women are involved in much more than baking cookies.

Some researchers have attempted to define different "styles" of grandparenting as one way to characterize what goes on when relating to a grandchild. There exists a cultural stereotype of the ideal grandparent which is best expressed by the French term *"parents de plaisanterie."* This refers to a style of grandparenting that involves closeness and informality, a style described as fun-seeking. Johnson (1983a) refers to the Auntie Mame image—playful, intermittently helpful, but with few obligations— as the role most contemporary grandmothers prefer. But this kind of relationship occurs only under specific and relatively rare circumstances. In their study of seventy sets of grandparents in Chicago, Neugarten and

Weinstein (1964) found five style types: fun-seekers (informal and playful); distant figures (those who are formal with rare contact); surrogate parents (providing upbringing, especially by grandmothers); reservoirs of family wisdom; and finally, formal relationships (similar to distant figure type, but with more frequent contact). The first two are most typical of younger grandparents, and the last of older ones. Those who play roles of surrogate parents or of reservoirs of wisdom are extremely rare. Finally, this study found little enjoyment in grandparenting; in fact, a third of the sample described the role as uncomfortable, disappointing, or unrewarding.

Although there are studies that conclude the relationship has many positive aspects, in general researchers find little evidence of closeness between grandparents and grandchildren (Cumming and Henry 1961). Nor do grandchildren look for role models or material support from grandparents, even though positive attitudes toward them are expressed. Robertson (1976) concluded this from her study of eighty-six blue-collar young adults who mainly expected some form of emotional gratification from the grandparents. In a study of grandparents' attitudes, Wood and Robertson (1978) found that although respondents claimed their grandchildren were very significant to them, interaction with friends was more predictive of high morale than interaction rates with grandchildren. In fact, frequency of contact with grandchildren is unrelated to grandparent morale (Kivnick 1984). This is also true for the relationship between adult children and their parents. Clearly, the impact that family relationships have for morale has little to do with the amount of contact.

What complicates the grandparent-grandchild relationship is the mediation of the parental generation which largely determines what the acceptable roles are in the relationship, and most important, how often there will be an opportunity to perform such roles (Robertson 1976). Based on a study of older widows, Lopata (1973) concludes that a satisfactory relationship between grandparent and grandchild is precluded if there is tension in the relationship with the parental generation. Another study attempting to deal with these issues (Nydegger 1981b) provides data on a sample of 260 middle-class men interviewed on their parenting experiences across their life cycle. She found that the age at which men begin their families has consequences which ripple throughout their lives. Men who become fathers later rather than earlier in life have much better relations with their children lasting into old age. Earlier fathers are likely to be too busy attempting to move up their career ladders to pay much attention to their children. A result of this poor relationship may be that they are not encouraged by their children to be involved grandfathers later in life. Research along these lines can provide the data base necessary for theoretical development of the life course perspective.

The fact is that grandparents see much less of their grandchildren than in earlier periods because of the increased mobility in modern society. This is also the conclusion of Kornhaber and Woodward (1981) who interviewed some six hundred grandparents and grandchildren (whom they have dubbed "grandorphans"). Some of their more striking findings are that only 5% of grandparents live with their grandchildren and only another 10% are within walking distance. Some 45% live more than one hundred miles away, and the majority of these are more than one thousand miles away. Despite the enormous importance Kornhaber and Woodward find in the link between grandparents and grandchildren for both, and the fact that a close relationship can reduce some of the alienation and antagonism increasingly more common in American family life, they found only 5% in their sample had close ties. Of the few grandparents who did have close relations with their grandchildren, it is interesting to note that they tended to be people who were highly sensitive to the feelings of others, very active people who related well to all ages and accepted new trends even though they might cherish a number of traditional values.

A further complication in performing the grandparent role is the high rate of divorce now characteristic of our society. With one out of every two first marriages ending in divorce, the grandparents whose child does not obtain custody could find access to their grandchildren completely blocked. Recently, distressed grandparents have had success in some states in obtaining legal visitation rights, and in one state, Michigan, a self-help group called "Grandparents Anonymous" has emerged to press for their rights (Porcino 1983). We will return to the problems of divorce and the elderly shortly.

Matthews and Sprey (1984) help us to summarize the results of a number of grandparent studies. Based on their interviews with thirty-seven grandparent couples, they conclude three factors must be considered basic to an understanding of the grandparent role: the marital status of the middle generation; the age differentials between grandparents, parents, and grandchildren; and geographic proximity. In her sample of fifty-nine white, middle-class grandmothers, Johnson (1985b) found that age (based on dichotomizing the sample between those younger and older than sixty-five) was by far the most important predictor of the grandparents' behavior. An additional complexity is the possibility of having multiple grandchildren, each one representing a distinct dyad. To assume a generalized grandparental role for a person who has more than one grandchild ignores the many differences that could exist between each of the dyads. Unfortunately, most studies have not accounted for this important factor (Kivnick 1984).

A relatively new phenomenon in family life is the startling increase in the number of four-generation families. Almost one-half of all people sixty-five or older who have living offspring are members of a four-generation family. And three-fourths of everyone eighty or older are great-grandparents (Shanas 1980). The role great-grandparents play in such families is especially ill-defined, a prime example of the roleless role, a characteristic considered typical of the status of old age in our society because of the absence of explicit socializing mechanisms (Burgess 1960; Rosow 1974). Often their children—i.e., the grandparents—find themselves in the role of caretaker for the elderly and frail parents. This situation can coincide with expectations of reduced family responsibilities as their own children have been launched and they are looking forward to retirement. Alternatively, they may still find themselves in a position of costly exchanges with their children as the latter attempt to establish their own families of procreation. Facing obligations simultaneously to both adult children and elderly parents has been referred to as the "generation crunch" or "life-cycle squeeze" (Oppenheimer 1981).

Retirement

Retirement has suffered from a terrible reputation among many of the most influential writers in the field. In her wide-ranging book on aging, the remarkable French intellectual, Simone de Beauvoir, provided a grim view of retirement: cursed with boredom, alienated from leisure time, men face a gloomy idleness which endangers their physical and intellectual balance (de Beauvoir 1973). Earlier writing in gerontology was hardly more encouraging. In a well-known survey of the field a generation ago, Burgess (1960) described the retired couple as imprisoned in a roleless role which could only negatively affect marriage because of the loss of status.

To what extent is this vision an accurate assessment? Here we cannot explore all its implications, but instead confine ourselves to looking at retirement in terms of how it affects family life. Despite the common assumption that work is a critical component in one's identity, there is very little evidence that retirement per se is linked to unhappiness, unless there is a financial need. But even lowered income need not affect the satisfaction that men derive from retirement (Campbell 1981; Shanas 1970). Based on data from national samples taken periodically over the past fifteen years, Campbell (1981) confirms that men have no regrets about retirement. Two out of three men report they were glad to retire when they did, and of the others, the majority wish they had retired earlier. Compared to men who are still working, in most cases younger men of course, the retired report less strain in their lives. Indeed, according to Campbell, there is a quality of serenity and unprecedented contentment in the lives of retired men.

Shanas (1970), working with a national probability sample of noninstitutionalized persons sixty-five or older, found that there was little evidence of the popular image regarding forced retirement. Most men who retired did so voluntarily. Only one-third of all retired men claimed they stopped work because they reached the compulsory retirement age or because their jobs were eliminated. Of her sample, 30% did claim they enjoyed nothing about their retirement, but these were typically men whose health problems limited their capacity to carry on a normal life.

How families adjust to retirement is related, of course, to the nature of the conjugal relationship that already exists. In a study of women whose husbands were fifty years or older, Fengler (1975) found that the wives' retirement orientation could be classified into three types: pessimists, optimists, and neutralists, with approximately a third falling into each category. The pessimists were concerned about what their husbands would do with so much spare time and feared their domestic sphere would be intruded upon. The optimists viewed retirement as the possibility of an exciting new life together. What is interesting in this study is the difference in the kin networks between optimists and pessimists in Fengler's study. Optimists were much less connected with their kin, visited their children much less frequently, and shared more of their leisure time interests with their spouses. Pessimists, on the other hand, enjoyed a much closer kin network, had less need for communication and sharing of recreational activities with their spouse. As Bott (1971) found in a classic study of kin networks, the more a married couple is encapsulated into a broader kin network, the less likely it is that there is a sense of closeness and sharing of a lot of activities with one's spouse.

What impact does retirement have on the marital relationship? A thoughtful study by Dressler (1973) provides some insights, although his sample is small (thirty-eight white couples ranging in age from sixty-one to over eighty) and includes only people from working-class backgrounds. These couples report little change in their relationship compared to pre-retirement, that is, when they were age fifty. Although over half found the transition a difficult one, this condition improved several months into the retirement period. Couples were interviewed jointly on a wide range of topics concerning their marital relationship, and in almost all areas the respondents reported high degrees of satisfaction. Only half the couples were willing to respond to questions on sexual relations, but those who did rated satisfaction with this lower than other areas of their relationship. The for-the-most-part positive view of marital relations conveyed by the respondents is somewhat dampened by the assessment made independently by the interviewers who sensed more marital conflict and tension than the couples reported. This exposes the difficulty of interpreting the results of a single interview encounter on highly sensitive topics.

Another survey of 1,560 persons over fifty from a small Ohio township provides some longitudinal data over a limited number of years (Atchley and Miller 1983). Respondents were interviewed on three occasions during the 1970s, but only 1,106 out of 1,560 responded to the initial survey, a sample loss of 29%, and by the third round, only 678 responded. Although large sample loss makes any interpretations highly speculative, the authors find retirement has neither a positive nor a negative effect on marital satisfaction for healthy, middle-class couples. This is consistent with other, more elaborate longitudinal studies where retirement had little or no effect on physical health, social activities, and attitudes of the retirees (Palmore et al. 1985). On the other hand, Atchley and Miller conclude that marriage does influence when one retires. Nonmarried men retire earlier because they are in poorer health and have less economic need to work longer compared to married men, the vast majority of whom retire at sixty-five. Conversely, nonmarried women are more likely to work beyond their sixty-fifth birthday because of economic need, while their married counterparts retire earlier than sixty-five in order to join their typically older husbands.

Cole (1984) reports that during the retirement years more satisfying adjustments are made in partner-centered marriages—that is, where the primary emphasis in the family is on the conjugal dyad as opposed to child-centered marriages where the emphasis is on the parent-child dyad. Partner-centered marriages enjoy more effective communication between spouses and are more likely to resolve conflicts in a manner that builds self-other esteem. Communication in general, however, does not appear to increase appreciably between spouses during the retirement stage despite the increased opportunities for contact (Keating and Cole 1980).

Until more longitudinal studies are available, it is difficult to determine how retirement affects the marital relationship over a number of years. As the life span gradually increases, longer periods of retirement living are necessarily to be expected. Heyman and Jeffers (1968) provide some indication of what the consequences of this extended retirement period might be. They found that the longer a couple lived in retirement, the higher the proportion of wives who regretted their husbands had stopped working. This points out the need to view retirement not simply as a status, but rather as involving potentially complex dynamics through the later years.

Widowhood and Divorce

Insofar as a marriage does not end in separation or divorce, then it is of course inevitable that one of the spouses will experience widowhood. Two factors create an enormous imbalance in the sex ratio of the widowed: the cultural tendency for men to marry younger women, a tendency that grows stronger the older the male is at the time of marriage, and the demographic reality of the greater longevity of women. Consequently, widowhood is overwhelmingly the experience of females. There are five widows to every widower in the United States; in total numbers, there were two million widowers and ten million widows in 1975 (Lopata 1979).

On the average, a woman can expect ten years of widowhood; for those women who reach seventy-five, over two-thirds are widowed.

The trauma of widowhood for women is now well-documented. Studies report on their severe loneliness, greater unhappiness compared to those who are married, increased death rate immediately following the death of a spouse, and their proneness to suicide (Burgess 1960; Parkes, Benjamin, and Fitzgerald 1969; Maddison and Viola 1968; Hyman 1983). An estimated 40% live on or below the poverty level (Porcino 1983). Because of their drop in status and life-style following their husband's death, they begin to idealize him as a means of maintaining some semblance of self-esteem. If a woman has been socialized to accept traditional sex role values, she may refrain from social activities without a male escort, thus further limiting any opportunities she might have of replacing her lost partner. Lopata (1979) found that even if widows do make an attempt to reconstruct their social life, they frequently feel like a fifth wheel in a world dominated by couples. If social contacts do exist with peer couples, widows find themselves the objects of fear and jealousy by married women because of the sexual interest exhibited by their husbands. Given the perceived availability of a widow, men are often blunt about or poorly disguise their sexual advances. These and other factors contrive to bring about a painful degree of isolation.

Once the initial shock is over, a period that can last anywhere from three months to two years (Silverman 1967), widows begin to recover from the trauma. This is especially true of those who are older (i.e., in their sixties rather than middle age) and have good health and a decent income (Clark and Anderson 1967). Some even report a more active social life once liberated from a controlling husband or the need to care for him during a period of severe illness prior to death. In another study of both widows and widowers (Bornstein et al. 1973) 109 subjects were interviewed one month after they had lost a spouse, and 35% were diagnosed as depressed. When they were reinterviewed twelve months later, 12 of the original 38 and 4 of the original nondepressed were now rated as depressed, a total of 17%. The authors note that the depressed subjects had fewer supportive children and less adequate financial and religious support. An interesting characteristic of the nondepressed was the greater likelihood that they had experienced a previous bereavement. It could well be that the experience of once having expended emotional energy in dealing with a loss aids one in confronting subsequent episodes of a similar nature.

Be that as it may, a sense of loneliness and other negative affects can persist beyond the initial trauma of loss. In fact, generally, the widowed have a significantly higher index on "negative feelings" than married people do, regardless of age and income levels (Harvey and Bahr 1974). In her study of 1,169 widows in Chicago, Lopata (1978) found that children were the only kin offering economic, service, or emotional support of any kind, and relatively little of that. She attributes the problems faced by widows to the isolated nuclear family existing with minimal support of extended kin and the restricted role allowed wives because of being bound to the household (Lopata 1979). As a result, they never develop the social skills necessary to reconstruct their social network or discover the available community resources they require once widowed. The more educated a woman is, according to Lopata, the more likely it is that she has the skills to develop friendships and commitments to voluntary associations which can be supportive during the period of adjustment.

If widows do live with their adult children, it tends to be with a no-longer- or never-married child (Lopata 1979). But, in fact, most widows live alone. The low percentage of widowed people living with their adult children can be partly attributed to a variety of difficulties it can create in our society. It normally means the widow must relocate to her child's residence, away from her own home and familiar contacts. As the guest in another's home, it is not always possible to carry on the life-style and daily routine to which one has become accustomed. And finally, conflict is likely to emerge with the spouse of a child, especially if this person is a daughter-in-law and she resents her husband's relationship with his mother (Lopata 1971).

How important is contact with family to the morale of the widowed? It is still not clear, despite the results obtained by Bornstein and colleagues (1973) mentioned above. It could be that income security is a much more powerful predictor of morale than levels of social interaction (Harvey and Bahr 1974). Often alternative institutions provide adequate surrogates to families. For example, Petrowsky (1976) found that widowed persons in Florida seem to use religious organizations as substitutes for lack of family involvement. And in a study of widows ranging in age from sixty-five to eighty-five, Arling (1976) concluded that friends were more important to morale than family. Some form of social support is surely critical for grieving widows, and there is increasing evidence that if this support is not available in the initial months of the bereavement process, there can be long-term negative consequences (Bankoff 1984).

Some researchers have argued that the negative impact of widowhood is much greater on men. Widowers share with widows most of the same characteristics that tend to be inimical to one's well-being. But in addition, they are frequently incapable of self-maintenance and their rates of physical illness, alcoholism, accidents, dissatisfaction with family life, mental breakdown, and suicide are much higher than both widows and married men (Lopata 1979; Hyman 1983). Despite these findings, there is disagreement regarding this difference in gender response to widowhood (Troll, Miller, and Atchley 1979). The national survey data analyzed by Campbell (1981) indicate that widows have higher scores on the negative affect scale than widowers. It seems to depend in part on precisely which factors one wishes to emphasize. Given the nature of a marriage market characterized by more women and greater acceptability of marriage to younger women, widowers are much more likely to remarry than widows (Cleveland and Gianturco 1976), or to live alone (Chevan and Korson 1972). On the other hand, it is generally thought true that widows are more likely to live with their children or relatives, although Treas (1975) insists that there is no difference between widows and widowers in this respect based on the 1970 census data. In fact, she found less than 5% of all households include a parent or parent-in-law of the household head.

Before considering remarriage in later life, we must examine briefly how the other means of breaking the marital bond, that is divorce and separation, affects the aged. With the explosion of the divorce rate among young and middle-aged couples in this country during the 1960s and 1970s, one can safely predict that many more divorced people will enter old age in the future (see Uhlenberg's data on divorce in chapter 9). Although the aged cohort still has the lowest divorce rate, nevertheless between 1960 to 1983 the rate more than doubled, from 32 to 70 per 1,000 married persons (U.S. Bureau of the Census 1983). In fact, Cherlin (1983) estimates that by the year 2000 one-fourth of those reaching old age will have experienced divorce.

Hyman (1983) has recently provided a cogent analysis of the differential impact of marriage, widowhood, and divorce or separation on the elderly. His data base is a national sample from surveys conducted annually by the National Opinion Research Center between 1972 and 1978. Most of his results are consistent with other studies on widowhood, although he finds the impact less negative than generally found. But most significant is the negative effect of divorce or separation compared to those who are married or widowed, and this is especially true of older men even though they do not suffer as severe financial losses as older women. With respect to such attitudinal measures as life satisfaction, misanthropy (anger directed at others), and anomia (meaninglessness and unpredictability of life), the divorced or separated show the most negative outlook, but this is less consistently true among elderly women. Similarly, various measures of social involvement—such as frequency of informal social interaction, membership in voluntary associations, church attendance, and use of mass media—show little difference between the married and the widowed, but considerably less involvement among the divorced or separated. Again the women in the latter group show greater variability. The conclusion is clear: divorce is hard on older people, especially men.

If we recall that older men have far greater opportunities for remarriage, one could infer that the divorced or separated might represent the least desirable partners because of personal characteristics not exclusively a consequence of their broken marriage, and indeed perhaps even contributing to its end. What is still needed is research that clearly specifies the impact of divorce at various stages in the family life cycle. It is still not clear how one who enters old age after being divorced for a number of years compares with those who divorce after passing sixty. Also, in comparing the widowed with the divorced, it is important to control for the number of years a person has been in the particular status.

With few exceptions, such as Johnson (1983a; 1985b), we know little about how the aged are affected by their adult children divorcing. Earlier we discussed some of the problems that grandparents have simply in terms of access to their grandchildren once such divorces occur. In addition, both financial and emotional support may be expected by the divorcing children, especially if a daughter is involved. On the other hand, Cherlin (1983) has suggested that divorce and remarriage could potentially expand the number of kin available to the elderly and thus have a positive effect. But there is too little research on reconstituted families to support this assertion.

Remarriage

Assuming that they desire such, what is the likelihood that older people can find a spouse? We have already indicated the great advantage elderly men have in the marriage market, so women's chances for marriage in later years are severely reduced. Uhlenberg reports in chapter 9 that men over sixty-five are eight times more likely to remarry than women over sixty-five. In examining the marriage certificates for 1970 in most states of the union, Treas and VanHilst (1976) found that of all marriages involving a spouse sixty-five or older, 20% of the grooms married someone younger than fifty-five, but this is true of only 3% of the brides. They also found that the divorced are more likely to remarry than the widowed—which is surprising, given the far greater negative impact of divorce reported in the Hyman (1983) study we discussed in the previous section. Overall, the least likely to wed in old age are those who have never married at all during their younger years.

Besides the demographic imbalance and double standard involved in marriage to younger people, a number of other factors can hinder the likelihood of remarriage for women. These include financial restraints, opposition of adult children, cultural notions of what is acceptable behavior for older people especially with regard to sexual expression, and reduced opportunities for meeting people socially, to name a few. These factors can also inhibit older men, but the impact of these constraints on them is much less severe. Treas and VanHilst (1976) also suggest that some ethnic and religious subcultures can affect the incidence of later life remarriage. This is a possible explanation for the differences found regionally in the remarriage rates; it tends to be much lower in the Northeast and North

Central states as compared with the South and the West. If a prospective spouse is found in later life, it is noteworthy that there seems to be no lesser value placed on the symbolic significance of the wedding ceremony.

What is the likelihood that later life marriages can succeed? There is still little research in this area, but we can report on one interesting study (McKain 1972) of one hundred couples married for at least five years at the time of the interview and where the husband was at least sixty-five at the time of marriage. McKain found that marital success was related to such factors as having an adequate income (that ever-present variable), being well-acquainted before the marriage (often including the period of previous marriages), enjoying the approval of friends and relatives (especially of children), having good health, and not living in a home that had belonged to either partner before the marriage.

For those who neither seek nor find an opportunity for remarriage, but nevertheless prefer some form of intimacy, the possibilities are severely limited by the cultural constraints older people impose on themselves in our society. Obviously, there is the possibility of nonmarital liaisons or cohabitation, but as we saw in the chapter on sexuality, many will reject this alternative. Nevertheless, Gebhard (1970) reports that 40% of divorcees and 25% of widows admit to postmarital sexual relations. Cavan (1973) argues that a number of alternatives other than remarriage could work for the elderly if they would accept a broader range of normative behavior; she suggests such alternatives as polygyny, group marriage, nonmarital cohabitation, communal living, and homosexual companionship. But there is little empirical support as yet for the acceptance of such "neogamous" alternatives to marriage among older people (Klemmack and Roff 1980). Yet it would be a delightful irony if the variety of experimentation with new social forms associated with the youth of the sixties would find its most useful expression among the elderly of our society.

Caretaking of Elders and Their Abuse

As the number and proportion of old people increases, particularly in the age cohort over eighty-five, more families will have to face the prospect of providing for the needs of an elderly relative in physical or mental decline (the problems of the oldest old are covered in detail in chapter 15). Either from a sense of obligation or the unavailability of a known alternative, many of these infirm aged are maintained by their families, most frequently by a spouse but also by, and in the home of, a child. It has been estimated that approximately 20% of the noninstitutionalized aged require some degree of caretaking on the part of other family members. Even in Great Britain, despite its comprehensive health care system, the bulk of care in the year before death is provided by relatives, especially by the daughters (Bowling and Cartwright 1982). In a study of 167 post-hospitalized elderly people in the San Francisco area, Johnson (1983b) found that the most comprehensive care, involving the least stress and ambivalence on the part of the caregiver, was provided by a spouse. Nevertheless, those in the sample who were unmarried and childless were the most likely to have built up the social and psychological resources to deal effectively with increasing dependence on others for care (Johnson and Catalano 1981).

Caring for a frail, incontinent, disoriented person unable to perform even the most prosaic daily routines can be a demanding task. One study found that two-fifths of those children caring for an aged parent carried out what was the equivalent of a full time job of custodial care (Treas 1977). And this is occurring at a time when, increasingly, both husband and wife are working outside the home. As in Great Britain, daughters in our society take primary responsibility for such care, and even in those cases where the son is the primary caregiver, his wife contributes equally to the effort. The consequences of this household situation have been painfully clear: a home in which an unmarried older person is cared for by younger family members is most vulnerable to disruption (Soldo and Myllyluoma 1983).

Several factors exacerbate the tensions created by providing this kind of daily care. To the extent that children do so mainly out of a sense of duty, and where there is no history of emotionally warm and reciprocal relations with parents, the effort is neither supported by any feelings of affection nor done willingly. If most of the care falls on the shoulders of one person, and there is little sharing of the burden by other family members either in or beyond the household, the caretaker will come to deeply resent the situation. Some have argued that the most important factor explaining a caring attitude and positive treatment of the elderly is the existence of a family support system, a factor we will encounter in other contexts as well. Without a wider support system, a caretaking family is vulnerable to a variety of pressures. If the amount and kind of care suddenly changes instead of increasing gradually, and this causes a major disruption in the organization of the household, the consequences can be disastrous for all concerned. Finally, regardless of the presence or absence of the above factors, any household wracked by poverty, substance abuse, or marital problems can push one into "granny bashing," as the British have come to call it.

The nature of abuse inflicted on the elderly varies greatly. Several types have been discussed in the literature: (1) physical abuse—where the elder is beaten, physically restrained and locked up, and even sexually (and thus incestuously) assaulted; (2) negligent abuse—whereby proper food and necessary medicine and supervision are denied; (3) exploitative abuse—which involves the theft of personal property and money, frequently the monthly social security check; and (4) psychological abuse—which ranges from verbal threats and intimidation to extreme social ostracism. It is this last type that is the most prevalent and is even considered by some to be the most devastating to the victim.

The elderly who find themselves in this kind of horrifying situation are among the most vulnerable and least visible people in our society. Despite the difficulties in demonstrating trends over time for these crimes, many researchers insist that there has been an alarming rise in the incidence of such abuse in recent years, and this has attracted the attention of the mass media, which occasionally report on the shocking details of particular incidents. According to estimates presented to congressional committees concerned with the aged, the number of cases of abusive behavior toward the elderly ranges from 600,000 to 1 million (Eastman 1984). Other estimates have ranged up to 2.5 million reported cases of abuse per year, involving one out of every ten older persons living with their families. Despite considerable consistency among the various studies available, the nature of the abuse problem has resisted the accumulation of accurate data on incidence, prevalence, and the groups at high risk (Douglass and Hickey 1983).

Whichever figure is closest to the truth, there is little disagreement that this is but the tip of the iceberg, for most cases of this kind of abuse go unreported. Since these elderly rarely leave home, they remain like prisoners with little or no contact with individuals able to intervene. In addition, the victims themselves are often unwilling or fearful to report their children to the authorities. For some, the perceived alternative might seem even worse, such as being carted off to a nursing home.

Who are the typical victims of this battering by family members? Although there are cases across the age, sex, social class, and ethnic spectrum of our society, usually it is a female who is over eighty and extremely vulnerable because of physical and mental impairment, and whose most common response to victimization is denial (Franklin Research Center 1980). The abuser, who is usually female, was probably abused herself as a child and might very well be abusing her own children at the same time. This sketchy profile of the abuser, however, is not supported by a study of 328 abuse cases in three northeastern states (Wolf, Godkin, and Pillemer 1984). Here the most likely abuser was a male, and there was little evidence of the victim having once abused his or her children.

Although no federal legislation exists on mandatory reporting of elder abuse, about one-fourth of the states have passed laws requiring professionals to report known cases under penalty of a fine. Communities are only beginning to provide support and services for families caring for infirm elderly, thus it is not known yet the extent to which this could relieve some of the pressure that leads to abusive treatment. There is little doubt, however, that a number of conditions can conspire to make the family one of the least desirable alternatives for the care of its frail elderly.

Comparison with Japan

Since most of the material covered in this chapter deals with the United States, it is important to recognize the dangers inherent in this relatively narrow perspective. The problem is, of course, that the findings obtained in any one society may be peculiar to its experience and thus it is inappropriate to generalize beyond it. We have made occasional references to European societies, but there is a considerable sharing of experience between ourselves and the industrialized countries of Western Europe. As a result there are many similarities in the situation of the aged. However, Japan is an industrialized society in which the nature of family life, among other aspects of culture, appears to be quite different. We may thus look to this country as a test case for some of the generalizations we have examined so far in this chapter.

Japan is a fascinating society for a variety of reasons. First of all, they became the first non-Western country to make a successful breakthrough into the realm of the advanced industrial societies. Because of the astonishing skill of the Japanese in competing economically with other industrial powers, their success has been received with a mixture of awe, envy, and even resentment by the rest of the world. While this economic miracle rapidly rebuilt Japan under the watchful gaze of outsiders, another change was also restructuring Japanese society, but received far less notice. That involved an unprecedented increase in the longevity of the Japanese people occurring since World War II (Plath 1980). Starting fairly far back in the pack, Japan has caught up with and now even exceeds the life expectancy rates of the United States, and as you read this they may well have reached the plateau of the countries in northern Europe. In fact, as of 1978, Japan had even exceeded the Scandinavian countries in the life expectancy for men with just under 73 years at birth and 14.63 at age 65 (Myers and Manton 1984). This veritable longevity explosion cannot help but create dislocations with some negative impact on the situation of the aged just as it did in other industrial countries.

Second, the Japanese have achieved the transition to an industrial power, a process that actually began in earnest during the last third of the nineteenth century, while maintaining much of their cultural distinctiveness. This is not surprising in and of itself, but for those who were examining the modernizing process in the West, what the Japanese retained from their traditional culture seemed inconsistent with or inappropriate for facilitating the growth of a modern society. Thus, when viewed technologically or from the structure of their national institutions, Japan is clearly an advanced industrial democracy. But when viewed in terms of their values, or from various psychological perspectives, or from the nature of their family life, the Japanese have characteristics unlike those of other peoples who have undergone the same transition. It is this distinctiveness that may well be crucial for their elderly people.

Palmore (1975) has provided perhaps the most important yet controversial account of the Japanese aged. He identifies three "social-psychological traits" which have impact on the role and treatment of the elderly. First, the Japanese have a great deal of national pride and are very sensitive to any kind of criticism. This has a number of consequences. Old people are motivated to continue working and make themselves useful to their family and community. Also, many consider it a matter of national honor to improve the situation of the elderly.

Second, the Japanese are greatly concerned with displays of politeness and deference toward superiors. This is related to their vertically organized society and the requirement to respect those above one in this hierarchy. In a classic study of Japanese national character Benedict (1946) pointed out the overriding importance of the system of obligation which, among other things, required unlimited duty to parents. That obligation continues even after death, for ancestor worship is a major element of their religious life. Thus, filial piety is a dominant motif of Japanese family relationships.

And third, aesthetic sensitivity is an important part of the Japanese temperament. Interestingly, many of the skills most admired for their aesthetic appeal—such as calligraphy, bonsai gardens, folk dancing, etc.— tend to be pursued by the elderly as hobbies. Thus, their activities are highly valued by younger people in the society. One would search in vain for an equivalent phenomenon in the United States. The cultivation of artistic hobbies does not exhaust the involvements of the elderly since a very large proportion continue to work after reaching retirement age. Compared to France (8%), Great Britain (9%), and the United States (18%), in 1980 some 41% of those sixty-five or older in Japan were still in the workforce.

There are also crucial tasks for grandparents to perform within the Japanese family. As both husband and wife typically work outside the household, especially in rural areas, the older generation is responsible for many of the household chores. They perform caretaker duties, supervise the children, and since co-sleeping is preferred in Japanese families (Caudill and Plath 1974), each grandparent normally sleeps with one of the children rather than with a spouse or alone. Finally, the aged have important religious functions to perform in the household, and are advisors in family matters, although in recent times this advice tends to be limited to traditional matters.

The foregoing should make clear that many Japanese live in what is called joint households, three-generation extended families living together. And in this respect they clearly differ considerably from other industrial societies. Compared to the United States, where in the 1980s somewhere between 10 and 15% of those sixty-five or older live with their adult children, in Japan that proportion was 75% in 1973. Even in Tokyo, the most modern and Western-influenced city, more than two-thirds live with their children. The large number of elderly living alone, typical of other industrial societies, is hardly present in Japan where 83% of those aged who are single live in joint households. When there is joint living in the United States or Western Europe, it is mostly with an unmarried adult child, but in Japan three-fourths of these joint households are with married children. Another striking difference is that in Japan most aged live with their son; in fact, four times as many as those who live with their daughter. This reflects the patrilateral bias in the expression of filial piety; upon marriage women tend to switch their allegiance to the husband's family and thus will be involved more with in-laws than their own family of orientation.

Based on attitudinal studies, the overwhelming majority of those living with their adult children prefer this living arrangement. Of the small number who don't, most want to live either in the same compound or in walking distance from their children. Finally, unlike older Americans, most elderly Japanese not living with their children would much prefer to do so. In fact, those living with children in Japan express greater happiness than those who are not. In general, there is much less expression of loneliness than found in the United States, Great Britain, and Denmark. When asked what the most important thing is for life satisfaction, older Japanese mention "family respect and care" second only to health.

The number of ways younger people display their respect and filial piety to the aged in Japan is legion. Indeed, it is possible to find in Japanese society examples of every type of deferential behavior found among a worldwide sample of societies (Silverman and Maxwell 1978). These types of deference include linguistic (honorific language used in addressing aged), spatial (given the seat of honor in household), victual (served first and given the choicest food, prepared according to their taste), presentational (younger person always must bow lower in greeting ritual), prestative (gifts for family chosen to please primarily the elderly), and celebrative (special celebration for everyone who reaches sixty-one years). Palmore does point out that respect for the aged is no longer automatic in Japan. The prerogatives of age are more likely to accrue to those who carry out their responsibilities and do so with fairness.

At the national level there is recognition of the need to support the elderly and give them recognition through ritual celebrations. For example, each year there is a national "Respect for Elders Day," similar in importance to our Mother's Day. At age sixty-five all receive free annual health examinations, and at seventy completely free medical expenses, except for the wealthy. In 1963 a national law for the welfare of the elders was passed in Japan which declares that elders shall be "loved and respected" and guaranteed a "wholesome and peaceful life." The equivalent legislation in the United States, the Older Americans' Act of 1965, also commits the government to assist the elderly in various ways, but it guarantees nothing and is silent on such issues as love and respect.

Palmore's analysis is not without its critics, both Western and Japanese. Those who disagree tend to find the same strains with the accompanying demeaned status of the aged in Japan as is found in other industrial societies, or if not quite the same, certainly heading rapidly in that direction. Kiefer (1983) points out the problems Japan has encountered in dealing with the care of the rapidly increasing number of frail and bedridden among the very old. But the most pessimistic view of aging in Japan can be found in the writings of Plath (1972, 1980). He claims that some Western students of Japanese culture have been overly impressed with the sociocentric nature of the society and the dependent, submerged ego. Instead, he emphasizes the diversity and individuation of the people, which is hardly surprising in a nation of over 100 million. His general argument is well taken: the Confucian ethic of respect for elders is subject to compromise by the realities of modern life. Plath admits having an axe to grind in presenting this darker side of Japanese life; he wishes to correct the overly romantic view of Japan often found in the West.

Despite these criticisms and reservations, gerontologists continue to find many traditional patterns supportive of the aged. Maeda (1983) recently reported that joint family living remains strong even in highly urbanized Japan, and the rate of decline in the proportion of such households is proceeding very slowly. Furthermore, despite the hardships it often entails, middle-aged children remain strongly committed to caring for their frail parents and tend not to seek alternative caretakers. It is not that Japan is any more successful in avoiding the social dislocations brought about by industrialism. It is their manner of dealing with such problems, and their concern with alleviating them, that conveys a strikingly distinct Japanese flavor of strong commitment and concern. Indeed, this same pattern of obligation to parents and social embeddedness within the family throughout the life cycle was found to be still ingrained among second- and third-generation Japanese-Americans living in Honolulu (Johnson 1977).

The role and treatment of the elderly in post-industrial Japan still appear quite different from the typical experience in the Western countries. Both Plath (1980) and de Beauvoir (1973) have argued persuasively that industrial society—with its dominant values of competition and achievement according to one's productivity outside the household—inevitably has led to the degrading position of the aged. Counter to this theory of modernization, the Japanese experience suggests that there are cultural forces that can mitigate the impact of the dominant economic order. In the case of Japan a commitment to traditional values—such as filial piety, the nature of obligation in social relationships, and a preference for an ordered hierarchy based partly on age—have conspired to give the elderly a number of opportunities to play useful roles and receive the requisite esteem from other members of the society.

How strong these forces are in Japanese society is, as stated, a matter of some debate. The likelihood that they will remain or even become stronger in the future will require continual monitoring. Given the nature of the Japanese, it could be the issue is already decided. Because of their extreme sensitivity to criticism, the very fact that such matters are being monitored could lead to highly favorable treatment of the aged. To do otherwise would be too grave an insult. If this is a valid argument, we have here a rather curious example of the positive impact of social science scrutiny.

Conclusion

In the major reviews that are available on the family life of older people—one for studies published during the sixties (Troll 1971) and one for the seventies (Streib and Beck 1980)—it is generally agreed that despite the accumulation of much useful descriptive data there has been little theoretical development. Putting these data within the framework of a life course perspective remains a major task still at hand, a task made more difficult given the lack of longitudinal studies and remaining empirical gaps in such areas as family life in the middle years.

As a result, many of the studies at hand do not deal adequately with the process of family life through the various stages that significantly affect individuals. Troll, Miller, and Atchley (1979) complain that studies of widowhood in particular emphasize the status rather than the process, and consequently we know little about the long-term versus short-term effects of the desolation caused by the death of a spouse. The same criticism holds for other status changes associated with older families such as grandparenthood, later life marriage, and caregiving.

Others argue that it is essential to have an adequate psychodynamic theory of adulthood phrased in terms of the varying needs of family members across the life course. Without such a theory it will be difficult to clarify such issues as the need for autonomy versus interdependence, as Cohler (1983) is attempting to do. His use of data from India and the discussion of the Japanese family in the previous section illustrate how cross-cultural comparisons can provide insight into how these needs are shaped by the basic values of particular societies. Comparative research, however, requires more than an occasional gesture toward the quaint customs in remote areas of the world. What is needed are systematic, large-scale comparisons of cultural elements and their psychological consequences, both at the finer-grained level of ethnic groups or subcultural enclaves as well as the molar level of national cultures.

Much is already known about the amount of contact between family members and the kind of mutual support occurring within the family network. We also have a fairly good understanding of how various statuses that typically emerge in later life—such as retiree, grandparent, widow—can affect the elderly. This understanding of later life statuses is heavily oriented toward the adjustment individuals make in terms of their well-being, whether that is measured by life satisfaction, morale, or happiness. Yet it remains unclear how the frequency of contact and the extent of intergenerational exchanges affect the well-being of the older family members. More generally, it is not possible to state the conditions under which family life either contributes to or detracts from the well-being of the elderly. This is more likely to occur if the global measures of well-being presently used are broken down so that each component of the measure refers to particular aspects of everyday life (Mancini 1983).

There is still much to learn about the interaction styles, the shifts in power relations, and the overall emotional tone of relations with elderly family members (Quinn and Hughston 1984). Most reviewers continue to bemoan the lack of qualitative studies that can provide this more subjective assessment of interpersonal relations. Nevertheless, a general portrait of later life families is emerging from studies in the United States and other industrialized countries. Although the outlines are blurred by the enormous differentiation of such societies, the picture is not nearly as grim as was once commonly believed. There are clearly conditions which all too frequently lead to poverty, loneliness, low morale, insult, abuse, and intolerable living conditions for a difficult-to-determine proportion of the elderly population. More typical, however, may be the number of aged who appear to lead socially varied and personally satisfying lives. And, even though the importance researchers attribute to kinship may be overestimated (Mancini 1983), family life is arguably the main contributor to these positive outcomes.

XI

COMMUNITY SETTINGS

Philip Silverman

Theory

In this chapter, we are concerned with the variety of community settings in which the elderly live. The concept of community encompasses a broad range of living environments from small, self-contained villages to the bustling neighborhoods of metropolitan areas. In its modern usage, it refers not only to the physical disposition of the environment but also the available community resources, such as social services and entertainment opportunities, and the interpersonal relations characteristic of the setting. To understand how people adapt to these environmental features, various theoretical models are emerging that attempt to view the person-environment interaction in a transactional mode (Carp 1976b). This means that the models seek a broader, more dynamic, multi-causal theory rather than a set of unidirectional predictions involving a given environmental stimulus leading to a particular individual response. There is considerable overlap in how these models are conceptualized. A brief overview of some better-known ones will provide guideposts for the discussion that follows.

The Loss Continuum Concept

Pastalan (1982) views aging as a progressive contraction of life-space associated with the common losses of later life. These losses include the dispersion of children, loss of social roles, decline in income, death of spouse and peers, decline in sensory acuity, and restricted mobility due to failing health. Some gerontologists have argued that because a person's life-space constricts, the immediate environment as encompassed by one's domicile and neighborhood takes on far greater importance, making the elderly acutely sensitive to even small environmental changes (Regnier 1983; Rowles and Ohta 1983).

One example of the importance of neighborhood and its resources is the finding that a block radius around the home is critical. Beyond this point the rate elderly people make trips for shopping and other purposes drops off sharply (M. P. Lawton, personal communication, 1985). This suggests that even small changes in the environment, if undertaken knowledgeably, can have significant payoffs for the aged in terms of their adaptive capacity. Indeed, Pastalan (1982) views his approach as less an academic theory than a practical means to bring about the environmental changes that facilitate the adaptation of people with decreasing competence.

Environmental Press Model

Lawton (1982) and his associates propose that behavior is a function of two interacting variables: (1) personal competence, including health, sensory-perceptual capacity, motor skills (strength and coordination), cognitive skills (such as measured by IQ tests), and ego strength; and (2) the environmental press, including both its social and physical dimensions. A given environment has a certain "demand character" of either high or low quality to which people must adapt behaviorally. Related to this model is the "environmental docility hypothesis," which states that the more limited an individual's competences, the greater the impact of environmental factors on that individual (Lawton and Simon 1968).

The concept of competence has an evaluative connotation that makes it difficult to measure (Lawton 1975). The model also recognizes the importance of "secondary incompetences," which are extraneous to the individual but, nevertheless, detract from the ability to deal with the environment. These include various social deprivations that often accompany old age and thus are experienced as reductions in competence. Among these are low income, social isolation, and the negative labeling accompanying ageism. The elderly internalize this external labeling and accept a pejorative self-concept, which in turn influences how they behave. A similar view has been stated by Kuypers and Bengston (1973) in their conceptualization of the "social breakdown syndrome."

Lawton's model requires the presence of a given balance between individual competence and environmental press for the maximum positive adaptation to occur. Thus, not only will an individual of limited competence have problems adapting to high environmental press, but also a highly competent person in a setting of weak environmental press will be understimulated and bored, and this too can lead to negative affect and maladaptive behavior. The model also incorporates the perception individuals have of their competences and the environment. These subjective variables, difficult as they are to measure, can be central in predicting behavior. Parr (1980) considers the perception of the environment as part of a larger set of variables concerned with how a person evaluates and experiences the environment, and these are best seen as mediating between personal competence and environmental press, on the one hand, and behavior on the other.

Lawton is well aware of the limitations in this and similar models at this relatively early stage of theoretical development. He recognizes that the absence of any generally accepted taxonomy of environments limits their usefulness. As a result, the environmental factors treated vary greatly from one study to the next.

Person-Environment Congruence Model

This approach differs from the previous two in that it does not focus on the losses suffered by the elderly. Like the environmental press model, however, it is concerned with individual competences, but construed more broadly as the satisfaction of needs (Kahana 1982). Personal needs of particular saliency in adapting to a given environment are: need for privacy, need for affective expression, preference for autonomy as opposed to being controlled, tolerance for ambiguity, preference for activity as opposed to disengagement, and capacity for impulse control. All of these have been shown to vary with age.

The elderly are considered to have highly individualistic personal needs and ideally these may be congruent with the environment. Kahana has specified which environmental characteristics either facilitate or hinder the satisfaction of particular needs. When there is dissonance between the environmental press and personal needs, and it is not possible to modify the press, then stress and discomfort necessarily follow. Kahana and Kahana (1983) have found in their research a diversity of coping patterns and environmental preferences. Thus, the emphasis is on a dynamic process involving a rather large set of interacting variables which they attempt to measure simultaneously.

Socioenvironmental Model

Gubrium (1973) considers his model an attempt to resolve the debate between the activity and disengagement theories, both of which he submits to an extended critique. In his terminology, one must take account of the "activity resources" the aged person utilizes in coping with the environment, both physical and social. Those activity resources found to be critical in coping with a given environment are health, wealth, and continuity of a social support system. With respect to the social environment, Gubrium gives emphasis to "activity norms," the repertoire of expectations as to what an aged person can and cannot do. Thus, given the particular mix of personal resources of the individual and the activity norms allowed by the social environment, a person adjusts to old age by resolving the tension between what is expected and what one is capable of expressing.

Unlike the other models, Gubrium's conception makes no provision for psychological characteristics.

It should be clear there is much in common among these various approaches. Work has hardly begun on this person-environment approach and as yet the results of various studies are not well systematized. As mentioned earlier, there is still no agreed-upon set of environmental factors that must be accounted for, and of course there can be only limited use of experimental designs in human behavior studies whereby the environment is carefully controlled. For the most part, one must be satisfied with correlational studies.

It is also not clear as yet if a developmental transition occurs with the coming of old age so that one must account for a distinct person-environment transaction occurring late in life (Rowles and Ohta 1983). Such a possibility is of obvious concern to a life course perspective, which has been little used in person-environment studies. With the main focus of such studies on the impact of different kinds of communities, there remain many unstudied aspects of the person-environment interaction. Nevertheless, the corpus of research does allow at least one unambiguous conclusion: *elderly people require an extremely broad range of living environments to satisfy the variety of personal needs they exhibit.*

Before turning to the studies of various community settings, we first examine two aspects of the immediate environment considered to have a critical impact on the elderly—housing and neighborhood. We then summarize what is known about how likely the elderly are to migrate to new community settings. Following this, the community studies are organized according to two intersecting dimensions—rural versus urban and age homogeneous versus heterogeneous settings. Each of these dimensions is in fact a continuum. For example, at one extreme the aged can achieve almost total segregation from other age cohorts by moving to isolated, self-contained retirement communities in the vast desert of the American Southwest, or they can live with adult children and continue to participate in the normal range of everyday community life. There are an infinite number of possibilities between these two extremes, so we choose some of the more salient points along the continuum where we are likely to find the largest proportion of elderly people.

Housing and Neighborhood

Over 20% of the households in the United States are headed by an elderly person, a rate that is higher and rising more rapidly than the proportion of old people in the total population. For a number of reasons, including the greater amount of time spent at home and in their neighborhoods (Struyk

1981), housing and its immediate setting can have a decisive effect on the life-style and well-being of older people.

As yet, no generally accepted measures of the need for housing are available. Estimates range as high as 30% for the proportion of elderly occupying housing that is deteriorating or sub-standard, although according to a 1978 survey, only 12% of aged-headed households were physically inadequate units (Brotman 1982). Based on longitudinal data for the years 1974 to 1979 collected in the National Annual Housing Survey, Zais and Thibodeau (1983) find that housing "filters down" in its characteristics if old people replace younger adults and "filters up" if younger adults replace the aged. Why this should be the case is not explained by the data,[1] but it does expose a structural constraint on providing adequate housing for the elderly.

The expense of housing is all too often the biggest drain on the financial resources of the aged. The fraction of income devoted to housing is substantially higher for them. Thirty-eight percent of the aged pay over 35% of their income for housing, while only 21% of the non-aged do so (Zais and Thibodeau 1983). According to Brotman (1982), almost 20% of aged-headed households pay a disproportionate part of their income for housing.

Furthermore, Golant (1984) claims that both the homeowners and the renters among the aged live in housing inappropriate for their declining personal resources and distinctive life-styles. Such housing has features designed to accommodate younger age cohorts whose needs for space are usually greater during earlier periods of their marital lives. As a result, aged homeowners often find themselves with homes designed with multiple levels and too large to clean and maintain. This problem is especially acute among the suburban elderly (Gutowski 1981).

It is important to realize that between 65 and 70% of all housing units headed by the elderly are owner-occupied. Indeed, homeownership represents the only widely held asset among older people (Brotman 1976). Their homes are typically older, in poorer condition, and located in the less desirable sections of the community, and thus have low market value. But compared to those aged who rent, homeowners enjoy a major saving. Eighty-six percent of those who own their home are free of any mortgage, whereas of those elderly who rent, half spend 30% or more of their incomes on housing. Also, according to the 1976 Annual Housing Survey, the condition of rented domiciles of the aged is poorer than that of homes owned by the aged (Lawton and Hoover 1981).

However, the objective conditions of housing are not always related to the level of the occupants' satisfaction with it. The attachment people have

---

1. Possible explanations for the filtering down of elderly housing include the greater difficulty older people have in undertaking repairs, lack of finances to have repairs done, and possible age discrimination in home improvement loans.

to their domiciles goes beyond functional factors to more complex ones like long-time familiarity, strength of informal social network, attachment to various aesthetic qualities, and others. And more satisfying alternatives may not be recognized by or available to people. Studies show that when people have options, they are less likely to be satisfied with their housing; if options are not apparent, they tend to express greater satisfaction with even poorly rated housing (Carp 1975).

The adequacy of housing cannot be evaluated without accounting for the larger environmental setting in which people live. In many communities the neighborhood becomes the arena in which most needs are satisfied and social interaction takes place, especially for the elderly. And as these needs change through the life course, a different set of environmental pressures are created by potential physical decrements, reduced incomes, and shifting social networks. As a result, housing must be seen within a matrix of transportation and shopping facilities, health care services, and recreational and social opportunities relevant to an older population (Carp 1976b).

The Annual Housing Surveys conducted by the U.S. Bureau of the Census through the 1970s provide useful information on the satisfaction with neighborhoods. The old people most satisfied with their neighborhoods are, not surprisingly, those of higher socioeconomic status, homeowners living in single-family dwellings, and residents of nonmetropolitan areas, that is, in communities of less than fifty thousand inhabitants. Curiously, there is only a modest relationship between the objective characteristics of a neighborhood, the neighborhood characteristics as perceived by older respondents, and measures of the well-being of these respondents (Lawton 1980). Generally, the aged complain less than younger cohorts about their neighborhood, perhaps due to the desire to reduce cognitive dissonance or the greater unwillingness to question the status quo, as suggested by Lawton. Thus, their subjective evaluations tend to be higher than the objective ones that the researchers claim to employ.

A recent study of one hundred elderly males in Boston conducted by the Veterans Administration provides insights into the factors relevant to neighborhood satisfaction (Jirovec, Jirovec, and Bosse 1985). The environmental characteristics that explained over half the variance were safety, beauty, space (degree of density), and antiquity. Consistent with other studies, the most important of these factors is safety, which alone explains one-third of the variance. We return to the issue of safety in the section dealing with the rural-urban dimension, but what is striking about these results is that the other characteristics are all, more or less, aesthetic ones. They concern aspects of people's perception of the environment, an area that is getting more attention from researchers. Neither the accessibility of resources nor higher concentrations of age peers were associated with neighborhood satisfaction, contradicting results found in other studies that we will discuss below. The message of this study is that if the aged have adequate housing, can feel physically protected, and then enjoy some degree of aesthetic satisfaction, other deficiencies in the environment may be more easily tolerated.

Other studies of neighborhood perception indicate that the elderly tend to recognize only those features of the environment that directly affect their lives. Based on data from a Los Angeles neighborhood, Regnier (1983) suggests that the feature that may be most important to them is what "social and interactive processes" are available in the neighborhood rather than the visual structure of the environment. This same neighborhood has been compared with one in the adjacent city of Long Beach by interviewing in each a sample of one hundred elderly people averaging over seventy years old (Walsh, Krauss, and Regnier 1981). The authors demonstrate that changes that may occur with age in cognitive capacity can also have a decisive impact on the response to the environment. They find positive correlations between the test scores on spatial cognitive ability and the accuracy with which respondents locate neighborhood landmarks and the distance they travel for goods and services. Thus, we are beginning to obtain more systematic findings relating specific cognitive abilities to the way in which the immediate environment is used.

Migration

In general, elderly people are less likely to move than younger people. In the five-year period between 1975 and 1980, some 21% (almost 5 million) of the noninstitutionalized elderly but over 48% of the under sixty-five population moved (U.S. Bureau of the Census 1984). Of the aged who moved, 57% did so within the same county, and only 20% moved to another state. Yet the number of interstate migrants has increased dramatically over the past three decades. For example, in 1980 the number of people sixty or over who moved to another state in the previous five years was over 1.6 million, a substantial increase over the previous decades. This is a migration rate of nearly double that of the national population increase for this age cohort (Flynn et al. 1985). There is every reason to believe that the trend in retirement migration will continue in the foreseeable future.

The major migration route of the aged in the United States is the well-documented movement from the populous northeastern and north central states to the Sun Belt. Between 1975 and 1980 about half of all interstate migrants sixty or older headed for five states, listed here in order of preference: Florida, California, Arizona, Texas, and New Jersey. Over the past three decades Florida has increased its dominance as a destination state, attracting over a quarter of the migrants in the 1975–80 period. Yet other states are increasing in popularity dramatically, especially Arizona and North Carolina, a Sun Belt state that entered the top ten destination states for the first time in 1980.

Despite the dominance of these trends, it is also important to recognize variations in this pattern. For example, the large northeastern states such as New York, New Jersey, and Pennsylvania, still receive a larger volume of elderly interstate migrants than the smaller Sun Belt states such as South Carolina, Alabama, Mississippi, Louisiana, and New Mexico (Flynn et al. 1985). Also, several areas that have a strong attraction for tourists in general are also drawing increasing numbers of elderly migrants from surrounding states; they include the Ozarks region in Arkansas and Missouri and the Olympic Peninsula in the state of Washington (Longino 1981). And finally, the phenomenon of "snow-birding" is also increasing in frequency. This refers to the seasonal migration to sunnier regions during the severe winter months, then returning home for the moderate seasons. Often this move is to areas closer to where the children of the elderly live (Rudzitis 1984).

The five states that sent the most older people to other states between 1975 and 1980 were New York, California, Illinois, Florida, and Ohio. Interestingly, two states among the top five that gave up the most also received the most, California and Florida. But the pattern in each is very different. California loses about the same number of elderly people as it gains, whereas Florida attracts more than four times as many as it loses. Furthermore, Florida benefits from the exchange, in that it gives up elderly who are older, poorer, less educated, and more dependent than those it receives. On the other hand, California is losing its attractiveness to younger retirees, receiving migrants who tend to be older and more dependent than those it gives up (Longino 1984). These characteristics of migrants are just as important as the volume, for they have profound effects on the housing required and the nature of community facilities that must be provided.

Kahana and Kahana (1983) have studied long-distance migration of the aged to Florida and Israel (although it is still unclear exactly what motivates people to migrate to foreign countries, they claim this is a trend that can be expected to increase). They found four types of well-adjusted voluntary "relocaters" in both Florida and Israel:

(1) Explorers—those who seek and often find a new life-style. These people view retirement as liberating, a time for new experiences. They are willing to take risks and do not give material comfort the highest priority.

(2) Helpers—those who find retirement difficult to adjust to, and thus seek meaningful substitutes for work. They engage in a lot of voluntary work as a way of satisfying their altruistic impulses.

(3) Fun seekers—those who view retirement as a well-earned vacation. They are drawn to warmer climates to pursue highly sociable, leisure-oriented life-styles.

(4) Comfort seekers—those who seek a relatively disengaged, quiet life-style in a warmer climate and an improved living environment. Often in frail health, they become involved in decorating and maintaining their new home or apartment.

All of the well-adjusted categories relocated because they were attracted to the new environment, the so-called pull factor. Those people in the sample found to be poorly adjusted were more likely to have relocated because of the push factor; that is, to avoid some negative aspect of their previous environment, such as living in a high crime area. Thus, Kahana and Kahana conclude, based on their congruence model discussed earlier, if migration is voluntary, the discontinuity with the previous setting can lead to enhanced congruence between personal needs and the environment.

Although we have been looking exclusively at the migration of older people, mobility rates and outcomes can be better understood as a phenomenon that varies through successive age cohorts and can be affected by decisions made earlier in life (Longino 1981). For example, short distance or local moves decline gradually through middle and later years, and only begin to increase again after age seventy-five, especially for widowed women. Interstate migration rates tend to jump for the sixty-five to seventy cohort, especially for men, presumably related to the increase in retirement. Interstate migrants are more likely to live in independent households and enjoy higher levels of socioeconomic status than local movers. In general, if one has moved little as an adult, it is less likely that a move will be made in the later years. These and other life course factors play a role in determining whether a new environment will be sought in old age.

Rural-Urban Dimension

The majority of elderly Americans live in metropolitan areas, the large cities and the suburban fringe that encircles them (see Table 9.4 in the chapter by Uhlenberg). Although this proportion has remained fairly stable over the past three decades, the distribution within the metropolitan subareas has changed significantly in recent years. Earlier, the aged were least represented in the suburbs. From 1950 to 1970, the proportion of all older people living in the suburbs increased from 12% to 21% (Gutowski 1981). However, the most recent data indicate they are now about equally distributed between central cities and suburbs of our metropolitan areas (Rudzitis 1984). This growth in the suburban areas has not occurred through in-migration, but instead primarily by the aging-in-place of those people who have fled to the suburbs since World War II.

Elderly people who live in our central cities must deal with some of the worst social problems in American society. They are concentrated in deteriorating and filthy neighborhoods, occupy high-cost though inadequate housing, endure the overcrowding and the jarring noise that are an inevitable part of urban life, and must survive on streets considered dangerous even for the hardiest of souls. Indeed, in study after study, the major problem faced by old people in urban areas is the fear of crime. The 1975 Harris survey (National Council on the Aging 1975) found that the highest proportion of people experiencing fear within one mile of their residence occurred in the sixty and older cohort living in large cities (over 250,000 inhabitants). No less than 71% of these elderly lived in fear, a greater proportion than younger cohorts in the same size cities, and considerably greater than aged cohorts living in smaller cities and rural areas. In fact, there is a strong lineal increase in fear of crime by size of community. The rural elderly are least likely to fear victimization, with only 19% expressing concern about crime. Between this survey and the 1981 Harris survey, the percentage of people sixty-five and older who considered crime a serious problem in their lives increased from 23% to 25%.

Because of its pervasive impact on elderly people living in urban areas, it is worth dwelling a bit on the problem of crime. We know from opinion polls that this is a problem that has become steadily worse since the 1940s, especially for the aged. In a study of 750 census tracts in Los Angeles, Kendig (1976) found that the highest rates of assault and fires were in tracts where older people are concentrated. The highest robbery rates occur in those tracts with the highest concentrations of elderly and/or poor people. Although nationwide the aged are less likely to be the victims of crimes in general, their rates are about the same as other age cohorts for "personal larceny with contact," that is, crimes such as purse snatching and pickpocketing. In one study the aged came out with substantially higher rates of victimization from this crime in ten of thirteen large cities. The worst city of all was San Francisco with a rate of 43 per 1,000 compared to a national average of 3.1 per 1,000 for all ages (Lawton 1980). Since this is a crime that occurs typically on the streets, the anxiety it engenders in old people is compounded by its unpredictability and uncontrollability. A further complication is the racial factor involved; 65% of all predatory crimes (robbery and personal larceny) against elderly whites are committed by black males, mostly youngsters. The black elderly are not spared victimization; they, along with those aged who are female and poor, have the greatest fear of crime.

Gubrium (1973) has attempted to explain the circumstances in which the elderly are most vulnerable to crime victimization. His Detroit study of 210 elderly people between the ages of sixty and ninety-four develops a four-fold typology of community contexts based on either high or low social homogeneity (whether or not one lives close to high concentrations of elderly people), and high or low residential proximity (whether living in multi-unit dwellings or single homes). Using this typology and concepts from his socioenvironmental model, Gubrium develops the following hypotheses: (1) The greater the social homogeneity (i.e., age concentration), the less vulnerable the aged are to crime. The reason for this is that social homogeneity provides increased local protectiveness. (2) In community settings of low social homogeneity, the aged are more likely to respond to crime victimization with fear; while in settings of high social homogeneity, the likely response is one of anger. (3) The elderly with high activity resources (see explanation of this concept in the section entitled "Socioenvironmental Model") are more vulnerable to victimization in settings of high social homogeneity because of their greater mobility; those with low activity resources are more vulnerable in settings of low social homogeneity. These hypotheses deserve elaboration and closer scrutiny; unfortunately, Gubrium provides only anecdotal data in support of their validity.

There is much about the impact of crime on the lives of the elderly that we still do not know. To what extent does the fear of crime force the urban aged to become prisoners in their own homes? How much does it influence the degree and kind of social participation? Does media coverage of sensational crimes, often dwelling on the details of brutal and heinous acts, influence the use of various neighborhood and community facilities? And does all this so intimidate people that it has a major effect on their overall well-being? Research is obviously needed here. At present the best hope of mitigating this problem lies in the demographic changes that are restructuring the population pyramid. As our society continues to age there will be a decreasing proportion of people in the population most likely to perpetrate crimes; that is, teenagers and young adults.

Despite these harsh circumstances, the positive side of urban living for the aged has been recognized also. Compared to rural aged, those in the central cities are less likely to live below the poverty line and more likely to enjoy better health, although the suburban elderly are the richest and the healthiest. The cities allow easier access to medical facilities, and the elderly there are more likely to visit a doctor (Lawton 1980); although this does not appear to hold for Canada where a study in Manitoba found no urban and rural differences in health care usage except for hospital admissions rate, which was higher for the rural sample (Shapiro and Roos 1984). In the United States the number and range of accessible social programs for the elderly are greatest in the cities and the availability of public transport to get to these services is more likely. Yet, Carp (1976b) has argued that the aged do not take advantage of the services available in the city because of severely reduced mobility; and Lopata (1975) found that in Chicago the elderly are poorly informed and make little use of services designed for them.

Finally, the opportunities for social interaction are probably greatest in the city. Cohler and Grunebaum (1981) claim that modern urban living fosters intergenerational relations and even dependence within families, facilitated by telephoning and easy access to mass transportation. Carrying this point beyond the family, a study in Chicago found the concentration of older people in certain areas of the city to be explained not by their desire to have greater accessibility to services, but rather by their desire to maintain links with members of their ethnic group (Rudzitis 1984). Generally, the elderly are much more likely to be found in the ethnic enclaves of the cities than in the so-called "geriatric ghettos."

As of 1980, about one-third of the aged in the United States lives in nonmetropolitan areas (U.S. Bureau of the Census 1984). Most of the rural aged are concentrated in the southern and north central regions of the United States (Harbert and Wilkinson 1985). Because of the continuous out-migration of young people from these areas, small towns now represent the highest concentration of elderly people as a proportion of the total population. In these towns 17% of the population are sixty-five or over. A very small percentage (3 to 5%) of the elderly actually live on farms. In addition to the out-migration of younger cohorts, recent decades have brought about a "migration turnaround" (Longino 1982) as the migration patterns of the elderly have begun to favor smaller communities.

Rural elderly have received much less attention in the literature than their urban counterparts whose problems have appeared so overwhelming. As a result, the more positive aspects of the rural setting for the elderly have been overdone at times. Their communities are far safer, there are often strong family and neighborly support networks, and they can enjoy high status in institutional spheres such as the church (Davis 1980). The maintenance of certain rural values, such as independence, hard work, freedom, responsibility, conservatism, and a desire for accomplishment are considered by White (1977) to be wholesome for adapting to old age. Rowles (1983) found in a small, Appalachian community a strong support system for elderly people not only within the neighborhood but also via telephone (a mode of communication also found common in other rural studies). Their network embraced a number of middle-aged people as well who acted as caretakers when necessary. The elderly were very much a part of the social life of the community, and they obtained considerable emotional support from their long attachment to a particular house and neighborhood. The author rated their subjective well-being as very high.

If the rural elderly have greater contact with relatives, it does not translate into a greater desire to live in the same household. In fact, there is some evidence that they are even less willing to live with a relative than the urban aged. In a study of rural Iowa reported by Powers, Keith, and Goudy (1981), it was found that older people preferred to move to a nursing home rather than live with a child or close relative. Furthermore, their review of longitudinal studies in the same state concludes that over time older people evince considerable emotional withdrawal from family contacts. The proportion who claim to receive their greatest satisfaction from contact with children decreases substantially, and such pastimes as hobbies and watching TV get higher ratings.

Many Americans hold a romantic view of rural life. This is stimulated in part by the bucolic scenes exploited by advertising and the popularity of television programs with appealing small town or agrarian families. Given the structure of the U.S. interstate highway system, most people have little or no contact with such areas, allowing the fantasy to be easily perpetuated. Be that as it may, there is a grim side of rural life for older Americans (Noll 1981). They are more likely to live in substandard housing, have lower incomes, are less educated, and are in greater need of medical facilities and social service programs. The strong conviction with which values such as independence and self-reliance are held, values that often co-occur with xenophobia and a strong distaste for anything smacking of outside interference, can negatively affect the use of existing services. In a longitudinal study of rural elderly in Iowa, Powers and Bultena (1974) conclude that the nonutilization of available services was not due to the absence of need, but instead could be explained by the desire to avoid a definition of self as old and a strong antipathy against accepting "charity." In many parts of rural America the common settlement pattern is highly dispersed; isolated homesteads are often many miles from towns with necessary amenities. Yet, based on 1970 census data, 30% of rural elderly had no automobile available. Although urban and suburban elderly are even less likely to have this available, the need for transportation is obviously greater in rural areas.

It remains unclear if these disadvantages of rural life are balanced by the positive attributes described above so that one can conclude such settings allow for greater well-being for the elderly than in urban areas. Lawton (1980) reports that studies by rural sociologists conclude that when health and income are controlled, there is no difference in life satisfaction by community size. It is equally difficult to find clear-cut differences with respect to other factors. For example, having a confidant is known to be a highly positive element in one's personal network (Lowenthal and Haven 1968), but according to the national sample interviewed by Harris in 1975, there is no difference in the proportion of elderly who have a confidant by community size (National Council on the Aging 1975). With respect to a family support system, there also appears to be little difference between urban and rural areas, but the results are inconsistent, pointing out an area where more research is needed.

Nevertheless, one can cite a number of instances where the advantages of rural life are evident. Zais and Thibodeau (1983) report that the rural elderly evaluate their neighborhood conditions more positively than the urban elderly, perhaps because social interaction with friends and neighbors is greater in the rural areas. There is also more interaction with younger age cohorts, and less expression of loneliness than is found in the larger communities. Lawton (1980) tentatively concludes that the quality of social interaction may not differ by community size, but the quantity is greater for those elderly living in rural areas. He suggests that this difference may be the factor that counteracts the erosion of psychological well-being due to the depriving features of rural life.

Age-Homogeneous Versus Age-Heterogeneous Dimension

Most old people live in age-heterogeneous settings where they are integrated with other age groups. The studies covered in the previous section on rural/urban differences basically are concerned with this segment of the population. But increasingly there is emerging in the more advanced industrial countries a variety of housing and community settings in which the elderly can segregate themselves to various degrees from other age cohorts. The impact of these age-homogeneous settings on the life of the aged has been a major research concern since the 1960s, and it is to these studies we now turn.

A bench mark for any discussion of living in an age-concentrated setting is the study by Rosow (1967) of several apartment buildings and retirement hotels in Cleveland. Rosow's sample of 1200 middle- and working-class aged was grouped into three categories according to the proportion of elderly people living in their dwelling unit. His major finding was that living near younger age cohorts does not encourage friendships; rather, the number of friends an elderly person has increases with the proportion of older neighbors. This effect occurs only with relatively high concentrations of the aged; when the proportion is below 50%, the effect on contacts is negligible. And it appears to have its greatest impact on older women whose social activity increases more dramatically with age-concentration than older men.

Rosow's results were consistent with studies using various measures of subjective well-being. For example, Messer (1968) found among a much smaller sample of 157 older public housing residents in Chicago that they enjoyed higher morale in the age-homogeneous settings. Further, such settings functioned as an alternative to the nurturance and affective support provided by family; morale remained high even among those aged with relatively little contact with their children. They did not feel neglected despite this lack of contact with children.

Subsequent studies have both supported and questioned these results. The work of Lawton (1980) and his colleagues confirms that age-concentration results in greater participation in social activities, higher levels of interaction with fellow tenants, and even greater satisfaction with housing. This holds not only for age-homogeneous settings at the level of the apartment building but also the city block. But these studies are not able to confirm the association found with morale or the impact such settings provide as an alternative to family relations. Carp (1976a) points out that although a limited number of age peers could adversely affect potential friendships, by restricting contacts with younger adults the potential for the establishment of social bonds along many other commonalities suffers. For some people these commonalities may be more important than age. Carp (1976b) also points out that the elderly studied by Rosow lived in an old, established neighborhood and had many distinctive characteristics besides the age-homogeneity factor.

It is important to note that Rosow's study does not actually deal with an age-segregated setting, but with apartment complexes housing varying proportions of elderly people. Since the beginning of federally-assisted housing programs in 1956, there are a number of facilities that admit only older people. Most of these are low-cost, high-rise apartment buildings. In the mid-seventies, it was estimated that about 3% of the aged lived in federally-assisted housing (Carp 1976b). At about the same time there were 466,000 public housing units occupied by the elderly, of which 200,000 were in age-segregated settings (Lawton 1979). Although difficult to count, there is by now an equal number of units for the aged funded by a variety of private organizations.

If we include settings such as retirement communities and congregate housing (to be discussed), approximately 6% of the elderly now live in planned housing that is age-segregated. Thus, the total number of settings that are completely age-homogeneous is not large as yet, and they are certainly much less available than in countries such as the Netherlands, Sweden, France, and West Germany. But the research undertaken in such settings deserves close scrutiny because of the likely expansion of this type of housing in the future. Also, there is increasing evidence that elderly people fare better in housing and neighborhoods that have higher proportions of their age peers (Lawton, Moss, and Moles 1984). For these reasons gerontologists have been especially interested in these settings. The following sections attempt to summarize this considerable literature.

Apartment Complexes for the Elderly

There have been several excellent studies of apartment complexes for the elderly. Large samples of tenants have been interviewed, and an extensive battery of social and psychological measures have been employed. This research has included longitudinal assessments both before and after the move to the complex, and frequently there have been interviews with matched samples of people who did not move, although it is obviously not possible to match randomly in anything but a controlled experimental setting.

The most notable of these studies is of Victoria Plaza in San Antonio, as reported in a number of publications (see especially, Carp 1966). In addition to baseline data, follow-up interviews are available for eight years following the initial occupancy. In general, the move to Victoria Plaza is associated with improved social and psychological well-being as well as lower rates of mortality and institutionalization. The residents had higher morale, enjoyed improved health, and increased their participation in social activities. Despite the highly positive results and the comparison with matched samples, Carp (1976b) does not eliminate the possibility that the residents represent a self-selection of the more aware and capable aged, buoyed by their opportunity to be included in such a visible experiment. Be that as it may, for the kind of people who do choose such residences, they are highly beneficial.

Similar results were obtained by other researchers, although the positive effects are less impressive than in the Carp study. Lawton and Cohen (1974) studied five separate urban housing sites in New Jersey and Pennsylvania, and took extra precautions in matching the residents with control groups. As in the Carp study they found the age-segregated settings had a favorable impact on several measures of well-being, but no measurable effect on morale or several social interactional variables. Unlike Carp, they found the move had a negative impact on functional health. Although there are several explanations for this difference (Lawton 1980), only further research can clarify how health is affected by these moves.

Messer (1967) was able to clarify other aspects of this issue by comparing two public housing projects, one limited to elderly residents, the other age-integrated. In the age-integrated setting, the morale of the old people was related to their level of social interaction, but these factors varied independently in the age-segregated setting. Messer claims that in the integrated setting, the standards of younger people prevailed, and this meant that the high levels of social involvement expected of all people were difficult for some of the elderly to meet. In the age-segregated project, however, the norms recognized that some older people prefer less social involvement.

Thus, Messer's research suggests that the advantage of age-homogeneous settings is the potential emergence of a distinctive and exclusive set of norms relevant to the elderly. Skills and characteristics that are sources of high social status in the outside world may be irrelevant to the aged in such settings, where new bases for social status emerge. This sort of analysis is more clearly apparent in studies employing qualitative techniques such as participant observation. In contrast to survey and other quantitative techniques, which are sometimes erroneously distinguished as more "data-based" (Lawton 1980) than qualitative approaches, those employing participant observation often allow greater insight into the more subjective realm, such as the basic values which are expressed through behavior. We now turn to a consideration of such studies.

One of the best-known participant observation studies is of a small apartment house for low income elderly in San Francisco where most of the forty-three residents were widows (Hochschild 1973). What impressed the author was the creation of community that had occurred among the residents. Because they lived only among their age peers, a fact that did not disturb them, a subculture had emerged distinctive to the occupants. They might not have had a great awareness of what was happening in the larger community, but they were well informed on events relevant to their lives. They kept track of birthdays and celebrated together; looked in on one another; shared information, shopping, and the cost of various products; and engaged in an enormous amount of communication, especially by telephone. Since the community that had emerged allowed new roles to replace those lost as the residents became old, Hochschild concludes that living among age peers mitigates against the isolation of the elderly so that they are much less likely to disengage.

Jacobs (1975) has reexamined Hochschild's data in conjunction with his own research in an age-segregated setting. Jacobs studied a high-rise apartment building located on a college campus in Syracuse, New York. Like the apartment house studied by Hochschild, the Syracuse site was a public housing project for working-class elderly. But it differed in that it was much larger (with over four hundred residents) and ethnically diverse, with obvious animosity toward the few black residents by many whites. It also housed people in fragile health and with physical limitations. This was resented by some who were afraid the residence would turn into a nursing home. Jacobs found a large proportion of the residents were apathetic, passive, and isolated. Thus, Jacobs concludes that a cohesive social identity cannot emerge simply by throwing people together who share the same age status, but that factors such as number, ethnicity, and health status, among others, can affect the pattern of social relations in ways that detract from the creation of community.

Although more properly belonging to the category of congregate housing, another study that focuses on the creation of community, is concerned with a French retirement home located near Paris (Ross 1977). The author also employed participant observation, but supplemented her data with formal observation and structured interviews, which could be analyzed statistically. The result is a well-rounded and thoughtful account of life in a modern fourteen-story residence occupied by some 127 retirees and spouses. The residents had many characteristics in common on entering the home, especially their working-class background in the construction industry and their unhappiness with their prior housing situation.

Ross is able to demonstrate that residents are socialized to a distinct social organization, with a status structure and norms relevant only within the home, and a sense of "we-feeling," with its own symbols and recognition of common fate. This community exists in spite of, or perhaps partly because of (if we accept Ross's analysis), the intense cleavage between Communist and non-Communist residents. Although these political allegiances were identities brought with them from the outside, they take on a new meaning relevant to the concerns and conflicts within the residence. Ross found that previous social status was for the most part unrelated to positions occupied within the residence. Nor was morale related to either their outside contacts or the amount of social activity they engaged in. A distinct community with its own norms had been created while still maintaining the particular French panache that characterized their life-style. Through the richness of the participant observation data, the peculiar temperament of the residents is conveyed.

The thrust of these data from a life course perspective point to the complex relationship that exists between previous experiences and the process of adjusting to old age. These experiences and the allegiances engendered do not become irrelevant, but they can take on quite different meanings if the social context is substantially altered.

While anthropologically-oriented researchers have tended to work with the concept of community creation, sociologists dealing with similar problems have employed the concept of an aged "subculture." As first developed by Rose (1962), such a subculture would emerge if old people were excluded from interaction with other groups in the population and where a "positive affinity" could develop because of common background, similar interests and problems, or some other basis of solidarity. In a study of three rather different age-homogeneous settings in the Midwest, Longino (1981) and his associates found that a subculture had emerged in each case, and this had a positive impact on residents who appeared to be doing much better than matched samples of elderly who did not live in such settings.

Retirement Communities

A more encompassing form of age-homogeneous living is represented by the growing number of retirement communities. Not only is the housing restricted to those of a given age level, but a whole community is designed to cater in varying degrees to the needs of the elderly. Sometimes such communities are adjacent to or part of larger metropolitan areas, and appear more like a separate housing development; and sometimes, they are geographically quite distinct with a varying complement of municipal facilities and services, as is more typically found in the southwestern states. The development of these communities has been due primarily to private sector investment. They provide relatively low cost, low density housing in a highly planned community context in which recreational facilities and leisure time pursuits are extensively provided. The architecture of the housing tends to be modified only minimally to accommodate a population with increasing physical deficits; thus, they tend to be inappropriate for those with severe disabilities.

Although such communities were first developed in Florida and rapidly spread throughout the Sun Belt states, they are increasingly appearing in the northeast and north central states. This trend reflects the preference for short-distance moves of many urban elderly who wish to avoid a total disruption of their network of family and friends. Heintz (1976) has provided a useful study of these communities in New Jersey where five separate retirement developments distributed in three counties were surveyed in 1975 to determine their impact on the larger communities to which they were attached. The profile she obtained of the residents may be considered typical of such communities: they are overwhelmingly white, relatively affluent and better educated, retired but formerly enjoyed occupations of high status; they represent the young-old in relatively good health, and tend to be married and living with spouse.

Heintz's survey data yield an attractive view of retirement community residents. She finds high levels of life satisfaction, and the longer the residency, the greater the satisfaction. A scant 6.9% wished to move, and usually this was because of some personal circumstance, like a death in the family. There was little evidence of disengagement. Social involvement both within and beyond the community is not affected by the move. In fact, a substantial number of people participate in the social, cultural, and political life of the wider community, providing labor for a variety of volunteer activities.

Similar results were found in a study of four retirement communities in Arizona. Bultena (1974) compared his sample of 322 respondents with a somewhat smaller sample of elderly people living in age-integrated circumstances in three Arizona cities. Those living in the retirement communities had higher life satisfaction, and this could not be explained by differences in age, income, education, occupation, or health status. The people who fared best in the retirement communities were those who preferred an active life-style with an emphasis on what he calls leisure and expressive roles. But for those who are more oriented to productive and instrumental roles typical of the larger society—that is, role definitions that are located in the work ethic—the age-homogeneous setting tended to have deleterious effects. To the extent that self-indulgence and pleasure-seeking could be defined as legitimate and dignified, residents fared well.

Turning now to qualitative studies, we find a much less appealing characterization of retirement communities. Jacobs (1974, 1975) employs participant observation techniques and a symbolic interactionist perspective in interpreting the data from "Fun City," a geographically isolated community located southeast of Los Angeles. The sociodemographic profile of the residents is comparable to the studies cited above, but Jacobs describes the typical resident as lonely, unhappy, and in despair. Although the usually rich complement of recreational facilities is available, participation is limited. Of the ninety-two clubs and organizations in a community of close to six thousand, no more than five hundred people are active. The largest segment of the population lead very isolated lives. They live far from other cities, and inter- and intra-city public transportation is poor. Although many claim they moved to the area to be closer to adult children living in the metropolitan spread of Southern California, they in fact have little contact with their families.

Jacobs is convinced that the prevalence of racist attitudes ensures the unlikelihood of any minority group members moving in; no blacks, Hispanics, or American Indians live in the community. Residents seem very concerned with maintaining a peaceful and tranquil life at the expense of allowing the development of a more diverse population or engaging in any social or political discussions that could create controversy. To the extent that Jacobs's description is accurate, Fun City appears to fit the environmental press model of Lawton (1975) and associates, whereby an imbalance exists between the relatively high personal competence levels of the residents and the low demand character of the environment. As a result, positive adaptation is less likely.

It is not clear why the quantitative-type survey studies cited earlier yield a much more positive view of retirement communities than the apathy and passivity found in Jacobs's data. Perhaps the qualitative technique with its emphasis on naturally occurring behavior allows a more meaningful assessment of subjective attitudes and emotional responses. Or it is possible that the discrepancy lies in the peculiar structural characteristics of Fun City—its size, isolation, and lack of stimulating environment except for the provision of recreational facilities. Jacobs's findings are clearly at odds with other assessments of retirement communities. Without further research these issues are difficult to resolve.

In any case, there remain divergent views regarding the desirability of such age-segregated settings. The positive view sees retirement communities as an opportunity for old people to escape the loneliness and danger of conventional community settings and establish new bases of social status relevant to their needs and values. The negative view is that such settings are abnormal (Jacobs writes about a "false paradise") and force people to withdraw from the diverse stimulation of the larger society and to pursue a highly regimented leisure-dominated life-style. In the view of Gray Panther leader Maggie Kuhn, such settings are playgrounds that can trivialize one's life. It could be that the uncongeniality that elderly people perceive in the larger society inclines them to choose a living context away from younger people, given that they have sufficient resources to manage the move, and can find a community with people of similar social and ethnic background. But it is clearly no panacea.

Congregate Housing

This form of age-homogeneous living has received increasing attention, although its relative novelty has made it more difficult to define. Somewhere between living totally independent of any organized support and living in an institutional setting (nursing homes, etc.), there exists a variety of circumstances whereby the elderly can live with some degree of protection and support. This has been variously called intermediate, communal, or community housing. The importance of congregate housing is that it provides an immensely important alternative to institutionalization for marginally independent people in need of a variety of supportive services to maintain their independence.

Brody (1977) has provided an assessment of the need for health and social services among elder Americans living at home. She estimates that about one-fourth of those sixty-five and over and more than half of those seventy-five and over living in the community require home care services of some nature. There should be a rapid increase in the volume of this need by 1990. Although most home care needs continue to be provided by family members, the availability of congregate facilities is essential for the growing number of elderly without a family support system capable of providing these services.

For more than thirty years Great Britain has led the way in developing a system of congregate housing. The United States has followed the British model, although it still lags far behind in the number of such units available. Typically, a complex will have self-contained apartments that are able to communicate with a central office in case of an emergency. For those who wish to make use of them, various support services are provided, such as meals, house cleaning, and shopping. A medical clinic with full-time nursing staff is usually on the premises. Whereas some facilities cannot accommodate the bedfast and severely handicapped, others provide life-long care regardless of physical and mental condition. Planned social activities are normally organized by staff in conjunction with the residents.

In a survey of shelter care facilities in Great Britain, Heumann and Boldy (1982) conclude on the basis of a preliminary analysis of data, that residents remain functionally independent longer, are more likely to avoid living in a total care institution, and "appear" [sic!] to live longer than the elderly living in conventional housing.

In a study of a congregate facility in the northeastern United States, using more informal data gathering techniques, Carlin and Mansberg

(1984) obtained similar positive results. The residents are described as remarkably active and admirable in their capacity for organizing an elaborate round of social activities. Factors that enhanced their cohesiveness and high level of involvement were the accessibility of a downtown area where many took advantage of urban amenities, provisions for participating in the management of the home, and a sense of pride and mutual concern for the home and the residents—what Ross (1977) called, in her study among working-class French, a "we-feeling." The authors also claim that an important advantage of such facilities is that they enhance relations with adult children by relieving them of the daily, onerous burdens they would have if their parents were completely dependent on them, and thereby making support from them far more likely during crises.

The developing trend of congregate housing has profound implications for the future. Carlin and Mansberg (1984) report on one study that estimated 3 million elderly in the United States are in need of some form of assisted-living arrangement. Without it they will inevitably end up in a nursing home unnecessarily. As the proportion and total number of old-old increases in the industrial societies, and with fewer children available as caregivers, it will be increasingly more difficult to provide the requisite institutional care. In fact, Heumann and Boldy (1982) claim that between 20% and 30% of those now in nursing homes could live independently if proper assistance were available. It allows for increased control over their lives despite some disabilities and presumably enhances a sense of worth and dignity.

However, determining the level of disability that will be accommodated in a given congregate setting has proven to be a sensitive matter. If the care and protection is overabundant for the needs of some, this could be detrimental to their maintaining a more active, stimulating life-style. For those who have only minor disabilities, the presence of extremely decrepit and disoriented fellow-residents can be strongly resented. As the care required by people increases with age, it is difficult, if not impossible, to find a point acceptable to all at which individuals no longer are accommodated without affecting the character of the setting. Lawton (1980) has suggested two models for congregate housing: a constant model, in which residents are expected to maintain essentially the same level of independence throughout their tenure in the home; and an accommodating model, in which increasing levels of care are provided, short of 24-hour medical attention.

Lawton's accommodating model is similar to the life care communities, which are designed to provide supportive and health care for the remainder of a person's life. They can accommodate people with an active, independent life-style as well as those who are bedridden. Thus, they offer an alternative to the retirement communities for those who seek a greater range of services. Such facilities tend to be expensive, requiring a large

entrance fee and monthly service charges. It is estimated that in the 1980s
there are three hundred such complexes in the United States housing more
than one hundred thousand elderly people (Office of Technology Assessment 1984). We can anticipate a substantial growth in these facilities in the
next decades, as those who can afford it will seek the security they offer.
An obvious need is to study longitudinally the life course of individuals
from the time they enter through subsequent moves to increasing levels of
care provided by this type of congregate living.

Single Room Occupancy (SRO) Hotels

Unlike those seeking support through some form of congregate housing,
there are elderly people who strongly prefer to maintain an independent
life-style, unfettered by any form of planned housing or institutional-like
constraints. The SRO hotel provides a viable alternative for poor people
who desire a high degree of autonomy, despite the obvious drawbacks of
living in some of the most dangerous and dilapidated areas of our inner
cities where most of these hotels are located. This is not strictly an age-
homogenous setting, in that the elderly living in these hotels often share
them with younger adults who tend to be more transient than the older
occupants. In the 1976 Annual Housing Survey, it is estimated that some
130,000 (about 0.6%) of elderly heads of families live in hotels (Lawton and
Hoover 1981). About two-thirds of these elderly are male and 88% are
single (Lawton 1980).

Based on a survey of thirty-two hotels in downtown San Diego, Erickson
and Ekert (1977) classify SROs into three types: (1) skid row hotels—
dominantly male occupants, the most deteriorated with the lowest income
residents, provide no housekeeping or maintenance; (2) working-class
hotels—almost exclusively male occupants, relatively clean and organized
with full-time maintenance staff and housekeeping services; and (3) middle-class hotels—almost equally divided between male and female occupants, more comfortable and expensive, and in addition to the maintenance and housekeeping services, they may offer board and organized
social activities. A sample of eighty-two residents were interviewed in
twelve of the hotels and they are described by the authors as extremely
self-reliant. Some of the reasons given for preferring the hotels as a domicile is the safety they provide, the privacy they allow, and the access to the
goods and services available in the downtown areas.

There have been several useful participant observation studies of SRO
hotels. Employing a grounded theory approach from the symbolic interactionist perspective in sociology, Stephens (1976) draws a picture of the
elderly in a Detroit slum hotel that gives credence not only to their tough-
minded independence, but also their tenacity and courage in surviving on

their own terms. Their life-style is characterized by mutual suspicion, isolation, depersonalization, and alienation from the conventional institutions of U.S. society. The attachment to family and work has been marginal throughout most of their lives. Yet they do establish interpersonal bonds when it is in their self-interest, and they can be extremely flexible in tolerating the disorder and unpredictability of city life. In addition to their monthly social security check, most have some hustle, usually illegal, as a major means of support. Although "losers" and carrying "tarnished identities" from the point of view of the larger society, these people have developed excellent coping skills while maintaining their autonomy in a dangerous environment.

In their study of ninety-six personal networks in ten midtown Manhattan hotels, Sokolovsky and Cohen (1983) provide a more precise analysis of the social contacts of elderly hotel dwellers. They argue that previous studies had usually underestimated the breadth of these contacts. The authors use an anthropological social network analysis, which combines questionnaire data with participant observation to both assess the accuracy of the questionnaire responses as well as determine the cultural meaning behind particular contacts. They found that respondents frequently minimize the volume of their social contacts, preferring to describe themselves as "loners," although they might actually have larger than average networks. Only two persons in the sample lacked any discernible personal network. The others had contacts often equally divided between those living in the hotel and outsiders. Almost 20% even communicated with family members on a weekly basis. Several characteristics of these networks—such as dispersion of the contacts and highly selective intimacy with a few of the safest contacts—reflect the ideal self-image of the residents; that is, their emphasis on self-sufficiency and independence and avoiding the penetration of societal institutions in their lives.

Several studies have attempted to show the extent to which a sense of community can be found even among these fiercely independent hotel dwellers. Ekert (1980) found the elderly residents who lived in the various SRO hotels in downtown San Diego thought of themselves as distinct from all other people in the neighborhood. They recognized such shared values as personal autonomy and minding one's own business; they were aware of the negative view of their world by outsiders, a view they did not share; and they recognized a common identity, a "we-feeling," distinct from the younger, transient residents in the hotels who were considered by the elderly residents as even more deviant (pimps, prostitutes, addicts, etc.). Ekert argues that these characteristics fulfill the notion of community as developed by Ross (1977) in her study of the French retirement home discussed earlier.

A similar community spirit can prevail among residents of a single hotel. Teski (1981) concluded this from a participant observation study of a middle-class retirement hotel in a deteriorated neighborhood of Chicago. Living in an atmosphere she described as "decadent elegance," the residents were able to create relationships of mutual support, activated especially by the women residents, and carried on despite their powerlessness in dealing with the hotel staff.

Most observers agree that such hotels play an important role in serving the poor and socially alienated elderly in U.S. society (Lawton 1980). For individuals who have pursued a private, autonomous existence for most of their lives and have the personality of loners (Ehrlich and Ehrlich 1982), SRO hotels provide a reasonable life-style alternative. But a number of factors make them either unsuitable or unavailable for the elderly. They become unsuitable because of the many deviant societal elements that also choose them, such as the mentally ill who have been de-institutionalized during recent decades. And they become unavailable because of urban redevelopment programs which deplete the number of hotels without the provision of an alternative that is affordable (Erickson and Ekert 1977). As a result, there have been serious shortages.

Some have blamed the proliferation of homeless people in recent years in the United States partly on the conversion of SRO hotels into high-priced condominium housing inaccessible to the poor. Sanjek (1984) reports that in New York City, 89% of the SRO rooms disappeared between 1970 and 1983 and were replaced in large measure by luxury housing. By the mid-1980s estimates of the number of homeless Americans ranged as high as 2 million, and many of them were older people. Some of the so-called shopping bag ladies (Rousseau 1981) intermittently live in SRO hotels when not domiciled in public bathrooms or on the street. These modern day foragers in urban America have been dubbed the "Grate Society" because some seek the warmth of hot air vents on the sidewalk for sleeping. In New York City fences have been erected around such grates to prevent access. And in other parts of the country, particularly California, one finds a growing antagonism toward, and even municipal laws passed against, homeless people sleeping in and foraging through the public domain. Given that the public shelters are frequently too dangerous for the elderly, who can be easy prey for their monthly government checks, it is not clear what alternatives exist for these poverty-stricken elderly.

Although Ekert (1980) provides some useful life course data through his analysis of life histories, well-designed longitudinal studies are not available for SRO hotel residents and homeless aged. More needs to be known regarding their social background, distinctive personality traits, health status, and hotel residency careers. And with increasing numbers living on the streets, it would be important to learn the connection between SRO residency and homelessness.

Alternative Living Arrangements

There are a number of other possibilities, some old and others only recently emerging, that allow the elderly some degree of separation from the larger society. They span a variety of living arrangements, from those that provide some form of sheltered care to ones where no such provisions are available. We order these according to the extent of supportive services available.

Community Housing for the Elderly

This has been called Intermediate Housing because it involves an element of sheltered care. It is a form of independent living for the elderly that provides readily accessible support if needed. Among the better known Community Housing experiments is a project developed by the Philadelphia Geriatric Center (PGC) in 1971. Several semi-detached homes adjacent to the center were renovated so that each set of three apartments shared certain living accommodations. Almost half the units were rented at reduced rates with the help of federal funding. A hot-line phone connects each apartment with PGC for use in case of medical or other emergencies. Other services, such as meals and housekeeping services, can be purchased from PGC at reduced prices.

During the early years of the project's existence, follow-up studies were conducted by PGC staff members after six months residency and then at yearly intervals. The findings indicate that the elderly in the Community Housing project did better than those in two control groups, one that had not moved and the other that had moved elsewhere (Brody and Liebowitz 1981). The Community Housing residents expressed higher morale, felt safer, and had an improved sense of privacy. They also enjoyed improvement in their neighborhood motility as well as their eating and sleeping habits.

House-Sharing

Since housing is the single largest budget item for people, this is especially helpful to those with limited incomes. In addition, it is a possible alternative for people who would otherwise live alone and are in need of some form of assistance (Porcino 1983). It is also one means of efficiently utilizing the excess space found in many homes owned by the aged. Some programs, such as SHARE (Senior Housing at Reduced Expense) in Nassau County on Long Island, attempt to match homeowners with homeseekers.

Communal Living or Cooperative Housing

Although still relatively rare in this country, some people are creating "intentional families." Sometimes they include individuals of various ages in order to maintain intergenerational bonds in a society where such relationships rarely exist outside of family contacts. Typically, residents pool their resources and share housekeeping chores, but each has a separate room. A similar concept well-known in Great Britain is called "sheltered housing."

A variation of this communal living is the Share-A-Home concept (Streib and Streib 1976; Streib 1982). This alternative began in Winter Park, Florida in 1969 and spread to several other cities after it had proven quite successful. It usually begins with a particular family charging others to share their home, usually with the condition that participants have to be ambulatory. If accepted by the "family members" after a 30-day trial period, one joins the collectively-owned-property group by sharing daily expenses and activities. Unlike a commune, however, there is a manager and a staff to care for various needs—meals, housekeeping, transportation, etc.

Elder Cottages and Accessory Apartments

These are creative alternatives that allow a modicum of independent living adjacent to the home of an adult child or other relative. Elder cottages, sometimes called echo housing units, were first developed in Australia where they are referred to as "granny flats." They are compact, portable structures that can be erected on the property of a family home and are designed to be easily installed and removed. Although prototypes are still being developed in the United States (Porcino 1983), a typical unit consists of three small rooms. Much more prevalent is the accessory apartment, whereby a single-family home is converted so that an apartment can be added while changing the outside appearance only minimally. The Census Bureau has estimated over 2.5 million units of this kind are in use in the United States. Both of these alternatives provide efficient and low cost housing, but they can be in violation of local zoning ordinances in some areas.

Boarding Homes

This is a rather old arrangement that still can be found, particularly in small-town America. These tend to be small, locally owned enterprises that may have difficulty surviving with increasing regulation by state and federal authorities. Streib (1982) considers the boarding home, where quality care is common, a superior alternative to a nursing home. But Lawton (personal communication 1985) strongly disagrees with this assessment, claiming that many old people are in boarding homes with terrible conditions or should be receiving nursing care unavailable in these homes.

Mobile Home Parks

This variant may be thought of as the white, working-class equivalent to a retirement community. There are some 12,000 trailer parks in the United States (Porcino 1983), with elderly people comprising some 17% of the occupants (Lawton 1980). In many of the trailer parks, the largest proportion of which are located in the rural areas of the Sun Belt states, over half the residents are retired. In 1980 slightly more than 5% of all households headed by an elderly person were mobile home households (U.S. Bureau of the Census 1984). This is a significant increase over previous figures, and it is anticipated that by the year 2000 some 8% of the aged will live in such homes (Struyk 1981).

Not a great deal is known about such living arrangements. Especially lacking is any longitudinal data, but there is a useful participant observation study of how older people are able to create a sense of community in one of these settings (Johnson 1971). On the other hand, a distinct lack of community creation was found in a Florida mobile home park where residents had no role in decision-making (Angrosino 1976). There is, in fact, increasing evidence from a variety of age-segregated settings that the absence of any input into the decision-making process hinders the development of a group identity.

Conclusion

Although much of the research covered in this review dealt with how old people fare in different environments, it is important to realize that living arrangements in old age are the outcome of a variety of decisions made throughout the life course. Decisions made regarding such diverse aspects of life as family size, kinship patterns, health care, and occupational opportunities all impact on later life. That impact is no less pronounced even though one is not conscious of their consequences for old age (Soldo and Brotman 1981). Furthermore, there is a body of research that indicates that the greater the disruption with adaptation made to the environment during earlier phases of the life course, the greater will be the risk of personal demoralization. And these disruptions can involve many aspects of culture, including life-style preferences, status markings, social activities, or network relationships.

It is generally accepted that the aged are more sensitive to the environment (Wiseman 1981). But it has been difficult to translate this broad axiom into a set of more specific but nontrivial generalizations. Along these lines Lawton (1975) did attempt to summarize how the personal competence of aging individuals interacts with environmental press, in the language of his theoretical model. Perhaps the most common generalization he found

in the literature is that, not surprisingly, the lower competency of individuals is associated with maladaptive behavior and negative effect. It is
also known that those with lowered competency are differentially sensitive
to environmental press. But without more specific operationalization of
environmental attributes, it is difficult to state precisely which of these
attributes is having the most impact. A second generalization is that environments of inappropriately high or low demand quality have a negative
impact on the aged. However, any increase or decrease in environmental
press causing a moderate departure from the adaptation level is experienced positively. This is both suggestive and important, but there is
need for much stronger empirical support.

Wiseman (1981) has discussed the various strategies for improving the
person-environmental fit. The first is to change an individual's level of
competence or personal resources. This is the most difficult to achieve, but
much more could be done to provide greater economic security and to
improve such services as medical delivery, counseling opportunities, and
educational programs for the aged. A second strategy is to change the
person's environment. This has been done with some degree of success
through relocation to age-homogeneous settings oriented toward the
needs of the elderly. But more attention must be given to the great majority
of elderly who are unwilling or otherwise unable to relocate. For them, the
focus should be on the neighborhoods and communities in which they
live. A third and final strategy is to facilitate environmental interactions for
the aged. This involves ensuring greater mobility through the provision of
transportation facilities (such as dial-a-ride), enhancing communications
capability (including the use of computers, which Wiseman doesn't mention), and increasing the opportunities for fantasy experiences. Little is
known about stimulating fantasies in later life, but if it were possible to
determine the environmental cues that trigger fantasy experiences, this
could prove to be a powerful form of expression for the elderly.

It is still not known whether certain developmental constraints related to
personality styles can affect the adaptation to the biological and social
changes that are experienced with aging (Lawton 1975). In this connection,
it is important to know more about the subjective meanings the elderly
have of their environment. Then this information needs to be reconciled
with the technically less difficult to obtain objective assessments of the
person-environment fit (Rowles and Ohta 1983). The development of more
holistic research designs inherent in the life course perspective can provide
this broader accounting of the total context. The danger in this approach,
however, is that the breadth leads to only platitudes and sterile conclusions. Therein lies the challenge for a better understanding of the
person-environment relationship.

XII

THE EFFECTS OF SOCIAL CLASS AND ETHNICITY ON THE AGING PROCESS

Linda Evers Cool

Prior to 1960, few scholars conducted research in the area of gerontology, and, of those who did, even fewer made any attempt to examine the particular situation of older ethnic group members. In spite of warnings that not all people have the same experiences while aging (e.g., Maddox 1969), research concerning the heterogeneity of older people was largely preempted by a focus on the unitary nature of the aging process itself and on the concomitant shared problems of all people as they grow older. In fact, homogeneity marked the research endeavor itself as most of the gerontological studies at that time were directed by the prevailing assumptions of the Activity and Disengagement theories, and thus focused on a single "problem" believed to be common to all older people—the quantity of social roles and activities available to and employed by the elderly.[1]

Other factors also came into play in the tendency to seek gerontological research topics in areas other than ethnicity. In some cases the individuals who otherwise might have been interested in conducting research in ethnicity lacked the necessary linguistic abilities to conduct research. In addition, members of the ethnic groups themselves often were suspicious of researchers who were not of their group, and there were (and are) few researchers who are also members of the ethnic groups they wish to examine.[2] Finally, at that time, social gerontology was still a relatively

---

1. For a brief discussion of these gerontological theories, see the Introduction to this volume.

2. The difficulties of conducting research among ethnic group members can be more severe than overcoming suspicions. Ransford (1976), for example, finds that different answers can be given to the same question depending on whether the researcher is or is not a member of the group under study. This is not to suggest that outsiders cannot study ethnicity; rather, researchers must be alert to the possibility of such problems and work to overcome them.

young field and many different aspects of the aging process were simultaneously demanding research attention.

As gerontologists have come to emphasize the diversity of the aging
experience, they have begun to focus their attention on ethnicity, social
class, and minority status as potentially important variables for analysis.
This interest on the part of gerontologists has coincided with increased
attention paid to the study of ethnicity and minority groups during the last
two decades by social scientists in general. With the civil rights movement
and the War on Poverty during the 1960s, there came a realization that
ethnic minorities were an emerging political force that would have to be
recognized, and funding for research on minority groups became available
(Markides 1982). However, in the process of "discovering" ethnicity,
gerontologists have encountered the same conceptual and theoretical problems that have plagued all researchers concerned with ethnicity: how to
define the concepts, how to distinguish the effects of ethnicity from those
of minority status and social class, and how to avoid providing an overly
homogeneous portrait of the particular ethnic groups in question. This
chapter will attempt to come to grips with some of these problems and to
provide an overview of current research concerning the effects of ethnicity
and social class on the aging process.

Definitions of Ethnicity, Minority Status, and Socioeconomic Class

One widely held perspective is that ethnicity must be viewed along with
class, sex, and age as an additional dimension of stratification in a multiple
hierarchy society such as those found among the modern, industrialized
nations. While few individuals question the validity of such a viewpoint,
the difficulty comes in trying to isolate the effects of each of these variables
(Markides 1982, 468). In an interesting paper, Holzberg claims that one
major reason for this problem is that much of the research on ethnicity has
focused on deprived minorities and that "investigators who are mostly not
anthropologists often failed to distinguish 'ethnic' or cultural factors from
the effects of social class and racial discrimination" (1982a, 250). These
variables are not mutually exclusive: minority status and its accompanying
discrimination at the hands of the larger society undoubtedly are major
contributors to lower socioeconomic class standing. However, we ought to
be able to isolate their varying effects on the aging process.

Ethnicity

In this chapter, the definition of ethnicity encompasses socially significant
characteristics of an aggregate of people within a larger sociocultural context (van den Berghe 1970, 10). Thus, ethnic groups are composed of sets of

individuals who interact and feel bonds of attachment to each other based on shared traits. Researchers interested in the topic of ethnicity may disagree on the exact definition of the concept or on the specific cultural forms that distinguish one ethnic group from another. However, most researchers probably would find that the following criteria contribute to a working definition of ethnicity (Cool 1986):

(1) A past-orientation that places emphasis on distinctive origins (whether real or putative) such as a shared history, common place of origin, language, etc.
(2) Current cultural and/or social distinctiveness (dress, religion, customs, values)
(3) The presence of a larger social context against which the ethnic differences stand in contrast and often in disagreement
(4) An extension of loyalties beyond the face-to-face interactions of a kin or locality grouping
(5) The situational nature of ethnicity whereby ethnic phenomena arise from other conditions of the social environment (including economic, ecological, and political factors) and are amenable to manipulation by individuals and groups
(6) The subjective nature of ethnicity which gives rise to different interpretations of its significance by individuals, both those within the ethnic group and those who stand outside
(7) The flexibility of ethnicity such that no perfect correlations can be found between ethnic categories on census forms and individuals' claims to ethnic status (for example, some individuals who exhibit all the characteristics of ethnic group membership refuse to categorize themselves as such)

As Barth's (1969) study of ethnic relations stressed, research emphasis on ethnicity most fruitfully focuses on how and why boundaries are maintained between groups rather than what makes up ethnic cultural content per se. These boundaries often are more social and psychological (feelings of loyalty and identity) in nature than material or geographical, for their delineation of collective differences comes as a result of both ascription and achievement from within and stereotyping from without. Ethnic ties are not manifested only in cultural forms (Levy 1975, 26). In fact, relying solely on these overt cultural forms or markers for ethnic identification may lead researchers astray. Each generation of ethnic members maintains its ethnic designation by virtue of ancestry and personal identification. Over time, some traditional cultural forms characteristic of a particular ethnic group may well disappear without damaging the group's viability as an ongoing collective entity. For example, distinctive dress often is one of the first external ethnic signs to disappear (Cronin 1970), and such a "loss" rarely affects the vitality of an ethnic group.

Some researchers have focused on an individual's ability to compartmentalize his or her ethnic identity and membership by "turning them on and off" (Little 1966; Nagata 1974; Cool 1980). It seems quite likely that an individual may ignore and/or disguise ethnic membership at times when he or she is occupied with other roles (such as raising a family or making a living) and yet still revitalize the ethnic identity and/or membership at a later date when he or she has lost or modified interim roles and identities. This perspective does not deny the possibility of the negative aspects of such an identity; rather it places emphasis on an individual's potential ability to manipulate the existing situation. Ethnicity thus becomes an adaptive strategy that might provide its older members an exploitable social identity, ongoing interpersonal relationships, and a support network that can be employed at a time in life when many people find that their social world is shrinking.

Thus, what holds an ethnic group together is not so much its cultural uniformity, its unbroken history of group or individual allegiance, or its geographical proximity. Rather, it is social coercion and sometimes individual choice that provide the cement for ethnic group relations. This is not to downplay the importance of cultural distinctiveness, such as differing value systems, in maintaining cohesion as an ethnic group. The cultural dimensions of ethnicity undoubtedly affect the aging process. As Schweitzer indicates, "That the aged face similar problems inherent in growing old is not as important as the fact that there are different and varied perceptions and solutions used to meet these perceptions" (1983, 177).

Minority Groups

In distinguishing minority status from ethnicity, Kolm notes that "the main focus of ethnic groups is on cultural continuity, while the focus of minority groups is mainly on equality regarding economic benefits, civil rights, political rights, etc." (1977, 25). Such a distinction may provide a starting point for analysis. However, it tends to overlook the close relationship between ethnicity and minority groups. In certain cases, ethnicity becomes the basis for discrimination and minority group standing at the hands of the dominant group. An early definition by the sociologist Wirth offered just such a view of a minority group: "A group of people who, because of their physical or cultural characteristics, are singled out from others . . . for special treatment and who therefore regard themselves as objects of collective discrimination" (Wirth 1945, 347).

Stanley Eitzen (1980) argues that the most crucial distinguishing trait of a minority group is its powerlessness in the hands of a dominant group. Here "minority" does not necessarily refer to the numerical sense of the term—hence, the attention paid to the minority status of women in the

United States in recent times (Jackson 1980; David and Brannon 1976). In fact, Eitzen notes that there are many possible bases for the creation of minority groups in contemporary societies: (1) race (genetic differences), (2) ethnicity (cultural differences), (3) religion, (4) poverty, (5) gender, (6) homosexuality, (7) old age, and (8) deformities or handicaps. Regardless of the particular basis for minority standing, such a status typically implies visible differentiation from the majority society, relative powerlessness, negative stereotyping, and discrimination.

Social Class

Theorists have tried for decades to reach a single definition of social class—to little avail, since the definitional criteria vary among researchers and among the various social classes themselves. One attempt, by the Polish sociologist Stanislaw Ossowski (1963), at least has arrived at outlining some aspects of class upon which most researchers appear to agree: (1) classes constitute parts of a larger system—one can define one social class only in relation to another, (2) class divisions determine access to privileges and discrimination not based on biological criteria, and (3) although most class systems are relatively open, membership in a particular class tends to be long term. In most sociological research in the United States, the concept of social class often encompasses three dimensions: income, education, and occupational status. Beyond these factors, many scholars note that classes tend to be arranged hierarchically so that some are inferior or superior to others, and such differential status often leads to a consciousness of one's bonds to and shared interests with others in a similar position. Dowd provides a definition of what he calls the "realist" viewpoint of social classes: ". . . groups possessed both of real and vital common economic interests and of a group-consciousness of their general position in the social scale" (Marshall quoted in Dowd 1983, 30). According to Dowd, although definitions of social class vary, the factor of relative power and control must be part of all of them (1983). Thus, the aspect of relative power/powerlessness becomes the point of intersection for the definitions of ethnicity, minority status, and social class.

Social class position and relative economic standing certainly help shape the life conditions of older people. In fact, Henretta and Campbell (1976) indicate that the factors that determine income in old age are essentially the same as those in earlier life. The social class system remains the same in old age and has similar effects on older as on younger people. Thus, social class position is central to later life because it is central to life in general; social class affects early socialization and therefore the values, attitudes, lifestyle, etc. of an individual are directly affected. Jackson (1980) indicates that differences in family support between black and white aged may be attributable largely to socioeconomic status, and she questions the hypothesis that familial support is stronger for aged minorities than for whites because of cultural differences. Thus, she notes that improved economic conditions for the minority aged (such as greater access to adequate housing) are correlated with increasing proportions of elderly minority group members living alone, just as higher economic status for other groups also is correlated with the elderly living in separate households (1980, 136). Cantor reports similar findings that socioeconomic status is a determinant of the support provided older persons in black, Hispanic, and white families:

> We do not know whether the decreased likelihood of assistance on the part of children as socioeconomic status increases is a response to the greater financial ability of the parent to provide for his own needs, or whether it reflects the greater geographic and psychological distance often associated with upward mobility and higher social status (Cantor 1979, 172).

Thus, Cantor remains convinced that rising socioeconomic status is the cause of the decreased assistance to elderly parents by children, but she is unsure whether such a change is "born of necessity" or "born of desire."

However, other research efforts report findings in direct contradiction to those discussed above. For example, Blau and associates (1979, 501) found that ethnicity exerts more powerful effects than either age or socioeconomic status on educational attainment, the timing of role exits, health and disability, activity, social supports, self-concepts, morale, economic dependency, and the need for public services among a large sample of Anglo, black, and Mexican-American Texans aged fifty-five and over. "The findings . . . indicate that race-ethnicity continues to constitute the most fundamental division in American society at the present time" (Blau et al. 1979, 518). In a more recent study, Mutran (1985) attempted to separate the effects of ethnic and socioeconomic variables on exchanges of help across generations in black and white families. In general, she found that black families were more involved in generational exchanges than white families. When she held socioeconomic class constant, the differences between black and white families began to lessen. However, in spite of such increasing similarities, Mutran found that black families still offered and received more intergenerational help than the white families in her sample.

Because of the contradictory nature of such findings, it remains very difficult, if not impossible, to separate the effects of ethnicity from those of social class on the aging process. Thus, it may be that ethnicity and class cannot be separated into two independent variables and should be considered as a complex single unit. "From this perspective, not only is the priority of class or ethnicity a false issue, but questions can be raised as to the soundness of dealing with ethnicity in isolation from class and vice versa" (Gelfand and Kutzik 1979, 357).

The Effects of Ethnicity on the Social Aging Process

The research on the relationship of ethnicity, social class, and aging has generated three major, and apparently contradictory, viewpoints regarding the mutual interference of ethnicity and the social aging process. First is the notion of double jeopardy—a viewpoint that asserts that minority or ethnic group membership and its accompanying powerlessness and economic deprivation serve only to heighten the problems encountered by older persons. On the other hand, some researchers argue that old age acts as a leveling mechanism. In other words, aging is by itself a sufficiently powerful and universal process to cut across any potential ethnic, racial, or socioeconomic boundaries differentiating older people. Finally, a third argument is that, far from being a solely negative influence on all older people, ethnicity may be a potential mitigating factor that can be employed as a buffer or mediating force against some of the problems (such as isolation, role loss, or lowered socioeconomic status) faced by older people.

The Double Jeopardy of Ethnicity and Old Age

In 1964, a publication by the National Urban League first employed the term "double jeopardy" to refer to the notion that certain elderly persons are doubly disenfranchised from the larger American culture by virtue of their minority/ethnic status as well as by their generally devalued position as elderly citizens. Markson has stated this viewpoint very clearly: "The combination of being old and ethnic . . . forms a distinct social category, albeit of heterogeneous individuals. They suffer from a double stigma, where they have perhaps been lifelong victims of ethnic prejudice and now are victims of ageism" (1979, 344). Jacquelyne Jackson (1970, 1971, 1980), in a series of reports, has extended the notion of double jeopardy to triple (old, poor, and minority status) and even to quadruple (black, female, old, and poor) jeopardy.

Certainly, the elderly members of American racial and ethnic groups constitute a numerical minority. According to Atchley (1985, 275), in 1980 over 92% of the older population of the United States was white, 7% was black, and the remaining 1% was composed of Asian Americans (0.8%), American Indians (0.3%), and "a smattering of other races." In addition, Atchley (1985, 281) notes that in 1980 about 2.5% of the American elderly population was of Spanish heritage—mainly Mexican, Puerto Rican, and Cuban.

Support for the double jeopardy notion comes from many different

TABLE 12.1. **Income and Perceived Health by Ethnicity, 1973**

	Blacks	Hispanics	Whites
Income (mean amount for ages 65–74)	$3,490	$3,360	$6,890
Health (% of those 65–74 who label their health as "poor" or "very poor")	27%	23.2%	4.0%

SOURCE: Bengston, V. L., and L. A. Morgan. 1983. Ethnicity and aging: A comparison of three ethnic groups. In *Growing old in different societies: Cross-cultural perspectives,* edited by Jay Sokolovsky, 160. Belmont, Calif.: Wadsworth Publishing. Reprinted with permission.

sources. The 1971 White House Conference on Aging found that the minority aged faced more social barriers than the white aged in terms of educational levels, income, quality of housing, rates of chronic illness, and average life expectancy (U.S. Senate 1971, 157–201). In 1978, the U.S. Senate's Special Committee on Aging found that poverty in the United States had declined among elderly whites but that "the number . . . and the percentage . . . of low-income aged Blacks and other races actually increased" (U.S. Senate Special Committee on Aging 1978, 151). In studies carried out in Los Angeles, Dowd and Bengston (1978) and Bengston and Morgan (1983) found support for the double jeopardy notion in that older blacks and Mexican Americans reported significantly lower incomes and poorer health than older whites (see Table 12.1).

Current figures for the income of elderly Asian Americans were not available. However, the median *family* income in 1980 was $22,075, the highest for *all* groups. Native Americans were the most deprived in terms of employment and income, and this pattern is sustained in old age: the median income for native Americans aged sixty-five and over was $1,654 for males and $1,162 for females (Cox 1984, 155). One must note that income disparities affect not only the person who is a salaried employee, but also those who retire and receive social security benefits. Because such benefits generally are based on past salaries, the amounts received from social security by the minority aged tend to be lower than those received by their white counterparts. Double jeopardy also appears to be at work in predicting the differential life expectancy patterns of various racial and ethnic groups. However, while the life expectancy patterns for minority populations clearly are unfavorable compared to those of white Americans at birth, by age sixty-five the differences become negligible (see Table 12.2).

When one compares the 1976 data to those of 1981, an interesting phenomenon appears. In the 1976 data, there appears to be a cross-over by age seventy-five where the life expectancy of older blacks is *greater* than

TABLE 12.2. **Life Expectancy by Age, Sex, and Race in 1976 and 1981**

| | 1976 | | | | 1981 | | | |
| | White | | Black | | White | | Black | |
Age	Male	Female	Male	Female	Male	Female	Male	Female
0	69.7	77.3	64.1	72.6	71.1	78.5	64.4	73.0
65	13.7	18.1	13.8	17.6	14.4	18.8	13.2	17.0
70	10.9	14.4	11.3	14.3	11.5	15.1	10.8	13.9
75	8.5	11.2	9.7	12.2	9.0	11.8	8.7	11.1
85	5.1	6.4	7.2	9.1	5.2	6.6	4.7	6.3

NOTE: For similar data with greater historical depth, see Table 9.2 of chapter 9 by Uhlenberg.

SOURCES: 1976 data are from Cox, H. 1984. *Later life: The realities of aging*, 156. Englewood Cliffs, N.J.: Prentice-Hall. 1981 data are from U.S. Bureau of the Census. 1985. *Statistical abstract of the United States: 1985* (105th ed.), 70. Washington, D.C.: Government Printing Office.

that of whites. A similar cross-over in life expectancy has been reported for the Pacific Asian and native American elderly (Cox 1984, 153). Little information exists as to the life expectancy patterns of elderly Hispanics (Cox 1984, 152). According to Roberts and Askew (1972), the mortality rate among Mexican American males was 1.66 times greater than that of Anglo males in 1950, but that rate had dropped to approximately the same level as Anglo males (1.12 times greater) by 1960. The same study reported the mortality rate for Mexican American females as 2.43 times greater than the Anglo female rate in 1950. This rate had dropped to 1.67 times higher than the Anglo female mortality rate by 1960.

There has been a great deal of discussion among researchers concerning the apparent cross-over of life expectancy among the elderly of different racial and ethnic groups. Some believe that it is a matter of census or measurement error. Others argue that such a cross-over does indeed occur and may represent a form of survival of the fittest among blacks and other minorities. That is to say, the living conditions of minority group members were so difficult that anyone who did survive into old age probably represented a biologically elite group and therefore could expect to live longer into old age: "The cross-over is a result of the differential early mortality which selects the least robust persons from the disadvantaged population at relatively earlier ages so that, at advanced ages, the disadvantaged population has proportionately more robust persons" (Manton 1980, 481). Finally, such a cross-over might be evidence indicating that factors encouraging the original differences in life expectancy between blacks and whites—differential nutrition or access to medical care, for example—are changing so as to induce greater similarity in life expectancy patterns (Jackson 1980, 84).

Interestingly enough, the cross-over seen in 1976 does not appear in 1981 (refer again to Table 12.2). In fact, although the racial differences in life expectancy are slight, they again appear to favor the white elderly. Once again, we are left to our own devices to explain this difference. Perhaps there is indeed census and/or measurement error. It may also be that the data in 1981 represent a temporary anomaly in the normal pattern. Or, perhaps Jackson (1980) is correct when she points out that life expectancy patterns may be changing in response to alterations in the environment of blacks throughout the course of their lives.[3]

In an interesting study concerning predictors for increased longevity, Palmore (1982) held age, sex, and race constant. In this way, he discovered that race or ethnicity per se had no measurable effect on life expectancy while indicators of socioeconomic status were moderate to strong predictors of increased longevity for men. While social class variables also predicted longevity among women, the relationship was not strong enough to be statistically significant. "Substantial research has shown that persons from higher socioeconomic groups have lower mortality, probably because they have better nutrition, housing, medical care, and the other good things that contribute to longer life" (Palmore 1982, 516).

Other evidence for double jeopardy appears in the negative attitudes held by those who control important support services for the elderly. Carter (1973) finds that psychiatrists (the vast majority of whom are white) display racism and ageism both in the kind of patients they choose to treat and in their lack of support for alternative systems of support for these people. Jackson (1973) also raises the theme of the mental health problems of the black elderly by indicating that not only does racism adversely affect the delivery of effective health-care resources, but variables negatively associated with aging and mental health (loss of a spouse, forced retirement, etc.) generally occur earlier and with greater frequency among blacks than among whites. Kart (1976) indicates that blacks are over-represented in state mental hospitals while white elderly are over-represented in nonprofit and private homes.

Finally, several researchers report an interesting twist to the double jeopardy notion of aging. The acceptance of stereotypes about minorities (especially those stereotypes that appear to be positive) actually may work against the minority aged. For example, Kim (1973) points to the stereotype of Asian Americans as the "model minority" because of their apparent economic and educational successes. Kim takes exception to the designation indicating that not only is this "model status" a myth unsupported by reality for the majority of Asian Americans, but it also is a convenient device to exclude them from benefiting from social programs. As a result,

3. For a further discussion of the first two explanations for this cross-over effect, see chapter 4 by Beall.

the burden for the care of the elderly is placed solely on their families because "everyone knows" that Chinese children must care for their parents due to the tradition of filial piety (Fuji 1976). However, Wu (1975) notes that in Los Angeles, the Mandarin-speaking elderly are victims of political, social, economic, and cultural changes, *including* a weakening in the concept of filial piety which undermines even this traditional source of support for the elderly.

Maldonado (1975) argues against the popular wisdom that assumes that aged Mexican Americans are properly cared for because of the extended family pattern. According to Maldonado, increased mobility and urbanization of younger Chicanos seriously threaten the roles and personal security provided to the elderly under the traditional extended family structure.

> Governmental social agencies, in "respecting the culture," may be avoiding their responsibility to provide services since they place responsibility on the Chicano family. At the same time, the agencies are not providing the family with the resources for making the needed services available to the aged (Maldonado 1975, 213).

An Assessment of the Double Jeopardy Hypothesis

In spite of such supporting documentation, the evidence from the research on the double jeopardy hypothesis is far from clear. As noted earlier, Bengston and Morgan (1983) find confirmation of the double jeopardy notion in income deprivation and health perceptions. But, the results of the other two variables that they tested (life satisfaction and social interaction) are not so clear: there was little difference found among members of the three ethnic groups on two measures of life satisfaction, tranquility and optimism, and the responses to the questions on social interaction were quite mixed. If the double jeopardy situation were indeed in effect, one would expect to see the white respondents reporting higher levels of both life satisfaction and social contact (see Table 12.3).

On these life satisfaction scores, little difference appeared between black and white respondents although Mexican Americans appeared to be less optimistic. Neither blacks nor Mexican Americans were found to be in less frequent contact with relatives than whites. In fact, the Mexican American respondents reported greater contact with their children and grandchildren than either the black or white respondents, and the black respondents reported more extensive contact with "other relatives" than members of the other two groups. Other studies report similar findings regarding the social contacts of minority group members. Ragan and Simonin (1977), for example, found that an equal percentage of black and Mexican American women in their sample said that they saw their adult children as often as they liked. In addition, Clemente, Rexroad, and Hursch (1975) found that black elderly are more likely to belong to church, social, and recreational groups than their white counterparts.

TABLE 12.3. **Tri-Ethnic Comparisons of Life Satisfaction and Social Interaction for Persons Aged 65–74**

Life Satisfaction	Blacks	Hispanics	White
Tranquility (mean score)	2.17	1.93	2.17
Optimism (mean score)	1.31	.98	1.43
Social Interaction			
Children (% who saw their children the week before)	68.8	85.2	79.9
Grandchildren (% who saw their grandchildren the week before)	75.6	82.9	73.1
Other relatives (% who saw other relatives the week before)	42.7	40.2	40.5
Friends or neighbors (% who saw friends or neighbors the week before)	50	31.6	75

SOURCE: Bengston, V. L., and L. A. Morgan. 1983. Ethnicity and aging: A comparison of three ethnic groups. In *Growing old in different societies: Cross-cultural perspectives,* edited by Jay Sokolovsky, 162. Belmont, Calif.: Wadsworth Publishing. Reprinted with permission.

In recent articles, Holzberg (1982a, 1982b) has provided an important critique of the double jeopardy notion. Her argument stresses that most of the evidence supporting double jeopardy comes from the study of *deprived* minority groups. Because of this focus, there tends to be a confounding of the effects of poverty, racial/ethnic discrimination, and cultural differences that might be attributed to ethnicity. According to Holzberg, these subcultures will also include "value-sets" (e.g., family support systems) of significance to the aging process. But her findings also imply that the value-sets that are characteristic of minorities are more the result of responses to socioeconomic deprivation than they are examples of longstanding cultural traditions. The strategies she describes are, therefore, class-based coping mechanisms rather than subcultural value-sets (Holzberg 1982a, 251). Finally, Holzberg points to this additional problem: that much of the research on minority aging has tended to deal with minority populations as if they were completely homogeneous entities in terms of individuals' experiences, income levels, and values.

According to our best knowledge at this point in the research endeavor, there is a double jeopardy of being old and a member of a minority group which operates in certain areas of some individuals' lives. But for the moment at least, it appears that double jeopardy cannot be considered an explanatory theory per se, but rather a description of existing conditions. Conclusive evidence either supporting double jeopardy or refuting it awaits careful research and new methodologies that can encompass the combined effects of social class and minority status.

Age as the Equalizer of Social Differences

A second major position to arise from research dealing with ethnicity and aging is the "age-as-leveler" hypothesis. Rather than viewing aging and minority status as two mutually reinforcing and *negative* influences on people's lives, this perspective argues that the aging process is so pervasive and powerful that it mediates any racial, ethnic, or social class differences that might exist among older people. From this viewpoint then, the problems faced by old people are seen as very similar regardless of particular differences among groups of people in a given society: "social class and race which seem important in youth evidently pass with time and fade when individuals are confronted with problems of survival" (Kent 1971, 49).

An early version of the age-as-leveler hypothesis was promoted by Burgess (1960). This pioneer of gerontological studies in industrialized societies argued that old age is a "roleless role"; that modern society provides no specific roles or activities for older people and leaves them to face a meaningless existence. Barron (1961) added to this picture of old age by focusing on the elderly as an unprivileged minority group. For him, low status and income are not just the facts of growing old, they are the inevitable destiny for those who reach age sixty-five. Arnold Rose (1965) argued that a unique subculture with its own life style, organizations, and political objectives was developing among older Americans. While he did note that one might expect to find some individuals less involved in such a subculture than others,

> the aging subculture is a general one that cuts across other subcultures—those based on occupation, religion, sex, and possibly even ethnic identification—that are characteristic of the middle-aged population. Insofar as older people are somewhat more likely to unite on the basis of age than on the basis of these other divisions, relatively speaking, they are likely to weaken the other subcultures as they substitute a new one for them (Rose 1965, 7).

Data from research support this age-leveling perspective as well. For example, Foner and Kertzer (1978) found age to be a "major organizing principle" in their study of preliterate African age-set societies. However, they also noted that other stratification principles such as social class, race, and sex may be more important in more complex societies. As indicated earlier, Dowd and Bengston (1978) and Bengston and Morgan (1983), in their studies of blacks, Mexican Americans, and whites in Los Angeles, found some leveling with age for several dimensions of life satisfaction and social interaction. Pampel (1981) found evidence of income leveling across age groups, with white males exhibiting the greatest income loss. He also found that inequality within the older population declined between 1947 and 1974, although he noted that substantial inequality remains.

David Gutmann has added an intriguing psychological-developmental dimension to the age-as-leveler hypothesis.[4] Essentially, Gutmann (1969, 1975) suggests that gender differences become neutralized as a normal part of the aging process. Although his conclusions are not accepted by all anthropologists, his research has led him to believe that behavioral differences between the sexes are associated with parenthood. When parental tasks are over, women and men are able to approximate "the normal androgyny of later life" (Gutmann et al. 1980, 122). If Gutmann is correct, the movement of aging men (who traditionally worked outside the home and served the major "breadwinner" role) away from active and competitive styles of behavior can be used to help explain status-leveling in old age for ethnic groups as well as for members of the majority culture.

An Assessment of the Age-as-Leveler Perspective

As was the case with the double jeopardy hypothesis, more data are needed before we can make a definitive assessment of the validity of the age-as-leveler perspective. Bengston and Morgan (1983) are correct in their emphasis on the fact that longitudinal studies are necessary if we are ever to approximate an understanding of the relative effects of aging as opposed to other forms of stratification. It may be that the general problems that older people face *are* similar. But this does not mean that all people respond to stimuli in exactly the same way. One must never lose sight of individuals' abilities to manipulate various aspects of their personal and social lives, including their ethnicity.

Ethnicity as a Source of Support

A series of studies by anthropologists in a variety of societies including the United States has raised the possibility that there has been an undue emphasis placed on the negative aspects of ethnic membership for the elderly. This research also raises the possibility that ethnicity may in fact offer elderly members opportunities for participation in formal and informal networks and serve as a source of on-going personal and social identities. It suggests as well that ethnic membership might provide two-way channels of communication and aid: older members teach younger members about the meaning of their ethnicity and younger members provide continued moral and physical support for the elderly. As Lozier and Althouse indicated, "successful aging is based on the continuing existence of a social system in which behavior toward elders has social significance and social consequences for juniors" (1974, 69).

4. For a more detailed discussion of Gutmann's work, see chapter 7 by Chiriboga and chapter 14 by Silverman.

This emerging perspective also helps explain the persistence of ethnicity and ethnic identity in the face of powerful assimilative forces in the larger society. Andrew Greeley (1974) uses the term "ethnogenesis" for this persistence. Ethnogenesis refers to a model of ethnic relations in which pressures to assimilate exist concomitantly with pressures to maintain ethnic identification. According to this model then, maintaining an ethnic identity becomes a device for expressing group interests and maintaining group solidarity. And, because the elderly are necessarily chronologically closer to a purported time of ethnic purity before the contamination of the larger society, they are evidently the ones who can offer "proof" of the validity of this identity.

Many of the anthropologists who conduct research concerning ethnicity as a potential source of support for elderly ethnic members at least implicitly have employed tenets of the life course perspective. Myerhoff (1978a), especially, was able to weave the theme of continuity into her study of older Jewish residents of Venice, California. For Myerhoff, the success of her elderly Jewish informants was due largely to the fact that they had made aging their life's career. Myerhoff stressed the point that persistence in life patterns and identities is crucial to a person's adaptation to old age. Such an emphasis on examining the meaning and context of the whole life course and the maintenance of continuity within it may help overcome some of the problems encountered in the double jeopardy and age-as-leveler perspectives outlined earlier.

A growing body of research indicates that ethnicity may be a potential source of support which older people may manipulate to mitigate some of the difficulties they encounter. To examine the findings of these research enterprises, it is helpful to view ethnicity as a multidimensional phenomenon encompassing at least three related components: cultural, personal, and behavioral/organizational.

The Cultural Component

The cultural heritage of ethnic members differs from that of the larger society in several ways; among them are value systems, world view, and normative structure. Certainly as individuals grow older, they carry with them a culture derived from group interactions and early socialization. In this respect, an ethnic value system can support older people by providing them a continuing set of beliefs as well as a place in the larger social system. And to the extent that older ethnic members remain committed to a pattern of evaluation and interaction different from that of the larger society, they should be better able to avoid the internalization of the larger society's attitudes toward them as older persons. This does not mean, of course, that ethnicity is a fail-safe investment against the negative self-perceptions that threaten many older people in industrialized societies.

However, its presence does provide an additional basis for shared understandings, self-identification, and group membership.

An ethnic group's historical uniqueness furnishes a context in which aging individuals can reinterpret the meaning of their own lives. In many ethnic groups throughout the world, youthful members currently are redefining their groups' histories, a fact that has important ramifications for the elderly members. Moore (1971, 90) provides a good example of this reinterpretation of history by young black Americans. In the past, many older blacks knew only frustration and failure as they tried to achieve the "American dream" in a hostile white society. In light of the pervasive image of "the land of equal opportunity," they blamed their lack of success on personal inadequacy. But young blacks' current reinterpretation of their people's collective problems, and their focus on the inequities of the larger society now offer these old people an opportunity to ascribe a more positive meaning to their apparent lack of success and to remove the stigma of individual failure and personal inadequacy. Younger blacks now acknowledge the difficult times their elders faced and assign them a kind of pioneer status in current efforts to eliminate discrimination.

Such efforts to review and reinterpret the subordinate group's history might facilitate the elderly's reinvention of those roles and power resources customarily allocated to their counterparts in more traditional societies. For example, Cool (1980) has found that elderly Corsicans have taken for themselves the role of guardians and teachers of traditional knowledge and customs. Young Corsicans who are interested in promoting their distinctiveness from the larger French population must turn to their elders for proof that such differences do (or did) exist. Holzberg's (1983) research among Jewish residents of the Toronto Baycrest Center also illustrates this tactic. Certain residents of the facility came up with the idea of documenting their own past experiences and they were able to obtain funding to support a project to collect and publish their memoirs. The residents themselves were convinced that their project was crucial:

> Recognizing that since the Holocaust they were the last remaining links to the social and cultural traditions of turn-of-the-century central and Eastern European Jewry . . . they kept repeating how their grandchildren would now have something concrete to remember them by and how it was important for these children to learn about their cultural roots (Holzberg 1983, 260–61).

The Personal Aspect of Ethnicity

Self-identity derives at least partly from the roles one assumes or is allowed to assume during the course of a lifetime. According to Royce (1982, 7), people obtain their personal ethnic identity from two sources: "one being the ethnic group itself [what defines the group to itself], the other the sense of solidarity that devolves upon groups that find themselves different from other groups or cut off from society." Hendel-Sebestyen (1979) found such a situation as she conducted research among older Jewish residents of a home for Jews of Spanish and Portuguese descent in New York City. Even though they find themselves in an institution, these older people carry with them their cultural and religious traditions and roles. In fact, because the center is dedicated to Jewish cultural and religious traditions, the residents are encouraged to maintain the roles and identities that marked their younger years. One must also note that the roles which these elderly residents assume are "not just the ones assigned to them by the organizational framework" (Hendel-Sebestyen 1979, 22). For example, the residents of the center form voluntary charitable organizations which approximate as closely as possible those in which they had participated prior to moving to the home. In addition, the residents actively participate in the running of a synagogue in the home—they select officers for its administration and assist in the hiring of the rabbi.

Cool (1981) has found a similar situation in which ethnicity provides an identity and accompanying roles different from age, gender, or occupation among noninstitutionalized elderly Portuguese residents of Santa Clara County, California. There, Portuguese and non-Portuguese necessarily mingle in school, on the job, and, to a certain extent, in their neighborhoods. However, the primary focus of attention of many Portuguese in Santa Clara County is their own church and their ethnic community—and this effectively excludes the non-Portuguese population. Both Portuguese and non-Portuguese are quick to point out this lack of association between the groups, and both account for it in terms of the preference that Portuguese have for their own traditions and the tendency of many to never learn English. Most elderly Portuguese who were interviewed do not perceive this lack of integration in the wider American society to be a problem. Rather, the majority live with or in close proximity to at least one child who is expected to provide any links that might be needed between the larger society and the elderly individual. Many of the elderly commented that they do not take part in the making of economic decisions, for most of these involve the unfamiliar outside world. Rather, they perceive their role to be more spiritual, in the sense that it revolves around teaching the young and carrying on the traditional culture as much as possible. The elders perceive this role to be all the more important in the face of desertions from the traditional ways on the part of the young who do speak English, attend schools, and are in most ways very Americanized. The young also acknowledge the importance of such teaching as they attempt to separate themselves from other ethnic groups in the region and to reassert their pride in their Portuguese heritage.

The Behavioral/Organizational Component of Ethnicity

The behavioral/organizational component of ethnicity includes distinctive values, beliefs, and norms that lead to actions and serve as the bases for social interaction and the rise of an ethnic group per se. Ethnic groups themselves exhibit a degree of social organization that ranges from relatively loose interpersonal networks that are based on a sense of shared origins and history, to formal corporate association whose economic and political institutions are defined by membership lists and clearly articulated goals. One "advantage" of ethnicity is that it can provide informal support networks to people of all ages who claim to be ethnic (Gelfand 1982, 105). In fact, Cohen (1978, 401) reports that a hypothesis which ought to be tested empirically is that "the greater the participation in ethnic group activities, the less persons feel alienated in contemporary society." While this hypothesis may help to explain why ethnicity continues to exist in the face of pressures to assimilate from the larger society, it also provides a clue as to the importance of ethnicity to the elderly ethnic member. Palmore (1982) already has noted that measures of organizational and nonfamilial activities are significant predictors of longevity. Thus, he suggests that interactions outside the neighborhood are more important for longevity than interactions with family: "those who had substantial involvement outside the neighborhood were an above average group who benefitted from the extra stimulation and gratifications of organizational activities" (Palmore 1982, 517).

Cuellar has found that senior citizen voluntary associations are providing both meaning in life and arenas for social interaction for elderly Chicanos in Los Angeles. This finding is especially compelling because voluntary associations of this kind are lacking for the most part in traditional Mexican rural societies (Cuellar 1978, 208) and therefore represent an adaptation to the new society that is *based on ethnicity* (emphasis mine) but for which there are no direct antecedents in the culture of origin.

> Within the framework of the voluntary association, some older Chicanos have learned new roles, acquired new information, and been socialized into an emergent age-based subculture. The voluntary association has also served as a social arena where its members have demonstrated their competences and abilities, have shared experiences, and have acquired new perspectives as well as some measure of prestige and power through the manipulation of available resources and social interaction (Cuellar 1978, 215).

Cuellar emphasizes that while these senior voluntary associations may not be based on a traditional culture per se, they are strongly based on common ethnic origins: pride in their cultural differences from the larger society, a special group history, and a history of discrimination at the hands of the larger society.

Cool (1980) has found that ethnic group membership may take at least three different forms among Corsicans living in Paris: (1) informal interpersonal networks based on a sentiment of brotherhood, friendship, or kinship, (2) quasi-groups which exist because of the availability of shared interests and a meeting place, and (3) formal associations with economic and/or political institutions defined by membership lists and articulated, collective goals. In addition, great diversity exists among individual Corsicans in terms of how they participate in these different sorts of networks and when they choose to involve themselves: some elderly Corsicans participate in all three levels of association, others in one or two, and some Corsicans choose not to participate at all. The emphasis here is placed on an individual's ability to manipulate his or her environment. "Ethnic affiliation is not . . . a universal panacea for the problems of old age. At best, it offers the possibility for personal involvement and group membership for those individuals who seek it out" (Cool 1980, 167).

An Assessment of the Ethnicity-as-Support Perspective

To reiterate, this perspective does not ignore or minimize the discrimination that minorities and ethnic groups have suffered at the hands of a larger society. However, it does indicate that ethnicity as a cultural system may be manipulated as may any other aspect of culture. Because of anthropology's traditional disciplinary focus on the study of the development, maintenance, and change of cultures, it is not surprising to find that the researchers who have adopted this position have been, by and large, anthropologists. And, because anthropologists tend to focus on comparisons of particular (often relatively small) groups of people, they often are able to avoid the creation of an overly homogeneous portrait of an ethnic group. However, the perspective must be tested adequately before it can be fully accepted. Longitudinal studies are needed to validate points raised about the long-term benefits of ethnicity for individuals. On-going studies of changes within particular groups themselves are needed to illustrate that current findings are not just artifacts of the particular climate of today. Similarly, more care must be taken to isolate the relative effects on the aging process of ethnicity, discrimination against members of minority groups by the larger society, and socioeconomic status.

Conclusion

This chapter began with definitions of ethnicity, minority status, and social class and raised questions about the relative effects of these three social aspects on the aging process. Although a great deal of recent research attention has focused on just these questions, there remains relatively little consensus as to the answers. Some researchers argue that one cannot separate ethnicity from social class, some argue that one or the other of these two variables is primordial in explaining variations in the aging process, while others argue that the mere fact of growing old takes precedence over all other aspects of a person's life.

Given the present state of our knowledge concerning the relationship of ethnicity, socioeconomic class, and minority status, it would be a mistake to assume that one of the three viewpoints described earlier is necessarily more correct than the others. Each has its own areas of support and its own weaknesses. However, there are ways to overcome some of the problem areas raised in the preceding discussion and to gain a better understanding of the relation of these three variables to the aging process: (1) Longitudinal research on individuals and their involvement in ethnic groups as well as longitudinal studies of the life course of ethnic groups themselves will offer a clearer picture of the long-term effects of ethnicity on older members today and in the future. (2) Careful research methodologies can control for the effect of social class in a number of ways. Controlled comparisons, *holding age and social class constant*, of different groups of older ethnic members would go a long way toward helping us evaluate the double jeopardy, age-as-leveler, and ethnicity as manipulative strategy viewpoints. One could also, for example, investigate the effects of race/ethnicity on social class by comparing the salaries of ethnic workers in particular occupations (one measure of socioeconomic status). (3) Attention must be paid to all kinds of ethnic groups, not just the deprived minorities, to gain a broader understanding of the relation of ethnicity to aging. (4) Internal differences within particular ethnic groups must be considered if a clearer picture is to emerge. (5) Researchers also must attempt to understand the difference between the *immigration* experience and ethnic membership. Longitudinal studies comparing generations of ethnic members could help here.

Obviously the research on stratification and aging has come a long way—we have learned a great deal and our methodologies are becoming increasingly sophisticated and powerful. But we also have a long way to go before we can make authoritative statements about the effects of ethnicity and social class on the aging process.

It is evident that a single homogeneous world culture is not necessarily the future condition of humanity. In fact, many scholars note that pluralistic societies are on the rise throughout the world. Thus, people within any given society must increasingly interact socially and politically with individuals who represent different ways of living and thinking. To the extent that most people will now be growing older in such pluralistic societies, it is particularly important that gerontologists understand how ethnic identity is manipulated by the elderly. The challenge of explaining the present and predicting the future of the elderly in complex societies has been made; it is up to us to meet it.

XIII

AGE IN CROSS-CULTURAL PERSPECTIVE

AN EVOLUTIONARY APPROACH

Rhoda H. Halperin

The Ethnography of Age

Age is a variable in the organization of all human cultures. This chapter is a review of age as a variable in the analysis of cultural systems (Kertzer and Keith 1984; Fortes 1984; Mayberry-Lewis 1984; Hammel 1984; Sokolovsky 1983; Holmes 1983; Keith 1979, 1980; Fry and Keith 1980). The concepts and questions presented are meant to stimulate further research by suggesting lines of inquiry with both theoretical and practical implications. In this exploratory essay then, I use age and the life course as focal points for revealing questions about the analysis of cultural systems, especially as they are changing rapidly in the postindustrial world economy. By analyzing specific ethnographic case materials I hope to shed light upon which segments and characteristics of the life course—childhood, adulthood, and particularly old age—are manifested generally and universally, and which are culture-specific.

Carl Eisdorfer (1981, xiii) points out that the "aging crisis" is not restricted to the industrialized West: "The massive increase in the numbers of aged is a world-wide phenomena." He points out that "the countries whose economies are least able to bear additional burdens—whose traditional social arrangements are experiencing the most rapid change—are precisely those that will shortly have to bear the double burden of many more dependent elders as well as many more dependent young children. In Africa, Latin America, and Asia the number of people over 60 will more than double before the year 2,000, putting a severe strain on social arrangements for meeting their needs" (1981, xiv).

I elaborate here upon a preliminary framework set forth in an earlier article (Halperin 1984). The framework is designed to facilitate comparative analysis by establishing an evolutionary model for dealing with pattern and variability in life course processes. While the earlier paper concentrated upon the economics of aging across cultures and across time, this chapter retains that focus and builds upon it. Since work roles almost always change with age, and since the organization of work for the elderly (as well as for other age groups) is and will be an increasingly difficult problem as populations grow older, emphasis upon economic processes is warranted. Examining the cross-cultural record makes it possible to question the often ethnocentric assumptions concerning the nonproductivity and resultant dependency of the elderly. Most importantly, the conditions under which the elderly become dependent members of society must be spelled out, for the circumstances under which people of different ages, old as well as young, retain or are able to obtain viable economic and social roles vary greatly across cultures and with time. Contemporary societies need creative solutions to the problem of the division of labor by age; it may even be possible to use knowledge of other cultures to restructure the division of labor so that the needs of society can be met. Positive life course patterns in other cultures can be used as models for inspiring creative solutions to problems that have faced humans in cultural systems for thousands of years. Also, the physical and mental health risks, especially for those people at the extreme ends of the life course, can, with some cross-cultural knowledge, be avoided by policymakers (Scheper-Hughes 1979).

Age is a critical variable for almost all processes in any culture. Individuals in all cultures grow older, change their productive tasks and later, their involvement in social life. The social units within which individuals produce, distribute, and consume their livelihood change with time and thus age. The fact that until very recently, age has been treated only serendipitously in most ethnographic studies is both a testimony to the relatively primitive state of the art, and a reflection of our own culture's denial of inevitable aging processes (Myerhoff 1978b). Aging processes are an intrinsic part of all cultures and are linked to social structures in variable and intricate ways.

The analysis of age as a variable in cultural systems depends greatly on the type of society under consideration. Before meaningful comparisons are drawn or generalizations made for processes of aging and life course, a framework within which comparisons can be carried out must be established. The perspective I will take is an evolutionary one. Generally, as cultures evolve from preindustrial egalitarian societies to highly stratified capitalist systems, age becomes less of an independent variable shaping cultural processes such as the division of labor for production, the structure of authority relations, patterns of deference, and access to knowledge; instead age becomes a dependent variable that is controlled by economic, technological, and ideological processes.

I use age in several ways. In some instances age refers to demographic age distribution, in others, individual chronological age, in still others, life course stage as culturally defined, or level of physical functionality. This last is particularly important in determining contributions to subsistence in societies that rely solely or primarily upon human muscular energy. Age also refers to chronological and ecological time periods such as yearly seasonal cycles or village life cycles of several years or more. Conceptualizing time is critical for understanding aging and cultural processes. As individuals age, their relationships in social and political units such as households, villages, and cities change. The social units themselves exist in historical time, and therefore change ecologically, demographically, and technologically.

In a sense then, to pose the question of age as a variable in any cultural process is to investigate time and social structure (Fortes 1949, 1984). As Fortes demonstrates, in what may now ironically be a timeless piece, neither the time factor nor the age factor in social structure is uniform in incidence. He distinguishes the functions of time: (1) as duration and/or simple sequence, (2) as continuity, and (3) as genetic or growth processes. The first is an extrinsic factor having no critical influence on the structuring of social events or organization. The second is an intrinsic and critical characteristic of some social events and is significant as an index of forces and conditions that remain constant or change over time. In the third, time is correlated with change within a frame of continuity. Fortes uses these distinctions to discuss the constant and variable features of Ashanti social structures, but his time concepts are applicable to any social structure; they are truly cross-cultural, comparative concepts.

Ideally, I would have liked to be consistent and use the word age with a single meaning. The data, and the nature of our language, however, do not allow it (Eckert 1984). It is possible, however, to use an evolutionary framework to find patterns delineating the relationships between age and fundamental processes of production, distribution, and consumption as well as patterns of social organization, social change, political organization, religious organization, and so on. To propose an evolutionary framework is not to exhaust the range of evolutionary types or to suggest a rigid typology of cultural systems. It is an attempt to use a familiar analytic scheme as a model for organizing questions which may lead to the addition of more detailed qualitative, and especially quantitative, data to an otherwise primarily descriptive and anecdotal ethnographic record concerning age as a variable in human cultural systems (Nag 1973).

If we assume that both the quality and the quantity of an individual's contribution to the life of a household, a village, or a nation changes over time, then the task becomes one of explaining the nature of the change. Who works, for how long, at what sorts of tasks in different societies? What does an understanding of the variation indicate about processes of livelihood, social organization, and the nature of cultural processes? Why, for example, are the elderly marginal in industrial economies and key resources in others? What kinds of institutions, relations of production and ecological settings in different cultures create economic and ritual importance for certain categories of individuals at particular points during the life course? Given the increased and increasing longevity of populations in industrial societies (Fries 1980), what are the implications, theoretical as well as practical, of long-term dependency of the old upon the young (Dohlinow 1984)?

An Evolutionary Framework

Aging processes are universal in human societies. The intersection of aging processes and other processes (biological, ecological, social, and political) in culture demands attention not only because individuals grow old, and change the nature of their activities, but also because social units (units of social structure such as kin groups) themselves change with time and thus mature. In some societies that maturation occurs within an individual's lifetime, in others over many generations. Households age and so do villages, cities, and nation-states.

Age touches every facet of social life, but it does so differently in different cultures. The ways in which social, economic, and political units change with age depend greatly upon the political, technological, and ecological contexts within which the units operate. In cultures that are demographically small, technologically simple, and politically egalitarian, age functions with sex as one of the two determinants of the division of labor in society. In most preindustrial cultures, age statuses function alongside those of kinship; often the two overlap to set patterns of labor division. In more complex and politically stratified social systems, age is only one of many principles dividing labor, and it is subordinate to social class.

Egalitarian societies with hunter-gatherer and horticultural technologies are the first type of society to be considered. The general questions framing the section are: How do people at different ages participate in social life? What kinds of contributions do people make? I then deal with ranked and stratified societies, first chiefdoms and then state-level societies with increasingly larger and more complex political units. By organizing the ethnographic material in an evolutionary framework, we can ask both general and particular questions. For example, once human societies become sedentary, how does age affect social life in general, and the division of labor in particular? What is the relationship between population size, the age pyramid, and the function of age in the overall social organization in preindustrial societies? How does the development of the state and class stratification affect social roles for people of different ages?

It should be noted that technology alone does not suffice to classify cultures as similar or different. Societies with horticultural technologies, for example, differ enormously along a range of variables, among them, population size, resource base, and degree of political centralization and ranking. At one end of the continuum, egalitarian horticultural societies such as those in the Amazon Basin, exhibit social structures which are, in many respects, similar to those of hunter-gatherers. At the other end of the pre-state continuum are horticultural societies such as the Trobrianders with much larger populations and a social organization closer to that of preindustrial states. Most peasant producers in nation-state systems practice some form of horticulture. In some cases, peasant households are smaller and more simply organized than households at the chiefdom level. The latter may comprise a clan, a group of clans, or a whole village population. Controlling for technology, the implications of the size of the social unit for the allocation of tasks among people of different ages needs further analysis.

Egalitarian Societies

Egalitarian societies are the oldest, smallest, and, technologically, most simple societies in the human cultural experience. Subsistence in egalitarian societies consists of hunting and foraging in demographically small, nomadic bands of extended families which cluster together or split apart according to the seasonal availability of resources. For most of our existence on earth as *Homo sapiens,* we lived as hunter-gatherers. Among contemporary foragers are the Eskimo, the Kalahari !Kung, and the Tiwi of Australia. Egalitarian social structures can also be found among semi-sedentary horticulturalists, populations utilizing slash and burn or shifting agriculture. Small villages relocate approximately every five years to replenish the soil and take advantage of new sources of meat and vegetables. Examples include some tropical horticultural groups in the Amazon Basin which combine hunting, fishing, and gathering with horticulture. Demographically, small-scale horticultural societies are comparable in many ways to foraging bands. A politics of consensus contributes to egalitarianism (Leacock 1978, 249). Economically, egalitarianism is manifested by the fact that no individual or group has differential access to resources. Because ranking and class stratification do not exist, there is no potential for control or monopolization of scarce resources. In these societies, the egalitarian social structure ensures itself by rules of reciprocity and redistribution manifested by food sharing and resource management; all members of a group have equal access to available food. In times of scarcity everyone goes without. To understand the role of age in egalitarian societies, these important definitional features must be taken into account.

If defined independently of subsistence strategy, political organization tends to reflect the allocation of resources and overall demographic adjust-

Elder Leader of the Yaquas: This man moved with the starving rem-
nants of his tribe to the Amazon area near Iquitos in eastern Peru.
Amazonian Indians remain vulnerable to the unrelenting and often
brutal expansion of Western, industrial culture into their areas. (Photographer: G. Pasha Turley)

ment better than does a classification according to technology. Using
political criteria to group cultures allows for analysis of cultural differences
in societies that are technologically alike but ecologically, and often demographically and politically, different. The Indians of the Northwest
Coast of North America are an example. Technologically, groups such as
the Tlingit, Haida, the Kwakiutl and the Coast Salish are hunter-gatherers,
but demographically they are large because of their extremely abundant
maritime environment. Politically they are by no means egalitarian; there is
now substantial evidence of economically important slavery on the
Northwest Coast with clear-cut ranked distinctions between owners (high-
ranking lineage heads), commoners, and slaves in precontact times (Mitchell and Donald 1985). The important point is that because of their elaborate
political structure, these groups are not comparable to egalitarian hunter-
gatherers. They look much more like ranked horticulturalists such as the

Trobrianders, and, therefore, for evolutionary purposes, must be treated as such (Fried 1967).

In short, an evolutionary framework requires a whole complex of interacting elements which result in a cultural unit. Such a framework can explain the similarities between Kwakiutl and Trobriand chiefs, including, perhaps, their age requirements. Because a population's size and its resource base figure so importantly in shaping the relationships between age and social organization, a clear and precise evolutionary framework is essential.

Hunter-Gatherers

Data on the life span for hunter-gatherers indicate some contradictory, or at least highly variable patterns. For example, while life expectancies for hunter-gatherers are low by modern European standards, they compare favorably with expectancies for displaced hunter-gatherers, many subsistence agriculturalists, and poor urban people in the tropics (Dunn 1968, 224). Richard Lee reports that among !Kung Bushmen of the Dobe area in a population of 466 individuals, no fewer than 46 individuals (17 men and 29 women) were over sixty years old, a ratio comparing favorably to the percentage of elderly in industrial populations (1968, 37). Howell (1979, 35) describes an eighty-two-year-old man whose hunting days were long since over, but who still had the ability to walk long distances when the group moved and who could still collect much of his own food. The fact that an older man can take on the traditionally female task of food collecting not only illustrates the viability of an elderly man but also the flexibility of the sexual division of labor (van den Berghe 1973). Among the !Kung, adolescents assume adult responsibility late in life; the young are not expected to provide food regularly for the group until they are married (between the ages of fifteen and twenty for girls, five years later for boys); approximately 40% of the population in camps contributes little to the food supply.

Biesele and Howell (1981) report that older men and women make up the core of a !Kung camp, and that because of their long-term association with a particular waterhole, the old maintain a stewardlike control over water and food resources in a region. They are resource managers who control rights to *the* critical resource: water. The aged also are repositories of essential technical knowledge concerning seasonal fluctuations in local resources, animal behavior, and the like. The elderly pass on their accumulated knowledge as part of their stewardship of gathering areas and hunting grounds. In order to exploit the Kalahari environment effectively with the technology at their disposal, the !Kung need the elderly's detailed knowledge of plant and animal life (Biesele and Howell 1981, 84).

Elderly !Kung engage in decision-making and gerontocide is rare. Lee says, "Long after their productive years have passed, the old people are fed and cared for by their children and grandchildren. The blind, the senile, and the crippled are respected for the special ritual and technical skills they possess" (1968, 36). Lee describes four elders at one waterhole who were totally or partially blind. Apparently this handicap did not prevent their active participation in decision-making and ritual curing. The !Kung allocate work to young and middle-aged adults; children, adolescents, and the elderly lead a life of relative leisure (Lee 1968, 36). For both ecological and technological reasons, !Kung food-getters must be adults who are old enough to be sufficiently knowledgeable about the locations of the various plants and animals, but not too young or old to walk sixteen kilometers or more a day, often while carrying at least one child in addition to the harvest (Draper 1976, 216).

The !Kung are highly selective in their food habits (Lee 1984, 44). Because of both the abundance and the variety of plant foods, they have two options in food strategy in any situation where the desirable foods are scarce: They may walk further in order to obtain the more desirable species, in which case the younger, more active camp members go farther afield to bring back the desired food. Alternatively they may remain closer to camp and exploit the least desirable plant species, in which case the older, more sedentary camp members collect the less desirable, but more easily obtained foods. Thus, the abundance and variety of plant species result in a flexible division of labor by age.

The subject of food taboos in relation to age is an important, but relatively unexamined topic; age significantly affects consumption patterns. For the !Kung, food taboos apply to younger people in the various stages of reproductive life. Often they are relaxed at the cessation of childbearing. The prohibition on ostrich egg consumption by males and females of reproductive age is a case in point. The eggs are reserved for the very young and the very old. In the !Kung folk system, ostrich eggs are believed to make reproductively active people crazy if they eat them; older people are said to be past the danger of having their minds affected by the rich food (Biesele and Howell 1981, 90). From a scientific viewpoint, the eggs are soft, high protein food that the taboo reserves for people who have difficulty chewing hard food, especially when grinding the plentiful mongongo nuts with mortar and pestle may be inconvenient—in short, the very young and the elderly.

The abundant environment of the Australian Tiwi hunter-gatherers is another case in which viable producers are relieved from active production roles. All males between the ages of fourteen and twenty-five absent themselves from food-production units for long periods of the year. After the age of twenty the young men do not contribute to household food production, but Hart and Pilling point out that "only a very well-off tribe could afford to allow so much time off from food production to all its young hunters" (1960, 95). Since Tiwi women contribute substantially to subsistence from a very young age, doing the great bulk of the food getting

(Goodale 1971, 38–39), the division of labor by sex—created in large part by matrilineal kinship, early betrothal, and polygyny—combined with the abundant maritime environment, permit leisure for males, both young and old. Were the Tiwi living in the Artic, the leisure of viable male producers would be out of the question, at least for most periods of the year.

Complementing the Tiwi data is Rose's study of the Groote Eylandt Aborigines of northern Australia, a maritime food collecting group in which "there was almost always meat (protein) of sea origin" (1960, 82). Here the distribution of food was carried out primarily by older men. Rose (1960, 87), arguing that polygyny is an economic necessity, shows that the incidence of polygyny among women varies considerably with age. He has suggested that rates of polygyny are higher for women in their childbearing years because the demands upon women are greatest at this point in the life course. Rose also argues that monogamously married women tend to die out sooner because they have difficulty supporting themselves without the help of co-wives.

The Eskimo represent a famous and opposite situation to that of the !Kung and the Tiwi. Hoebel has argued that gerontocide was general among the Eskimos because they were unable to sustain the old in times of stress (1954, 76–79). Citing numerous anecdotes illustrating requests for death from old people, Hoebel states that gerontocide, invalicide, and suicide are manifestations of the same postulate that underlies infanticide: a harsh life with a small margin of safety. People who cannot contribute their full share to productive activities forfeit the right to live (1954, 76).

In sum, the role of age in egalitarian hunting and gathering societies is more a function of resource availability than of any other variable. Whereas ecology does not seem to affect the overall egalitarian division of labor by sex among hunter-gatherers, environmental scarcity or abundance does limit how many nonproducing consumers, young and old, a society can afford, both in the long and the short run. For hunter-gatherers, relationships between people in different age cohorts are qualitatively different from those in other types of cultures. There may be more similarities between kin-based societies in this respect than differences. Having demonstrated that the elderly are essential for the maintenance of foraging societies and not just tolerated or allowed to survive, it would be important to examine what happens when the population of elders becomes so low that certain tasks cannot be performed. Do younger band members compensate? If so, does the birth rate go up? Do more children need to be produced to provide the needed labor? Do bands merge to acquire elders? How are the band movements then affected? How does the proportion of elderly affect the relationships between bands and sedentary agricultural groups? If elders are regarded as conservative culture preservers, one could argue that the higher the proportion of the elderly the less likely the bands would have been to evolve into tribes.

Egalitarian Horticulturalists

Egalitarian horticultural societies consist of small, semisedentary, village populations that relocate every five or six years. The Sharanahua and the Cashinahua of lowland South America are two examples (Kensinger et al. 1975; Siskind 1973). Newly settled villages may coexist with older, more mature ones with full-blown gardens near the end of their productive cycle. New villages require a great deal of energy to clear and plant the new gardens as well as to maintain the village by hunting and gathering until the gardens have begun to produce. Once the gardens begin yielding food, gathering subsides. The longer a group stays in an area the more uncertain hunting becomes. At the end of the village life cycle resources may be hunted and gathered out and the soil less productive. Thus, just before the village moves, the population may be nutritionally stressed, such that mortality rates rise. As different subsistence activities become more or less prominent, the division of labor will change accordingly.

As males and females age, the division of labor by sex changes. For both men and women, age may reverse traditional economic roles as they are defined by sex. For example, Sharanahua extended family households contain a minimum of two adult males and two adult females. When elderly Sharanahua males are too old to hunt, they work in the gardens; older women supervise the work of older men and younger women (Siskind 1973, 82). The Mundurucu of the Brazilian Amazon Basin have different expectations of women at different points in the life course. During childbearing years, women should be passive, retiring, and demure; male company is not sought, and males and females occupy separate physical and social domains. By contrast, postmenopausal women can sit anywhere, with males or with females, and men will defer to an older woman by making room for her. Older women may also speak freely and with credence and authority that may influence people's behavior (Murphy and Murphy 1974, 105–6). Within households, senior women coordinate the work of groups of female kin (Murphy and Murphy 1974, 13–20); young girls begin contributing to the economy much earlier than do boys. Seven-year-old girls will monitor one-year-old siblings. While similar patterns of older and younger sibling relationships are found among hunter-gatherers, it is difficult to picture a seven-year-old carrying a one-year-old for long gathering expeditions. Male Mundurucu children begin small-scale hunting around the age of ten. Adult hunting begins at the age of fourteen (Murphy and Murphy 1974, 75). The sedentary base seems to provide the young and the old much more opportunity to contribute to the economy. Perhaps this occurs because of the population's short life span. Murphy and Murphy note that grandparents take care of children, if they are still alive (1974, 173).

The degree to which the physical nature of tasks imposes limitations upon people in different stages of the life course remains a problem for analysis. We know that cultures deal very differently with the same biological processes when it comes to allocating tasks around reproduction. How flexible can cultures be when it comes to the division of labor by age? Does the biology of aging impose the same kind of limitations upon work in all cultures, or do cultures vary just as much in their ways of allocating tasks to the elderly as they do in allocating tasks to childbearers?

Hammond and Jablow (1976) address some of these issues in small-scale kin-based societies and imply that it may be easier for elderly women to maintain productive work in the domestic sphere than it is for men to act effectively in the public sphere. While women may not expend as many calories per minute as men, their work in many societies begins at a younger age and lasts well into old age. Women's economic life centers upon the household and is intimately bound up with the work of other women. Only extreme senility or death ends a woman's working life.

> An industrious and clever girl is undoubtedly a credit to her own kinfolk, especially her mother, and she will be an asset to her husband. In her own household she will go on using those skills she learned as a girl. With the passage of time she may delegate some of the tasks to growing daughters and daughters-in-law, and eventually even to granddaughters. As an older woman she may thus be relieved of the more arduous work, but she is never completely idle. Whatever work the old woman does is important to her self-esteem. Her self-image demands that she continue as a productive member of the community as long as she can (Hammond and Jablow 1976, 66–68).

This passage raises the issue of whether the inherent flexibility of work in the domestic sphere contributes to the longevity of women. With sedentary life comes a marked distinction between public and domestic domains in the lives of men and women. Without making assumptions either about the exclusivity of these domains for the sexes, or about the ranking of the domains on a single prestige scale, we can ponder the implications of the public-domestic dichotomy for the allocation of tasks according to age.

For horticultural societies, warfare may play a significant part in fixing the age ratios of the population. While Polgar (1972, 206) estimates that warfare seldom kills more than 10% of males of reproductive age, Chagnon studied one Yanomamo village in which nearly 50% of the males were killed in war (Chagnon 1974). As populations grow larger and denser they are also subject to infectious diseases, many of which, such as malaria and tuberculosis, are not in and of themselves life-threatening but which, when combined with other conditions such as malnutrition, can cause early death. All of this points to a shorter life span for many horticultural peoples than for hunter-gatherers.

To summarize, for egalitarian horticulturalists, sedentary life has a greater effect upon the division of labor by age than it does upon the division of
labor by sex. The sexual division of labor looks very much like that for
hunter-gatherers but the age division is quite different. People in sedentary
economies begin work at a much earlier age and they remain working
much longer.

For all horticultural societies, the use of root crops and grains results in
closer birth spacing (Draper 1975; Kolata 1974). With sedentization and
increased population size, certain infectious diseases such as measles,
mumps, rubella, and smallpox, begin to become significant. In the long
run, nutritional well-being tends to go down, fertility rates go up, life
spans shorten, and infant mortality rates increase (Cockburn 1971). In the
short run, however, there is some evidence that children and old people
fare better in a sedentary context than they do as members of a nomadic
foraging culture (Handwerker 1983). Howell reports, for example, that
!Kung families who, in the 1960s were burdened by the sick or handicapped or by many children or elderly, had a tendency to congregate at
Bantu cattle posts. Healthy !Kung tended to gain weight on the high calorie
diet provided there (1979, 50). It should be noted though that the !Kung
contact with the Bantu agriculturalists involves the !Kung in relations with
a culture that is several steps up the evolutionary ladder. How do these
patterns affect age as a principle of social organization? More precisely,
how do these factors affect the proportions of young and old in the
population and in turn the allocation of people among social activities? We
know that prolonged survival of incapacitated individuals, young or old, is
less likely in nomadic than in sedentary populations (Dunn 1968, 224).

Ranked Horticultural Societies

For ranked horticultural societies the relationship between age systems,
kinship structures, and political life is more complicated because the populations are much larger and the overall division of labor is more complex.
The prominence of ceremonial exchange organized by big men and chiefs,
creates a political and religious context for examining age in these societies.
Both big men, who achieve power by creating a loyal following, and chiefs,
who take over existing offices by virtue of their kinship rank, are the focal
points for elaborate redistributive exchanges of goods and services. If we
ask the following questions we can begin to gain some new insights into
social structure and political organization: How old does one have to be to
function effectively as a big man or a chief? Can a young chief marshall
more resources by virtue of his kinship rank than a young big man whose
kinship status may carry him less far in achieving his goals? Oliver says
that Siuai men of Melanesia gain wealth and renown because of what they
do beyond subsistence, not because of their vitality, economic solidarity,

general knowledge or age (1955, 73). Insofar as it may take time to marshall sufficient resources to engage in activities beyond subsistence, older men certainly have an advantage. Oliver describes a kind of generalized reciprocity between young and old:

> While age by itself does not command great respect in Siuai, the offspring are usually tenderly affectionate toward aging parents, demonstrating by word and deed that they feel an obligation for their welfare. If the parents occupy the same hamlet or neighboring hamlets, the son or daughter will oft times perform much of the work of clearing and cultivating their parent's garden. Or, if they live too far apart for that, they usually take along baskets of food when they return for visits. As explained: "When we were children they fed and cared for us well; and now that they are aged we repay by giving food to them. For, if we did not, they would surely starve" (Oliver 1955, 209).

For the Siuai there is clearly a high correlation between age and high rank as an active feast-giver and leader. Highest ranking leaders have been involved in competitive feasting for some twenty-five years previously (Oliver 1955, 390). Young leaders start out with substantial support from kin.

A comparable ranked society is that of the Coast Salish of the Northwest Coast of the United States, and a similar pattern of kin support for leaders who grow powerful with age can be found. In the precontact period, all political and economic leadership was in the hands of the old. In order to become a powerful elder, however, a person had to have seniority in a large and wealthy family (Amoss 1981, 33). Coast Salish adults were named teknonymously, suggesting that generational position defined the most important roles (Amoss 1981, 230). Generational position, combined with high kinship rank, creates the prerequisites for leaders to engage in the elaborate redistributive feasts (potlatches) for which many groups on the Northwest Coast are famous.

In premodern times the elderly among the Coast Salish were valued for special skills in food procurement and processing, knowledge of house building, and canoe making. They were repositories of knowledge and ritual prestige. They also made important contributions to group solidarity by holding together the extended family households (Amoss 1981, 227). Under modern economic conditions, the production and consumption unit is the nuclear household, not the extended one. Yet old men and women maintain prestige and social rank through their control of scarce information about the old ritual practices and through the spiritual power people believe they possess. Amoss argues that with change, the position of the elderly has improved:

The issue is not social change per se, but whether social change allows old people opportunities to reestablish themselves in useful roles. . . . People were considered old when they could no longer perform the full range of adult tasks appropriate to their sex and age. When men could no longer hike miles to kill game and pack it home again, and when women found it hard to bend and stoop and pick berries or dig roots, they would begin to shift the major part of these jobs to younger relatives and turn to tasks reserved for older people (Amoss 1981, 228).

Many of the taboos that applied to people in their youth were waived for the elderly.

Women past childbearing age could no longer pollute hunters or their gear, nor would they contaminate the berry patches or offend the salmon. Old men no longer had to observe the discipline of sexual abstinence and fasting that were incumbent on active hunters and fishermen. Certain foods forbidden for the young were reserved for the old. With the raising of these restrictions new avenues of spiritual power opened up to both men and women. The old were often caretakers for people in dangerous liminal states—successful spirit questers, girls at menarche, women in childbirth, warriors returned from battle, mourners, and recently dead. A grand-mother was an ideal attendant for a girl at her first menstruation, because she was not only wise, experienced, and concerned about her granddaugh-ter but also impervious to the girl's sacred contagion (Elmendorf 1960, 439, cited in Amoss 1981, 231).

Old people also have a virtual monopoly over the other ritual roles that control the welfare of others (Ostor 1984; Sankar 1984). "Shamans, who have the power to inflict fatal illness and cure it, are all old. Mediums, who can see ghosts and who officiate after funerals, when food is burned to placate the ghosts, are also old men or old women" (Amoss 1981, 241).

There are two points to be made in summary. The first is that the roles of elders in ranked societies do not necessarily diminish with change. Amoss's case supports a general critique of the conventional wisdom on age and modernization (Foner 1984a). The cross-cultural record indicates that while social and economic change clearly affects all age strata in a society, it often affects each one differently (Foner 1984b, 211). It is not necessarily the case that gains for one generation represent losses for another. Secondly, the function of age in ranked horticultural societies contrasts greatly with the patterns seen above for egalitarian horticultural-ists. Whereas age and kinship status complement one another in egalitar-ian societies, with age possibly superceding kinship, in ranked societies age is always in some way, if not subordinate to, embedded in the kinship system.

Age-Set Systems: Africa

In African age-set societies, age is a formalized principle of social organization which explicitly regulates the allocation of social roles (Foner and Kertzer 1978, 1979; Kertzer and Madison 1981). At a designated point in the life course, people become members of a named group of their peers and they spend the remainder of their lives as group members, formally making transitions through a series of age-graded roles together with their fellow age-set members (Kertzer and Madison 1981). It is important to distinguish age sets from age grades. Whereas all societies have age grades, which are different culturally defined stages of the life course (childhood, adolescence, adulthood, old age), each with more or less clearly defined social roles, not all societies have age sets, which are actual groups of people who recognize common membership in a named grouping based on common age (Kertzer and Madison 1981). Kertzer and Madison examine the intersection of age and sex as principles of social differentiation by analyzing women's age sets among the Latuka, an East African kin-based agricultural chiefdom of some 150,000 people living in twenty-four permanent villages. For the Latuka, both men and women past a certain age, belong to an age set. The groupings are not based on kinship or wealth, but exclusively upon age. Within age sets there is no stratification for either sex. The age system is used to organize collective labor for individuals and for the chief and involves men and women in the middle two of the four age grades in Latuka society (Kertzer and Madison 1981).

The larger question is that of the relative importance of principles of sex, age, and kinship in allocating roles to individuals and to groups. What is the relationship, for example, between age-set systems and unilineal descent systems (Ritter 1980)? Are age grades categories of producers, categories of productive activities, or categories of specialists? Do the variables of age and kinship complement and crosscut one another? Or, do age and kinship function in different domains of culture? Which casts a wider net of relationships, age or kinship, and what bearing does the network have upon social life? Does one's kinship status function differently at different points of the life course? Evans-Pritchard contends that age is expressed in a kinship idiom (1940, 258). Gulliver says for the Jie "[A]lthough the age group is only a weak corporate group . . . nevertheless bonds of friendly equality between members of a group cut across the parochialism of clan and settlement to provide a wider network of personal links than kinship and neighborhood afford" (1965, 186).

State Systems, Peasants, and Proletarians

At the state level, age functions very differently than it does in kin-based egalitarian or ranked societies. With the development of class stratification systems based upon private property, age becomes a dependent variable, subordinate to class in the structuring of cultural processes. The higher a person's social class, the greater is longevity. In most instances longevity is inversely related to a person's actual contribution to subsistence. That is, the greater one's ability to extract surplus from subordinates, the longer one lives. Yet, ironically perhaps, the higher the social class the lower the status of the elderly. In state-level societies class becomes the independent variable for dividing tasks in society. Again, age affects cultural processes differently, depending upon the units of social organization, and the political and economic contexts within which the units function.

One of the most sensitive descriptions of age as a variable in rural agrarian (peasant) societies is Conrad Arensberg's classic study, *The Irish Countryman* (1968). In the Irish family farm household, both children and the elderly contribute to the subsistence base, the former as performers of small tasks such as errand running and child minding, the latter as managers and decision-makers. Young and middle-aged adults perform the heavy physical work under the aegis of older males and females. As long as a married man's father is present in the household, that man is a "boy" who is socially and economically subservient to his father. Thus, even a forty-five-year-old married man is not, in the Irish peasant social structure, an economically viable adult. Similarly, women in this patrilocal system are under the wing of a mother-in-law. This has its benefits, for example, providing help with child care and relief from many responsibilities while pregnant, but it also has its emotional costs. The system provides a role for the elderly, while at the same time giving essential help to young adults (see also Streib 1972; Scheper-Hughes 1979).

The leisure time of hunter-gatherers is something peasants cannot afford. Rural agrarian societies in state systems are subject to many outside demands. The pressure to bring products to market on a certain day and the vagaries of the market-determined pricing system are only two such pressures. Meeting these demands requires a great deal of labor which must be recruited from all available sources. It is not surprising then, that peasants take children out of school to help with the harvest. Whereas hunter-gatherers can subsist without the labor of the very young and the very old, the primary peasant producers, young and middle-aged adults, need all the help they can get to produce their subsistence, distribute the products effectively, and reproduce their labor force. The help comes from children and the elderly. The Irish countryman's farm is a well-functioning system which is a viable adaptation to the larger political and economic context within which the family farm must operate.

Judith Friedlander's (1976) description of the multiple economic roles of a sixty-five-year-old grandmother and head of a household in Hueyapan, Mexico raises several questions regarding age and the division of labor in peasant households and villages. As a small landowner, subsistence agriculturalist, market woman, and curandera (curer), Doña Zeferina plays a variety of social and economic roles. These roles are public, but not political. Her work contrasts greatly with that of her thirty-two-year-old daughter-in-law who labors only in the domestic sphere of food preparation and child care. How typical is Doña Zeferina, her household, and its division of labor by age? While large-scale statistical data are missing for this particular village, I suspect that the Hueyapan case, in which childbearing women perform domestic work and older women play economic roles outside of the domestic domain, is not at all atypical.

Analysis of the extent to which age ratios within households influence the allocation of work to domestic or public domains would require the collection of new data. The relationship between reproductive patterns and work outside the domestic sphere also merits further exploration. We know that many peasant women work in public spheres, such as markets, during their childbearing years, but the conditions under which they are able to do so are not known. Household life cycles and the needs of households at particular stages are likely to be significant determinants of how old the major producers or income earners will be (Durrenberger 1984, Minge-Kalman 1977).

Peasant villages have numerous mechanisms for rendering household consumption units economically viable. Colombian peasants "loan" grandchildren to their grandparents (Kagan 1980, 71). The children provide labor and social support to keep the old people independent. The arrangement also provides subsistence relief for the grandchild's nuclear family. With one less mouth to feed, the other children will receive better nourishment. This arrangement presumes, however, that the labor of the child on loan is, at least temporarily, not needed in his nuclear household and acts to redistribute labor in the village. Neighborhood ties may also function to insure the maintenance of the elderly. Kagan describes a woman with four children in Bojaca who takes an elderly neighbor, with whom no kin ties were shared, into her household to help with her work (1980, 71).

Households in virtually all rural agrarian villages in state systems must have access to cash. Young men and women provide much of it, often by becoming wage laborers outside of the village. For peasant economies in which the household is the smallest productive unit and in which wage labor is predominant, age operates differently than it does in household-based, subsistence economies. When young adults, particularly women, leave their village-based kinship systems to work in towns and cities, their economic and emotional viability may be severely compromised by the absence of younger or elderly women to provide childcare. The dependent and often exploitative relationships created between spouses, combined with the inaccessibility of the family farm as a source of subsistence goods and reserve labor, presents hardships for recent migrants. Anna Rubbo (1975) describes the plight of poor women of childbearing age once they give up subsistence production in rural villages to become workers on commercial plantations in a Colombian frontier town. The society has become age segregated to meet the exigencies of agrarian capitalism. Teenagers and the elderly are left behind in villages; young adults and small children must cope without traditional economic and social supports. Concomitantly, the village economy is undermined as more and more productive adults leave the rural areas.

The "peasant-to-worker transition" in rural agrarian economies presents critical issues regarding age and economic change (Beckford 1972; Minge-Kalman 1978; Holmes 1982). Among these are issues of work loads for older adults whose children have left the village for educational and/or economic reasons, and are not available to work. Some peasant-to-worker transition strategies are based on child labor. When households are under economic stress, children will be sent as migrant laborers. Cole and Katz (1973) describe groups of children from South Tyrol who appeared in the Kindermarkt of South Germany where they were known to be auctioned off for a summer's work. Their earnings were negligible but their absence meant one less mouth to feed.

Processes of colonialism, modernization, development, and incorporation into the world economy have many ramifications which differentially affect age groups. For example, as industrially manufactured goods begin to replace traditional craft items, not only are whole occupations eliminated, but apprenticeship relationships common in precolonial periods also become extinct. Apprenticeships provide important roles for the elderly as well as training for youths. For much of Africa and Latin America, traditional weaving, both for males and females is no longer done. For adolescent Ben'ekie males in Zaire, idleness and unemployment replace weaving apprenticeships (Fairley 1981). For the older people to whom young men traditionally would have been apprenticed, occupational status is lowered. My own fieldwork in the West Indies shows a similar pattern. Few job opportunities exist, especially for male adolescents of the lower classes. While females can usually work as market women or as servants in the domestic domain, adolescent males, who have not attained full adult status, yet are not dependent children, have few if any economic opportunities. In Grenada, older adolescent males may be employed as shop tenders, but such jobs often require minimal literacy and transportation to the capital. Even if the former conditions can be met, the jobs are extremely scarce. Expectations of upward mobility increase daily as radios and, in many parts of Latin America, television sets appear in barrio dwellings. As peasant villages come increasingly into contact with modern industrial societies and traditional age and sex statuses are undermined, the role of male adolescents changes from important subsistence producer into often frustrated consumer—frustrated because, unlike their female counterparts, males have few sources of income other than those that are illegal.

In sum, we find a great deal of variation in peasant societies regarding the treatment of people, young and old, and in the significance of age as a variable in the allocation of social and economic roles. Accounting for the variation is a difficult task, but we can identify some key factors. For example, the position of individuals and villages in the national stratification system and the degree to which people and groups are integrated into the market economy are two critical factors. These two go hand in hand. The more insulated a village is from the market economy and the more self-sufficient, the tighter the kin network, and the stronger the support system for people of all ages.

Age and Politics

The question of age and its relationship to the occupation of political office, the nature of political structure, recruitment, and succession to political office is in need of analysis (Cohen 1984). Mesoamerican cargo systems provide one of the few contexts within which age and politics have been discussed. Cargos, or civil-religious hierarchies, are organized in a ladder-like arrangement such that a man first occupies those offices lower in the hierarchy and proceeds to move up into increasingly more expensive and more prestigious positions. The timing of a person's career is critical. As a man ages, his position in the hierarchy changes. Late entrance into the system can prevent mobility within it.

One of the most complete descriptions of a cargo system, and one that includes age as a variable, is Frank Cancian's (1965) account of Zinacantan, and I will draw extensively upon it here. Zinacantan is a township with 7,650 Tzotzil-speaking Maya Indians in the highlands of the state of Chiapas in Mexico. Zinacantecos are primarily corn farmers who buy and sell corn and other cash crops in exchange for cotton, metal tools, and other staples in the Ladino city of San Cristobal. Occupying a religious office requires individuals to spend large sums to sponsor religious celebrations for Catholic saints. An incumbent receives no pay because his work is regarded as service to the community: public works, settling disputes, and managing relationships between the community and the nation-state of Mexico.

Cancian states clearly that Zinacantan is not a typical civil religious hierarchy in which an individual alternates between civil and religious offices and in which the office holders serve for a year and then give the office to another man. The cargo system is almost entirely religious, with civil offices filled by different recruitment mechanisms. There are thirty-four religious cargos at the lowest level, twelve offices at the second level, six at the third, and two on the fourth and final level of the religious hierarchy. Thus, the system becomes increasingly selective at higher levels. The highest offices represent the apex of the social structure; only the wealthy can afford the most expensive cargos. In Zinacantan none of the civil offices count for progress up the ladder of religious cargos (Cancian 1965, 22). A high civil office can be held by someone who is relatively young and unimportant; a *presidente* can be in his late twenties. Of the six *presidentes* who served between 1952 and 1963, four were younger than thirty when they entered office (1965, 25). The system of recruitment for religious offices is entirely different and age is extremely important; men under thirty never hold high religious offices.

Cancian has formulated models for predicting the age and conditions under which cargos are taken. In one model the assumption is that at least 90% of the men take cargos. Since life expectancy in Zinacantan is relatively short, and since a person must take the cargos in hierarchical order, a delay of the first cargo until age forty-five, for example, will probably prevent a person from ever reaching the highest level (1965, 168). A second model postulates a constant age of the first cargo and analyzes the results. Since the population of Zinacantan is increasing, under the second model's conditions the proportion of men who will never take a first cargo will increase (1965, 169). The important point about Cancian's analysis is that it is one of few to use age as a condition in a formal model. Cancian uses the model to compare postulated conditions with actual conditions. Such formal models that include age as a component could add greatly to the precision as well as to the time depth of political analyses. The models would provide ways of systematizing the data by comparing expected conditions with observable facts.

Aging in Rural America

Aging in rural America is a topic that has received little systematic attention from an anthropological perspective (van Willigen 1985). Until recently, anthropologists have concentrated upon fieldwork abroad, leaving the United States for sociologists to investigate. Such an academic division of labor has not only created artificial boundaries between disciplines but it has precluded a comparative perspective so essential for understanding patterns and variability in aging processes in the rural parts of complex societies. Life course patterns in rural America are very similar to patterns in other areas of both the industrial and preindustrial world. Our research in rural Kentucky (Halperin and Schaiper n.d.) indicates that approximately a century ago rural Kentucky society was organized in three-generation, family-farm households that were self-sufficient economically while at the same time organized in hamlets with a dispersed settlement pattern.

Technological changes have drastically affected the division of labor by sex and age in rural Kentucky. We have done a pilot study documenting changes in the division of labor by sex and age on farms producing burley tobacco in an eastern Kentucky county. Burley tobacco is one of the most common varieties of tobacco, and it is the most important cash crop grown in eastern Kentucky. After 1950, changes in tobacco technology combined with changes in market incentives to cause drastic alterations in the size and organization of production units, both landholdings and labor groups. Changes in the division of labor occurred so that inequalities between the sexes and between generations intensified with innovations in tobacco technology. The tobacco economy changed from one in which not only did men and women participate equally in production processes, but also senior household members (third generation) involved themselves vigorously in all phases of production, to an economy in which adult male household heads controlled production and carried the major responsibility of the farm. After 1950, women, children, and senior members of the households participated only seasonally or marginally in tobacco production.

Before 1950, the contributions of women, children, and senior household members were essential in the production of burley tobacco. Mechanical aids were minimal, and the highly intensive nature of burley tobacco production made hand labor a necessity for every phase of production (i.e., for approximately ten months out of the year). During most phases of tobacco production, with the exception of plowing, tasks were generally shared by all household residents. All capable members of the family farm worked toward a common goal—securing their sole cash resource for the year. Before 1950, children worked side by side with their parents and grandparents. The money received from the tobacco crop was used to purchase staples that could not be raised on the family farm (e.g., material for clothing, shoes, salt, and the like). The pattern then consisted of a three-generation family economy. In the period before 1950, the fact that both sexes and all ages participated in a complementary and interdependent manner in tobacco production fostered interdependence among generations.

Wherever new technology was utilized, it was typically by the adult men of the burley farms. This increasing reliance and control of technology by the adult male farmers displaced the work normally contributed by farm women (wives), farm children, and the grandparent generation during the preharvest season. In some phases of tobacco production even the adult male farmer's labor was displaced as a specialist possessing technical expertise and expensive machinery might be called in (Stovall 1972; Shugars and Gavett 1972).

A second and much more subtle transformation was also occurring throughout the county. The family farm household was becoming increasingly dependent upon a market economy. From 1850 to approximately 1930 the farmers in eastern Kentucky were engaged in a full-scale subsistence economy. Before heavy reliance on purchased staples, the subsistence economy was highly diversified and very secure; the division of labor by age and sex was one of complementarity and interdependence. Nearly everyone farmed. Garden produce that could not be stored in the root cellar or saved by some other insulating device in the field—for example, dirt mounding—was canned at harvest. Pigs butchered in autumn supplied the family with their primary protein source. Cattle provided various dairy products; chickens were kept primarily for their eggs rather than for their meat. Under the skilled guidance of the elderly, utilization of wild resources also contributed significantly to subsistence. Children trapped rabbits in snares and dead-falls baited with apples; they also fished for catfish and bass. Older children hunted squirrels with ammunition purchased with cash from the sale of the tobacco crop. Squirrel and dumpling stew was a favorite. Occasionally venison was eaten. Finally various greens, nuts such as hickory, wild blackberries, raspberries, pawpaws, and persimmons seasonally contributed to the farm family's diet. By the time mechanization of burley tobacco was introduced, the subsistence economy had already declined significantly and people relied on cash generated from tobacco sales. This meant that the contributions of women, children, and the elderly to the subsistence economy had already been shifted to the cash crop: tobacco. Once removed, they could not go back to subsistence production. This issue is critical in discussing age and gender roles in production processes.

Life histories (Halperin and Schaiper n.d.) indicate three phases in the evolution of rural economy in eastern Kentucky. Each phase manifests a different division of labor by age and sex and a different contribution of people through the life course. The three phases can be summarized as follows:

Phase I: *Subsistence based economy (1800–1900)*
             —equality of gender roles
             —active and vital participation of
               children and elderly
             —flexible and interdependent division of labor
               (seasonally based)
Phase II: *Entrance of cash crop (1865–1950)*
             —equality of gender roles
             —active and vital participation of children and elderly
             —subsistence based economy declining
             —beginning of specialized division of labor
Phase III: *Mechanization and market dependence (1950+)*
             —shift in sex role equality toward male dominance
             —elimination of roles for children and elderly in rural
               economy
             —rise in number of hired hands: adult males and females

Overall, the roles for the elderly, and the importance of children in the rural economy, declined with the increase in the utilization of new technology. Concomitantly, the rural economy became increasingly integrated into and dependent upon the market as a source of both subsistence goods, staples, and services. The socioeconomic status of all individuals declined as a rural proletariat developed and as people migrated to the cities to become marginally employed or unemployed entirely. While rural Kentucky had existed in a market economy for at least a century before mechanization, the eastern part was protected from its vagaries by a stable subsistence base. Now, the subsistence base is severely weakened and the quality of life, particularly for the elderly in these rural areas, is declining accordingly.

Conclusion

Kertzer has pointed out that, the

> ways in which societies cope with the problems of assigning different roles to individuals through their life course, and ways in which individuals cope with this experience compose one of the basic problems of social organization. . . . Anthropology has never ignored this issue, but it has been dealt with fragmentally rather than systematically. Thus we have compendia of life-course stages, we have studies of childhood socialization and the roles of the aged, but few are the studies that address the whole aging process in a comprehensive, theoretical framework, identifying implications for social organization as well as personal adjustment, identifying sources of strain, sources of change in the system, and the relationship between formal norms and actual behavior (1978, 369).

In this chapter, I have used an evolutionary framework to develop a consistent set of factors that can be used to define the political and demographic contexts in which age can be understood as a variable in cross-cultural analysis.

At the most general level, we can say that the relationship between age and cultural processes is basically similar among all kin-based societies, both egalitarian and ranked. Property-based, state-level societies begin to manifest different patterns and relationships depending upon the context within which the units of social organization are found. Since there is both greater specialization as well as clearly indicated socioeconomic stratification in these societies, the elderly will fare better or worse depending upon how they fit into and contribute to the overall division of labor. The same can be said of children, teenagers, and adults. The relative contribution of people in different age cohorts, in turn, will depend upon the kinds of social and economic units within which they carry out their lives and livelihoods.

Within a set of general evolutionary types some further distinctions can be made. For hunter-gatherers, abundant environments seem to exempt both the very young and the very old from productive activities and seem to permit a considerable amount of leisure time for people of all ages. Thus Sahlins's notion of "the original affluent society" (1972). It should be clear, however, that "affluence" as it is manifested by leisure is a result of several interrelated variables: abundant environments, egalitarian social organization, consensus politics, flexible division of labor by sex, and simple technology. None of these, singly or even in pairs would bring about affluence or leisure. In harsher environments, such as those inhabited by the Polar Eskimo, the luxury of idleness is much less affordable, and the elderly must not only be able to move with the group, a *sine qua non* in all hunting-gathering societies, they must also contribute positively to the group without creating a drain on the group's resources. Thus the !Kung or the Tiwi can afford to support elders who are blind or crippled, but the Eskimo cannot. In the Tiwi case the marriage system and the division of labor by age allow both the elderly and young males to be idle. At the hunting-gathering level, some sex role reversal also occurs with age as in the case of elderly !Kung males who take on female tasks of gathering.

In contrast to hunter-gatherers, members of both egalitarian and ranked horticultural societies begin working at a much earlier age and maintain production for most of their lives. This is particularly true of women. Girls in sedentary societies can care for young children without having to carry them on long gathering expeditions. Since weaning foods are plentiful, children nurse for shorter periods of time and thus can be separated from their mothers at a much younger age.

In horticultural societies, aging seems to reverse the traditional sexual division of labor in a much more accentuated fashion than at the hunting-gathering level. Both men and women can take on the productive and distributive roles of the opposite sex. Brown has argued that cross-culturally, middle age lifts restrictions upon women and confers upon them rights to exercise authority over certain kinsmen. She also notes the importance of older women in food distribution and in the enterprise of food preparation (1982, 154).

For kin-based societies the lack of specialization in the division of labor overall seems to enable people of all ages to match their skills and abilities with the various necessary tasks required by the annual round. All men and women are food producers, and to varying degrees, food distributors. Interestingly, the separation of producers from distributors occurs earlier in human cultural evolution than does the separation of producers and nonproducers. This is because age and sex statuses act to create these distinctions before class distinctions develop. The skills a young boy performs before puberty may be the very ones he needs in old age. Work groups in kin-based societies are often heterogeneous in age. Older and younger men and women commonly work together. Mat weaving in Samoa, for example, involves women of all ages; fishing brings together old and young men (Holmes 1972, 75). Fishing, for the Eskimo, brings together the old and young of both sexes. Such arrangements in pre-industrial societies make it possible to learn new skills and to change qualitatively the nature of one's work as one proceeds through the life course. In highly specialized postindustrial societies such qualitative changes cannot be accomplished easily. Once a person is unable to work at a specialized task, work must cease altogether. This is one of the many reasons why the elderly become isolated from production processes in industrial societies. It is important to recognize, however, for preindustrial societies, that the elderly are not more respected because of their revered position in the extended family. Rather, the basic interdependent and flexible nature of the division of labor, what Durkheim called organic solidarity, makes it possible for both young and old to make valuable contributions in preindustrial societies.

State-level societies present different issues for understanding age and social organization. Probably the two most critical, and often related, factors impinging on age and social organization are the class position of the individual and the unit of production within which the individual works. Modernization processes have greatly affected the economic activities of people of all ages, some positively, many negatively (Cowgill and Holmes 1972). Indigenous peasant agriculturalists in closed-corporate peasant communities (Wolf 1966b) operate in ways that are similar to horticulturalists in stateless kin-based societies. Links to larger political and economic entities through relations of patronage and brokerage create different economic functions for old and young. Once young men from tribal and peasant societies leave their indigenous groups and acquire wealth by using channels outside the traditional system, patterns of kin-based seniority become undermined or, in some cases, destroyed. We can see in the Kentucky case that the shift from subsistence production to wage labor creates many stresses for children, young adults, and for elderly members of extended families. For the elderly, subsistence patterns may become diluted, severely altered, or destroyed by the combination of new technology and increased cash cropping. For children and young adults in many areas of the world, the absence of extended family members in areas where wage labor is prevalent creates serious shortages of caregivers and severe reductions in general social and economic support.

The issue of intergenerational political and economic relationships must be examined cross-culturally. While an ideology of reciprocity probably always prevails to some extent between generations, the facts of reciprocity may be quite different. In state-level societies with private property, the dynamics of intergenerational exchange (Salamon and Lockhart 1980) will be different from exchange and power processes in pre-state societies, in which the elderly control knowledge but not privately held resources. While intergenerational exchanges of goods and services are important in all societies, once societies develop private property and resources are no longer controlled by kin groups, the importance of intergenerational exchange is altered.

There seems to be little question that in societies in which kin are the basic means of economic support, insurance in old age, and buffers against starvation and destitution, exchanges of goods and services between people of varying ages and life cycle stages are absolutely essential for the viability of the group. Such societies encompass a range of evolutionary types. The importance of intergenerational exchanges as the key survival strategy is also heightened when the group is near the bottom of a class-stratification system. A striking example is Carol Stack's (1974) description of reciprocal exchange networks among poor urban blacks. Old women in particular are critical to the maintenance of the network because they care for children and allow younger female adults to work. An interesting point here is that women seem to provide the core of the network. Men operate in peer groups (Liebow 1967) in which certain kinds of reciprocal exchanges take place, but because males and females have very different ways of articulating with the larger society, the patterns of exchange for males and females are very different.

Patterns of adaptation tend to repeat themselves in different cultural contexts. That patterns of production and reciprocal exchange in urban ghettos operate according to principles of generalized reciprocity should not be surprising; neither should the key child-care roles played by older siblings and older women. Kin-based economies still function within industrial societies and there is increasing evidence that a hidden economy based on nonmarket principles is on the increase. The giving of food to elderly people by senior citizens' centers is one example (Myerhoff 1978a). Teenagers will need to create new survival strategies in our own culture as unemployment rises. Elderly people on fixed incomes will also need new strategies, mutual aid systems perhaps, or reciprocal exchange systems of social and economic support which will provide needed goods and services. The role governmentally organized redistributive systems play in industrial societies in providing needed goods and services to age groups that are economically marginal remains to be fully explored.

To summarize, we can see a diversity of adaptations, economic and social, in stratified state-level economies and, consequently, different patterns of age and social organization. If extended family production and consumption units are subsistence based, without wage labor, children and the elderly are viable, indeed essential, contributors to the maintenance of the unit. Once subsistence patterns are interrupted and extended family production units are no longer viable, the roles of people of all ages change drastically.

If there is a watershed for marking the diminished roles of the elderly as well as children in cultural evolution, it is the breakup of the extended family as a basic unit of social and economic organization (Cowgill and Holmes 1972; Holmes 1983, 172–73). That it may be possible to reconstitute the extended family, under certain conditions, is shown clearly in Carol Stack's study (1974; see also Martin and Martin 1978). Whether or not the extended family can be preserved in other contexts, such as in rural Kentucky, and whether or not modernization can be geared toward the viability of units of social organization in such a way that children, adults, and seniors alike can play important social and economic roles, remains for future analysis.

Matilda White Riley has identified four myths and fallacies about aging (1978, 42): (1) most old people are not (as the myth has it) destitute, dependent, or residing in nursing homes; (2) most are not seriously disabled; (3) work productivity does not invariably decline in old age; and (4) most old people *do* feel adequate. Most are satisfied with their roles. Barbara Myerhoff has stated, quite forcefully, that aging is a more variable process than is child development:

> [I]f any generalizations can be made, they point to the great variety of styles and forms of aging in different cultural settings. Here one is struck by diversity rather than uniformity, by variation rather than universality. The studies that are available suggest that social scientists must be as diligent in including the role of cultural factors in aging as they are in including them in studies of child rearing and childhood. Not all anthropologists may agree, but in the opinion of many the data point towards malleability of the human organism and the significant role of nonbiological factors: in other words, culture appears to explain more of the peculiarities and idiosyncrasies of aging than do factors that are attributable to a "common humanity." In comparison with old age, infancy and childhood display striking patterning and regularity in part because of predictable and inevitable physiological events (Myerhoff 1978b, 152).

An evolutionary framework provides a systematic way of supporting Myerhoff's idea that aging and roles of the aged are highly variable. Many cultural systems require interdependence as well as flexibility with the age division of labor.

In complex societies the units of social organization vary greatly even within social strata; the aging process varies accordingly. In extended family households of different ethnic groups and social classes, the elderly play a variety of roles from farm managers to household managers to child caregivers. Children in extended families are needed helpers in a range of tasks. Idleness is unknown for a child in an extended-family farm household. As the physical capabilities of children increase with adolescence they become more valued as workers. In extended rural farm families children know that they must learn from elders in order to survive in later years (Silverman and Maxwell 1983). An incremental increase in task complexity occurs with increasing physical strength. There is no clear-cut separation between childhood as leisure time or as a time for schooling, and adulthood as the appropriate time for physical labor.

When families nucleate and generations reside separately, the roles of people at the extreme ends of the life course either disappear entirely or are so severely diminished as to be insignificant. Myerhoff's descriptions of elderly Jews who live alone, their problems when they are taken in by relatives, and the function of the community center as a replacement for the extended family illustrate some of the transitions that occur in the roles of the elderly when units of social organization and residence change. When upward mobility, especially movement into professions, is coupled with nuclear family structures, generations are separated not only by age and (often) geographic distances, but also by education and the concomitant changes in social class (Myerhoff 1978a). In industrial societies, with increases in social class position and in the amount of formal schooling, nuclear families show much more marked separations between childhood and adulthood. Whereas in rural contexts children are considered to be preparing gradually for adulthood and work roles, in urban, industrial settings childhood is prolonged as long as possible to prevent entrance into the work force. Elderly are also retired early in this context. It should be noted, however, that the now controversial idea of retirement at age sixty-five presupposes employment in a capitalist and/or governmental agency in a postindustrial state-level society. From a cross-cultural perspective the arbitrary removal from the workplace or prevention of entrance into the workplace in industrial societies is an anomaly.

Myerhoff's statement that "there are no universal criteria for life stages, nor are there even universal divisions of a crude sort" (1978b, 155), is highlighted by examining the life course in an evolutionary perspective. While there is not space here to elaborate this in full, it is clear that there are no universals regarding the life course in the cross-cultural record.

The diversity of social and economic roles that people play at different ages across cultures serves to illustrate Matilda White Riley's point "that aging is not inevitably prescribed, that there is no pure process of aging, that the ways in which children enter kindergarten, or adolescents move into adulthood, or older people retire are not preordained. In this view, the life course is not fixed but widely flexible" (1978, 39).

The tendency in Western European culture to translate biological universals into cultural ones is certainly widespread but unsupported in the cross-cultural record. The statement by Meyer Fortes that age must be understood as stages of maturation that are separate from biology or chronology cannot be underscored too strongly:

> The life cycle is made up of stages of *maturation* or growth along the gradient of biological age. . . . The cross-cultural evidence is that stages of maturation are identified, named, culturally defined, and built into the social structure in all societies. The number of stages that are so recognized—Shakespeare's well-known seven are an instance—varies from society to society (Fortes 1984).

The very idea of defining stages at all is culturally determined. How the number of stages actually varies can be illuminated by understanding cultures in an evolutionary framework. We are seeing the definition of life course stages undergoing revision and redefinition in many cultures. The challenge facing our modern world system is one of using knowledge of the redefined life course to improve the quality of life for people of all ages. There is much work to be done.

XIV

COMPARATIVE STUDIES

Philip Silverman

An essential way of gaining a better understanding of any phenomenon is through the comparative method. No generalization about human behavior should be accepted unless tested in the natural laboratory of the world's cultures. This is a truism few would dispute, yet the amount of comparative research in gerontology is relatively meager. By comparing a number of different populations in a variety of settings, we can better determine which properties old people share in common as an inevitable consequence of changes through the life span—that is, changes due to the maturational effect—and which properties vary because of divergent cultural and/or environmental conditions. The goal is far from a modest one, since it would then be possible to specify more adequately the conditions that hinder or facilitate the elderly leading fuller and richer lives.

There are several types of comparative research used in the study of the aged. One favored by sociologists and developmental psychologists is the approach of cross-national studies. Most frequently this involves carrying out a survey among a sample of individuals in several countries, employing either questionnaires, interviews, or psychological tests. The study by Shanas and colleagues (1968), mentioned in the chapter on family life, which compared responses from a sample of elderly in Great Britain, Denmark, and the United States, is an example of this kind of research. Some cross-national studies use aggregate data, such as population censuses, institutional records, or archival materials from a variety of sources to compare the elderly in various countries. Although different priorities in aggregating data from one country to the next often make comparisons difficult, the problems are amplified when newly emerging third world countries are included, where conditions for collecting such data are not always favorable. Be that as it may, several cross-national studies will be pertinent to the material in this chapter.

The comparative approaches preferred by anthropologists emphasize the totality of behavior among all human populations, and sometimes even closely related species. Their focus is on the concept of culture, that common repertoire of meanings that people construct and that, hopefully, provides significance to their lives. Thus, a culture or society refers to any population sharing this system of meanings, and is used in comparative studies as a case to be compared with similar such cases. Although it has been difficult to determine how similar these cases should be in terms of size, degree of social differentiation, or condition of political autonomy before acceptable comparisons can be made, care is usually given to use comparable units of analysis, whether they be individuals, families, communities, or broader geographic units.

The two comparative approaches favored by anthropologists are cross-cultural and holocultural studies. Cross-cultural has been a term used to refer to any study involving the comparison of more than one culture, but more recently the term has been specialized to refer to small-scale comparisons. Such studies are limited to relatively few cultures, and the comparison attempts to preserve the richness of the data distinctive of each culture included in the analysis. The type of analysis favored in such studies is a qualitative one which, in some cases, is based on interpreting the intrinsic meaning of behavior rather than attempting to isolate variables that can be organized into causal sequences. Typically, the samples used in cross-cultural studies are fortuitous, selected because of the convenience of the data.

In contrast, holocultural studies are more likely to include much larger and more systematic samples, ideally ones that represent the diversity of all cultures in the world. Hypotheses are tested quantitatively, based on variables that have been operationalized according to a fixed set of alternative categories that allow for statistical proofs. Although much rarer, qualitative techniques have also been developed for analyzing data from a large sample of societies (Maxwell and Maxwell 1980a). Since holocultural studies use data collected by others, most usually the ethnographers who provide descriptive accounts of small-scale cultures, this is a form of secondary analysis. Given this remoteness from the primary data collection, such studies create formidable problems of validity and reliability, technical problems that will not be dealt with here. Nevertheless, the potential for universally valid generalizations remains a powerful incentive for researchers to overcome or, at the very least, minimize these problems.

The development of data banks beginning in the 1930s and then accelerating with the advent of computers has given wider access to data systematically organized for a large number of cultures. Of primary importance in the development of holocultural studies has been the Human Relations Area File (HRAF), a continuously expanding data bank of now several hundred cultures, in which data are filed according to a large number of cultural categories, including several that are pertinent to the role and treatment of the aged, yet retrievable within the context of the published material of the particular culture. In fact, one of the very first studies to use this data bank (Simmons 1945) became a landmark in the cross-cultural study of the aged. Simmons worked at a time when sampling procedures were primitive, careful operationalization of variables often ignored, and statistical testing inadequate. But he looked at a wide range of behavior by and toward the elderly and threw out a lot of useful ideas about what determined their status and treatment. His work and that of the other founders of the HRAF provided the foundation for all subsequent holocultural studies and the eventual development of more adequate data files of anthropological materials. In this chapter we concentrate on the findings from some of the more recent of these studies.

Respect for the Elderly: The Modernization Hypothesis

A major concern of comparative studies in gerontology has been to determine how well the aged fare in different settings. Historians provide temporal depth to our view of aging by tracing the changes that have occurred primarily in Western societies of Europe and their extensions overseas, whereas anthropologists focus on cultural differences by providing accounts of the aged in primarily non-Western, nonindustrial societies throughout the world. In both cases, these comparative studies have attempted to apply or confront some version of modernization theory in seeking an explanation for the differences that are found in the role and treatment of the aged. This theory, which can be viewed as an extension of the evolutionary perspective of the previous chapter, offered a highly useful framework for a macro-level analysis appropriate for comparisons between societies or within a society at different historical stages. Whereas most theories tended to explain patterns of aging in terms of psychological variables and individual adjustment, modernization theory made possible the inclusion of structural factors in looking at aging, factors that affect the overall organization and the level of differentiation of the society (Hendricks 1982). As such the theory had much to recommend it.

The Impact of Modernization on the Elderly

Modernization is a process of change that has been most closely associated with the Industrial Revolution, a revolution that began during the later half of the eighteenth century in Western Europe and continues to spread fitfully (and often unsuccessfully, based on Western criteria) to the rest of the world. It is a process that is most closely identified with the exploitation of new sources of energy, which brought about the factory production associated with industrialization. But, in addition, it refers to such changes as urbanization, growth of mass education, spread of mass media, bureaucratization, increasing political participation, and secularization. Two corollaries of these processes are the widespread dissemination of information and a significant increase in mobility, both geographically, to different areas in the world, and hierarchically, to different class levels in the society.

These factors neither occurred simultaneously, nor necessarily proceeded in the same order. Furthermore, as this is a continuously unfolding process, societies are invariably at different stages in the modernization process, thus making comparisons between societies sometimes misleading. Given this complexity, researchers emphasize differing aspects of the modernization process so that comparisons between studies are frequently not possible. Nevertheless, a common approach has been to divide societies into one of two categories, traditional or modern, and then to compare the two. As we shall see, this procedure is fraught with difficulties.

Modernization has had a profound effect on the entire life course. The very way a life cycle is conceptualized is altered by the onset of these changes. Certain stages in the life cycle, considered irrelevant or of minor cultural significance in nonindustrial societies—such as adolescence or middle age—become well recognized and agonized-about in modern societies. Also, as discussed in the previous chapter by Rhoda Halperin, the emergence of a modern society transformed the later years of life profoundly. From the very earliest analysis of old age by modern social scientists, the impact of modernization was thought to have had a negative effect on the elderly. In classic theoretical statements by Durkheim ([1893] 1964) and Weber ([1922] 1968) (although neither was particularly concerned with aging per se) both contrasted the position of the elderly in traditional society, where they played active and often powerful roles, with their situation in modern society, where their power and prestige were at best negligible.

This view was carried forth by more recent research. Some twenty-five years ago an important cross-national study, comparing data from six Western European countries (Burgess 1960), blamed the impact of modernizing trends for the low status of the aged. Burgess based his conclusions on the changes wrought by modernization, but he had no data from the preindustrial period in these countries as a point of comparison. He simply infers that times were once better for old people.

Perhaps the most elaborate statement of the modernization hypothesis can be found in Cowgill and Holmes (1972). This cross-cultural study attempts to draw a number of conclusions from the data presented on fourteen societies. Their major hypothesis is that modernization tends to decrease the "relative status" of the aged and undermine their security. From this they derive some twenty-two propositions concerned with the effects of modernization. The data from these societies tended to support their propositions, even though the writers of the individual chapters were not made aware of the propositions. They did find exceptions to their major hypothesis, which they attribute to historical peculiarities. In Ireland, Israel, and Russia, all of which occupy in this study the modern end of the continuum with Austria, Norway, and the United States, the status of the elderly remained high because of maintenance of traditional values and/or the persistence of traditional family structure.

It is important to note that the examples of what Cowgill and Holmes call preliterate societies are actually studies of tribal groups within nation-states of Africa that are themselves in various degrees and with varying success committed to modernizing their respective countries. Of the four transitional societies, two are indigenous Indian communities of Mexico and the United States, again two countries at very different stages of the modernizing process. And the seven modern societies are all nation-states ranging from Ireland, one of the least industrialized countries of Europe, to the United States, a highly pluralistic, postindustrial society. These very different examples of societies exist contemporaneously but are arranged on a scale so that the preliterate are equated with the preindustrial versions of the modern societies. In addition to these differences in the type of societal units being compared, one must be aware of the cross-sectional nature of these comparative data that are used to make statements about social process. Ideally, more comparable units are preferable, such as a comparison of specific communities with similar characteristics within each country. That is not to say that comparisons which must necessarily compromise these ideals are unhelpful, but their limitations must be recognized.

Following the publication of the Cowgill and Holmes (1972) volume, Donald Cowgill (1974) provided an elaboration of the modernization theory. He considers four aspects of modernization to be most salient in devaluing the status of the aged:

(1) Advances in health technology—This led to larger populations and greater longevity, which generated competition in the labor force between young and old, and resolved itself by pressuring the elderly into retirement from valued positions.

(2) Advances in economic technology—Technological advances in economic production and distribution create new jobs mostly filled by younger members of society, making the traditional skills of the elderly obsolete, leading to further pressure for retirement.

(3) Urbanization—The young migrate to the cities, leaving the elderly to maintain a rural way of life considered increasingly archaic and undesirable.

(4) Extension of mass education—The young are provided with increasing opportunities to become educated in a modernizing society, and this inevitably gives them the knowledge and skills relevant to the contemporary situation and unavailable to the elderly.

The combined consequences of these aspects of modernization are the emergence of a value system that glorifies youth, the dependency of the aged in a cultural context where the work ethic and self-reliance are typically valued, and the social and intellectual segregation of the elderly from the rest of society. As will be seen, the validity of many elements in this argument has been questioned vigorously.

Several cross-national studies have helped to specify more precisely the relationship between modernization and the status of the aged. Palmore and Manton (1974) analyzed aggregate data from a time period around 1960 collected in thirty-one countries. The sample represented a reasonable distribution of developing and industrial countries throughout the world, although it included only one country, Ghana, from Africa. As indicators of modernization they use gross national product (GNP), percent of the total labor force that is in the non-agricultural sector, and several indicators relating to the proportion with education. All of these can be equated with the aspects of modernization that Cowgill (1974) expected to affect the status of the elderly. A so-called Equality Index was constructed with the data from these variables; this is determined by the proportion of both men and women sixty-five or over who are employed, occupy various occupational categories, and attain educational levels comparable to the adults between the ages of twenty-six and sixty-four in the respective countries. The authors recognize that this index is not a direct measure of prestige; their assumption is that, given a comparable occupational and educational position with the other adult members of the society, the aged should not be subject to low esteem.

Palmore and Manton find that the status of the aged declines with modernization, but the productivity indicator (GNP) is much less important than the shift away from agricultural occupations and increased educational opportunity. The most interesting finding, however, had to do with the most advanced of the modernized countries. If all the countries in the sample are ordered according to degree of modernization, the relationship with the status of the aged is not a linear one, but rather has a J-shaped curve. That is, when a country reaches a certain advanced level of modernization, the equality index begins to rise. In other words, the discrepancy between the aged and the younger adults begins to narrow for the occupational and educational measures. This is not found, however, for the employment one; even in advanced countries the increasing trend to retirement continues unabated. Taking all the variables into consideration, these data suggest that the changes taking place in the most advanced, postindustrial societies reverse the trend toward increasingly lower status of the elderly.

Palmore and Manton do recognize that traditional values could maintain the status of the elderly in the face of modernization. They mention as a possibility the Confucian ethic as such a tradition, and the position of the aged in Japanese society was discussed in the chapter on family life. But their recognition of potential negative cases has not relieved them of criticism. Fischer (1978) claims they left out countries which did not fit their model, and they confounded their results by including education as both an independent and dependent variable. These are persuasive criticisms, but the suggestiveness of the results warrants further explorations along similar lines, preferably with less indirect measures of prestige.

Other cross-national studies approach the modernization hypothesis by means of survey data. Bengston and his colleagues (1975) analyze interviews from 5,450 men between the ages of eighteen and thirty-two based on samples from six countries. Their hypothesis is that favorable attitudes toward aging and the aged are inversely related to (1) societal modernization and (2) individual modernity. The first refers to the same type of broad-scale variable discussed by Cowgill and used in the Palmore and Manton study. The second refers to characteristics of individuals who have been exposed to industrial technology and urban settings. The dependent variable has to do with attitudes people express, based on responses to three questions regarding the worth of elderly people, obligations toward them, and their feelings about growing old. The responses obtained in the three more traditional and less Westernized countries (India, Bangladesh, and Nigeria) were compared with those of the more modern ones (Argentina, Chile, and Israel).

The authors found confirmation for the first part of the hypothesis but not the second. Negative attitudes toward the aged and aging were inversely related to the degree of societal modernization. However, at the individual level, they found evidence in the direction opposite to their hypothesis; that is, the greater the modernity of an individual, the more positive his attitudes toward aging and the aged. Interpreting attitudinal data can be tricky. Does it mean that individuals with modern characteristics are more likely to fulfill their obligations to old people? Or are such people more likely to respond to such attitudinal questions in a more "sophisticated" way, one that they consider more socially acceptable? Although we cannot resolve this issue here, this study adds a new dimension to the theory by exposing the lack of synchronization between modernization and modernity, at least as far as the expression of attitudes is concerned.

Critique of Modernization Theory

There has been an avalanche of criticism directed at the modernization hypothesis, mostly by historians and anthropologists. Historians insist that it is very difficult to find a Golden Age in preindustrial Europe when old folks were venerated and lived in blissful contentment. For example, the evidence from England (Quadagno 1982) and France (Stearns 1977) supports at best an ambivalent attitude, at worst, utter contempt for old age. In tracing the course of old age throughout American history, Fischer (1978) concludes that the most hopeful statement one can make is that the condition of the aged became better in some ways and worse in others.

Anthropologists are especially critical of the undifferentiated way modernization theorists treat traditional societies. They are sensitive to the enormous diversity of culture among nonindustrial societies. To characterize these societies as having essentially the same cultural patterns for the role and treatment of the aged is grossly inadequate, as the previous chapter by Rhoda Halperin clearly demonstrates. A good summary of the limitations of the modernization model is provided by Nancy Foner (1984b) who supplies examples in both nonindustrial and industrial societies that do not fit the expected pattern of high status before and low status after. Furthermore, Goldstein and Beall (1981) have demonstrated that even without direct penetration of an industrial economy, rural areas can be affected substantially. They show how modernization indirectly influenced the economic and cultural life of the agricultural Sherpas of Nepal so that the situation of the elderly became wretched despite the high social status that Buddhist culture confers on the old.

These limitations are important to recognize. But the exceptions one can find in this, and almost any, generalization can be stultifying unless there are more powerful theoretical alternatives available. Obviously, the modernization hypothesis requires elaboration so that the inadequate before-after model incorporates broader processes of change. Additional factors relevant to the situation of elderly people need to be brought into the analysis. Several suggestions have been made which will be covered in the conclusion section of this chapter. First, however, an examination of several holocultural studies will help broaden the framework for a more adequate modernization model.

Respect for the Elderly: Resource Control

Holocultural studies of the status of the aged, although influenced by the modernization hypothesis, generally have taken a broader tack. Since the samples used in such studies are heavily weighted toward what modernization theorists collectively call traditional societies, and are usually treated as an undifferentiated set in their "before" category, the theoretical perspectives have necessarily taken into account more abstract or wider ranging variables than those associated with the "after," or modern, category. One can subsume most of these variables under the general category of resource control, and generalizations are phrased in terms of an association between the presence of a particular kind of resource control enjoyed by the aged and the respect they are accorded in the society. Simmons

(1945) had essentially the same idea in mind when he concluded that respect for the aged is found where they have some "asset," such as knowledge, skill, control over property, or the exercise of some ritual function. But he acknowledged the analysis was hampered by the difficulty encountered in measuring prestige, a term that is used synonymously with respect and esteem.

Following the early work of Simmons, a preliminary attempt was made by Maxwell and Silverman (1970) to state specific hypotheses and measure more carefully several variables considered pertinent to the position of the aged. As part of a general theoretical statement dealing with the nature and distribution of information in a culture, we hypothesized that the esteem in which the aged are held varies directly with the degree of control they maintain over informational resources. A second hypothesis derived essentially from modernization theory; it stated that under conditions of rapid social change, caused by contact with more dominant cultures as occurs in colonial situations or coincident to industrialization, the information of the elderly becomes rapidly obsolete and this contributes to their loss of esteem. Only the first hypothesis was tested with a convenience sample of twenty-six cultures in the HRAF, chosen on the basis of the richness of data available on old people.

Informational control was measured by six different modes (to be explained shortly) of conveying information in social situations. The twenty-six cultures were then arranged on a scale constructed according to the number of different modes of conveying information the elderly employed in a particular society. This measure of the amount of information control was then related to the esteem in which they were held, based on twenty-four items of either positive or negative treatment they received from other members of society. A linear relationship was found between the degree of information control by the elderly and the amount of esteem they received.

Subsequently, these hypotheses were tested with a more adequate sample and more precise measures of the variables. The Standard Cross-Cultural Sample (Murdock and White 1969) consists of 186 societies chosen to represent all known cultural diversity in the world and, at the same time, to avoid the inclusion of societies considered too similar because of their geographical closeness or historical connection. The data for each society are also pinpointed with reference to a particular community from which the data were collected and the specific years the fieldwork was done. In most cases the time frame was chosen to coincide with the period just prior to substantial penetration by outside influences, such as subjugation by a colonial power.

Drawing upon this systematic sample Silverman and Maxwell (1983) drew a 55% subsample from the 186 and found sufficient data on the elderly to include 95 societies in their analysis. A somewhat revised in-

formational control variable was employed, consisting of seven information processing categories:

(1) Administration—when elders make decisions to coordinate the action of
others
(2) Consultation—when elders provide information requested by others
(3) Arbitration—when elders are expected to resolve conflict between individuals and groups
(4) Reinforcement—when elders compliment, advise, or admonish people
on their behavior
(5) Entertainment—when elders are involved in expressive performances
such as storytelling, reciting myths, and making music
(6) Teaching—when elders instruct in formal settings that are periodically
scheduled, as in schools
(7) Instruction—when elders instruct in informal settings at the request of
individuals; usually this involves passing on knowledge of skills

It is important to consider a number of additional resource control
variables relevant to determining the status of the aged. These include
resources also thought to confer power on individuals who control them
and in turn earn the esteem of other members of society. They are:

(1) Control of material resources—elders own property, money, or articles
of symbolic and aesthetic value
(2) Control over social resources—for our purposes, this included any
rights elders had over the adoption or buying of children, or priorities
over the choice of spouses
(3) Control over supernatural resources—any special powers the elders
possess for manipulating the universe, such as communicating with
spirits, causing natural disasters, or curing the misfortunes of others.

A more rigorous effort was made to operationalize the dependent variable, the esteem in which the old people are held. Whereas the information
processing variable refers to the behavior of the aged, esteem refers to the
behavior of others toward the aged that is designed to enhance their
physical well-being, maximize their self-image, or dramatize in some fashion the respect and appreciation they enjoy. We developed a "deference
index" (Silverman and Maxwell 1983) whereby all such behavior found in
the literature could be subsumed under one of the following categories:

(1) Spatial deference—elders given preferred position, such as a seat or area
in a home
(2) Victual deference—elders given preferences in food and drink
(3) Linguistic deference—through speech or writing the elders are deferred
to

(4) Service deference—any kind of work performed for the benefit of elders, such as cooking and housekeeping

(5) Celebrative deference—any ritual or ceremony to dramatize the social worth of being an elder

(6) Prestative deference—bestowing gifts on persons because they are elders

(7) Presentational deference—any modification of appearance or bodily position required in the presence of elders, such as kneeling or wearing only modest attire, etc.

Using statistical techniques that allow for the analysis of multiple independent and dependent variables, and combining the scores for both elderly men and women, the categories of information processing were shown to be significantly related to the deference index. This confirmed the results of the early study (Maxwell and Silverman 1970). But this time the analysis went further by including the additional resource control variables. They were added to the list of information processing items and then run as an expanded set of independent variables against the deference index. The newly added items also contribute to the overall relationship with the dependent variables, which is not especially surprising. However, significantly, the most important contribution made to the correlation is by three of the information processing items—administration, consultation, and reinforcement. All three, especially administration, have a greater impact on the overall correlation with the deference items than control over material and social resources. Thus, the control of information variables are a more powerful predictor of esteem than the control over material, social, and supernatural resources.

But what are the social conditions that promote the involvement of elders in information processing, which in turn is able to predict the esteem they receive? Two antecedent factors were theorized as important in determining how information is managed in a society and, consequently, how that affects the role played by old people: (1) Community isolation refers to a condition in which there is a relative lack of information entering a community. There would be few links with external groups and institutions in such a community. (2) Social rigidity denotes a condition in which there is a relative lack of communication within the community because of social or physical barriers that hinder contact between groups and various categories of people. These barriers could exist between castes, religious groups, or men and women (see also Young and Bacdayan 1965).

With respect to the first factor, we hypothesized a linear relationship between community isolation and information processing among the elderly. This is actually another version of the modernization hypothesis, for an isolated community is by definition not participating in this global process. Because such communities have little outside contact, there is a

An Honored Elder: This woman from the village of Decs in southern Hungary is in her early eighties. Because of her exceptional skill in weaving, the government has bestowed on her the title of Master of Hungarian Folk Art. She receives a monthly stipend and is expected to pass on her skill to others. (Photographer: Thomas Lazar)

low rate of informational turnover. Under such conditions, the knowledge old people acquire through life experiences is more likely to remain useful. Using a number of different measures of community isolation, we attempted to test this hypothesis. The only correlation was found when the penetration of mass media was used as the measure of community isolation, but it was not in the predicted direction. In other words, the greater the exposure to mass media, which in general was not at a very high level for any of the cases in our sample, the more likely that old people were involved in information processing.

Initially, this seemed inconsistent with the modernization hypothesis and the results obtained in cross-cultural and cross-national studies. After a more thorough examination of the data, it became obvious that our results were based on a consideration of only those societies classified as traditional by modernization theorists. Although there were clearly significant differences in the type and complexity of economic and social organization, all the societies in our sample were nonindustrial or, at most, traditional agrarian communities within a country where some segments of the economy were industrializing. The most modern of the cases was a rural Japanese community studied in the 1950s. Thus, it would appear that at a middle range level of differentiation—approximately the level of rural, peasant communities that have some degree of penetration by the larger society—the aged are maximally involved in information processing. This is consistent with the claim made by Simmons (1945) that the prestige of the aged is highest in those societies falling in the middle range of cultural development.

It is now possible to view these findings in relation to other studies. Our sample is truncated approximately at the point of social differentiation at which the Palmore and Manton (1974) sample begins. Ours deals with only traditional communities, theirs deals with modern nation-states at different points in their modernizing quest. Their sample may be thought of as an extension of ours, despite the fact each used different units of analysis; community in one, nation in the other. Presumably, if our sample had included communities from countries in which modernization trends had become more deeply imbedded, we would have seen the control of information among the elderly diminish and, concomitantly, a decrease in their prestige. Then, with the development of the postindustrial societies, the trends begin to reverse themselves somewhat. Thus, when taking account of the full range of complexity in human societies, from hunter-gatherers to the postindustrial world of high technology, the status of the aged has a bimodal distribution, with the most recent trend in the direction of increasing prestige or, perhaps more accurately, concern for their welfare.

But there are other factors that can affect the esteem enjoyed by the elderly. Let us return to the second antecedent factor, social rigidity. In communities where there are communicational barriers among the constituent groups and social categories, we expected to find greater control of information by the elderly. Because they are either less threatening or, because of age, better known by the members of other groups in the community, the elderly can more easily penetrate whatever barriers to communication exist and thus provide a critical channel for giving and receiving information. Furthermore, as suggested by Cool (1980), the aged may best represent for the members of the particular group they belong to the characteristics and qualities that make them different from the other community groups. Because the aged can reflect continuity with the distinctive history or life-style of the group (whether in terms of their kinship, religious, occupational, or other affiliation), they can contribute useful information and provide a focus for the maintenance of solidarity among the members of the group.

We indexed social rigidity by the presence of the following cultural items: (1) subcommunity endogamy; (2) economic, political or religious activities organized at the family or subcommunity levels; (3) exclusive male or female activities or associations; and (4) restrictions on the movement and/or behavior of women. In testing the hypothesis, we found that the societies with communities high on social rigidity also have old people who are heavily involved in information processing.

How this factor of social rigidity combines with community isolation to affect the position of old people still requires exploration. Slater (1964) has pointed out, based on examining Simmons's (1945) data, that the societies in which the aged have high prestige are generally authoritarian and collectivistic, have hereditary castes or classes, include decision-making processes at the extended-family level, and typically are governed by monarchs or restricted councils of oligarchs. This sounds like the type of society commonly found at the middle range of cultural development where the trend away from community isolation has not yet reached the point of making the informational role of the aged obsolete. Conceivably, then, a high level of social rigidity can combine with a moderate level of community isolation to maximize the involvement of elders in informational processing, which in turn is rewarded by the community holding them in high esteem. It also implies that despite low levels of community isolation, where outside penetration related to the modernization process has substantially influenced the nature of community life, it is possible that the prestige of the aged can remain high as long as community life is characterized by social rigidity. This may help explain the many exceptions researchers have found to the modernization hypothesis.

Other holocultural studies lend support to some elements in the above argument. In a bivariate analysis based on a sample of 135 societies from the HRAF, McArdle and Yeracaris (1981) found that when the elderly are engaged in valued activities, they are more highly respected than when only nonvalued activities are available to them. The elderly are defined as engaging in valued activities if they are involved in the economy or maintain lawful authority over all the people. They are categorized as receiving high respect based on the presence of any one of several items that fit the categories of service, victual, and celebrative deference as used by Silverman and Maxwell (1978, 1983).

In the McArdle and Yeracaris study, the different items of valued activities and respect for the elderly are not combined to form a composite measure; thus, it would be difficult to rate each society according to the overall presence of these variables. However, their analysis is enhanced by controlling for a third variable—type of family organization. They found that the relationship between valued activity and respect holds only in societies that are organized in independent nuclear families. The elderly are more likely to be respected in societies with extended families, but this respect is less likely to be contingent on the kind of activities they engage in. They conclude that, regardless of whether or not the aged are engaged in valued activities, the extended family is more suited to caring for the elderly because of greater opportunities to maintain a high degree of emotional interaction among family members. By controlling for additional third variables, they also demonstrate that respect can occur without performing socially valued activities where leisure time is available to the elderly for interaction with others and where they no longer are responsible for maintaining social control, which allows them to develop affective rather than only instrumental relationships with others. But the data in support of these conclusions are less convincing.

What kind of activities are the elderly particularly involved in? Eleanor Maxwell (1975) used the qualitative techniques based on grounded theory (Glaser and Strauss 1967) to examine the data on the role of the aged in forty-five societies in the Standard Cross-Cultural Sample. She found the aged particularly active in three kinds of rituals: life cycle rituals (such as ceremonies at birth, puberty, marriage, and death), work cycle rituals, and power displays (usually involving control over supernatural powers). Thus, the elderly are particularly important in expressive displays that are designed to maintain social solidarity for what Naroll (1983) calls the "moralnet," which refers to the largest primary group from whom an individual learns moral ideas, norms, and values.

Finally, Tom Sheehan (1976) analyzed data from forty-seven societies selected from the Standard Cross-Cultural Sample of Murdock and White (1969). Although he presents no statistical tests of his findings, he concludes that the lowest esteem for the elderly is found in the simplest socioeconomic structures, such as in nomadic societies, and the highest esteem in the more complex peasant societies. Nevertheless, comparison with the data from other holocultural studies is hampered by Sheehan's broad definition of esteem. He defines it as the interaction of a decision-making role or resource control and the quality of received behavior. In other words, it includes both the behavior of the elderly as well as behavior directed at them by others. This highlights the technical problems researchers have encountered in dealing with such protean concepts as esteem. There is still need for better measures of this crucial variable.

Contempt for the Elderly

As we have seen, a major objection to modernization theory has been the evidence for the disparaging treatment of the aged in nonindustrial societies. Although ill-treatment is commonly found in the ethnographic record, the measures used to index this form of behavior vary considerably and, as a result, there is disagreement regarding precisely how widespread it is. For example, in the study by McArdle and Yeracaris (1981) discussed in the previous section, 46 of the 135 societies in their sample, or 34%, were found to have low respect for the elderly; the remaining ones were classified as having high respect. Significantly, whenever they encountered treatment modes that reflected both high and low respect in the same society, these cases were dropped from the sample. We are not told how many societies were dropped for this reason.

The findings of Glascock and Feinman (1980) paint a gloomier picture. They conclude that nonsupportive treatment of the elderly is even more commonly found than supportive treatment; only 48% of the societies in their sample had supportive treatment, whereas 58% had nonsupportive treatment (which is close to the 61% of the societies in which the elderly receive some form of negative treatment found by Maxwell, Silverman, and Maxwell 1982). Although the Glascock and Feinman sample is considerably smaller than the one used by McArdle and Yeracaris (1981), it is derived from the carefully selected HRAF Probability Sample Files of sixty societies chosen for holocultural comparisons (Naroll, Michik, and Naroll 1976). They also find that in every society where nonsupportive treatment is found, the attitude toward the aged is one of respect. By demonstrating how important it is to distinguish between attitude and behavior, they provide a useful reminder of the critical difference between real and ideal culture.

There is evidence in a number of societies of both supportive and nonsupportive treatment of the elderly. This is hardly surprising even in less differentiated, preindustrial societies, where any one of several factors can account for mistreatment. Firstly, some families or subgroups within the same community may be more or less indifferent to the situation of the elderly. Secondly, when catastrophic events engulf a society, like warfare or natural calamities, the needs of the old can easily be neglected. And finally, variation in treatment may depend on the condition of the aged person. Having to deal daily with mental and physical decrepitude does not bring out the best in people, as we saw in chapter 10 in the section on caretakers.

Glascock and Feinman (1981) have fastened upon this last point as an explanation for why both supportive and nonsupportive treatment occur in the same society. Using the HRAF Probability Sample File mentioned above, they find that 26% of the fifty-seven societies distinguish between intact or young-old, and decrepit or old-old. They then hypothesize that societies making a distinction between intact and decrepit aged will also have both supportive and nonsupportive treatment of the aged. This occurs because the members of society provide support for the aged while they are still intact, but when decrepitude sets in, this support is withdrawn dramatically. Presumably, it is obvious why this occurs, for no particular explanation is given for this type of mean-spirited behavior. Glascock and Feinman claim their hypothesis is supported, since all the societies that have both supportive and nonsupportive treatment also make the distinction between intact and decrepit aged. However, their tabular data show that the intact/decrepit distinction is also made in an equal number of societies that do not have both supportive and nonsupportive behavior. But their point is well taken: old age is not an undifferentiated cultural category even in nonindustrial society. We will return to the fate of the decrepit in the section on death and dying.

In dealing with the same problem, Silverman and Maxwell (1984) started from a basic assumption regarding the nature of social life as it affects old age. It is possible that contradictory factors operating in some societies may lead to an ambivalent attitude or differing responses to the aged. Because of this ambivalence, there exists both positive and negative treatment either by the same people in different situations or only certain categories of people who are more highly stressed by the contradictory factors. We found that 20% of our sample of ninety-five societies (see discussion of this sample in the previous section) had high scores for both positive and negative treatment. Positive treatment was measured by the deference index of seven categories (which are defined in the previous section). Negative treatment was measured by combining some eighteen distinct acts of disparaging behavior into three differently weighted sets: (1) mild contempt—excluding elderly from participation in some aspect of community life; (2) moderate contempt—acts indicative of loss of status, such as face-to-face insults or suffering downward mobility; and (3) severe contempt—acts of genuine deprivation, such as lack of food provision or abandonment.

After running a number of ecological and social variables, we did not find any significant relationships with the presence of both positive and negative treatment of the aged, although the relationship was nearly significant when run with the variable of the type of household family. Recall that one of the findings of McArdle and Yeracaris (1981) was that in societies with extended family households, the aged received high respect whether or not they engaged in valued activities. But in societies with nuclear family households, high respect came only with carrying out valued activities. If extended family structures provide a powerful context for the positive treatment of the elderly, then it is conceivable that under certain conditions other factors could compromise the strength of this relationship. In pursuing this argument, we controlled for household family structure, and found a significant relationship between the presence of social stratification and evidence of both negative and positive treatment of the elderly, but only in the context of extended family households.

Thus, we find that in some contexts old people continue to live in extended family households, although the society is sufficiently stratified that a status hierarchy of classes or other social strata exists outside the kinship system. The source of the stratification may be indigenous or may be due to changes taking place due to modernization. Regardless of its source, this combination sets up two opposing value tendencies, one based on kinship solidarity and the other on the desire for social mobility, for any system of social stratification allows for opportunities, however modest, to move up the status hierarchy. This in turn leads to both positive and negative treatment accorded the elderly in the same society. It should be added that more work is required before this line of argument can be well substantiated. Eventually, it may be possible to incorporate it into a more sophisticated modernization model.

In the preceding discussion we were looking for the social conditions that could explain the negative treatment of the elderly. Alternatively, it is possible to approach the problem from a cognitive, or attitudinal, perspective by examining the reasons given in the ethnographic accounts for why the aged are treated poorly. As part of the same project discussed in the previous paragraph, Maxwell and Maxwell (1980b) have analyzed data on the complaints made about the elderly. These complaints can be viewed as expressive of attitudes toward them. Each instance of complaint was associated with one or more acts of negative treatment toward an elderly person. All complaints were classified into eight categories:

(1) Physical deterioration—loss of strength exclusive of sexual potency; sickness and decrepitude
(2) Mental deterioration—senility, mental weakness, offensive behavior
(3) Devalued appearance—wrinkles, gray hair, sagging breasts, ugliness
(4) Lack or loss of skills—also obsolescence of skills
(5) Lack or loss of wealth
(6) Hoarding of wealth
(7) Acquisition of negative traits—especially the involvement in witchcraft or sorcery
(8) Loss of family support system—especially the lack or loss of children

These eight reasons were considered an independent variable and run against the eighteen kinds of negative treatment acts as the dependent variable. A multiple regression analysis showed that the category with the strongest predictive power is lack of a family support system, which is able to explain 21% of the variance. Of the remaining variance, devalued appearance and physical deterioration each explain an additional 14%. None of the other five categories can explain more than 4% of the remaining variance. The total amount of variance explained is 59%.

It is interesting to note that physical deterioration does not explain the greatest proportion of variance, although by virtue of its occurrence in 25% of the societies in the sample, it has the highest frequency of all categories. Thus, decrepitude is a factor but not the most important one, as argued by Glascock and Feinman (1981), in the overall negative treatment of the elderly. Surprisingly, physical appearance was the second most important in explaining the variance. The Maxwells suggest that appearance may be a far more important component of one's social self than has been recognized, perhaps because people don't like to talk about such matters. This includes behavioral scientists who have done few studies of the differential destinies of beautiful and ugly people. It is an issue that clearly deserves more attention.

Thus, what has proven to be the most important protection for the elderly against callous treatment is a family support system. Although this had been documented previously in industrial societies, these data suggest that we have some justification to consider this a cultural universal.

Aging Women and Men

We have now seen that the treatment of the aged varies enormously from one culture to the next, ranging from veneration, through indifference, to callousness and active contempt. Given this variation, what can we say about the relative fate of aging women and men? As with so many characteristics associated with the aging process, esteem in later years differs substantially by gender. Based on the data from his earlier work published in 1945, Simmons (1960) found considerably more evidence for respect directed at old men than old women. He points out that whenever elderly females are respected in a society, it is extremely rare that elderly males would not be respected; conversely, respect for males is no assurance that females are also so treated. Old men tend to get prestige in societies with patrilineal descent, herding (pastoral) economies, agricultural economies, where the food supply is constant, and where property rights are deeply entrenched. Old women tend to get prestige in hunter-gatherer economies and where there is matrilineal descent, although a more recent study with modern sampling techniques (Whyte, 1978) did not find any important benefits in matrilineal societies for women in general, except for the greater likelihood that they have control over property. Also, women do better in agricultural as opposed to herding societies; the agricultural societies Simmons refers to here are more than likely horticultural economies where women make a major contribution to subsistence.

Silverman and Maxwell (1978) did a preliminary analysis on thirty-four societies from the Standard Cross-Cultural Sample, selected to provide a balanced geographical distribution of societies throughout the world. Their findings are consistent with Simmons on the relative respect given old men and women. But the various categories of esteem used in their study allow for a more detailed analysis. Only six of the seven deference items could be used because it was not possible to make gender distinctions for the celebrative deference category (see definition of categories in resource control section of this chapter).

TABLE 14.1. **Percentage of Societies Having Types of Deference for Elderly Men and Women**

Type of deference	Percentage of societies where type of deference is present by gender	
	Men	Women
Service	56	59
Victual	76	38
Spatial	56	35
Linguistic	71	29
Prestative	44	26
Presentational	53	18
	n = 34	

NOTE: Data based on Silverman, P., and R. J. Maxwell. 1978. How do I respect thee? Let me count the ways. *Behavior Science Research* 13(2): 91–108.

Table 14.1 summarizes the frequency of the various categories of deference as they occur in the sample. Only service deference is more common for old women, and even then the difference is negligible. In all other categories men get deference in far more societies than women. Typically, the categories have a frequency substantially greater for men, in some cases occurring in more than twice as many societies as for women. If one looks at the distribution closely, women do better in the first three categories listed in the table. Together these represent, for the most part, one or another form of custodial deference, where something is done to enhance the physical well-being of the people who receive it. In contrast, the lower three categories in the table represent what we may call symbolic deference, where appreciation of the elders is dramatized to them in some fashion, but it has no direct consequences for their physical well-being. Thus, we can conclude that elderly women come close to elderly men in receiving deference in support of basic custodial care which typically occurs within the immediate family, but women are very much less likely to receive the kind of public, ceremonial displays associated with symbolic deference that can be a powerful facilitator of self-esteem.

These gender differences in status were also found in a recent study using quite different techniques (Baker 1985). This was not a comparative study, but instead a sample of 334 U.S. students between the ages of seventeen and thirty-five, with a median age of somewhat over twenty. The students were presented with a list of some twenty-eight age and sex combinations and asked to make a status rating on a seven point scale from "far below average" to "far above average." Ratings were obtained for both sexes from ages five to one hundred. Through the life span, an inverted U curve of status was found; that is, status begins very low, then rises sharply during adolescence, peaks around thirty, and then a slow but increasingly accelerated decline occurs until ninety.

Most interesting in these results is the gender difference that occurs through the life span. The status of males and females remains about the same through adolescence, but then begins to diverge sharply as males are accorded higher status until the divergence reaches a peak in middle age, after which the difference gradually closes as the status ratings become virtually the same for both sexes from eighty to ninety years old. Surprisingly, the sex or the age of the students did not significantly affect their ratings. An unexpected finding was the upward trend in status occurring after ninety; Baker found that one-hundred-year-old men and women gained considerable status, especially the men. His explanation is the scarcity of centenarians; like quintuplets, they are honored by virtue of being rare. Can this also explain why the centenarian men are more highly prized? Perhaps, but one would expect the status disadvantage of being female would be lost at this august point in time. It would be interesting to have comparative data and samples with a broader age span than was possible in this useful study.[1]

Despite the unfavorable comparison with men, the status of women increases substantially across the life span, and in contrast to Baker's results from North American culture, it may be more typical cross-culturally for it to remain high through old age. Based on an examination of the role of women in a number of cultures, Judith Brown (1982) concludes that their lives improve with the coming of middle age. She defines middle-aged women as mothers who are not yet aged but who have adult offspring. Although the impact on women's lives varies from moderate to dramatic, there is overwhelming evidence of three positive changes: (1) fewer restrictions—menstrual taboos and other restrictions required by their sexuality no longer apply, deference to male authority is loosened, and a greater variety of public settings are made available to them; (2) a gain in authority over specified kinsmen—they acquire the right to command the labor of and make important decisions for younger family members; and (3) new opportunities for achievement and recognition beyond the household—this is especially true in religious and ceremonial activities.

Brown explains the increased status women achieve in middle age as the inevitable consequence of having adult children. More than any other kinship dyad, mother-adult child relations are governed by a characteristic set of norms found without exception cross-culturally; that is, grown children ideally should support and show respect for their mothers. Fur-

1. Although no details are provided on the sample in Baker's study, it is likely Canadian. He is a professor of sociology at a university in British Columbia.

thermore, in a number of societies, this bond with adult offspring is reinforced by the mother's right to control the preparation and distribution of food in the household. Although she presents a number of supportive examples for her conclusions, there is no systematic test provided for these generalizations.

Anthropologists are masters at finding exceptions to almost any generalization, and this one has not escaped that inevitable fate. According to Jeanine Anderson (1982), the model does not fit the realities of poverty among Latin American peasants and marginal urban groups, situations where it is difficult to find any improvement in the security and well-being of middle-aged women. More importantly, Molly Dougherty (1982) points out that Brown's theory ignores the relatively large proportion of women in all cultures who remain childless or have no children surviving to adulthood. By including such women in the analysis, it may be possible to demonstrate which of the two factors is most closely related to status change, having grown children or the diminished sexual desirability and reproductive capacity of women in middle age. David Gutmann (1982), for one, doubts that the increased status is due to the bond with adult children or based on the importance of food distribution, as argued by Brown. However, he does agree that the fortunes of an older woman are dependent on the success of her son, and she is valued for her role as sponsor and legitimizer of his ambitions. Taking these criticisms into account, we have in Brown's work several important generalizations that deserve to be translated into testable hypotheses.

Several comparative studies suggest support for various elements of Brown's ideas. In a holocultural study of thirty societies, which were reasonably distributed over the world's culture areas, except for the underrepresentation of South American societies, Bart (1969) found that the status of women went up in mid-life in seventeen societies and down in only two (presumably, the data were insufficient in the remainder of the cases). Her indices of status are very close to Brown's three factors of positive change listed above. Bart found that the position of women improves in middle age in societies with extended family residential units, "explicit roles" for grandmother and mother-in-law, concern over reproduction, and extensive menstrual taboos. The last two factors probably relate to the obsessive concern with the control over female sexuality found in many societies, which then relaxes for women in the postmenopausal period. In four of the seventeen societies where women's status increases, they also gain participation in governmental affairs. This is most common in African societies.

In another study of forty-six peasant societies throughout the world, Michaelson and Goldschmidt (1971) found these communities were typified by an "androcentric" economic structure, one in which the father's role is authoritarian and the mother's indulgent, and there are weak affective ties between spouses. In this context, strong bonds are maintained between mother and son, which in later years leads to an increase in her powers, although at the expense of normally strained relations with the daughter-in-law.

Finally, a study of five Israeli subcultures provides a link between the adjustment of middle-aged women and modernization. Datan, Antonovsky, and Maoz (1985) conducted a broad-scale survey of 1,146 women from Israeli subcultures that were ordered along a continuum from most to least modern: immigrant Jews from Central Europe, Turkey, Persia, and North Africa, and Israeli born Muslim Arabs. The authors find that the life course of women in traditional subcultures more closely approximates the biological life cycle, while those in modern subcultures are relatively more independent of it. In traditional subcultures women marry sooner, bear more children over a longer life span, and are more likely to respect elaborate taboos relating to menstruation, pregnancy, and childbirth. Yet, despite great differences in fertility and control of conception, all groups were unanimous in welcoming the cessation of fertility. The authors interpret this as evidence for a maturational change; that is, an inevitable response of women that cannot be explained in terms of culture.

A finding not anticipated by Datan, Antonovsky, and Maoz was that neither a linear nor an inverse relationship was found between adjustment in middle age and the degree of modernization of the subculture, as predicted by contending theories. Instead, the relationship proved to be curvilinear; the women reporting the highest levels of psychological well-being were the most traditional (Muslim Arabs) and most modern (Central European Jews) subcultures, and those with the lowest levels were from the remaining three transitional subcultures where the greatest cultural discontinuity was experienced. Despite the use of quite different data bases and units of analysis, it is possible to interpret these findings as consistent with those of Palmore and Manton (1974) discussed earlier. It also points to the contexts in which the positive changes occurring for women in middle age, as posited by Brown (1982), may not hold.

One of the five theoreticians of personality reviewed in chapter 7 is David Gutmann. Because his work is influential in characterizing gender role changes in later life—for example, Brown (1982) considered his explanations the most satisfactory—and because his supportive data are cross-cultural, we return to his ideas in this context. Gutmann ([1969] 1974; 1985) hypothesizes a universal psychological pattern in aging which occurs regardless of the constraints set by particular cultures. This involves a diminishing need for fathers and mothers to continue expressing typically masculine (active, aggressive, and competitive) and feminine (passive, receptive, and nurturant) behavior in the postparental years. Once no longer responsible for the physical and emotional security of children, they are free to indulge in behavior typical of the other sex but denied them earlier because of the parental division of labor imposed upon them by child-rearing and required for the survival of the species.

As a result, postparental women seek out and create more powerful roles; Gutmann (1985) talks about the "protean potency" of older women and their androgynous, sexually bimodal behavior. They may not occupy positions of formal dominance, but their behavior becomes more aggressive and their role more that of a matriarch. For their part, the men become more passive, affiliative, and "feminine" in their strivings. As a result, the once distinct gender personality types converge in later life. Gutmann has used psychological projective tests in several cultural settings to support his argument. Thematic Apperception Test protocols have been collected among Navajo in the American Southwest, Highland and Lowland Maya of Meso-America, Druze of Israel and Syria, and in urban United States (Kansas City). In addition, longitudinal data collected from both Navajo and Druze suggest that these distinct personality profiles are psychological changes within individuals rather than cohort differences.

Gutmann's ideas find some support in the ethnographic research from various parts of the world. In a cross-cultural study of sexual stratification, both Schlegel (1977) and Smock (1977) find gender distinctions becoming muted or even disappearing as people age. Even in male-dominated societies, like the Comanche in North America, the Mundurucú in South America, and the Ewe of West Africa, women who have reached menopause fill important decision-making roles otherwise restricted to men.

On the other hand, at least one anthropologist has taken rather sharp exception to the construct of universal later life androgyny. Corinne Nydegger (1984) has criticized Gutmann's findings on several counts: limited samples, at times equivocal results from the projective protocols, the lack of confirmation when nonprojective techniques are used, and the mixing up of psychodynamic, behavioral, and social structural levels of analysis in assembling his evidence. Others have found Gutmann's theory simply another misguided, sexist view of an unsentimental and unappealing older female figure, although Gutmann interprets this later life reversal as demonstrating that there is nothing inherently "masculine" or "feminine" in personality, and sees it as, rather, a result of constraints imposed by parenting during the younger adult years. These disagreements notwithstanding, the notion that personality qualities diverge during earlier life stages and then converge in old age remains a fascinating hypothesis that deserves more careful examination in a wide range of cultural contexts.

Grandparents

Grandparenthood is a social role defined in terms of one's generational position in the family. Although normally associated with old age, its occurrence in the life course can encompass a much broader age range, as was discussed in the section on grandparenthood in chapter 10. In examining the life course as a cultural category that is defined differently across societies, Fry and Keith (1982) discuss patterns of age differentiation, several of which are relevant to a consideration of grandparenthood. They examined qualitatively data from the sixty societies in the HRAF Probability Sample Files as well as selected ethnographic monographs with particularly rich data on the aged. Their preliminary search yielded four common patterns of age differentiation, which they state as hypotheses to be tested more systematically:

(1) As societies become more differentiated, the categories of age groupings also become more elaborate. For example, less complex societies are unlikely to have a category for adolescence or middle age. The notion of childhood as a life stage distinct from adulthood is a relatively recent development in Western civilization (Ariès, 1962). Thus, the pattern of the differentiation of age groupings obviously relates to the evolutionary and modernization perspectives. In this context, it is relevant to mention holo-cultural research that has attempted to find common patterns in the definition of old age cross-culturally (Glascock and Feinman 1981). Although only 62% of the societies in their sample included explicit data on the subject, the most common means of defining old age was by the change in social role. Depending on which social role is focused upon, including grandparenthood, old age is differentially determined cross-culturally.

(2) Spatial separation of age groups is common. In almost half the societies examined, residential separation by age was the norm. Fry and Keith do not indicate how often the segregation of the elderly cohort occurs, but they claim the recent development of segregated housing for the old in industrial societies can occur in a variety of cultural contexts. This naturally has consequences for relations with grandchildren.

(3) During those life stages when individuals are least likely to be in positions of power, such as youth and old age, the saliency of age is greatest and the equality among peers most likely. During those stages of social maturity when individuals are typically in positions of power, groupings based on other criteria—such as kinship groupings, religious or political affiliations—are more likely to be given priority.

(4) A cross-age alliance occurs among alternate generations. A common feature of social life, particularly in societies with elaborate age set organizations, is the alliance between old and young, grandparent and grandchild, at times in opposition to the middle generation. Adjacent generation relations tend to be characterized by authority or, in some cases, competition. But alternate generation relations are more likely to be characterized by affect and indulgence. Fry and Keith point out that this alliance between young and old can be found in U.S. society, and it is part of the ideology of the Gray Panther organization.

However, alternate generation warmth and affection is not found universally. Apple (1956) analyzed data on the nature of grandparenthood from a sample of seventy-five societies, which unfortunately overrepresented Africa and underrepresented South America. Based on the work of the British anthropologists A. R. Radcliffe-Brown and S. N. Nadel, Apple argued that the grandparent role is determined by the way authority is distributed in the family. Among other things, this can affect differentially relations with each set of grandparents. The major hypothesis for which she found support was that an indulgent, close, friendly relationship between grandparents and grandchildren existed when the grandfather is dissociated from family authority (the situation which normally exists in U.S. society). Conversely, when the grandfather is involved in the family authority structure, relations with grandchildren are formal and more distant. Thus, the social structure of kinship relations must be considered in understanding the link between grandparent and grandchild.

Has the role of grandparent been affected by modernization? Profoundly, according to Naroll (1983). Using data from a study of 128 societies by Williams (1972), Naroll finds that in the large majority of pre-industrial, small-scale societies, the elders (more specifically, the grandparents) are charged with providing moral guidance to the young. In the ten modern industrial societies in the sample, this traditional role is weakened or completely absent. Naroll attributes many ills of modern society to the absence of older members in the extended family passing on a set of core values related to the moral order.

Death and Dying

By the latter decades of the twentieth century in the United States and other Western industrial countries, communities had all but abandoned the elaborate traditions that were once part of funeral rituals. Despite the well-recognized need to mourn and express grief for the deceased, more typical today is the hiding or minimizing of death from those closest to it, including the dying person (Rosenblatt, Walsh, and Jackson 1976). This is especially true in the American South. Where once the funeral ritual demanded considerable time, energy, and money, even from people of modest means, it has now become a short, superficial necessity to be defrayed as inexpensively as possible.

Despite this trend, the former elaborateness can be revitalized in special cases, such as the death of someone who enjoys particular esteem in the community. When such a person recently died in Alabama, the funeral service took place in one church hooked electronically to two others in order to accommodate the thousands of mourners. The funeral procession was estimated to be three miles long, consisting of more than three hundred cars and six buses which drove in caravan for sixty miles from Tuscaloosa, where the service occurred, to Birmingham, where the deceased was laid to rest. Some claimed it was the biggest funeral in the South in many years. Why such a fuss for an elderly, retired person? Paul "Bear" Bryant, for years the successful and popular head football coach at the University of Alabama, had died. A colleague eulogized him as one of the greatest men of the century (*Los Angeles Times* 1/27/83, 1/29/83). It was a vivid expression of contemporary American values.

One can find similar examples in nonindustrial societies. In a classic study on death written around the turn of the century, Hertz ([1907] 1960) relates how the death of a chief or high-ranking person in Borneo reverberates throughout the community, but the death of a child, slave, or stranger passes almost unnoticed. These examples underscore how the response to death may represent the most sensitive measure of status available to us. As the ultimate human condition and yet, according to Lévi-Strauss (1974), the arch-enemy of humanity, death is an opportunity to express what is most valued by the living. Because the emotions it arouses vary enormously throughout the world, the dying and death of old people may provide important insights into their position in society. We are concerned here with comparative studies exclusively; a more comprehensive treatment of this topic can be found in the final chapter.

We begin by situating the elderly relative to other members of society with respect to measures of violent and deliberate death. Raoul Naroll (1983) has provided useful cross-national data on suicide and murder rates based on a 1975 United Nations report. The sample is unfortunately limited almost exclusively to European societies and their extensions beyond the continent. Japan is the only Asian country in the sample, and there is no representative from Africa or the Muslim Near East. Nevertheless, there is remarkable variability in these rates among the countries in the sample, although no explanation is provided for these differences.

Naroll's data indicate that in most modern countries the suicide rate is considerably higher for the aged. The suicide rate for people over sixty-five is expressed as a percentage of the rate for people between the ages of twenty-four and forty-four years; thus an elder suicide ratio of 100 would mean they have exactly the same rate of suicide as the younger cohort. Only six of the thirty-three countries in the sample have ratios below 100 for elder suicide; they are Poland, Ireland, Northern Ireland, Iceland, Chile, and Barbados, which reports no suicides among its small elderly population. The countries with the highest ratios are Israel (leading easily with 529), Bulgaria (471), Spain (387), and Japan (329). If there is anything this last group of countries has in common, it might be, paradoxically, the high esteem in which the aged are held. The United States falls about in the middle of the pack, close to the Scandinavian countries, with a ratio of 131.

Naroll also provides U.S. data on the changing suicide rates among men throughout the life course. Beginning in childhood the rate goes up steadily until it dips slightly between fifty-five and sixty-five years, but then rises sharply again from seventy to eighty, finally ending in a slight dip at eighty-five years. We also know that the suicide rate is much higher for older men than older women. It may well be that the rate fluctuates downward in late middle age for men because they tend to reach the apex of their earning power and authority between fifty-five and sixty-five years. It then rises sharply with the onset of old age, perhaps due to the loss of status coincident to retirement or, possibly, because of increased health problems. Whatever the reasons causing the increase among the young-old, they do not appear to affect those few who reach the most advanced ages. We need only be reminded of the status bestowed on long-lived people which may provide longevity with its own reward.

Turning to the murder rates, they show a surprisingly high ratio of elders who are homicide victims compared to their younger age cohorts. Using the same measure as with the suicide rate, twenty of the thirty-two countries reported in the United Nations data have higher rates of murder for the elderly than for those between twenty-four and forty-four years old. At the top, far beyond any other country, is France with an astonishing ratio of 847, followed by Norway (177), Czechoslovakia (175), and New Zealand (153). The crime-ridden United States is among the twelve countries that have a lower murder rate for elderly than for the younger cohort, with a ratio of only 41. Other countries below 100 include Finland (80), Spain (79), Sweden (78), and Australia (72). Little wonder that Naroll suggests no explanations; there is no obvious pattern to this distribution. Here we have what appears to be an important cultural difference in how elderly people fare in a society, which still requires a convincing explanation.

Murdering old people is called gerontocide, which encompasses not only killing but also abandoning them, including their exposure to the natural elements. Heinous as this act may seem, it is surprisingly common. Holocultural studies have been fairly consistent in their estimates of how widespread this phenomenon is cross-culturally. Simmons's (1945) early study reports a somewhat higher rate than subsequent estimates; for example, the proportion of societies in his sample with evidence of killing the elderly stood at just under 30%. He also found that old women were much more likely to be the victims. There was evidence of the killing of old men in 18% of the seventy-one societies in his sample, compared to 27% for old women. Abandonment of the aged was even more prevalent; 26% abandoned old men, and a surprisingly high 35% abandoned old women. Simmons concludes that these practices occur in nomadic societies, where the climate is severe and the food supply irregular, and the subsistence economy is nonagricultural. All these explanations appear reasonable, indeed most had been previously mentioned in the anthropological literature. He does not suggest any explanation for the clear preference for doing in elderly females.

Maxwell and Silverman (1987) found gerontocide to be present in a little over 20% of their sample of ninety-five societies. Geographically, the highest proportions were in aboriginal North America and Africa, each with about one-third of their societies having this custom. Most of our results did not support Simmons's conclusions. Using more sensitive measures of climate, we found that societies located in areas with harsh climates tended to practice gerontocide, but the relationship was not significant. This was also true of nomadic societies, although seminomadic societies had the highest proportion of all. Contrary to Simmons, we found an inverse relationship between gerontocide and the presence of an irregular food supply. We argued that where such irregularity existed the elderly are more likely to be tolerated because of the information they possess concerning subtle details of food production or the skills required for the food search. The only conclusion of Simmons we confirmed was that gerontocide was more likely to occur in nonagricultural societies. Related to this is an inverse relationship with social complexity as measured by social stratification; that is, the less stratified a society is, the more likely for gerontocide to occur.

We then looked at basic features of family life. It is possible to divide kinship systems into two basic types: collateral and lineal. Collateral systems are those in which relations are traced along both mother's and father's side so that all living relatives are included. In such a system members of society cannot by divided into discrete groups of kinsmen. In a lineal kinship system, relations are traced along only one line of descent, so that either mother's or father's side is excluded. These so-called unilineal systems generate discrete kinship groups, called either clans or lineages. Although she presents no systematic data, Barbara Myerhoff (1978b) claims that in lineal systems the aged have great authority and status. These tend to be societies with ancestor worship, and because elders are linked with ancestors, who are thought of as simply an extension of the older generation, they (the elders) are honored regardless of their personal qualities or the particular emotional attitude felt toward them.

We have not been able to find any relationship between ancestor worship and the status or authority of the elderly. But we did find that 39% of the societies with collateral kinship systems commit gerontocide, whereas only 9% of those with lineal systems do so; the relationship turned out highly significant. The key seemed to be that the lineal types are organized into kinship groups with strong bonds of solidarity among members, both living and dead, for that matter. To murder someone who is practically an ancestor is simply too disruptive. On the other hand, where social bonds are more fluid and there are no corporate kinship groups, as in collateral systems, the commitment among individuals is less binding, and thus it is, possibly, more acceptable to people.

Other than the corporate kinship groups in the lineal systems mentioned above, there are a number of ways by which people organize themselves into exclusive groups. It seems reasonable to assume that such a group, regardless of what principle it is organized upon, could create such a strong commitment among all its members that ridding itself of its elderly, no matter how irksome they might be, would be rendered unthinkable. Recall that in the study discussed in the section on resource control in this chapter (Silverman and Maxwell 1982), we found the control of information by the aged was related to social rigidity, which refers to communicational barriers within a community. The corporate family groups which typically organize a variety of activities for their members represents one index of social rigidity. Thus, a socially rigid community is one that has a number of groups or social categories that within themselves have a great deal of solidarity and a unified image of who they are. We found an inverse relationship between communities that were socially rigid and the presence of gerontocide. Only 13% of the societies high on social rigidity practice gerontocide, whereas 30% of those low on this index do; this proved to be a significant relationship.

The linkage between group solidarity and treatment of the elderly can be further specified by introducing a motivational factor. In the study by Maxwell and Maxwell (1980b) discussed in the section on contempt for the elderly, the various complaints made against the elderly were analyzed in terms of their relative importance. In the ethnographic literature, these complaints often justified or were a prelude to the mistreatment old people endured. It is possible to think of these complaints as an expression of attitudes that provide the motivation for members of the community to behave in certain ways toward the elderly. Although this must be considered a somewhat rough measure of motivation, it allows us to bring the more remote social structural characteristics discussed in the previous paragraph down to the individual level. By so doing we may gain some insight into how the decision is made to murder an elderly community or, more typically, family member.

In our analysis of the motive for gerontocide (Maxwell, Silverman, and Maxwell 1982), we found that the kind of complaint that correlates significantly with killing and abandoning the elderly is complaining about their physical weakness. This is consistent with the findings of Anthony Glascock (1982) who shows that most societies make a distinction between the intact and the decrepit aged, and once someone falls in the later category, it is common to draw "death-hastening" behavior. Since we found gerontocide to be related to nonagricultural societies, we expected to find a correlation between these subsistence types and complaints about physical weakness, and we did.

We argued that in nonagricultural societies, which include hunters and gatherers, herders (pastoral societies), and the seminomadic horticultural-ists, it is more likely that from time to time dramatic efforts are required by the work routine. Whereas true agricultural work tends to be more plod-ding and requires perseverence, the nonagricultural economies may de-pend occasionally on sudden and relatively brief bursts of strength and endurance. Such efforts may be precisely the ones a weakened elderly person is least capable of undertaking. Consequently, an ethic emerges that renders them more dispensable. This point is made most clearly in the anthropological literature by Allan Holmberg (1969) in his study of the Siriono Indians of Bolivia, a group of seminomadic hunters and gatherers:

> Since status is determined largely by immediate utility to the group, the inability of the aged to compete with younger members of the society places them somewhat in the category of excess baggage. Having outlived their usefulness they are relegated to a position of obscurity. Actually the aged are quite a burden. They eat but are unable to hunt, fish, or collect food; they sometimes hoard a young spouse, but are unable to beget children; they move at a snail's pace and hinder the mobility of the group. . . . When a person becomes too ill or infirm to follow the fortunes of the band, he is abandoned to shift for himself (Holmberg 1969, 224–25).

One should not conclude from this that the aged play an insignificant role in nonagricultural societies. In the previous chapter Rhoda Halperin has demonstrated their essential contribution to hunting and gathering societies. But such systems still may be too fragile to deal with decrepitude. While recognizing that we may no longer require sudden physical ex-ertions on the part of our decrepit elderly in postindustrial societies, at what point life is no longer worth living has become a serious social issue again. Some form of gerontocide continues to exist, curiously a phenom-enon most typically found in societies with the least and the most sophisti-cated technologies.

Conclusion

Most of the comparative studies covered in this review deal with some aspect of the status of the elderly in various societies. Many concepts are found in the literature to refer essentially to the same phenomenon: status, prestige, esteem, social honor, and others. Why has so much concern focused on this issue? It has been argued that more than anything else in life, more than money and material goods, humans hunger for self-esteem, and seeking prestige is the main way to obtain and maintain this sense of self-worth (Barkow 1975).

A number of methodological problems are inherent in comparative research. The major challenge is to create variables that are standardized so that they can be compared across cultures, but at the same time have validity within each of the cultures (Fry and Keith 1980). There are probably an infinite number of ways that old people can be accorded esteem by other members of society. The problem lies in finding some equivalence among different acts of esteem so that they can be reduced to a manageable set for analysis.

Another problem is dealing with the variation among individuals that occurs in even the least differentiated cultures. Christine Fry (1980) points out that, as the task of ethnographers is to build models of behavior for a given setting, they cannot be faulted for ignoring variation. When dealing at the macrolevel of comparisons between cultures, one must assume that the differences within a given setting are not as great as those between settings. One must be content to capture the most typical expression of the behavior without forgetting that a variety of alternatives to this typicality also finds expression even in the most undifferentiated societies. These alternatives may be critically important for certain kinds of analyses, but only rarely can they be accounted for if the study design is large-scale comparisons.

There is also the problem of the difference between what people say they do and believe, and what their actual behavior is—what anthropologists have called the difference between the ideal and the real culture. This is not just a problem in comparative research but of all attitudinal surveys where extrapolations are made to actual behavior. Glascock and Feinman (1980) have claimed that in nonindustrial societies there is a difference between the attitude stated by individuals and the actual treatment accorded the aged. Of course, there is no reason to believe that this discrepancy would be any less remarkable in industrial societies. They do well to point out the possible confusion between attitude and behavior, but in their effort to call attention to this, they may have exaggerated the seriousness of the problem. But the point is well taken, for it is not always clear from ethnographic accounts if the ethnographer is reporting on an act actually observed (and at what frequency?) or on standards expressed by informants but never actually observed by the researcher.

One has little choice but to accept statements of behavior by the ethnographer as actually existing. Further confidence can be gained by using the samples now available that are based on a careful culling of the best ethnographic accounts. An alternative is to undertake comparative studies whereby data collection occurs within a common framework or protocol so that the researcher in each cultural setting is collecting data comparable to that of all others. This was the strategy of Whiting and Whiting (1975) in the well-known Six Culture Study concerned with parenting, child care, and children's behavior. However, this is obviously an extremely expensive technique, and given the present state of research funds in the social sciences, we are not likely to see much of this in the immediate future.

As we have seen, the theoretical thread that runs through much of the comparative research is modernization theory. This is not surprising since it is a theory that offers an integrated framework for viewing patterns of aging both comparatively and historically (Hendricks 1982). But the danger with such a macrostructural approach is that when it is used incautiously, it oversimplifies and even falsifies what is, in fact, a complex process. Alternatives to modernization theory are necessary to supplement it and provide a more contextual frame for the changes affecting the aging process. Anne Foner (1982), in a general statement, has pointed out the importance of sources of change other than modernization which must be accounted for. Goldstein, Schuler, and Ross (1983) have demonstrated with data from the Hindu Nepalese of Kathmandu that economic and social changes only remotely related to modernization have been detrimental to the aged. Even though the elderly live within the extended family, intergenerational relations are very poor and many traditional tensions have been exacerbated in recent years. Thus, even the vaunted extended family, which appeared to be such a positive factor for the treatment of the elderly in several of the comparative studies covered earlier, cannot be considered invariably a safe haven in old age.

In order to retrieve it from the many critics, Ashenbaum and Stearns (1978) have suggested several broad modifications to modernization theory. These include the recognition of stages in the modernization process, each with varying effects over time and impacting on different age groups in dissimilar ways. Their point is well taken. Preindustrial society was neither utopia nor purgatory for the aged, and with the onset of modernization, their condition improved in some respects and deteriorated in others. For the most part, the task remains to specify more precisely how this complex process unfolded.

XV

THE LIVING DEAD
CULTURAL CONSTRUCTIONS OF
THE OLDEST OLD

Andrea Sankar

A new sociodemographic category has been created and it is causing policymakers and popular theorists great concern. The oldest old, those eighty-five and older, are the fastest growing group in the population (Manton and Soldo 1985). In 1940 only .3% of the total population was eighty-five and older. Since then, this sector of the population has been experiencing significant increases, so that by 1960 it had expanded by 154% (Rosenwaike 1985). However, it was not until the 1980 census that the numbers involved became significant: by 1982, the number of oldest old stood at 2.5 million or 1.1% of the total population (*Wall Street Journal* 7/30/84). If this rate of increase continues, the oldest old are expected to number 5.1 million in 2000, about 2% of all Americans, and by 2050 more than 16 million people will be eighty-five and older, constituting 5.2% of the population (Manton and Soldo 1985).

The emergence of the oldest old has been greeted with dismay. The *Wall Street Journal* (7/30/84) asks, "Should Care Be Rationed?" while others discuss "Can We Afford the Oldest Old?" The National Institute on Aging has made studying the oldest old a top priority, and the Health Care Financing Administration views this segment of the population with greatest concern.

Almost uniformly the oldest old are popularly described as a group of sick, depressed, alone, and very needy individuals (*Wall Street Journal* 7/30/84). In this respect they epitomize all that American culture fears about aging. The film "Cocoon" is a graphic demonstration of this fear. In the film, residents of a nursing home in Florida by chance encounter aliens who have the ability to rejuvenate them. Almost all of the elderly characters are depicted as frail, sick, bored, unhappy with their lot in life, and sexually frustrated. The elderly characters literally jump at the chance to

345

become young. The most noteworthy aspect of this otherwise unremark-
able film is the extreme nature of the stereotype it depicts. The ultimate
symbol of the rejuvenation and banishment of old age is the return of
sexuality and end of disease for a central character. This film says a great
deal about the level of anxiety with which the successful, young, Holly-
wood male producers view aging. The oldest old can be expected to evoke
the most extreme form of this stereotype and provide, therefore, an
illuminating case study in the cultural construction of aging.

Any new phenomenon that occurs within society is interpreted, made
sense of, or constructed using the systems of meaning already operative
within a culture. This construction or interpretation may change over time
as new information makes specific and therefore differentiates aspects of
the event, for example, establishes how the new is similar to and different
from preconceived ideas. In studying a new group such as the oldest old,
one can learn much about the culture through its manner of construing this
new phenomenon, and one can begin to understand the new group itself.
In analyzing health and health care needs of the oldest old, I shall attempt
to disentangle the various cultural constructs used to interpret the oldest
old, such concepts as autonomy, work, fear of death, individualism, and
old age, and to analyze some of the theories accounting for this group and
its potential impact on American society and culture. An analysis of the
cultural response to the oldest old will be a voyage into uncharted waters;
for the United States is one of the first cultures (Japan is another) to be
confronted with such a large group of extremely old people.

I shall focus on three interrelated elements of the cultural construction of
the oldest old: (1) the assumption that chronological age alone constitutes a
sufficient criterion to identify a homogeneous group; (2) the imputed
causal link between old age and disease; and (3) the labeling of the oldest
old as "needy."

The Homogeneity of the Oldest Old

Policymakers and popular writers have been quick to adopt the demographic projections of the oldest old as proxy measures for the cost of
medical care and the kinds and extent of formal health care services this
group will require. The assumption is that the oldest old will be sick, frail,
alone, and depressed. The stereotype of the elderly as a uniformly needy
and sick population is a strong one in American culture. Significant attempts on the part of researchers to modify this stereotype (Neugarten
1974, 1982) have merely succeeded in shifting the stereotype to those more
advanced in years, releasing the "young old," (sixty-five to seventy-five)
and "old old" (seventy-five to eighty-four) and encapsulating the oldest old
(eighty-five-plus) (Binstock 1985). Despite the arguments of Neugarten

Centenarian Celebration: John Langham is celebrating his one hundredth birthday with his friend Julia who is ninety-nine. They live in Pioneers' Home in Prescott, Arizona. (Photographer: Jay Langham)

(1974, 1982) and Binstock (1981, 1985), stereotypes concerning the elderly remain strong.

Consider for example the case of nursing homes. Popular impressions of families abandoning their elderly members to nursing homes persist. Although Liang and Tu (1986) have recently demonstrated that while the incidence rate for nursing home placement (i.e., the percentage of those sixty-five and older in residences on any one day) may be only 5%, the prevalence rate (total risk in a lifetime) is 25% for those sixty-five and older, the belief exceeds these increased risk data. A careful examination of nursing home residents reveals that the risk of placement is not at all evenly distributed throughout the population; that it is, in fact, highly specific (see Johnson, this volume). Weissert (1985) identifies several factors that discriminate nursing home residents: more than 90 percent of nursing home patients are dependent in activities of daily living (ADL) (i.e., bathing, dressing, toileting, continence, transferring, or eating), and two-thirds are unmarried. Only about one million people nationwide who are living in the community are dependent in ADL, and of these more than half are married. Thus the potential candidates for nursing home placement are a select group.

These findings are particularly significant for, as Weissert (1985) demonstrates, some researchers, along with the general public, continue to hold that nursing home placement is a serious threat to many elderly. This assumption then structures research questions designed to establish the cost-effectiveness of community as opposed to institutional care. Research based on these assumptions seeks to demonstrate that community care can keep people out of nursing homes in a cost-effective manner. A firm grasp of the specificity of the nursing home population should indicate that such comparisons are inappropriate, that the risk of nursing home placement is not evenly distributed in the population and therefore, that community-based care must be evaluated by criteria other than avoidance of nursing home placement.

A similar kind of indiscriminate categorization takes place in many discussions of health care costs for the elderly. Images abound of the growing numbers of elderly devouring greater and greater shares of the gross national product (Estes 1986). Again a few basic principles are needed to separate the actual phenomenon from the stereotyping taking place. To begin with, the elderly are blamed for the rising cost of health care. In fact, 70% of rising health care costs are attributable to inflation, 25% to increased intensity of care, and only 3% to demographic aging (Health Care Financing Administration 1983, cited in Estes 1986). To be sure, when one examines the distribution of health care costs, the elderly account for a disproportionate share (32.7%) (Fuchs 1984). The association between increased health care utilization and the elderly is, however, in large part misleading for, as Fuchs argues, it is not old age itself that accounts for increased health care utilization but nearness to death. It has been demonstrated that approximately 5% of the Medicare population account for 30% of the costs (Lubitz and Prihoda 1984) and these 5% are in the last year of life. Because the oldest old, those eighty-five and older, have on the average six years to live, their nearness to death concentrates mortality within a few years. However, this concentration of mortality is not the result of the accumulation of years but of the nearness to death (Fuchs 1984). This point is important because it helps establish the significance of the heterogeneity of the aging population. As we shall see, the sheer number of years an individual has lived does affect health and consequently nearness to death, yet the effect is not one of a predetermined march toward disease, disability, and death; other factors besides number of years since birth determine the susceptibility to disease in most cases.

The first aspect of the cultural construction of the oldest old that I have analyzed is the uniformity or stereotypical nature of the approach to the oldest old. The next point I will consider has helped to structure this uniform stereotypic response.

Death, Disease, and Old Age

Stereotyping implies a prejudicial, usually negative, response to a perceived group. This response is primarily rooted in the perceiver's context rather than in characteristics of the group being stereotyped. In the case of racial prejudice in the United States such a response serves to focus attention on an outside threat and away from systemic factors creating unequal access to opportunities and resources within society. In the case of the elderly, and in particular the oldest old, around whom the stereotypes of aging are now coalescing, we need to ask what factors in the perceiver promote the stereotyping response to this group, or more basically, the perception of those eighty-five and older as members of a group at all?

The old as a group symbolize the loss of key elements of the American cultural character. Clark and Anderson's work (1967) on aging and culture illustrated how the perceived loss of autonomy, independence, and, one should add, sexuality, attractiveness, and power, make the status of "old" a threat to the cultural ideal of the self-made, white, middle-aged male executive. Notions of autonomy, power, and aggressive sexuality dominate images of the desired public persona (Cancian 1985). Although it is true that some people sixty-five and older may have lost these attributes, other groups, such as children, do not possess them either, and a good number of people of either gender would not characterize themselves as powerful. So why are these primarily seen as negative characteristics of the elderly?

Examining another characteristic of old age, the proximity of death, helps to explain the strength of the sense of loss or decrement. The myth that anyone can obtain wealth, power, even beauty if they work hard enough is a strong one in American culture. For example, the frequent reiteration of this myth has contributed significantly to Ronald Reagan's popularity. Those individuals who do not possess the attributes of the cultural ideal, or children who are not yet expected to have such attributes can live in the hope that they might still acquire them through hard work, self-change, or luck. The elderly, because of their proximity to death, are—so to speak—out of the race, they can never catch up. Thus, old age is an extreme threat because not only does it represent the loss of what has been obtained but also the end of hope for what might be obtained; furthermore, the fantasies that are sustained by examples of older entrepreneurs like Colonel Sanders are ruled out in considering the oldest old for whom there can be no future fantasies.

The image of old age as the end of opportunity and loss of ability and status is created in part by the withdrawal from the work force of those sixty-five and older and in part by the image of disease and disability which contribute to the stereotype of aging. Any stereotype is, of course, constructed from elements of truth. Disability and disease are more prevalent at older ages. Yet these problems are by no means a pervasive characteristic of the elderly at sixty-five or even at eighty-five. In fact, the greatest heterogeneity in health status is found in the oldest population groups (Minaker and Rowe 1985). Despite the existence of a significant proportion of those eighty-five and older who are in good health (i.e., no ADL impairment), the stereotype of old age as disease remains. Part of the power of the old age stereotype derives from the fact that the losses associated with old age are perceived as natural; that is, that they are part of nature and that there is little we can do about them. This image draws its strength from the diagnostic schema of Western medicine (Sankar 1984) which seeks for specific causes for physical ailments. When it cannot find a specific cause, it attributes a problem to nature. Thus, physicians either from ignorance, confusion, or stereotyping attribute that which they cannot explain in their elderly patients to old age (Minaker and Rowe 1985; Sankar 1984).

Genuine confusion within the scientific establishment concerning the relationship between age and disease contributes to the negative association. The debate over the causal nature of the aging process asks whether old age itself is a disease, and if so are all the oldest old likely to be sick and disabled? Although in most situations subtle academic debates over the nature of causality do not normally affect the average person, in the case of the etiology of the disabilities of the oldest old, such debates will be significant; for, their outcome will help structure public policy and inform popular images and stereotypes. We will examine the sides of this debate as it affects the oldest old both to better understand the nature of this elderly population group and to illustrate the workings of cultural categories within scientific debate.

Data directly relevant to the health status of the oldest old are difficult to obtain because (1) the oldest old are widely scattered within the population; (2) until recently census data aggregated all those eighty and older; and (3) cause of death on death certificates in this group is often listed simply as old age. Therefore to understand the nature of health in the oldest old and to appreciate the needs they may have and the services they require we must turn to indirect sources of data. In developing an explanatory model for changes in the mortality rate, Golini and Egidi (1984, cited in Manton and Soldo 1985) argue that reasonable changes in the case fatality rate and the duration of a disease could explain changes in disease incidence. That is, if the duration of a disease like cancer is increased by one year over its initial two year survival rate, the prevalence of the disease will increase by 50%. As our clinical management of the major killer diseases like cancer, heart disease, and hypertension improves, we can expect to see an increase in the prevalence of those diseases as the number of people who die from them in the short run declines.

The theoretical premise underlying this explanation of sickness and old age is that morbidity and mortality rates are linked. That is, a change in morbidity rates will change mortality rates, that mortality or age at death is not fixed. I shall return to the significance of the point in a moment. The basic premise of this theory is that old age itself does not presuppose disease. Recent research supports this theory by demonstrating that many of the physiological changes associated with age can be attributed to age-related pathological changes and not to the aging processes themselves (Riley and Bond 1983).

The physiologic changes associated with aging have a complex and by no means unidirectional relationship to the disease process. Because of some of the changes associated with normal aging, some diseases are less likely to occur or are less severe at older ages (Minaker and Rowe 1985): for instance, Lupus or multiple sclerosis rarely strike older people; breast cancer, when it occurs among elderly women, appears to be less virulent. On the other hand, because age-related changes reduce the function of many bodily organs, the elderly individual is at increased risk of disease in those organs. It is this age-related change in organ capacity that helps explain the increased frailty of the elderly and their consequent susceptibility to disease. Decreased pulmonary function and decreased response of the immune system are particularly significant factors predisposing the elderly individual to disease (Minaker and Rowe 1985). In a few isolated incidents, the aging process itself has pathological consequences. Such problems as cataracts and arteriosclerosis are caused by normal aging processes. Some would include menopause in this list. However, the pathological nature of menopause has been questioned; and its inclusion as a disease has been attributed to the medicalization of normal life processes (Kaufert 1984; Locke 1982).

According to the theory that links morbidity and mortality, one's risk of serious disease and death is related to a morbid state not to age. Morbidity is more prevalent among the elderly partly because of loss of organ capacity produced by the process of aging and partly because of increased exposure to environmental toxins. The progress of the aging process varies significantly from individual to individual as does exposure to the environment. Thus, asserting a link between morbidity and mortality implies that the number of years since birth is not the criterion determining onset of disease and death. In other words, old age itself, except in the few already specified examples, does not constitute a disease. Consequently, many of the problems attributable to old age may be ameliorated, controlled, or wiped out with advances in medical science and better preventive practices. Old age need not be, and indeed for many is not, a time of disease and disability.

The idea that disease and disability need not be associated with old age has found an effective spokesman in the person of cardiologist James Fries. Fries argues (1980, 1983) that the natural life span of the human species is eighty-five years, and any deaths prior to this time are premature and preventable. At age eighty-five, if one lives right, Fries argues, the body will fall apart like the "one-hoss shay" of Oliver Wendell Holmes, and death will result. Fries bases his argument on Hayflick's discovery of a finite number of species cell doublings (which in the human skin amounts to approximately eighty-five years) and on observations of life tables which, if viewed from birth on, appear to become rectangular at age eighty-five (1980, 1983). There are some problems with these basic arguments. First, Hayflick's work has only been proven relevant to the growth of cells in the laboratory; second, a close examination of the tail of the life curve demonstrates a substantial extension as the current population figures on the eighty-five and older population confirm. Despite these problems, Fries's argument based on the contention that individuals should die of old age and therefore that there is no connection between morbidity and mortality, is an appealing one to many people, especially popular health and fitness writers.

Ironically, the conceptual basis supporting Fries's theory of a fit and healthy old age draws heavily on the cultural constructs that account for the negative stereotype of old age. Fries has, in effect, extended the cultural constructs of autonomy, individualism, and control over the environment into old age. These central constructs, which form the modal cultural identity, have previously been limited to the middle-aged who exercise political, social, and economic power. It is the loss of these attributes and the loss of the possibilities of obtaining these attributes that help create the negative stereotype associated with the elderly. Fries's ideas offer a substitute for the loss of power, prestige, and sexuality—control over one's body, individual responsibility for one's health, power over disease and disability. By disassociating morbidity from mortality Fries can argue that all death prior to the species set limit of eighty-five is premature and hence preventable. As in the theory that links morbidity and mortality, Fries's theory implies more attention to prevention of disease. In this theory, last minute heroics would be ruled out because the potential to extend life beyond eighty-five should not exist, and such attempts at an earlier point in the life should be made redundant through proper preventive practices. The negative implications of this theory, which conflicts with the linkage of morbidity and mortality, lie elsewhere.

Fries (1980) writes that he tells his patients "use it or lose it"; that is, keep active and your body will not age, become inactive and you face the possibility of loss of functional capacity. There are two important assumptions here. The first is that if you do use it you won't lose it—that is, continued activity provides more control over the aging process. Although regular activity has been shown to be related positively to mortality rates (Paffenberger et al. 1986), there is little conclusive evidence that it retards aging. Attention to regular physical activity is part of a life-style. This life-style often is associated with the middle class and includes access to resources such as better prenatal care, better nutrition, better medical care, more education, and reduced exposure to environmental toxins. It also implies control over one's time and the environment in which to pursue this regular activity.

This leads to the second implication of Fries's statement, namely, that the individual has responsibility for his or her health. Such reasoning ignores the significant impact of genetics (Manton and Soldo 1985), cohort effects (Riley and Bond 1983), and environmental exposures on the aging process (Minaker and Rowe 1985). It also assumes a uniform rate of aging which indirectly justifies the age-based stereotyping of the elderly. Variations in the aging rate cannot all be tied to disease (Minaker and Rowe 1985; Manton and Soldo 1985; Soldo and Manton 1985), therefore the potential prevention of disease, while making a significant impact on aging processes, cannot make them uniform. For that to occur, we will need interventions in the basic aging processes, which are estimated to be at least thirty years away (Manton and Soldo 1985).

The Fries approach of "use it or lose it" appeals to the American culture and has been widely accepted. It has several serious flaws, however: (1) demographics show the eighty-five and older population is expanding quickly enough to make the rectangularization of the life curve impossible, which disproves the notion that our species specific age limit is eighty-five; (2) the theory posits individual control over the aging process, which research findings on the variability of aging demonstrate is an unrealistic goal; (3) it assumes individual responsibility for health and ignores the impact of environment, class, race, or gender; and (4) it implies a homogeneity of the aging process, which is inaccurate.

The Oldest Old as "Needy"

The cultural construction of the elderly as a group, a diseased and disabled group, is similar to other disease categories (such as women's problems) in that the disease label helps account for a disempowered and marginal status. Like women's problems, this popular category is used by physicians when a clear-cut explanation for a problem eludes them (Minaker and Rowe 1985; Sankar 1984). The study of old age in American culture, however, represents a singular opportunity to move beyond the analysis of disease categorization and cultural relationships represented in the work done on women (e.g., Horton 1984) and examine how such categories operate within the larger cultural domain including economics, politics, and public policy. A brief discussion of the stereotype of the elderly as "needy" will begin to illustrate how a more extensive cultural analysis focusing on old age might proceed.

Closely linked to the stereotype of old age as a disease state is that of the elderly as needy. Until recently the elderly were categorized as the "deserving poor." For the young old this stereotype is slowly being replaced by that of the "affluent elderly," another detrimental characterization (Estes 1986). The oldest old are still considered to be the "deserving poor." Although it is estimated this group will require 19.8 million units of long term care services, a growth of 12.9 million units from the current base (Soldo and Manton 1985), because of their physical frailty, low income, age of their children/caregivers, primarily single status, and high risk of cognitive impairment, these sizeable estimated increases do not in themselves adequately account for the negative label of needy. The basically negative image of the elderly as needy implies they require everything from society and give nothing or little in return. Even "deserving poor" represents only a slight modification of the stereotype. Discussions of the five generation family are especially noteworthy in depicting the oldest old as extremely needy (Shanas 1980). Rarely is any mention made of the potentially positive aspects of such a family structure, only the burden on the caregiver is highlighted. Images of neediness are linked directly to the stereotype of a diseased and disabled population.

In several works, Estes (1979, 1984, 1986) analyzes the social construction of need among the elderly and its impact on public policy. She demonstrates how this construction of need justifies what she calls the "aging enterprise" whose beneficiaries are primarily the administrators and bureaucrats associated with special programs designed to meet the needs of the elderly. She argues that the problems that create need among the elderly are not so much disease and disability as the social problems of poverty, unemployment, racism, and sexism (65.19% of black and 59.3% of Hispanic elderly are near the poverty level, and 71% of poor elderly are women [New York Times 5/29/85]), which plague the rest of society. Such factors as inflation followed by recession, public policies, and a labor market that discriminates against the elderly, deprive them of adequate work or income. According to Estes, these factors, not health, create need.

Estes argues that a powerful medical lobby has encouraged funding for basic biological research into the process and cause of aging, ignoring the causes of disease and disability. This focus on biological research helps sustain the notion that the problems of aging are biological ones which can therefore be cured by biomedical interventions. Indirectly, the focus on biological aging is an attempt to prolong life and triumph over death, a quest the Chinese alchemists have pursued for millennia. The elderly are made to bear the consequences of a cultural fear of death; consequences that result in an allocation of resources to meet needs that may be more a projection of fears of the middle-aged than actual problems confronting an elderly individual.

Detailed analysis of the requirements of long term care services for this population has established that the oldest old are by no means uniformly needy; and that, in part, those requiring services can be accurately distinguished and described. Soldo and Manton (1985) rank order the following descriptions of the oldest old who will need formal services: those living with nonrelatives are most likely to require formal services when impairments in activities of daily living (ADL) and instrumental activities of daily living (IADL) (e.g., reaching) are both present; for those alone need comes when ADL impairments and medical needs are present; for those frail women living with spouses, services are needed when incontinence is added to ADL and IADL needs and medical problems; and for those cared for by other relatives, usually adult children, services are not required until both supervision and incontinence problems are added to IADL and ADL impairments and medical problems. So far our ability to specify the dimensions of specific needs has done little to modify the popular stereotype of needy, and in the case of the oldest old, of "extreme need."

Conclusion

A brief comparison with another cultural construction of old age will illustrate both the variability and hence subjectivity of cultural constructions of old age and throw into relief the negativity of the American view. In Japan the decreased physical capacity and general slowing down associated with age and especially with advanced old age, do not constitute a threat to culturally valued personal attributes, as they do in the United States. From a general perspective this inhibits the formation of negative stereotypes concerning the elderly. It also has a specific impact on actual care practices. For example, because Japanese do not highly value personal independence, the activity regimen of skilled nursing homes is not focused on maintaining a patient's functional independence. Instead, staff devote considerable energies to socializing with patients, touching them, and in general making them feel they are in a family (Campbell 1984). The fact that they are no longer independent individuals is not seen as a threat. Although there is concern about the resources that long term care consumes, the Japanese have not isolated the elderly into a group separate from society.

It is true that the United States is one of the first cultures to confront such a large and extremely elderly population. It is also true that we cannot yet predict how healthy the oldest old will be, and consequently, how much of a drain on social resources. However, a full 29% of the ninety and older women living in the community have no ADL impairments (Manton and Soldo 1985). Clearly they are a special group of physically fit people. Possibly prevention efforts will increase the heterogeneity of the elderly population and hence the illness burden (Manton and Soldo 1985). Possibly that increase in morbidity could be a cohort effect and we could move on to future generations of healthier elderly (Verbrugge 1984). The diversity of future scenarios and the complexity of the current situation are blurred together by the cultural construction of the oldest old that depicts them as a group that is diseased, disabled, and needy. Given the trend toward an aging society and the clearly negative and threatening image associated with such a movement, we need to understand in greater detail the fundamental aspects of our culture that contribute to the creation of such stereotypes. This is essential not only for the theoretical self-knowledge it provides but also for facilitating a smoother transition to an aging culture.

XVI

MENTAL DISORDERS AMONG THE ELDERLY
DEMENTIA AND ITS SOCIO-CULTURAL CORRELATES

J. Neil Henderson

The latter decades of life hold many events that test the coping skills acquired in previous life stages. Eric Pfeiffer (1973) has characterized the senium as a "season of loss" in which many inevitable changes occur in one's social environment and physical body. However, it is not known exactly how many elderly people successfully cope with inevitable changes of the latter years, nor conversely, how many people are sufficiently stressed by the sequelae of survivorship into the sixth decade or beyond to produce physical or mental disorder. Generating accurate epidemiological statistics regarding mental disorders is difficult due to variant nosological categories and clinical diagnostic or assessment technologies operating concurrently with common geriatric features such as atypical presentation of disease. For example, cases of depression in an elderly person may be identified only retrospectively through the unfortunately high rates of suicide, particularly among elderly males, but escape early detection due to the atypical presentation of depression without sadness. Moreover, the phenomenon of "nonpresentation" exists in which older people show a greater willingness to tolerate noxious symptoms both physically and mentally because of close identification with the value of rewards for youth and penalty for age. Therefore, many elderly people sit at home and suffer silently with symptoms, physical or mental, simply because they feel that no better can be expected in old age.

Nosological and diagnostic difficulties notwithstanding, it has been estimated that approximately 15% of the sixty and older population suffers from some form of significant mental health problem (Pfeiffer 1977a). In a 1964 study by Kay, Beamish, and Roth in Newcastle-upon-Tyne, England, a total prevalence rate for mental health disorders was 263 per 1000 persons sixty-five and over. More recently, Allan and Brotman (1981) and Kay and Bergmann (1980) report approximately a 25% frequency of psychological problems in elderly people. Organic brain syndromes have been reported at a rate of 56 per 1000 persons sixty-five and over (Liptzin 1982).

More specifically, the common geropsychiatric afflictions include dementia, depression, paranoia, and hypochondriasis. Although the primary focus of this chapter is on dementia of the Alzheimer's type, other psychiatric disorders, such as depression, are sufficiently prevalent to merit some brief discussion of the current literature. Complete and thorough volumes addressing mental disorders in the elderly can be found in Belsky (1984) and Zarit (1980).

Depression and Other Geropsychiatric Afflictions

Depression in the older person particularly deserves careful scrutiny because it is quite treatable. However, it is very often overlooked or unrecognized because of atypical presentations or confusion with normal age-related changes (Gurland 1976; Becker 1974; Epstein 1976). According to Dagon (1984), difficulties in diagnosing depression in the older person relate specifically to the atypical presentation which symptomatically may present as a pseudodementia, anger without sadness, self injury or accident proneness, substance abuse, somatic preoccupations, or paranoia. The atypical or masked depression occurs in cases where casual observation suggests that the patient's mood is not sad or does not show other obvious depressive symptomatology. Nevertheless, due to the common occurrence of depression in the elderly, it is worth considering detection of depression with screening inventories, or searching for depressive symptoms other than depressed affect including vegetative symptoms such as weight loss, crying spells, diurnal variation in mood, and sleep disturbance. However, sleep disturbance as a symptom can be problematic, in that elderly people normally lose stage three and four sleep and may have altered sleep patterns in the absence of any other pathological indicators.

It is particularly important to distinguish dementia from depression because of the treatability of depression. The common overlapping symptom is apparent memory loss, which in the presence of advanced age may cause the clinician, family member, or patient to leap to a false conclusion of dementia. In depression, memory loss is more accurately described as lack of concentration. Briefly, depression has several indicators distinguishing it from dementia: abrupt onset, relatively short duration, and a constancy of mood. When asked a question, depressed patients tend to answer with "don't know" rather than attempt to make a correct response. They will also highlight disabilities, and have a history that shows the depressed mood occurring prior to changes in apparent memory capabilities (Ham and Marcy 1983).

The significance of depression among elderly people is underscored by the Duke Longitudinal Study, in which 20–25% of subjects could be diagnosed as depressed at any one time, and over time approximately 60% of the subjects could be identified as having experienced a depressive episode (Gianturco and Busse 1978). Furthermore, Stenbeck (1980) reports that in almost all cases of suicide among elderly people, depressive symptoms were present antecedent to the event. Detection and treatment of depression in the elderly person is particularly important because suicide attempts will be "successful" in comparison to adolescent rates (Wells 1979).

Recent work in the affective disorders has refined the nosological category of depression into three distinct syndromes: depression (as described above), demoralization, and depletion (Dagon n.d.). According to Dagon, demoralization, is often experienced as sadness associated with stress or a loss. It is characteristically short in duration and is similar to grief reactions. Depletion is characterized by progressive emotional exhaustion in which the person does not have the energy to invest in significant others or themselves. "It (depletion) is different from depression in which the decision making part of the self is paralyzed and self esteem is lowered" (Dagon 1984, 31). The depletion syndrome can be seen in its extreme form among POWs and concentration camp survivors.

Other types of psychiatric disorder in old age include paranoia and hypochondriasis. Paranoid ideation has been described along a continuum of intensity: suspiciousness, transitional paranoid reaction, paraphrenia (late onset, no schizophrenic symptoms), and paranoia with schizophrenic symptoms (Eisdorfer 1980). Savage and colleagues (1977) reported a prevalence rate of 11% for an aged community sample showing mild signs of paranoid ideation. Such people contend that some force external to themselves has control of their destiny.

Paranoia may be related to normal or pathological sensory changes such as hearing impairment. Hearing has been referred to as the "social sense" and changes or severe loss in one's hearing capacity can be manifest in paranoid thinking and behavior. Also, paranoid thought may be associated with a depressive episode in which delusions may appear. Thus, the paranoid behavior may stem from external changes in the biopsychosocial environment including social isolation, general insecurity, and solitary living (Pfeiffer 1973).

Hypochondriasis can also be associated with depression, as well as being a means of attracting attention or creating more stimuli in the psychosocial environment. Of 152 depressed patients over age sixty, 65.7% of the men and 62% of the women had hypochondriacal symptoms (Busse and Blazer 1980). Although hypochondriasis may be considered nothing more than a nuisance to families and practitioners, suicide attempts are much more frequent among hypochondriacs than those without such symptoms. Busse and Blazer (1980) consider elderly people to be at greater risk for hypochondriacal symptoms than younger adults because of the multiple chronic physical diseases which can manifest themselves in older adults.

The Dementia Epidemic

As Richard Besdine suggests, "Human brain function is precious and unique, and deranged intellect is feared more than death by most people" (1982, 97). Unfortunately, Alzheimer's disease thoroughly disorders intellect and is the "number one health problem of the next century" (Belsky 1984, 231) and a "disorder which now confronts the world as a major challenge to public health" (Henderson 1986, 3). Alzheimer's disease is a term which is currently in the public spotlight via television, movies, and popular press accounts of its course and resultant problems. The portrayals in these accounts are sufficiently effective in highlighting the problems experienced as a result of Alzheimer's disease so that the word itself has made the transition from a technical medical diagnostic taxon to a folk medical concept that replaces "senility" and is at risk of popular over-use. In fact, some are lead to perceive that a virtual epidemic of Alzheimer's disease is underway. While Alzheimer's disease does not fit a classical definition of an epidemic, it is correct that more cases of Alzheimer's disease are occurring in the industrialized nations than ever before. This trend will continue because more people than ever before live to the age of risk. Age-specific prevalence rates show that 4% of the population aged sixty-five or older have Alzheimer's disease at any one time. However, at age seventy-five it has increased to 10–15% and continues upward until the ages of eighty to eighty-five where it reaches 20–25% (Mortimer 1983; Mortimer, Schuman, and French 1981).

The impact of Alzheimer's disease and related dementias does not fall on one person but has a diffusion pattern starting with the victim and moving to the primary caregiver, other family members and friends, and the service delivery system in terms of diagnostic services and ongoing medical care. Other service delivery systems affected by the presence of Alzheimer's disease include case management services, family support groups, and respite care services. The impact is felt even in private industry. For example, nursing homes now are developing dementia-specific care units felt to respond more effectively to the symptomology presented by the dementia patient and to gain a competitive edge in attracting a new patient/disease market. This new development in long-term care management of dementia is currently uncharted and proceeding by trial and error.

The human factor cost and social service cost directly lead to economic costs. While it is difficult to project a future cost for dementing disorders, some indirect picture can be obtained from looking at nursing home expenditures. In 1973, nursing home expenditures were $7 billion annually, while in 1979 they had risen to $18 billion annually. By 1990, nursing home expenditures are expected to rise to $76 billion annually (Pfeiffer 1985). It is important to note that 60–70% of nursing home patients suffer from Alzheimer's disease or a related dementia (Tomlinson, Blessed, and Roth 1970; Blazer 1980).

Although Alzheimer's disease is a specific diagnostic taxon, it by no means encompasses all forms of dementia. In Reisberg's (1981) discussion of prevalence rates, Alzheimer's disease is reported as the most common type of dementing disease, constituting 50% of all cases. Next in prevalence is multi-infarct dementia which has a prevalence rate of 15% of all cases. Multi-infarct dementia results from brain cell loss due to lesions produced by numerous "strokes" throughout the cerebral cortex. Clinically, the symptomatology of Alzheimer's disease and multi-infarct dementia are very similar. However, Alzheimer's disease is characterized by an evenly paced, gradual deterioration of cognitive function, while multi-infarct dementia is more likely to have a step-wise decline in which plateaus of no change are linked by rapid and remarkable declines in cognitive function. Furthermore, the same patient may have a "mixed" type of both Alzheimer's disease and multi-infarct dementia as is found in 25% of cases.

About 8% of cases are pseudodementias attributable to correctable environmental sources, but if left untreated could result in permanent brain cell loss. Also, rare types of dementia account for less than 2% of all cases. These include Pick's disease, Creutzfeld-Jakob's disease, Huntington's chorea, kuru and Binswanger's disease. All of these are comparatively rapid in course and/or have obvious inheritability.

Popular nomenclature, including government reports, often uses "Alzheimer's disease" to mean all types of dementia. Even though symptomatology is similar for the two most common dementias, differential and more accurate use of terms is desirable, particularly for epidemiologic research and, clinically, for disease management. For example, a case of dementia of the multi-infarct type would put the clinician on alert to closely evaluate and monitor hypertension and medications.

Sociomedical History of Alzheimer's Disease

Using Western culture as a point of reference, Torack (1983) provides a history beginning at 500 B.C. of references to aberrant behavior among elderly people, which probably represented in many cases some form of dementing disorder. Cohen (1983) provides a similar short history but with greater emphasis on present nomenclatures.

Wang (1977), however, provides a comprehensive overview of the history, definition, and usage of dementia including the term "Alzheimer's disease." *Demens* is derived from Latin and means "out of one's mind." It received specific psychiatric usage in the late 1800s by becoming synonymous with virtually all mental disease producing aberrant behavior. Also, a description of short term memory loss in older people was published by James C. Prichard in 1835. Prichard termed the syndrome "incoherence" or "senile dementia." Soon, however, neurological advances led to the pathophysiologic elucidation of diseases characterized by neuronal depopulation and the paper by Alois Alzheimer in 1907 describing a case of "pre-senile dementia." In the first decades of the 1900s "senile dementia" was used synonomously with "senile psychosis." In the 1940s "dementia" was used to describe a syndrome and also to describe a specific diagnosis. By the 1950s, "dementia" was seldom used as a diagnostic taxon, and the 1952 Diagnostic and Statistical Manual of Mental Disorders introduced "chronic brain syndrome" to replace "senile dementia." It was under the taxon "chronic brain syndrome" that Alzheimer's disease was included. However, the term "dementia" has been reintroduced to refer generically to various kinds of organic brain diseases. Now that it is possible to distinguish different kinds of dementing disorders, more specific terminology has been introduced such as "senile dementia of the Alzheimer's type" in contradistinction to multi-infarct dementia, Pick's disease, Creutzfeld-Jakob, etc. It is now more common to eliminate "senile" and simply use "dementia of the Alzheimer's type."

Dementia of the Alzheimer's Type

The pathophysiologic changes of Alzheimer's disease center about the death of brain cells. The specific structural changes found in the Alzheimer's patient are neurofibrillary tangles and senile plaques. In fact, normally functioning elderly individuals show both of these structural changes without clinical symptoms severe enough to warrant a diagnosis of a disease process (Kay 1977; Terry and Wisniewski 1977; Roth 1980). Neurofibrillary tangles and senile plaques are part of the cellular correlates to the macro-behavior changes seen in Alzheimer's patients. The severity of a case of Alzheimer's disease is related to the number of both tangles and plaques (Terry, Gonatas, and Weiss 1964), although some evidence suggests otherwise (Ball 1983). Neurofibrillary tangles are also known as (1) "paired helical protein filaments" or "PHFs" due to their physical configuration, and (2) "Alzheimer's neurofibrillary tangles" are known as "NFT's" (Igbal and Wisniewski 1983). They are found in the cerebral cortex with concentrations in the hippocampus, which is the structural part of the brain associated with short term memory (Reisberg 1981).

The source of neurofibrillary tangles is unknown. They may be derived from intracellular structures such as neurofilaments and neurotubules which together constitute neurofibrils (Reisberg 1981; Besdine 1982). Neurofibrils run throughout the neuron and extend from one dendrite to another. The pathological tangles are most often found in the cytoplasm near the nucleus. Senile plaques are found in the same areas of the brain as neurofibrillary tangles, but unlike tangles, can be found in non-human animal brains. Senile plaques consist of immunoglobulin chains which in clusters form a protein of the amyloid type. Immunoglobulin chains are the antibody result of antigenic material (such as a virus) (Reisberg 1981; Wisniewski 1983).

According to Besdine (1982), other structural changes in the Alzheimer's brain include cytoplasmic neuronal granulovacuolar degeneration (i.e., fluid-filled membrane-bounded "holes" in neurons) and loss of dendrites.

Case Assessment

Barry Reisberg (1983) has developed a seven-stage Global Deterioration Scale. Stage 1 is characterized by no cognitive decline and essentially normal cognitive function. Stage 2 shows very mild cognitive decline with evidence of forgetfulness such as forgetting the location of familiar objects or names of familiar people. The patient is likely aware of the memory deficit and is concerned about symptoms. In the third stage, mild cognitive declines are present and clear-cut confusional states occur such as losing direction when traveling. Also, other people easily recognize the patient's deficits. Retention of new information, either read or heard, is compromised, and denial and compensating behavior are commonly observed in the patient. Stage 4 is characterized by moderate cognitive decline and shows definite confusion at clinical interview. At this stage, patients commonly make mistakes of three or more on the Kahn, Goldfarb, and Pollack (1960) mental status questionnaire which provides an index of mental functioning. However, the patient usually is fairly well oriented to time, person, and familiar people.

In the fifth stage, the patient shows moderately severe cognitive decline. This stage clinically is identified as "early dementia" in which the patient now requires constant assistance with activities of daily living such as clothing selection, knowledge of telephone number and address, and the names of familiar people and places. Severe cognitive decline marks the sixth stage, when the patient is clinically classed in "middle dementia." Patients may make five to ten errors on the Kahn, Goldfarb, and Pollack (1960) mental status questionnaire. In this stage, personality and emotional changes begin to be noticeable. These behaviors are often very disturbing to the caregivers and include delusional behavior, obsessive symptoms, anxiety, agitation, occasionally violent behavior, and abulia (i.e., loss of will). Lastly, in stage 7, very severe cognitive declines are apparent. Clinically, this is "late dementia" characterized by loss of linguistic abilities and incontinence of bladder and bowel. It is common for the patient to become totally bedfast due to the loss of locomotor ability.

The clinical impression is that death of the patient is preceded by a sharp decline in the person's health status. Some practitioners have made the clinical observation that such health status changes predate the patient's death by about six months. The Alzheimer's victim is often statistically recorded as a death from bronchopneumonia or cardiopulmonary failure when, in fact, the gradually deteriorating brain is the ultimate cause.

Epidemiology

The epidemiology of Alzheimer's disease and other dementias is currently lacking in detail and specificity. Primary reasons for this are differences in definitions of dementia, diagnostic protocols, and the insidious onset of the disease which makes early stage cases difficult to detect. Gruenberg (1978) discusses a series of problems in epidemiologic testing for both descriptive and analytic studies. These include the determination of age-specific annual incidence as a continuous or discontinuous curve, determination of sex ratio at various age groups, the influence of physical environment, the influence of rural/urban environment, and specific individual factors such as personality, birth order, race, and gene pool membership. Answers to these questions may not only create a more complete epidemiologic pattern for this disease but also suggest a means of modification or, ultimately, prevention.

Although there appears to be little differential risk by sex, the prevalence of dementia in the general population varies greatly with age cohort. For example, 5–8% of noninstitutionalized persons sixty-five and over have been found with moderate to severe dementia (Kay and Bergmann 1980). Mortimer and Schuman (1981) summarize eight European studies conducted during the last thirty years that show severe dementia prevalence rates ranging from 1.3% to 6.2% of the sixty-five and older population. Those with milder impairments range from 6.2% to 15.4%. Wang (1977) reports seventeen international studies most of which are from Europe but include the United States as well as Japan and China. In these studies the rate of severe dementia in the roughly sixty-plus population is 4.8% and mild dementia is 10.14%. The studies reported range in time from 1948 to 1975. The data for the United States show for age group sixty-five and older a rate of 7.1% for severe cases and 24.7% for mild cases in 925 community dwelling subjects (Pfeiffer 1975). Goldman (1984) compares Japan, England, and Denmark by comparable age categories. In the eighty-plus age group, the cumulative risk in Japan is 19.8%, in England, 22.0%, and in Denmark, 13.2%. While the cross-national prevalence rates are quite disparate *within* each age group due to variant diagnostic criteria, there is strong cross-national confirmation of an increase in the prevalence of dementia with increasing age. This further underscores Gruenberg's (1978) salient commentary that simply citing a 5–8% prevalence rate for Alzheimer's disease and other dementias is nearly meaningless given that the variance in prevalence from age sixty to ninety-five is so great.

Most dementia victims in the United States are cared for at home (Kay and Bergmann 1980; U.S. Department of Health and Human Services 1984). Nonetheless, the greatest concentration of cases is found in the nation's nursing homes. Blazer (1980) reports that 70% of nursing home patients are suffering from some form of dementia, most of which would be Alzheimer's disease.

The impact of Alzheimer's disease and related dementias at the individual and national level is and will continue to be substantial. For example, Wang (1977) reports that an estimated 3 million elderly people in the United States alone suffer from severe and mild dementia. Moreover, the elderly population should increase by 43% by the year 2000, and with that increase should come an additional 50% increase in the number of elderly people with dementing disorders.

Diagnostic Protocol for Determining Alzheimer's Disease

Although thorough discussion of the diagnostic protocol for determining the presence of Alzheimer's disease or other types of dementing disorders is beyond the scope of this chapter, certain principles and directions of action merit discussion. First, the only infallible diagnostic technique for Alzheimer's disease in a living patient is a brain biopsy (Glenner 1982). Since such an invasive procedure is seldom warranted, a diagnosis by exclusion typically suffices for a reasonably accurate diagnostic protocol. A thorough "ruling out process" should leave the clinician with a 90–95% rate of correct diagnoses. Ham and Smith (1983) provide a listing of investigations usable in evaluating the patient presenting with confusion or short term memory loss. First, the clinician should rule out all possible reversible causes for the confusion. These include a vast array of possible causes including drugs, emotional illness, metabolic or endocrine disorders, normal or abnormal sensory changes, environmental changes, nutritional problems, normal pressure hydrocephalus, tumors, other trauma to the brain or central nervous system, infection, atherosclerosis, anemia, and alcoholism.

Each of these categories of possible causes of confusion, which are treatable, has specific investigations indicated. For example, when assessing metabolic or endocrine system function, the clinician would be looking for possible thyroid disease, dehydration, hypoglycemia, renal failure, and many other possibilities for which treatment is available. Because geriatric patients often exhibit "altered presentation" of common diseases, it is particularly worthwhile to note that infections and even constipation can produce symptoms of confusion in the elderly person, which may lead to the erroneous assumption of a dementing disorder.

As always, the patient's history must be thorough. However, it is often helpful to have the patient's primary caregiver available for verification of the patient-elicited history. Next, the mental status of the patient can be quickly assessed using technologies like the Short Portable Mental Status Questionnaire (Pfeiffer 1974), in which the patient is asked to respond to ten questions testing for orientation to time, place, self, and intellectual functioning. There is also a scale for determining the level of seriousness of cognitive deficit on four dimensions: intact, mild impairment, moderate impairment, severe impairment. Such brief questionnaires are not diagnostic but do yield quick clinical results for determining level of mental functioning (cf. Kahn, Goldfarb, and Pollack 1960; Blessed, Tomlinson, and Roth 1968; Mattis 1976).

If the patient's medical work-up shows no cause for the presenting symptoms of confusion or memory loss, and a history has been obtained that gives a profile of insidious onset and gradual, steady worsening, a diagnosis of dementia of the Alzheimer's type would be warranted.

Sociocultural Management Issues

Alzheimer's disease has a far-reaching impact on society in both human and economic terms. The dependencies that Alzheimer's disease produces in the elderly adult precipitate many kinds of supportive services such as in-home care assistance, adult daycare, respite care, acute hospital care, and institutional care. The number of professionals, paraprofessionals, and family members involved in the management of a single case of Alzheimer's disease can be staggering. The question that is seldom asked, however, is, "How are the *illness* problems of Alzheimer's disease generated or exacerbated by the sociocultural environment in which this disease exists?" This question is particularly relevant in terms of cross-cultural comparative study and inter-ethnic and intra-ethnic studies regarding differential response to the symptoms of Alzheimer's disease.

Several sociocultural factors exist in this society that worsen the impact of Alzheimer's disease on the individual, family, and nation. First, the predominance of the medical model of care must be considered as a cultural product. For example, "senility" is still present as an operational construct in the minds of many practitioners who will attempt diagnosis and treatment of Alzheimer's disease. The medical model further perpetuates an acute care orientation emphasizing treatment with rapid cessation of symptoms. With a chronic disease like dementia, acute care orientations fail and lead to frustrated practitioners (Comfort 1983). The practitioner is trained to cure and yet is increasingly confronted with an incurable disease. In addition, there is a unidisciplinary treatment approach employed in the presence of a bioculturally complex, lengthy disease process. The Alzheimer's patient and his/her family experience this disease in a medical culture oriented to in-patient, acute care facilities staffed by practitioners who have little medical education in geriatrics and interdisciplinary team management using a health service system that is largely unarticulated in the provision of services, thereby leading to suboptimal care.

Other sociocultural correlates of Alzheimer's disease center on kinship structure, migration patterns, and values regarding division of labor and sex roles as these impinge on in-home caregiving. The nuclear family organization in America concentrates human resources and financial resources in a relatively small number of people. As the family grows and ages, marriage or postadolescent age result not in the inclusion of new members into the residence but a reduction of on-site human resources via the establishment of new and separate residences in which to start again the cycle of concentrated resources. The postmarital neolocal residence pattern causes burden-bearing to be placed on the intact spouse or, secondarily, another family member. The concentrated burden-bearing is further intensified by postadolescent dispersion of kindred via geographic migration away from the nuclear family for educational opportunities, occupational opportunities, or in late life, retirement which may lead to migration to the Sun Belt. In each of these cases, kinsmen physically distance themselves from the caregiving site and caregiving role performance potentials.

The implication of these kinship structure effects, postmarital residence patterns, and postadolescent migration patterns can be seen when compared with a society in which such patterns are reversed. For example, consider an extended family organization that uses either patrilocal or matrilocal postmarital residence patterns, and has a value system that promotes permanence of residence regardless of opportunities that would otherwise disperse the kinship group. Although definitely not a panacea, it may be that under these circumstances caregiving burdens would be diffused within the concentrated on-site system of potential caregivers, resulting in improved care of the patient, improved mental health of the caregiver, and less reliance on institutional care.

The American traditional division of labor and sex roles can be understood as a cohort effect, which may change in future generations. The current cohort of Alzheimer's disease patients and families were socialized during a time in which discrete sex role patterns were instilled. Thus, a husband and wife in their latter years living independently in a home but with the wife experiencing the debilitation of Alzheimer's disease, means the husband will be the primary caregiver even though he may possess a very meager role repertoire of domestic duties. Even though such activities can be learned, there may be a reluctance on the part of the male to participate fully in what he perceives as a woman's duty, the result being psychological conflict and/or suboptimal care of the demented spouse. However, as our sociocultural milieu changes over time, subsequent generations of elderly people who have a modified socialization experience regarding sex role division of labor may bring to the Alzheimer's disease experience a more balanced capacity for caregiver roles or other supportive household services regardless of the sex of the dementing spouse.

The special difficulties imposed by the sociocultural environment on those families coping with Alzheimer's disease is dramatically accentuated by the spontaneous emergence of mutual aid societies specifically designed for Alzheimer's disease patients and family members. Such mutual aid societies typically go under the rubric of a "support group." The development of Alzheimer's disease support groups can be seen as a cultural product that emerged in response to the deficits of an acute care medical system and nuclear family kinship system unable to meet the salient needs of a population experiencing a chronic, debilitating brain disease. In fact, the informally organized Alzheimer's support groups developed by Ms. Bobbie Glaze in the early 1970s have led to a nationally incorporated network: the Alzheimer's Disease and Related Disorders Association.

Alzheimer's disease support groups function socially as fictive kinship groups. They arise in a culture in which fragmented kinship networks are typical and serve to supplement the immediate, face-to-face interactions and assistance that could occur were it not for kindred dispersion. Support groups also function to fill gaps created by the acute care medical system in the long-term management of the disease. One of the discrete internal functions of support groups is to provide knowledge as well as the sharing of techniques for in-home management of the demented patient (Middleton 1984). The in-home caregiver can also look to guidebooks to help develop the role of caregiver (Mace and Rabins 1981; Powell and Courtice 1983), while professionals begin to evaluate the impact of caregiving on the caregiver (Zarit, Orr, and Zarit 1985). Ultimately, Alzheimer's disease support groups create a facsimile of a healing community in which the population is brought together by a common experience related to brain failure in an effort to better cope with this drastic and unpredictable change in the latter years of their lives.

Alzheimer's Disease, Support Groups, Ethnicity: A Latin Example

While aging and ethnicity as a topic of exploration has received increasing attention in recent years, the cluster of aging, ethnicity, and dementia has lagged far behind. Ramon Valle (1981) in a very thorough article on minority response to late life dementias points out that while minority populations as a group tend to have a shortened life expectancy compared to white populations, the longevity crossover effect causes the numbers of

Hispanics and blacks age sixty-five and over to approach the magnitude of the white elderly population. Therefore, the concern about the increasing prevalence of Alzheimer's disease among minority populations is a very real one. Valle points out several areas for further investigation:

(1) Exploring the impact of greater exposure of minority populations to high risk

(2) Examination of illness-producing jobs which may cause differential exposure to noxious environmental elements possibly linked to dementing disorders

(3) An investigation of younger age cohorts in minority populations on the effect of deleterious life conditions of these minority groups as they survive into old age

(4) Relative to the crossover effect, studies should be done to determine if the "survivor cohort" shows differential rates of Alzheimer's disease

Valle also poses other questions regarding biophysical effects such as diet, use of folk medicines, differential effects of biochemical agents in minority populations, and the effect of gene pool source on risk factors.

In an informal survey conducted by the author of twenty-three anthropologists professionally involved with aging and minority issues throughout the United States, not a single response was gathered regarding instances of extending Alzheimer's support group intervention into ethnic communities. Also, key people in the professional and volunteer aging networks were contacted in New York, San Francisco, Los Angeles, Memphis, San Antonio, Miami, and Tampa where significant ethnic populations live and where Alzheimer's disease support groups are in operation. They, too, reported no specific plan for incorporation or extension of services to minority caregivers and nearly zero participation in the existing groups by ethnic populations. It is not surprising that the 1981 White House Conference on Aging specifically targeted blacks and Hispanics as ethnic groups whose informal mental health care systems were inadequately understood and in need of strengthening.

The inadequate understanding of mental health issues among Hispanics in general is found in the fiction of the 1950s that Hispanics were less prone to psychiatric problems. Bacerra, Karno, and Escobar (1982) have corrected this view in a volume that focuses on Hispanics and mental health issues relating to sociocultural influence, major syndromes, and service delivery strategies all specifically tailored to various Hispanic populations.

Stereotypes about ethnic elderly populations have been noted for virtually all major ethnic groups in the United States (New, Henderson, and Padgett 1985). Specific to Hispanics, David Maldonado (1985) has indicated that policies must be based on an accurate appraisal of real life circumstances for the various Hispanic populations. Also, Maldonado notes that

Hispanic age cohorts respond differently to service delivery options. For example, the older Hispanic population who developed coping strategies during pre-civil rights decades will have a greater reliance on self-sufficiency leading to underuse or misuse of the service delivery system. On the other hand, the adult children of these elderly Hispanic people were socialized in this society during or after civil rights reform and have a more active response to existing service delivery systems. The age cohort effect has a significant influence on family support group intervention for Alzheimer's disease patients.

A Latin Alzheimer's Support Group Example

A step toward improving the understanding of differential ethnic response to Alzheimer's disease has taken place in a Latin population in Tampa, Florida. The Latin community of the Tampa area is situated in two portions of the city historically related to the development of hand-rolled cigar industries which moved from Cuba, to Key West, and then to Tampa. This industry developed in the late 1800s and early 1900s. The Latin population by census tracts are most concentrated in Ybor City and west Tampa, both of which are parts of the city of Tampa, Hillsborough County, Florida.

In 1980 the Hispanic population aged sixty-five and over was 12.9% in Hillsborough County, of which Tampa is the county seat. Using the 1980 census figures for this study and a mid-range 15% prevalence rate it was estimated that at any one time there would be almost 1200 Hispanic Alzheimer's victims in the county.

A project was developed by the author and a colleague, Lillian Middleton, at the University of South Florida's Suncoast Gerontology Center to establish an Alzheimer's disease support group in the Tampa Latin community. The Tampa Bay area has an Alzheimer's support group affiliated with the national Alzheimer's Disease and Related Disorders Association but its users are predominantly white, middle-class people. In order to facilitate entry of the project into the Latin community, the assistance of a Latin, bilingual worker in the Senior Daycare Center in Ybor City, was solicited for participation in the project as group facilitator and liaison between the non-Hispanic research project staff and the community.

This project tests the appropriateness and utility of support group intervention among Hispanic populations. Some investigators suggest that group psychotherapy, which is akin to family support group intervention, is prone to failure among Hispanics due to members' concerns about privacy (del Valle and Usher 1982). However, del Valle and Usher note that with proper empathy from group leaders such concerns can be overcome. Other specialists agree that there are positive outcomes of Hispanic psychotherapy group meetings. For example, Acosta reports that while group psychotherapy among Hispanic people is not currently common, it "can be a powerful modality in treating the Spanish speaking Hispanic patients" (1982, 195). Becerra, Karno, and Escobar state even more positively that:

> one type of treatment strategy that has proven very useful with the Spanish speaking Hispanic has been group psychotherapy. The group acts as a support system that facilitates the disclosure of private experiences that many Hispanics find difficult to communicate outside the family or community setting. The all Hispanic group serves to promote greater identity and cohesion among the group members. The similarity in culture and lifestyle provide an environment that is conducive to openness, understanding and change (1982, 11).

The findings of this thirty-four-family project are consistent with the predictions that the support group will constitute a fictive kinship network in itself. Thus, the support group serves as a form of extended family with a problem focus on coping with Alzheimer's disease. According to Escobar and Randolph (1982) the extended kinship network is a primary social resource among Hispanics, and there is strong reliance on the *"concepto de la familia"* as a key element in Hispanic culture.

Maldonado's (1985) suggestion that Hispanic populations differentially respond to available helping services by age cohorts has been very clearly observed in the Latin Alzheimer's Support Group. The most active members are adult daughters and sons of parents who are coping with a spouse with Alzheimer's disease. The older generation Hispanics thus far seldom attend the group except when specifically brought by their daughters or sons. Furthermore, when knowledge of additional community resources are made known to the parent generation, arrangements for such resources are negotiated through the adult daughters or sons in the group.

The prominence of the Latin kinship and family dynamic structure is very clear in issues related to burden-bearing and responsibility. The foremost of these is the sex biased pattern of familial transmission of responsibility for care of the demented patient. Members commonly report that women are expected to provide care for the demented person, whether it is a spouse or parent, or parent-in-law. When the Latin family has males and females "available" for providing the major burden-bearing responsibility, it is the female who is expected to provide that type of care (Spector 1979). In fact, women in general are more likely than men to perform caregiving tasks regardless of ethnicity (Ory et al. 1985). However, these Latin women report that role prescriptions for caregiving tasks and women involve a sociocultural demand perceived as far exceeding that of their Anglo counterparts. One informant reported that during the life of the patient (her father), her mother and she would be expected to provide the bed and body care (see Gubrium 1975) for the patient, but that when death occurred, her brothers who live nearby would take charge because now it entered a business domain, namely the funeral as a financial matter and public display.

If the family does not have a consanguineal female to provide bed and body care for the patient, these duties will be assigned to an affine, notably a nearby daughter-in-law. This provides a source for a variety of intrafamilial irritations. For example, many Hispanic parents are concerned that their adult children may disengage from family responsibilities with the parents. In fact, a daughter-in-law is often the target of great hostility because she has removed the son from the immediate purview of the family arena (del Valle and Usher 1982). Nonetheless, the daughter-in-law may be pressed into service to her in-laws.

Alzheimer's disease carries with it symptoms that the general public would interpret as characteristic of someone who is "crazy." The stigma attached to mental disorders is well known within this culture and many others. Escobar and Randolph report that, "for many Hispanics, mental illness is still seen as a dreaded affliction akin to 'mal de Sangre' or 'bad blood' " (1982, 411). Concern with a family member being perceived as "crazy" is a common one in the Latin Alzheimer's Support Group meetings. There is often a personal crusade launched to be sure that friends and family understand that Alzheimer's disease is an organic disease and therefore not under the control of the individual, thus relieving the patient and family of any social stigma.

There are also two related ethics within the Latin community that can interrupt the benefit of a support group as an intervention mode. These are (1) the "sin of gossip" and (2) the tabu of revealing personal matters in public arenas (del Valle and Usher 1982). Parents who are providing care to a spouse sometimes attend support group meetings with their adult children. In these cases, parents commonly sit silently, leaving the younger generation to proceed along behavioral pathways more in line with American, middle-class whites. The adult daughter or son is often explicit in private interviews about his/her parent's cultural values of preserving a proper image of the family in public settings. It is as if the adult offspring are the cultural brokers of information and services from the support group to their aged parents.

Folk medical practices are not discussed in the group setting. Likewise, in individual interviews in the homes, informants deny using any specific folk remedies. In Ybor City, however, there are *botanicas* which sell a variety of folk medicines including herbal remedies as well as spiritualist and occult paraphernalia. Inquiries at these shops reveal the presence of materials frequently sold for old people who are suffering a memory decline. Spiritualists or occult beliefs are not revealed in the Latin Alzheimer's Support Group settings, although del Valle and Usher (1982) report that such topics eventually emerged in their Latin psychotherapeutic groups.

Discussion

The sixteen months of the Latin Alzheimer's Support Group project has shown that a significant Hispanic population is in need of family support group services to assist in coping with Alzheimer's disease in the family. Initially, there was some skepticism that there was a service population for such a support group. However, with minimal effort the project revealed a few dozen Latin people impacted by Alzheimer's disease who were not users of the well-publicized Alzheimer's disease support group in Tampa.

The project has illuminated various issues. First, there is a definite benefit to the family member participating in an ethnic-specific Alzheimer's disease support group. As Acosta (1982) has termed it, the group becomes a "mini-community." The issue of cultural relevance is critical particularly if the initiators of such projects are non-Hispanics. Likewise, the formation of an alliance with an indigenous member of the Hispanic community who is bilingual and has some knowledge of the aging services network is very critical. Also, the use of ethnic-specific media for announcing the group to the community proved to be a very useful vehicle for ethnic-specific communication.

Second, the experience of this project shows that those attracted to the Latin Alzheimer's Support Group were middle-class, bilingual Latins. It appears that support groups are most attractive to middle-class, middle-level educated people. Moreover, those attending the group are very likely the adult daughters or sons of the parent who is coping with a dementing spouse.

Third, it has been helpful to perceive the adult children as the brokers of information and cultural styles of receiving health care assistance on behalf of their elderly parents. The bulk of the group members bridge the cultural gap associated with the project initiators from the University Medical Center to their parents whose interactional patterns with "authorities" cause them to appear quiet and passive relative to their adult children.

In overview, the concept of ethnic-specific dementia support groups is one that requires continued problem-focused research. Research activities should center on further knowledge of the epidemiology of Alzheimer's disease in ethnic populations, and the variable impact of support group intervention by socio-economic class and age cohort. Furthermore, the potential negative effects of support group formation must be explored. For example, observing a trend in the reduction of Federal assistance programs (Maldonado 1985), David Maldonado (personal communication 1985) considers support groups which rely totally on the personal resources of their members a nonservice strategy. Also, involvement in a support group can generate expectations of mutual reciprocity among group members who may be already operating at their physical and financial resource limit and, therefore, perceive the interactions with group members as an additional stress. Nonetheless, the weight of the literature on Hispanic group psychotherapy and the experience of the Latin Alzheimer's Support Group project show that such interventions have a therapeutic role in promoting the health and well-being of Hispanic caregivers to Alzheimer's disease patients when developed and maintained in a culturally sensitive manner.

Summary

More people live longer today than at any other time in hominid history. Life performance data of hominids from a few million years ago to the present show that the dramatic increase in life performance began in only the last few decades of the twentieth century. This is a precedent-setting phenomenon that rapidly takes us on an uncharted course into the human frontier.

The elderly person of today may encounter two major mental health problems: (1) depression, which is treatable; and (2) Alzheimer's disease, a mysterious, slow killer. Studies show that the majority of elderly people will experience a clinical depression during their elder years, but relatively few cases will be recognized or treated. On the other hand, a majority of elderly people will *not* have Alzheimer's disease, although that minority which does will be detected but *not* cured because no cure yet exists.

The hope of the future is to improve recognition of depression and treat cases pharmacologically and psychotherapeutically, as indicated, with age as no barrier. For Alzheimer's disease, symptom treatment may come before the discovery of its etiology. Numerous pharmacologic agents are being tested world-wide for symptom treatment, but as of this writing, nothing near a "breakthrough" exists.

Overall, pioneers in the mental health of the elderly are faced with an enormous need for new knowledge to make the recent leap in life performance a human experience worth performing.

XVII

THE INSTITUTIONAL SEGREGATION OF THE AGED

Colleen Leahy Johnson

While there is much variation cross-culturally in the status and prestige accorded to the elderly, one finds striking parallels in attitudes toward the totally dependent aged. All societies make a distinction between old age and this final stage of helplessness. Reviews of the anthropology of aging conclude that there are no happy solutions, and this portion of the elderly population is everywhere viewed as a burden (Amoss and Harrell 1981). Even in societies where elderly are accorded high status, old age, when accompanied by dependency and loss of competence, is viewed as distressing and burdensome. For example, in Japan, a country long noted for the endurance of its values on filial piety in the face of rapid Westernization, this last stage of life is described as "the hateful age" (Plath 1983). Virtually everywhere then, loss of physical and economic resources, when accompanied by decrepitude, undermines one's status and prestige.

Solutions to these problems of this second stage of old age in small-scale societies range from murder or assistance in dying, to abandonment, to insulting, demeaning treatment, to grudging support. By the best estimates, 20 to 30% of the cultures reviewed by Glascock and Feinman (1981) either abandon or kill the decrepit elderly. Simmons notes how common various harmful practices are: "Among all people a point is reached in aging at which time any further usefulness appears to be over. Senility may be the suitable label for the 'overaged,' 'the sleeping period,' 'the age-grade for dying,' or the 'already dead' " (1960, 87). Although the numbers of individuals who reach this period of life are few in small-scale societies, some provisions are made to limit the resources granted to those

NOTE: Portions of this chapter were drawn from *The Nursing Home in American Society* by Colleen L. Johnson and Leslie Grant, Johns Hopkins University Press, Baltimore, Maryland, 1985. I wish to thank Leslie Grant for his assistance on an earlier draft of this paper.

375

who can no longer contribute to the welfare of others. (For a fuller discussion of gerontocide, see chapter 14 by Silverman.)

The most common solution to this problem in Western societies is the institutional segregation of the aged, a tack that is quite rare in most cultures. With Westernization, however, one is beginning to find citations in the literature that describe nursing homes in less developed societies (Delaney 1981; Rhoads and Holmes 1981). Most reports suggest that the appearance of this family substitute is not related to changes in filial values, but rather results from social and economic factors over which families have no control. These societies are beginning to experience some of the forces now having an impact on industrial societies. In a period of demographic transition in which life expectancy has recently been considerably extended, their populations have increasing numbers of dependent elderly.

Most significant to these changes when one is considering the "over-aged" is the fact that the largest gains in life expectancy are being made by the seventy-five-years-and-over group. Von Mering and O'Rand (1981) point out that the aging process is different now since significantly larger numbers experience their bodies to the limits of its functioning. While biomedical technologies have provided the opportunity to further prolong life, parallel advances have not been made in addressing the dependencies stemming from widespread chronic diseases. With increasingly large numbers of elderly in this final stage of dependency, the family, social services, and health care system have become overtaxed (Johnson and Grant 1985). Usually as a last resort, the problems of dependency are dealt with through the custodial care of the elderly in institutional settings. By the best estimates of Western capitalist countries, approximately 4–6% of the aged are cared for in such settings (Shanas et al. 1968).

In the United States today, there are over 18,000 nursing homes which house 1.4 million individuals. These institutions have been described as "houses of death," "human junkyards," "warehouses for the dying," or "travesties on the word home." While there is ample justification for such epitaphs, there is also evidence that the quality of nursing homes has actually improved in recent years (Dunlop 1979). This fact is reassuring given the fact that while only 5% of the elderly are housed in nursing homes at any one time, at least 25% will die there (Kovar 1977). The number of nursing home beds has more than doubled in the past twenty years and far exceeds the numbers of beds for acute care hospitals. This quantum leap in statistics can be traced to various factors—changes in family structure, easier access to institutional care, increased longevity, and changing attitudes regarding nursing homes.

Although nursing facilities are increasingly referred to as long-term care facilities, I will use that term interchangeably with the more common and colloquial term, the nursing home. Goffman (1961) has pointed out that the appellation "home" connotes an effort by society to offer replacement for the care and protection of the family. Such could hardly be farther from the case, for due to a series of historical and contemporary processes, the nursing home has come to resemble acute-care hospitals rather than places to live.

In the following, I will trace the origins and development of the nursing home in this country, the population it serves, its functions as an institution within a cultural framework and in the context of other institutions in our society—the family, the health care system, and the political institution which determines policies for the funding and regulation of nursing homes. While it cannot be assumed that the United States is more likely to institutionalize its elderly than other countries, there are several factors that together make the nursing home a very necessary institution in our society and one that is functionally integrated with other institutions.

The Cultural Framework of Institutional Care

An anthropological analysis of institutional care seems particularly appropriate at this time, for the population served presents a marked contradiction to American values and sentiments. In fact, there is a longstanding adversarial relationship between this institution and the public. Most people view nursing homes as uniformly bad without recognition of the important generic functions they fulfill. As a result, somewhat conflicting and inconsistent ideologies and reform strategies are evident. Health planners such as Kane and Kane (1982) point to the need to examine national values, for they are not only reflected in individual actions but in public policies which determine the allocation of financial resources.

One source of these ideological differences can be traced to the particular difficulty Americans have in tolerating chronic states of helplessness and dependency. This ambivalence exists despite the fact that our family system and the health care system are generally not structured to handle prolonged dependency of adults. Although nursing homes are needed to house the ever increasing numbers of dependent elderly, such an option is also in contradiction to humanitarian values and the current spirit of reform. The cultural contradictions are reflected by the confusion at the level of federal policy making, where there is not yet even agreement as to whether the long-term care of the elderly is a public or a private responsibility, or whether priorities should be placed upon long-term institutional or community care.

Suggested reforms also reflect value dilemmas. There are competing platforms for change—those which favor deinstitutionalization of the older population or "deinstitutionalizing the institution" by finding means to improve the quality of institutional care (Johnson and Grant 1985). The mental health movement of the 1960s offers an interesting parallel to the attempts today to prevent the institutionalization of the elderly or to deinstitutionalize those who may be able to live in the community. Similar humanitarian reforms in the 1960s resulted in the deinstitutionalization of thousands of chronic mental patients, many of whom now populate our inner-city streets, often without homes or needed outpatient services. Apparently the mental health services designed to serve these chronic patients either did not materialize or are instead serving those with acute psychiatric conditions (Goldman and Morrissey 1985). If comprehensive community services for the elderly are not in place, reforms in patterns of institutional care will create similar problems. Despite these previous experiences, however, most planners concentrate their energies on finding community alternatives, and surprisingly there are fewer reforms in place to improve the quality of institutional care.

Value dilemmas are also evident in attitudes toward illness itself. The long-term and incurable dependency of many chronic conditions is a violation of our most cherished values and sentiments. Such a fate is invariably viewed as abhorrent. For example, our dominant values place demands on individuals to be independent, instrumentally active, self-reliant, and in control of one's life. Ever larger numbers of older Americans are failing to live up to these demands and thus are anathema to those who espouse these values. These people who are alarmed at the idea of institutionalization include not only the general population, but also the elderly themselves who may be seriously at risk of institutionalization. As Margaret Clark (1969) points out, they are placed in an unsatisfactory situation of either having to deny their dependency or recriminating themselves for being dependent. Thus, it is not surprising that the deleterious effects of institutionalization begin during the admissions process when psychological declines have been observed (Tobin and Lieberman 1976). These problems may be associated with the stigma of moving into a socially undesirable status.

Most interestingly, the abhorrence of dependency is also observed among the leaders in gerontology and in the political action groups of the elderly. They tend to espouse an upbeat, optimistic philosophy. In fact, these activists often point an accusatory finger at social and behavioral scientists who write of disengagement and physical and psychological decline. They point out correctly that most elderly are healthy, active, and socially involved, but they also tend to overlook the plight of the overaged and the dependent. Social science research on the negative events in the aging process has even been described as "the social construction of reality" in which conceptual and empirical works are selectively used to create a misleading view of the aged (Estes 1979). In other words, even researchers, in their high valuation of health and independent functioning rather than illness and dependency, are reflecting American values on optimism and self-mastery.

Another interest group who on occasion view dependency in old age as an anathema come from the health care system and the health promotion/disease prevention movement (Fries and Crapo 1981). Those who espouse these views point out the advantages of self-mastery as a key factor to longevity. If one exercises self-control and adheres to a proper diet, exercise, and life-style, one will live longer. Thus, self-reliance is equated with life itself, and illness is equated with human frailties and lack of self-control. This assignment of responsibility for one's health and illness to the patients who are dependent implies that individuals must take the blame for their plight.

Also in keeping with our value system is the high valuation of medical approaches geared at curing acute illnesses rather than managing long-term incurable diseases. Not surprisingly then, the organization of the nursing home has incorporated many features of the acute care system (Kane and Kane 1978). Unlike most European countries, in fact, the long-term care system in general is financed and organized along the lines of hospitals rather than places to live. Even in the financing of long-term care, this bias is evident, for the most liberal benefits are available for acute care and skilled nursing care rather than psychosocial services (Johnson and Grant 1985).

American values that emphasize mastery over nature and instrumental activism are consistent with the emphasis in medical training and clinical practice on technological interventions aimed at curing acute illnesses. The patients with chronic illness, who cannot be cured, become an accusation of failure to the physician. Such attitudes often lead to therapeutic nihilism and a neglect of the patients with chronic conditions, particularly those in institutional settings (Strauss 1975). Despite the fact that most nursing homes are organized and financed as a health service, the mean time a physician spends with a nursing home patient is less than half a minute a day (California State Department of Health 1977). As Vladeck (1980) suggests, the organization of the nursing home based upon the medical model essentially means a medical model without a physician.

The health care system usually works together with the family in dealing with the dependency of acute illnesses and preventing the perpetuation of the sick role (Parsons and Fox 1952). Because the nuclear family is a highly vulnerable unit that is unable to deal with the prolonged dependency of an adult member, the health profession potentially plays an important role during periods of acute illnesses. The physician takes over responsibility and satisfies the dependency needs of the patient under controlled situations. The patient is permitted to assume the sick role but only temporarily, for all are working together to encourage the transition to independence.

Despite the fact that illness and dependence are also a threat to the families of chronic patients, these processes in which the health care system and the family work together do not usually take place. The problem does not lie in the motivation of family members; the attitudes and sentiments of children and immediate family members are not usually questioned. Nevertheless, the dependency of an adult family member is not only a contradiction in our values, but it is also a situation in which the resources of the family may be taxed to the limit. Competing commitments of children and frequently the failing health of a spouse often prevent the family from providing needed home care. Without the collaboration of formal systems of support then, the family's toleration of dependency and the burdens of care finally breaks down (Johnson and Catalano 1983).

Cultural mechanisms are used to deal with the problems generated by large numbers of dependent individuals whose status is incongruent with their values and who are labeled as socially undesirable. There are two quite different types of solutions. One is the search for alternatives to institutionalization, and a second and more common solution is one used with similar incurable health problems of the past. With leprosy and with mental illness, Western societies have founded institutions, not to suppress them, but to keep it at a safe distance (Foucault 1965). Another interpretation comes from Phillip Slater (1970) who describes the "toilet assumption" to problems in our society. In his view, Americans deal with pressing social problems by "flushing" them out of sight.

The Origin and Development of the Nursing Home

A review of the origin and development of the contemporary nursing home suggests how this form of organization evolved (Cohen 1975; Dunlop 1979; Johnson and Grant 1985). For one thing, the institution has become a repository for those who were previously served in other types of settings. Even from colonial times, custodial care was provided to serve the pauper. Almshouses, orphanages, and poor farms were provided at the local level to serve the poor as well as the mentally ill, the blind, and the chronically ill who had no families. In other words, over much of this country's history, the solution to poverty and other social problems was some form of institutional care.

Even until the 1920s, few older people actually lived in these poorhouses—roughly 50,000, or 0.6% of the over-sixty-five population. An equal number lived in charitable private homes for the aged, the forerunners of the contemporary voluntary nursing home. In fact, until relatively recently, more older people resided in mental hospitals than in nursing homes. With the passage of the Social Security Act of 1935, the characteristics of the institutionalized population began to change. This legislation specifically prevented those in institutions from receiving retirement income, so only those who needed custodial care went to nursing homes. The remainder, who ordinarily would have been institutionalized, were able to remain in the community until they became dependent. Dunlop (1979) concludes that in a relatively short time, many boarding homes and homes for the aged were transformed into institutions serving a far sicker population of older people. While public institutions remained as last refuges for the poor, they also began to take on the characteristics of chronic disease hospitals.

Today nursing homes also serve those previously cared for in acute-care hospitals. Until World War II, few nursing homes provided more than token nursing care; the very sick were cared for in acute-care hospitals. While the affluent were usually cared for in their homes, hospitals were also refuges for the poor. It is only in recent years that hospitals have become specialized treatment centers with high technology to treat acute illness. With these changes, the chronically ill elderly were shunted to nursing homes, which were also undergoing changes. During the 1960s, legislation such as the Hill-Burton Act and Medicare and Medicaid imposed standards that transformed nursing homes into "mini-hospitals" in which many of the functions of the medical model of care were also adopted.

The deinstitutionalization of patients in mental hospitals added another population to nursing homes that was also served elsewhere. While the deinstitutionalization movement was made possible by the use of psychoactive drugs and was encouraged as an economy move, it was also humanely believed that the older psychiatric patient would be better cared for in a nursing facility (Stotsky 1973). Thus between 1940 and 1970, the percentage of persons aged sixty-five and older cared for in mental institutions declined 36%, while the proportion in old age institutions increased 105% (Manard, Kart, and van Gils 1975).

The contemporary nursing home, then, has changed dramatically from a small-scale institution serving the poor and disabled to a more technologically complex, formal organization which now also cares for those formerly treated in acute-care hospitals and mental institutions. In the process, the model of care increasingly used has been a medical model designed for acute illness rather than one that takes into account the nature of chronic illness and its special treatment needs. It has become increasingly evident that such a model is incongruent with the population the nursing home serves. The Kanes, outspoken critics of the contemporary nursing home, have pointed out that "in the United States, although not in many European countries, institutional care of the elderly is conceived and financed as a health service, even though institutional placement provides a complete social context for an individual and obviously constitutes a rather dramatic intervention" (1978, 913).

Who Is Institutionalized?

A combination of demographic and social factors work in combination with our value system in the determination of who is likely to be institutionalized. Obviously, increasing longevity has rapidly increased the numbers in advanced old age. For example, the average American who reaches a sixty-fifth birthday can expect to live sixteen more years. Women can expect to live longer than men; for example, of all white women who celebrate their seventy-fifth birthday, 78% will live to eighty years of age (Kovar 1977). These old old have a high incidence of chronic diseases, and after the age of seventy-five years, almost half have some limitation on their activities of daily living. Over eighty-five years of age, that proportion reaches almost two-thirds of the age group.

Such impairment, however, does not necessarily result in being institutionalized. For every old person in an institution, there are at least two individuals with a similar level of impairment who are able to live in the community. Thus, to identify the "at risk" population, one must go beyond functional ability to examine the social characteristics—age, gender, minority status and family characteristics—factors that are far more important determinants of who goes into institutions.

In examining the place of residence before institutionalization, one finds that over half of those entering a nursing home come from other institutions—32% from acute-care hospitals and 22% from mental hospitals (National Center for Health Statistics 1977). The most important shared characteristic is age, with 72% of the residents being seventy-five years old or older. Because of gender differences in longevity, 69% of the residents are female and 63% are widowed or never married. There is also a high proportion of residents who had lived alone or with a nonrelative before relocation or who had no children. The distribution by race is also significant; a disproportionate number, 96%, are white, which may suggest that minorities have difficulty gaining access to institutional care (Manard, Kart, and van Gils 1975).

Marital status is probably the most significant variable. The unmarrieds face the most serious risk of institutionalization (Health Care Financing Administration 1981). A government study found that gender differences in risks of institutionalization are less prominent when examined in the context of both age and marital status. Both widowed and single men *and* women are the most likely to be institutionalized. The presence of children and other family members also appears to prevent institutionalization, but their role is less prominent than that of a spouse (Johnson 1985a).

A pressing concern stems from the question, how many are institutionalized needlessly? At first glance, it appears that most of the residents have disabilities of such severity that independent living is threatened. According to another government survey (Kovar 1977), 49% cannot see to read a newspaper, 35% are incontinent, 35% cannot speak on the telephone, and 31% are chairbound or bedfast. A high percentage, 63%, are described as senile in this report. Other estimates suggest that from 40% to 80% of the nursing home residents also have that label. Thus, one can conclude that cognitive deterioration poses one of the most serious threats to continued community living.

Studies of the misuse of nursing homes do not find an excessive propensity to institutionalize the elderly needlessly. Perhaps 17% to 25% are in institutions because they do not have alternative supports in the community (Abdellah 1978). Up to one-third, however, are in the wrong level of care (Dunlop 1979). Usually they are at a higher level of care, a situation often traced to financial incentives making skilled nursing care more profitable. In any case, most researchers conclude that individuals are in institutions because they lack formal and informal supports (Johnson and Grant 1985).

The Family's Role in Institutionalization

In all, family status is the single most important factor related to risk of institutionalization. Contrary to the common myth of family abandonment, very few families reject their elderly. Very few elderly are without any relative, and the majority are in contact with family members. Of the 80% who have children, only 18% live with a child, a decline from 36% in 1957 (Shanas 1979). In any case, about three quarters of the over-sixty-five population are in at least weekly contact. Although the number who live together has declined in recent years, the number in frequent contact has increased (Shanas 1979).

Despite these optimistic reports, demographic constraints to family support are prominent (Treas 1977). The pressures on the family are also considerably magnified, because of the structure of the family and the dominant American values on the individual's obligation to family. The elderly today have fewer children (1.2 daughters in comparison to 3.0 in 1900). Today is also an era of the vanishing spinster; unlike the past, these daughters are much more likely to be married, to have children, and to work. Since more and more elderly live into advanced old age, children are also commonly past middle age themselves. In fact, one study found that 40% of the applicants to a nursing home had at least one child sixty years or older (Brody 1977).

In any case, the presence of children does not mean they are free to help their parent remain in the community (Johnson 1983b). There is considerable evidence that children are unable to provide comprehensive supports, although most experience anxiety at the possibility that such a situation would arise. The gender differences in longevity also undermine the capacity of a spouse to provide supports. After seventy-five years of age, when needs for supports markedly increase, only 22% of the women are married in comparison to 68% of the men. An unusually high proportion of the women, 43%, live alone after seventy-five years, which suggests a high risk situation for them (Soldo 1980).

It bears repeating that our value system strongly emphasizes the independence of children from the family of orientation and a strong respect for the privacy of the nuclear family. Since the elderly, as products of our culture, also espouse such values and express horror at the possibility of becoming dependent, they often go to extraordinary means to preserve their independence. Thus, when the final stage of decrepitude is reached, the elderly themselves are often the ones who insist upon the institutional option. Undoubtedly the values on independence in the face of the realities of dependency and helplessness are a source of personal and interpersonal conflict (Johnson and Catalano 1983).

In summary, it should be emphasized that the issue of the family's role in the process of institutionalization does not relate to problems of motivation. In fact, there is considerable evidence that families go to great lengths and make heroic efforts to keep their elderly in the community. Rather, there is little depth of support potential in our family structure. The family rarely functions as a unit; instead, one individual is available to care for an elderly member at any one time. Shanas (1979) has characterized this situation as "the principle of substitution." If one is married, he relies upon a spouse; if one is widowed, she relies upon a child; and if one is childless, another relative is usually available. With increased kinship distance one must go outside the family to secure a caregiver, however, the risk of institutionalization increases.

Most informed observers conclude that the nursing home is an important and necessary institution in our society, for it permits the families of the dependent elderly to go about their normal lives without having to make radical adjustments in order to care for an individual who can no longer care for himself. Such realities are often neglected by reformers who are likely to favor the concentration of resources on retaining the dependent in the community. If, however, widespread access to institutional care were denied and comprehensive formal services were not in place, many children and other relatives would have to make drastic changes in their lives in order to care for the dependent elderly.

The Institution's Impact on Its Residents

The isolation and segregation of individuals who are sources of public problems have resulted in the development of the total institution, which by definition is, "a place of residence and work where like-minded individuals, cut off from the larger society for an appreciable period of time, together lead an enclosed, formally administered round of life" (Goffman 1961, 1). These facilities include those such as nursing homes which care for the harmless who can no longer care for themselves. Others, such as leprosoria, care for the incapacitated who pose a threat to society. Others, such as jails, protect society from the dangerous, while still others, such as boarding schools, are task centered or are retreats from the world.

Detailed and restrictive controls, regimentation, loss of privacy, and the breakdown of barriers between life activities have all been associated with "institutional effects," the harmful effects on individuals. The nursing home as a total institution provides an extreme contrast to living within a family. Most residents upon entering do not expect to leave. They are entering an institution because they can no longer care for themselves and have no family member to care for them. The move itself very likely breaks down one's accustomed social activities. The new residence will be inferior in quality in terms of independence, privacy, convenience, and the familiarity of one's own home (Kasl 1972). Individuals are likely to be surrounded by those who are cognitively impaired. If they have retained their mental functioning, being surrounded by such impaired individuals would have detrimental effects.

Over the years researchers have studied the effects of institutionalization. These include physical and psychological effects. Physically the effects are found to be quite harmful. One-third of the residents die within their first year of entrance, while another third die within three years. There is also evidence that iatrogenic illnesses result from institutionalization. For example, the most common preadmission diagnoses are cardiovascular disease, cerebro-vascular disease, and arthritis, while in contrast, the most common postadmission diagnoses are infections of the urinary tract, bedsores, and upper respiratory infections. As Vladeck concludes "These are diseases, not of age and frailty, but of inadequate institutional care" (1980, 19). There is also evidence that drugs are overused, often as a source of social control and as a means to ease the burdens on the staff.

Iatrogenic psychological effects have also been observed. Depersonalization is common; it is a process by which one's personal talents and resources wither with disuse. Depression, apathy, and lack of initiative reflect a process of estrangement from the outside world (Sommer and Osmond 1961). Thus there is now sufficient research to identify what factors in institutional care create the harmful effects. For example, these effects have been found to vary depending upon the "totality" of the institution. "Totality" refers to the degree of privacy provided, the rigidity of scheduling and controls, the access to private property, and the extent of isolation from the outside world (Coe 1965).

With the aged, it is sometimes difficult to single out the causes and effects. Some researchers maintain that the characteristics of the residents upon entering the institution, more than the effects of the institutional living, account for the high prevalence of harmful effects (Tobin and Lieberman 1976). Even the admission process itself entails loss and feelings of separation which can undermine one's mood. The relocation to an institution, then, involves a stressful life event, which is often associated with adverse effects.

These areas of research indicate that some harmful effects can be moderated by several means. The relocation effects can be ameliorated by making the move predictable and by giving the individual some control over the events taking place (Schultz and Brenner 1977). Once in the institution, some steps can be taken to provide more privacy, a more personalized environment and greater links to the outside community. More adequate medical and psychiatric care and social activities that encourage sensory stimulation are also needed. In other words, efforts can be made to deinstitutionalize the institution rather than deinstitutionalizing individuals, many of whom would find enormous hurdles to community living. It appears, however, that most reforms are directed toward preventing institutionalization rather than addressing the deficiencies of institutional care.

Public Policy and the Form of Institutional Care

A history of the nursing home indicates that increasingly, federal policy has designated the nursing home as the repository of most of the elderly who require long-term institutional care. Recent policies at the federal level determine who will finance long-term care, what kind of services will be provided, and who is eligible (Johnson and Grant 1985). Although current reforms are largely geared to providing community alternatives to institutional living, the funding bias in public policy today favors expensive solutions—acute care over long-term care and institutional care over community care. For example, the one source of benefits uniformly available to everyone is Medicare, a health care insurance program which pays for much of acute care and one hundred days of nursing home care. Only a small proportion of federal dollars for medical care goes for nursing home care—9% of the total federal spending for nursing homes and 2% of Medicare dollars. Nevertheless, the federal government spends an ever increasing amount on medical care and less, proportionately, on social services.

The Medicaid program is designed to pay for long-term institutional care. This is a cost-sharing program with the states, so there is a great deal of variability from state to state on eligibility and the quality of care. One must be medically indigent or medically needy to qualify for Medicaid. Among those who require institutional care, it is not uncommon to find many who "spend down" until assets are gone to pay for long-term nursing home care services. Public policy is congruent with our value system; for example, children are independent of any responsibilities to assist their parents financially. In any case, far more money from the Medicaid program goes to nursing home care, 40% of the budget, than goes to home health care. With current dominance of medical interventions over social service interventions, the nursing home, as noted above, has come to resemble hospitals rather than home-like environments.

There are numerous problems in the present system, many of which arise because of the value emphasis on acute care (Kane and Kane 1978). The escalating costs are the most common source of concern. Of all rising health costs, the greatest increase is in long-term care. Yet financing policies still limit access to less medically-oriented community services (Butler and Newacheck 1981). The New Federalism or the decentralization of federal programs was an attempt to limit growth in these programs by transferring responsibility to local and state governments. Such attempts have some deleterious effects on efforts to improve the quality of institutional care. Consumer activist groups have fewer resources if also decentralized. Moreover, local politicians are more easily swayed by interest groups competing for economic resources, making any attempts at reform more politicized.

At this point, there is not even agreement among policymakers as to whether the long-term care of the elderly is a public or private responsibility (Kutza 1981). Currently the private sector responds to the initiatives of the public sector because of financial incentives. There has tended to be a patchwork of reforms and an escalation of services without addressing the underlying problems. Consequently, one of the most important ideological issues has not been resolved, a situation that raises numerous problems (Farrow et al. 1981).

Most commonly now, community alternatives center on programs incorporating case management, a service that coordinates already available community services. Some critics suggest that these new programs may come to serve a new population rather than those most at risk of institutionalization. In reality, most residents in nursing homes are white women, over the age of seventy-five years who have outlived their natural support system. Those with families are usually seriously functionally or cognitively impaired and have entered a nursing home only after having been cared for by their families. They are not likely candidates for services under these reform movements. By most yardsticks, the majority of the nursing home residents appear to need that level of care.

Conclusions

Throughout the history of the United States, the public's approach to the problems of the poor and dependent has been institutional solutions involving the removal of these individuals from public visability. Nevertheless, there has been a longstanding public view that nursing homes are uniformly bad without consideration of the fact that these institutions provide substitutes for the family and other primary groups which formerly served dependent adults. With a family system that has difficulty tolerating dependency needs of its adult members, and with a health care system in which most resources go to acute rather than long-term care, the nursing home becomes an important "last resort" for those who cannot care for themselves.

In this analysis, I have suggested that the manner in which the problems of the dependent elderly are addressed in our society relate to our value system. The differing views and dilemmas in regard to institutional care at both the public and the personal level reflect the incongruence between our values and realistic problems in late life. Even in the current era of reform, questions on the basic issues of institutionalization have not yet been fully addressed. Do we solve the problems of dependent elderly by further encouraging their isolation and segregation in institutional settings? Or should these individuals remain in the community where everyone is expected to function independently? Or will a humane and comprehensive support system fully meet their dependency needs, a system that also takes into consideration the longstanding ambivalence Americans have in the face of adult dependency?

XVIII

DEATH AND DYING

Richard A. Kalish

Being human means being mortal, and being mortal means that we each face the inevitability of our own death. Being human also means that the dying process occurs in many ways, and that the beliefs and expectations and assumptions that each of us makes about death differ greatly from the beliefs and expectations and assumptions held by others. Being human also means that we grieve, but the grief of each of us varies as a function of who we are and for whom, or for what, we grieve.

Many factors affect the dying process, the meanings of death and of being dead, and grieving, ranging from one's religious value system to responsiveness to pain to family-support systems to the nature of the conditions causing the death. In this chapter, we will examine some of these factors, but through the lens of being elderly which, itself, is a major influence. The remainder of this chapter will consist of three major sections: definitions and their significance, the meanings of death, and the process of dying and the nature of grieving. The underlying theme of the chapter will be the meanings of death for older persons.

Before continuing, however, a comment. This chapter will focus primarily on concepts and ideas, and it will present many statements that are generalities, albeit presumably valid generalities. It does not offer adequate consideration of the individual terminally-ill elderly person. Yet, in the lives of most people, it is the individual that matters most, and valid generalities are much less important. Therefore, it becomes necessary to read these materials for what they are and to apply them to individual situations only with full consideration of the uniqueness of those individual situations.

Definitions

There are three groupings of terms that require definition, even though you use these terms all the time and, with rare exception, you use them correctly. The odds are high, however, that you have seldom if ever carefully considered the implications of the terms' meanings. These groupings are: aging and being elderly; death, dying, and dead; and grief, mourning, and bereavement.

Aging and Being Elderly

Aging is a process; being elderly or old or a senior is a status or, in sociological terms, a position in society. This difference is clear, but defining each term precisely is a difficult, perhaps impossible, task. For example, when does aging begin? At conception? Birth? Or not until the decremental aspects of development outweigh the more positive maturational changes? Or when maximum height and maximum potential cognitive functioning have been attained?

Also, when does being elderly or old begin? Do we use chronological age or functional capacity or social roles (e.g., work roles, family roles) or attitudes or physical appearance or health? And once you have decided on the framework within which to determine whether any given person is elderly or old (and do these words mean exactly the same thing or not quite the same thing?), what is the exact age marker or boundary? If you prefer a chronological definition, would you select sixty or sixty-two or sixty-five or seventy? Or, if you look to work role, would you select retirement? And what if the person accepts another job two years later: does that mean he or she is no longer old? Or if becoming a grandparent is a major part of your definition, how do you classify those who become grandparents in their late thirties? If you use functional capacity, as so many people want to do, what particular capacities are you including and how do you determine the level at which each capacity has lost sufficient function so that the person is defined as old?

Sometimes being old is a joint function of more than one criterion, such as chronological age, functional capacity, and health. Thus, a healthy, functioning sixty-five-year-old is not elderly, but a healthy functioning seventy-five-year-old or an unhealthy, poorly-functioning sixty-five-year-old is elderly.

Social policies don't help much with these definitions. Thus, social security is for older people, but the earliest one can begin to receive payments is age sixty-two, while maximum benefits don't accrue until sixty-five; however, if you are working for pay, you may forfeit some benefits, but not if you are seventy-two years old. That is, if you are healthy enough to work between ages sixty-two and 71.9, you aren't really old, but if you are healthy enough to work at age 72.0, you are old. In England, it becomes muddled in a different fashion: women can receive full retirement pensions earlier than men, presumably because wives are younger than their husbands and this permits them to retire simultaneously; however, if pensions are for the elderly, this would suggest that women age faster than men, whereas we know that in terms of health and functional capacity, they age more slowly.

In the final analysis, the definitions of aging and of elderly or old are arbitrary, with legitimate bases for disagreement. Most important is knowing the definitions used by the person to whom you are talking or whose book you are reading. Sometimes even having different definitions is not important, but at other times it is. If you are developing health-education services for family members of older dying persons, and you don't have sufficient funds to cover costs of services to all applicants, you may need to decide whom to serve and whom to turn down on the basis of their meeting your organization's definitions of *older* and of *dying*.

Death, Dying, and Dead

Death is the transition between being alive and being dead; dying, like aging, is a process; and dead, like old, is a status. Each of these terms produces its own set of difficulties when we attempt to develop precise definitions.

For example, when does the process of dying begin? How do you know it has begun? Does it inevitably end at death? What is someone who is labeled "dying" and then recuperates fully: can you still say that person was dying or must you say that "it was believed he/she was dying" or words that indicate uncertainty? Your aunt says that your uncle is dying, and the physician says he is dying, but your uncle says that he is not dying; he recovers and dies ten years later of something else. When you refer to the earlier period, can you legitimately say that he was dying? We can, of course, say that he was critically ill, but that doesn't have the same meaning as dying.

When does death occur? The most familiar operational definition is when the heart has ceased to beat for a designated period of time, but occasionally the cessation of brain function, sometimes called brain death, is used instead. For brain death to occur, the four following criteria proposed by the Harvard University Medical School must all be met: (1) unreceptivity and unresponsivity, (2) no movements or breathing, (3) no reflexes, and (4) flat encephalogram (measurement of brain waves); all four need to be evaluated on two occasions, at least twenty-four hours apart (cited in Veatch 1976).

And, since death is the transition from being alive to being dead, what is the nature of being dead? Is it abiding with God? Does it permit the continuing existence to know what is going on on earth? Is it perpetual peace that surpasses all understanding? Does it include any forms of conscious awareness? Does the existence subsequently return to earth in another living form? If so, can this form have knowledge of its previous forms? Or is it extinction? Nothingness? And will one ever reemerge from being dead, that is, be reborn? After death, are you recognizable as you? If so, and your mother died at thirty-three and you died at eighty-three, will she appear young and you appear old? These questions cannot be answered in the abstract, but only in terms of one's belief systems, especially one's religious beliefs and values.

Once again, differing definitions often don't matter at all, but sometimes they do. In the summer of 1986, in totally unrelated incidents, two women were maintained on life-support systems so that the fetus each was carrying could become viable. If these women had been declared dead, the life-support systems would have been turned off, and the fetuses would inevitably have died. (At this writing, one fetus is still living, while the other died within twenty-four hours of the time at which the life-support system was turned off.) Also, if either woman had been declared dead, her health insurance company would have ceased payments, and her life insurance company would have begun to process payment to her heirs. A funeral would probably have been conducted, and she would have been buried or perhaps cremated. However, neither woman was declared dead on the usual bases; both remained technically alive until their infants could be delivered.

Grief, Mourning, and Bereavement

Grief is a feeling or emotion; mourning is a form of behavior; bereavement is a status. You are bereaved when someone considered close to you has died. Bereavement can also occur with the death of a beloved pet, the death of a powerful or influential person you never met (ask people, if you don't recall, what happened when John F. Kennedy and Martin Luther King were killed), or even at the sale of an automobile or a house to which you were deeply attached.

If the loss or death causes such affective reactions as depression or sadness, cognitive expressions such as disbelief and confusion, and behavioral responses such as sleep disturbances, loss of appetite, restlessness, crying, and difficulty in concentration (Worden 1982), you are probably grieving.

Mourning behavior includes attending the funeral, visiting the grave, canceling social engagements out of respect for the dead person, and lighting a candle in memory.

As you undoubtedly expect by now, each of these terms has its gray area. How close does a friend or relative have to be to have you acknowledged as bereaved? If your sister dies, and you neither grieve nor mourn, are you still bereaved? How do you know when I'm grieving? I may pretend to grieve, when I actually feel detached; and if my role-playing or acting is good enough, you will believe I'm grieving. How much grief does a person have to feel to be referred to as grieving? Any amount at all? Or a medium amount or a large amount, whatever these expressions mean? And is it mourning behavior when I sit under a tree away from everyone else and think back over the good times the dead person and I had together? These are just a few of the complexities to be dealt with in order to understand with clarity the concepts/terms under discussion.

In Other Cultures

For the most part, we accept ambiguity in concepts when we speak and when we write, and only on occasion do we misunderstand each other regarding the eight terms outlined above. When heated controversies arise concerning definitions, the basis for the controversy is usually a policy or value that requires a particular definition, rather than the definition itself. That is, in order to reduce social security payments, we state that people are not really old until they are sixty-seven, so we could postpone maximum benefits to that age. Or a young man who is comatose and undoubtedly going to die soon is defined as dead so that his heart can be used for a transplant. Your definitions of old and of life and death follow from other deeply held beliefs.

In other words, with some exceptions, we all share the same cultural meanings for these terms: they are part of a shared symbol system or meaning system. Assuming that we all speak English, are essentially Western in our cultural outlook, and are part of the Judaic-Christian tradition—and these assumptions will not always be valid—we share, relatively speaking, most definitions. When we step outside these boundaries, we often find that others use what appear to be the same words and concepts that we are using, but with very different meanings.

In defining *old*, the tendency in Western societies is to use chronological age, while simultaneously acknowledging its inadequacies. In large part, this is because policies that depend on certain individuals being old, such as pension plans and health-care services or membership in a senior center or residence in a housing project, cannot tolerate ambiguity. Functional capacity and health can be the determinants of *old* when personalized decisions are made, for example, "Father is really old" or "As long as I continue to exercise, I won't get old," or even in situations that involve only a handful of people. However, just consider the financial cost and general confusion if the Internal Revenue Service evaluated every person individually in providing the extra deduction for being old, which is now based strictly on chronological age.

Neugarten's differentiation into young-old and old-old (1974) was actually an attempt to utilize a functional-capacity base for making policy and other decisions. It is certainly not without precedent, since there is a lengthy history of differentiating healthy and functioning elderly from the frail elderly; these categories have sometimes been described as "green" elderly and "dry" elderly, and they date back at least as far as Hippocrates (Stearns 1976).

However, other divisions can be found. Among the Melanesians, the term *mate* includes the very sick, the very old, and the dead; the word *toa* refers to all other living persons. The most important distinction is between these two groupings, not between the living and the dead as in our culture. Further complicating this picture, the Melanesians view the life one lives prior to *mate* and the life one has after death as having many qualities in common (Counts and Counts 1985a).

For other Oceanic societies, life is viewed as being based on a life force that may leave the body during sleep or illness, suggesting that sleep, illness, and death are kindred states, in distinction to the state in which all three are absent. This also means that death is experienced long before the "final" death is experienced, so that death is initially not permanent. One of the outcomes of this form of definition is that seriously ill people may be neglected, since their condition is seen as comparable to being dead (Counts and Counts 1985a). This becomes an extension of social death (Glaser and Strauss 1964; Kalish 1985), in which Person A views Person B as functionally dead when the latter becomes cognitively impaired, extremely ill, or institutionalized, and Person A reacts to Person B in terms of this perception. It would seem, however, that the Oceanic version of social death acts more powerfully on members of the community than the Western version.

In contrasting other Western societies with the United States, observed differences are less significant, but they nonetheless exist. The word for death in French is *la morte;* in Spanish, it is *el muerte.* In English, the concept refers to a transition state or event, but in French and Spanish, the concept elicits much more of a visual image or personification; it is both more sinister and more mystical. So, although the dictionary meanings are the same, the affective associations differ.

Even the process of dying is defined differently in different cultures. Among the Kaliai, "the people . . . are prepared to diagnose as potentially fatal any fever or internal pain or illness that does not respond readily to treatment" (Counts and Counts 1985a, 150). The individuals themselves decide that they are dying, and they participate in the behavior and rituals usually prescribed for the dying. However, it is important to keep in mind that being dead does not mean that one remains dead; they need not return as a frightening ghost, although this can occur, or even as a helpful ghost, which also occurs, but as someone who still has a vital role to perform (Counts and Counts 1985b).

Also varying from society to society are the mourning rituals and definitions of the status of bereavement. These have been described in literally hundreds or even thousands of reports, with an excellent summary of the earlier literature in Simmons (1945). Whether the emotion of grief is experienced differently in different societies is more difficult to determine. Obviously, both personality development and personal relationships vary from culture to culture, so adult children of dying elderly parents may be more detached in one community than in another. What is more problematic is whether the inner experience and feelings associated with the death of a loved one also differ in the same fashion. You can tell me how you feel and I can tell you how I feel, and if we use the same language, a shared symbol system, we may intuitively "know" that we are feeling the same emotions, but "knowing" when major cultural differences are involved is much less likely to occur.

The Meanings of Death

Death has many meanings, and these vary from culture to culture and among individuals within cultures. In this section, some of these meanings will be explored, with particular reference to the elderly: death as a boundary, death as the thief of meaning, death as the basis for fear and anxiety, the changing meanings of life, and death as having conflicting meanings. The section ends with a discussion of cultural differences in the meanings of death.

Death as a Boundary

Whether you define death as a transition, as extinction, or in some other fashion, death is usually seen as an end, a boundary, for your on-earth existence in its present form. And when the end of a time period is imminent, we have a strong tendency to pay greater attention to the use of the remaining time and to organize it more effectively than we had been doing. As we come closer to these boundaries, we often continue to reorganize our time. For example, as your undergraduate college career nears its end, you are likely to continue to change your plans for what you want to do during the remaining months, weeks, and days. In effect, when you have lots of time, you anticipate doing lots of things; when that future time shrinks, you find yourself developing priorities. Consider how your behavior and life-style might differ if you could assume 350 additional years of life rather than 50 or 60 more years: would you continue your present educational plans or change them? Would you remain in your present marriage or whatever your most intimate relationship is, or would you extend increased effort to improve the relationship, or would you leave the relationship? Would you try to learn another foreign language? Would you exert extra energy to become a computer expert?

So one meaning of death is that of a boundary that serves to organize the

time within the boundary. For older people, the end is closer and, therefore, more salient and compelling. In fact, research shows with considerable consistency that older people think more often about their death than
younger persons. In one study, 29% of those over sixty thought about their
death every day, compared to 15% under forty, and 11% between forty and
sixty (Kalish and Reynolds 1981).

Death as the Thief of Meaning

Philosophically, each of us knows that we may die any day, any moment,
but in contemporary times, the statistical probability of death prior to our
later years is very low. In earlier centuries, death occurred almost randomly across the life cycle, with lots of deaths being recorded for infants and
very young children and for women during childbirth. With wars and
epidemics, and with little knowledge of maternal and infant health or of
good health practices in general, death rates were high in all age groups.

Today it is primarily the elderly who die in Western cultures, although
this is much less the case in developing nations and in many societies
around the world. French author Philippe Ariès (1974) believes that people
in earlier times lived every day to the fullest, because they knew that death
really did occur to people of all ages. In contemporary times, we are so
certain of long life that we easily let many days slip by, so that fulfillment is
often postponed until the later years when illness or limited finances may
restrict our chances of doing what we had expected to do.

If Ariès is correct, it would follow that today's elderly face greater
pressures within themselves to find the satisfactions that they had been
postponing, compared to the elderly of two centuries ago. Erikson (1963)
proposes that the stage conflict of the later years is that of maintaining ego
integrity in the face of so much potential for despair. And one of the bases
for despair is that the knowledge that death is no longer decades away
creates questions of what things mean (i.e., why bother earning money or
learning photography or traveling or doing much of anything, since death
will come so soon that the activities will have no meaning).

Death as the Basis for Fear and Anxiety

Although the elderly think about death more frequently than younger
persons, they seem less fearful and more accepting of death, even of their
own death. Once again, the research evidence is fairly consistent (e.g.,
Bengston, Cuellar, and Ragan 1977; Kalish and Reynolds 1981; Keller,
Sherry, and Piotrowski 1984). And there are good reasons for older people
to have less fear.

First, older people are more likely than younger people to have chronic health conditions that are painful and discomforting and that interfere with their enjoyment of life and, sometimes, with their ability to perform normal life tasks easily. Further, these conditions are not going to be ameliorated by time or treatment.

Second, whatever their present financial status, it is not likely to improve.

Third, the probabilities are high that they have lost close friends and family members through serious illness, incapacitation, and death. Further, some elderly are reluctant to establish new relationships because they wish to avoid the pain produced by the eventual deaths of these individuals also.

Fourth, the odds are fairly high that their spouse has died or is ill and requires a great deal of care (this is much more likely to be the case for women than for men). Although some elderly, especially men, remarry when a long-term marriage or other relationship is broken by death, new replacement relationships can seldom provide the same level of intimacy, closeness, and understanding. Further, remarriage to another elderly person may lead one of the partners into another round of caring for a seriously-ill, eventually terminally-ill, spouse, and many older people prefer to avoid this possibility.

Fifth, for most elderly, the important tasks of life have been completed. They have reared their children and enjoyed their grandchildren; their careers are often over and most of them are no longer working full time for remuneration; they have long since given up their fantasies of reforming the world, so that any earlier political or social activism is now a memory. And the dream is fading or has faded: they have come to terms with not being a famous novelist, a wealthy industrialist, a successful politician, a renowned designer, or the winner of the county-fair baking contest. They have also given up their dreams for their children, although some may remain for the grandchildren.

Sixth, they have experienced the deaths of many others; they have thought about death and have talked about death. In a very real way, they have worked through their fear regarding their own death. That is, they have had the opportunity to deal with the prospect of their own death, to develop spiritual values that—whatever the specific values may be—are comforting.

And they know that if they don't die soon of this, they will die a little later of that. To modify a familiar expression, much of their future is behind them. It isn't that they want to die, but that they are ready to die. Compared to younger adults, they are more likely to have made out a will, made funeral arrangements, paid for a cemetery plot, and arranged for someone to handle their affairs after their death (Kalish and Reynolds 1981; Riley and Foner 1968).

The Changing Meaning of Life

When we examine the previous paragraphs, it becomes obvious that we aren't so much discussing feelings about death as feelings about life. However, we can no more understand the meaning of death without understanding the meaning of life than we can understand the meaning of tall without understanding the meaning of short.

Perhaps a major basis for the reduced fear of death in the later years is that, for many elderly persons, the value of and satisfaction from living are not as great, and the future is not as promising as in earlier times. In addition, their life is viewed as less valuable to others and to society in general. The elderly, especially the ill elderly, the elderly with diminished functional competence, and the very old, offer less to their communities, and their younger friends and family members may already have begun to disengage, to pull back both in terms of social contacts and affectional involvements, so that when death does occur, the emotional pain and the practical dislocations are not so great. In effect, death is easier because the losses produced by death are less valuable and meaningful.

In reading this, please keep in mind that the discussion is in terms of generalities and does not accurately describe every older person. A few elderly are eager for death; others continue to find immense richness in life and are still exploring their world and experimenting with new ideas and new ways of doing things and new things to do into their eighties and occasionally nineties; and some, while not desiring death, have lost much of their ability to be excited with life.

Other Meanings of Death

This discussion has not exhausted the possible meanings of death. For example, death is seen by some people as a punishment, initially as a punishment for the transgressions of Adam and Eve in the Garden of Eden, and subsequently as a punishment for sin or immoral behavior or, sometimes, immoral thoughts. However, death can also be seen as a reward: the good die young; he is at peace with God. The Hopi Indians believed that kindness, good thoughts, and peace of mind led to a long life; for the Berber, deceit was punished by a shorter life (Simmons 1945).

In one study of four ethnic communities in Los Angeles (black, Hispanic, Japanese-American, and Anglo), over half of the respondents over age sixty-five and about 30% of younger respondents agreed with the statement, "Most people who live to be ninety years or older must have been morally good people" (Kalish and Reynolds 1981). A similar view was espoused by the Managalase, an Oceanic society; they believe that simply remaining alive into old age is a sign of strength of "soul," and their elderly are treated with more respect than in most societies (McKellin 1985). It would be interesting to see whether those individuals in our society who believe that most very old people are morally good respect the elderly more than those who disagree with the statement.

And, of course, death means loss. Some losses have been discussed earlier in this chapter, and others undoubtedly occur to you. Among the most significant losses that are brought about by death are the loss of experiencing, the loss of people you love and care about (and the unhappiness that comes from knowing they will feel pain from losing you), the loss of control of your self *(sic)* and your environment, the loss of competence, the loss of capacity to complete projects and carry out plans, the loss of things, the loss of body, and the loss of the dream (Kalish 1985).

Before leaving this topic, one other matter deserves consideration. It is my belief that each of us allocates to himself or herself an approximate number of years of life that are his or her due. That is, "I am entitled to live until sixty-five" or seventy-five or eighty-five. This is not a precise number of years, nor does it remain the same throughout life. However, it is part of seeing life as fair or what social psychologists refer to as a just-world view. When an individual sees death as imminent many years prior to this entitled length of life, he or she feels cheated out of his/her birthright. If the number of years of expected life is exceeded, then death does not cheat him or her, but is—in a sense—playing by the rules. Since many elderly have already lived beyond the number of years they believed themselves entitled to live, it is now all right to die.

For whom is death more painful: the elderly person whose life has been, on the whole, rich and rewarding, or the elderly person whose life has seldom been happy or satisfying? Although this could be argued either way, it seems as though the former dies "an easier death." While he or she has more to lose, it is possible to look back on a life that has essentially been satisfying and to feel that the life had been well-lived. On the other hand, the individual whose life had seldom been satisfying views death as removing the only opportunities for life to provide rewards, that is, future time. Here again the issue of birthright appears, except it no longer involves length of life but the very substance of life. It would seem, then, that the better use you make of life at all ages, the more gracefully you will age, the more accepting you will be of your own old age, and the more effectively you will cope with your eventual death.

Meanings of Death in Other Cultures

The meaning of death varies from culture to culture on many dimensions. For example, the size of a society can influence its perceptions of death (Jorgensen 1985). In large Western societies, with their hospitals and long-term care institutions, death can reach almost the level of an abstraction: it occurs in antiseptic institutions, hidden away from the view of all except a very few professionals, with the body either never being seen again or being seen only after having been remodeled into a presumably lifelike form for the wake or funeral. And since it is usually the elderly who die, they have already become less important to others and to society in general by virtue of having disengaged from many of the roles and tasks that make death socially and psychologically destructive.

On the other hand, in small societies, with only a few hundred people, every death affects every person in the society. Deaths occur more randomly across the life span, so that it is impossible to designate one age-group as people-who-will-die and to treat them accordingly. And the elderly live in more intimate contact with the nonelderly than in developed societies. In addition, the dying process is much more likely to be in the home or very close to it, so that segregation of the elderly-dying from others in the community rarely occurs.

Extremely important in this regard is the nature of existence after death. In one community, it was believed that the elderly who had been mis-treated could punish the offender after death (Lepowsky 1985). In another, death for the elderly marked the end of their participation in society, with the assumption that their magical powers had "consume(d)" them and no longer kept them from death. For younger people, however, death meant that their magic was not sufficiently strong to protect them from death; however, because their death was more disruptive to the society as a whole, leaving an extensive network of roles, relationships, and obliga-tions untended, it was believed that after death, the spirits of the young would remain active in assisting kinsmen and women (McKellin 1985). Obviously, death is a transition to another form of existence for both these societies.

The Anggor, a New Guinea tribe, see death as the final separation of two components of the individual: the *vital spirit* and the consciousness or personality. When alive, the personality is in charge, but after death, the life spirit takes control. Since their powers in death are great and they do not behave rationally, these spirits can harm the community, and the Anggor will call on protective spirits to help them (Huber 1972). There may be parallel meanings in Western culture; for example, why do we use such heavy tombstones and what is the meaning of *rest in peace?*

Most societies in the world believe in ghosts, although these ghosts are more likely to be helpful than destructive (Simmons 1945). However, the living usually need to propitiate these ghosts in whatever ways the belief systems dictate, ranging from offering them prayers to behaving in ways that the deceased would presumably approve.

Since life and death are seen by many societies as less distinct from each other than they are seen in Western cultures, this will influence the mean-ings of death. If death is essentially a continuation of life, perhaps in an improved form, then death might not be frightening. Or, putting it another way, one's own death might not be fear-provoking, while the death of another might create fear because of not knowing what the dead person is going to do.

The Process of Dying and Bereavement

The emphasis in this chapter has been on the meanings of death, but we will also discuss, although fairly briefly, the process of dying and bereavement, with particular reference to the elderly. The elderly who are dying or who are bereaved share many characteristics with nonelderly dying and bereaved individuals, but they also differ in significant ways, and we will focus on the differences.

The Process of Dying

Even a cursory examination of the causes of death for the elderly, in relationship to the causes of death of the nonelderly, indicates that the process of dying for older persons differs in important ways from the process for younger persons. Having made that statement, it becomes important to emphasize that these differences need to be seen as tendencies and do not refer to all elderly or all nonelderly.

The old die of chronic diseases, primarily heart disease, stroke, and cancer; younger people are much more likely to die from accidents. The chronic illnesses of the elderly incapacitate before they kill; their trajectories often display a slow decline, leading eventually to death. Because older people are more likely than younger people to die of chronic disease, their dying process differs in the following ways:

(1) Financial costs are often higher because of the need for long-term care.
(2) Their need for health care and for human care is greater for the same reason.
(3) They have a greater potential for leading a relatively normal life during the early part of the dying process.
(4) They have a longer period to contemplate their own death and during which they can make plans for it.
(5) They have more opportunity to see old friends or to visit important places.
(6) They are more likely to die in institutions, in part because of the illness from which they are dying and in part because of physical and cognitive changes that may be unrelated to their terminal illness. For this reason, also, the elderly are more likely to be confused or comatose prior to their death, which greatly influences the care they receive, whether in a hospital, at home, or in a long-term-care facility.
(7) More elderly, especially elderly women, die without a spouse or brother/sister to participate in their care, thus making them more dependent on their adult children (Kalish 1985).

All in all, it would appear that elderly take longer to die and are more likely to die in isolation from the individuals who were most important to them in their middle years.

Adding to their difficulties is what is termed "the social value of life," which refers to the value others place on a person's life. Factors that contribute to high social value include competence, ability to contribute to society, education and verbal fluency, health, vigor and energy, sexuality, wealth, knowledge and skills, and ability to participate in reciprocal social relationships. The elderly, and the dying elderly in particular, have these qualities only in limited degrees, yet these are the qualities that make people attractive to others. Therefore, the dying elderly are not as compelling as dying younger persons, and as a result they often receive less care and less adequate care. As Weisman says, "The terminally aged may be as helpless as a child, but they seldom arouse tenderness" (1972, 144).

Improvements in the Care of Older Dying Persons

Considerable improvement in the care of dying elderly persons has been observed during the past fifteen years. This improvement has stemmed from several sources, in addition to the increased knowledge of medical science. One of the most visible improvements in the care of the dying is the advent of the hospice movement. Hospice, as is often said, is not so much an institution for care as a philosophy of care, offered to individuals who have been determined to be terminal by their physicians (Koff 1980). Hospice programs vary a great deal as to whether they offer in-patient and out-patient services or only the latter, but they all share the policy of providing high quality human care for individuals for whom medical treatment no longer offers hope. Initially hospices emphasized care for nonelderly patients, but they now include the elderly as well.

A second basis for improvement has come from what Kastenbaum (1981) has termed the "death-awareness movement," which has led to the trend for health caretakers and others to be more aware of the need for personal satisfactions and to place less emphasis on the strictly medical issues in the dying process. The hospice movement is an important part of this trend.

Third, over the last twenty years, we have experienced a great increase in the number of books, research studies, articles in both popular media and professional journals, university courses, workshops and lectures, and so forth. This has increased the general level of awareness of the importance of good medical and personal care for terminally-ill older persons, which, in turn, has increased the willingness of patients and their family members to become more active in determining their own treatment program and of health caretakers to provide more effective human care. Probably the best-known of all persons in the field is Elisabeth Kübler-

Ross, a psychiatrist whose first book on death and dying has become a classic in the field and a sustained best-seller (Kübler-Ross 1969).

However, in the final analysis, it may well be the *zeitgeist*, the spirit of the times, that needs to be examined in order to understand the bases for improved sensitivity to the personal needs of the terminally-ill elderly. It is likely that the 1980s have seen a general movement away from viewing science and technology as leading to the ultimate in health care; instead, the importance of the personal relationships between the health caretakers and the ill person and the spiritual well-being of that individual have asserted themselves as being primary goals. At the same time the rights of persons who are helpless and vulnerable received increased attention, and most certainly many dying elderly were both helpless and vulnerable.

In addition, a new form of concern with the meaning of life led to questioning the generally accepted working assumption that any opportunity for existence was worth any amount of physical pain, emotional suffering, and financial cost. In one instance, a physician recommended painful back surgery for a man whose colon cancer was expected to cause his death within a relatively few weeks. The right-to-die began to be promulgated as a legitimate right of certain individuals who were extremely ill, usually terminally ill, and in pain. At the same time certain hazards were recognized in regard to using this right-to-die as an excuse for not giving these individuals the quality of health and personal care that they deserved.

One outcome of questioning the earlier assumptions was the development of *the living will,* a document that a person could sign while fully competent indicating the circumstances under which he or she would request that special medical procedures *not* be used to sustain life. Many states have adopted this document as either binding or advisory, although the conditions for its enforcement vary considerably from state to state. It is assumed that many thousands of older people have a living will filed with their physician and/or family members.

Thus, the dying process of the elderly differs in many ways from the dying process of the nonelderly, including the conditions that cause death, the death trajectory, the attitudes of health and personal caretakers, the attitudes of the elderly themselves, the extent of institutional care, the availability of family members to provide care, and so forth.

The Bereaved Elderly

The circumstances under which the elderly become bereaved also differ from those experienced by younger persons. Younger people are most likely to grieve the death of a parent or grandparent, while the elderly are most likely to grieve the death of a spouse or brother or sister. Since women outlive men by several years, on average, women are more often the ones to grieve: wives for husbands, sisters for brothers.

In fact, just over half of all women over age fifty-four are widows, and the proportion goes up to 70% among women over seventy-five; widows outnumber widowers 6:1 among those sixty-five to seventy-five, and the ratio is nearly 5:1 for those over seventy-five (Brotman 1982). Obviously, the death of a spouse for an individual in his or her sixties or seventies leads to very different kinds of stress, life changes, new role expectations, and so forth, than the death of a parent for someone twenty years younger. Even when comparisons are made across age groups for the death of a person in the same role, the effects differ considerably. That is, the death of a parent of a sixty-year-old has a different impact on the adult child than the death of a parent of a forty-year-old.

Older widows and widowers, especially the former, are unlikely to remarry. They anticipate fewer years of life and, perhaps, prefer to cherish the memory of the dead spouse rather than attempt to enter a new marriage at this point (Raphael 1983). This does not mean that they avoid new relationships, but that they avoid those requiring the commitment of marriage. Also, since men usually marry younger women, elderly widowers have a wide range of women—widowed, divorced, and never-married—from whom to select a companion, a lover, or a wife; conversely, older widows have relatively few available men, especially with the societal norms encouraging women to select men who are older and men to select women who are younger.

In many Western nations, certainly including the United States and Canada, there is so much emphasis on independence and autonomy that older widows and widowers frequently state that they prefer living alone to burdening their children with their presence as residents in the home. In most instances they do live alone, occasionally with a brother or sister, as long as they remain reasonably self-sufficient; that is, as long as they can drive, cook and keep house, find friends, and feel and be physically safe and secure.

As they become more frail and more confused (although most elderly do not become confused, many do), their adult children begin to contemplate other arrangements, ranging from sharing households to residing in some form of protected or assisted environment. In some instances, the elderly themselves make arrangements for these futures while they are still fully competent. For example, a healthy elderly couple will purchase a unit in a continuing care retirement community; when one member of the couple dies, usually the husband, the survivor is in a setting that offers some degree of protection against loneliness, criminal victimization, inactivity, undue vulnerability to health problems and costs, and reduced functional capacity.

Another difference between the bereavement of the elderly and of the nonelderly is that the death of an older person is not unexpected, and since many of the deaths take place over an extended period of time, the spouse has the opportunity both to provide care and to begin the grieving process. This is similar to the adult child whose elderly parent dies, but is very different from those less familiar, but still fairly frequent, occurrences when the spouse of a nonelderly person dies.

Concluding Comments

Very little can be said about virtually all elderly that does not also describe some nonelderly. Perhaps the one such statement that can be made is that most elderly in this society experienced the stock market crash of 1929 and the subsequent depression as teenagers or adults, while no one who is not at least sixty-five years old has had that experience.

In reviewing the discussion in this chapter, it becomes apparent that the emphasis has been on differences between the elderly and the nonelderly, rather than the similarities that also are evident. And among the most important conclusions that we have drawn are the following: death has different meanings for the elderly; they die of different illnesses in different settings; and they grieve for the loss of different relationships.

CONTRIBUTORS

CYNTHIA BEALL, associate professor of anthropology at Case Western Reserve University in Cleveland, Ohio, conducts research in the Himalayas and the Andes on social and physical environmental factors influencing the biological processes of growth, development and aging.

DAVID CHIRIBOGA is currently director of the Clinical Gerontology Program at the University of Texas Medical Branch, Galveston, Texas. His research interests center on the study of social stressors and transitions from a life-span perspective.

LINDA EVERS COOL is associate professor of anthropology and chair of the Department of Anthropology/Sociology at Santa Clara University. She has conducted research in two French regions (the island of Corsica and Brittany) and among Portuguese-Americans in California. Her research interests include cross-cultural studies of the aging process, ethnicity, regionalism, and the Mediterranean European culture area.

DEIRDRE A. KRAMER is an assistant professor in the Psychology Department at Rutgers University. Her interests include social cognitive development in adulthood, especially as it pertains to the solution of real-life interpersonal problems, and theoretical and metatheoretical issues in life-span research.

RHODA HALPERIN is associate professor of anthropology and psychiatry at the University of Cincinnati. She has edited and authored books and articles in economic anthropology, the political economy of peasants, and age and economic organization.

J. NEIL HENDERSON is an assistant professor in psychiatry and coordinator of the Division of Education and Training at the University of South Florida's Suncoast Gerontology Center for Health and Long Term Care. His current research projects include staff, family, and patient responses to dementia-specific care units in nursing homes, and family response to Alzheimer's disease and similar dementias in ethnic populations.

COLLEEN L. JOHNSON is on the faculty of the Medical Anthropology Program, University of California, San Francisco. She has published extensively on ethnic families and the late-life family, and is the author of two recent books, *Growing Up and Growing Old in Italian American Families* and

407

The Nursing Home in American Society. Currently she is conducting research on marital instability and late-life family ties.

RICHARD A. KALISH is dean of External Degree Programs at Antioch University. His extensive writings, including 14 books, emphasize death and loss.

PETER J. MAYER is research assistant professor in the Department of Radiation Oncology, SUNY-Health Science Center in Brooklyn, New York, where he is studying DNA repair in aging human lymphocytes.

MARY JANE MOORE is associate professor at San Diego State University. Her current research interests include menarche, menopause, and longevity; human lactation; and demography of southern Appalachian communities.

DANA J. PLUDE is assistant professor in the Department of Psychology, University of Maryland. His research interests include attentional, perceptual, and cognitive processes across the life span.

DIANE E. RYKKEN is a lecturer in computer science at California State University at Sacramento. She has also taught developmental psychology, human sexuality, and aging.

ANDREA SANKAR is a lecturer in the School of Public Health and a research scientist in the Department of Anthropology, University of Michigan. She has published numerous articles on health and aging. Her research interests include: the role of family factors in caregiving outcomes for Alzheimer's and cancer patients; communication and decision-making in home care; the impact of prospective payment on the community system of care; and health and aging policy in the People's Republic of China.

PHILIP SILVERMAN is professor of anthropology and chair of the Department of Sociology/Anthropology at California State College, Bakersfield. He has conducted research in rural communities in eastern Canada and among the Lozi of Zambia. His research interests include holocultural studies of aging, ethnicity and aging, and tribal-national relations in Africa.

PETER UHLENBERG is associate professor of sociology at the University of North Carolina, Chapel Hill, engaged in research on demography of the older population and demography of children. He is particularly interested in the changing meaning of old age in American society.

REFERENCES

Abbott, M. H., E. A. Murphy, D. R. Bolling, and H. Abbey. 1974. The familial component in longevity. A study of offspring of nonagenarians, II. Preliminary analysis of the completed study. *Johns Hopkins Medical Journal* 134:1–16.

———. 1978. The familial component in longevity—a study of offspring of nonagenarians: III. Intrafamilial studies. *American Journal of Medical Genetics* 2:105–20.

Abdellah, F. G. 1978. Long term care policy issues: Alternatives to institutional care. *Annals of the American Academy of Political and Social Sciences* 438:28–39.

Abeles, R. P., and M. W. Riley. 1976–1977. A lifecourse perspective on later years of life: Some implications for research. *Social Science Research Council Annual Report*, pp. 1–16.

Abrahams, J. P., W. J. Hoyer, M. F. Elias, B. Bradigan. 1975. Gerontological research in psychology published in the *Journal of Gerontology*, 1964–1974: Perspectives and progress. *Journal of Gerontology* 30:668–73.

Acosta, F. X. 1982. Group psychotherapy with Spanish-speaking patients. In *Mental health and Hispanic Americans: Clinical perspectives*, edited by R. Becerra, M. Karno, and J. Escobar. New York: Grune & Stratton.

Acsadi, G., and J. Nemeskeri. 1970. *History of human life span and mortality*. Budapest: Akademiai Kiado.

Adams, C. B., and B. F. Turner. 1985. Reported change in sexuality from young adulthood to old age. *Journal of Sex Research* 21(2):126–41.

Adelman, R. C., and G. S. Roth, eds. 1982. *Testing the theories of aging*. Boca Raton, Fla.: CRC Press.

Ade-Ridder, L., and T. H. Brubaker. 1983. Quality of long-term marriages. In *Family relationships in later life*, edited by T. H. Brubaker. Beverly Hills: Sage Publications.

Albrecht, R. 1962. The role of older people in family rituals. In *Aging around the world*. Vol. 1, *Social and psychological aspects of aging*, edited by C. Tibbetts and W. Donahue. New York: Columbia University Press.

Aldous, J., and R. Hill. 1965. Social cohesion, lineage type, and intergenerational transmission. *Social Forces* 43:471–82.

Allan, C., and H. Brotman. 1981. *Chartbook on aging in America*. Washington, D.C.: 1981 White House Conference on Aging.

Allport, G. 1937. *Pattern and growth in personality*. New York: Holt, Rinehart & Winston.

Alpaugh, P., and J. E. Birren. 1977. Variables affecting creative contributions across the adult life span. *Human Development* 20:240–48.

Alzheimer, A. 1907. Über eine eigenartige Erkrankung der Hirninde. *Allgemeine Zeitschrift für Psychiatrie und Psychisch-Gerichtliche Medizin* 64:146–48.

Amoss, P. T. 1981. Coast Salish elders. In *Other ways of growing old*, edited by P. T. Amoss and S. Harrell. Stanford: Stanford University Press.

Amoss, P., and S. Harrell, eds. 1981. *Other ways of growing old*. See Amoss, 1981.

Anderson, J. 1982. Comments on J. K. Brown's "Cross-Cultural Perspectives on Middle-Aged Women." *Current Anthropology* 23(2):148–49.

Andres, R. 1980. Influence of obesity on longevity in the aged. In *Aging, cancer, and cell membranes,* edited by C. Borek, C. Fenoglio, and D. W. King. New York: Thieme-Stratton.

———. 1985. Mortality and obesity: The rationale for age specific height-weight tables. In *Principles of geriatric medicine,* edited by R. Andres, E. Bierman, and W. Hazzard. New York: McGraw Hill.

Angrosino, M. V. 1976. Anthropology and the aged: A preliminary community study. *The Gerontologist* 16(2):174–80.

Apple, D. 1956. The Social structure of grandparenthood. *American Anthropologist* 58(4):656–63.

Arensberg, C. 1968. *The Irish countryman: An anthropological study.* New York: Peter Smith.

Ariès, P. 1962. *Centuries of childhood: A social history of family life.* Translated from the French by R. Baldick. New York: Knopf.

———. 1974. *Western attitudes toward death: From the middle ages to the present.* Translated by P. N. Ranum. Baltimore: Johns Hopkins University Press.

Arling, G. 1976. The elderly widow and her family, neighbors, and friends. *Journal of Marriage and the Family* 38(November):757–68.

Arluke, A., and J. Levin. 1984. Another stereotype: Old age as a second childhood. *Aging* (August–September):345.

Arluke, A., J. Levin, and J. Suchwalko. 1984. Sexuality and romance in advice books for the elderly. *Gerontologist* 24(4):415–18.

Armstrong, D., R. S. Sohol, R. G. Cutler, and T. F. Slater. 1984. *Free radicals in molecular biology, aging and disease.* New York: Raven Press.

Ashenbaum, W. A., and P. N. Stearns. 1978. Old age and modernization. *The Gerontologist* 18(3):307–12.

Aso, R., and M. Yasutomi. 1974. Urinary and sexual disturbances following radical surgery for rectal cancer and pudendal nerve block as a countermeasure for urinary disturbance. *American Journal of Proctology.* 25:60–70.

Atchley, R. C. 1985. *Social forces and aging.* Belmont, Calif.: Wadsworth Publishing.

Atchley, R. C., and S. J. Miller. 1983. Types of elderly couples. In *Family relationships in later life.* See Ade-Ridder and Brubaker, 1983.

Baker, P. M. 1985. The status of age: Preliminary results. *Journal of Gerontology* 40(4):506–8.

Ball, M. 1983. Granulovacuolar degeneration. In *Alzheimer's disease,* edited by B. Reisberg. New York: Free Press.

Baltes, P. B. 1979. Life-span developmental psychology: Some converging observations on history and theory. In *Life-span development and behavior.* Vol. 2, edited by P. B. Baltes and O. G. Brim, Jr. New York: Academic Press.

Baltes, P. B. and M. Baltes. 1980. Plasticity and variability in psychological aging: Methodological and theoretical issues. In *Aging and the CNS,* edited by C. Guerski. Berlin: Schering.

Baltes, P. B., F. Dittmann-Kohli, and R. A. Dixon. 1984. New perspectives on the development of intelligence in adulthood: Toward a dual-process conception and a model of selective optimization with compensation. In *Life-span development and behavior.* Vol. 6, edited by P. B. Baltes and O. G. Brim, Jr. New York: Academic Press.

Baltes, P. B., H. W. Reese, and L. P. Lipsitt. 1980. Life-span developmental psychology. *Annual Review of Psychology* 31:65–100.

Bancroft, J. 1983. *Human sexuality and its problems.* Edinburgh: Churchill Livingstone.

Bandura, A. 1982. Self-efficacy in human agency. *American Psychologist* 37:122–47.

Bankoff, E. A. 1984. The long-term consequences of social support for newly widowed women. Paper presented at the Sunbelt Social Network Conference, February, Phoenix, Arizona.

Barash, D. 1983. *Aging: An exploration.* Seattle: University of Washington Press.

Barron, M. L. 1961. *The aging American.* New York: Thomas Y. Crowell.

Bart, P. B. 1969. Why women's status changes in middle age: The times of the social ferris wheel. *Sociological Symposium* 3:1–18.

Barth, F. 1969. *Ethnic groups and boundaries.* Boston: Little, Brown and Company.

Barzel, U. S., S. R. Gambert, and P. D. Tsitouras. 1983. Endocrinology and metabolism in the elderly. In *Contemporary geriatric medicine.* Vol. 1, edited by S. R. Gambert. New York: Plenum Medical Book Co.

Beall, C. 1984. Theoretical dimensions of a focus on age in physical anthropology. In *Age and anthropological theory,* edited by D. I. Kertzer and J. Keith. New York: Cornell University Press.

―――. n.d. Nutrition and variation in biological aging. In *Nutrition in anthropology,* edited by F. E. Johnston. New York: Alan R. Liss. Forthcoming.

Becerra, R., M. Karno, and J. I. Escobar, eds. 1982. *Mental health and Hispanic Americans.* See Acosta, 1982.

Becker, J. 1974. *Depression: Theory and research.* Washington, D.C.: V. H. Winston.

Beckford, G. L. 1972. *Persistent poverty: Underdevelopment in plantation economies of the third world.* New York: Oxford University Press.

Beller, S., and E. Palmore. 1974. Longevity in Turkey. *Gerontologist* 14:373–76.

Belloc, N. B. 1973. Relationship of health practices and mortality. *Preventive Medicine* 2:67–81.

Benedict, R. 1946. *The chrysanthemum and the sword.* Boston: Houghton Mifflin.

Benet, S. 1974. *Abkhasians: The long-living people of the Caucasus.* New York: Holt, Rinehart & Winston.

Bengston, V. L., J. B. Cuellar, and P. K. Ragan. 1977. Stratum contrasts and similarities in attitudes toward death. *Journal of Gerontology* 32:76–88.

Bengston, V. L., J. J. Dowd, D. H. Smith, and A. Inkeles. 1975. Modernization, modernity, and perceptions of aging: A cross-cultural study. *Journal of Gerontology* 30(6):688–95.

Bengston, V. L., and L. A. Morgan. 1983. Ethnicity and aging: A comparison of three ethnic groups. In *Growing old in different societies: Cross-cultural perspectives,* edited by J. Sokolovsky. Belmont, Calif.: Wadsworth Publishing.

Bengston, V. L., E. B. Olander, and A. A. Haddad. 1976. The "generation gap" and aging family members: Toward a conceptual model. In *Time, roles, and self in old age,* edited by J. F. Gubrium. New York: Human Sciences Press.

Bengston, V. L., M. N. Reedy, and C. Gordon. 1985. Aging and self-conceptions: Personality processes and social contexts. In *Handbook of the psychology of aging.* 2d ed., edited by J. E. Birren and K. W. Schaie. New York: Van Nostrand Reinhold.

Benjamin, H. 1983. The role of the physician in the sex problems of the aged. In *Advances in sex research,* edited by H. G. Beigel. New York: Harper & Row.

Bennet, J. W. 1980. Management style: A concept and a method for the analysis of family-operated agricultural enterprise. In *Agricultural decision making,* edited by P. F. Barlett. New York: Academic Press.

―――. 1982. *Of time and the enterprise: North American family farm management in a context of resource marginality.* Minneapolis: University of Minnesota Press.

Berezin, M. A. 1978. Sex and old age: A review of the literature. In *Normal psychology of the aging process,* edited by N. E. Zinberg and I. Kaufman. New York: International Universities Press.

Berg, C. A., and R. J. Sternberg. 1984. People's implicit theories of intelligence over the adult years. Paper presented at the 37th annual meeting of the Gerontological Society, November, San Antonio, Texas.

———. 1985. Toward a triarchic theory of intellectual development during adulthood. *Developmental Review* 5:334–70.

Bergman, M. 1971. Hearing and aging. *Audiology* 10:164–71.

Berkman, L. R., and S. L. Syme. 1979. Social networks, host resistance, and mortality: A nine year follow-up study of Alameda County residents. *American Journal of Epidemiology* 1009:186–204.

Berman, E. M., and H. I. Lief. 1976. Sex and the aging process. In *Sex and the life cycle*, edited by W. W. Oaks, G. A. Melchiode, and I. Ficher. New York: Grune & Stratton.

Besdine, R. 1982. Dementia. In *Health and disease in old age*, edited by J. Rowe and R. Besdine. Boston: Little, Brown and Company.

Biesele, M., and N. Howell. 1981. "The old people give you life": Aging among Kung hunter-gatherers. In *Other ways of growing old*. See Amoss, 1981.

Binstock, R. H. 1972. Interest-group liberalism and the politics of aging. *Gerontologist* 12:265–80.

———. 1981. The aging as a political force: Images and reality. In *Aging: A Challenge to science and social policy*. Vol. 2 of *Medicine and social science*, edited by A. J. J. Gilmore, A. Svanberg, M. Marois, W. M. Beattie, and J. Piotrowski. London: Oxford University Press.

———. 1985. The oldest old: A fresh perspective or compassionate ageism revisited? *Milbank Memorial Fund Quarterly* 63(2):420–51.

Birren, J. E. 1965. Age changes in speed of behavior: Its central nature and physiological correlates. In *Behavior, aging, and the nervous system*, edited by A. T. Welford and K. W. Schaie. Springfield, Ill.: Charles C. Thomas.

———. 1969. Age and decision strategies. In *Decision making and age: Interdisciplinary topics in gerontology*. Vol. 4, edited by A. T. Welford and J. E. Birren. Basel, Switzerland: S. Karger.

Birren, J. E., R. C. Casperson, and J. Botwinick. 1950. Age changes in pupil size. *Journal of Gerontology* 5:267–71.

Birren, J. E., and V. J. Renner. 1977. Research on the psychology of aging. In *Handbook of the psychology of aging*, edited by J. E. Birren and K. W. Schaie. New York: Van Nostrand Reinhold.

Black, F. O. 1979. The aging vestibular system. In *Special senses in aging: A current biological assessment*, edited by S. S. Han and D. H. Coons. Ann Arbor: University of Michigan Press.

Blackfield-Cohen, J., and J. A. Brody. 1981. The epidemiologic importance of psychosocial factors in longevity. *American Journal of Epidemiology* 114:451–61.

Blanchard-Fields, F. 1981. Cognitive functioning in adulthood: A case for adaptive progression. Paper presented in *Adaptation and competence in adulthood: Perspective for the 80s*, organized by F. Blanchard-Fields and D. A. Kramer, at the Biennial Meeting of the Society for Research on Child Development, April, Boston.

Blau, Z. S. 1981. *Aging in a changing society*. 2d ed. New York: Franklin Watts.

Blau, Z. S., G. T. Oser, and R. C. Stephens. 1979. Aging, social class, and ethnicity: A comparison of anglo, black, and Mexican-American Texans. *Pacific Sociological Review* 22(40):501–25.

Blazer, D. 1980. The epidemiology of mental illness in late life. In *Handbook of geriatric psychiatry*, edited by E. Busse and D. Blazer. New York: Van Nostrand Reinhold.

Blessed, G., B. Tomlinson, and M. Roth. 1968. The association between quantitative measures of dementia and of senile change in the cerebral grey matter of elderly subjects. *British Journal of Psychiatry* 114:797–811.

Blieszner, R., S. L. Willis, P. B. Baltes. 1981. Training research in aging on the fluid ability of inductive reasoning. *Journal of Applied Developmental Psychology* 2:247–65.

Bloch, A., J. Maeder, and J. Haissly. 1975. Sexual problems after myocardial infarction. *American Heart Journal* 90:536–37.

Block, J. 1971. *Lives through time.* Berkeley: Bancroft.

Bobrow, D. G., and D. A. Norman. 1975. Some principles of memory schemata. In *Representation and understanding: Studies in cognitive science,* edited by D. G. Bobrow and A. Collins. New York: Academic Press.

Bohannon, P. 1980. Time, rhythm, and pace. *Science 80,* 1(3):18, 20.

Bornstein, P. E., P. J. Clayton, J. A. Halikas, W. L. Maurice, and E. Robbins. 1973. The depression of widowhood after thirteen months. *British Journal of Psychiatry* 122:561–66.

Bosse, R., and C. L. Rose, eds. 1984. *Smoking and aging.* Lexington, Mass.: Lexington Books.

Bott, E. 1971. *Family and social networks.* 2d ed. New York: Free Press.

Botwinick, J. 1977. Intellectual abilities. In *Handbook of the psychology of aging.* See Birren and Renner, 1977.

———. 1978. *Aging and behavior.* 2d ed. New York: Springer Publishing.

Bowers, L. M., R. R. Cross, and F. A. Lloyd. 1963. Sexual function and urologic disease in the elderly male. *Journal of the American Geriatrics Society* 11:647–52.

Bowling, A., and A. Cartwright. 1982. *Life after a death: A study of the elderly widowed.* London: Tavistock Publications.

Brackenridge, R. D. C. 1985. *Medical selection of life risks: A comprehensive guide to life expectancy for underwriters and clinicians.* 2d ed. New York: Macmillan, Nature Press.

Bradley, R. M. 1979. Effects of age on the sense of taste: Anatomical considerations. In *Special senses in aging.* See Black, 1979.

Branch, L., and A. Jette. 1984. Personal health practices and mortality among the elderly. *American Journal of Public Health* 74:1126–29.

Brenner, J., J. Bearman, and B. Brown. 1985. Re: Mortality of widowed vs. married. *American Journal of Epidemiology* 122:721–22.

Brent, S. B., and D. Watson. 1980. Aging and wisdom: Individual and collective aspects. Paper presented at the 33rd Annual Meeting of the Gerontological Society, November 23, San Diego, California.

Breslow, L., and J. E. Enstrom. 1980. Persistence of health habits and their relationship to mortality. *Preventive Medicine* 9:469–83.

Brim, O. G., Jr., and J. Kagan. 1980. Constancy and change: A review of the issues. In *Constancy and change in human development,* edited by O. G. Brim, Jr. and J. Kagan. Cambridge: Harvard University Press.

Brim, O. G., Jr., and C. D. Ryff. 1980. On the properties of life events. In *Life-span development and behavior.* Vol. 3, edited by P. B. Baltes and O. G. Brim, Jr. New York: Academic Press

Broderick, C. 1978. Sexuality and aging: An overview. In *Sexuality and aging,* edited by R. L. Solnick. Los Angeles: University of Southern California Press.

Brody, E. M. 1977. *Long-term care of older people: A practical guide.* With two guest chapters by S. J. Brody. New York: Human Services Press.

Brody, E. M., and B. Liebowitz. 1981. Some recent innovations in community living arrangements for older people. In *Community housing choices for older Americans,* edited by M. P. Lawton and S. L. Hoover. New York: Springer Publishing.

Bromley, D. E. 1967. Age and sex differences in the serial production of creative conceptual responses. In *Journal of Gerontology* 22:32–42.

Bronfenbrenner, U. 1977. Toward an experimental ecology of human development. *American Psychologist* 52:513–31.

Brotman, H. B. 1976. Every tenth American: The "problem" of aging. In *Community planning for an aging society*, edited by M. P. Lawton, R. J. Newcomer, and T. O. Byerts. Stroudsburg, Pa.: Dowden, Hutchinson and Ross.

———. 1982. *Every ninth American: 1982 edition.* An analysis for the Chairman of the Select Committee on Aging. House. 97th Cong., 2d Sess. Washington, D.C.: Government Printing Office.

Brown, G. W., and T. Harris. 1978. *Social origins of depression: A study of psychiatric disorder in women.* London: Tavistock Publications.

Brown, J. K. 1975. Iroquois women: An ethnohistoric note. In *Toward an anthropology of women*, edited by R. Reiter. New York: Monthly Review Press.

———. 1982. Cross-cultural perspectives on middle-aged women. *Current Anthropology* 23(2):143–56.

Bryant, E. S., and M. El-Attar. 1984. Migration and redistribution of the elderly. *The Gerontologist* 24(6):634–40.

Bultena, G. L. 1969. Life continuity and morale in old age. *The Gerontologist* 9:251–53.

———. 1974. Structural effects on the morale of the aged: A comparison of age-segregated and age-integrated communities. In *Late life: Communities and environmental policy*, edited by J. F. Gubrium. Springfield, Ill.: Charles C. Thomas.

Burch, P. R. J. 1983. Blood pressure and mortality in the very old. *Lancet* 2:853.

Burgess, E. W. 1960. Introduction. In *Aging in western societies*, edited by E. W. Burgess. Chicago: The University of Chicago Press.

Busse, E. and D. Blazer. 1980. Disorders related to biological functioning. In *Handbook of geriatric psychiatry.* See Blazer, 1980.

Butler, L., and P. Newacheck. 1981. Health and social factors relevant to long term care policy. In *Policy options in long-term care*, edited by J. Meltzer, F. Farrow, and H. Richman. Chicago: University of Chicago Press.

Butler, R. N. 1963. The life review: An interpretation of reminiscence in the aged. *Psychiatry* 26:65–76.

———. 1967. The destiny of creativity in later life: Studies of creative people and the creative process. In *Psychodynamic studies on aging*, edited by S. Levin and R. J. Kahana. New York: International Universities.

Butler, R. N., and M. I. Lewis. 1976. *Sex after sixty: A guide for men and women for their later years.* New York: Harper & Row.

Calder-Marshall, A. 1960. *The sage of sex: A life of Havelock Ellis.* New York: G. P. Putnam.

California State Department of Health. 1977. *Skilled nursing and intermediate care facilities.* Annual Report. Office of Statewide Health Planning and Development.

Camp, C. J. 1981. The use of fact retrieval vs. inference in young and elderly adults. *Journal of Gerontology* 36:715–21.

Campbell, A. 1981. *The sense of well-being in America: Recent patterns and trends.* New York: McGraw-Hill.

Campbell, R. 1984. Nursing home and long-term care in Japan. *Pacific Affairs* 51(1):78–89.

Cancian, F. 1965. *Economics and prestige in a Maya community: The religious cargo system in Zinacantan.* Stanford: Stanford University Press.

Cancian, F. M. 1985. Gender politics: Love and power in the private and public spheres. In *Gender and the life course*, edited by A. Rossi. New York: Aldine Publishing.

Cantor, M. H. 1975. Life space and the social support system of the inner city elderly of New York. *The Gerontologist* 15(1):23–27.

———. 1979. The informal support system of New York's inner-city elderly: Is ethnicity a factor? In *Ethnicity and aging*, edited by D. Gelfand and A. Kutzik. New York: Springer Publishing.

Carlin, V. F., and R. Mansberg. 1984. *If I live to be 100 . . . Congregate housing for later life*. West Nyack, N.Y.: Parker Publishing.

Carp, F. M. 1966. *The future for the aged*. Austin: University of Texas Press.

———. 1975. Ego-defense or cognitive consistency effects on environmental evaluation. *Journal of Gerontology* 30:707–11.

———. 1976a. Urban life style and life-cycle factors. In *Community planning for an aging society*. See Brotman, 1976.

———. 1976b. Housing and living environments of older people. In *Handbook of aging and the social sciences*, edited by R. H. Binstock and E. Shanas. New York: Van Nostrand Reinhold.

Carter, J. 1973. Psychiatry's insensitivity to racism and aging. *Psychiatric Opinion* 10(6):21–25.

Catron, L., D. A. Chiriboga, S. Krystal. 1980. Divorce at midlife: Psychic dangers of the liminal period. Part I. Empirical considerations. *Maturitas* 2:131–39.

Caudill, W., and D. W. Plath. 1974. Who sleeps by whom? Parent-child involvement in urban Japanese families. In *Culture and personality: Contemporary readings*, edited by R. A. Levine. Chicago: Aldine Publishing.

Cavan, R. S. 1973. Speculations on innovations to conventional marriage in old age. *Gerontologist* 13:409–11.

Cavanaugh, J. C. 1983. Comprehension and retention of televised programs by 20- and 60-year-olds. *Journal of Gerontology* 38:190–96.

———. 1984. Effects of presentation format on adults' retention of televised programs. *Experimental Aging Research* 10:51–53.

Cavanaugh, J. C., D. A. Kramer, J. D. Sinnott, C. J. Camp, and R. P. Markley. 1985. On missing links and such: Interfaces between cognitive research and everyday problem solving. *Human Development* 28:146–68.

Cerella, J. 1985. Age-related decline in extrafoveal letter perception. *Journal of Gerontology* 40(6):727–36.

Cerella, J., L. W. Poon, and D. M. Williams. 1980. Age and the complexity hypothesis. In *Aging in the 1980's: Psychological issues*, edited by L. W. Poon. Washington, D.C.: American Psychological Association.

Chagnon, N. 1974. *Studying the Yanomamo*. New York: Holt, Rinehart & Winston.

Chance, J., T. Overcast, and S. J. Dollinger. 1978. Aging and cognitive regression: Contrary findings. *Journal of Psychology* 98:177–83.

Chayanov, A. V. 1966. *Chayanov on the theory of peasant economy*, edited by D. Thorner, B. Kerblay, and R. E. F. Smith. Homewood, Ill.: Richard D. Irwin for the American Economic Association.

Cherlin, A. J. 1981. *Marriage, divorce, remarriage*. Cambridge: Harvard University Press.

———. 1983. A sense of history: Recent research on aging and the family. In *Aging in society: Selected reviews of recent research*, edited by M. W. Riley, B. B. Hess, and K. Bond. Hillsdale, N.J.: Lawrence Erlbaum.

Chevan, A. and J. H. Korson. 1972. The widowed who live alone: An examination of social and demographic factors. *Social Forces* 51(1):45–53.

Chiriboga, D. A. 1979. Conceptualizing adult transitions: A new look at an old subject. *Generations* 4:4–6.

————. 1981. The psychology of middle age. In *Modern perspectives in the psychiatry of middle age,* edited by J. G. Howells. New York: Brunner/Mazel.

————. 1984. Social stressors as antecedents of change. *Journal of Gerontology* 39(4):468–77.

————. 1985. Stress and personal continuity. Paper presented at the annual meeting of the Gerontological Society of America, November, San Antonio, Texas.

Chiriboga, D. A., and L. Cutler. 1980. Stress and adaptation: Life span perspectives. In *Aging in the 1980's.* See Cerella, Poon, and Williams, 1980.

Christenson, C. V., and J. H. Gagnon. 1965. Sexual behavior in a group of older women. *Journal of Gerontology* 0:351–56.

Clark, M. 1969. Cultural values and dependency in later life. In *Dependence and old people,* edited by R. Kalish. Ann Arbor: University of Michigan, Occasional papers in Gerontology.

Clark, M. and B. Anderson. 1967. *Culture and aging: An anthropological study of older Americans.* Springfield, Ill.: Charles C. Thomas.

Clark, R. W. 1971. *Einstein: The life and times.* New York: Avon Books.

Clark, R. L., and J. J. Spengler. 1980. *The economics of individual and population aging.* Cambridge: Cambridge University Press.

Clausen, J. A. 1972. The life course of individuals. In *Aging and society.* Vol. 3, *A sociology of age stratification,* edited by M. W. Riley, M. Johnson, and A. Foner. New York: Russell Sage Foundation.

————. 1986. *The life course: A sociological perspective.* Englewood Cliffs, N.J.: Prentice-Hall.

Clayton, V. 1982. Wisdom and intelligence: The nature and function of knowledge in the later years. *International Journal of Aging and Human Development* 15:315–21.

Clayton, V. P., and J. E. Birren. 1980. The development of wisdom across the life-span: A re-examination of an ancient topic. In *Life-span development and behavior,* Vol. 3. See Brim and Ryff, 1980.

Clemente, F., P. A. Rexroad, and C. Hursch. 1975. The participation of the black aged in voluntary associations. *Journal of Gerontology* 30:469–72.

Cleveland, W. P., and D. T. Gianturco. 1976. Remarriage probability after widowhood: A retrospective method. *Journal of Gerontology* 31(1):99–103.

Coatsworth, E. 1976. *Personal geography: Almost an autobiography.* Brattleboro, Vt.: The Stephen Greene Press.

Cockburn, T. A. 1971. Infectious diseases in ancient populations. *Current Anthropology* 12:45–62.

Coe, E. 1965. Self-conception and institutionalization. In *Older people and their social world,* edited by A. Rose and W. Peterson. Philadelphia: F. A. Davis.

Cogan, D. G. 1979. Vision: Introduction. In *Special senses in aging.* See Black, 1979.

Cohen, E. 1975. An overview of long-term care facilities. In *A social work guide to long-term care facilities,* edited by E. Brody. Rockville Md.: National Institute of Mental Health.

Cohen, G. D. 1983. Historical views and evolution of concepts. In *Alzheimer's disease.* See Ball, 1983.

Cohen, R. 1978. Ethnicity: Problem and focus in anthropology. In *Annual Review of Anthropology,* edited by B. J. Siegel 7:379–403.

————. 1984. Age and culture as theory. In *Age and anthropological theory.* See Beall, 1984.

Cohen, T., and L. Gitman. 1959. Oral complaints and taste perception in the aged. *Journal of Gerontology* 14:294–98.

Cohler, B. J. 1983. Autonomy and interdependence in the family of adulthood: A psychological perspective. *The Gerontologist* 23(1):33–39.

Cohler, B. J., and H. U. Grunebaum. 1981. *Mothers, grandmothers and daughters: Personality and child-care in three-generation families*. With the assistance of D. M. Robins. New York: Wiley & Sons.

Colarusso, C. A., and R. A. Nemiroff. 1979. Some observations and hypotheses about the psychoanalytic theory of adult development. *International Journal of Psychoanalysis* 60:59–72.

Cole, C. L. 1984. Marital quality in later life. In *Independent aging: Family and social systems perspectives*, edited by W. H. Quinn and G. A. Hughston. Rockville, Md.: Aspen Systems Corporation.

Cole, J. W., and P. S. Katz. 1973. Knecht to Arbiter: The proletarianization process in South Tyrol. *Studies in European Society* 1:39–66.

Comfort, A. 1979. *The Biology of Senescence*. 3d ed. New York: Elsevier.

———. 1980. Sexuality in later life. In *Handbook of mental health and aging*, edited by J. E. Birren and R. B. Sloane. Englewood Cliffs, N.J.: Prentice-Hall.

———. 1983. Foreword. In *Primary care geriatrics*, edited by R. Ham. Boston: John Wright.

Commons, M. L., F. A. Richards, and C. Armon. 1984. *Beyond formal operations: Late adolescent and adult cognitive development*. New York: Praeger.

Commons, M. L., F. A. Richards, C. Armon, and J. D. Sinnott. n.d. *Beyond formal operations 2: The development of adolescent and adult thinking and perception*. New York: Praeger. Forthcoming.

Cool, L. 1980. Ethnicity and aging: Continuity through change for elderly Corsicans. In *Aging in culture and society*, edited by C. L. Fry. New York: J. F. Bergin Publishers.

———. 1981. Ethnic identity; A source of community esteem for the elderly. *Anthropological Quarterly* 54:179–89.

———. 1986. Ethnicity: Its significance and measurement. In *New methods for old age research*, edited by C. L. Fry and J. Keith. South Hadley, Mass.: Bergin & Garvey Publishers.

Corby, N., and R. L. Solnick. 1980. Psychosocial and physiological influences on sexuality in the older adult. In *Handbook of mental health and aging*. See Comfort, 1980.

Cornelius, S. W., and S. R. Kenny. 1982. *Academic and everyday intelligence in adulthood and old age*. Unpublished manuscript. Cornell University.

Corsini, R. J. 1977. Introduction. In *Current personality theories*, edited by R. J. Corsini. Itasca, Ill.: F. E. Peacock Publishers.

Corso, J. R. 1977. Auditory perception and communication. In *Handbook of the psychology of aging*. See Birren and Renner, 1977.

———. 1981. *Aging sensory systems and perception*. New York: Praeger.

———. 1984. Auditory processes and age: Significant problems for research. *Experimental Aging Research* 10:171–74.

Counts, D. A., and D. R. Counts. 1985a. Introduction: Linking concepts aging and gender, aging and death. In *Aging and its transformations*, edited by D. A. Counts and D. R. Counts. Lanham, Md.: University Press of America.

———. 1985b. I'm not dead yet! Aging and death: Process and experience in Kaliai. In *Aging and its transformations*. See Counts and Counts, 1985a.

Coward, R., and G. Lee, eds. 1985. *The Elderly in Rural Society*. New York: Springer Publishing.

Cowgill, D. O. 1972. A theory of aging in cross-cultural perspectives. In *Aging and modernization*, edited by D. O. Cowgill and L. D. Holmes. New York: Appleton-Century-Crofts.

————. 1974. The aging of populations and societies. *The Annals of the American Academy of Political and Social Science*, 415(September):1–18.

Cowgill, D. O., and L. D. Holmes, eds. 1972. *Aging and Modernization*. New York: Appleton-Century-Crofts.

Cox, H. 1984. *Later life: The realities of aging*. Englewood Cliffs, N.J.: Prentice-Hall.

Craik, F. I. M. 1977. Age differences in human memory. In *Handbook of the psychology of aging*. See Birren and Renner, 1977.

Craik, F. I. M., and M. Byrd. 1981. Aging and cognitive deficits: The role of attentional resources. In *Aging and cognitive processes*, edited by F. I. M. Craik and S. E. Trehub. New York: Plenum.

Cronin, C. 1970. *The sting of change*. Chicago: University of Chicago Press.

Cuber, J. F., and P. B. Harroff. 1963. The more total view: Relationships among men and women of the upper middle class. *Marriage and Family Living* 25(May):130–42.

Cuellar, J. 1978. El senior citizens club: The older Mexican-American in the voluntary association. In *Life's career-aging: Cultural variations on growing old*, edited by B. Myerhoff and A. Simič. Beverly Hills: Sage Publicatons.

Cumming, E., and W. Henry. 1961. *Growing old*. New York: Basic Books.

Cumming, E., and D. M. Schneider. 1961. Sibling solidarity: A property of American kinship. *American Anthropologist* 63:498–507.

Cutler, R. G. 1975. Evolution of human longevity and the genetic complexity governing aging rate. *Proceedings of the National Academy of Sciences* 72:4664–68.

————. 1976. Evolution of longevity in primates. *Journal of Human Evolution* 5:169–202.

————. 1978. Evolutionary biology of senescence. In *The biology of aging*, edited by J. A. Behnke, C. E. Finch, and G. B. Moment. New York: Plenum.

————. 1980. Evolution of human longevity. *Advances in Pathobiology* 7:73–79.

————. 1984. Antioxidants, aging, and longevity. In *Free radicals in biology*, Vol. 6, edited by W. A. Pryor. New York: Academic Press.

Dagon, E. 1984. Demoralization, depletion, and depression in elderly nursing home patients. In *Mental health and aging: A curriculum guide to nursing home caregivers*, edited by J. N. Henderson and E. Pfeiffer. Tampa: University of South Florida, Suncoast Gerontology Center.

————. 1987. Depression in the nursing home. In *Principles and practice of nursing home care*, edited by P. Katz and E. V. Calkins. New York: Springer Publishing. Forthcoming.

Datan, N., A. Antonovsky, and B. Maoz. 1985. Tradition, modernity and transitions in five Israeli subcultures. In *In her prime: A new view of middle-aged women*, edited by J. K. Brown and V. Kerns. South Hadley, Mass.: Bergin & Garvey Publishers.

David, D. S., and R. Grannon, eds. 1976. *The forty-nine percent majority: The male sex role*. Reading, Mass.: Addison-Wesley Publishing.

Davies, D. 1975. *The centenarians of the Andes*. Garden City, N.Y.: Anchor Press, Doubleday.

Davies, L. J. 1977. Attitudes toward old age and aging as shown by humor. *Gerontologist* 17(3):220–26.

Davis, K. C. 1980. The position and status of black and white aged in rural Baptist churches in Missouri. *The Journal of Minority Aging* 5(3):242–48.

Dean, S. R. 1966. Sin and social security. *Journal of the American Geriatrics Society* 14:935–38.

de Beauvoir, S. 1973. *The coming of age*. Translated by P. O'Brian. Originally published in French under the title *La vieillesse* in 1970. New York: Warner Paperback Library.

Delaney, W. 1981. Is Uncle Sen insane? Pride and humor in a northern Thailand home for the elderly. *International Journal of Aging and Human Development* 13(2):137–50.

del Valle, A. G., and M. Usher. 1982. Group therapy with aged Latino women: A pilot project and study. *Clinical Gerontologist* 1:51–58.

Demming, J. A., and S. L. Pressey. 1957. Tests "indigenous" to the adult and older years. *Journal of Counseling Psychology* 4:144–48.

Dempster, A. P. 1972. Functional age and age-related measures. *Aging and Human Development* 3:195–96.

De Nigola, P., and M. Peruzza. 1974. Sex in the aged. *Journal of the American Geriatrics Society* 22(8):380–82.

Dennis, W. 1966. Creative productivity between the ages of 20 and 80 years. *Journal of Gerontology* 21:1–18.

Denos, V., and A. Jacke. 1981. When you care enough: An analysis of attitudes toward aging. *Gerontologist* 21(2):209–14.

Deutscher, I. 1964. The quality of post-parental life: Definitions of the situation. *Journal of Marriage and the Family* 26:52–59.

DiLollo, V., J. L. Arnett, and R. V. Kruk. 1982. Age-related change in rate of visual information processing. *Journal of Experimental Psychology: Human Perception and Performance* 8:225–37.

Dittmann-Kohli, F., and P. B. Baltes. n.d. Toward a neofunctionalist conception of adult intellectual development: Wisdom as a prototypical case of intellectual growth. In *Beyond formal operations: Alternative endpoints to human development*, edited by C. Alexander and E. Langer. Forthcoming.

Dixon, R. A., D. A. Kramer, and P. B. Baltes. 1985. Intelligence: Its life-span development. In *Handbook of intelligence: Theories, measurements and applications*, edited by B. B. Wolman. New York: Wiley & Sons.

Dohlinow, P. 1984. The primate: Age, behavior, and evolution. In *Age and anthropological theory*. See Beall, 1984.

Domey, R. G., R. A. McFarland, and E. Chadwick. 1960. Dark adaptation as a function of age and time: II. A derivation. *Journal of Gerontology* 15:267–79.

Dougherty, M. 1978. An anthropological perspective on aging and women in the middle years. In *The anthropology of health*, edited by E. Bauwens. St. Louis: C. V. Mosby.

———. 1982. Comments on J. K. Brown's "Cross-cultural perspectives on middle-aged women." *Current Anthropology* 23(2):149–50.

Douglass, R. L., and T. Hickey. 1983. Domestic neglect and abuse of the elderly: Research findings and a systems perspective for service delivery planning. In *Abuse and maltreatment of the elderly: Causes and interventions*. Boston: John Wright-PSG.

Dowd, J. 1983. Social exchange, class, and old people. In *Growing old in different societies*. See Bengston and Morgan, 1983.

Dowd, J., and V. L. Bengston. 1978. Aging in minority populations: An examination of the double jeopardy hypothesis. *Journal of Gerontology* 33:427–36.

Draper, P. 1975. !Kung women: Contrasts in sexual egalitarianism in foraging and sedentary contexts. In *Toward an anthropology of women*. See Brown, 1975.

———. 1976. Social and economic constraints on child life. In *Kalahari hunter-gatherers*, edited by R. B. Lee and I. DeVore. Cambridge: Harvard University Press.

Dressler, D. M. 1973. Life adjustment of retired couples. *International Journal of Aging and Human Development* 4:335–49.

Dunlop, B. D. 1979. *The growth of nursing home care*. Lexington, Mass.: Lexington Books.

Dunn, F. L. 1968. Epidemiological factors: Health and disease in hunter-gatherers. In *Man the hunter*, edited by R. B. Lee and I. DeVore. Chicago: Aldine Publishing.

Dupre, G., and P.-P. Rey. 1973. Reflections on the pertinence of a theory of the history of exchange. *Economy and Society* 2:131–63.

Durkheim, E. [1893] 1964. *The division of labor in society*. Translated by G. Simpson. New York: The Free Press of Glencoe.

Durrenberger, E. P., ed. 1984. *Chayanov, peasants and economic anthropology*. New York: Academic Press.

Duvall, E. 1977. *Marriage and family development*. 5th ed. Philadelphia: J. B. Lippincott.

Dychtwald, K. 1981. Liberating aging: An interview with Maggie Kuhn. In *The holistic health lifebook*, compiled by the Berkeley Holistic Health Center. Berkeley: And/Or Press.

Eastman, P. 1984. Elders under siege. *Psychology Today* 18(1):30.

Eckert, P. 1984. Age and linguistic change. In *Age and anthropological theory*. See Beall, 1984.

Edwards, A. E., and J. R. Husted. 1976. Penile sensitivity, age, and sexual behavior. *Journal of Clinical Psychology* 32:697–700.

Ehrlich, P., and I. F. Ehrlich. 1982. SRO elderly: A distinct population in a viable housing alternative. In *Aging and the human condition*, edited by G. Lenoff-Caravaglia. New York: Human Sciences Press.

Eisdorfer, C. 1980. Paranoia and schizophrenic disorders in later life. In *Handbook of geriatric psychiatry*. See Blazer, 1980.

———. 1981. Introduction. In *Other ways of growing old*. See Amoss, 1981.

———. 1983. Conceptual modes of aging: The challenge of a new frontier. *American Psychologist* 38:197–202.

Eitzen, D. S. 1980. *Social problems*. Boston: Allyn & Bacon.

Ekert, J. K. 1980. *The unseen elderly: A study of marginally subsistent hotel dwellers*. San Diego: The Campanile Press, San Diego State University.

Elder, G. H., Jr. 1974. *Children of the Great Depression*. Chicago: University of Chicago Press.

———. 1981. History and the life course. In *Biography and society*, edited by D. Berteaux. Beverly Hills: Sage Publications.

———. 1985. Perspectives on the life course. In *Life course dynamics: Trajectories and transitions, 1968–1980*, edited by G. H. Edler, Jr. Ithaca, N.Y.: Cornell University Press.

Ellis, W. J., and J. T. Grayhack. 1963. Sexual function in aging males after orchiectomy and estrogen therapy. *Journal of Urology* 89:895–99.

Engen, T. 1977. Taste and smell. In *Handbook of the psychology of aging*. See Birren and Renner, 1977.

Epstein, L. J. 1976. Depression in the elderly. *Journal of Gerontology* 31:278–82.

Erickson, R., and K. Ekert. 1977. The elderly poor in downtown San Diego hotels. *The Gerontologist* 17(5):440–46.

Erikson, E. H. 1963. *Childhood and society*. 2d ed. New York: W. W. Norton & Company.

———. 1968. *Identity: Youth and crisis*. New York: W. W. Norton & Company.

———. 1969. *Gandhi's truth: On the origins of militant nonviolence*. New York: W. W. Norton & Company.

———. 1975. *Life history and the historical moment*. New York: W. W. Norton & Company.

———. 1978. Reflections on Dr. Borg's life cycle. In *Adulthood*, edited by E. H. Erikson. New York: W. W. Norton & Company.

———. 1980. *Identity and the life cycle.* New York: W. W. Norton & Company.

———. 1982. *The life cycle completed.* New York: W. W. Norton & Company.

Escobar, J., and E. Randolph. 1982. The Hispanic and social networks. In *Mental health and Hispanic Americans.* See Acosta, 1982.

Estes, C. 1979. *The aging enterprise.* San Francisco: Jossey-Bass.

———. 1986. The aging enterprise; In whose interests? *International Journal of Health Services* 16(2):243–51.

Estes, C. L., L. Gerard, J. Zones, and J. Swan. 1984. *Political economy, health and aging.* Boston: Little, Brown & Company.

Evans-Pritchard, E. E. 1940. *The Nuer.* Oxford: Oxford University Press.

Fairley, N. 1981. *The economic roles of male teenagers: The case of Zaire.* Paper presented to the Central States Anthropological Society, Cincinnati.

Farrow, F., T. Joe, J. Meltzer, and H. H. Richman. 1981. The framework and directions for change. In *Policy options in long-term care.* See Butler and Newacheck, 1981.

Featherman, D. L. 1981. The life-span perspective in social science research. In *Policy outlook: Science, technology and the issues of the eighties. Sources*—Vol. 2. A Report from the American Association for the Advancement of Science. Washington, D.C.: Government Printing Office.

Feldman, H. 1964. Development of the husband-wife relationship. Preliminary report, Cornell studies of marital development: Study in the transition to parenthood. Department of Child Development and Family Relationships. New York State College of Home Economics. Cornell University.

Fengler, A. P. 1975. Attitudinal orientations of wives toward their husbands' retirement. *International Journal of Aging and Human Development* 6:139–52.

Finch, C. E., and L. Hayflick, eds. 1977. *Handbook of the biology of aging.* 1st ed. New York: Van Nostrand Reinhold.

Finch, C. E., and E. L. Schneider. 1985. *Handbook of the biology of aging.* 2d ed. New York: Van Nostrand Reinhold.

Finkle, A. L. 1976. Sexual aspects of aging. In *Geriatric psychiatry: A handbook for psychiatrists and primary care physicians,* edited by L. Bellak and J. B. Karasu. New York: Grune & Stratton.

Finkle, A. L., M. I. Tobenkin, and S. J. Karg. 1959. Sexual potency in aging males. I. Frequency of coitus among clinic patients. *Journal of the American Medical Association* 170(12):113–15.

Fischer, D. H. 1978. *Growing old in America.* New York: Oxford University Press.

Fiske, M., and D. Chiriboga. 1985. The interweave of societal and personal change in adulthood. In *Lifespan and change in gerontological perspective,* edited by J. Munnichs, P. Mussen, and E. Olbrich. New York: Academic Press.

Flynn, C. B., C. F. Longino, Jr., R. F. Wiseman, and J. C. Biggar. 1985. The redistribution of America's older population: Major national migration patterns for three census decades, 1960–1980. *The Gerontologist* 25(3):292–96.

Foner, A. 1982. Perspectives on changing age systems. In *Aging from birth to death: Sociotemporal perspectives.* Vol. 2, edited by M. W. Riley, R. S. Abeles, and M. P. Teitelbaum. Boulder, Colo.: Westview Press.

———. 1986. *Aging and old age: New perspectives.* Englewood Cliffs, N.J.: Prentice-Hall.

Foner, A., and D. Kertzer. 1978. Transitions over the life course: Lessons from age-set societies. *American Journal of Sociology* 83:1081–1104.

———. 1979. Intrinsic and extrinsic sources of change in life-course transitions. In *Aging from birth to death: Interdisciplinary perspectives,* edited by M. W. Riley. Boulder, Colo.: Westview Press.

Foner, N. 1984a. Age and social change. In *Age and anthropological theory*. See Beall, 1984.

———. 1984b. *Ages in conflict: A cross-cultural perspective on inequality between old and young*. New York: Columbia University Press.

Fortes, M. 1949. Time and social structure: An Ashanti case study. In *Social structure*, edited by M. Fortes. Oxford: Oxford University Press.

———. 1984. Age, generation, and social structure. In *Age and anthropological theory*. See Beall, 1984.

Foster, D., L. Klinger-Vartabedian, and L. Wispé. 1984. Male longevity and age differences between spouses. *Journal of Gerontology* 39:117–20.

Foucault, M. 1965. *Madness and civilization: A history of insanity in the age of reason*. New York: Pantheon Books.

Fozard, J. L., W. Ernst, B. Bell, R. A. McFarland, and S. Podolosky. 1977. Visual perception and communication. In *Handbook of the psychology of aging*. See Birren and Renner, 1977.

Frank, G. 1980. Life histories in gerontology: The subjective side to aging. In *New methods for old age research*, edited by C. L. Fry and J. Keith. Chicago: Center for Urban Policy, Loyola University of Chicago.

Franklin Research Center. 1980. *Elder abuse*. Washington, D.C.: U.S. Department of Health and Human Services.

Freeman, J. T. 1971. Sexual aspects of aging. In *The care of the geriatric patient*, edited by E. V. Cowdry and F. U. Steinberg. St. Louis: C. V. Mosby.

———. 1961. Sexual capacities in the aging male. *Geriatrics* 16:37–43.

Freud, S. 1965. *New introductory lectures on psychoanalysis*. Translated by J. Strachey. New York: W. W. Norton & Company.

Fried, M. 1967. *The evolution of political society*. New York: Random House.

Friedlander, J. 1976. *Being Indian in Hueyapan*. New York: St. Martin's Press.

Fries, J. F. 1980. Aging, natural death, and the compression of morbidity. *New England Journal of Medicine* 303:130–35.

———. 1984. The compression of morbidity: Miscellaneous comments about a theme. *The Gerontologist* 24:354–59.

Fries, J. F., and L. Crapo. 1981. *Vitality and aging*. San Francisco: W. H. Freeman.

Fry, C. L. 1980. Cognitive anthropology and age differentiation. In *New methods for old age research*. See Frank, 1980.

———, ed. 1981. *Dimensions: Aging, culture, and health*. New York: Praeger.

———. 1983. Temporal and status dimensions of life cycles. *International Journal of Aging and Human Development* 17(4):281–300.

———. 1985. Culture, behavior and aging in the comparative perspective. In *Handbook of the psychology of aging*. See Bengston, Reedy, and Gordon, 1985.

Fry, C. L., and J. Keith. 1980. Introduction. In *New methods for old age research*. See Frank, 1980.

———. 1982. The life course as a cultural unit. In *Aging from birth to death*. See A. Foner, 1982.

Fuchs, V. 1984. Reflections on aging, health, and medical care. *Milbank Memorial Fund Quarterly* 62(2):142–46.

Fujii, S. M. 1976. Elderly Asian Americans and use of public services. *Social Casework* 57(30):202–7.

Funk, J. 1985. Postformal cognition and musical composition. Paper presented in *Beyond formal operations: The development of adolescent and adult thought and reasoning*, organized by M. L. Commons, June, Harvard University.

Furlow, W. L. 1977. Inflatable penile prosthesis: Mayo clinic experience with 175 patients. *Urology* 13(2):1661–70.

Futterweit, W., M. Molitch, J. Morley, and R. S. Cherlin. 1984. Is there a male climacteric? *Medical Aspects of Human Sexuality* 18(4):147–71.

Gardner, E. F., and R. H. Monge. 1977. Adult age differences in cognitive abilities and educational background. *Experimental Aging Research* 3:337–83.

Garrison, R. J., M. Feinleib, W. P. Castelli, and P. McNamara. 1983. Cigarette smoking as a confounder of the relationship between weight and long-term mortality. *Journal of the American Medical Association* 249:2199–2203.

Gebhard, P. 1970. Postmarital coitus among widows and divorcees. In *Divorce and after*, edited by P. Bohannon. Garden City, N.Y.: Doubleday.

Gelfand, D. E. 1982. *Aging: The ethnic factor.* Boston: Little, Brown and Company.

Gelfand, D. E., and A. J. Kutzik. 1979. Conclusion: The continuing significance of ethnicity. In *Ethnicity and Aging.* See Cantor, 1979.

George, L. K., and S. J. Weiler. 1981. Sexuality in middle and late life: The effects of age, cohort, and gender. *Archives of General Psychiatry* 38:919–23.

Gergen, K. J. 1977. Stability, change, and chance in human development. In *Lifespan developmental psychology: Dialectical perspectives on experimental research*, edited by N. Datan and H. W. Reese. New York: Academic Press.

Gerry, R., and H. Wisniewski. 1977. Structural aspects of aging of the brain. In *Cognitive and emotional disturbance in the elderly.* Chicago: Yearbook Medical Publishers.

Gescheider, G. A. 1985. *Psychophysics: Method and theory.* 2d ed. Hillsdale, N.J.: Lawrence Erlbaum.

Gianturco, D. T., and E. W. Busse. 1978. Psychiatric problems encountered during the long-term study of normal aging volunteers. In *Studies in geriatric psychiatry*, edited by A. D. Issacs and F. Post. New York: Wiley & Sons.

Glascock, A. P. 1982. Decrepitude and death-hastening: The nature of old age in third world societies. In *Aging and the aged in the third world: Part I*, edited by J. Sokolovsky. Publication Number 22 of *Studies in Third World Societies* 22:43–66.

Glascock, A. P., and S. L. Feinman. 1980. Toward a comparative framework: Propositions concerning the treatment of the aged in non-industrial societies. In *New methods for old age research.* See Frank, 1980.

———. 1981. Social asset or social burden: Treatment of the aged in non-industrial societies. In *Dimensions.* See Fry, 1981.

Glaser, B. G., and A. L. Strauss. 1964. The social loss of dying patients. *American Journal of Nursing* 64:119–21.

———. 1967. *The discovery of grounded theory: Strategies for qualitative research.* Chicago: Aldine Publishing.

Glenner, G. 1982. Alzheimer's disease (senile dementia). *Journal of the American Geriatrics Society* 30:59–62.

Glueck, C. J., P. Gartside, R. W. Fallat, J. Sielski, and P. M. Steiner. 1976. Longevity syndromes: Familial hypobeta and familial hyperalpha lipoproteinemia. *Journal of Laboratory and Clinical Medicine* 88:941–57.

Glueck, C. J., P. S. Gartside, P. M. Steiner, M. Miller, T. Todhunter, J. Haaf, M. Pucke, M. Terrani, R. W. Fallat, and M. L. Kashyap. 1977. Hyperalphalipoproteinemia and hypobetalipoproteinemia in octogenarian kindreds. *Atherosclerosis* 27:387–406.

Goffman, I. 1961. *Asylums.* Garden City, N.Y.: Anchor Books.

Golan, N. 1986. *The perilous bridge: Helping clients through mid-life transitions.* New York: The Free Press.

Golant, S. M. 1984. Factors influencing the nighttime activity of old persons in their community. *Journal of Gerontology* 39(4):485–91.

Golde, P., and N. A. Kogan. 1959. A sentence completion procedure for assessing attitudes toward old people. *Journal of Gerontology* 14:355–60.

Goldman, H., and J. Morrissey. 1985. The alchemy of mental health policy: Homelessness and the fourth cycle of reform. *American Journal of Public Health* 75(7):727–31.

Goldman, R. 1984. The epidemiology and demography of dementia. *Psychiatric Annals* 14:169–74.

Goldstein, M. C., and C. M. Beall. 1981. Modernization and aging in the third and fourth world: Views from the rural hinterland in Nepal. *Human Organization* 40(81):48–54.

Goldstein, M. C., S. Schuler, and J. L. Ross. 1983. Social and economic forces affecting intergenerational relations in extended families in a third world country: A cautionary tale from South Asia. *Journal of Gerontology* 38(6):717–24.

Golini, A., and V. Egidi. 1984. Effect of morbidity changes on mortality and population size and structures. In *Methodologies for collection and analysis of mortality rates,* edited by J. Vallin, J. H. Pollard, and L. Heligman. Liege, Belgium: International Union for the Scientific Study of Populate.

Gonda, J., M. Quayhagen, and K. W. Schaie. 1979. New tests for old people. Paper presented at the 87th annual meeting of the American Psychological Association, September, New York.

Goodale, J. C. 1971. *Tiwi wives.* Seattle: University of Washington Press.

Goodwin, F. K. 1971. Behavioral effects of L-Dopa in man. *Seminars in Psychiatry* 3:477–92.

Gould, R. L. 1978. *Transformation: Growth and change in adult life.* New York: Simon & Schuster.

Grant, C. 1969. Age differences in self-concept from early adulthood through old age. *Proceedings of the 77th Annual Convention of the American Psychological Association,* 4:717.

Graziadei, P. P. C. 1971. The olfactory mucosa of vertebrates. In *Handbook of sensory physiology.* Vol. 4, edited by L. M. Beidler. New York: Springer Publishing.

Greeley, A. 1974. Ethnicity in the United States. New York: Wiley & Sons.

Green, D. M., and J. A. Swets. 1966. *Signal detection theory and psychophysics.* New York: Wiley & Sons.

Greenberg, L. J., and E. J. Yunis. 1978. Histocompatibility determinants, immune responsiveness and aging in man. *Federation Proceedings* 37:1258–61.

Griffith, J. E. 1985. *How older Americans live: An analysis of census data.* Prepared for the Special Committee on Aging, United States Senate, 99th Cong., 1st Sess. Washington, D.C.: Government Printing Office.

Griffitt, W. 1981. Sexual intimacy in aging marital partners. In *Aging: Stability and change in the family,* edited by R. W. Fogen, E. Hatfield, S. B. Kiesler, and E. Shanas. New York: Academic Press.

Groth, A. N., and W. E. Hobson. 1985. Child molesting. *Medical Aspects of Human Sexuality* 19(5):218–26.

Gruenberg, E. 1978. Epidemiology. In *Aging.* Vol. 7, *Alzheimer's disease: Senile dementia and related disorders,* edited by R. Katzman, R. D. Terry, and K. L. Bick. New York: Raven Press.

Gubrium, J. F. 1973. *The myth of the golden years: A socio-environmental theory of aging.* Springfield, Ill.: Charles C. Thomas.

———. 1975. *Living and dying at Murray Manor.* New York: St. Martin's Press.

Gulliver, P. H. 1965. The Jie of Uganda. In *Peoples of Africa,* edited by J. L. Gibbs. New York: Holt, Rinehart & Winston.

Gurland, B. 1976. The comparative frequency of depression in various adult age groups. *Journal of Gerontology* 31:283–92.

Gutmann, D. L. 1964. An exploration of ego configurations in middle and later life. In *Personality in middle and later life,* edited by B. Neugarten. New York: Atherton.

———. 1969. The country of old men: Cross-cultural studies in the psychology of later life. In *Occasional papers in gerontology,* edited by W. Donahue. Ann Arbor: Institute of Gerontology, University of Michigan.

———. [1969] 1974. Alternatives to disengagement: The old men of the highland Druze. In *Culture and personality.* See Caudill and Plath, 1974.

———. 1975. Parenthood: A key to the comparative study of the life cycle. In *Life-span developmental psychology: Normative life crises,* edited by N. Datan and L. H. Ginsberg. New York: Academic Press.

———. 1977. The cross-cultural perspective: Notes towards a comparative psychology of aging. In *Handbook of the psychology of aging.* See Birren and Renner, 1977.

———. 1979. Use of informal and formal supports by white ethnic aged. In *Ethnicity and aging.* See Cantor, 1979.

———. 1982. Comments on J. K. Brown's "Cross-Cultural Perspectives of Middle-Aged Women." *Current Anthropology* 23(2):151.

———. 1985. Beyond nurture: Developmental perspectives on the vital older woman. In *In her prime.* See Datan, Antonovsky, and Maoz, 1985.

Gutmann, D., J. Grunes, and B. Griffin. 1980. The clinical psychology of later life: Developmental paradigms. In *Lifespan developmental psychology: Transitions of aging,* edited by N. Datan and N. Lohman. New York: Academic Press.

Gutowski, M. 1981. Housing-related needs of the suburban elderly. In *Community housing choices for older Americans.* See Brody and Liebowitz, 1981.

Haan, N. 1981. Common dimensions of personality development: Early adolescence to middle life. In *Present and past in middle life,* edited by D. H. Eichorn, J. A. Clausen, N. Haan, M. P. Honzig, and P. H. Mussen. New York: Academic Press.

Haan, N., and D. Day. 1974. A longitudinal study of change and sameness in personality development: Adolescence to later adulthood. *International Journal of Aging and Human Development* 5:11–39.

Habib, J. 1985. The economy and the aged. In *Handbook of aging and the social sciences.* 2d ed., edited by R. H. Binstock and E. Shanas. New York: Van Nostrand Reinhold.

Halperin, R. H. 1972. Duality reconsidered: Some measures of womanhood in the Caribbean. Paper presented to Northeastern Anthropological Association, Albany, New York.

———. 1975. *Administration agraria y trabajo: Un caso de la economia politica Mexicana.* Mexico City: Instituto Nacional Indigenista.

———. 1980. Ecology and mode of production; Seasonal variation and the division of labor by sex among hunter-gatherers. *Journal of Anthropological Research* 36:379–99.

———. 1982. New and old in economic anthropology. *American Anthropologist* 84:339–49.

———. 1984. Age in cultural economics: An evolutionary approach. In *Age and anthropological theory.* See Beall, 1984.

Halperin, R., and D. Schaiper. n.d. *Age, gender, and technology: Changing units of production on tobacco farms in eastern Kentucky.* Unpublished manuscript.

Halsell, G. 1976. *Los viejos: Secrets of long life from the sacred valley.* Emmaus, Pa.: Rodale Press.

Ham, R., and M. Marcy. 1983. Depression in the elderly. In *Primary care geriatrics.* See Comfort, 1983.

Ham, R., and M. Smith. 1983. The confused elderly patient. In *Primary care geriatrics.* See Comfort, 1983.

Hamilton, G. V. 1939. Changes in personality and psychosexual phenomena with age. In *Problems of aging,* edited by E. V. Cowdry. Baltimore: Williams & Wiklins.

Hamilton, J., and G. Mestler. 1969. Mortality and survival: Comparison of eunuchs with intact men and women in a mentally retarded population. *Journal of Gerontology* 24:395–411.

Hammel, E. 1984. Age in the Fortesian coordinates. In *Age and anthropological theory.* See Beall, 1984.

Hammond, D., and A. Jablow. 1976. *Women in cultures of the world.* Reading, Mass.: Cummings.

Handwerker, W. P. 1983. The first demographic transition: An analysis of subsistence choices and reproductive consequences. *American Anthropologist* 85:5–27.

Harbert, A. S., and C. W. Wilkinson. 1985. Growing old in rural America. In *Aging.* 4th ed., edited by H. Cox. Guilford, Conn.: Dushkin Publishing Group.

Hareven, T. K., ed. 1978. *Transitions: The family and the life course in historical perspective.* New York: Academic Press.

Hareven, T. K., and K. J. Adams. 1982. *Aging and life course transitions: An interdisciplinary perspective.* New York: Guilford Press.

Harkins, S. W., and C. R. Chapman. 1976. Detection and decision factors in pain perception in young and elderly men. *Pain* 2:253–64.

———. 1977. The perception of induced dental pain in young and elderly women. *Journal of Gerontology* 32:428–35.

Harper, J. A. 1983. Coronary heart disease—an epidemic related to diet? *American Journal of Clinical Nutrition* 37:669–81.

Hart, C. W., and A. R. Pilling. 1960. *The Tiwi of northern Australia.* New York: Holt, Rinehart & Winston.

Harvey, C. D., and H. M. Bahr. 1974. Widowhood, morale and affiliation. *Journal of Marriage and the Family* 36:97–106.

Havighurst, R. J. 1952. *Developmental tasks and education.* New York: D. McKay.

Hayflick, L. 1982. Biological aspects of aging. In *Biological and social aspects of mortality and the length of life,* edited by S. H. Preston. Liege, Belgium: Ordina Editions.

Haynes, S., A. McMichael, and H. Tyroler. 1977. Survival after early and normal retirement. In *Second conference on the epidemiology of aging,* edited by S. Haynes and M. Feinleib. N.I.H. Pub. No. 80-969. Washington, D.C.: U.S. Government Printing Office.

———. 1978. Survival after early and normal retirement. *Journal of Gerontology* 33:269–78.

Hazzard, W. R. 1985. The sex differential in longevity. In *Principles of geriatric medicine,* edited by R. Andres, E. Bierman, and W. Hazzard. New York: McGraw Hill.

Health Care Financing Administration. 1981. *Long term care: Background and future directions.* HCFA Publications No. 81-10047. Washington, D.C.: U.S. Department of Health, Human Services.

Hegeler, S., and M. M. Mortensen. 1977. Sexual behavior in elderly males. In *Progress in sexology,* edited by R. Gemme and C. C. Wheeler. New York: Plenum.

Heikinheimo, R. J., M. V. Haavisto, M. K. Koivunen, K. J. Matila, and S. A. Rajala.

1985. Mortality and high haematocrit in the very aged. *Age and Aging* 14:159–62.

Heiman, J. R. 1976. Issues in the use of psychophysiology to assess females sexual dysfunction. *Journal of Sex and Marital Therapy* 2(3):197–204.

Heintz, K. M. 1976. *Retirement communities: For adults only.* New Brunswick, N.J.: Rutgers—The State University of New Jersey, Center for Urban Policy Research.

Hellerstein, H. E., and E. H. Friedman. 1969. Sexual activity and the post coronary patients. *Medical Aspects of Human Sexuality* 3:70.

Helsing, K. J., and M. Szklo. 1981. Mortality after bereavement. In *American Journal of Epidemiology* 114:41–52.

———. 1985. Re: Mortality of widowed vs. married. The authors reply. *American Journal of Epidemiology* 122:722–23.

Hendel-Sebestyen, G. 1979. Role diversity: Toward the development of community in a total institutional setting. *Anthropological Quarterly* 52:19–28.

Henderson, A. S. 1986. The epidemiology of Alzheimer's disease. *British Medical Bulletin* 42:3–10.

Hendricks, J. 1982. The elderly in society: Beyond modernization. *Social Science History* 6(3):321–45.

Henretta, J., and R. Campbell. 1976. Status attainment and status maintenance: A study of stratification in old age. *American Sociological Review* 41:981–92.

Hermanova, H. W. 1983. Human sexuality and aging. In *Aging in the eighties and beyond: Highlights of the twelfth international congress of gerontology*, edited by M. Bergener, U. Lehr, E. Lang, and R. Schmitz-Scherzer. New York: Springer Publishing.

Hertz, R. [1907] 1960. *Death and the right hand.* Translated by R. Needham and C. Needham. Glencoe, Ill.: The Free Press.

Hertzog, C. 1980. Applications of signal detection theory to the study of psychological aging: A theoretical review. In *Aging in the 1980's.* See Cerella, Poon, and Williams, 1980.

Heumann, L., and D. Boldy. 1982. *Housing for the elderly: Planning and policy formulation in Western Europe and North America.* London: Croom Helm.

Heyman, D., and F. C. Jeffers. 1968. Wives and retirement: A pilot study. *Journal of Gerontology* 23:488–96.

Hill, R., and P. Mattessich. 1979. Family development theory and life-span development. In *Life-span development and behavior*, Vol. 2. See Baltes, 1979.

Hinchcliffe, R. 1962. The anatomical locus of presbycusis. *Journal of Speech and Hearing Disorders* 27:301–10.

Hirschi, T., and M. Gottfredson. 1983. Age and the explanation of crime. *American Journal of Sociology* 89(3):552–84.

Hite, S. 1976. *The Hite report.* New York: Macmillan.

Hochschild, A. R. 1973. *The unexpected community.* Englewood Cliffs, N.J.: Prentice-Hall.

Hoebel, E. A. 1954. *The law of primitive man.* Cambridge: Harvard University Press.

Holloway, C., and S. A. Youngblood. 1985–86. Survival after retirement. *International Journal of Aging and Human Development* 22:45–54.

Holmberg, A. R. 1969. *Nomads of the long bow.* Garden City, N.Y.: Natural History Press.

Holmes, D. R. 1982. *A Peasant-worker model in a northern Italian context.* Unpublished manuscript.

Holmes, L. D. 1972. The role and status of the aged in a changing Samoa. In *Aging and modernization.* See Cowgill, 1972.

———. 1980. Anthropology and age: An assessment. In *Aging in culture and society.* See Cool, 1980.

———. 1983. *Other cultures, elder years: An introduction to cultural gerontology.* Minneapolis: Burgess Publishing.

Holmes, T., and R. Rahe. 1967. The social readjustment rating scale. *Journal of Psychosomatic Research* 11:213–18.

Holzberg, C. S. 1982a. Ethnicity and aging: Anthropological perspectives on more than just the minority elderly. *The Gerontologist* 22(30):249–57.

———. 1982b. Ethnicity and aging: Rejoinder to a comment by Kyriakos S. Markides. *The Gerontologist* 22(6):471–72.

———. 1983–84. Anthropology, life histories, and the aged: The Toronto Baycrest Center. *International Journal of Aging and Human Development* 18(4):255–75.

Hooper, F. H., J. Fitzgerald, and D. Papalia. 1971. Piagetian theory and the aging process: Extensions and speculations. *International Journal of Aging and Human Development* 2:3–20.

Hoover, R., A. Laman, P. Cole, and B. MacMahon. 1976. Menopausal estrogens and breast cancer. *New England Journal of Medicine* 295(8):401–5.

Horn, J. L. 1976. Human abilities: A review of research and theory in the early 1970s. *Annual Review of Psychology* 17:437–82.

Horton, C. F. 1984. Women have headaches, men have backaches! Patterns of illness in an Appalachian community. *Social Science and Medicine* 19(6):647–54.

Howard, D. 1983. *Cognitive psychology: Memory, language, and thought.* New York: Macmillan.

Howell, N. 1979. *Demography of the Dobe !Kung.* New York: Academic Press.

Hoyer, W. J., and D. J. Plude. 1980. Attentional and perceptual processes in the study of cognitive aging. In *Aging in the 1980's: Psychological issues.* See Cerella, Poon, and Williams, 1980.

———. 1982. Aging and the allocation of attentional resources in visual information processes. In *Aging and human visual function,* edited by R. Sekuler, D. Kline, and K. Dismukes. New York: Alan R. Liss.

———. 1985. Attentional factors and visual function. *Geriatric Ophthalmology* 1:32–37.

Hoyer, W. J., C. L. Raskind, and J. P. Abrahams. 1984. Research practices in the psychology of aging: A survey of research published in the *Journal of Gerontology,* 1975–1982. *Journal of Gerontology* 39:44–48.

Hrdy, S. B. 1981. "Nepotists" and "altruists": The behavior of old females among macaques and langur monkeys. In *Other ways of growing old.* See Amoss, 1981.

Huber, P. S. 1972. Death and society among the Anggor of New Guinea. *Omega* 3:233–43.

Hulicka, I. M. 1967. Age differences in retention as a function of interference. *Journal of Gerontology* 22:180–84.

Hultsch, D. F., and R. A. Dixon. 1983. The role of pre-experimental knowledge in text processing in adulthood. *Experimental Aging Research* 9:17–22.

Hutchinson, I. W., III. 1975. The significance of marital status for morale and life satisfaction among lower-income elderly. *Journal of Marriage and the Family* 34(2):287–93.

Hyman, H. H. 1983. *Of time and widowhood: Nationwide studies of enduring effects.* Durham, N.C.: Duke University Press.

Igbal, K., and H. K. Wisniewski. 1983. Neurofibrillary tangles. In *Alzheimer's disease.* See Ball, 1983.

Jackson, J. J. 1970. Aged Negroes: Their cultural departures from statistical stereotypes and rural-urban differences. *Gerontologist* 10:140–45.

———. 1971. Compensatory care for the black aged. *Minority aged in America*. Occasional paper #10. Ann Arbor: University of Michigan Press.

———. 1973. Help me somebody! I's an old black standing in the need of institutionalizing! *Psychiatric Opinion* 10(6):6–16.

———. 1980. *Minorities and aging*. Belmont, Calif.: Wadsworth Publishing.

Jacobs, J. 1974. *Fun City: An ethnographic study of a retirement community*. New York: Holt, Rinehart & Winston.

———. 1975. *Older persons and retirement communities*. Springfield, Ill.: Charles C. Thomas.

Jacquard, A. 1982. Heritability of human longevity. In *Biological and social aspects of mortality and the length of life*, edited by S. H. Preston. Liege, Belgium: Ordina Editions.

James, W. 1950. *The principles of psychology*, Vol. 1. New York: Dover.

Janis, I. L., and L. Mann. 1977. *Decision making: A psychological analysis of conflict, choice, and commitment*. New York: The Free Press.

Jaques, E. 1970. *Work, creativity, and social justice*. London: Heinemann.

Jarvik, L. F., A. Falik, F. J. Kallman, I. Lorge. 1960. Survival trends in a senescent twin populations. *American Journal of Human Genetics* 12:170–79.

Jerger, J. 1973. Audiological findings in aging. *Advances in Oto-Rhino-Laryngology* 20:115–24.

Jirovec, R. L., M. M. Jirovec, and R. Bosse. 1985. Environmental determinants of neighborhood satisfaction among urban elderly men. *The Gerontologist*, 24(3):261–65.

Johnson, C. L. 1977. Interdependence, reciprocity and indebtedness: An analysis of Japanese-American kinship relations. *Journal of Marriage and the Family* 36(May):351–63.

———. 1983a. A cultural analysis of the grandmother. *Research on Aging* 5(4):547–67.

———. 1983b. Dyadic family relations and social support. *The Gerontologist* 23(4):377–83.

———. 1985a. The impact of illness on late-life marriages. *Journal of Marriage and the Family* 44(February):165–72.

———. 1985b. Grandparenting options in divorcing families: An anthropological perspective. In *Grandparenthood*, edited by V. L. Bengston and J. F. Robertson. Beverly Hills: Sage Publications.

Johnson, C. L., and D. J. Catalano. 1981. Childless elderly and their family supports. *The Gerontologist* 21(6):610–618.

———. 1983. A longitudinal study of family supports. *The Gerontologist* 23(6):612–18.

Johnson, C. L., and L. Grant. 1985. *The nursing home in American society*. Baltimore: Johns Hopkins University Press.

Johnson, O. R., and A. Johnson. 1975. Male/female relations and the organization of work in a Machiguenga community. *American Ethnologist* 2:634–48.

Johnson, S. K. 1971. *Idle haven: Community building among the working class retired*. Berkeley: University of California Press.

Jokinen, K. 1973. Presbycusis VI: Masking of speech. In *Acta Oto-Laryngologica* 76:426–30.

Jones, M. C., N. Bayley, J. W. Macfarlane, and M. P. Honzik, eds. 1971. *The course of human development*. New York: Wiley & Sons.

Jorgensen, D. 1985. Femsap's last garden: A telefol response to mortality. In *Aging and its transformations*. See Counts and Counts, 1985a.

Jung, C. G. 1933. *Modern man in search of a soul.* New York: Harcourt Brace.
———. 1953. On the psychology of the unconscious. In *Collected works. Vol. 7, Two essays on analytical psychology.* New York: Pantheon Books.
———. 1954. Marriage as a psychological relationship. In *Collected works. Vol. 17, The development of personality.* New York: Pantheon Books.
———. 1960. The stages of life. In *Collected works, Vol. 8, The structure and dynamics of the psyche.* New York: Pantheon Books.
Kagan, D. 1980. Activity and aging in a Colombian peasant village. In *Aging in culture and society.* See Cool, 1980.
Kagan, J., and H. Moss. 1962. *Birth to maturity: A study in psychological maturation.* New York: Wiley & Sons.
Kahana, E. 1982. A congruence model of person-environment interaction. In *Aging and the environment: Theoretical approaches,* edited by M. P. Lawton, P. G. Windley, and T. O. Byerts. New York: Springer Publishing.
Kahana, E. and B. Kahana. 1983. Environmental continuity, futurity, and adaptation of the aged. In *Aging and milieu: Environmental perspectives on growing old,* edited by G. D. Rowles and R. J. Ohta. New York: Academic Press.
Kahn, R. L., and T. C. Antonucci. 1980. Convoys over the life course: Attachment, roles, and social support. In *Life-span development and behavior,* Vol. 3. See Brim and Ryff, 1980.
Kahn, R. L., A. I. Goldfarb, M. Pollack, and A. Peck. 1960. Brief objective measures for the determination of mental status in the aged. *American Journal of Psychiatry* 117:326–28.
Kalish, R. A. 1985. *Death, grief, and caring relationships.* 2d ed. Monterey, Calif.: Brooks/Cole.
Kalish, R. A., and D. K. Reynolds. 1981. *Death and ethnicity: A psychocultural study.* Farmingdale, N.Y.: Baywood Publishing.
Kallman, F. J., and G. Sander. 1948. Twin studies on aging and longevity. *The Journal of Heredity* 39:349–57.
Kane, R. I., and R. A. Kane. 1978. Care of the aged: Old problems in need of new solutions. *Science* 200(May 26):913–19.
———. 1982. *Values and long-term care.* Lexington, Mass.: Lexington Books.
Kaplan, A., E. Glanville, and R. Fischer. 1965. Cumulative effect of age and smoking on taste sensitivity in males and females. *Journal of Gerontology* 20:334–37.
Kaplan, H. S., and C. J. Sager. 1971. Sexual patterns at different ages. *Medical Aspects of Human Sexuality* 5(6):10–23.
Karacan, I., F. B. Scott, P. J. Salis, S. L. Attia, J. C. Ware, A. Altinel, and R. L. Williams. 1977. Nocturnal erections, differential diagnosis of impotence and diabetes. *Biological Psychiatry* 12(3):373–80.
Kart, C. S., and B. L. Beckham. 1976. Black-white differentials in the institutionalization of the elderly. *Social Forces* 54(4):901–10.
Kasl, S. 1972. Physical and mental health effects of involuntary relocation and institutionalization of the elderly—A review. *American Journal of Public Health* 62:377–84.
Kassel, V. 1966. Polygyny after 60. *Geriatrics* 21:214–18.
Kastenbaum, R. J. 1981. *Death, society, and human experience.* 2d ed. St. Louis: C. V. Mosby.
Katz, M. B. 1982. Families and early industrialization: Cycle, structure, and economy. In *Aging from birth to death.* See A. Foner, 1982.
Kaufert, P. A. 1985. Midlife in the Midwest: Canadian women in Manitoba. In *In her prime.* See Datan, Antonovsky, and Maoz, 1985.

Kausler, D. H. 1982. *Experimental psychology and human aging*. New York: Wiley & Sons.

Kay, D. 1977. The epidemiology and identification of brain deficit in the elderly. In *Cognitive and emotional disturbance in the elderly*, edited by C. Eisdorfer and R. Friedel. Chicago: Yearbook Medical Publishers.

Kay, D., P. Beamish, and M. Roth. 1964. Old age mental disorders in Newcastle-upon-Tyne: Part 1. A study of prevalence. *British Journal of Psychiatry* 110:146–58.

Kay, D., and K. Bergmann. 1980. Epidemiology of mental disorders among the aged in the community. In *Handbook of mental health and aging*. See Comfort, 1980.

Keating, N., and P. Cole. 1980. What do I do with him 24 hours a day? Changes in the housewife role after retirement. *The Gerontologist* 20:84–89.

Keith, J. 1979. The ethnography of old age. *Anthropological Quarterly* 52:1–6.

———. 1980. The best is yet to be: Toward an anthropology of age. In *Annual review of anthropology*, edited by B. Siegel. Palo Alto, Calif.: Annual Reviews.

———. 1982. *Old people as people: Social and cultural influences on aging and old age*. Boston: Little, Brown and Company.

Keith, J., and D. I. Kertzer. 1984. Introduction. In *Age and anthropological theory*. See Beall, 1984.

Keller, J. W., D. Sherry, C. Piotrowski. 1984. Perspectives on death: A developmental study. *Journal of Psychology* 116:137–42.

Kendig, H. 1976. Neighborhood conditions of the aged and local government. *The Gerontologist* 16:148–56.

Kenshalo, D. R. 1977. Age changes in touch, vibration, temperature, kinesthesis, and pain sensitivity. In *Handbook of the psychology of aging*. See Birren and Renner, 1977.

Kensinger, K. M., P. Rabineau, H. Tanner, S. G. Ferguson, and A. Dawson. 1975. *The Cashinahua of eastern Peru*. Vol. 1 of *Brown University studies in anthropology and material culture*. Providence, R.I.: Brown University Press.

Kent, D. P. 1971. The Negro aged. *Gerontologist* 11:48–50.

Kent, S. 1975. The intimate relationship between the urinary system and sexual function. *Geriatrics* June:138–43.

Kertzer, D. 1978. Theoretical developments in the study of age-group systems. *American Ethnologist* 5:368–74.

———. 1982. Generation and age in cross-cultural perspective. In *Aging from birth to death*. See A. Foner, 1982.

———. 1983. Generation as a social problem. *Annual Review of Sociology* 9:125–49.

Kertzer, D. I., and J. Keith, eds. 1984. *Age and anthropological theory*. Ithaca, N.Y.: Cornell University Press.

Kertzer, D. I., and O. B. B. Madison. 1981. Women's age-set systems in Africa: The Latuka of southern Sudan. In *Dimensions*. See Fry, 1981.

Kiefer, C. W. 1983. Care of the aged in Japan. Paper presented at the Social Science Research Council Conference on Health and Illness in Japan. Chicago, Illinois.

Kim, B.-L. D. 1973. Asian-Americans: No model minority. *Social Work* 18:44–53.

Kinsey, A. C., W. B. Pomeroy, and C. E. Martin. 1948. *Sexual behavior in the human male*. Philadelphia: W. B. Saunders Co.

———. 1953. *Sexual behavior in the human female*. Philadelphia: W. B. Saunders Co.

Kirkwood, T. B. L. 1985. Comparative and evolutionary aspects of longevity. In *Handbook of the biology of aging*. See Finch and Schneider, 1985.

Kitchener, K. S. 1983. Cognition, metacognition, and epistemic cognition. A three-level model of cognitive processing. *Human Development* 26:222–32.

Kivnick, H. Q. 1984. Grandparents and family relations. In *Independent aging*. See Cole, 1984.

Klemmack, D. L., and L. L. Roff. 1980. Heterosexual alternatives to marriage: Appropriateness for older persons. *Alternative Lifestyles* 3(2):137–48.

Kline, D. W., and J. E. Birren. 1975. Age differences in backward dichoptic masking. *Experimental Aging Research* 1:17–25.

Kline, D. W., and F. Schieber. 1981. Visual aging: A transient/sustained shift? *Perception & Psychophysics* 29:181–82.

———. 1985. Vision and aging. In *Handbook of the psychology of aging*. See Bengston, Reedy, and Gordon, 1985.

Kline, D. W., and J. Szafran. 1975. Age differences in backward monoptic visual noise masking. *Journal of Gerontology* 30:307–11.

Koff, T. H. 1980. *Hospice: A caring community*. Cambridge, Mass.: Winthrop.

Kogan, N. 1973. Creativity and cognitive style: A life span perspective. In *Life-span developmental psychology: Personality and socialization*, edited by P. B. Baltes and K. W. Schaie. New York: Academic Press.

Kolata, G. B. 1974. !Kung hunter-gatherers: Feminism, diet, and birth control. *Science* 85:932–34.

Koplowitz, H. 1984. A projection beyond Piaget's formal-operations stage. In *Beyond formal operations*. See Commons, Richards, and Armon, 1984.

Kornhaber, A., and K. Woodward. 1981. *Grandparents/grandchildren: The vital connection*. Garden City, N.Y.: Anchor Press/Doubleday.

Koslov, V. 1984. Longevity in Abkhasia. *The Gerontologist* 24:446.

Kovar, J. 1977. Elderly people: The population 65 years and over. In *Health: United States 1976–1977*. U.S. Department of Health Education and Welfare, DHEW publications No. (HRA) 77-121232, 3–25.

Kramer, D. A. 1983a. Post-formal operations? A need for further conceptualization. *Human Development* 26:91–105.

———. 1983b. *Structural and developmental features of relativistic and dialectical thought*. Unpublished doctoral dissertation, Temple University.

———. 1984. *A study of wisdom-related processes in adults of varying ages: A proposal*. Unpublished manuscript available from author.

———. 1985. The development of awareness of contradiction across the lifespan and the question of post-formal operations. Presented in *Beyond formal operations*. See Funk, 1985.

Kramer, D. A., and F. Dittmann-Kohli. 1984. A taxonomy of tasks in cognitive aging: An action-in-context approach. Paper presented at the 37th annual meetings of the Gerontological Society, November, San Antonio, Texas.

Kramer, D. A., and D. S. Woodruff. 1984. Categorization and metaphoric processing in young and older adults. *Research on Aging* 6:271–86.

———. 1986. Relativistic and dialectical thought in three adult age groups. *Human Development* 29:280–90.

Kripke, D. F., and D. Wingard. 1985. Mortality risk factors in the elderly. *American Journal of Public Health* 75:788–89.

Kübler-Ross, E. 1969. *On death and dying*. New York: Macmillan.

Kuhn, D., N. Pennington, and B. Leadbeater. 1983. Adult thinking in developmental perspective. In *Life-span development and behavior*, edited by P. B. Baltes and O. Brim. New York: Academic Press.

Kuhn, M. 1976. Sexual myths surrounding the aging. In *Sex and the life cycle*. See Berman and Lief, 1976.

Kutza, E. 1981. Allocating long-term-care services. In *Policy options in long-term care*. See Butler and Newacheck, 1981.

Kuwabara, T. 1975. The maturation process of the lens cell: A morphologic study. *Experimental Eye Research*, 20:427–43.

Kuypers, J. A., and V. L. Bengston. 1973. Social breakdown and competence: A model of normal aging. *Human Development* 16:181–201.

———. 1984. Perspectives on the older family. In *Independent aging*. See Cole 1984.

Labouvie, E. W. 1975. The dialectical nature of measurement activities in the behavioral sciences. *Human Development* 18:396–403.

Labouvie-Vief, G. 1977. Adult cognitive development: In search of alternative interpretations. *Merrill Palmer Quarterly* 23:227–63.

———. 1982. Dynamic development and mature autonomy. A theoretical prologue. *Human Development* 25:161–91.

———. 1985. Intelligence and cognition. In *Handbook of the psychology of aging*. See Bengston, Reedy, and Gordon, 1985.

Labouvie-Vief, G., and M. J. Chandler. 1978. Cognitive development and life-span developmental theory: Idealistic versus contextual perspectives. In *Life-span development and behavior*. Vol. 1, edited by P. B. Baltes. New York: Academic Press.

Labouvie-Vief, G., and D. A. Schell. 1982. Learning and memory in later life: A developmental view. In *Handbook of developmental psychology*, edited by B. Wolman and G. Stricker. Englewood Cliffs, N.J.: Prentice-Hall.

Lachman, R., J. L. Lachman, and E. C. Butterfield. 1979. *Cognitive psychology and information processing: An introduction*. Hillsdale, N.J.: Lawrence Erlbaum.

La Fontaine, J. S. 1978. Introduction. In *Sex and age as principles of social differentiation*, J. S. La Fontaine. New York: Academic Press.

Lamy, P., and M. Kitler. 1971. Drugs and the geriatric patient. *Journal of the American Geriatrics Society* 19(1):23–33.

Lancaster, J. B. 1985. Evolutionary perspectives on sex differences in the higher primates. In *Gender and the life course*. See Cancian, 1985.

Larsson, L. 1982. Aging in mammalian skeletal muscle. In *The aging motor system*, edited by J. A. Mortimer, F. J. Pirozzolo, and G. J. Maletta. New York: Praeger.

Laslett, P. 1976. Societal development and aging. In *Handbook of aging and the social sciences*. See Carp, 1976b.

La Torre, R. A., and K. Kear. 1977. Attitudes toward sex in the aged. *Archives Sexual Behavior* 6:203–13.

Lawton, M. P. 1975. Competence, environmental press, and adaptation. In *Theory development in environment and aging*, edited by P. G. Windley, T. O. Byerts, and F. G. Ernst. Washington, D.C.: The Gerontology Society.

———. 1979. How the elderly live. In *Environmental context of aging: Life-styles, environmental quality, and living arrangements*, edited by T. O. Byerts, S. C. Howell, and L. A. Pastalan. New York: Garland STPM Press.

———. 1980. *Environment and aging*. Monterey, Calif.: Brooks/Cole Publishing.

———. 1982. Competence, environmental press, and the adaptation of older people. In *Aging and the environment*. See Kahana, 1982.

Lawton, M. P., and J. Cohen. 1974. The generality of housing impact on the well-being of older people. *Journal of Gerontology* 29:194–204.

Lawton, M. P., and S. L. Hoover. 1981. Introduction. In *Community housing choices for older Americans*. See Brody and Liebowitz, 1981.

Lawton, M. P., M. Moss, and E. Moles. 1984. The supra-personal neighborhood context of older people: Age heterogeneity and well-being. *Environment and Behavior* 16(1):89–109.

Lawton, M. P., and B. Simon. 1968. The ecology of social relationships in housing for the elderly. *The Gerontologist* 8:108–15.

Layton, B. 1975. Perceptual noise and aging. *Psychological Bulletin* 82:875–83.

Leacock, E. 1978. Women's status in egalitarian society: Implications for social evolution. *Current Anthropology* 19:247–75.

Leaf, A. 1973a. Unusual longevity: The common denominators. *Hospital Practice* 8:75–87.

———. 1973b. Getting old. *Scientific American* 229:45–52.

———. 1982. Long-lived populations: Extreme old age. *Journal of the American Geriatrics Society* 38:485–87.

Lee, G. R. 1978. Marriage and morale in later life. *Journal of Marriage and the Family* 40(February):131–39.

Lee, R. B. 1968. What hunters do for a living, or how to make out on scarce resources. In *Man the hunter*. See Dunn, 1968.

———. 1979. *The !Kung San: Men, women, and work in a foraging society*. Cambridge: Cambridge University Press.

———. 1984. *The Dobe !Kung*. New York: Holt, Rinehart & Winston.

Lehman, H. C. 1953. *Age and achievement*. Princeton, N.J.: Princeton University Press.

Lemere, F., and J. W. Smith. 1973. Alcohol-induced sexual impotence. *American Journal of Psychiatry* 130:212–13.

Lepowsky, M. 1985. Gender, aging, and dying in an egalitarian society. In *Aging and its transformation*. See Counts and Counts, 1985a.

Lerner, R. M., and N. A. Busch-Rossnagel, eds. 1981. *Individuals as producers of their development: A life-span perspective*. New York: Academic Press.

Levinson, D. 1978. *The seasons of a man's life*. New York: Knopf.

Lévi-Strauss, C. 1974. *Tristes tropiques*. Translated from the French by J. Weightman and D. Weightman. New York: Atheneum.

Lew, E. A., and L. Garfinkel. 1979. Variations in mortality by weight among 750,000 men and women. *Journal of Chronic Diseases* 32:563–76.

Lewis, M. 1980. Developmental theories. In *Handbook on stress and anxiety*, edited by I. L. Kutash, L. B. Schlesinger, and Associates. San Francisco: Jossey-Bass.

Lewis, R. A. 1979. Macular degeneration in the aged. In *Special senses in aging*. See Black, 1979.

Liang, J., and E. J.-C. Tu. 1986. Estimating lifetime risk of nursing home residency: A further note. *The Gerontologist* 26(5):560–63.

Liebow, E. 1967. *Tally's corner*. Boston: Little, Brown and Company.

Lifton, R. J. 1971. Protean man. *Archives of General Psychiatry* 24:298–301.

Lindsay, P. H., and D. A. Norman. 1977. *Human information processing: An introduction to psychology*. New York: Academic Press.

Lints, F. A. 1978. *Genetics and aging*. Basel, Switzerland: S. Karger.

Liptzin, B. 1982. Psychiatric aspects of aging. In *Health and disease in old age*. See Besdine, 1982.

Little, V. C. 1983. Introduction: Cross-national reports on elder care in developed and developing countries. *The Gerontologist* 23(6):573–75.

Livson, N. 1973. Developmental dimensions of personality: A life-span formulation. In *Life-span developmental psychology*. See Kogan, 1973.

Locke, M. 1982. Models and practice in medicine: Menopause as syndrome or life transition. *Culture, Medicine and Psychiatry* 6:261–80.

Longino, C. F., Jr. 1981. Retirement communities. In *The dynamics of aging*, edited by F. J. Berghorn, D. E. Schafer, and Associates. Boulder, Colo.: Westview Press.

———. 1982. Changing aged nonmetropolitan migration patterns, 1955–60 and 1965–70. *Journal of Gerontology* 37(2):228–34.

————. 1984. Migration winners and losers. *American Demographics* 6(December):27–29, 45.

Lopata, H. Z. 1971. Widows as a minority group. *The Gerontologist* 11(1, part 2):67–77.

————. 1973. *Widowhood in an American city.* Cambridge, Mass.: Schenkman Publishing.

————. 1975. Support systems of elderly urbanites: Chicago of the 1970's. *The Gerontologist,* 15(1):35–41.

————. 1978. Contributions of extended families to the support systems of metropolitan area widows: Limitations of the modified kin network. *Journal of Marriage and the Family* 40(May):355–64.

————. [1977] 1979. Widows and widowers. In *The age of aging: A reader in social gerontology,* edited by A. Monk. Buffalo, N.Y.: Prometheus Books.

Los Angeles Times. 1983. Bear Bryant has left his legacy on sidelines. January 27, Part III:1, 10–11.

————. 1983. 8,000 mourners pay last tribute to Bryant. January 29, Part III:1, 13.

Lovejoy, C. O., R. S. Meindl, T. R. Pryzbeck, T. S. Barton, K. G. Heiple, and D. Kotting. 1977. Paleodemography of the Libben Site, Ottawa County, Ohio. *Science* 198:291–93.

Lowenthal, M. F., and D. Chiriboga. 1973. Social stress and adaptation: Toward a lifecourse perspective. In *The psychology of adult development and aging,* edited by C. Eisdorfer and M. P. Lawton. Washington, D.C.: American Psychological Association.

Lowenthal, M. F., and C. Haven. 1968. Interaction and adaptation: Intimacy as a critical variable. *American Sociological Review* 33(1):20–30.

Lowenthal, M. F., M. Thurnher, and D. Chiriboga. 1975. *Four stages of life: A comparative study of women and men facing transitions.* San Francisco: Jossey-Bass.

Lubitz, J., and R. Prihoda. 1984. The use and costs of medicare services in the last 2 years of life. *Health Care Financing Review* 5(3):117–31.

Maas, H., and J. Kuypers. 1974. *From thirty to seventy.* San Francisco: Jossey-Bass.

Mace, N., and P. Rabins. 1981. *The 36-hour day.* Baltimore: Johns Hopkins University Press.

Madden, D. J., and R. D. Nebes. 1980. Aging and the development of automaticity in visual search. *Developmental Psychology* 16:377–84.

Maddison, D. and A. Viola. 1968. The health of widows in the year following bereavement. *Journal of Psychosomatic Research* 12:297–306.

Maddox, G. 1969. Growing old: Getting beyond the stereotypes. In *Foundations of practical gerontology,* edited by R. Boy and C. Oakes. Columbia: University of South Carolina Press.

Maddox, G. L., and R. T. Campbell. 1985. Scope, concepts, and methods in the study of aging. In *Handbook of aging and the social sciences.* See Habib, 1985.

Madigan, F. 1957. Are sex mortality differentials biologically caused? *Milbank Memorial Fund Quarterly* 35:202–23.

Maduro, R. 1974. Artistic creativity and aging in India. *International Journal of Aging and Human Development* 5:303–27.

Maeda, D. 1983. Family care in Japan. *The Gerontologist* 23(6):579–83.

Makinodan, T. 1977. Immunity and aging. In *Handbook of the biology of aging.* See Finch and Hayflick, 1977.

Maldonado, D. 1975. The Chicano aged. *Social Work* 20(3):213–16.

————. 1985. The Hispanic elderly: A socio-historical framework for public policy. *Journal of Applied Gerontology* 4:18–27.

Malik, M. O. A. 1979. Sudden coronary deaths associated with sexual activity. *Journal of Forensic Sciences* 24(1):216–20.

Malinowski, B. 1978. *Coral gardens and their magic*. New York: Dover.

Manard, B., C. Kart, and D. van Gils. 1975. *Old-age institutions*. Lexington, Mass.: Lexington Books.

Mancini, J. A. 1983. Research on family life in old age: Exploring the frontiers. In *Family relationships in later life*. See Ade-Ridder and Brubaker, 1983.

Mann, A. E. 1975. *Paleodemographic aspects of the South African australopithecines*. Philadelphia: University of Pennsylvania Publications in Anthropology, No. 1.

Manton, K. G. 1980. Sex and race specific mortality differentials in multiple cause of death data. *The Gerontologist* 20:480–93.

———. 1982. Changing concepts of morbidity and mortality in the elderly population. *Milbank Memorial Fund Quarterly* 60(2):183–244.

Manton, K. G., S. S. Poss, and S. Wing. 1979. The black/white mortality crossover. *The Gerontologist* 19:291–300.

Manton, K. G., and B. J. Soldo. 1985. Dynamics of health changes in the oldest old: New perspectives and evidence. *Milbank Memorial Fund Quarterly* 63(2):206–85.

Markides, K. S. 1982. Ethnicity and aging: A comment. *The Gerontologist* 22(6):467–70.

———. 1983. Mortality among minority populations: A review of recent patterns and trends. *Public Health Reports* 98:252–60.

Markides, K. S., and R. Machalek. 1984. Selective survival, aging and society. *Archives of Gerontology and Geriatrics* 3:207–22.

Markson, E. 1979. Ethnicity as a factor in the institutionalization of the ethnic elderly. In *Ethnicity and aging*. See Cantor, 1979.

Marris, P. 1974. *Loss and change*. New York: Random House.

Marshall, L. 1981. Auditory processing in aging listeners. *Journal of Speech and Hearing Disorders* 46:226–40.

Martin, E. P., and J. M. Martin. 1978. *The black extended family*. Chicago: University of Chicago Press.

Martin, G. M. 1985. Genetics of human disease, longevity and aging. In *Principles of geriatric medicine*, edited by R. Andres, E. Bierman, and W. Hazzard. New York: McGraw Hill.

Massie, E., E. F. Rose, J. C. Rupp, and R. W. Whelton. 1969. Viewpoints: Sudden death during coitus—fact or fiction. *Medical Aspects of Human Sexuality* 3(6):22–26.

Masters, W. H., and V. E. Johnson. 1966. *Human sexual response*. Boston: Little, Brown and Company.

———. 1970. *Human sexual inadequacy*. Boston: Little, Brown and Company

———. 1981. Sex and the aging process. *Journal of the American Geriatrics Society* 29(9):385–90.

Matthews, S. H., and J. Sprey. 1984. The impact of divorce on grandparenthood: An exploratory study. *The Gerontologist* 24(1):41–47.

Mattis, S. 1976. Mental status examination for organic mental syndrome in the elderly patient. In *Geriatric psychiatry*. See Finkle, 1976.

Mauss, M. 1966. Essai sur le don: Forme et raison de l'échange dans les sociétés archaiques. In *Sociologie et Anthropologie*. Paris: Presses Universitaires de France.

Maxwell, E. K. 1975. Dynamic aspects of ritual performance: A resource in decline? Paper presented at the 28th Annual Meeting of the Gerontological Society of America, October 26–30, Louisville, Kentucky.

Maxwell, E. K., and R. J. Maxwell. 1980a. Search and research in ethnology: Continuous comparative analysis. *Behavior Science Research* 15:219–43.

———. 1980b. Contempt for the elderly: A cross-cultural analysis. *Current Anthropology* 21(4):569–70.

Maxwell, R. J., and P. Silverman. 1970. Information and esteem: Cultural considerations in the treatment of the aged. *International Journal of Aging and Human Development* 1(4):361–92.

———. 1987. Gerontocide. In *The content of culture*, edited by R. Bolton. New Haven, Conn: HRAF Press.

Maxwell, R. J., P. Silverman, and E. K. Maxwell. 1982. The motive for gerontocide. In *Aging and the aged in the third world: Part I*, edited by J. Sokolovsky. Publication Number 22 of *Studies in Third World Societies* 22:67–84.

Mayberry-Lewis, D. 1984. Age and kinship: A structural view. In *Age and anthropological theory*. See Beall, 1984.

Mayer, P. J. 1982. Evolutionary advantage of the menopause. *Human Ecology* 10:477–94.

Mazess, R., and S. Foreman. 1979. Longevity and age exaggeration in Vilcabamba, Ecuador. *Journal of Gerontology* 34:94–98.

Mazess, R., and R. W. Mathisen, 1982. Lack of unusual longevity in Vilcabamba, Ecuador. *Human Biology* 54:517–24.

McArdle, J. L., and C. Yeracaris. 1981. Respect for the elderly in preindustrial societies as related to their activity. *Behavior Science Research* 16(3 and 4):307–39.

McCrae, R. R., and P. T. Costa, Jr. 1984. *Emerging lives. Enduring dispositions: Personality in adulthood.* Boston: Little, Brown and Company.

McCreary, C. P. 1979. Criminality and the aging. In *Psychopathology of aging*, edited by O. J. Kaplan. New York: Academic Press.

McFarland, R. A., and M. B. Fisher. 1955. Alterations in dark adaptation as a function of age. *Journal of Gerontology* 10:424–28.

McFarland, R. A., A. B. Warren, and C. Karis. 1958. Alterations in critical flicker frequency as a function of age and light: Dark ratio. *Journal of Experimental Psychology* 56:529–38.

McKain, W. 1967. Are they really that old? *The Gerontologist* 7:70–73, 80.

McKain, W. C., Jr. 1972. A new look at older marriages. *The Family Coordinator* 21(1):61–69.

McKee, J. P., and W. S. Turner. 1961. The relation of drive ratings in adolescence to CPI and EPPS scores in adulthood. *Vita Humana* 4:1–9.

McKellin, W. H. 1985. Passing away and loss of life: Aging and death among the Managalase of Papua New Guinea. In *Aging and its transformations*. See Counts and Counts, 1985a.

McNeely, R. L., and J. L. Cohen, eds. 1983. *Aging in minority groups.* Beverly Hills: Sage Publications.

Mead, M. 1961. *Coming of age in Samoa.* New York: Morrow Quill Paperbacks.

Medawar, P. B. 1952. *An unsolved problem of biology.* London: H. K. Lewis.

Medvedev, Z. A. 1974. Caucasus and Altay longevity: A biological or social problem? *The Gerontologist* 14:381–87.

Melzack, R. 1973. *The puzzle of pain.* New York: Basic Books.

Merriam, A. P. 1971. Aspects of sexual behavior among the Bala. In *Human sexual behavior: Variations in the ethnographic spectrum*, edited by D. S. Marshall and R. C. Suggs. New York: Basic Books.

Messer, M. 1967. The possibility of an age-concentrated environment becoming a normative system. *The Gerontologist* 7:247–51.

———. 1968. Age grouping and the family status of the elderly. *Sociologist and Social Research* 52(3):271–79.

Michaelson, E. J. and W. Goldschmidt. 1971. Female role and male dominance among peasants. *Southwestern Journal of Anthropology* 27:330–52.

Middleton, L. 1984. *Alzheimer's family support groups.* Tampa: University of South Florida, Suncoast Gerontology Center.

Miller, G. 1980. Male-female longevity: Comparisons among the Amish. *Journal of the Indiana State Medical Association* 73:471–73.

Miller, G., and D. Gerstein. 1983. The life expectancy of non-smoking men and women. *Public Health Reports* 98:343–49.

Minaker, K., and J. Rowe. 1985. Health and disease among the oldest old: A clinical perspective. *Milbank Memorial Fund Quarterly* 63(2):324–49.

Minge-Kalman, W. 1977. On the theory and measurement of domestic labor intensity. *American Ethnologist* 4:273–84.

————. 1978. Household economy during the peasant-to-worker transition in the Swiss Alps. *Ethnology* 17:183.

Mischel, W. 1981. *Introduction to personality.* 3d ed. New York: Holt, Rinehart & Winston.

Money, J., and A. A. Ehrhardt. 1972. *Man & woman boy & girl: The differentiation and dimorphism of gender identity from conception to maturity.* Baltimore: Johns Hopkins University Press.

Mitchell, D., and L. Donald. 1985. Some economic aspects of Tlingit, Haida, and Tsimshian slavery. In *Economic anthropology,* edited by B. L. Isaac. Greenwich, Conn.: JAI Press.

Moody, H. R. 1983. Wisdom and the search for meaning. Paper presented at the 36th Annual Meeting of the Gerontological Society, November, San Francisco.

Moore, J. W. 1971. Situational factors affecting minority aging. *The Gerontologist* 11:88–93.

Moore, M. J. 1981. Physical aging: A cross-cultural perspective. In *The dynamics of aging.* See Longino, 1981.

Morgan, L. A. 1981. Aging in a family context. In *Aging: Prospects and issues.* 3d ed., edited by R. H. Davis. Los Angeles: Andrus Gerontology Center, University of Southern California Press.

Morley, J. E. 1984. Impotence due to hypothyroidism. *Medical Aspects of Human Sexuality* 18(2):124–30.

Mortimer, J. A. 1983. Alzheimer's disease and senile dementia: Prevalence and incidence. In *Alzheimer's disease.* See Ball, 1983.

Mortimer, J. A., F. J. Pirozzolo, and G. T. Maletta. 1982. *The Aging Motor System.* New York: Praeger.

Mortimer, J., and L. Schuman, eds. 1981. *The epidemiology of dementia.* New York: Oxford University Press.

Mortimer, J., L. Schuman, and R. French. 1981. Epidemiology of dementia. In *The epidemiology of dementia.* See Mortimer and Schuman, 1981.

Mundy-Castle, A. C. 1953. An analysis of central response to photic stimulation in normal adults. In *Electroencephalography and Clinical Neurophysiology* 5:1–22.

Murdock, G. P., and D. R. White. 1969. Standard cross-cultural sample. *Ethnology* 8:320–69.

Murphy, C. 1979. The effect of age on taste sensitivity. In *Special senses in aging.* See Black, 1979.

Murphy, E. A. 1979. Genetics of longevity in man. In *The genetics of ageing,* edited by E. L. Schneider. New York: Plenum Press.

Murphy, Y., and R. F. Murphy. 1974. *Women of the forest.* New York: Columbia University Press.

Mutran, E. 1985. Intergenerational family support among blacks and whites. *Journal of Gerontology* 40:382–89.

Myerhoff, B. 1978a. *Number our days.* New York: Simon & Schuster.

———. 1978b. Aging and the aged in other cultures: An anthropological perspective. In *The anthropology of health.* See Dougherty, 1978.

———. 1984. Rites and signs of ripening: The interwining of ritual, time, and growing older. In *Age and anthropological theory.* See Beall, 1984.

Myers, G. C., and K. G. Manton. 1984. Recent changes in the U.S. age at death distribution: Further observations. *The Gerontologist* 24(6):572–75.

Naessen, R. 1971. An enquiry on the morphological characteristics of possible changes with age in the olfactory region of man. *Acta Oto-Laryngologica* 71:49–62.

Nag, M. 1973. Anthropology and population: Problems and perspectives. *Population Studies* 27:59–68.

———. 1976. The economic view of children in agricultural societies: A review and a proposal. In *Culture, natality, and family planning,* edited by J. F. Marshall and S. Polgar. Chapel Hill: University of North Carolina Press.

Nagata, J. A. 1974. What is a Malay? Situational selection of ethnic identity in a plural society? *American Ethnologist* 1:331–50.

Naroll, R. 1983. *The moral order: An introduction to the human situation.* Beverly Hills: Sage Publications.

Naroll, R., G. L. Michik, and F. Naroll. 1976. *Worldwide theory testing.* New Haven, Conn.: HRAF Press.

National Center for Health Statistics. 1976. *Vital statistics of the U.S.* Vol. 2, Sec. 5, Life tables. DHHS Pub. No. (PHS) 80–1101. Washington, D.C.: U.S. Government Printing Office.

———. 1977. *Utilization of nursing homes.* Vital and Health Statistics, Series 13, No. 28. DHEW Publication Number (HRA) 77–1779. Washington, D.C.: U.S. Government Printing Office.

———. 1985. *Vital statistics of the United States, 1982.* Vol. 2, Sec. 6, Life tables. DHHS Pub. No. (PHS) 84–1104. Washington, D.C.: U.S. Government Printing Office.

National Council on the Aging. 1975. *The myth and reality of aging in America.* Survey conducted for NCOA by L. Harris and Associates. Washington, D.C.: National Council on the Aging.

———. 1981. *Aging in the eighties: America in transition.* A survey conducted for NCOA by L. Harris and Associates. Washington, D.C.: National Council on the Aging.

National Urban League. 1964. *Double jeopardy: The older Negro in America today.* New York: National Urban League.

Neisser, U. 1976. *Cognition and reality.* San Francisco: Freeman.

Nesselroade, J. R., and H. W. Reese, eds. 1973. *Life span developmental psychology: Methodological issues.* New York: Academic Press.

Netting, R. M. 1977. *Cultural ecology.* Menlo Park, Calif.: Benjamin/Cummings.

Neugarten, B. L. 1964. Summary and implications. In *Personality in middle and late life.* See Gutmann, 1964.

———. 1974. Age groups in American society and the rise of the young old. *Annals of the American Academy of Political and Social Science* 415:187–98.

———. 1977. Personality and aging. In *Handbook of the psychology of aging.* See Birren and Renner, 1977.

———. 1982. Policy for the 1980's: Age or need entitlement? In *Age or need,* edited by B. L. Neugarten. Beverly Hills: Sage Publications.

―――. 1985. Interpretative social science and research on aging. In *Gender and the life course*. See Cancian, 1985.

Neugarten, B. L., and N. Datan. 1973. Sociological perspectives on the life cycle. In *Life-span developmental psychology*. See Kogan, 1973.

Neugarten, B. L., and D. Gutmann. 1968. Age-sex roles and personality in middle age: A thematic apperception study. In *Middle age and aging*, edited by B. L. Neugarten. Chicago: Chicago University Press.

Neugarten, B. L., and K. K. Weinstein. 1964. The changing American grandparent. *Journal of Marriage and the Family* 26:199–204.

Neugarten, B. L., V. Wood, R. J. Kraines, and B. Loomis. 1968. Women's attitudes toward the menopause. In *Middle age and aging*. See Neugarten and Gutmann, 1968.

New, P. K., J. N. Henderson, and D. K. Padgett. 1985. Aging, ethnicity and the public: Policy implications. *Journal of Applied Gerontology* 4:1–5.

Newman, G., and C. R. Nichols. 1960. Sexual activities and attitudes in older persons. *Journal of the American Medical Association* 173(1):33–35.

Newman, J. L., M. S. Attig, and D. A. Kramer. 1983. Do sex-role appropriate materials influence the Piagetian performance of older adults? *Experimental Aging Research* 9:197–202.

New York Times. 1986. Help for women, old and young. Editorial, May 27.

Nieschlag, E. 1979. The endocrine function of the human testis in regard to sexuality. *Sex, hormones and behavior. CIBA Foundation Symposium* 62:183–208.

Noelle-Neumann, E. 1984. Der Zweifel am Verstand Wertewandel am Beispiel der Normen des rationalen Verhaltens. In *Die Stellung der Wissenschaft in der modernen Kultur*, edited by Helmut Engler. Mainz: V. Hase und Koehler.

Noll, P. F. 1981. Federally assisted housing programs for the elderly in rural areas: Problems and prospects. In *Community housing choices for older Americans*. See Brody and Liebowitz, 1981.

Norman, D. A., and D. Bobrow. 1975. On data-limited and resource-limited processes. *Cognitive Psychology* 7:44–64.

Nutrition Week. 1984. Unique table published on life expectancy. *Nutrition Week*, January 5, 1985, 6.

Nuttall, R. L. 1972. The strategy of functional age research. *Aging and Human Development* 3:149–52.

Nydegger, C. N. 1981a. On being caught up in time. *Human Development* 24:1–12.

―――. 1981b. The ripple effect of paternal timing. Paper presented at the Gerontological Society of America Meeting, November, Toronto.

―――. 1982. Strategies of life course analysis. Paper presented in Symposium, The Art of Research, at the 81st Annual Meetings of the American Anthropological Association, December, Washington, D. C.

―――. 1984. Androgyny and aging: A conceptual and methodological critique. Paper read at the 13th Annual Meeting of the Society for Cross-Cultural Research, February 17–19, Boulder, Colorado.

Nydegger, C. N., and L. Mitteness. 1979. Transitions in fatherhood. *Generations* 4(Summer):14–15.

Office of Technology Assessment. 1984. *Technology and aging in America*. Washington, D.C.: Government Printing Office.

Oliver, D. 1955. *A Solomon Island society*. Boston: Beacon Press.

Olsho, L. W., S. W. Harkins, and M. L. Lenhardt. 1985. Aging and the auditory system. In *Handbook of the psychology of aging*. See Bengston, Reedy, and Gordon, 1985.

Olson, L., C. Caton, and M. Duffy. 1981. *The elderly and future economy*. Lexington, Mass.: Lexington Books.

Oppenheimer, V. K. 1981. The changing nature of life-cycle squeezes: Implications for the socioeconomic position of the elderly. In *Aging*. See Griffitt, 1981.

Ory, M. G., T. F. Williams, M. Emr, B. Lebowitz, P. Rabins, J. Salloway, T. Sluss-Radbaugh, E. Wolff, and S. Zarit. 1985. Families, informal supports, and Alzheimer's disease. *Research on Aging* 7:623–44.

Ossowski, S. 1963. *Class structure in social consciousness*. Translated by S. Patterson. London: Routledge and Kegan Paul.

Ostor, A. 1984. Chronology, category, and ritual. In *Age and anthropological theory*. See Beall, 1984.

Overton, W. F., and H. W. Reese. 1973. Models of development: Methodological implications. In *Life-span developmental psychology*. See Nesselroade and Reese, 1973.

Paar, J. 1980. The interaction of persons and living environments. In *Aging in the 1980's*. See Cerella, Poon, and Williams, 1980.

Paffenberger, R. S., Jr., R. T. Hyde, A. L. Wing, and C.-C. Hsieh. 1986. Physical activity, all cause mortality and longevity of college alumni. *New England Journal of Medicine* 314(10):605–13.

Palmore, E. B. 1971. Attitudes toward aging as shown by humor. *The Gerontologist* 11:181–86.

———. 1975. *The honorable elders. A cross-cultural analysis of aging in Japan.* Durham, N. C.: Duke University Press.

———. 1982. Predictors of the longevity difference: A 25-year follow-up. *The Gerontologist* 22(6):513–18.

———. 1984. Longevity in Abkhazia: A reevaluation. *The Gerontologist* 24:95–96.

———. 1984. Palmore dissents. *The Gerontologist* 24:446.

Palmore, E. B., B. M. Burchett, G. G. Fillenbaum, L. K. George, and L. M. Wallman. 1985. *Retirement: Causes and consequences.* New York: Springer Publishing.

Palmore, E. B., and K. Manton. 1974. Modernization and status of the aged: International correlations. *Journal of Gerontology* 29(2):205–10.

Pampel, F. 1981. *Social change and the aged: Trends in the United States.* Lexington, Mass.: Lexington Books.

Papalia, D., and D. Bielby. 1974. Cognitive functioning in middle and old age adults: A review of research based on Piaget's theory. *Human Development* 17:424–43.

Papalia-Finlay, D., J. Blackburn, E. Davis, M. Dellmann, and P. Roberts. 1980–81. Training cognitive functioning in the elderly—inability to replicate previous findings. *International Journal of Aging and Human Development* 12:111–17.

Parasuraman, R., and D. R. Davies. 1984. *Varieties of attention.* New York: Academic Press.

Parkes, C. M. 1972. *Bereavement: Studies of grief in adult life.* New York: International Universities Press.

Parkes, C. M., R. Benjamin, and R. A. Fitzgerald. 1969. Broken heart: A statistical study of increased mortality among widowers. *British Medical Journal* 1:740–43.

Parsons, T., and R. Fox. 1952. Illness, therapy and the modern American family. *Journal of Social Issues* 13(4):31–44.

Pastalan, L. A. 1982. Research in environment and aging: An alternative to theory. In *Aging and the environment*. See Kahana, 1982.

Pearl, R., and J. R. Miner. 1935. Experimental studies in the duration of life. XIV. The comparative mortality of certain lower organisms. *Quarterly Review of Biology* 10:60.

Pearl, R., and R. D. Pearl. 1934a. *The ancestry of the long-lived.* Baltimore: Johns Hopkins University Press.

——. 1934b. Studies on human longevity. VI. The distribution and correlation of variation in the total immediate ancestral longevity of nonagenarians in relation to the inheritance factor in duration of life. *Human Biology* 6:98–222.

Pearlin, L. 1980. Life-strains and psychological distress among adults. In *Themes of love and work in adulthood,* edited by N. J. Smelser and E. H. Erikson. Cambridge: Harvard University Press.

Pearlin, L. I., and M. A. Lieberman. 1979. Social sources of emotional distress. In *Research in community and mental health,* edited by R. Simmons. Greenwich, Conn.: JAI Press.

Pepper, S. C. 1942. *World hypotheses.* Berkeley, Calif.: University of California Press.

Peskin, H., and Livson, N. 1981. Uses of the past in adult psychological health. In *Present and past in middle life.* See Haan, 1981.

Petrowsky, M. 1976. Marital status, sex, and the social networks of the elderly. *Journal of Marriage and the Family* 38(November):749–56.

Pfeiffer, E. 1969. Geriatric sex behavior. *Medical Aspects of Human Sexuality* 3(7):19, 22–28.

——. 1973. Mental disorders in later life—affective disorders; Paranoid, neurotic, and situational reactions. In *Mental illness in later life,* edited by E. Busse and E. Pfeiffer. Washington, D.C.: American Psychiatric Association.

——. 1975. A short portable mental status questionnaire for the assessment of organic brain deficit in elderly patients. *Journal of the American Geriatric Society* 23:433–41.

——. 1977a. Psychopathology and social pathology. In *Handbook of the psychology of aging.* See Birren and Renner, 1977.

——. 1977b. Sexual behavior in old age. In *Behavior and adaptation in late life.* 2d ed., edited by E. W. Busse and E. Pfeiffer. Boston: Little, Brown and Company.

——. 1978. Sexuality in the aging individual. In *Sexuality and aging.* See Broderick, 1978.

——. 1985. Policy issues in long term care. In *Issues in long-term care and Alzheimer's disease.* Tampa: University of South Florida, Suncoast Gerontology Center.

Pfeiffer, E., and G. C. Davis. 1972. Determinants of sexual behavior in middle and old age. *Journal of the American Geriatrics Society* 20:151–58.

Pfeiffer, E., A. Verwoerdt, and G. C. Davis. 1972. Sexual behavior in middle life. *American Journal of Psychiatry* 128:1262–67.

Pfeiffer, E., A. Verwoerdt, and H. Wang. 1968. Sexual behavior in aged men and women. Part I. Observations on 254 community volunteers. *Archives of General Psychiatry* 19:753–58.

Pitskhelauri, G. A. n.d. *The longliving of Soviet Georgia.* Translated in 1982. New York: Human Sciences Press.

Plath, D. W. 1972. Japan: The after years. In *Aging and modernization.* See Cowgill, 1972.

——. 1980. *Long engagements: Maturity in modern Japan.* Stanford: Stanford University Press.

——. 1983. Ecstasy years—Old age in Japan. In *Growing old in different societies.* See Bengston and Morgan, 1983.

Plemons, J. K., S. L. Willis, and P. B. Baltes. 1978. Modifiability of fluid intelligence in aging: A short-term longitudinal training approach. *Journal of Gerontology* 33:224–31.

Plude, D. J., and W. J. Hoyer. 1981. Adult age differences in visual search as a function of stimulus mapping and information load. *Journal of Gerontology* 36:598–604.

———. 1985. Attention and performance: Identifying and localizing age deficits. In *Aging and human performance*, edited by N. Charness. London: Wiley & Sons.

———. 1986. Age and the selectivity of visual information processing. *Journal of Psychology and Aging* 1:4–10.

Plude, D. J., W. J. Hoyer, and J. Lazar. 1982. Age, mapping, and response complexity in visual search. *Experimental Aging Research* 8:99–102.

Plude, D. J., D. B. Kaye, W. J. Hoyer, T. A. Post, M. J. Saynisch, and M. V. Hahn. 1983. Adult age differences in visual search as a function of information load and target mapping. *Developmental Psychology* 19:508–12.

Polanyi, K. 1957. The economy as instituted process. In *Trade and market in the early empire*, edited by K. Polanyi, C. Arensberg, and H. W. Pearson. New York: Free Press.

Polgar, S. 1972. Population history and population policies from an anthropological perspective. *Current Anthropology* 13:203–11.

Pollack, R. H., and B. M. Atkeson. 1978. A life-span approach to perceptual development. In *Life-span development and behavior*. Vol. 1, edited by P. B. Baltes. New York: Academic Press.

Poon, L. W. 1985. Differences in human memory with aging: Nature, causes, and clinical implications. In *Handbook of the psychology of aging*. See Bengston, Reedy, and Gordon, 1985.

Poon, L. W., and J. L. Fozard. 1978. Speed of retrieval from long-term memory in relation to age, familiarity, and datedness of information. *Journal of Gerontology* 33:711–17.

Popper, K. R. 1963. What is dialectic? In *Conjectures and refutations: The growth of scientific knowledge*, edited by K. R. Popper. London: Routledge and Kegan Paul.

Porcino, J. 1983. *Growing older, getting better: A handbook for women in the second half of life*. Reading, Mass.: Addison-Wesley Publishing.

Posner, M. I., and S. J. Boise. 1971. Components of attention. *Psychological Review* 78:391–408.

Powell, L. and K. Courtice. 1983. *Alzheimer's disease: A guide for families*. Reading, Mass.: Addison-Wesley Publishing.

Powers, E. A., and G. L. Bultena. 1974. Correspondence between anticipated and actual uses of public services by the aged. *Social Service Review* 48:245–54.

Powers, E. A., P. M. Keith, and W. J. Goudy. 1981. Family networks of the rural aged. In *The family in rural society*, edited by R. T. Coward and W. M. Smith, Jr. Boulder, Colo.: Westview Press.

Precht, W. 1979. Vestibular mechanisms. *Annual Review of Neuroscience* 2:265–89.

Preston, S. H. 1985. Children and the elderly in the U.S. *Scientific American* 251(6):44–49.

Prichard, J. C. 1935. *A Treatise on insanity and other disorders affecting the mind*. London: Sherwood, Gilbert, and Piper.

Protinsky, H., and G. Hughston. 1978. Conservation in elderly males. *Developmental Psychology* 14:114.

Quadagno, J. 1982. *Aging in early industrial society: Work, family, and social policy in nineteenth-century England*. New York: Academic Press.

Quinn, W. H., and G. A. Hughston. 1984. Introduction. In *Independent aging*. See Cole, 1984.

Ragan, P. K., and M. M. Simonin. 1977. *Black and Mexican-American aging: A Selected bibliography*. Los Angeles: Andrus Gerontology Center, University of Southern California.

Rajala, S., M. Haavisto, and R. Mattilaik. 1983. Blood pressure and mortality in the very aged. *Lancet* 2:520–21.

Ransford, H. E. 1976. On isolation, powerlessness and violence. In *The research experience,* edited by M. P. Golden. Itasca, Ill.: F. E. Peacock Publishers.

Raphael, B. 1983. *The anatomy of bereavement.* New York: Basic Books.

Reese, H. W., and W. F. Overton. 1970. Models of development and theories of development. In *Life-span developmental psychology: Research,* edited by L. R. Goulet and P. B. Baltes. New York: Academic Press.

Reese, H. W., and D. Rodeheaver. 1985. Problem solving and complex decision making. In *Handbook of the psychology of aging.* See Bengston, Reedy, and Gordon, 1985.

Reff, M. E., and E. L. Schneider, eds. 1982. *Biological markers of aging.* Bethesda: NIH Publication No. 82-2221.

Regnier, V. 1983. Urban neighborhood cognition: Relationships between functional and symbolic community elements. In *Aging and milieu.* See Kahana and Kahana, 1983.

Reisberg, B. 1983. Clinical presentation, diagnosis, and symptomatology of age-associated cognitive decline and Alzheimer's disease. In *Alzheimer's disease.* See Ball, 1983.

Rhoads, E., and L. Holmes. 1981. Samoa mapulfagalele, Western Samoa's home for the aged—A cultural enigma. *International Journal of Aging and Human Development* 13(2):121–36.

Richards, O. W. 1977. Effects of luminance and contrast on visual acuity, ages 16 to 90 years. *American Journal of Optometry and Physiological Optics* 54:178–84.

Richmond, J. 1977. The foolishness and wisdom of age: Attitudes toward the elderly as reflected in jokes. *Gerontologist* 17(3):210–19.

Riegel, K. R. 1975. Adult life crises: A dialectic interpretation of development. In *Life span development psychology.* See Gutmann, 1975.

Riley, M. W. 1976. Social gerontology and the age stratification of society. In *The sociology of aging,* edited by R. C. Atchley and M. M. Seltzer. Belmont, Calif.: Wadsworth Publishing.

———. 1978. Aging, social change, and the power of ideas. *Daedalus* 197:39–52.

———. 1979. Introduction. In *Aging from birth to death: Interdisciplinary perspectives,* edited by M. W. Riley. Boulder, Colo.: Westview Press.

———. 1985. Age strata in social systems. In *Handbook of aging and the social sciences.* See Habib, 1985.

Riley, M. W., and K. Bond. 1983. Beyond ageism: Postponing the onset of disability. In *Aging in society: Selected reviews of recent research,* edited by M. W. Riley, B. B Hess, and K. Bond. Hillsdale, N.J.: Lawrence Erlbaum.

Riley, M. W., and A. Foner, in association with M. E. Moore, B. Hess, and B. K. Roth. 1968. *Aging and society.* Vol. 1, *An inventory of research findings.* New York: Russell Sage Foundation.

Riley, M. W., M. Johnson, and A. Foner. 1972. Introduction. In *Aging and society.* See Clausen, 1972.

Ritter, M. L. 1980. The conditions favoring age-set organization. *Journal of Anthropological Research* 36:87–104.

Roberts, R., and A. Askew. 1972. A consideration of mortality in three subcultures. *Health Services Reports* 87:262–70.

Robertson, J. F. 1976. Significance of grandparents: Perceptions of young adult grandchildren. *The Gerontologist* 16(2):137–40.

Robinson, D. W., and G. J. Sutton. 1979. Age effects in hearing: A comparative analysis of published threshold data. *Audiology* 18:320–34.

Rockstein, M., ed. 1974. *Theoretical aspects of aging.* New York: Academic Press.

Roe, A. 1972. Maintenance of creative output through the years. In *Climate for creativity*, edited by C. W. Taylor. New York: Pergamon Press.

Roodin, P. A., J. Rybash, and W. J. Hoyer. 1984. Affect in adult cognition: A constructivist view of moral thought and action. In *Emotion in adult development*, edited by C. Z. Malatesta and C. E. Izard. Beverly Hills: Sage Publications.

Rosaldo, M. Z. 1974. Women, culture, and society: A theoretical overview. In *Women, culture, and society*, edited by M. Z. Rosaldo and L. Lamphere. Stanford: Stanford University Press.

Rose, A. M. 1962. The subculture of the aging: A topic for sociological research. *The Gerontologist* 2(3):123–27.

———. 1965. The subculture of the aging: A framework for research in social gerontology. In *Older people and their social worlds*, edited by A. M. Rose and W. Peterson. Philadelphia: F. A. Davis Company.

Rose, F. G. G. 1960. *Classification of kin, age structure, and marriage amongst the Groote Eylandt Aborigines: A study in method and theory of Australian kinship*. Oxford: Pergamon Press.

Rose, M. R., and P. M. Service. 1985. Evolution of aging. *Review of Biological Research in Aging* 2:85–98.

Rosenblatt, P. C., R. P. Walsh, and D. A. Jackson. 1976. *Grief and mourning in cross-cultural perspective*. New Haven, Conn.: HRAF Press.

Rosenmayr, L. 1968. Family relations of the elderly. *Journal of Marriage and the Family* 30(November):672–80.

Rosenmayr, L., and E. Koeckeis. 1963. Propositions for a sociological theory of aging and the family. *International Social Science Journal* 15(3):410–42.

Rosenwaike, I. 1979. A new evaluation of U.S. census data on the extremely aged. *Demography* 16:279–88.

———. 1985. A demographic portrait of the oldest old. *Milbank Memorial Fund Quarterly* 63(2):187–205.

Rosenwaike, I., and S. Preston. 1984. Age overstatement and Puerto Rican longevity. *Human Biology* 56:503–25.

Rosman, A., and P. Rubel. 1970. Potlatch and Sagali: The structure of exchange in Haida and Trobriand societies. *Transactions of the New York Academy of Sciences* 32:732–42.

———. 1978. Exchange as structure, or why doesn't everyone eat his own pigs? In *Research in economic anthropology*, edited by G. Dalton. Greenwich, Conn.: JAI Press.

Rosow, I. 1967. *Social integration of the aged*. New York: Free Press.

———. 1974. *Socialization to old age*. New York: Free Press.

———. 1982. Intergenerational perspectives on aging. In *Aging and the human condition*. See Ehrlich and Ehrlich, 1982.

Ross, E. A. 1985. A note on the demographic concomitants of sedentism. *American Anthropologist* 87:380–82.

Ross, J. K. 1977. *Old people, new lives*. Chicago: The University of Chicago Press.

Ross, M. D. 1979. Effects of aging on the otoconia. In *Special senses in aging*. See Black, 1979.

Rossman, I. 1978. Sexuality and aging: An internist's perspective. In *Sexuality and aging*. See Broderick, 1978.

Roth, M. 1980. Aging of the brain and dementia: An overview. In *Aging. Vol. 13, Aging of the brain and the dementia*, edited by L. Amaducci, A. Davison, and P. Antuono. New York: Raven Press.

Rothstein, F. 1979. Two different worlds: Gender and industrialization in rural Mexico. In *New directions in political economy: An approach from anthropology,* edited by M. B. Leons and F. Rothstein. Westport, Conn.: Greenwood Press.

Rousseau, A. M. 1981. *Shopping bag ladies: Homeless women talk about their lives.* New York: Pilgrim Press.

Rowan, R. L. 1985. Sexual effects of prostatectomy. *Medical Aspects of Human Sexuality* 19(6):120–24.

Rowles, G. D. 1983. Geographical dimensions of social support in rural Appalachia. In *Aging and milieu.* See Kahana and Kahana, 1983.

Rowles, G. D., and R. J. Ohta. 1983. Emergent themes and new directions: Reflection on aging and milieu research. In *Aging and milieu.* See Kahana and Kahana, 1983.

Royce, A. P. 1982. *Ethnic identity: Strategies of diversity.* Bloomington: Indiana University Press.

Rubbo, A. 1975. The spread of capitalism in rural Colombia. In *Toward an anthropology of women.* See Brown, 1975.

Rubin, I. 1963. Sex over 65. In *Advances in sex research,* edited by H. G. Beisel. New York: Harper & Row.

———. 1965. *Sexual life after sixty.* New York: Basic Books.

Rudzitis, G. 1984. Geographical research and gerontology: An overview. *The Gerontologist* 24(5):536–42.

Sacher, G. A. 1957. Relation of lifespan to brain and body weight in mammals. In *CIBA foundation colloquia on aging.* Vol. 5, *The Lifespan of Animals,* edited by G. E. W. Wolstenholme and M. O'Connor. London: J. & S. Churchill.

———. 1975. Maturation and longevity in relation to cranial capacity in hominid evolution. In *Antecedents of man and after.* Vol. 1, *Primates: Functional morphology and evolution,* edited by R. Tuttle. The Hague: Mouton.

———. 1976. Evolution of the entropy and information terms governing mammalian longevity. *Interdisciplinary Topics in Gerontology* 9:69–82.

Sahlins, M. 1972. *Stone age economics.* Chicago: Aldine Publishing.

Salamon, S., and V. Lockhart. 1980. Land ownership and the position of elderly in farm families. *Human Organization* 39:324–31.

Salthouse, T. A. 1980. Age and memory: Strategies for localizing the loss. In *New directions in memory and aging,* edited by L. W. Poon, J. L. Fozard, L. S. Cermak, D. Arenberg, and L. W. Thompson. Hillsdale, N.J.: Lawrence Erlbaum.

———. 1982. *Adult cognition: An experimental psychology of human aging.* New York: Springer-Verlag.

———. 1985. Speed of behavior and its implications for cognition. In *Handbook of the psychology of aging.* See Bengston, Reedy, and Gordon, 1985.

Sanday, P. R. 1974. Female status in public domain. In *Women, culture, and society.* See Rosaldo, 1974.

Sanjek, R. 1984. *Crowded out: Homelessness and the elderly poor in New York City.* New York: The Coalition for the Homeless.

Sankar, A. 1984. "It's just old age": Old age as a diagnosis in American and Chinese medicine. In *Age and anthropological theory.* See Beall, 1984.

Savage, R. L., P. Gaber, N. Britton, and A. Cooper. 1977. *Personality adjustment in the aged.* New York: Academic Press.

Schaie, K. W. 1977–78. Toward a stage theory of adult cognitive development. *International Journal of Aging and Human Development* 8:129–36.

———. 1984. Historical time and cohort effects. In *Life-span developmental psychology: Historical and generational effects,* edited by K. A. McCluskey and H. W. Reese. New York: Academic Press.

Schaie, K. W., and I. A. Parham. 1977. Cohort-sequential analyses of adult intellectual development. *Developmental Psychology* 13:649–53.

Schaier, A. H., and V. G. Cicirelli. 1976. Age differences in humor comprehension and appreciation in old age. *Journal of Gerontology* 3:577–82.

Schaiper, D. 1985. The changing division of labor in the production of burley tobacco. Paper presented to the Central States Anthropological Society, Louisville, Kentucky.

Schank, R. C., and R. P. Abelson. 1977. *Scripts, plans, goals, and understanding: An inquiry into human knowledge structures.* Hillsdale, N.J.: Lawrence Erlbaum.

Scheibel, A. B. 1978. Structural aspects of the aging brain: Spine systems and the dendritic arbor. In *Aging.* Vol. 1, *Alzheimer's disease: Senile dementia and related disorders,* edited by R. Katzman, R. D. Terry, and K. L. Bick. New York: Raven Press.

Schemper, T., S. Voss, and W. S. Cain. 1981. Odor identification in young and elderly persons: Sensory and cognitive limitations. *Journal of Gerontology* 36:446–52.

Scheper-Hughes, N. 1979. *Saints, scholars and schizophrenics: Mental illness in rural Ireland.* Berkeley: University of California Press.

Schiffman, S. 1979. Changes in taste and smell with age: Psychophysical aspects. In *Special sense in aging.* See Black, 1979.

Schlegel, A. 1977. Toward a theory of sexual stratification. In *Sexual stratification: A cross-cultural view,* edited by A. Schlegel. New York: Columbia University Press.

Schlossberg, N. K. 1981. A model for analyzing human adaptation to transition. *The Counseling Psychologist* 9(2):2–18.

———. 1984. *Counseling adults in transition: Linking practice with theory.* New York: Springer Publishing.

Schluderman, E., and J. P. Zubek. 1962. Effect of age on pain sensitivity. *Perceptual and Motor Skills* 14:295–301.

Schon, M., and A. M. Sutherland. 1983. The relationship of pituitary hormones to sexual behavior in women. In *Advances in sex research.* See Benjamin, 1983.

Schonfield, D. 1974. Translations in gerontology—from lab to life: Utilizing information. *American Psychologist* 29:796–801.

Schuknecht, J. 1974. *Pathology of the ear.* Cambridge: Harvard University Press.

Schultz, R., and B. Brenner. 1977. Relocation of the aged; A review and theoretical analysis. *Journal of Gerontology* 32:323–33.

Schweitzer, M. M. 1983. The elders: Cultural dimensions of aging in two American Indian communities. In *Growing old in different societies.* See Bengston and Morgan, 1983.

Scribner, S. 1984. Mind and action. Colloquium presented at Rutgers University, November 2.

Sears, R. 1977. Sources of life satisfactions of the Terman gifted men. *American Psychologist* 32:119–28.

Sears, P., and A. Barbee. 1977. Careers and life satisfaction among Terman's gifted women. In *The gifted and the creative: A fifty year perspective,* edited by J. Stanley, W. George, and C. Solano. Baltimore: Johns Hopkins University Press.

Sex Information and Education Council of U.S. 1970. *Sexuality and man.* New York: Charles Scribners Sons.

Selye, H. 1956. *The stress of life.* New York: McGraw-Hill.

Shanas, E. 1970. Health and adjustment in retirement. *Gerontologist* 10:19–21.

————. 1979. Social myth as hypothesis: The case of family relations of old people. *The Gerontologist* 19(1):3–9.

————. 1980. Older people and their families: The new pioneers. *Journal of Marriage and the Family* 42(1):9–15.

Shanas, E., P. Townsend, D. Wedderburn, H. Friis, P. Milhøj, and J. Stehouwer. 1968. *Older people in three industrial societies.* New York: Atherton Press.

Shapiro, E. and L. L. Roos. 1984. Using health care: Rural/urban differences among the Manitoba elderly. *The Gerontologist* 24(3):270–74.

Sheehan, T. 1976. Senior esteem as a factor of socioeconomic complexity. *The Gerontologist* 16(5):433–52.

Shiffrin, R. M., and W. Schneider. 1977. Controlled and automatic human information processing: II. Perceptual learning, automatic attending, and a general theory. *Psychological Review* 84:127–90.

Shugars, O. K., and E. E. Gavett. 1972. Changing technology in tobacco production. In *Social and economic issues confronting the tobacco industry in the 1970s,* edited by A. F. Bordeaux and R. H. Brannon. Lexington: University of Kentucky Press.

Silverman, P. and R. J. Maxwell. 1978. How do I respect thee? Let me count the ways: Deference towards elderly men and women. *Behavior Science Research,* 13(2):91–108.

————. 1983. The significance of information and power in the comparative study of the aged. In *Growing old in different societies.* See Bengston and Morgan, 1983.

————. 1984. Behavioral indices of sentiments toward the elderly. Paper read at the 13th Annual Meeting of the Society for Cross-Cultural Research, February 17–19, Boulder, Colorado.

Silverman, P. R. 1967. Services to the widowed: First steps in a program of preventive intervention. *Community Mental Health Journal* 3(1):37–44.

Simič, A. 1982. Aging in the United States: Achieving new understanding through foreign eyes. In *Aging,* edited by A. Kolker and P. I. Ahmed. New York: Elsevier.

Simmons, L. W. 1945. *The role of the aged in primitive society.* New Haven: Yale University Press.

————. 1960. Aging in preindustrial societies. In *Handbook of social gerontology,* edited by C. Tibbitts. Chicago: The University of Chicago Press.

Simon, J. R. 1968. Signal processing as a function of aging. *Journal of Experimental Psychology* 78:76–80.

Simonton, D. K. 1983. Creative productivity and age: A mathematical model based on a two-step cognitive process. *Developmental Review* 3:97–111.

Simopoules, A., and T. Van Itallie. 1984. Body weight, health, and longevity. *Annals of Internal Medicine* 100:285–95.

Sinnott, J. D. 1975. Everyday thinking and Piagetian operativity in adults. *Human Development* 18:430–43.

————. 1984. Postformal reasoning: The relativistic stage. In *Beyond formal operations.* See Commons, Richards, and Armon, 1984.

————. 1985. General systems theory: A rationale for the study of everyday memory. Presented at the Talland Conference on Memory and Aging, "Cognition in Everyday Life," Cape Cod.

Siskind, J. 1973. *To hunt in the morning.* New York: Oxford University Press.

Slater, P. E. 1964. Cross-cultural view of the aged. In *New thoughts on old age,* edited by R. Kastenbaum. New York: Springer Publishing.

————. 1970. *The pursuit of loneliness.* Boston: Beacon Press.

Smith, D. C., R. Prentice, D. J. Thompson, and W. L. Herman. 1975. Association of exogenous estrogen and endometrial carcinoma. *New England Journal of Medicine* 293(23):1164–67.

Smock, A. C. 1977. Modernization of women's position in the family in Ghana. In *Sexual stratification*. See Schlegel, 1977.

Snyder, E. E., and E. Spreitzer. 1976. Attitudes of aging toward non-traditional sexual behavior. *Archives of Sexual Behavior* 5:249–54.

Sokolovsky, J., ed. 1983. *Growing old in different cultures*. See Bengston and Morgan, 1983.

Sokolovsky, J., and C. Cohen. 1983. Networks as adaptation: The cultural meaning of being a "loner" among the inner-city elderly. In *Growing old in different societies*. See Bengston and Morgan, 1983.

Soldo, B. J. 1980. America's elderly in the 1980's. *Population Bulletin* 35(4):1–47.

Soldo, B. J., and H. B. Brotman. 1981. Housing whom? In *Community housing choices for older Americans*. See Brody and Liebowitz, 1981.

Soldo, B. J., and K. B. Manton. 1985. Health status and service needs of the oldest old: Current patterns and future trends. *Milbank Memorial Fund Quarterly* 63(2):286–319.

Soldo, B. J., and J. Myllyluoma. 1983. Caregivers who live with dependent elderly. *The Gerontologist* 23(6):605–11.

Solnick, R. L. 1978. Sexual responsiveness, age, and change: Facts and potential. In *Sexuality and aging*. See Broderick, 1978.

Solnick, R. L., and J. E. Birren. 1977. Age and male erectile responsiveness. *Archives of Sexual Behavior* 6(1):1–9.

Solso, R. L. 1979. *Cognitive Psychology*. New York: Harcourt Brace Jovanovich.

Sommer, R., and H. Osmond. 1961. Symptoms of institutional care. *Social Problems* 8:254–62.

Spanier, G. B., R. A. Lewis, and C. L. Coles. 1975. Marital adjustment over the family life cycle: The issue of curvilinearity. *Journal of Marriage and the Family* 37:263–75.

Spector, R. 1979. Health and illness in the Hispanic-American community. In *Cultural diversity in health and illness*, edited by R. Spector. New York: Appleton-Century-Crofts.

Spirduso, W. W. 1975. Reaction and movement time as a function of age and physical activity level. *Journal of Gerontology* 30:435–40.

———. 1980. Physical fitness, aging, and psychomotor speed: A review. *Journal of Gerontology* 35:850–65.

———. 1982. Physical fitness in relation to motor aging. In *The aging motor system*, edited by J. A. Mortimer, F. J. Pirozzolo, and G. J. Maletta. New York: Praeger.

Spoor, A. 1967. Presbycusis in relation to noise induced hearing loss. *International Audiology* 6:48–57.

Stack, C. 1974. *All our kin*. New York: Harper & Row.

Starr, B. D., and M. B. Weiner. 1981. *Sex and sexuality in the mature years*. New York: Stein & Day.

Stearns, P. N. 1977. *Old age in European society*. London: Croom Helm.

Steere, G. H. 1981. The family of the elderly. In *Dynamics of aging*. See Longino, 1981.

Steffl, B. M. 1978. Sexuality and aging: Implications for nurses and other helping professionals. In *Sexuality and aging*. See Broderick, 1978.

———. 1984. Sexuality and aging. In *Handbook of gerontological nursing*, edited by B. M. Steffl. New York: Van Nostrand Reinhold.

Stenbeck, A. 1980. Depression and suicidal behavior in old age. In *Handbook of mental health and aging*. See Comfort, 1980.

Stephens, Joyce. 1976. *Loners, losers, and lovers: Elderly tenants in a slum hotel.* Seattle: University of Washington Press.

Sternbach, R. A. 1978. *The psychology of pain.* New York: Raven Press.

Stini, W. A. 1985. Growth rates and sexual dimorphism in evolutionary perspective. In *The analysis of prehistoric diets,* edited by R. I. Gilbert and J. H. Mielke. New York: Academic Press.

Stotsky, B. 1973. Extended care and institutional care: Current trends, methods, and experience. In *Mental illness in later life,* edited by E. Busse and E. Pfeiffer. Washington, D.C.: American Psychiatric Association.

Stovall, J. C. 1972. An overview of social and economic issues confronting the tobacco industry in the 1970s. In *Social and economic issues confronting the tobacco industry in the 1970s,* edited by A. F. Bordeaux and R. H. Brannon. Lexington: University of Kentucky Press.

Strathern, A. 1971. *The rope of moka: Big-men and ceremonial exchange in Mount Hagen.* Cambridge: Cambridge University Press.

Strathern, M. 1972. *Women in between.* New York: Seminar Press.

Strauss, A. L. 1975. *Chronic illness and the quality of life.* St. Louis: C. V. Mosby.

Strehler, B. 1977. *Time, cells, and aging.* 2d ed. New York: Academic Press.

Streib, G. F. 1965. Intergenerational relations: Perspectives of the two generations on the older parent. *Journal of Marriage and the Family* 27(November):469–76.

———. 1972. Old age in Ireland: Demographic and sociological aspects. In *Aging and modernization.* See Cowgill, 1972.

———. 1982. The continuum of living arrangements: Traditional, novel, and pragmatic alternatives. In *Aging and the human condition.* See Ehrlich and Ehrlich, 1982.

Streib, G. F., and R. W. Beck. 1980. Older families: A decade review. *Journal of Marriage and the Family* 42(November):937–56.

Streib, G. F., and R. B. Streib. 1976. Communes and the aging. In *Age in society,* edited by A. Foner. Beverly Hills: Sage Publications.

Streib, G. F., and W. E. Thompson. 1960. The older person in a family context. In *Handbook of social gerontology.* See Simmons, 1960.

Struyk, R. J. 1981. The changing housing and neighborhood environment of the elderly: A look at the year 2000. In *Aging: Social change,* edited by S. B. Kiesler, J. N. Morgan, and V. K. Oppenheimer. New York: Academic Press.

Sussman, M. B. 1976. The family life of old people. In *Handbook of aging and the social sciences.* See Carp, 1976b.

Sviland, M. A. P. 1978. A program of sexual liberation and growth in the elderly. In *Sexuality and aging.* See Broderick, 1978.

Swedlund, A. C., R. S. Meindl, J. Nydon, and M. I. Gradie. 1983. Family patterns in longevity and longevity patterns of the family. *Human Biology* 55:115–219.

Swensson, R. G. 1980. A two-stage detection model applied to skilled visual search by radiologists. *Perception and Psychophysics* 27:11–16.

Tarail, M. 1962. Sex over 65. *Sexology* 28:440–45.

Terry, R., N. Gonatas, and M. Weiss. 1964. Ultrastructural studies in Alzheimer's presenile dementia. *American Journal of Pathology* 44:269–97.

Teski, M. 1981. *Living together: An ethnography of a retirement hotel.* Washington, D.C.: University Press of America.

The Wall Street Journal. 1984. The oldest old: More people live into 80's and 90's; The strain in social services and relatives will rise. July 30, 1984.

Thomas, J. T., N. C. Waugh, and J. L. Fozard. 1978. Age and familiarity in memory scanning. *Journal of Gerontology* 33:528–33.

Thompson, W. E., and G. F. Streib. 1961. Meaningful activity in a family context. In

Aging and leisure: A research perspective into the meaningful use of time, edited by R. W. Kleemeier. New York: Oxford University Press.

Tobin, S., and M. Lieberman. 1976. *Last home of the aged*. San Francisco: Jossey-Bass.

Tomlinson, B., G. Blessed, and M. Roth. 1970. Observations on the brains of demented old people. *Journal of Neurological Science* 11:205–42.

Torack, R. M. 1983. The early history of senile dementia. In *Alzheimer's disease*. See Ball, 1983.

Treas, J. 1975. Aging and the family. In *Aging: Scientific perspectives and social issues*, edited by D. S. Woodruff and J. E. Birren. New York: D. Van Nostrand.

———. 1977. Family support system for the aged: Some social and demographic considerations. *The Gerontologist* 17(6):486–91.

Treas, J., and A. VanHilst. 1976. Marriage and remarriage rates among older Americans. *The Gerontologist* 16(2):132–36.

Troll, L. 1971. The family of later life: A decade review. *Journal of Marriage and the Family* 33(May):263–90.

Troll, L. E., S. J. Miller, and R. C. Atchley. 1979. *Families in later life*. Belmont, Calif.: Wadsworth Publishing.

Troll, L. and J. Smith. 1976. Attachment through the life span: Some questions about dyadic relations in later life. *Human Development* 3:156–71.

Tsitouras, P. D., C. E. Martin, and S. M. Harman. 1982. Relationship of serum testosterone to sexual activity in healthy elderly men. *Journal of Gerontology* 37(3):288–93.

Turner, V. 1967. *The forest of symbols: Aspects of Ndembu ritual*. Ithaca, N.Y.: Cornell University Press.

Uberoi, J. P. S. 1962. *The politics of the Kula Ring: An analysis of the findings of Bronislaw Malinowski*. Manchester: Manchester University Press.

Ueno, M. 1963. The so-called coital death. *Japanese Journal of Legal Medicine* 17:535.

United Nations. Department of Economic and Social Affairs. 1978. *Statistical yearbook: 1977*. New York: United Nations.

———. Department of International Economic and Social Affairs. 1983. *Demographic yearbook*. New York: United Nations.

U.S. Bureau of the Census. 1983. *Household and family characteristics: March 1983*. Current Population Reports, P-20, No. 388. Washington, D.C.: Government Printing Office.

———. 1984. *Demographic and socioeconomic aspects of aging in the United States*. Current Population Reports, Series P-23, No. 138. Washington, D.C.: Government Printing Office.

———. 1985. *Statistical abstract of the United States: 1985* (105th ed.). Washington, D.C.: Government Printing Office.

U.S. Department of Health and Human Services. 1984. *Alzheimer's disease*. DHHS Publication #(ADM) 84-1323.

U.S. Senate. Special Committee on Aging. 1971. *The multiple hazards of age and race: The situation of aged black in the U.S.* Washington, D.C.: Government Printing Office.

———. 1978. *Single room occupancy: A need for national concern*. Washington, D.C.: Government Printing Office.

Vaillant, G. 1977. *Adaptation to life*. Boston: Little, Brown and Company.

Valle, R. 1981. Natural support systems, minority groups, and the late life dementias: Implications for service delivery, research, and policy. In *Aging*. Vol. 15, *Clinical aspects of Alzheimer's disease and senile dementia*, edited by N. Miller and G. Cohen. New York: Raven Press.

Van Arsdale, P. W. 1980. The measurement of age. In *New methods for old age research*. See Frank, 1980.

Van den Berghe, P. 1970. *Race and ethnicity*. New York: Basic Books.

———. 1973. *Age and sex in human society: A biological perspective*. Belmont, Calif.: Wadsworth Publishing.

Van der Laan, F. L., and W. J. Oosterveld. 1974. Age and vestibular function. *Aerospace Medicine* 45:540–47.

van Gennep, A. [1906] 1960. *The rites of passage*. Translated by E. Mourry. London: Routledge & Kegan Paul.

van Willigen, J., T. A. Arcury, and R. G. Cromley. 1985. Tobacco men and factory hands: The effects of migration turnaround and decentralized industrialization on the social lives of older people in a rural Kentucky county. *Human Organization* 44:50–57.

Veatch, R. M. 1976. *Death, dying, and the biological revolution*. New Haven, Conn.: Yale University Press.

Verbrugge, L. M. 1984. Longer life but worsening health? Trends in health and mortality of middle-aged and older persons. *Milbank Memorial Fund Quarterly* 62(3):475–519.

———. 1985. Gender and health: An update on hypotheses and evidence. *Journal of Health and Social Behavior* 26:156–82.

Verillo, R. T., and V. Verillo. 1985. Sensory and perceptual performance. In *Aging and human performance*, edited by N. Charness. London: Wiley & Sons.

Verville, E., and N. Cameron. 1946. Age and sex differences in the perception of incomplete pictures by adults. *Journal of Genetic Psychology* 68:149–57.

Verwoerdt, A., E. Pfeiffer, and H. S. Wang. 1969a. Sexual behavior in senescence. Changes in sexual activity and interest in aging men and women. *Journal of Geriatric Psychiatry* 2:163.

———. 1969b. Sexual behavior in senescence. II. Patterns of sexual activity and interest. *Geriatrics* 24(2):137–54.

Vladeck, B. C. 1980. *Unloving care: The nursing home tragedy*. New York: Basic Books.

Von Mering, O., and A. O'Rand. 1981. Illness and the organization of health care; A sociocultural perspective. In *Dimensions*. See Fry, 1981.

Waaler, H. T. 1984. Height, weight, and mortality; The Norwegian experience. *Acta Medica Scandinavica Supplementum* 679:1–56.

Wake, S. B., and M. J. Sporakowski. 1972. An intergenerational comparison of attitudes toward supporting aged parents. *Journal of Marriage and the Family* 34(February):42–48.

Waldron, I. 1983. Sex differences in human mortality: The role of genetic factors. *Social Science and Medicine* 17:321–33.

Walford, R. L. 1983. *Maximum life span*. New York: W. W. Norton.

Walsh, D. A. 1982. The development of visual information processes in adulthood and old age. In *Aging and human visual function*. See Hoyer and Plude, 1982.

Walsh, D. A., I. K. Krauss, and V. A. Regnier. 1981. Spatial ability, environmental knowledge, and environmental use. In *Spatial representation and behavior across the life span: Theory and application*, edited by L. S. Lipen, A. H. Patterson, and N. Newcombe. New York: Academic Press.

Waltzman, S. A., and T. B. Karasu. 1979. Sex in the elderly. In *On Sexuality: Psychoanalytic Observations*, edited by T. B. Karasu and C. W. Socarides. New York: International Universities Press.

Wang, H. S. 1977. Dementia of old age. In *Aging and dementia*, edited by W. L. Smith and M. Kinsbourne. New York: Spectrum.

Washburn, S. L. 1981. Longevity in primates. In *Aging—Biology and behavior*, edited by J. L. McGaugh and S. B. Kiesler. New York: Academic Press.

Wasow, M., and M. B. Loeb. 1978. Sexuality in nursing homes. In *Sexuality and aging*. See Broderick, 1978.

Weale, R. A. 1963. *The aging eye*. London: H. K. Lewis.

————. 1982. Senile ocular changes, cell death, and vision. In *Aging and human visual function.* See Hoyer and Plude, 1982.

Weber, M. [1922] 1968. *Economy and society: An outline of interpretive sociology.* Edited by G. Roth and C. Wittich. Translated from the German by E. Fischoff and others. New York: Bedminster Press.

Weg, R. B. 1978. Physiology and sexuality in aging. In *Sexuality and aging.* See Broderick, 1978.

Weiler, S. J. 1981. Aging and sexuality and the myth of decline. In *Aging.* See Griffitt, 1981.

Weiner, A. 1976. *Women of value, men of renown.* Austin: University of Texas Press.

Weisman, A. D. 1972. *On dying and denying.* New York: Behavioral Publications.

Weiss, K. M. 1981. Evolutionary perspectives on human aging. In *Other ways of growing old.* See Amoss, 1981.

Weiss, N. S., D. R. Szekely, and D. F. Austin. 1976. Increasing incidence of endometrial cancer in the United States. *New England Journal of Medicine* 294; 1259–62.

Weissert, W. 1985. Seven reasons why it is so difficult to make community-based long-term care cost-effective. *Health Services Research* 20(4):423–33.

Welford, A. T. 1977. Motor performance. In *Handbook of the psychology of aging.* See Birren and Renner, 1977.

————. 1980. Sensory, perceptual, and motor processes in older adults. In *Handbook of mental health and aging.* See Comfort, 1980.

————. 1984. Between bodily changes and performance: Some possible reasons for slowing with age. *Experimental Aging Research* 10:73–88.

————. 1985. Changes of performance with age: An overview. In *Aging and human performance,* edited by N. Charness. London: Wiley & Sons.

Wells, C. E. 1979. Pseudodementia. *American Journal of Psychiatry* 136:7.

White, C. B. 1982. Sexual interest, attitudes, knowledge, and sexual history in relation to sexual behavior in the institutionalized aging. *Archives of Sexual Behavior* 11(6):491–502.

White, M. A. 1977. Values of elderly differ in rural setting. *Generations* 2(3):6–7.

Whiting, B. B., and J. W. M. Whiting. 1975. *Children of six cultures: A psychocultural analysis.* Cambridge: Harvard University Press.

Whyte, M. K. 1978. *The status of women in preindustrial societies.* Princeton, N.J.: Princeton University Press.

Williams, G. C. 1957. Pleiotropy, natural selection, and the evolution of senescence. *Evolution* 11:398–411.

Williams, M. V. 1980. Receiver operating characteristics: The effect of distribution on between-group comparisons. In *Aging in the 1980's.* See Cerella, Poon, and Williams, 1980.

Williams, T. R. 1972. *Introduction to socialization: Human culture transmitted.* St. Louis: C. V. Mosby.

Willis, S. L., and P. B. Baltes. 1980. Intelligence in adulthood and aging: Contemporary issues. In *Aging in the 1980's.* See Cerella, Poon, and Williams, 1980.

Wilson, P. J. 1969. Reputation and respectability: A suggestion for Caribbean ethnology. *Man* 4:70–84.

————. 1971. Caribbean crews: Peer groups and male society. *Caribbean Studies* 10:18–34.

Wingard, D. L. 1982. The sex differential in mortality rates. *American Journal of Epidemiology* 115:205–16.

Wingard, D. L., and L. F. Berkman. 1983. Mortality risk associated with sleeping patterns among adults. *Sleep* 6:102–7.

Wingard, D. L., L. F. Berkman, and R. J. Brand. 1982. A multivariate analysis of health-related practices. *American Journal of Epidemiology* 116:765–75.

Wingfield, A., L. W. Poon, L. Lombardi, and D. Lowe. 1985. Speed of processing in normal aging: Effects of speech rate, linguistic structure, and processing time. *Journal of Gerontology* 40:579–85.

Winn, R. L., and N. Newton. 1982. Sexuality in aging: A study of 106 cultures. *Archives of Sexual Behavior* 11(4):283–98.

Wirth, L. 1945. The problem of minority groups. In *The science of man in the world crisis*, edited by R. Linton. New York: Columbia University Press.

Wiseman, R. F. 1981. Community environments for the elderly. In *The dynamics of aging*. See Longino, 1981.

Wisniewski, H. K. 1983. Neuritic (senile) and amyloid plaques. In *Alzheimer's disease*. See Ball, 1983.

Wolanski, N. 1982. Urbanization and life span. *Current Anthropology* 23:579–80.

Wolf, E. 1960. Glare and age. *Archives of Ophthalmology* 64:502–14.

———. 1967. Studies on the shrinkage of the visual field with age. *Highway Research Record* 167:1–7.

Wolf, E. R. 1966a. Kinship, friendship, and patron-client relations in complex societies. In *The social anthropology of complex societies*, edited by M. Banton. ASA Monographs. London: Tavistock.

———. 1966b. *Peasants*. Englewood Cliffs, N.J.: Prentice-Hall.

Wolf, R. S., M. A. Godkin, and K. A. Pillemer. 1984. Elder abuse and neglect: Final report from three model projects. Submitted to the Massachusetts Executive Office of Elder Affairs. Worcester, Mass.: University Center on Aging, University of Massachusetts Medical Center.

Wolfe, A. 1977. The supranational organization of production: An evolutionary perspective. *Current Anthropology* 18:615–36.

Wood, P. K. 1983. Inquiring systems and problem structure: Implications for cognitive development. *Human Development* 26:249–65.

Wood, V. and J. F. Robertson. 1978. Friendship and kinship interaction: Differential effect on the morale of the elderly. *Journal of Marriage and the Family* 40(May):367–75.

Worden, J. W. 1982. *Grief counseling and grief therapy*. New York: Springer Publishing.

Wright, L. L., and J. W. Elias. 1979. Age differences in the effects of perceptual noise. *Journal of Gerontology* 34:704–8.

Wu, F. Y. 1975. Mandarin-speaking aged Chinese in the Los Angeles area. *Gerontologist* 15(3):271–75.

Yarnell, J. W. G., A. S. St. Leger, I. C. Balfour, and R. B. Rusell. 1979. The distribution, age effects, and disease associations of HLA antigens and other blood group markers in a random sample of an elderly population. *Journal of Chronic Diseases* 32:555–62.

Yin, I-C. and M. Shine. 1985. Misinterpretations of increases in life expectance in gerontology textbooks. *Gerontologist* 25:78–82.

Young, F. W., and A. A. Bacdayan. 1965. Menstrual taboos and social rigidity. *Ethnology* 4:225–40.

Yuan, I-C. 1933. The influence of heredity upon the duration of life in man based on a Chinese geneology from 1365 to 1914. *Human Biology* 4:41–68.

Zais, J. P., and T. G. Thibodeau. 1983. *The elderly and urban housing*. Washington, D.C.: The Urban Institute Press.

Zarit, S. 1980. *Aging and mental disorders*. New York: Free Press.

Zarit, S., N. Orr, and J. Zarit. 1985. *The hidden victims of Alzheimer's disease: Families under stress*. New York: New York University Press.

Ziel, H. K., and W. Finkle. 1975. Increased risk of endometrial carcinoma among users of conjugated estrogens. *New England Journal of Medicine* 293(23):1167–70.

INDEX

Abkhasians, 73, 74, 76–78

Abuse of elderly persons, 226–27. *See also* Crimes against elderly persons

Accessory apartments of elderly persons, 260

Accumulation of wastes theory of aging, 33–34. *See also* Biological theories of aging; Cellular theories of aging

Activity norms, defined, 236

Activity theory of aging, defined, 6–7

Actuarial theories of aging, 79–84

Adaptation, defined, 5

Adaptive theories of aging, 59, 60, 66, 68, 70. *See also* Biological theories of aging; Evolutionary theories of aging

Adult-centered cognition theory of aging, 115, 128; defined, 116, 117; traditional cognition theory of aging compared to, 117, 121–22, 123, 132

Affectional solidarity, 207, 210–11, 212

Africa, age-set societies in, 297

Age-as-leveler theory of aging, 269, 275–76

Age effect, 11

Age-homogeneous housing, 247–48, 336. *See also specific types of housing*

Ageism, 160

"Age-pigment," 33–34

Age-set societies, 7, 297

Age stratification theory of aging, 7–8

Aging, defined, 390, 391

Aging, theories of. *See specific theories*

Aging of the population, defined, 187

Agrarian societies, 195; elderly persons in, 245, 298–301, 302–305, 307, 310, 330. *See also* Rural areas

Alcohol consumption of elderly persons, 86, 91, 177

Allocation, defined, 108

Alzheimer's disease, 20, 360–61; caretakers for, 367–68; causes of, 362–63; diagnosis of, 365, 366; history of, 361–62; influence on nuclear families of, 367, 368; in minority groups, 368–74; sociocultural aspects of, 366–68; support groups for, 368, 369, 370–74; symptoms of, 361, 363–64

Analytic theory of aging. *See* Traditional cognition theory of aging

Androgens, 167, 169

Androgyny of elderly persons, 334–35

Anemia of elderly persons, 176

Anthropological theories of aging, 73–79

Anti-depressants, 177

Antioxidants, 58, 59

Apartment complexes for elderly persons, 248–51

Aphrodisiacs, 177–78

Appearance of elderly persons, 329–30

Apprenticeships, 300

Arizona, elderly persons in, 196, 240–41

Asian Americans, 272–73

Associational solidarity, 206–10

Assumptive worlds, 156

Ataxia telangiectasia, 25

Auditory system of elderly persons, 100–102, 359. *See also* Sensory function of elderly persons

Autoimmunity of elderly persons, 38, 39

Average life span, 54–55, 65–66

Baby boom, 186, 190

Barbiturates, 177

Basal metabolic rate, 36, 56, 58

Beauvoir, Simone de, 218

Behavior, defined, 235

Bereavement of elderly persons, 392, 403–405

"Big bang" theory of aging, 52. *See also* Evolutionary theories of aging

Binswanger's disease, 361

Biological age: causes of, 51–53; characteristics of, 6, 11, 20–22, 41–42; defined, 18, 51

Biological theories of aging, 17–18, 23, 24–26. *See also specific theories*

Birth cohorts, defined, 183

"Blind spots" of elderly persons, 100

Boarding homes of elderly persons, 260

Body size and weight, 91; life span's relationship to, 56, 58, 60–62

Boredom of elderly persons, 178, 181

Brain death, defined, 391